Fodor's 2016

SOUTHERN
CALIFORNIA

Excerpted from *Fodor's California 2016.*

WELCOME TO SOUTHERN CALIFORNIA

Balmy weather, blissful beaches, Hollywood glamour—Southern California delivers fun and relaxation year-round. Outdoor enthusiasts revel in the natural beauty and excellent outdoor activities in the dramatic Mojave Desert and iconic Yosemite National Park, and at relaxing Palm Springs resorts. Beachgoers are drawn to the seemingly endless strands that line the stunning coast. For urban culture-vultures, trendy Los Angeles and sunny San Diego hold a wealth of treasures, including movie studio tours, America's preeminent zoo, and superb restaurants.

TOP REASONS TO GO

★ **Cool Cities:** San Diego's bay, Los Angeles's movie lore, Palm Springs' spa resorts.

★ **Beaches:** For swimming, surfing, or tanning, the beaches can't be beat.

★ **Feasts:** Cutting-edge cuisine, food trucks, fusion flavors, farmers' markets.

★ **Theme Parks:** From Disneyland to LEGOLAND, SoCal has some of the biggest and best.

★ **Outdoor Adventures:** Hiking, golfing, and national park excursions are all excellent.

★ **Road Trips:** The Pacific Coast Highway offers spectacular views and thrills aplenty.

Fodor's SOUTHERN CALIFORNIA 2016

Publisher: Amanda D'Acierno, *Senior Vice President*

Editorial: Arabella Bowen, *Editor in Chief*; Linda Cabasin, *Editorial Director*

Design: Tina Malaney, *Associate Art Director*; Chie Ushio, *Senior Designer*; Ann McBride, *Production Designer*

Photography: Jennifer Arnow, *Senior Photo Editor*; Jennifer Romains, *Photo Researcher*

Production: Linda Schmidt, *Managing Editor*; Evangelos Vasilakis, *Associate Managing Editor*; Angela L. McLean, *Senior Production Manager*

Maps: Rebecca Baer, *Senior Map Editor*; David Lindroth and Mark Stroud *Cartographers*

Sales: Jacqueline Lebow, *Sales Director*

Marketing & Publicity: Heather Dalton, *Marketing Director*; Katherine Punia, *Publicity Director*

Business & Operations: Susan Livingston, *Vice President, Strategic Business Planning*; Sue Daulton, *Vice President, Operations*

Fodors.com: Megan Bell, *Executive Director, Revenue & Business Development*; Yasmin Marinaro, *Senior Director, Marketing & Partnerships*

Copyright © 2016 by Fodor's Travel, a division of Random House LLC

Writers: Sarah Amandalore, Michele Bigley, Cheryl Crabtree, Maren Dougherty, Casey Hatfield-Chiotti, Mary James, Ron James, Kathy A. McDonald, Steve Pastorino, Joan Patterson, Jeff Terich, Claire Deeks van der Lee, Bobbi Zane

Editors: Luke Epplin, Salwa Jabado, Teddy Minford

Editorial Contributors: Daniel Mangin, Nicholas McNallen, Kristan Schiller, Amanda Theunissen

Production Editor: Evangelos Vasilakis

ISBN 978-1-101-87850-7

ISSN 1543-1037

All details in this book are based on information supplied to us at press time. Always confirm information when it matters, especially if you're making a detour to visit a specific place. Fodor's expressly disclaims any liability, loss, or risk, personal or otherwise, that is incurred as a consequence of the use of any of the contents of this book.

SPECIAL SALES

This book is available at special discounts for bulk purchases for sales promotions or premiums. For more information, e-mail specialmarkets@penguinrandomhouse.com

PRINTED IN THE UNITED STATES OF AMERICA

10 9 8 7 6 5 4 3 2 1

CONTENTS

MAPS

ABOUT THIS GUIDE

Fodor's Recommendations

Everything in this guide is worth doing—we don't cover what isn't—but exceptional sights, hotels, and restaurants are recognized with additional accolades. **Fodor's Choice★** indicates our top recommendations; and **Best Bets** call attention to notable hotels and restaurants in various categories. Care to nominate a new place? Visit Fodors.com/contact-us.

Trip Costs

We list prices wherever possible to help you budget well. Hotel and restaurant price categories from **$** to **$$$$** are noted alongside each recommendation. For hotels, we include the lowest cost of a standard double room in high season. For restaurants, we cite the average price of a main course at dinner or, if dinner isn't served, at lunch. For attractions, we always list adult admission fees; discounts are usually available for children, students, and senior citizens.

Hotels

Our local writers vet every hotel to recommend the best overnights in each price category, from budget to expensive. Unless otherwise specified, you can expect private bath, phone, and TV in your room. For expanded hotel reviews, facilities, and deals visit Fodors.com.

Top Picks

★ Fodor's Choice

Listings

- ✉ Address
- 📨 Branch address
- ☎ Telephone
- 📠 Fax
- 🌐 Website
- 📧 E-mail
- 🎟 Admission fee
- 🕒 Open/closed times
- [M] Subway
- ✥ Directions or Map coordinates

Hotels & Restaurants

- 🏨 Hotel
- 🛏 Number of rooms
- 🍽 Meal plans
- ✕ Restaurant
- ✍ Reservations
- 👔 Dress code
- 💳 No credit cards
- [$] Price

Other

- ⇨ See also
- ☞ Take note
- 🏌 Golf facilities

Restaurants

Unless we state otherwise, restaurants are open for lunch and dinner daily. We mention dress code only when there's a specific requirement and reservations only when they're essential or not accepted. To make restaurant reservations, visit Fodors.com.

Credit Cards

The hotels and restaurants in this guide typically accept credit cards. If not, we'll say so.

EUGENE FODOR

Hungarian-born Eugene Fodor (1905–91) began his travel career as an interpreter on a French cruise ship. The experience inspired him to write *On the Continent* (1936), the first guidebook to receive annual updates and discuss a country's way of life as well as its sights. Fodor later joined the U.S. Army and worked for the OSS in World War II. After the war, he kept up his intelligence work while expanding his guidebook series. During the Cold War, many guides were written by fellow agents who understood the value of insider information. Today's guides continue Fodor's legacy by providing travelers with timely coverage, insider tips, and cultural context.

1

EXPERIENCE
SOUTHERN
CALIFORNIA

WHAT'S NEW IN SOUTHERN CALIFORNIA

Foodie's Paradise

Great dining is a staple of the California lifestyle, and a new young generation of chefs is challenging old ideas about preparing and presenting great food. The food-truck frenzy continues to fuel movable feasts up and down the state. Diners are also embracing the pop-up concept, where guest chefs offer innovative menus in unconventional settings for a limited time. These pop-up engagements are hosted anywhere from inside a warehouse to outside in a field. Visitors can look for local pop-ups listed on foodie websites such as Eater (⊕ *www.eater.com*).

California chefs continue to shop locally for produce and farmer-sourced meat, and many restaurants proudly display their vendors on the menu.

Family Fun

California's theme parks work overtime to keep current and attract patrons of all ages. LEGOLAND California Resort keeps expanding with additional attractions such the LEGOLAND Water Park and its 250-room LEGO-theme hotel.

Disneyland also continues to grow. The relatively new Cars Land section is a must for big and little kids. Fans of Elsa, Anna, and Olaf will also take delight in the incorporation of *Frozen*-themed elements around the park.

Both kids and adults will be fascinated by the creatures at the Monterey Bay Aquarium.

Wine Discoveries

California offers oenophiles ample opportunities for new discoveries beyond Napa and Sonoma. In the hillsides of San Diego County, the Ramona Valley AVA is seeing an increasing number of visitors, and the boutique wineries in the hillsides of Malibu are garnering attention.

All Aboard

Riding the rails can be a satisfying experience, particularly in California where the distances between destinations sometimes run into the hundreds of miles. The best trip is on the luxuriously appointed Coast Starlight, a long-distance train with sleeping cars that runs between Seattle and Los Angeles, passing some of California's most beautiful coastline as it hugs the beach. For the best surfside viewing, get a seat or a room on the left side of the train and ride south to north.

Amtrak also has frequent Pacific Surfliner service between San Diego and Los Angeles, and San Diego and Santa Barbara. These are coach cars, but many of the trains have been upgraded and are comfortable and convenient, especially if you want to get off and on the train at several destinations—Anaheim near Disneyland, Downtown Los Angeles, coastal Ventura, Santa Barbara, and San Luis Obispo.

Homegrown Hospitality

Agritourism in California isn't new, but it is on the rise, with farm tours and agricultural festivals sprouting up everywhere. In the Central Valley, America's number-one producer of stone fruit, you can travel themed tourist routes and tour herb gardens, fruit orchards, organic dairies, and pumpkin patches.

State of the Arts

California's beauty-obsessed citizens aren't the only ones opting for a fresh look these days: its esteemed art museums are also having a bit of work done. The Los Angeles County Museum of Art (LACMA) keeps expanding its Wilshire Boulevard campus following the 2010 opening of the Renzo Piano–designed Resnick Pavilion.

PLANNER

WHEN TO GO

Because they offer activities indoors and out, the top California cities rate as all-seasons destinations. Ditto for Southern California's coastal playgrounds.

Death Valley and Joshua Tree National Park are best appreciated in spring when desert blooms offset their austerity and temperatures are still manageable. Yosemite is ideal in late spring because roads closed in winter are reopened, and the park's waterfalls—swollen with melting snow—run fast. Autumn is "crush time" in all the wine destinations. Ski resorts typically open around Thanksgiving (they sometimes remain in operation into June).

Climate

It's difficult to generalize about the state's weather beyond saying that precipitation comes in winter and summer is dry in most places. As a rule, inland regions are hotter in summer and colder in winter, compared with coastal areas, which are relatively cool year-round. Fog is a potential hazard any day of the year in coastal regions. Day and nighttime temperatures can also vary greatly. In August, Palm Springs' thermometers can soar to 110°F at noon, and drop to 75°F at night.

CAR TRAVEL

Driving may be a way of life in California, but it isn't cheap (gas prices here are usually among the highest in the nation). It's also not for the fainthearted; you've surely heard horror stories about L.A.'s freeways, but even the state's scenic highways and byways have their own hassles. For instance, on the dramatic coastal road between San Simeon and Carmel, twists, turns, and divinely distracting vistas frequently slow traffic; in rainy season, mudslides can close the road altogether.

On California's notorious freeways, other rules apply. Nervous Nellies must resist the urge to stay in the two slow-moving lanes on the far right, used primarily by trucks. To drive at least the speed limit, get yourself in a middle lane. If you're ready to bend the rules a bit, the second lane (lanes are numbered from 1 starting at the center) moves about 5 mph faster. But avoid the far-left lane (the one next to the carpool lane), where speeds range from 75 mph to 90 mph.

AIR TRAVEL

Around Los Angeles, there are several airport options to choose from. LAX, the world's sixth-busiest airport, gets most of the attention—and not usually for good reasons. John Wayne Airport (SNA), about 25 miles south in Orange County, is a solid substitute—especially if you're planning to visit Disneyland or Orange County. You might also consider Bob Hope Airport (BUR) in Burbank (close to Hollywood and its studios) or Long Beach Airport (LGB), convenient if you're catching a cruise ship. San Diego's Lindbergh International Airport (SAN) is located minutes from the Gaslamp Quarter, Balboa Park and Zoo, and the cruise ship terminal.

WHAT'S WHERE

The following numbers refer to chapters.

3 San Diego. San Diego's Gaslamp Quarter and early California–themed Old Town have a human scale—but big-ticket animal attractions like the San Diego Zoo pull in visitors.

4 Orange County and Catalina Island. A diverse destination with premium resorts and restaurants, strollable waterfront communities, and kid-friendly attractions.

5 Los Angeles. Go for the glitz of the entertainment industry, but stay for the rich cultural attributes and communities.

6 The Central Coast. Three of the state's top stops—swanky Santa Barbara, Hearst Castle, and Big Sur—sit along the scenic 200-mile route. A quick boat trip away lies scenic Channel Islands National Park.

7 Monterey Bay Area. Postcard-perfect Monterey, Victorian-flavored Pacific Grove, and exclusive Carmel all share this stretch of California coast. To the north, Santa Cruz boasts a boardwalk, a UC campus, ethnic clothing shops, and plenty of surfers.

8 The Inland Empire. The San Bernardino Mountains provide seasonal escapes, and the Temecula Valley will challenge your ideas of "California Wine Country."

9 Palm Springs and the Desert Resorts. Golf on some of the West's most challenging courses, lounge at fabulous resorts, check out mid-century-modern architectural gems, and trek through primitive desert parks.

10 Joshua Tree National Park. Proximity to major urban areas—as well as world-class rock climbing and nighttime celestial displays—help make this one of the most visited national parks.

11 The Mojave Desert. Material pleasures are in short supply here, but Mother Nature's stark beauty more than compensates.

12 Death Valley National Park. America's second-largest national park is vast, beautiful, and often the hottest place in the nation.

13 The Central Valley. Travelers along Highway 99 will enjoy attractions like Fresno's Forestiere Underground Gardens, the wineries of Lodi, and white-water rafting on the Stanislaus River.

14 The Southern Sierra. In the Mammoth Lakes region, sawtooth mountains and deep powdery snowdrifts create the

state's premier conditions for skiing and snowboarding.

15 Yosemite National Park. The views immortalized by photographer Ansel Adams—towering granite monoliths, verdant glacial valleys, and lofty waterfalls—are still camera-ready.

16 Sequoia and Kings Canyon National Parks. The sight of ancient redwoods towering above jagged mountains is breathtaking.

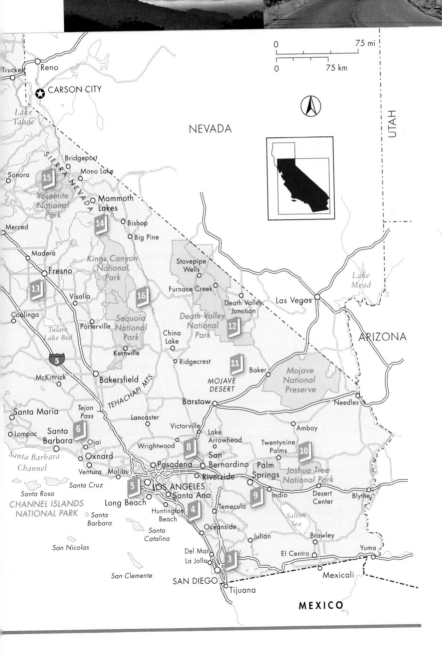

SOUTHERN CALIFORNIA TODAY

The People

California is as much a state of mind as a state in the union—a kind of perpetual promised land that has represented many things to many people. In the 18th century, Spanish missionaries came seeking converts and gold. In the 19th, miners rushed here to search for gold. And, in the years since, a long line of Dust Bowl farmers, land speculators, hippies, migrant workers, dot-commers, real estate speculators, and would-be actors have come chasing their own dreams.

The result is a population that leans toward idealism—without necessarily being as liberal as you might think. (Remember, this is Ronald Reagan's old stomping ground.) And despite the stereotype of the blue-eyed, blond surfer, California's population is not homogeneous either. Ten million people who live here (more than 27% of Californians) are foreign born. Almost half hail from Latin American countries; another third emigrated from Asia, following the waves of Chinese workers who arrived in the 1860s to build the railroads and subsequent waves of Indochinese refugees from the Vietnam War.

The Politics

What's blue and red and green all over? California: a predominantly Democratic state with an aggressive "go green" agenda. Democratic Governor Jerry Brown, who was elected to the office for the second time in 30 years, is moving the progressive agenda ahead with policies that make California the greenest state in the nation, supporting more green construction, wind farms, and solar panels.

The Economy

Leading all other states in terms of the income generated by agriculture, tourism, entertainment, and industrial activity, California has the country's most diverse state economy. Moreover, with a gross state product of more than $2 trillion, California would be one of the top 10 economies *in the world* if it were an independent nation.

Due to its wealth ($61,094 median household income) and productivity, California took a large hit in the 2007 recession, but the Golden State's economic history is filled with boom and bust cycles—beginning with the mid-19th-century gold rush that started it all. Optimists already have their eyes on the next potential boom: high-tech and bioresearch, "green companies" focused on alternative energy, renewables, electric cars, and the like.

The Culture

Art and culture thrive in San Diego. Balboa Park alone holds 15 museums, opulent gardens, and three performance venues, in addition to the San Diego Zoo. The Old Globe Theater and La Jolla Playhouse routinely originate plays that capture coveted Tony Awards in New York.

But California's *real* forte is pop culture, and L.A. and its environs are the chief arbiters. Movie, TV, and video production have been centered here since the early 20th century. Capitol Records set up shop in L.A. in the 1940s, and this area has been instrumental in the music industry ever since. And while these industries continue to influence national trends, today they are only part of the pop culture equation.

The Parks and Preserves

Cloud-spearing redwood groves, snow-tipped mountains, canyon-slashed deserts, primordial lava beds, and a seemingly endless coast: California's natural diversity is staggering—and efforts to protect it started early. Yosemite, the first national park, was established here in 1890, and the National Park Service now oversees 32 sites in California (more than in any other state). When you factor in 280 state parks—which encompass underwater preserves, historic sites, wildlife reserves, dune systems, and other sensitive habitats—the number of acres involved is almost as impressive as the topography itself.

Due to encroaching development and pollution, keeping these natural treasures in pristine condition is an ongoing challenge. For instance, Sequoia and Kings Canyon (which is plagued by pesticides and other agricultural pollutants blown in from the San Joaquin Valley) has been named America's "smoggiest park" by the National Parks Conservation Association, and the Environmental Protection Agency has designated it as an "ozone nonattainment area with levels of ozone pollution that threaten human health."

There is no question that Californians love their 280 state parks. Nearly every park has its grass-roots supporters, who volunteer to raise money, volunteer as rangers, and work other jobs to keep the parks open.

The Cuisine

California gave us McDonald's, Denny's, Carl's Jr., Taco Bell, and, of course, In-N-Out Burger. Fortunately for those of us with fast-clogging arteries, the state also kick-started the organic food movement. Back in the 1970s, California-based chefs put American cuisine on the culinary map by focusing on freshly prepared seasonal ingredients.

Today, this focus has spawned the "locavore" or sustainable food movement—followers try to only consume food produced within a 100-mile radius of where they live, since processing and refining food and transporting goods over long distances is bad for both the body and the environment. This isn't much of a restriction in California, where a huge variety of crops grow year-round. Some 350 cities and towns have certified farmers' markets—and their stalls are bursting with a variety of goods. California has been America's top agricultural producer for the last 50 years, growing more fruits and vegetables than any other state. Dairies and ranches also thrive here, and fishing fleets harvest fish and shellfish from the rich waters offshore.

SOUTHERN CALIFORNIA TOP ATTRACTIONS

Big Sur Coastline

(A) A drive along Highway 1 through the winding Big Sur Coastline is hard to beat. With towering forests on one side and rocky seaside cliffs on the other, drivers must take care not to become distracted by the spectacular ocean views. While the vistas are stunning from the road, travelers will be rewarded by short detours to visit elephant seals, relax on secluded beaches or hike through the redwoods.

Balboa Park

(B) What's not to like about San Diego's Balboa Park? A huge space in the heart of downtown where you can spend a whole day, the park is filled with open green lawns, great play areas for kids, colorful gardens, historic fountains, and beautiful Spanish-style buildings that are more than 100 years old. Fifteen museums display collections ranging from natural history to fine art and photography, from sports to classic cars to science.

Disneyland Resort

(C) Billed as the happiest place on earth, a trip to Disneyland is indeed a dream come true for many. Built in 1955, Disneyland is the original Disney amusement park. Today, the Anaheim resort has grown to include Disneyland, Disney's California Adventure, Downtown Disney, and three Disney hotels. Its close proximity to Los Angeles and San Diego makes it easy to incorporate a visit into almost any Southern California itinerary.

Hollywood

(D) Visitors can't help but be star-struck while wandering the Hollywood Walk of Fame, standing at the epicenter of Hollywood and Vine, or gazing up at the famous Hollywood sign. No trip to Hollywood would be complete without a visit to one of the studios that makes the magic happen, such as Paramount Pictures, Universal Studios Hollywood, or Warner Bros. Studios.

Yosemite National Park

(E) Nature looms large here, both literally and figuratively. In addition to hulking Half Dome, the park is home to El Capitan (the world's largest exposed granite monolith, rising 3,593 feet above the glacier-carved valley floor) and Yosemite Falls (North America's tallest cascade). In Yosemite's signature stand of giant sequoias—the Mariposa Grove—even the trees are Bunyanesque. Needless to say, crowds can be supersize, too.

San Diego Zoo

(F) The world-renowned San Diego Zoo is a must-see for adults and kids alike. Set in 100 acres within Balboa Park, the zoo is admired for its conservation efforts. Famous for its giant panda research, the zoo's resident pandas are the stars of the show. Other popular exhibits include the polar bear plunge, the gorilla and orangutan environments, and the newly redesigned koala habitat.

Mission Santa Barbara

Santa Barbara is the most beautiful of the 21 remaining settlements along California's Mission Trail. Originally built in 1786, the Mission is home to an excellent collection of Native American and Spanish/Mexican colonial art. Santa Barbara has many more attractions to warrant a visit, including the red-tiled architecture of its walkable downtown, and an excellent wine region.

Palm Springs and Beyond

In this improbably situated bastion of Bentleys and bling, worldly pleasures rule. Glorious golf courses, tony shops and restaurants, decadent spa resorts—they're all here. Fans of mid-century modernist architecture will love the many gems on display in Palm Springs. Solitude seekers can still slip away to nearby Joshua Tree National Park or Anza-Borrego Desert State Park.

QUINTESSENTIAL SOUTHERN CALIFORNIA

The Beach

California's beach culture is, in a word, legendary. Of course, it only makes sense that folks living in a state with a 1,264-mile coastline (a hefty portion of which sees the sun upward of 300 days a year) would perfect the art of beachgoing. True aficionados begin with a reasonably fit physique, plus a stylish wardrobe of flip-flops, bikinis, and wet suits. Mastery of at least one beach skill—surfing, boogie boarding, kayaking, Frisbee tossing, or looking fab while catching rays—is also essential. As a visitor, though, you need only a swimsuit and some rented equipment for most sports. You can then hit the beach almost anywhere, thanks to the California belief in coastal access as a birthright. The farther south you go, the wider, sandier, and sunnier the beaches become.

The Automobile

Americans may have a love affair with the automobile, but Californians have an out-and-out obsession. Even when gas prices rev up and freeway traffic slows down, their passion burns as hot as ever. You can witness this ardor any summer weekend at huge classic- and custom-car shows held statewide. Even better, you can feel it yourself by taking the wheel. Trace an old stagecoach route through the mountains above Santa Barbara on Highway 154; track migrating whales up the coast to Big Sur; or take 17-Mile Drive along the precipitous edge of the Monterey Peninsula. Highway 1 runs almost the entire length of the state, hugging the coast most of the way.

Californians live in such a large and splashy state that they sometimes seem to forget about the rest of the country. They've developed a distinctive culture all their own, which you can delve into by doing as the locals do.

The Wine

If California were a country, it would rank as the world's fourth-largest wine producer, after Italy, France, and Spain. In those countries, where *vino* is barely considered an alcoholic beverage, wine drinking has evolved into a relaxing ritual best shared with friends and family. A modern, Americanized version of that mentality integrates wine into daily life in California, and there are many places to sample it. You can find great wineries around Santa Barbara County, San Luis Obispo, and Monterey Bay. Winery tours and tastings will show you what all the buzz is about.

The Outdoors

One of California's greatest assets—the mild year-round weather enjoyed by most of the state—inspires residents to spend as much time outside as they possibly can. They have a tremendous enthusiasm for every imaginable outdoor sport and fresh-air adventures are extremely popular. But the California-alfresco creed is more broadly interpreted, and the general rule when planning any activity is "if it can happen outside, it will!" Plein air vacation opportunities include dining on patios, decks, and wharves; shopping in street markets or elaborate open-air malls; hearing almost any kind of music at moonlight concerts; touring the sculpture gardens that grace major art museums; and celebrating everything from gay pride to garlic at outdoor fairs.

SOUTHERN CALIFORNIA'S TOP EXPERIENCES

Ride a Wave

Surfing—which has influenced everything from fashion to moviemaking to music—is a quintessential California activity. You can find great surf breaks in many places along the coast, but one of the best places to try it is Huntington Beach. Lessons are widely available. If you're not ready to hang 10, you can hang out at "Surf City's" International Surfing Museum or stroll the Surfing Walk of Fame.

Think Globally, Eat Locally

Over the years California cuisine has evolved from a mere trend into a respected gastronomic tradition: one that pairs local, often organic or sustainable, ingredients with techniques inspired by European, Asian, and, increasingly, Indian and Middle Eastern cookery.

See Eccentric Architecture

California has always drawn creative and, well, eccentric people. And all that quirkiness has left its mark in the form of oddball architecture that makes for some fun sightseeing. Begin by touring Hearst Castle—the beautifully bizarre estate William Randolph Hearst built above San Simeon. Scotty's Castle, a Moorish confection in Death Valley, offers a variation on the theme, as does Marta Becket's one-woman Amargosa Opera House.

Get Behind the Scenes

In L.A. it's almost obligatory to do some Hollywood-style stargazing. Cue the action with a behind-the-scenes tour of one of the dream factories. (Warner Bros. Studios' five-hour deluxe version, which includes lunch in the commissary, is just the ticket for cinephiles.) Other must-sees include the Dolby Theater, permanent home to the Cirque du Soleil and Academy Awards; Grauman's Chinese Theatre, where celebs press feet and hands into cement for posterity's sake; Hollywood Boulevard's star-paved Walk of Fame; and the still-iconic Hollywood sign.

People-Watch

Opportunities for world-class people-watching abound in California. Hang around L.A.'s Venice Boardwalk, where chain-saw jugglers, surfers, fortune-tellers, and well-oiled bodybuilders take beachfront exhibitionism to a new high (or low, depending on your point of view). The result is pure eye candy.

SOUTHERN CALIFORNIA'S BEST ROAD TRIPS

THE ULTIMATE ROAD TRIP

CALIFORNIA'S LEGENDARY HIGHWAY 1

by Cheryl Crabtree

One of the world's most scenic drives, California's State Route 1 (also known as Highway 1, the Pacific Coast Highway, the PCH) stretches along the edge of the state for nearly 660 miles, from Southern California's Dana Point to its northern terminus near Leggett, about 40 miles north of Fort Bragg. As you travel south to north, the water's edge transitions from long, sandy beaches and low-lying bluffs to towering dunes, craggy cliffs, and ancient redwood groves. The ocean changes as well; the relatively tame and surfable swells lapping the Southern California shore give way to the frigid, powerful waves crashing against weatherbeaten rocks in the north.

HIGHWAY 1 TOP 10

- Santa Monica
- Santa Barbara
- Hearst San Simeon State Historical Monument
- Big Sur
- Carmel
- 17–Mile Drive
- Monterey
- San Francisco
- Marin Headlands
- Point Reyes National Seashore

Give yourself lots of extra time to pull off the road and enjoy the scenery

STARTING YOUR JOURNEY

You may decide to drive the road's entire 660-mile route, or bite off a smaller piece. In either case, a Highway 1 road trip allows you to experience California at your own pace, stopping when and where you wish. Hike a beachside trail, dig your toes in the sand, and search for creatures in the tidepools. Buy some artichokes and strawberries from a roadside farmstand. Talk to people along the way (you'll run into everyone from soul-searching meditators, farmers, and beatniks to city-slackers and working-class folks), and take lots of pictures. Don't rush—you could easily spend a lifetime discovering secret spots along this route.

To help you plan your trip, we've broken the road into three regions (Santa Monica to Carmel, Carmel to San Francisco, and San Francisco to Fort Bragg); each region is then broken up into smaller segments—many of which are suitable for a day's drive. If you're pressed for time, you can always tackle a section of Highway 1, and then head inland to U.S. 101 or I-5 to reach your next destination more quickly.

WHAT'S IN A NAME?

Though it's often referred to as the Pacific Coast Highway (or PCH), sections of Highway 1 actually have different names. The southernmost section (Dana Point to Oxnard) is the Pacific Coast Highway. After that, the road becomes the Cabrillo Highway (Las Cruces to Lompoc), the Big Sur Coast Highway (San Luis Obispo County line to Monterey), the North Coast Scenic Byway (San Luis Obispo city limit to the Monterey County line), the Cabrillo Highway again (Santa Cruz County line to Half Moon Bay), and finally the Shoreline Highway (Marin City to Leggett). To make matters more confusing, smaller chunks of the road have additional honorary monikers.

Just follow the green triangular signs that say "California 1."

HIGHWAY 1 DRIVING

- Rent a convertible. (You will not regret it.)
- Begin the drive north from Santa Monica, where congestion and traffic delays pose less of a problem.
- Take advantage of turnouts. Let cars pass you as you take in the ocean view and snap a picture.
- Mind your manners: Don't tailgate or glare at other drivers.
- If you're prone to motion sickness, take the wheel yourself. Focusing on the landscape outside should help you feel less queasy.
- If you're afraid of heights, drive from south to north so you'll be on the mountain rather than the cliff side of the road.
- Driving PCH is glorious during winter, but check weather conditions before you go as landslides are frequent after storms.

HIGHWAY 1: SANTA MONICA TO BIG SUR

Hearst Castle

THE PLAN

Distance: approx. 335 miles

Time: 3-5 days

Good Overnight Options: Malibu, Santa Barbara, Pismo Beach, San Luis Obispo, Cambria, Carmel

SANTA MONICA TO MALIBU (approx. 26 miles)

Highway 1 begins in Dana point, but it seems more appropriate to begin a PCH adventure in **Santa Monica.** Be sure to experience the beach culture, then balance the tacky pleasures of Santa Monica's amusement pier with a stylish dinner in a neighborhood restaurant.

MALIBU TO SANTA BARBARA (approx. 70 miles)

The PCH follows the curve of Santa Monica Bay all the way to **Malibu** and **Point Mugu,** near **Oxnard.** Chances are you'll experience *déjà vu* driving this 27-mile stretch:

Santa Monica

mountains on one side, ocean on the other, opulent homes perched on hillsides; you've seen this piece of coast countless times on TV and film. Be sure to walk out on the **Malibu Pier** for a great photo opp, then check out **Surfrider Beach,** with three famous points where perfect waves ignited a worldwide surfing rage in the 1960s.

After Malibu you'll drive through miles of protected, largely unpopulated coastline. Ride a wave at **Zuma Beach,** scout for offshore whales at **Point Dume State Beach,** or hike the trails at **Point Mugu State Park.** After skirting Point Mugu, Highway 1 merges with U.S. 101 for about 70 miles before reaching **Santa Barbara.** A mini-tour of the city includes a visit to the magnificent Spanish **Mission Santa Barbara** and a walk down hopping **State Street to Stearns Wharf.**

SANTA BARBARA TO SAN SIMEON (approx. 147 miles)

North of Santa Barbara, Highway 1 morphs into the Cabrillo Highway, separating from and then rejoining U.S. 101. The route winds through rolling vineyards and rangeland to **San Luis**

Santa Barbara

Obispo, where any legit road trip includes a photo stop at the quirky **Madonna Inn.** Be sure to also climb the humungous dunes at **Guadalupe-Nipomo Dunes Preserve.**

In downtown San Luis Obispo, the **Mission San Luis Obispo de Tolosa** stands by a tree-shaded creek edged with shops and cafés. Highway 1 continues to **Morro Bay** and up the coast. About 4 miles north of Morro Bay, you'll reach **Cayucos,** a classic old California beach town with an 1875 pier, restaurants, taverns, and shops in historic buildings.

The road continues through **Cambria** to solitary Hearst San Simeon State Historical Monument, better known as **Hearst Castle**—the art-filled pleasure palace at **San Simeon.** Just four miles north of the castle, elephant seals grunt and cavort at the **Piedras Blancas Elephant**

Big Sur

TOP 5 PLACES TO LINGER

- Point Dume State Beach
- Santa Barbara
- Hearst Castle
- Big Sur/Julia Pfeiffer Burns State Park
- Carmel

Seal Rookery, just off the side of the road.

SAN SIMEON TO CARMEL (approx. 92 miles)

Heading north, you'll drive through **Big Sur,** a place of ancient forests and rugged shoreline stretching 90 miles from San Simeon to **Carmel.** Much of Big Sur lies within several state parks and the 165,000-acre **Ventana Wilderness,** itself part of the **Los Padres National Forest.** This famously scenic stretch of the coastal drive, which twists up and down bluffs above the ocean, can last hours. Take your time.

At **Julia Pfeiffer Burns State Park** one easy but rewarding hike leads to an iconic waterfall off a beachfront cliff. When you reach lovely **Carmel,** stroll around the picture-perfect town's mission, galleries, and shops.

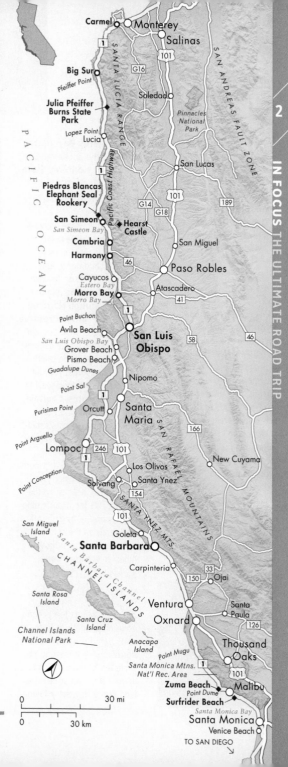

HIGHWAY 1: CARMEL TO SAN FRANCISCO

San Francisco

THE PLAN

Distance: approx. 123 miles

Time: 2-4 days

Good Overnight Options: Carmel, Monterey, Santa Cruz, Half Moon Bay, San Francisco

CARMEL TO MONTEREY
(approx. 4 miles)

Between **Carmel** and **Monterey,** Highway 1 cuts across the base of the Monterey Peninsula. Pony up the toll and take a brief detour to follow famous **17-Mile Drive,** which traverses a surf-pounded landscape of cypress trees, sea lions, gargantuan estates, and the world famous **Pebble Beach Golf Links.** Take your time here as well, and be sure to allow lots of time for pulling off to enjoy the gorgeous views.

If you have the time, spend a day checking out the sights in **Monterey,** especially the kelp forests and bat rays of

the **Monterey Bay Aquarium** and the adobes and artifacts of **Monterey State Historic Park.**

MONTEREY TO SANTA CRUZ (approx. 42 miles)

From Monterey the highway rounds the gentle curve of Monterey Bay, passing through sand dunes and artichoke fields on its way to **Moss Landing** and the **Elkhorn Slough National Estuarine Marine Preserve.** Kayak near or walk through the protected wetlands here, or board a pontoon safari boat—don't forget your binoculars. The historic seaside villages of **Aptos, Capitola,** and **Soquel,** just off the highway near the bay's midpoint, are ideal stopovers for beachcombing, antiquing, and hiking through redwoods. In boho **Santa Cruz,** just 7 miles north, walk along the **wharf,** ride the historic roller coaster on the **boardwalk,** and perch on the cliffs to watch surfers peel through tubes at **Steamer Lane.**

SANTA CRUZ TO SAN FRANCISCO (approx. 77 miles)

Highway 1 hugs the ocean's edge once again as it departs Santa Cruz and runs northward past a string of secluded beaches and small towns. Stop and stretch your legs in the tiny, artsy town

Davenport cliffs, Devenport

of **Davenport,** where you can wander through several galleries and enjoy sumptuous views from the bluffs. At **Año Nuevo State Park,** walk down to the dunes to view gargantuan elephant seals lounging on shore, then break for a meal or snack in **Pescadero** or **Half Moon Bay.**

FRIGID WATERS

If you're planning to jump in the ocean in Northern California, wear a wetsuit or prepare to shiver. Even in summer, the water temperatures warm up to just barely tolerable. The fog tends to burn off earlier in the day at relatively sheltered beaches near Monterey Bay's midpoint, near Aptos, Capitola and Santa Cruz. These beaches also tend to attract softer waves than those on the bay's outer edges.

Half Moon Bay

TOP 5 PLACES TO LINGER

- 17-Mile Drive
- Monterey
- Santa Cruz
- Año Nuevo State Reserve
- Half Moon Bay

From Half Moon Bay to **Daly City,** the road includes a number of shoulderless twists and turns that demand slower speeds and nerves of steel. Signs of urban development soon appear: mansions holding fast to Pacific cliffs and then, as the road veers slightly inland to merge with Skyline Boulevard, boxlike houses sprawling across **Daly City** and **South San Francisco.**

Golden Gate Nat'l. Recreation Area

San Francisco

Daly City

Pacifica

South San Francisco

San Francisco Bay

Moss Beach

Pillar Point
Half Moon Bay

El Granada

San Mateo

Hayward

Half Moon Bay

Belmont

San Gregorio

Palo Alto

Pescadero Point

Pescadero

Mountain View

Santa Clara

Bolsa Point

Pigeon Point

Año Nuevo State Park

Point Año Nuevo

Pacific Coast Highway

Boulder Creek

Saratoga

Los Gatos

San Jose

Davenport

The Forest of Nisene Marks State Park

Santa Cruz

Soquel

Capitola

Aptos

Watsonville

Monterey Bay

Elkhorn Slough National Estuarine Marine Preserve

Moss Landing

Castroville

17-Mile Drive

Cypress Point

Pacific Grove

Salinas

Pebble Beach

Carmel Bay

Monterey

Carmel

Carmel Valley

0   10 mi

0   10 km

Point Sur

Big Sur

HIGHWAY 1: SAN FRANCISCO TO FORT BRAGG

Mendocino Coast Botanical Garden

Point Reyes National Seashore

THE PLAN

Distance: 177 miles

Time: 2-4 days

Good Overnight Options: San Francisco, Olema, Bodega Bay, Gualala, Mendocino, Fort Bragg

SAN FRANCISCO

The official Highway 1 heads straight through **San Francisco** along 19th Avenue through **Golden Gate Park** and the **Presidio** toward the **Golden Gate Bridge.** For a more scenic tour, watch for signs announcing exits for 35 North/Skyline Boulevard, then Ocean Beach/The Great Highway (past Lake Merced). The Great Highway follows the coast along the western border of San Francisco; you'll cruise past entrances to the **San Francisco Zoo, Golden Gate Park,** and the **Cliff House.** Hike out to **Point Lobos** or **Land's End** for awesome vistas, then drive through **Lincoln Park** and the **Palace of the Legion of Honor** and follow El Camino del Mar/Lincoln Boulevard all the way to the Golden Gate Bridge.

The best way to see San Francisco is on foot and public transportation. A **Union Square** stroll—complete with people-watching, window-shopping, and architecture-viewing—is a good first stop. In **Chinatown,** department stores give way to storefront temples, open-air markets, and delightful dim-sum shops. After lunch in one, catch a **Powell Street cable car** to the end of the line and get off to see the bay views and the antique arcade games at **Musée Mécanique** (the gem of otherwise mindless **Fisherman's Wharf**). For dinner and live music, try cosmopolitan **North Beach.**

SAN FRANCISCO TO POINT REYES

(approx. 37 miles)

Leaving the city the next day, your drive across the Golden Gate Bridge and a stop at a **Marin Headlands** overlook will yield memorable views (if fog hasn't socked in the bay). So will a hike in **Point Reyes National Seashore,** farther up Highway 1 (now called Shoreline Highway). On this wild swath of coast you'll likely be able to claim an unspoiled beach for yourself. You should expect company, however, around the lighthouse at the tip of Point Reyes because year-round views—and seasonal elephant seal- and whale-watching—draw crowds. If you have time, poke around tiny Olema, which has some excellent restaurants.

POINT REYES TO MENDOCINO

(approx. 131 miles)

Passing only a few minuscule towns, this next stretch of Highway 1 showcases the northern coast in all its rugged glory. The reconstructed compound of eerily foreign buildings at **Fort Ross State Historic Park** recalls the era of Russian fur trading in California. Pull into **Gualala** for an espresso, a sandwich, and a little human contact before rolling onward. After another 50 miles of tranquil state beaches and parks you'll return to civilization in **Mendocino.**

Golden Gate Bridge

Point Reyes National Seashore

TOP 5 PLACES TO LINGER

- San Francisco
- Marin Headlands
- Point Reyes National Seashore
- Fort Ross State Historic Park
- Mendocino

MENDOCINO TO FORT BRAGG

(approx. 9 miles)

Exploring Mendocino you may feel like you've fallen through a rabbit hole: the weather screams Northern California, but the 19th-century buildings—erected by homesick Yankee loggers—definitely say New England. Once you've browsed around the artsy shops, continue on to the **Mendocino Coast Botanical Gardens;** then travel back in time on the **Skunk Train,** which follows an old logging route from **Fort Bragg** deep into the redwood forest.

Leggett
Rockpoint
Westport
Laytonville
Fort Bragg
Mendocino Coast Botanical Gardens
Caspar
Mendocino
Little River
Willits
Albion
Elk
Navarro
Calpella
Point Arena
ANDERSON VALLEY
Philo
Ukiah
Manchester
Boonville
Point Arena
Anchor Bay
Yorkville
Hopland
Gualala
Kelseyville
Stewarts Point
Cloverdale
Horseshoe Cove
Salt Point State Park
Geyserville
Fort Ross State Hist. Park
Fort Ross
Healdsburg
Jenner
Duncan Point
Carmet
Santa Rosa
Calistoga
Bodega Bay
Sebastopol
Bodega Head
Bodega Bay
Tomales Point
Tomales
Tomales Bay
Marshall
Inverness
Petaluma
Sonoma
Point Reyes
Point Reyes Station
Drakes Bay
Olema
BOLINAS RIDGE
Point Reyes National Seashore
San Rafael
Bolinas
Bolinas Bay
Mt. Tamalpais
Stinson Beach
Richmond
Muir Beach
Marin Headlands
Golden Gate Nat'l. Rec. Area
Sausalito
Golden Gate Park
San Francisco
Oakland
FARALLON ISLANDS
PACIFIC OCEAN
Pacific Coast Highway

0   15 mi
0   15 km

GREAT ITINERARIES

SOUTHERN CALIFORNIA WITH KIDS, 7 DAYS

SoCal offers many opportunities to entertain the kids beyond the Magic Kingdom. LEGOLAND is a blast for kids 12 and under, and families can't beat the San Diego Zoo, and San Diego's historic Old Town.

Days 1–2: Disneyland

(45 minutes by car from LAX to Disneyland.)

Get out of Los Angeles International Airport as fast as you can. Pick up your rental car and head south on the I-405 freeway, which can be congested day or night, toward Orange County and **Disneyland.** Skirt the lines at the box office with advance-purchased tickets in hand and storm the gates of the Magic Kingdom. You can cram the highlights into a single day, but if you get a two-day ticket and stay the night you can see the parade and visit **Downtown Disney** before heading south. The **Grand Californian Hotel** is a top choice for lodging within the Disney Resort. If tackling Disneyland after a long flight is too much, head south from LAX to the surfer's haven at **Huntington Beach,** where you can relax at the beach and spend the night in one of several beachfront hotels before heading inland to Anaheim the next morning.

Day 3: LEGOLAND

(1 to 1½ hours by car from Huntington Beach or Anaheim, depending on traffic.)

Get an early start for your next rollercoaster ride at **LEGOLAND,** about an hour's drive south of Huntington Beach via the Pacific Coast Highway. Check into the **LEGOLAND Hotel** or the **Sheraton Carlsbad Resort & Spa;** both offer direct access to the park. LEGOLAND has a water park and aquarium in addition to the LEGO-based rides, shows, and roller coasters. The little ones can live out their fairy-tale fantasies and bigger ones can spend all day on waterslides, shooting water pistols, driving boats, or water fighting with pirates.

Day 4: La Jolla and San Diego

(La Jolla is just over an hour's drive from Carlsbad along scenic S21, or 40 minutes on the I-5 freeway; Downtown San Diego is a 20-minute drive from La Jolla.)

Take a leisurely drive south to San Diego by using the "old road," the original Pacific Coast Highway that hugs the shore all the way. It's a slow drive through Leucadia, Encinitas, Solana Beach, and Del Mar, all of which are popular surfing beaches. When you get to **La Jolla,** swing around the cove to see one of the area's most beautiful beaches. Look, but don't go in the water at the Children's Pool, as it's likely to be filled with barking seals. The **Birch Aquarium at Scripps** here offers a look at how scientists study the oceans.

Hop onto I–5 and head for Downtown **San Diego.** Go straight for the city's nautical heart by exploring the restored ships of the **Maritime Museum** at the waterfront in Downtown. Victorian buildings—and plenty of other tourists—surround you on a stroll through the **Gaslamp Quarter,** but the 21st-century is in full swing at the **Westfield Horton Plaza** retail and entertainment complex. Plant yourself at a Downtown hotel and graze your way through the neighborhood's many restaurants.

Day 5: San Diego Zoo

(10 minutes by car from Downtown San Diego.)

Malayan tapirs in a faux-Asian rain forest, polar bears in an imitation Arctic, and pandas frolicking in the trees—the **San Diego Zoo** maintains a vast and

varied collection of creatures in a world-renowned facility comprised of meticulously designed habitats. Come early, wear comfy shoes, and stay as long as you like.

Day 6: SeaWorld and Old Town
(From Downtown San Diego, both Sea-World and Old Town are 10 minutes by car.)

Two commercial and touristy sights are on the agenda today. **SeaWorld**, with its walk-through shark tanks, can be a lot of fun if you surrender to the experience. Also touristy, but with genuine historical significance, **Old Town** drips with Mexican and early Californian heritage. Soak it up in the plaza at **Old Town San Diego State Historic Park**, then browse the stalls and shops at **Fiesta de Reyes** and along San Diego Avenue. Unwind after a long day with dinner and margaritas at one of Old Town's many Mexican restaurants.

Day 7: Departure from San Diego or Los Angeles
(San Diego Airport is 10 minutes by car from Downtown. Depending on traffic, allow 2½–4 hours to drive from Downtown San Diego to LAX.)

Pack up your Mouseketeer gear and give yourself ample time to reach the airport. San Diego International Airport lies within a 10-minute drive from Old Town. Although you'll be driving on freeways the entire way to LAX, traffic is always heavy and you should allot at least a half day to get there.

PALM SPRINGS AND THE DESERT, 5 DAYS

The Palm Springs area is paradise for many. Most go for more than a good tan or to play golf on championship courses. Expect fabulous and funky spas, a dog-friendly atmosphere, and sparkling stars at night.

Day 1: Palm Springs
(Just over 2 hours by car from LAX, without traffic.)

Somehow in harmony with the harsh environment, mid-century-modern homes and businesses with clean, low-slung lines define the **Palm Springs** style. Although the desert cities comprise a trendy destination with beautiful hotels, fabulous multicultural food, abundant nightlife, and plenty of culture, a quiet atmosphere prevails. The city seems far away when you hike in hushed **Tahquitz** or **Indian Canyon**; cliffs and palm trees shelter rock art, irrigation works, and other remnants of Agua Caliente culture. If your boots aren't made for walking, you can always practice your golf game or indulge in some sublime or funky spa treatments at an area resort instead. Embrace the Palm Springs vibe and park yourself at the retro **Orbit In Hotel** or the legendary **Parker Palm Springs.** Alternatively, base yourself at the desert oasis, **La Quinta Resort,** about 40 minutes outside of downtown Palm Springs.

Day 2: Explore Palm Springs
(The Aerial Tram is 15 minutes by car from central Palm Springs. Plan at least a half-day for the excursion.)

If riding a tram up an 8,516-foot mountain for a stroll or even a snowball fight above the desert sounds like fun to you, then show up at the **Palm Springs Aerial Tramway** before the first morning tram leaves (later, the line can get discouragingly long). Afterward stroll through the **Palm Springs Art Museum** where you can see a shimmering display of contemporary studio glass, an array of enormous Native American baskets, and significant works of 20th-century sculpture by Henry Moore and others. After all that walking you may be ready for an early dinner. Nearly every restaurant in Palm Springs offers a happy hour, when you can sip a cocktail and nosh on a light entrée, usually for half price. Using your hotel as a base, take a few day-trips to discover the natural beauty of the desert.

Day 3: Joshua Tree National Park
(1 hour by car from Palm Springs.)

Due to its proximity to Los Angeles and the highway between Las Vegas and coastal cities, **Joshua Tree** is one of the most popular and accessible of the national parks. You can see most of it in a day, entering the park at the town of Joshua Tree, exploring sites along **Park Boulevard,** and exiting at **Twentynine Palms.** With its signature trees, piles of rocks, glorious spring wildflowers, starlit skies, and colorful pioneer history, the experience is a bit more like the Wild West than Sahara sand dunes.

Day 4: Anza-Borrego Desert State Park and the Salton Sea
(About 2 hours by car from Palm Springs.)

The **Salton Sea,** about 60 miles south of Palm Springs via I-10 and Highway 86S, is one of the largest inland seas on earth. This new sea, formed by the flooding of the Colorado River in 1905, attracts thousands of migrating birds and bird-watchers every fall. **Anza-Borrego Desert State Park** is the largest state park in California, with 600,000 acres of mostly untouched wilderness; it offers one of the best spring-wildflower displays in California and also displays a large collection of life-size bronze sculpture of animals that roamed this space millions of years ago. **Borrego Springs,** a tiny hamlet, lies in the center of it all. The desert is home to an archeological site, where scientists continue to uncover remnants of prehistoric animals ranging from mastodons to horses.

Day 5: Return to L.A.
(LAX is just over 2 hours by car from Palm Springs without traffic, but the drive often takes significantly more time. Allow plenty of extra time if catching a flight.)

If you intend to depart from LAX, plan for a full day of driving from the desert to the airport. Be prepared for heavy traffic at any time of day or night. If possible, opt to fly out of Palm Springs International or LA/Ontario International Airport instead.

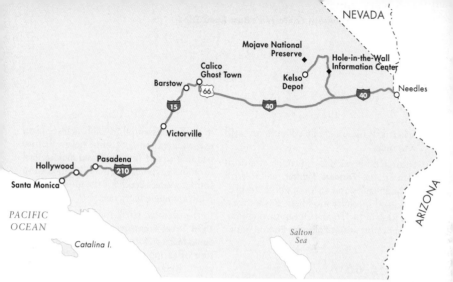

HOORAY FOR HOLLYWOOD, 4 DAYS

If you are a movie fan, there's no better place to see it all than L.A. Always keep your eyes out for a familiar face: you never know when you might spot a celebrity.

Day 1: Los Angeles

As soon as you land at LAX, make like a local and hit the freeway. Even if L.A.'s top-notch art, history, and science museums don't tempt you, the hodgepodge of art deco, Beaux-Arts, and futuristic architecture begs at least a drive-by. Heading east from Santa Monica, Wilshire Boulevard cuts through a historical and cultural cross section of the city. Two stellar sights on its Miracle Mile are the encyclopedic **Los Angeles County Museum of Art** and the fossil-filled **La Brea Tar Pits.** Come evening, the open-air **Farmers Market** and its many eateries hum. Hotels in Beverly Hills or West Hollywood beckon, just a few minutes away.

Day 2: Hollywood and the Movie Studios

(Avoid driving to the studios during rush hour. Studio tours vary in length—plan at least a half-day for the excursion.)

Every L.A. tourist should devote at least one day to the movies and take at least one studio tour in the San Fernando Valley. For fun, choose the special-effects theme park at **Universal Studios Hollywood;** for the nitty-gritty, choose **Warner Bros. Studios.** Nostalgic musts in Hollywood include the **Walk of Fame** along **Hollywood Boulevard** and the celebrity footprints cast in concrete outside **Grauman's Chinese Theatre** (now known as the TCL Chinese Theater). When evening arrives, the Hollywood scene boasts a bevy of trendy restaurants and nightclubs.

Days 3 and 4: Beverly Hills and Santa Monica

(15–20 minutes by car between destinations, but considerably longer in traffic.)

Even without that extensive art collection, the **Getty Center's** pavilion architecture, hilltop gardens, and frame-worthy L.A. views make it a dazzling destination. Descend to the sea via Santa Monica Boulevard for lunch along **Third Street Promenade,** followed by a ride on the historic carousel on the pier. The buff and the bizarre meet at **Venice Beach Oceanfront Walk** (strap on some Rollerblades if you want to join them!). **Rodeo Drive** in Beverly Hills specializes in exhibitionism with a heftier price tag, but voyeurs are still welcome.

Splurge on breakfast or brunch at a posh café in the **Farmers Market**, then stroll through aisles and aisles of gorgeous produce and specialty food before you take a last look at the Pacific Ocean through the camera obscura at **Palisades Park** in Santa Monica.

ROUTE 66 AND THE MOJAVE DESERT, 4 DAYS

Route 66 was the original road trip and California the ultimate destination. The Mother Road travels west from the Arizona border, skirting the Mojave Desert before passing through Los Angeles and ending at the Pacific Ocean. What makes this journey so compelling is actually what it lacks. Desolate stretches of road through windswept towns are reminders of the tough conditions faced by Dust-bowl pioneers, while faded neon signs and abandoned motels offer nostalgic glimpses of Route 66's heyday. Nearby, the solitary beauty of the Mojave National Preserve beckons with its volcanic rock formations, Joshua trees, and seemingly endless sand dunes.

Day 1: Santa Monica

By reversing the typical Route 66 journey and traveling from west to east, you can hit the road upon arrival at LAX, or spend a few days exploring Los Angeles first. Starting your journey off in **Santa Monica** may feel a bit like eating your dessert first. For road-trippers on Route 66, reaching the Pacific Ocean after a long dusty drive through the desert was certainly a treat. The official end of Route 66 is marked with a plaque in **Palisades Park**, on a bluff overlooking **Santa Monica State Beach**. Soak

in the quintessential SoCal beach scene on the wide expanse of sand below before heading to the famous **Santa Monica Pier**. From here, you can rent a bike and cruise south to **Venice Beach** for the ultimate people-watching experience.

In the evening, stroll the pedestrian-only **Third Street Promenade** and neighboring **Santa Monica Place** mall for a good selection of shopping, dining, and entertainment. Relax in luxury at the legendary **Shutters on the Beach**. Or, in keeping with the true Route 66 spirit, opt for the more modest motor lodge vibe of the **Sea Shore Motel**.

Day 2: Hollywood and Pasadena
(1½ hours by car from Santa Monica to Pasadena and another 1½–2 hours by car to Victorville.)

Heading inland through **Beverly Hills** and **Hollywood**, the remnants of Route 66 are easily overshadowed by the surrounding glitz and glamour. A stop at the **Hollywood Museum** or the **Hollywood Walk of Fame** will help transport you back in time to Tinseltown's golden age.

The route continues through **Pasadena**, with its stately homes and spacious gardens. Fans of Craftsman architecture won't want to miss a tour of the **Gamble House**, while a stroll around **Old Town Pasadena** is a great way to stretch your legs and grab a bite to eat.

Depending on your interests and how much sightseeing you've done, you might choose to stay in Pasadena for the night to enjoy a wider choice of dining and lodging options. Or, head to **Victorville** to maximize time on Route 66 tomorrow.

PACIFIC
OCEAN

Day 3: Route 66

(Barstow to Needles is 2 hours by car along I–40. However, add several more hours to trace Route 66. Plan on spending 1–2 hours at the Calico Ghost Town.)

Today is all about the drive. Hit the road early if you didn't spend the night in Victorville. First stop is the **California Route 66 Museum** in **Victorville**, where you'll learn all about the history of the Mother Road. Be sure to pick up a copy of their self-guided tour book and consult one of the many Route 66–related websites, such as ⊕ *www.historic66.com,* to help you navigate the old road as it crosses back and forth alongside Interstate 40 between Barstow and Needles. Abandoned service stations, shuttered motels, and faded signs dot the desert landscape in various states of alluring decay. Grab a meal at the famous **Baghdad Café** in Barstow. For a non–Route 66 related diversion spend a few hours exploring **Calico Ghost Town,** a restored old mining town just north of Barstow. In the evening, catch a flick at the **Skyline Drive-In Theatre.**

Accommodations in this area are mostly of the chain-motel variety. Victorville, Barstow, and Needles are your best bets for lodging.

Day 4: Mojave National Preserve

(There are several access points to the park along I–15 and I–40. Kelso Dunes Visitor Center is about 1½ hours by car from either Barstow or Needles. Stick to the major roads in the park, which are either paved or gravel—others require four-wheel drive.)

In the morning, head north from Route 66 into the beautiful and remote landscape of the **Mojave National Preserve.** Reaching the top of the stunning golden **Kelso Dunes** requires some athleticism, but your efforts will be rewarded with incredible scenery and the eerie sounds of "singing" sand. If you spent the night in Needles, explore the volcanic gas formations of **Hole-in-the-Wall** first. Farther north in the park, the Cima Road will bring you to the Teutonia Peak Trailhead and the largest concentration of Joshua trees in the world. Visitor centers at **Kelso Depot** and **Hole-in-the-Wall** provide information on additional sights, hiking trails, and campgrounds in the park.

There are several options for the next leg of your journey. You can drive back to Los Angeles in about 3 hours or drive onward to **Las Vegas** even faster. If you have more time, you can continue north and spend a few days in **Death Valley National Park,** or head south towards **Joshua Tree** and **Palm Springs** before making your way back to **Los Angeles.**

SANTA BARBARA WINE COUNTRY, 3 DAYS

It has been over a decade since the popular movie *Sideways* brought the Santa Barbara wine country to the world's attention, and interest in this wine growing area continues to grow. On this trip you will explore one of the most beautiful cities in the West, enjoy time along the gorgeous coast, and then head inland for a delightful wine-tasting adventure. This itinerary makes a perfect add-on to a trip to Los Angeles, or for those driving the coastal route between Los Angeles and San Francisco.

Day 1: Santa Barbara
(2 hours by car from LAX to Santa Barbara without traffic.)

Santa Barbara is a gem, combining elegance with a laid-back coastal vibe. It provides a tranquil escape from the congestion of Los Angeles, and a dose of sophistication to the largely rural central coast.

Start your day at the beautiful **Old Mission Santa Barbara**, known as the "Queen" of the 21 missions that comprise the California Mission Trail. From here, head to the waterfront and spend some time enjoying the wide stretch of sand at **East Beach** and a seafood lunch at one of the restaurants on **Stearns Wharf.**

Next stop is a tour of the **Santa Barbara County Courthouse** and the beautiful red-tile roofed buildings of the surrounding downtown. Don't miss the incredible views from the top of the courthouse tower.

Back on the ground, enjoy superb shopping along **State Street** and consider kicking off your wine tour early with some tastings along the **Urban Wine Trail**, a collection of tasting rooms spread over a few blocks between downtown and the beach. Enjoy the lively dining and nightlife scene downtown, or head towards tony **Montecito** for an elegant dinner or overnight stay at the ultra-exclusive (and expensive) **San Ysidro Ranch.**

Day 2: Santa Rita Hills, Lompoc, and Los Olivos
(Without stops, this route takes about 2 hours by car. Plan to linger, and to detour down side roads to reach the wineries.)

Take the scenic drive along the coast on Highway 101 before heading inland towards Buellton. Exit onto Santa Rosa Road to begin your loop through the Santa Rita Hills. This area's cooler climate produces top-notch Chardonnay and Pinot Noir. Vineyards line the loop as you head out on Santa Rosa Road and return on Highway 246 towards Buellton. **Lafond Winery and Vineyards, Alma Rosa Winery,** and **Ken Brown Wines** are just a few of the wineries found along this route. Don't miss a stop at the so-called **Lompoc Wine Ghetto**, located midway around the route. Several tasting rooms are clustered together in an industrial park downtown including well-regarded producers such as **Stolpman** and **Longoria.**

Back on Highway 101, head north about 6 miles before exiting towards **Los Olivos.** Here you can park the car and spend the rest of the day exploring on foot. Tasting rooms, galleries, boutiques and restaurants have made this former stagecoach town quite wine-country chic. **Carhartt Vineyard** and **Daniel Gehrs** are just two of the producers with tasting rooms in town.

Los Olivos is a good base to overnight in, or stay just outside of town at the lovely **Ballard Inn.** Or, dine at the chic locavore **Root 246** restaurant and stay at the **Hotel Corque** in nearby **Solvang.**

Days 3: Solvang, Foxen Canyon, and the Santa Ynez Valley
(The drive from Santa Ynez to Santa Barbara is about 45 minutes by car via Hwy. 154.)

Start the next morning with pastries at the Danish town of **Solvang,** 10 minutes south of Los Olivos. The collection of windmills and distinct half-timber architecture of this village is charming, even if it is touristy. Spend some time exploring the town before hitting the road.

The towns of Los Olivos, Santa Ynez, and Solvang are located just a few minutes apart, with wineries spread between them in an area known as the Santa Ynez Valley. Heading north from Los Olivos, the Foxen Canyon wine trail extends all the way to Santa Maria. Expect some backtracking along your route today as you wind between the towns and venture into Foxen Canyon. The tour at **Firestone Vineyard** is worthwhile, but very popular. The tasting rooms throughout the Santa Ynez region can get crowded, but there are plenty to choose from—if you see a

tour bus parked outside one winery, just keep driving to the next one. Don't blink or you might miss the tiny town of **Santa Ynez** itself, but it is worth a wander or a stop for lunch.

When you've had your fill of the wine region, take scenic Highway 154 over the San Marcos Pass and back to Santa Barbara. Wind down the day with a stroll along the beach, and perhaps one last glass of wine at sunset.

MONTEREY BAY, CARMEL, AND BIG SUR, 4 DAYS

In a nutshell, this drive is all about the jaw-dropping scenery of the Pacific Coast. Visitors pressed for time often make the drive from Monterey through Big Sur in one day. However, those who linger will be rewarded with more time to venture off the road and to enjoy the solitude of Big Sur once the day-trippers have gone.

Day 1: Monterey

Monterey, with its federally protected national marine sanctuary and its world-renowned aquarium, is the perfect spot to kick off your tour of the coast. Start the day with a visit to the enthralling **Monterey Bay Aquarium.** Exhibits such as the dramatic three-story kelp forest near the entrance give you a true sense of the local marine environment. For an even closer encounter, take to the water yourself on a kayak or whale watching tour. While undoubtedly touristy, the shops and galleries of **Cannery Row** still make for an interesting diversion and it's fun to watch the colony of sea lions at **Fisherman's Wharf**. There are plenty of excellent dining and lodging choices within walking distance of downtown, so enjoy a seafood dinner and an evening stroll before hitting the road the next morning.

Day 2: 17-Mile Drive and Carmel-By-The-Sea
(The 17-Mile Drive's Pacific Grove entrance gate is 15 minutes by car from Monterey.)

If your visit falls between October and March, begin your drive with a quick detour to visit the migrating monarch butterflies at the **Monarch Grove Sanctuary** in the charming Victorian town of **Pacific Grove**.

Enter the scenic **17-Mile Drive** through the tollgate off Sunset Drive in Pacific Grove. This scenic road winds its way along the coast through a hushed and refined landscape of stunning homes and the renowned golf links at **Pebble Beach**. Perhaps the most famous (and photographed) resident is the **Lone Cypress**, which has come to symbolize the solitude and natural beauty of the coast. Even though the drive is only 17 miles, plan on taking your time. If you stop for lunch or souvenir shopping, enquire about a refund on the entry toll.

Upon exiting the drive, continue south to the charming town of **Carmel-by-the-Sea**. Spend the afternoon browsing the town's boutiques and galleries before walking to **Carmel Beach** for sunset and dinner at one of the many fine restaurants here. Similarly, there is no shortage of stylish, but pricey, lodging. Venture outside of the village for less expensive accommodation.

Day 3: Big Sur
(30 minutes by car.)

The coastal drive through **Big Sur** is justifiably one of the most famous stretches of road in the world. The winding curves, endless views and scenic waypoints are the stuff of road trip legend. Keep your camera handy, fill up the tank and prepare to be wowed. Traffic can easily back up along the route and drivers should take caution navigating the road's twists and turns. While you will only drive about 30 miles today, allow several hours for hikes and stops.

Heading into Big Sur you will first come upon the extremely photogenic **Bixby Creek Bridge**. Pull over in the turnout on the north side of the bridge to get that perfect shot. About 10 miles down the road look for a small cluster of services known as Big Sur Village just before the entrance to **Pfeiffer Big Sur State Park**, the perfect place to stop for a hike.

One mile south of the park, watch carefully for the sharp turnout and unmarked road leading to **Pfeiffer Beach**. Following the unpaved road 2 miles toward the sea you may question whether you are lost, but your perseverance will be rewarded when you reach the secluded beach with its signature rocky arch just offshore. Don't miss it!

There are several lodging options around this portion of Big Sur, ranging from rustic to luxurious. If room rates at the legendary **Post Ranch Inn** are not in your budget, consider splurging on the nine-course tasting menu at its spectacular cliff-side **Sierra Mar** restaurant instead. Alternatively, the

2

terrace at **Nepenthe** offers decent food and gorgeous views at a lower price point. Be sure to check the time for sunset when making your dinner reservation.

Day 4: Big Sur to Cambria
(About 2 hours by car. Allow ample time for hiking and 2 hours to tour Hearst Castle.)

Start the morning off with a hike in **Julia Pfeiffer Burns State Park,** popular for its waterfall tumbling dramatically into the sea. Back on the road, several scenic overlooks will beckon as you head through the southern stretch of Big Sur. Treasure hunters should consider a stop at **Jade Cove.**

As you enter **San Simeon,** don't miss the **Piedras Blancas Elephant Seal Rookery.** Depending on your timing, you might catch a late afternoon tour at **Hearst Castle.** If not, you can make a reservation for a tour early the following morning. End the day with a walk at **Moonstone Beach** in the town of **Cambria,** 10 miles south of the castle and overnight in one of the reasonably priced lodgings here.

From here, you can continue your travels south through the central coast to **Santa Barbara.** Or head inland to visit the **Paso Robles** wine region before returning to Monterey via Highway 101.

SAN DIEGO

WELCOME TO SAN DIEGO

TOP REASONS TO GO

★ **Beautiful beaches:** San Diego's shore shimmers with crystalline Pacific waters rolling up to some of the prettiest stretches of sand on the West Coast.

★ **Good eats:** Taking full advantage of the region's bountiful vegetables, fruits, herbs, and seafood, San Diego's chefs dazzle and delight diners with inventive California-colorful cuisine.

★ **History lessons:** The well-preserved and recon-structed historic sites in California's first European settlement help you imagine what the area was like when explorers first arrived.

★ **Stellar shopping:** The Gaslamp Quarter, Seaport Village, Coronado, Old Town, La Jolla . . . no matter where you go in San Diego, you'll find great places to do a little browsing.

★ **Urban oasis:** Balboa Park's 1,200 acres contain world-class museums and the San Diego Zoo, but also well-groomed lawns and gardens and wild, undeveloped canyons.

1 Downtown. San Diego's Downtown area is delight-fully urban and accessible, filled with walkable A-list attractions like the Gaslamp Quarter and the waterfront.

2 Balboa Park. San Diego's cultural heart is where you'll find most of the city's museums and its world-famous zoo.

3 Old Town and Uptown. California's first permanent European settlement is now preserved as a state historic park in Old Town. Uptown is composed of several smaller neighborhoods that showcase a unique blend of historical charm and modern urban community.

4 Mission Bay and Beaches. Home to 27 miles of shoreline, this 4,600 acre aquatic park is San Diego's monument to sports and fitness. SeaWorld lies south of the bay.

5 La Jolla. This luxe, bluff-top enclave fittingly means "the jewel" in Spanish. Come here for fantastic upscale shopping and unspoiled stretches of the coast.

6 Point Loma and Coronado. Home to the Hotel Del, Coronado's island-like isthmus is a favorite celebrity haunt. Visit the site of the first European landfall on Point Loma.

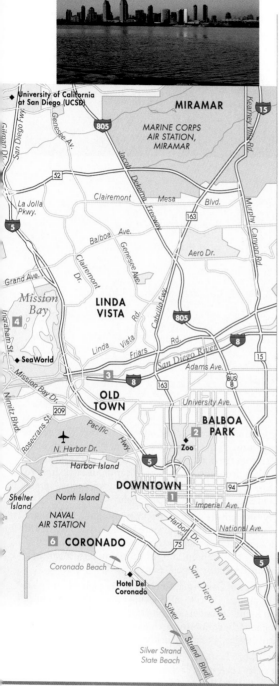

GETTING ORIENTED

3

Exploring San Diego may be an endless adventure, but there are limitations, especially if you don't have a car. San Diego is more a chain of separate communities than a cohesive city, and many of the major attractions are miles apart. Walking is good for getting an up-close look at neighborhoods like the Gaslamp Quarter, but true Southern Californians use the freeways that criss-cross the county. Interstate 5 runs a direct north–south route through the coastal communities from Orange County in the north to the Mexican border. Interstates 805 and 15 do much the same inland. Interstate 8 is the main east–west route. Routes 163, 52, and 94 serve as connectors.

Updated by Claire Deeks van der Lee, Maren Dougherty, Casey Hatfield-Chiotti, Mary Hellman James, Ron James, Jeff Terich, and Bobbi Zane

San Diego is a vacationer's paradise, complete with idyllic year-round temperatures and 70 miles of pristine coastline. Recognized as one of the nation's leading family destinations, with LEGOLAND and the San Diego Zoo, San Diego is equally attractive to those in search of art, history, world-class shopping, and culinary exploration. San Diego's beaches are legendary, offering family-friendly sands, killer surf breaks, and spectacular scenery. San Diego's cultural sophistication often surprises visitors, as the city is better known for its laid-back vibe. Tourists come for some fun in the sun, only to discover a city with much greater depth.

San Diego is a big California city—second only to Los Angeles in population—with a small-town feel. San Diego's many neighborhoods offer diverse adventures: from the tony boutiques in La Jolla to the yoga and surf shops of Encinitas; from the subtle sophistication of Little Italy to the flashy nightlife of the Downtown Gaslamp Quarter, each community adds flavor and flair to San Diego's personality.

San Diego County also covers a lot of territory, roughly 400 square miles of land and sea. To the north and south of the city are its famed beaches. Inland, a succession of chaparral-covered mesas is punctuated with deep-cut canyons that step up to forested mountains, separating the coast from the arid Anza-Borrego Desert.

Known as the birthplace of California, San Diego was claimed for Spain by explorer Juan Rodríguez Cabrillo in 1542 and eventually came under Mexican rule. You'll find reminders of San Diego's Spanish and Mexican heritage throughout the region—in architecture and place-names, in distinctive Mexican cuisine, and in the historic buildings of Old Town.

In 1867 developer Alonzo Horton, who called the town's bay front "the prettiest place for a city I ever saw," began building a hotel, a plaza, and prefab homes on 960 Downtown acres. A remarkable number of these buildings are preserved in San Diego's historic Gaslamp Quarter today. The city's fate was sealed in the 1920s when the U.S. Navy, impressed by the city's excellent harbor and temperate climate, decided to build a destroyer base on San Diego Bay. Today, the military operates many bases and installations throughout the county (which, added together, form the largest military base in the world) and continues to be a major contributor to the local economy.

PLANNING

WHEN TO GO

San Diego's weather is so ideal that most locals shrug off the high cost of living and relatively lower wages as a "sunshine tax." Along the coast, average temperatures range from the mid-60s to the high 70s, with clear skies and low humidity. Annual rainfall is minimal, less than 10 inches per year.

The peak season for sun seekers is July through October. In July and August, the mercury spikes and everyone spills outside. From mid-December to mid-March, whale-watchers can glimpse migrating gray whales frolicking in the Pacific. In spring and early summer, a marine layer hugs the coastline for much or all of the day (locals call it "June Gloom"), which can be dreary and disappointing for those who were expecting to bask in Southern California sunshine.

GETTING HERE AND AROUND

AIR TRAVEL

The major airport is San Diego International Airport (SAN), called Lindbergh Field locally. Major airlines depart and arrive at Terminal 1 and Terminal 2; commuter flights identified on your ticket with a 3000-sequence flight number depart from a third commuter terminal. A red shuttle bus provides free transportation between terminals.

Airport San Diego International Airport ✉ *3225 N. Harbor Dr., off I-5,* ☎ *619/400-2400* ⊕ *www.san.org.*

Airport Transfers Cloud 9/SuperShuttle ✉ *123 Caminio de la Riena,* ☎ *800/974-8885* ⊕ *www.cloud9shuttle.com.* **San Diego Transit** ☎ *619/233-3004* ⊕ *transit.511sd.com.*

BUS AND TROLLEY TRAVEL

Under the umbrella of the Metropolitan Transit System, there are two major transit agencies in the area: San Diego Transit and North County Transit District (NCTD). The bright-red trolleys of the San Diego Trolley light-rail system operate on three lines that serve Downtown San Diego, Mission Valley, Old Town, South Bay, the U.S. border, and East County. The trolley system connects with San Diego Transit bus routes—connections are posted at each trolley station.

San Diego Transit bus fares range from $2.25 to $5; North County Transit District bus fares are $1.75. You must have exact change in coins and/or bills. Pay upon boarding. Transfers are not included; the

$5 day pass is the best option for most bus travel and can be purchased on board.

San Diego Trolley tickets cost $2.50 and are good for two hours, but for one-way travel only. For a round-trip journey or longer, day passes are available for $5.

Bus and Trolley Information North County Transit District ☎ 760/966-6500 ⊕ www.gonctd.com. **San Diego Transit** ☎ 619/233-3004 ⊕ transit.511sd.com. **Transit Store** ✉ 102 Broadway ☎ 619/234-1060 ⊕ www.sdmts.com.

CAR TRAVEL

A car is necessary for getting around greater San Diego on the sprawling freeway system and for visiting the North County beaches, mountains, and Anza Borrego Desert. Driving around San Diego County is pretty simple: most major attractions are within a few miles of the Pacific Ocean. Interstate 5, which stretches from Canada to the Mexican border, bisects San Diego. Interstate 8 provides access from Yuma, Arizona, and points east. Drivers coming from the Los Angeles area, Nevada, and the mountain regions beyond can reach San Diego on I–15. During rush hour there are jams on I–5 and on I–15 between I–805 and Escondido.

There are border inspection stations along major highways in San Diego County. Travel with your driver's license, and passport if you're an international traveler, in case you're asked to pull into one.

TAXI TRAVEL

Fares vary among companies. If you are heading to the airport from a hotel, ask about the flat rate, which varies according to destination; otherwise you'll be charged by the mile (which works out to $15 or so from any Downtown location). Taxi stands are at shopping centers and hotels; otherwise you must call and reserve a cab. The companies listed *below* don't serve all areas of San Diego County. If you're going somewhere other than Downtown, ask if the company serves that area.

Taxi Companies Orange Cab ☎ 619/223-5555 ⊕ www.orangecabsandiego. com. **Silver Cabs** ☎ 619/280-5555 ⊕ www.sandiegosilvercab.com. **Yellow Cab** ☎ 619/444-4444 ⊕ www.driveu.com.

TRAIN TRAVEL

Amtrak serves Downtown San Diego's Santa Fe Depot with daily trains to and from Los Angeles, Santa Barbara, and San Luis Obispo. Amtrak trains stop in San Diego North County at Solana Beach and Oceanside. Coaster commuter trains, which run between Oceanside and San Diego Monday through Saturday, stop at the same stations as Amtrak as well as others. The frequency is about every half hour during the weekday rush hour, with four trains on Saturday. One-way fares are $4 to $5.50, depending on the distance traveled. The Sprinter runs between Oceanside and Escondido, with many stops along the way.

Metrolink operates high-speed rail service between the Oceanside Transit Center and Union Station in Los Angeles.

Information Amtrak ☎ 800/872-7245 ⊕ www.amtrak.com. **Coaster** ☎ 760/966-6500 ⊕ www.gonctd.com/coaster. **Metrolink** ☎ 800/371-5465 ⊕ www.metrolinktrains.com.

TOURS

BIKE TOURS

Biking is popular in San Diego. You can find trails along the beach, in Mission Bay, and throughout the mountains.

Secret San Diego. Taking in spectacular views of the beach, bay, and skyline, these bike rides, offered by Where You Want to Be Tours, cover everything from historic neighborhoods to historic Highway 101. The walking tours and Rent-a-Local custom tours are popular options as well. ⊠ *611 K St., #B224,* ☎ *619/917–6037* ⊕ *www.wheretours.com* ✉ *From $45.*

BOAT TOURS

Visitors to San Diego can get a great overview of the city from the water. Tour companies offer a range of harbor cruises, from one-hour jaunts to dinner and dancing cruises. In season, whale-watching voyages are another popular option.

Flagship Cruises and Events. One- and two-hour tours of the San Diego harbor loop north or south from the Broadway Pier throughout the day. Other offerings include dinner and dance cruises, brunch cruises, and winter whale-watching tours. ⊠ *990 N. Harbor Dr., Embarcadero,* ☎ *619/234–4111* ⊕ *www.flagshipsd.com* ✉ *From $23.*

H&M Landing. From mid-December to March, this outfitter offers three-hour tours to spot migrating gray whales just off the San Diego coast. From June to October, six-hour cruises search for the gigantic blue whales that visit the California coast in summer. Winter gray whale cruises are offered daily; summer blue whale tours are available Thursday, Saturday, and Sunday. ⊠ *2803 Emerson St.,* ☎ *619/222–1144* ⊕ *www.hmlanding.com* ✉ *From $45.*

Hornblower Cruises & Events. One- and two-hour cruises around San Diego harbor depart from the Embarcadero several times a day and alternate between the northern and southern portion of the bay. If you're hoping to spot some sea lions, take the North Bay route. Dinner and brunch cruises are also offered, as well as whale-watching tours in winter. ⊠ *970 N. Harbor Dr.,* ☎ *619/234–8687, 800/668–4322* ⊕ *www.hornblower.com* ✉ *From $23.*

San Diego Seal Tours. This amphibious tour drives along the Embarcadero before splashing into the San Diego Harbor for a cruise. The 90-minute tours depart from Seaport Village year-round, and from outside the Maritime Museum seasonally. Call for daily departure times and locations. ⊠ *500 Kettner Blvd., Embarcadero,* ☎ *619/298–8687* ⊕ *www.sealtours.com* ✉ *$39.*

Seaforth Boat Rentals. For those seeking a private tour on the water, this company can provide a skipper along with your boat rental. Options include harbor cruises, whale-watching, and sunset sails. Seaforth has five locations and a diverse fleet of sail and motorboats to choose from. ⊠ *1641 Quivira Rd., Mission Bay,* ☎ *888/834–2628* ⊕ *www.seaforthboatrental.com* ✉ *From $225.*

BUS AND TROLLEY TOURS

For those looking to cover a lot of ground in a limited time, narrated trolley tours include everything from Balboa Park to Coronado. To venture farther afield, consider a coach tour to the desert, Los Angeles, or even Baja, Mexico.

DayTripper. Single- and multiday trips throughout Southern California, the Southwest, and Baja depart from San Diego year-round. Popular day trips include the Getty Museum, and theater performances in Los Angeles. Call or check website for pickup locations. ☎ *619/299–5777, 800/679–8747 ⊕ www.daytripper.com ⌨ From $75.*

Five Star Tours. Private and group sightseeing bus tour options around San Diego and beyond include everything from the San Diego Zoo to Brewery tours and trips to Baja, Mexico. ✉ *1050 Kettner Blvd., ☎ 619/232–5040 ⊕ www.fivestartours.com ⌨ From $48.*

Old Town Trolley Tours. Combining points of interest with local history, trivia, and fun anecdotes, this hop-on, hop-off trolley tour provides an entertaining overview of the city and offers easy access to all the highlights. The tour is narrated, and you can get on and off as you please. Stops include Old Town, Seaport Village, the Gaslamp Quarter, Coronado, Little Italy, and Balboa Park. The trolley leaves every 30 minutes, operates daily, and takes two hours to make a full loop. ☎ *619/298–8687 ⊕ www.trolleytours.com/san-diego ⌨ From $35.10.*

San Diego Scenic Tours. Half- and full-day bus tours of San Diego and Tijuana depart daily, and some include a harbor cruise. Tours depart from several hotels around town. ☎ *858/273–8687 ⊕ www. sandiegoscenictours.com ⌨ From $38.*

WALKING TOURS

Several fine walking tours are available on weekdays or weekends; upcoming walks are usually listed in the *San Diego Reader.*

Coronado Walking Tours. Departing from the Glorietta Bay Inn at 11 am Tuesday, Thursday, and Saturday, this 90-minute stroll through Coronado's historic district takes in the island's mansions, old Tent City, the Hotel del Coronado, and the castles and cottages that line the beautiful beach. Reservations are recommended. ✉ *1630 Glorietta Blvd., ☎ 619/435–5993 ⊕ coronadowalkingtour.com ⌨ $12.*

Gaslamp Quarter Historical Foundation. Two-hour walking tours of the downtown historic district depart from the William Heath Davis House at 11 am Tuesday, Thursday, and Saturday. ✉ *410 Island Ave., ☎ 619/233–4692 ⊕ www.gaslampquarter.org ⌨ $15.*

Balboa Park Offshoot Tours. On Saturday at 10 am, free, hour-long walks start from the Balboa Park Visitor Center. The tour's focus rotates weekly, covering topics such as the park's history, palm trees, and desert vegetation. Reservations are not required, but no tours are scheduled between Thanksgiving and the New Year. ✉ *1549 El Prado, Balboa Park, ☎ 619/239–0512 ⊕ www.balboapark.org ⌨ Free.*

Urban Safaris. Led by longtime San Diego resident Patty Fares, these two-hour Saturday walks through diverse neighborhoods like Hillcrest, Ocean Beach, and Point Loma are popular with tourists and locals alike. The tours, which always depart from a neighborhood coffee-house, focus on art, history, and ethnic eateries, among other topics. Reservations are required, and private walks can be arranged during the week. ☎ *619/944–9255* ⊕ *www.walkingtoursofsandiego.com* ✄ *$10.*

VISITOR INFORMATION

For general information and brochures before you go, contact the San Diego Tourism Authority, which publishes the helpful *San Diego Visitors Planning Guide.* When you arrive, stop by one of the local visitor centers for general information.

Citywide Contacts San Diego Tourism Authority ☎ *619/232–3101* ⊕ *www. sandiego.org.* **San Diego Tourism Authority International Visitor Information Center** ✉ *1140 N. Harbor Dr., Downtown,* ☎ *619/236–1212* ⊕ *www. sandiego.org.*

EXPLORING SAN DIEGO

DOWNTOWN

Nearly written off in the 1970s, today Downtown San Diego is a testament to conservation and urban renewal. Once derelict Victorian storefronts now house the hottest restaurants, and the *Star of India,* the world's oldest active sailing ship, almost lost to scrap, floats regally along the Embarcadero. Like many modern U.S. cities, Downtown San Diego's story is as much about its rebirth as its history. Although many consider Downtown to be the 16½-block Gaslamp Quarter, it's actually comprised of eight neighborhoods, including East Village, Little Italy, and Embarcadero.

GASLAMP QUARTER

Considered the liveliest of the Downtown neighborhoods, the Gaslamp Quarter's 4th and 5th avenues are peppered with trendy nightclubs, swanky lounge bars, chic restaurants, and boisterous sports pubs. The Gaslamp has the largest collection of commercial Victorian-style buildings in the country. Despite this, when the move for Downtown redevelopment gained momentum in the 1970s, there was talk of bulldozing them and starting from scratch. In response, concerned history buffs, developers, architects, and artists formed the Gaslamp Quarter Council to clean up and preserve the quarter. The majority of the quarter's landmark buildings are on 4th and 5th avenues, between Island Avenue and Broadway.

WORTH NOTING

Gaslamp Museum at the William Heath Davis House. The oldest wooden house in San Diego houses the Gaslamp Quarter Historical Foundation, the district's curator. Before developer Alonzo Horton came to town, Davis, a prominent San Franciscan, had made an unsuccessful attempt to develop the waterfront area. In 1850 he had this prefab saltbox-style house, built in Maine, shipped around Cape Horn and assembled in San Diego (it originally stood at State and Market streets). Ninety-minute walking tours of the historic district leave from the house on Saturday

Be sure to enjoy a walk along San Diego's lovely waterfront sometime during your visit.

at 11 am and cost $15. If you can't time your visit with the tour, a self-guided tour map is available for $2. ✉ *410 Island Ave., at 4th Ave., Gaslamp Quarter,* ☎ *619/233–4692* ⊕ *www.gaslampquarter.org* ✉ *$5* ⊙ *Tues.–Sat. 10–5, Sun. noon–4.*

EMBARCADERO

The Embarcadero cuts a scenic swath along the harbor front and connects today's Downtown San Diego to its maritime routes. The bustle of Embarcadero comes less these days from the activities of fishing folk than from the throngs of tourists, but this waterfront walkway, stretching from the Convention Center to the Maritime Museum, remains the nautical soul of the city. There are several seafood restaurants here, as well as sea vessels of every variety—cruise ships, ferries, tour boats, and navy destroyers.

A huge revitalization project is underway along the northern Embarcadero. The overhaul will create a wide esplanade with gardens, shaded pavilions, and public art installations along the water as well as a new information center building. In mid-2014, San Diego unveiled the new Waterfront Park located adjacent to the County Administration Building. This 12-acre expanse includes a large green space, sprawling children's play area, and a spectacular interactive fountain that's perfect for cooling off on hot sunny days.

TOP ATTRACTIONS

FAMILY

Fodor's Choice

★

Maritime Museum. From sailing ships to submarines, the Maritime Museum is a must for anyone with an interest in nautical history. This collection of restored and replica ships affords a fascinating glimpse of San Diego during its heyday as a commercial seaport.

Highlights

The jewel of the collection, the *Star of India*, is often considered a symbol of the city. An iron windjammer built in 1863, the *Star of India* made 21 trips around the world in the late 1800s, when it traveled the East Indian trade route, shuttled immigrants from England to New Zealand, and served the Alaskan salmon trade. Saved from the scrap yard and painstakingly restored, the *Star of India* is the oldest active iron sailing ship in the world.

The popular HMS *Surprise,* purchased in 2004, is a replica of an 18th-century British Royal Navy frigate and was used in the Academy Award–winning *Master and Commander: The Far Side of the World.*

The museum's headquarters are on the *Berkeley,* an 1898 steam-driven ferryboat, which served the Southern Pacific Railroad in San Francisco until 1958. Its ornate detailing carefully restored, the main deck serves as a floating museum, with permanent exhibits on West Coast maritime history and complementary rotating exhibits.

Two submarines are featured at the museum: a *Soviet B-39* "Foxtrot" class submarine and the USS *Dolphin* research submarine. Take a peek at the harbor from a periscope, get up close with the engine control room, and wonder at the tight living quarters onboard.

Tips

Weekend sails (and Friday in summer) on the *Californian,* typically from noon to 4, cost $60 for adults; buy tickets online or at the museum on the day of sail. Arrive at least an hour early on sunny days for a spot onboard.

Cruise San Diego Bay for only $5 plus museum admission on the 1914 Pilot boat. The 45-minute narrated tours are offered at several times.

Partnering with the museum, the renowned yacht America also offers sails on the bay, and whale-watching excursions in winter. Times and prices vary.

Parties of eight or more should call ahead for special group admission and a guided two-hour tour. Exploring the submarines requires climbing through several midsize hatches; wear flat shoes and pants.

Keep an eye out for the workshop onboard the Berkley where volunteers build extraordinary model ships. ⊠ *1492 N. Harbor Dr., Embarcadero,* ☎ *619/234–9153* ⊕ *www.sdmaritime.org* ⊠ *$16 includes entry to all ships except Californian, $5 more for Pilot Boat Bay Cruise* ☉ *Daily 9–8.*

Fodor's Choice ★ **Museum of Contemporary Art San Diego (MCASD).** At the Downtown branch of the city's contemporary art museum (the original is in La Jolla), explore the works of international and regional artists in a modern, urban space. The Jacobs Building—formerly the baggage building at the historic Santa Fe Depot—features large gallery spaces, high ceilings, and natural lighting, giving artists the flexibility to create large-scale installations. MCASD's collection includes many Pop Art, minimalist, and conceptual works from the 1950s to the present. The museum showcases both established and emerging artists in temporary exhibitions, and has permanent, site-specific commissions by Jenny Holzer and Richard

Serra. ■TIP→ Admission, good for seven days, includes the Downtown and La Jolla locations. ✉ *1100 and 1001 Kettner Blvd., Downtown,* ☎ *858/454–3541* ⊕ *www.mcasd.org* 🎫 *$10; free 3rd Thurs. of the month 5–7* ⊗ *Thurs.–Tues. 11–5; 3rd Thurs. until 7.*

FAMILY

Fodor'sChoice

★

The New Children's Museum (NCM). The NCM blends contemporary art with unstructured play to create an environment that appeals to children as well as adults. The 50,000-square-foot structure was constructed from recycled building materials, operates on solar energy, and is convection-cooled by an elevator shaft. It also features a nutrition- and eco-conscious café. Interactive exhibits include designated areas for toddlers and teens, as well as plenty of activities for the entire family. Several art workshops are offered each day, as well as hands-on studios where visitors are encouraged to create their own art. The studio projects change frequently and the entire museum changes exhibits every 18 to 24 months, so there is always something new to explore. The adjoining 1-acre park and playground is across from the convention center trolley stop. ✉ *200 W. Island Ave., Embarcadero,* ☎ *619/233–8792* ⊕ *www.thinkplaycreate.org* 🎫 *$10, 2nd Sun. each month free 10–4* ⊗ *During school year: Mon. and Wed.–Sat. 10–4, Sun. noon–4, closed Tues.; summer hours: Mon.–Sat. 10–4, Sun. noon–4.*

FAMILY

Seaport Village. You'll find some of the best views of the harbor at Seaport Village, three bustling shopping plazas designed to reflect the New England clapboard and Spanish Mission architectural styles of early California. On a prime stretch of waterfront the dining, shopping, and entertainment complex connects the harbor with hotel towers and the convention center. Specialty shops offer everything from a kite store and swing emporium to a shop devoted to hot sauces. You can dine at snack bars and restaurants, many with harbor views.

Live music can be heard daily from noon to 4 at the main food court. Additional free concerts take place every Sunday from 1 to 4 at the East Plaza Gazebo. If you happen to visit San Diego in late November or early December, you might be lucky enough to catch Surfing Santa's Arrival and even have your picture taken with Santa on his wave. In late March or early April, the Seaport Buskers Fest presents an array of costumed street performers. The **Seaport Village Carousel** (rides $3) has 54 animals, hand-carved and hand-painted by Charles Looff in 1895.

Across the street, the newly opened **Headquarters at Seaport District** converted the historic police headquarters into several trendsetting shops and restaurants, including the local *Urban Beach House* for surfer-chic apparel, alongside outposts of Mario Batali's *Pizzeria Mozza* and L.A. celeb boutique *Kitson.*

Seaport Village's shops are open daily 10 to 9 in winter and 10 to 10 in summer; a few eateries open early for breakfast. The Headquarters' shops are open Monday to Saturday from 10 to 9, and 10 to 8 on Sunday; restaurants may have extended hours. ✉ *849 W. Harbor Dr., Downtown,* ☎ *619/235–4014 office and events hotline* ⊕ *www. seaportvillage.com.*

Fodor'sChoice

★

USS Midway Museum. After 47 years of worldwide service, the retired USS *Midway* began a new tour of duty on the south side of the Navy pier in 2004. Launched in 1945, the 1,001-foot-long ship was the largest in the world for the first 10 years of its existence. The most visible landmark on the north Embarcadero, it now serves as a floating interactive museum—an appropriate addition to the town that is home to one-third of the Pacific fleet and the birthplace of naval aviation. A free audio tour guides you through the massive ship while offering insight from former sailors. As you clamber through passageways and up and down ladder wells, you'll get a feel for how the *Midway*'s 4,500 crew members lived and worked on this "city at sea."

Though the entire tour is impressive, you'll really be wowed when you step out onto the 4-acre flight deck—not only the best place to get an idea of the ship's scale, but also one of the most interesting vantage points for bay and city skyline views. An F-14 Tomcat jet fighter is just one of many vintage aircraft on display. Free guided tours of the bridge and primary flight control, known as "the Island," depart every 10 minutes from the flight deck. Many of the docents stationed throughout the ship served in the Navy, some even on the *Midway*, and they are eager to answer questions or share stories. The museum also offers multiple flight simulators for an additional fee, climb-aboard cockpits, and interactive exhibits focusing on naval aviation. There is a gift shop and a café with pleasant outdoor seating. This is a wildly popular stop, with most visits lasting several hours. △ **Despite efforts to provide accessibility throughout the ship, some areas can only be reached via fairly steep steps; a video tour of these areas is available on the hangar deck.** ✉ *910 N. Harbor Dr., Embarcadero,* ☎ *619/544–9600* ⊕ *www.midway.org* ✈ *$20* ☉ *Daily 10–5; opens at 9:30 in July and Aug.; last admission 4 pm.*

EAST VILLAGE

The most ambitious of the Downtown projects is East Village, not far from the Gaslamp Quarter, and encompassing 130 blocks between the railroad tracks up to J Street, and from 6th Avenue east to around 10th Street. Sparking the rebirth of this former warehouse district was the 2004 construction of the San Diego Padres' baseball stadium, PETCO Park. As the city's largest Downtown neighborhood, East Village is continually broadening its boundaries with its urban design of red-brick cafés, spacious galleries, rooftop bars, sleek hotels, and warehouse restaurants.

LITTLE ITALY

Unlike many tourist-driven communities, the charming neighborhood of Little Italy is authentic to its roots, from the Italian-speaking residents to the imported delicacies. The main thoroughfare—from India Street to Kettner Boulevard—is filled with lively cafés, gelato shops, bakeries, and restaurants. Art lovers can browse gallery showrooms, while shoppers adore the Fir Street cottages. Home to many in San Diego's design community, Little Italy exudes a sense of urban cool.

BALBOA PARK AND SAN DIEGO ZOO

Overlooking Downtown and the Pacific Ocean, 1,200-acre Balboa Park is the cultural heart of San Diego. Ranked as one of the world's best parks by the Project for Public Spaces, it's also where you can find most of the city's museums, art galleries, the Tony Award–winning Old Globe Theatre, and the world-famous San Diego Zoo. Often referred to as the "Smithsonian of the West" for its concentration of museums, Balboa Park is also a series of botanical gardens, performance spaces, and outdoor playrooms endeared to the hearts of residents and visitors alike.

Thanks to the "Mother of Balboa Park," Kate Sessions, who suggested hiring a landscape architect in 1889, wild and cultivated gardens are an integral part of the park, featuring 350 species of trees. What Balboa Park would have looked like had she left it alone can be seen at Florida Canyon (between the main park and Morley Field, along Park Boulevard)—an arid landscape of sagebrush, cactus, and a few small trees.

In addition, the captivating architecture of Balboa's buildings, fountains, and courtyards gives the park an enchanted feel. Historic buildings dating from San Diego's 1915 Panama–California International Exposition are strung along the park's main east–west thoroughfare, El Prado. The parkland across the Cabrillo Bridge, at the west end of El Prado, is set aside for picnics and athletics. East of Plaza de Panama, El Prado becomes a pedestrian mall and ends at a footbridge that crosses over Park Boulevard, to rose and desert gardens.

TOP ATTRACTIONS

Bea Evenson Fountain. A favorite of barefoot children, this fountain shoots cool jets of water upwards of 50 feet. Built in 1972 between the Fleet Center and Natural History Museum, the fountain offers plenty of room to sit and watch the crowds go by. ⊠ *East end of El Prado, Balboa Park,* ⊕ *www.balboapark.org.*

Fodor's Choice ★ **Botanical Building.** The graceful redwood-lath structure, built for the 1915 Panama–California International Exposition, now houses more than 2,000 types of tropical and subtropical plants plus changing seasonal flower displays. Ceiling-high tree ferns shade fragile orchids and feathery bamboo. There are benches beside miniature waterfalls for resting in the shade. The rectangular pond outside, filled with lotuses and water lilies that bloom in spring and fall, is popular with photographers. ⊠ *1549 El Prado, Balboa Park,* ☎ *619/239–0512* ⊕ *www.balboapark.org* ⊠ *Free* ☉ *Fri.–Wed. 10–4.*

Cabrillo Bridge. The official gateway into Balboa Park soars 120 feet above a canyon floor. Pedestrian-friendly, the 1,500-foot bridge provides inspiring views of the California Tower and El Prado beyond. ■ **TIP→ This is a great spot for a photo capturing a classic image of the park.** ⊠ *On El Prado, at 6th Ave. park entrance, Balboa Park,* ⊕ *www.balboapark.org.*

FAMILY
Fodor's Choice ★ **Carousel.** Suspended an arm's length away on this antique merry-go-round is the brass ring that could earn you an extra free ride (it's one of the few carousels in the world that continue this bonus tradition). Hand-carved in 1910, the carousel features colorful murals, big-band

music, and bobbing animals including zebras, giraffes, and dragons; real horsehair was used for the tails. ⊠ *1889 Zoo Pl., behind zoo parking lot, Balboa Park,* ☎ *619/239–0512* ⊕ *www.balboapark.org* ⊠ *$2.50* ⊙ *Mid-June–Labor Day, 11–5:30 daily; Labor Day–Mid-June, 11–5:30 weekends and school holidays.*

Fodor'sChoice
★

Inez Grant Parker Memorial Rose Garden and Desert Garden. These neighboring gardens sit just across the Park Boulevard pedestrian bridge and offer gorgeous views over Florida Canyon. The formal rose garden contains 2,500 roses representing nearly 200 varieties; peak bloom is usually in April and May. The adjacent Desert Garden provides a striking contrast, with 2.5 acres of succulents and desert plants seeming to blend into the landscape of the canyon below. ⊠ *2525 Park Blvd., Balboa Park,* ⊕ *www.balboapark.org.*

Japanese Friendship Garden. A koi pond with a cascading waterfall, a tea pavilion, and a large activity center are highlights of the park's authentic Japanese garden, designed to inspire contemplation and evoke tranquillity. You can wander the various peaceful paths and meditate in the traditional stone and Zen garden. The development of an additional 9 acres is well underway, with several acres already open and the rest scheduled for completion in 2015. The expanded garden features a cherry tree grove and, when complete, a traditional teahouse, which will be the crown jewel of this serene escape. ⊠ *2215 Pan American Rd., Balboa Park,* ☎ *619/232–2721* ⊕ *www.niwa.org* ⊠ *$6* ⊙ *Daily 10–4:30, last admission at 3:30.*

Mingei International Museum. The name "Mingei" comes from the Japanese words *min,* meaning "all people," and *gei,* meaning "art." Thus the museum's name describes what's found under its roof: "art of all people." The Mingei's colorful and creative exhibits of folk art feature toys, pottery, textiles, costumes, jewelry, and curios from around the globe. Traveling and permanent exhibits in the high-ceilinged, light-filled museum include everything from a history of surfboard design and craft to the latest in Japanese ceramics. The gift shop carries items related to major exhibitions as well as artwork from various cultures worldwide, such as Zulu baskets, Turkish ceramics, and Mexican objects. ⊠ *House of Charm, 1439 El Prado, Balboa Park,* ☎ *619/239–0003* ⊕ *www.mingei.org* ⊠ *$8* ⊙ *Tues.–Sun. 10–5.*

Palm Canyon. Enjoy an instant escape from the buildings and concrete of urban life in this Balboa Park oasis. Lush and tropical, with hundreds of palm trees, the 2-acre canyon has a shaded path perfect for those who love walking through nature. ⊠ *South of House of Charm, 1549 El Prado, Balboa Park, .*

FAMILY
Reuben H. Fleet Science Center. Interactive exhibits here are artfully educational and for all ages: older kids can get hands-on with inventive projects in the Tinkering Studio, while the five-and-under set can be easily entertained with interactive play stations like the Ball Wall and Fire Truck in the center's Kid City. The IMAX Dome Theater, which screens exhilarating nature and science films, was the world's first, as was the Fleet's "NanoSeam" (seamless) dome ceiling that doubles as a planetarium. ⊠ *1875 El Prado, Balboa Park,* ☎ *619/238–1233* ⊕ *www.*

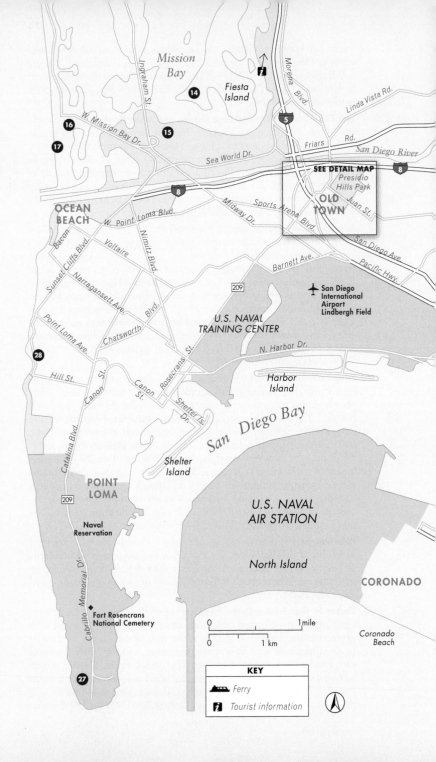

3

rhfleet.org 🖵 *Gallery exhibits $13; gallery exhibits and 1 IMAX film $17, or 2 IMAX films $24* ⊙ *Daily 10–5.*

Fodor'sChoice   **San Diego Museum of Art.** Known primarily for its Spanish baroque and
★   Renaissance paintings, including works by El Greco, Goya, Rubens, and van Ruisdael, San Diego's most comprehensive art museum also has strong holdings of South Asian art, Indian miniatures, and contemporary California paintings. The museum's exhibits tend to have broad appeal, and if traveling shows from other cities come to town, you can expect to see them here. Free docent tours are offered throughout the day. An outdoor Sculpture Court and Garden exhibits both traditional and modern pieces. Enjoy the view over a craft beer and some locally sourced food in the adjacent Panama 66 courtyard restaurant. ✉ *1450 El Prado, Balboa Park,* ☏ *619/232–7931* ⊕ *www.sdmart.org* 🖵 *$12* ⊙ *Mon., Tues., and Thurs.–Sat. 10–5, Sun. noon–5.*

FAMILY   **San Diego Zoo.**
Fodor'sChoice   *See the highlighted listing in this chapter.*
★

Fodor'sChoice   **Spanish Village Art Center.** More than 200 local artists, including glass-
★   blowers, enamel workers, woodcarvers, sculptors, painters, jewelers, and photographers work and give demonstrations of their craft on a rotating basis in these red tile–roof studio-galleries that were set up for the 1935–36 Exposition in the style of an old Spanish village. The center is a great source for memorable gifts. ✉ *1770 Village Pl., Balboa Park,* ☏ *619/233–9050* ⊕ *www.spanishvillageart.com* 🖵 *Free* ⊙ *Daily 11–4.*

Fodor'sChoice   **Spreckels Organ Pavilion.** The 2,400-bench-seat pavilion, dedicated in
★   1915 by sugar magnates John D. and Adolph B. Spreckels, holds the 4,518-pipe Spreckels Organ, the largest outdoor pipe organ in the world. You can hear this impressive instrument at one of the year-round, free, 2 pm Sunday concerts, regularly performed by civic organist Carol Williams and guest artists—a highlight of a visit to Balboa Park. On Monday evenings from late June to mid-August, internationally renowned organists play evening concerts. At Christmastime the park's Christmas tree and life-size Nativity display turn the pavilion into a seasonal wonderland. ✉ *2211 Pan American Rd., Balboa Park,* ☏ *619/702–8138* ⊕ *spreckelsorgan.org.*

OLD TOWN AND UPTOWN

San Diego's Spanish and Mexican roots are most evident in Old Town and the surrounding hillside of Presidio Park. Visitors can experience settlement life in San Diego from Spanish and Mexican rule to the early days of U.S. statehood. Nearby Uptown is composed of several smaller neighborhoods near Downtown and around Balboa Park: the vibrant neighborhoods of Hillcrest, Mission Hills, Mission Valley, University Heights, North Park and South Park showcase their unique blend of historical charm and modern urban community.

OLD TOWN

As the first European settlement in Southern California, Old Town began to develop in the 1820s. But its true beginnings took place on a nearby hillside in 1769 with the establishment of a Spanish military

Continued on page 66

Polar bear, San Diego Zoo

LIONS AND TIGERS AND PANDAS:
The World-Famous San Diego Zoo

From cuddly pandas and diving polar bears to 6-ton elephants and swinging great apes, San Diego's most famous attraction has it all. Nearly 4,000 animals representing 800 species roam the 100-acre zoo in expertly crafted habitats that replicate the animals' natural environments. While the pandas get top billing, there are plenty of other cool creatures to see here, from teeny-tiny mantella frogs to two-story-tall giraffes. But it's not all just fun and games. Known for its exemplary conservation programs, the zoo educates visitors on how to go green and explains its efforts to protect endangered species.

SAN DIEGO ZOO TOP ATTRACTIONS

Underwater viewing area at the Hippo Trail

❶ Children's Zoo (Discovery Outpost). Goats and sheep beg to be petted, and there is a viewer-friendly nursery where you may see baby animals bottle-feed and sleep peacefully in large cribs.

❷ Monkey Trails and Forest Tales (Lost Forest). Follow an elevated trail at treetop level and trek through the forest floor observing African mandrill monkeys, Asia's clouded leopard, the rare pygmy hippopotamus, and Visayan warty pigs.

❸ Orangutan and Siamang Exhibit (Lost Forest). Orangutans and siamangs climb and swing in this lush, tropical environment lined with 110-foot-long and 12-foot-high viewing windows.

Polar Bear Plunge

Skyfari West

PARK WAY

Express Bus Stop

Arctic Trader

POLAR RIM

Express Bus Sto

Elephar Odysse Entran

Ituri Forest Outpost

PANDA CANYON

Giant Panda Research Station

PARK WAY

LOST FOREST

Albert's Restaurant

Treehouse Trader

Treehouse Cafe

Treetops Room

Panda Shop

Hua Mei Co

Monkey Trail

Gorilla Exhibit

Scripps Aviary

Parker Aviary

Owens Aviary

Greenzoo Coffee Co.

Hippo Trail

Tiger Trail

Monkey Trail

Orangutan and Siamang Exhibit

CENTER STREET

Fern Canyon Trail

Orangutan Trail

EASY STREET

Tiger Trail

Wegeforth Bowl

First Aid & Nursing Station

Jungle Java

Bus Tour Loading

FRONTSTREET

DISCOVERY OUTPOST

Reptile House

Safari Kitchen

Zootari Photos

Front St. Photos

Cinnamon Tree

Lagoon Terrace

Rondavel Room

Clark Theater

Poppy's Patio

Front St. Cafe

Kidstore

Flamingo Sandwich Co.

Rondavel Room

Insect House

Skyfari East

Zoofari Party Area

San Diego Zoo Store

ENTRANCE

Warner Administration Center

Petting Zoo

Children's Zoo

Fisher Price Discovery Playground

Otto Center

Balboa Park Railroad (Miniature Train)

P

❹ Scripps, Parker, and Owens Aviaries (Lost Forest). Wandering paths climb through the enclosed aviaries where brightly colored tropical birds swoop between branches inches from your face.

❺ Tiger Trail (Lost Forest). The mist-shrouded trails of this simulated rainforest wind down a canyon. Tigers, Malayan tapirs, and Argus pheasants wander among the exotic trees and plants.

❻ Hippo Trail (Lost Forest). Glimpse huge but surprisingly graceful hippos frolicking in the water through an underwater viewing window and buffalo cavorting with monkeys on dry land.

❼ Gorilla Exhibit (Lost Forest). The gorillas live in one of the zoo's bioclimatic zone exhibits modeled on their native habitat with waterfalls, climbing areas, and an open meadow. The sounds of the tropical rain forest emerge from a 144-speaker sound system that plays CDs recorded in Africa.

❽ Sun Bear Forest (Asian Passage). Playful beasts claw apart the trees and shrubs that serve as a natural playground for climbing, jumping, and general merrymaking.

❾ Giant Panda Research Station (Panda Canyon). An elevated pathway provides visitors with great access

Lories at Owen's Aviary

to the zoo's most famous residents in their side-by-side viewing areas. The adjacent discovery center features lots of information about these endangered animals and the zoo's efforts to protect them.

❿ Polar Bear Plunge (Polar Rim). Watch polar bears take a chilly dive from the underwater viewing room. There are also Siberian reindeer, white foxes, and other Arctic creatures here. Kids can learn about the Arctic and climate change through interactive exhibits.

⓫ Elephant Odyssey. Get a glimpse of the animals that roamed Southern California 12,000 years ago and meet their living counterparts. The 7.5-acre, multispecies habitat features elephants, California condors, jaguars, and more.

⓬ Koala Exhibit (Outback). The San Diego Zoo houses the largest number of koalas outside Australia. Walk through the exhibit for photo ops of these marsupials from Down-Under curled up on their perches or dining on eucalyptus branches.

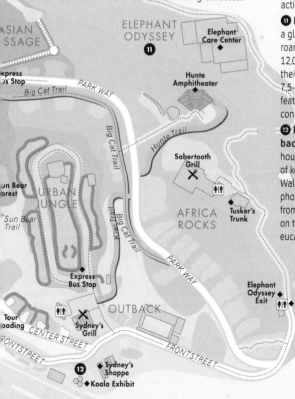

MUST-SEE ANIMALS

❶ GORILLA

This troop of primates engages visitors with their human-like expressions and behavior. The youngsters are sure to delight, especially when hitching a ride on mom's back. Up-close encounters might involve the gorillas using the glass partition as a backrest while peeling cabbage. By dusk the gorillas head inside to their sleeping quarters, so don't save this for your last stop.

❷ ELEPHANT

Asian and African elephants coexist at the San Diego Zoo. The larger African elephant is distinguished by its big flapping ears—shaped like the continent of Africa—which it uses to keep cool. An elephant's trunk has over 40,000 muscles in it—that's more than humans have in their whole body.

❸ GIANT PANDA

The San Diego Zoo is well-known for its giant panda research and conservation efforts, and has had five successful panda births. You'll likely see parents Bai Yun ("White Cloud") and Gao-Gao ("Big-Big") with their youngest baby Xiao Liwu ("little gift").

❹ KOALA

While this collection of critters is one of the cutest in the zoo, don't expect a lot of activity from the koala habitat. These guys spend most of their day curled up asleep in the branches of the eucalyptus tree—they can sleep up to 20 hours a day. Although eucalyptus leaves are poisonous to most animals, bacteria in koalas' stomachs allow them to break down the toxins.

❺ POLAR BEAR

The trio of polar bears is one of the San Diego Zoo's star attractions, and their brand-new exhibit gets you up close and personal. Visitors sometimes worry about polar bears living in the warm San Diego climate, but there is no cause for concern. The San Diego-based bears eat a lean diet, thus reducing their layer of blubber and helping them keep cool.

DID YOU KNOW?

Bamboo is the panda's dietary staple—they can consume 84 pounds of it a day—and the zoo grows 69 species of bamboo to ensure they have plenty of variety.

PLANNING YOUR DAY AT THE ZOO

Left: Main entrance of the San Diego Zoo. Right: Sunbear

PLANNING YOUR TIME

Plan to devote at least a half-day to exploring the zoo, but with so much to see it is easy to stay a full day or more.

If you're on a tight schedule, opt for the guided **35 minute bus tour** that lets you zip through three-quarters of the exhibits. However, lines to board the busses can be long, and you won't get as close to the animals.

Another option is to take the **Skyfari Aerial Tram** to the far end of the park, choose a route, and meander back to the entrance. The Skyfari trip gives a good overview of the zoo's layout and a spectacular view.

The **Elephant Odyssey**, while accessible from two sides of the park, is best entered from just below the Polar Rim. The extremely popular **Panda exhibit** can develop long lines, so get there early.

The zoo offers several entertaining **live shows** daily. Check the website or the back of the map handed out at the zoo entrance for the day's offerings and showtimes.

BEFORE YOU GO

■ To avoid ticket lines, purchase and print tickets online using the zoo's Web site.

■ To avoid excessive backtracking or a potential meltdown, plan your route along the zoo map before setting out. Try not to get too frustrated if you lose your way, as there are exciting exhibits around every turn and many paths intersect at several points.

■ The zoo offers a variety of program extras, including behind-the-scenes tours, backstage pass animal encounters, and sleepover events. Call in advance for pricing and reservations.

AT THE ZOO

■ Don't forget to explore at least some of the exhibits on foot—a favorite is the lush Tiger Trail.

■ If you visit on the weekend, find out when the Giraffe Experience is taking place. You can purchase leaf–eater biscuits to hand feed the giraffes!

■ Splurge a little at the gift shop: your purchases help support zoo programs.

■ The zoo rents strollers, wheelchairs, and lockers; it also has a first-aid office, a lost and found, and an ATM.

Fern Canyon, San Diego Zoo

GETTING HERE AND AROUND
The zoo is easy to get to, whether by bus or car.

Bus Travel: Take Bus No. 7 and exit at Park Boulevard and Zoo Place.

Car Travel: From Downtown, take Route 163 north through Balboa Park. Exit at Zoo/Museums (Richmond Street) and follow signs.

Several options help you get around the massive park: express buses loop through the zoo and the Skyfari Aerial Tram will take you from one end to the other. The zoo's topography is fairly hilly, but moving sidewalks lead up the slopes between some exhibits.

QUICK BITES
There is a wide variety of food available for purchase at the zoo from food carts to ethnic restaurants such as the Pan-Asian **Hua Mei Cafe.**

One of the best restaurants is **Albert's** ($), near the Gorilla exhibit, which features grilled fish, homemade pizza, and fresh pasta along with a full bar.

SERVICE INFORMATION

✉ 2920 Zoo Dr., Balboa Park

☎ 619/234–3153; 888/697–2632 Giant panda hotline

🌐 www.sandiegozoo.org

Gorilla

SAN DIEGO ZOO SAFARI PARK

About 45 minutes north of the zoo in Escondido, the 1,800-acre San Diego Zoo Safari Park is an extensive wildlife sanctuary where animals roam free—and guests can get close in escorted caravans and on backcountry trails. This park and the zoo operate under the auspices of the San Diego Zoo's nonprofit organization; joint tickets are available.

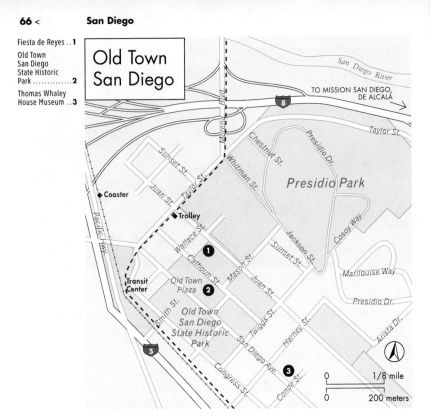

outpost and the first of California's missions, San Diego de Alcalá. In 1774 the hilltop was declared a *presidio reál*, a fortress built by the Spanish Empire, and the mission was relocated along the San Diego River. Over time, settlers moved down from the presidio to establish Old Town. A central plaza was laid out, surrounded by adobe and, later, wooden structures. San Diego became an incorporated U.S. city in 1850, with Old Town as its center. In the 1860s, however, the advent of Alonzo Horton's New Town to the southeast caused Old Town to wither. Efforts to preserve the area began early in the 20th century, and Old Town became a state historic park in 1968.

Today Old Town is a lively celebration of history and culture. The Old Town San Diego State Historic Park re-creates life during the early settlement, while San Diego Avenue buzzes with art galleries, gift shops, festive restaurants, and open-air stands selling inexpensive Mexican handicrafts.

TOP ATTRACTIONS

FAMILY

Fodor's Choice

★

Fiesta de Reyes. North of San Diego's Old Town Plaza lies the area's unofficial center, built to represent a colonial Mexican plaza. The collection of more than a dozen shops and restaurants around a central courtyard in blossom with magenta bougainvillea, scarlet hibiscus, and other flowers in season reflects what early California might have looked like from

1821 to 1872. Shops are even stocked with items reminiscent of that era. Mariachi bands and folklórico dance groups frequently perform on the plaza stage—check the website for times and upcoming special events. ■ TIP→ Casa de Reyes is a great stop for a margarita and some chips and guacamole. ✉ *4016 Wallace St., Old Town*, ☎ *619/297–3100* ⊕ *www.fiestadereyes.com* ⊗ *Shops daily 10–9.*

FAMILY
Fodor's Choice
★

Old Town San Diego State Historic Park. The six square blocks on the site of San Diego's original pueblo are the heart of Old Town. Most of the 20 historic buildings preserved or re-created by the park cluster around **Old Town Plaza,** bounded by Wallace Street on the west, Calhoun Street on the north, Mason Street on the east, and San Diego Avenue on the south. The plaza is a pleasant place to rest, plan your tour of the park, and watch passersby. San Diego Avenue is closed to vehicle traffic here.

Some of Old Town's buildings were destroyed in a fire in 1872, but after the site became a state historic park in 1968, reconstruction and restoration of the remaining structures began. Five of the original adobes are still intact. The tour pamphlet available at Robinson-Rose House gives details about all the historic houses on the plaza and in its vicinity; *a few of the more interesting ones are noted below.* Several reconstructed buildings serve as restaurants or as shops purveying wares reminiscent of those that might have been available in the original Old Town.

Racine & Laramie, a painstakingly reproduced version of San Diego's first cigar store in 1868, is especially interesting. Free tours depart daily from the Robinson-Rose House at 11 and 2. *2737 San Diego Ave.* ■ TIP→ The covered wagon located near the intersection of Mason and Calhoun streets provides a great photo opp.

Casa de Estudillo. San Diego's first county assessor, Jose Antonio Estudillo, built this home in 1827 in collaboration with his father, the commander of the San Diego Presidio, José Maria Estudillo. The largest and most elaborate of the original adobe homes, it was occupied by members of the Estudillo family until 1887. It was purchased and restored in 1910 by sugar magnate and developer John D. Spreckels, who advertised it in bold lettering on the side as "Ramona's Marriage Place." Spreckels's claim that the small chapel in the house was the site of the wedding in Helen Hunt Jackson's popular novel *Ramona* had no basis; that didn't stop people from coming to see it, however. *4001 Mason St.*

Cosmopolitan Hotel and Restaurant. A Peruvian, Juan Bandini, built a hacienda on this site in 1829, and the house served as Old Town's social center during Mexican rule. Albert Seeley, a stagecoach entrepreneur, purchased the home in 1869, built a second story, and turned it into the Cosmopolitan Hotel, a way station for travelers on the daylong trip south from Los Angeles. It later served as a cannery before being revived (a few times over the years) as a hotel and restaurant. *2660 Calhoun St.*

Robinson-Rose House. Facing Old Town Plaza, this was the original commercial center of Old San Diego, housing railroad offices, law offices, and the first newspaper press. Built in 1853 but in ruins at the end of the 19th century, it has been reconstructed and now serves as the park's visitor center. Inside are a model of Old Town as it looked in 1872 as well as various historic exhibits. Apparently ghosts came with the rebuild, as the house is now considered haunted. Just behind the Robinson-Rose House is a replica of the Victorian-era Silvas-McCoy house, originally built in 1869. *4002 Wallace St.*

Seeley Stable. Next door to the Cosmopolitan Hotel, the stable became San Diego's stagecoach stop in 1867 and was the transportation hub of Old Town until 1887, when trains became the favored mode of travel. The stable houses horse-drawn vehicles, some so elaborate that you can see where the term "carriage trade" came from. Also inside are Western memorabilia, including an exhibit on the California vaquero, the original American cowboy, and a collection of Native American artifacts. *2630 Calhoun St.*

Also worth exploring: The San Diego Union Museum, Mason Street School, Wells Fargo History Museum, First San Diego Courthouse, Casa de Machado y Silvas Commercial Restaurant Museum, and the Casa de Machado y Stewart. Ask at the visitor center for locations. ⊠ *Visitor Center (Robinson-Rose House), 4002 Wallace St., Old Town,* ☎ *619/220–5422* ⊕ *www.parks.ca.gov* 🖅 *Free* ☉ *Oct.–Apr., Mon.– Thurs. 10–4, Fri.–Sun. 10–5; May–Sept., daily 10–5; hrs may vary at individual sites.*

Thomas Whaley House Museum. A New York entrepreneur, Thomas Whaley came to California during the gold rush. He wanted to provide his East Coast wife with all the comforts of home, so in 1857 he had Southern California's first two-story brick structure built, making it the oldest double-story brick building on the West Coast. The house, which served as the county courthouse and government seat during the 1870s, stands in strong contrast to the Spanish-style adobe residences that surround the nearby historic plaza and marks an early stage of San Diego's "Americanization." A garden out back includes many varieties of prehybrid roses from before 1867. The place is perhaps most famed, however, for the ghosts that are said to inhabit it. You can tour on your own during the day, but must visit by guided tour starting at 5 pm. The evening tours are geared toward the supernatural aspects of the house. They are offered every half hour, with the last tour departing at 9:30 pm, and last about 45 minutes. ⊠ *2476 San Diego Ave., Old Town,* ☎ *619/297–7511* ⊕ *www.whaleyhouse.org* 🖅 *$6 before 5 pm, $10 after 5* ☉ *Sept.–May, Sun.–Tues. 10–5, Thurs.–Sat. 10–9:30; June–Aug., daily 10–9:30.*

HILLCREST

The large retro Hillcrest sign over the intersection of University and 5th avenues makes an excellent landmark at the epicenter of this vibrant section of Uptown. Strolling along University Avenue between 4th and 6th avenues from Washington Street to Robinson Avenue will reveal a mixture of retail shops and restaurants. A few blocks east, another interesting stretch of stores and restaurants runs along University Avenue to Normal Street. Long established as the center of San Diego's gay community, the neighborhood bustles both day and night with a mixed crowd of shoppers, diners, and partygoers. If you are visiting

Hillcrest on Sunday between 9 and 2 be sure to explore the Hillcrest Farmers Market.

MISSION VALLEY

Although Mission Valley's charms may not be immediately apparent, it offers many conveniences to visitors and residents alike. The Mission Basilica San Diego de Alcalá provides a tranquil refuge from the surrounding suburban sprawl.

TOP ATTRACTIONS

Fodor's Choice ★ **Mission Basilica San Diego de Alcalá.** It's hard to imagine how remote California's earliest mission must have once been; these days, however, it's accessible by major freeways (I-15 and I-8) and via the San Diego Trolley. The first of a chain of 21 missions stretching northward along the coast, Mission San Diego de Alcalá was established by Father Junípero Serra on Presidio Hill in 1769 and moved to this location in 1774. In 1775, it proved vulnerable to enemy attack, and Padre Luis Jayme, a young friar from Spain, was clubbed to death by the Kumeyaay Indians he had been trying to convert. He was the first of more than a dozen Christians martyred in California. The present church, reconstructed in 1931 following the outline of the 1813 church, is the fifth built on the site. It measures 150 feet long but only 35 feet wide because, without easy means of joining beams, the mission buildings were only as wide as the trees that served as their ceiling supports were tall. Father Jayme is buried in the sanctuary; a small museum named for him documents mission history and exhibits tools and artifacts from the early days; there is also a gift shop. From the peaceful, palm-bedecked gardens out back you can gaze at the 46-foot-high *campanario* (bell tower), the mission's most distinctive feature, with five bells. Mass is celebrated on the weekends. ⊠ *10818 San Diego Mission Rd., Mission Valley,* ✛ *From I-8 east, exit and turn left on Mission Gorge Rd., then left on Twain Rd.; mission is on right* ☎ *619/281-8449* ⊕ *www.missionsandiego.com* ▧ *$5, $3-$5 audio tours* ⊗ *Daily 9-4:30; check website for mass times.*

NORTH PARK

Named for its location north of Balboa Park, this evolving neighborhood is home to an exciting array of restaurants, bars, and shops. High-end condominiums and local merchants are often cleverly disguised behind historic signage from barbershops, bowling alleys, and theater marquees. The stretch of Ray Street near University Avenue is home to several small galleries. With a steady stream of new openings in the neighborhood, North Park is one of San Diego's top dining and nightlife destinations.

MISSION BAY AND THE BEACHES

Mission Bay and the surrounding beaches are the aquatic playground of San Diego. The choice of activities available is astonishing, and the perfect weather makes you want to get out there and play. If you're craving downtime after all the activity, there are plenty of peaceful spots to relax and simply soak up the sunshine.

Mission Bay welcomes visitors with its protected waters and countless opportunities for fun. The 4,600-acre Mission Bay Park is the place for water sports like sailing, stand-up paddleboarding, and waterskiing. With 19 miles of beaches and grassy areas, it's also a great place for a picnic. One Mission Bay caveat: swimmers should note signs warning about water pollution; on occasions when heavy rains or other events cause pollution, swimming is dangerous.

Mission Beach is a famous and lively fun zone for families and young people both; if it isn't party time at the moment, it will be five minutes from now. The pathways in this area are lined with vacation homes, many for rent by the week or month.

North of Mission Beach is the college-packed party town of Pacific Beach, or "PB" as locals call it. The laid-back vibe of this surfer's mecca draws in free-spirited locals who roam the streets on skateboards and beach cruisers. The energy level peaks during happy hour, when PB's cluster of nightclubs, bars, and 150 restaurants open their doors to those ready to party.

TOP ATTRACTIONS

FAMILY
Fodor's Choice
★
Belmont Park. The once-abandoned amusement park between the bay and Mission Beach Boardwalk is now a shopping, dining, and recreation complex. Twinkling lights outline the **Giant Dipper,** an antique wooden roller coaster on which screaming thrill-seekers ride more than 2,600 feet of track and 13 hills (riders must be at least 4 feet, 2 inches tall). Created in 1925 and listed on the National Register of Historic Places, this is one of the few old-time roller coasters left in the United States. The **Plunge,** an indoor swimming pool, was the largest—60 feet by 125 feet—saltwater pool in the world at the time it opened, also in 1935; it's had freshwater since 1951. Johnny Weismuller and Esther Williams are among the stars who were captured on celluloid swimming here.

Other Belmont Park attractions include miniature golf, a video arcade, bumper cars, a tilt-a-whirl, and an antique carousel. The rock wall challenges both junior climbers and their elders. Belmont Park also has the most consistent wave in the county at the **Wave House,** where the FlowRider provides surfers and bodyboarders a near-perfect simulated wave on which to practice their skills. ⊠ *3146 Mission Blvd., Mission Bay,* ☎ *858/488–1549 for rides* ⊕ *www.belmontpark.com* ✉ *Unlimited ride day package $29 for 48" and taller, $18 for under 48"; individual ride tickets also available* ◷ *Park opens at 11 daily, ride operation varies seasonally.*

Fodor's Choice
★
Mission Bay Park. San Diego's monument to sports and fitness, this 4,600-acre aquatic park has 27 miles of shoreline including 19 miles of sandy beaches. Playgrounds and picnic areas abound on the beaches and low, grassy hills. On weekday evenings, joggers, bikers, and skaters take over. In the daytime, swimmers, water-skiers, windsurfers, anglers, and boaters—some in single-person kayaks, others in crowded powerboats—vie for space in the water. ⊠ *2688 E. Mission Bay Dr., off I-5 at Exit 22 East Mission Bay Drive, Mission Bay,* ☎ *858/581–7602 Park Ranger's Office* ⊕ *www.sandiego.gov/park-and-recreation* ✉ *Free.*

Fodor's Choice **Mission Beach Boardwalk.** The cement pathway lining the sand from the
★ southern end of Mission Beach north to Pacific Beach is always bustling with activity. Cyclists ping the bells on their beach cruisers to pass
walkers out for a stroll alongside the oceanfront homes. Vacationers
kick back on their patios, while friends play volleyball in the sand. The
activity picks up alongside Belmont Park and the WaveHouse, where
people stop to check out the action on the FlowRider wave. ⊠ *Alongside
the sand from Mission Beach Park to Pacific Beach, Mission Beach,* .

FAMILY **SeaWorld San Diego.** One of the world's largest marine-life amusement
parks, SeaWorld is spread over 189 tropically landscaped bay-front
acres—and it seems to be expanding into every available square inch
of space, with new exhibits, shows, and activities. The park offers a
variety of amusement rides, some on dry land and others that will leave
riders soaking wet.

The majority of SeaWorld's exhibits are walk-through marine environments. Kids get a particular kick out of the **Shark Encounter,** where
they come face to face with sand, tiger, nurse, bonnethead, black-tipped,
and white-tipped reef sharks by walking through a 57-foot clear acrylic
tube that passes through the 280,000-gallon shark habitat. **Turtle Reef**
offers an incredible up-close encounter with the green sea turtle, while
the moving sidewalk at **Penguin Encounter** whisks you through a colony
of nearly 300 macaroni, gentoo, Adelie, and emperor penguins. Various
freshwater and saltwater aquariums hold underwater creatures from
around the world.

SeaWorld's highlights are its large-arena entertainments. You can get
front-row seats if you arrive 30 minutes in advance, and the stadiums
are large enough for everyone to get a seat in the off-season. The show
Blue Horizons combines dolphins, pilot whales, tropical birds, and
aerialists in a spectacular performance.

The **Dolphin Interaction Program** gives guests the chance to interact
with SeaWorld's bottlenose dolphins in the water. The hour-long program (20 minutes in the water), during which visitors can feed, touch,
and give behavior signals, costs $215.

The San Diego 3-for-1 Pass ($149 for adults, $119 for children ages 3
to 9) offers seven consecutive days of unlimited admission to SeaWorld,
the San Diego Zoo, and the San Diego Zoo's Safari Park. This is a good
idea, because if you try to get your money's worth by fitting everything
in on a single day, you're likely to end up tired and cranky. Many hotels,
especially those in the Mission Bay area, also offer SeaWorld specials
that may include rate reductions or two-day entry for the price of one.

There is no shortage of dining options inside SeaWorld, from burgers
at Café 64, to Italian fare at Mama Stella's Pizza Kitchen, BBQ at the
Calypso Bay Smokehouse, or baked goods at Seaside Coffee and Bakery.
Note: Theme parks like SeaWorld have been criticized by animal welfare
groups. They argue that the conditions and treatment of marine life kept
in captivity are harmful for the animals, and that human interaction
further exacerbates this. A bill in California's state legislature in 2014
proposed a ban on killer whale shows: it was sent back for further study.

✉ *500 SeaWorld Dr., near west end of I–8, Mission Bay,* ☎ *800/257–4268* ⊕ *www.seaworldparks.com* 💲 *$84 adults, $78 kids; parking $15* ⊙ *Daily 10–dusk; extended hrs in summer.*

LA JOLLA

La Jollans have long considered their village to be the Monte Carlo of California, and with good cause. Its coastline curves into natural coves backed by verdant hillsides covered with homes worth millions. La Jolla is both a natural and cultural treasure trove. The upscale shops, galleries, and restaurants of La Jolla Village satisfy the glitterati, while secluded trails, scenic overlooks, and abundant marine life provide balance and refuge.

Although La Jolla is a neighborhood of the city of San Diego, it has its own postal zone and a coveted sense of class; the ultrarich from around the globe own second homes here—the seaside zone between the neighborhood's bustling Downtown and the cliffs above the Pacific has a distinctly European flavor—and old-money residents maintain friendships with the visiting film stars and royalty who frequent the area's exclusive luxury hotels and private clubs.

The Native Americans called the site La Hoya, meaning "the cave," referring to the grottoes that dot the shoreline. The Spaniards changed the name to La Jolla (same pronunciation as La Hoya), "the jewel," and its residents have cherished the name and its allusions ever since.

TOP ATTRACTIONS

Fodor's Choice ★ **Museum of Contemporary Art San Diego.** Driving along Coast Boulevard, it is hard to miss the mass of watercraft jutting out from the rear of the Museum of Contemporary Art San Diego (MCASD) La Jolla location. *Pleasure Point* by Nancy Rubins is just one example of the mingling of art and locale at this spectacular oceanfront setting.

Highlights

The oldest section of La Jolla's branch of San Diego's contemporary art museum was originally a residence, designed by Irving Gill for philanthropist Ellen Browning Scripps in 1916. In the mid-1990s the compound was updated and expanded by architect Robert Venturi, who respected Gill's original geometric structure and clean Mission-style lines while adding his own distinctive touches. The result is a striking contemporary building that looks as though it's always been here.

The light-filled Axline Court serves as the museum's entrance and does triple duty as reception area, exhibition hall, and forum for special events, including the glittering Monte Carlo gala each September, attended by the town's most fashionable folk. Inside, the museum's artwork gets major competition from the setting: you can look out from the top of a grand stairway onto a landscaped garden that contains permanent and temporary sculpture exhibits as well as rare 100-year-old California plant specimens and, beyond that, to the Pacific Ocean.

California artists figure prominently in the museum's permanent collection of post-1950s art, but the museum also includes examples of every major art movement through the present—works by Andy Warhol,

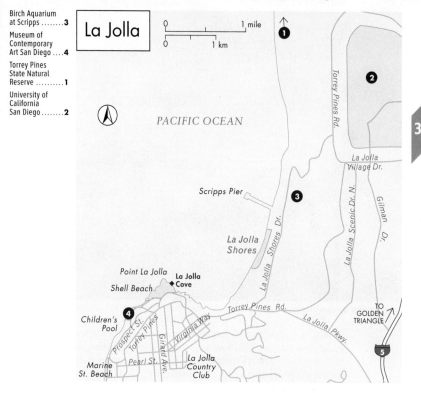

Robert Rauschenberg, Frank Stella, Joseph Cornell, and Jenny Holzer, to name a few. Important pieces by artists from San Diego and Tijuana were acquired in the 1990s. The museum also gets major visiting shows.

Tips

Be sure to also check out MCASD's downtown branch; admission is good for seven days and valid at both locations. Get in free the third Thursday of every month from 5 to 7. Informative and insightful exhibit tours are offered free of charge weekends at 2 (downtown on Saturday, and in La Jolla on Sunday), and on the third Thursday of the month at 5:30. Head to the museum's X Store for unique cards and gifts. The pleasant courtyard at the museum café is a great spot to relax and recharge. ⊠ *700 Prospect St., La Jolla,* ☎ *858/454–3541* ⊕ *www.mcasd. org* ✉ *$10, good for 1 visit here and at MCASD downtown within 7 days; free 3rd Thurs. of month 5–7* ⊙ *Thurs.–Tues. 11–5; 3rd Thurs. of month 11–7.*

Fodor's Choice **Torrey Pines State Natural Reserve.** *Pinus torreyana,* the rarest native pine
★ tree in the United States, enjoys a 1,700-acre sanctuary at the northern edge of La Jolla. About 6,000 of these unusual trees, some as tall as 60 feet, grow on the cliffs here. The park is one of only two places in the world (the other is Santa Rosa Island, off Santa Barbara) where the Torrey pine grows naturally. The reserve has several hiking trails

A surfer prepares to head out before sunset at La Jolla's Torrey Pines State Beach and Reserve.

leading to the cliffs, 300 feet above the ocean; trail maps are available at the park station. Wildflowers grow profusely in spring, and the ocean panoramas are always spectacular. When in this upper part of the park, respect the restrictions. Not permitted: picnicking, smoking, leaving the trails, dogs, alcohol, or collecting plant specimens.

You can unwrap your sandwiches, however, at Torrey Pines State Beach, just below the reserve. When the tide is out, it's possible to walk south all the way past the lifeguard towers to Black's Beach over rocky promontories carved by the waves (avoid the bluffs, however; they're unstable). **Los Peñasquitos Lagoon** at the north end of the reserve is one of the many natural estuaries that flow inland between Del Mar and Oceanside. It's a good place to watch shorebirds. Volunteers lead guided nature walks at 10 and 2 on most weekends. ⊠ *12600 N. Torrey Pines Rd., La Jolla,* ✛ *N. Torrey Pines Rd. exit off I–5 onto Carmel Valley Rd. going west, then turn left (south) on Coast Hwy. 101,* ☎ *858/755–2063* ⊕ *www.torreypine.org* ⬛ *Parking $12–$15* ☾ *Daily 8–dusk; visitor center has shorter hrs.*

WORTH NOTING

University of California at San Diego. The campus of one of the country's most prestigious research universities spreads over 1,200 acres of coastal canyons and eucalyptus groves, where students and faculty jog, bike, and rollerblade to class. If you're interested in contemporary art, check out the **Stuart Collection of Sculpture**—18 thought-provoking, site-specific works by artists such as Nam June Paik, William Wegman, Niki de St. Phalle, Jenny Holzer, and others arrayed around the campus. UCSD's **Price Center** has a well-stocked, two-level bookstore—the largest in San Diego—and a good coffeehouse, Perks. Look for the postmodern **Geisel Library**, named for longtime La Jolla residents Theodor "Dr. Seuss" Geisel and his wife, Audrey. Bring quarters for the parking meters, or cash or a credit card for the parking structures, because free parking is only available on weekends. ⊠ *Exit I–5 onto La Jolla Village Dr. going west; take Gilman Dr. off-ramp to right and continue on to information kiosk at campus entrance on Gilman Dr., La Jolla,* ☎ *858/534–4414 campus tour information* ⊕ *www.ucsd.edu* ☉ *90-min campus tours Sun. at 2 from South Gilman Information Pavilion; reserve before 4 pm Thurs.*

FAMILY **Birch Aquarium at Scripps.** Affiliated with the world-renowned Scripps Institution of Oceanography, this excellent aquarium sits at the end of a signposted drive leading off North Torrey Pines Road and has sweeping views of La Jolla coast below. More than 60 tanks are filled with colorful saltwater fish, and a 70,000-gallon tank simulates a La Jolla kelp forest. A special exhibit on sea horses features several examples of the species, plus mesmerizing sea dragons and a sea horse nursery. Besides the fish themselves, attractions include a gallery based on the institution's ocean-related research, and interactive educational exhibits on a variety of environmental issues. ⊠ *2300 Expedition Way, La Jolla,* ☎ *858/534–3474* ⊕ *www.aquarium.ucsd.edu* 🖃 *$17* ☉ *Daily 9–5; last entry at 4:30.*

POINT LOMA AND CORONADO WITH HARBOR AND SHELTER ISLANDS, AND OCEAN BEACH

Although Coronado is actually an isthmus, easily reached from the mainland if you head north from Imperial Beach, it has always seemed like an island and is often referred to as such. To the west, Point Loma protects the San Diego Bay from the Pacific's tides and waves. Both Coronado and Point Loma have stately homes, sandy beaches, private marinas, and prominent military installations. Nestled between the two, Harbor and Shelter islands owe their existence to dredging in the bay.

POINT LOMA

The hilly peninsula of Point Loma curves west and south into the Pacific and provides protection for San Diego Bay. Its high elevations and sandy cliffs provide incredible views, and make Point Loma a visible local landmark. Its maritime roots are evident, from its longtime ties to the U.S. Navy to its bustling sport fishing and sailing marinas. The funky community of Ocean Beach coexists alongside the stately homes of Sunset Cliffs and the honored graves at Fort Rosecrans National Cemetery.

TOP ATTRACTIONS

FAMILY

Fodor's Choice

★

Cabrillo National Monument. This 160-acre preserve marks the site of the first European visit to San Diego, made by 16th-century explorer Juan Rodríguez Cabrillo. Cabrillo landed at this spot on September 15, 1542. Today the site, with its rugged cliffs and shores and outstanding overlooks, is one of the most frequently visited of all the national monuments.

The **visitor center** presents films and lectures about Cabrillo's voyage, the sea-level tide pools, and migrating gray whales. **Interpretive stations** have been installed along the walkways that edge the cliffs. The moderately steep **Bayside Trail**, 2½ miles round-trip, winds through coastal sage scrub, curving under the cliff-top lookouts and taking you ever closer to the bay-front scenery. You cannot reach the beach from this trail; you must stick to the path to protect the cliffs from erosion and yourself from thorny plants and snakes—including rattlers. Sights along the way include prickly pear cacti and yucca, black-eyed Susans, fragrant sage, and maybe a lizard, rabbit, or hummingbird. The climb back is long but gradual, leading up to the **Old Point Loma Lighthouse.**

The western and southern cliffs of Cabrillo National Monument are prime whale-watching territory. A sheltered **viewing station** has wayside exhibits describing the great gray whales' yearly migration from Baja California to the Bering and Chukchi seas near Alaska. High-powered telescopes help you focus on the whales' waterspouts. Whales are visible on clear days from late December through early March, with the highest concentration in January and February. More-accessible sea creatures (starfish, crabs, anemones) can be seen in the **tide pools** at the foot of the monument's western cliffs. Drive north from the visitor center to Cabrillo Road, which winds down to the Coast Guard station and the shore. ⊠ *1800 Cabrillo Memorial Dr., Point Loma,* ☎ *619/557–5450* ⊕ *www.nps.gov/cabr* ☜ *$5 per car, $3 per person on foot/bicycle, entry good for 7 days* ☉ *Daily 9–5.*

Fodor's Choice
★ **Sunset Cliffs.** As the name suggests, the 60-foot-high bluffs on the western side of Point Loma south of Ocean Beach are a perfect place to watch the sun set over the sea. To view the tide pools along the shore, use the staircase off Sunset Cliffs Boulevard at the foot of Ladera Street.

The dramatic coastline here seems to have been carved out of ancient rock. The impact of the waves is very clear: each year more sections of the cliffs are posted with caution signs. Don't ignore these warnings—it's easy to slip in the crumbling sandstone, and the surf can be extremely rough. The small coves and beaches that dot the coastline are popular with surfers drawn to the pounding waves. The homes along the boulevard—pink stucco mansions beside shingled Cape Cod–style cottages—are fine examples of Southern California luxury. ⊠ *Sunset Cliffs Blvd., Point Loma, .*

OCEAN BEACH

At the northern end of Point Loma lies the chilled-out, hippyesque town of Ocean Beach, commonly referred to as "OB." The main thoroughfare of this funky neighborhood is dotted with dive bars, coffeehouses, surf shops, and 1960s diners. OB is a magnet for everyone from surfers to musicians and artists. Fans of OB applaud its resistance to "selling out" to upscale development, whereas detractors lament its somewhat scruffy edges.

Ocean Beach Pier. This T-shape pier is a popular fishing spot and home to the Ocean Beach Pier Café and a small tackle shop. Constructed in 1966, it is the longest concrete pier on the West Coast and a perfect place to take in views of the harbor, ocean, and Point Loma peninsula. Surfers flock to the waves that break just below. ⊠ *1950 Abbott St., Ocean Beach, .*

SHELTER ISLAND

In 1950 San Diego's port director decided to raise the shoal that lay off the eastern shore of Point Loma above sea level with the sand and mud dredged up during the course of deepening a ship channel in the 1930s and '40s. The resulting peninsula, **Shelter Island,** became home to several marinas and resorts, many with Polynesian details that still exist today, giving them a retro flair. This reclaimed peninsula now supports towering palms and resorts, restaurants, and side-by-side marinas. A long sidewalk runs past boat brokerages to the hotels and marinas that line the inner shore, facing Point Loma. On the bay side, fishermen launch their boats and families relax at picnic tables along the grass, where there are fire rings and permanent barbeque grills.

HARBOR ISLAND

Following the successful creation of Shelter Island, in 1961 the U.S. Navy used the residue from digging berths deep enough to accommodate aircraft carriers to build **Harbor Island**. Restaurants and high-rise hotels dot the inner shore of this 1½-mile-long man-made peninsula adjacent to the airport. The bay's shore is lined with pathways, gardens, and scenic picnic spots. The east-end point has killer views of the Downtown skyline.

CORONADO

As if freeze-framed in the 1950s, Coronado's quaint appeal is captured in its old-fashioned storefronts, well-manicured gardens, and charming **Ferry Landing Marketplace.** The streets of Coronado are wide, quiet, and friendly, and many of today's residents live in grand Victorian homes handed down for generations. Naval Air Station North Island was established in 1911 on Coronado's north end, across from Point Loma, and was the site of Charles Lindbergh's departure on the transcontinental flight that preceded his famous solo flight across the Atlantic. Coronado's long relationship with the U.S. Navy and its desirable real estate have made it an enclave for military personnel; it's said to have more retired admirals per capita than anywhere else in the United States.

Coronado is accessible via the arching blue 2.2-mile-long San Diego–Coronado Bay Bridge, which handles some 68,000 cars each day. The view of the harbor, Downtown, and the island is breathtaking, day and night. Until the bridge was completed in 1969, visitors and residents relied on the Coronado Ferry, which today has become quite popular with bicyclists, who shuttle their bikes across the harbor and ride Coronado's wide, flat boulevards for hours.

TOP ATTRACTIONS

FAMILY **Coronado Ferry Landing.** This collection of shops at Ferry Landing is on a smaller scale than the Embarcadero's Seaport Village, but you do get a great view of the downtown San Diego skyline. The little bayside shops and restaurants resemble the gingerbread domes of the Hotel Del Coronado. **Bikes and Beyond** (☎ *619/435–7180 ⊕ hollandsbicycles. com*) rents bikes and surreys, perfect for riding through town and along Coronado's scenic bike path. ✉ *1201 1st St., at B Ave., Coronado,* ☎ *619/435–8895 ⊕ www.coronadoferrylandingshops.com.*

San Diego's myriad coastal trails and paths provide great views of natural and man-made wonders alike.

Fodor's Choice **Hotel Del Coronado.** The Del's distinctive red-tile roofs and Victorian
★ gingerbread architecture have served as a set for many movies, political
meetings, and extravagant social happenings. It's speculated that the
Duke of Windsor may have first met the Duchess of Windsor Wallis
Simpson here. Eleven presidents have been guests of the Del, and the
film *Some Like It Hot*—starring Marilyn Monroe, Jack Lemmon, and
Tony Curtis—used the hotel as a backdrop.

The Hotel Del, as locals call it, was the brainchild of financiers Elisha
Spurr Babcock Jr. and H. L. Story, who saw the potential of Coronado's
virgin beaches and its view of San Diego's emerging harbor. It opened
in 1888 and has been a National Historic Landmark since 1977. The
History Gallery displays photos from the Del's early days, and books
elaborating on its history are sold, along with logo apparel and gifts,
in the hotel's 15-plus shops.

Although the pool area is reserved for hotel guests, several surrounding dining patios make great places to sit back and imagine the scene
during the 1920s, when the hotel rocked with good times. Behind the
pool area, an attractive shopping arcade features a classic candy shop
as well as several fine clothing and accessories stores. A lavish Sunday
brunch is served in the Crown Room. During the holidays, the hotel
hosts Skating by the Sea, an outdoor beachfront ice-skating rink open
to the public. ■**TIP➔** Whether or not you're staying at the Del, enjoy a
drink at the Sun Deck Bar and Grill in order to gaze out over the ocean—
it makes for a great escape.

Tours of the Del are $15 per person and take place on Monday, Wednes-
day, and Friday at 10:30, and weekends at 2; reservations are required.

✉ *1500 Orange Ave., at Glorietta Blvd., Coronado,* ☎ *619/435–6611, 619/437–8788 tour reservations (through Coronado Visitor Center)* ⊕ *www.hoteldel.com.*

Fodor'sChoice
★

Orange Avenue. Comprising Coronado's business district and its villagelike heart, this avenue is surely one of the most charming spots in Southern California. Slow-paced and very "local" (the city fights against chain stores), it's a blast from the past, although entirely up to date in other respects. The military presence—Coronado is home to the U.S. Navy Sea, Air and Land (SEAL) forces—is reflected in shops selling military gear and places like **McP's Irish Pub,** at No. 1107. A family-friendly stop for a good, all-American meal, it's the unofficial SEALs headquarters. Many clothing boutiques, home-furnishings stores, and upscale restaurants cater to visitors with deep pockets, but you can buy plumbing supplies, too, or get a genuine military haircut at **Crown Barber Shop,** at No. 947. If you need a break, stop for a latte at the sidewalk café of **Bay Books,** San Diego's largest independent bookstore, at No. 1029. ✉ *Orange Ave., near 9th St., Coronado, .*

WORTH NOTING

Glorietta Bay Inn walking tour. The former residence of John Spreckels, the original owner of North Island and the property on which the Hotel Del Coronado stands, is now a popular hotel. On Tuesday, Thursday, and Saturday mornings at 11 the Glorietta Bay Inn is the departure point for a fun and informative 1½-hour walking tour of a few of the area's 86 officially designated historic homes. It includes—from the outside only—some spectacular mansions and the Meade House, where L. Frank Baum, author of *The Wizard of Oz,* wrote additional Oz stories. ✉ *1630 Glorietta Blvd., Coronado,* ☎ *619/435–3101, 619/435–5993 tour information* ◰ *$12.*

BEACHES

San Diego's beaches have a different vibe from their northern counterparts in neighboring Orange County and glitzy Los Angeles farther up the coast. San Diego is more laid-back and less of a scene. Cyclists on cruiser bikes whiz by as surfers saunter toward the waves and sunbathers bronze under the sun, be it July or November.

Even at summer's hottest peak, San Diego's beaches are cool and breezy. Ocean waves are large, and the water will be colder than what you experience at tropical beaches—temperatures range from 55°F to 65°F from October through June, and 65°F to 73°F from July through September.

Finding a parking spot near the ocean can be hard in summer, but for the time being, unmetered parking is available at all San Diego city beaches.

Pay attention to signs listing illegal activities; undercover police often patrol the beaches. Smoking and alcoholic beverages are completely banned on city beaches. Drinking in beach parking lots, on boardwalks, and in landscaped areas is also illegal. Glass containers are not permitted on beaches, cliffs, and walkways, or in park areas and adjacent parking lots. Littering is not tolerated, and skateboarding is prohibited at some beaches. Fires are allowed only in fire rings or elevated barbecue grills. Although it may be tempting to take a sea creature from a tide pool as a souvenir, it may upset the delicate ecological balance, and it's illegal, too.

Lifeguards are stationed at city beaches from Sunset Cliffs up to Black's Beach in the summertime, but coverage in winter is provided by roving patrols only. When swimming in the ocean, be aware of rip currents, which are common in California shores.

San Diego's beaches are well maintained and very clean during summertime, when rainfall is infrequent. Pollution is generally worse near river mouths and storm-drain outlets, especially after heavy rainfall. Call San Diego's Lifeguard Services at ☎ 619/221–8824 for a recorded message that includes pollution reports along with surfing and diving conditions.

Beaches are listed geographically, south to north.

CORONADO

FAMILY **Silver Strand State Beach.** This quiet beach on a narrow sand-spit allows visitors a unique opportunity to experience both the Pacific Ocean and the San Diego Bay. The 2.5 miles of ocean side is great for surfing and other water sports while the bay side, accessible via foot tunnel under Highway 75, has calmer, warmer water and great views of the San Diego skyline. Lifeguards and rangers are on duty year-round, and there are places for biking, volleyball, and fishing. Picnic tables, grills, and fire pits are available in summer, and the Silver Strand Beach Cafe is open Memorial Day through Labor Day. The beach is close to Loews Coronado Bay Resort and the Coronado Cays, an exclusive community popular with yacht owners and celebrities. You can reserve RV sites ($65 beach; $50 inland) online (⊕ *www.reserveamerica.com*). Three day-use parking lots provide room for 800 cars. **Amenities:** food and drink, lifeguards, parking (fee), showers, toilets. **Best for:** walking, swimming, surfing. ⊠ *5000 Hwy. 75, 4.5 miles south of city of Coronado, Coronado, California, United States* ☎ 619/435–5184 ⊕ *www. parks.ca.gov/?page_id=654* 🅿 *Parking $10, $30 motorhome.*

FAMILY **Coronado Beach.** This wide beach is one of San Diego's most picturesque
Fodor'sChoice thanks to its soft white sand and sparkly blue water. The historic Hotel
★ Del Coronado serves as a backdrop, and it's perfect for sunbathing, people-watching, and Frisbee tossing. The beach has limited surf, but it's great for boogie-boarding and swimming. Exercisers might include Navy SEAL teams or other military units that conduct training runs on beaches in and around Coronado. There are picnic tables, grills, and popular fire rings, but don't bring lacquered wood or pallets. Only natural wood is allowed for burning. There's also a dog beach on the north end. There's free parking along Ocean Boulevard, though it's often hard to snag a space. **Amenities:** food and drink, lifeguards, showers, toilets. **Best for:** walking, swimming. ⊠ *Ocean Blvd., Between S. O St. and Orange Ave., Coronado,* ✛ *From the San Diego–Coronado bridge, turn left on Orange Ave. and follow signs.*

MISSION BAY, AND LA JOLLA

MISSION BAY

FAMILY **Mission Beach.** With a roller coaster, artificial wave park, and hotdog stands, this 2-mile long beach has a carnival vibe and is the closest thing you'll find to Coney Island on the West Coast. It's lively year-round but draws a huge crowd on hot summer days. A wide boardwalk paralleling the beach is popular with walkers, joggers, roller skaters, rollerbladers, and bicyclists. To escape the crowds a bit, head to South Mission Beach. It attracts surfers, swimmers, and scantily clad volleyball players, who often play competitive pick-up games on the courts near the N. Jetty. The water near the Belmont Park roller coaster can be a bit rough but makes for good boogie boarding and body surfing. For parking, you can try for a spot on the street, but your best bets are the two big lots at Belmont Park. **Amenities:** lifeguards, parking (no fee), showers, toilets. **Best for:** swimming, surfing, walking. ⊠ *3000 Mission Blvd., parking near roller coaster at West Mission Bay Dr., Mission Bay,* ⊕ *www. sandiego.gov/lifeguards/beaches/mb.shtml.*

Pacific Beach/North Pacific Beach. This beach, known for attracting a young college-age crowd, runs from the northern end of Mission Beach to Crystal Pier. The scene here is lively on weekends, with nearby restaurants, beach bars, and nightclubs providing a party atmosphere. In P.B. (as the local call it) Sundays are known as "Sunday Funday," and pub crawls can last all day. So although drinking is no longer allowed on the beach, it's still likely you'll see people who have had one too many. The mood changes just north of the pier at North Pacific Beach, which attracts families and surfers. Although not quite pillowy, the sand at both beaches is nice and soft, which makes for great sunbathing and sand-castle building. ■ TIP➔ **Kelp and flies can be problem on this stretch, so choose your spot wisely.** Parking at Pacific Beach can also be a challenge. A few coveted free angle parking spaces are available along the boardwalk, but you'll most likely have to look for spots in the surrounding neighborhood. **Amenities:** food and drink, lifeguards, parking (no fee), showers, toilets. **Best for:** partiers, swimming, surfing. ⊠ *4500 Ocean Blvd., Pacific Beach,* ⊕ *www.sandiego.gov/lifeguards/ beaches/pb.shtml.*

Tourmaline Surfing Park. Offering slow waves and frequent winds, this is one of the most popular beaches for beginning surfers, longboarders, windsurfers, and kiteboarders. The 175-space parking lot at the foot of Tourmaline Street normally fills to capacity by midday. Just like Pacific Beach, Tourmaline has soft, tawny colored sand, but when the tide is in the beach becomes quite narrow, making finding a good sunbathing spot a bit of a challenge. **Amenities:** seasonal lifeguards, parking (no fee), showers, toilets. **Best for:** windsurfing, surfing. ⊠ *600 Tourmaline St., Pacific Beach,* .

LA JOLLA

Fodor's Choice **Windansea Beach.** With its rocky shoreline and strong shore break, Windansea stands out among San Diego beaches for its dramatic natural beauty. It's one of the best surf spots in San Diego County. Professional surfers love the unusual A-frame waves the reef break here creates.

Although the large sandstone rocks that dot the beach might sound like a hindrance, they actually serve as protective barriers from the wind, making this one of the best beaches in San Diego for sunbathing. The beach's palm-covered surf shack is a protected historic landmark, and a seat here at sunset may just be one of the most romantic spots on the West Coast. The name Windansea comes from a hotel that burned down in the late 1940s. You can usually find nearby street parking. **Amenities:** seasonal lifeguards, toilets. **Best for:** sunset, surfing, solitude. ⊠ *Neptune Pl. at Nautilus St., La Jolla,* ⊕ *www.sandiego.gov/lifeguards/beaches/windan.shtml.*

Marine Street Beach. This wide expanse of white sand is famous for bodysurfing due to its powerful shore break, but it also teems with sunbathers, swimmers, walkers, joggers, and folks just out for the incredible views. The sand is soft and fluffy and feels wonderful as it squishes through your toes. Swimmers need to beware; waves break in extremely shallow water and you need to watch out for riptides. There are no amenities at the beach, but picnic tables, showers, and toilets are available at the nearby cove. **Amenities:** lifeguards. **Best for:** solitude, swimming, walking. ⊠ *Marine St. at Vista Del Mar Ave., 3 blocks west of La Jolla Blvd., La Jolla, .*

FAMILY
Fodor'sChoice
★

La Jolla Cove. This shimmering blue-green inlet surrounded by cliffs is what first attracted everyone to La Jolla, from Native Americans to the glitterati. "The Cove," as locals refer to it, beyond where Girard Avenue dead-ends into Coast Boulevard, is marked by towering palms that line a promenade where people strolling in designer clothes are as common as Frisbee throwers. Ellen Browning Scripps Park sits atop cliffs formed by the incessant pounding of the waves and offers a great spot for picnics with a view. The Cove has beautiful white sand that is a bit course near the water's edge, but the beach is still a great place for sunbathing and lounging. At low tide, the pools and cliff caves are a destination for explorers. This is also the best place in San Diego for snorkeling, and snorkelers can spot bright-orange Garibaldi fish and other marine life in the waters of the **San Diego–La Jolla Underwater Park Ecological Reserve.** The cove is also a favorite of rough-water swimmers. **Amenities:** lifeguards, showers, toilets. **Best for:** snorkeling, swimming, walking. ⊠ *1100 Coast Blvd., east of Ellen Browning Scripps Park, La Jolla,* ⊕ *www.sandiego.gov/lifeguards/beaches/cove.shtml.*

FAMILY **La Jolla Shores.** This is one of San Diego's most popular beaches due to its wide sandy shore, gentle waves, and incredible views of La Jolla peninsula. There's also a largy grassy park, and adjacent to La Jolla Shores lies the **San Diego La Jolla Underwater Park Ecological Reserve,** 6,000 acres of protected ocean bottom and tide lands. The white powdery sand at La Jolla Sands is some of San Diego's best, and several surf and scuba schools teach here. Kayaks can also be rented nearby. A concrete boardwalk parallels the beach, and a boat launch for small vessels lies 300 yards south of the lifeguard station at Avenida de Playa. Arrive early to get a parking spot in the lot at the foot of Calle Frescota. **Amenities:** lifeguards, parking (no fee), showers, toilets. **Best for:** surfing, swimming, walking. ✉ *8200 Camino del Oro, 2 miles north of downtown La Jolla, La Jolla,* ⊕ *www.sandiego.gov/lifeguards/beaches/shores.shtml.*

Fodor'sChoice ★ **Torrey Pines State Beach and Reserve.** With sandstone cliffs and hiking trails adjacent to the beach rather than urban development, Torrey Pines State Beach feels far away from the SoCal sprawl. The beach and reserve encompasses 1,600 acres of sandstone cliffs and deep ravines, and a network of meandering trails leads to the wide, pristine beach below. Along the way enjoy the rare Torrey pine trees, found only here and on Santa Rosa Island, offshore. Guides conduct tours of the nature preserve on weekends. Torrey Pines tends to get crowded in summer, but you'll find more isolated spots heading south under the cliffs leading to Black's Beach. Smooth rocks often wash up on stretches of the beach making it a challenge, at times, to go barefoot. If you can find a patch that is clear of debris, you'll encounter the nice soft, golden sand San Diego is known for. There is a paid parking lot at the entrance to the park but also look for free angle parking along N. Torrey Pines Rd. **Amenities:** lifeguards, parking (fee), showers, toilets. **Best for:** swimming, surfing, walking. ✉ *12600 N. Torrey Pines Rd.,* ☎ *858/755–2063* ⊕ *www.torreypine.org* 🖾 *Parking $12–$15 per vehicle depending on day and season.*

NORTH COUNTY BEACHES

DEL MAR

FAMILY **Del Mar Beach.** This famously clean 2-mile-long beach is the perfect place for long barefoot walks and sunbathing due to its extremely fine, soft sand and lack of seaweed and other debris. Del Mar Beach is also a great place for families. It has year-round lifeguards and areas clearly marked for swimming and surfing. Depending on the swell, you may see surfers at the 15th Street surf break; volleyball players love the courts at the beach's far north end. The section of beach south of 15th is lined with cliffs and tends to be less crowded than Main Beach, which extends from 15th north to 29th. Leashed dogs are permitted on most sections of the beach, except Main Beach, where they are prohibited from June 15 through the Tuesday after Labor Day. For the rest of the year, dogs may run under voice control at North Beach, just north of the River Mouth, also known locally as Dog Beach. Food, hotels, and shopping are all within an easy walk of Del Mar beach. Parking costs from $1.50 to $3 per hour at meters and pay lots on Coast Boulevard and along Camino Del Mar. **Amenities:** food and drink, lifeguards, parking (fee), showers, toilets. **Best for:** swimming, walking. ✉ *Main Beach, 1700 Coast Blvd.; North Beach 3200–3300 Camino Del Mar, Del Mar, California, United States* ☎ *858/755–1556* ⊕ *www.delmar. ca.us/203/Beaches-Parks.*

ENCINITAS

Swami's. The palms and the golden lotus-flower domes of the nearby Self-Realization Center temple and ashram earned this picturesque beach, also a top surfing spot, its name. Extreme low tides expose tide pools that harbor anemones, starfish, and other sea life. The only access is by a long stairway leading down from the cliff-top Seaside Roadside Park, where there's free parking. On big winter swells, the bluffs are lined with gawkers watching the area's best surfers take on—and be taken down by—some of the county's best big waves. The beach has flat, packed sand and can accumulate seaweed and some flies, so if lying out is your main objective you might want to head north to Moonlight Beach. Offshore, divers do their thing at North County's underwater park, Encinitas Marine Life Refuge. Sea Cliff, the small park next to the Swami's parking lot, offers shade trees, picnic tables, barbecues, and clean bathrooms. **Amenities:** lifeguards, parking (no fee), showers, toilets. **Best for:** snorkeling, surfing, swimming. ⊠ *1298 S. Coast Hwy. 101 (Rte. S21), 1 mile north of Cardiff, Encinitas, California, United States.*

WHERE TO EAT

San Diego's proximity to Mexico makes it an attractive destination for anything wrapped in a tortilla, but there's so much more. While most of the top restaurants offer seasonal California fare, San Diego also boasts excellent ethnic cuisines available at all prices.

As elsewhere in the United States, the San Diego dining scene has moved toward using sustainable, locally sourced meat, seafood, and produce—and providing good value. This emphasis on affordability is often presented as early or late-night dining specials, but also extends to the wine lists, where smart sommeliers are offering more wines from value regions like France's Loire and Languedoc, and countries like Chile and South Africa. *Use the coordinate (✛ A1) at the end of each listing to locate a site on the corresponding map.*

PRICES

Meals in San Diego popular dining spots can be pricey, especially in areas like La Jolla, the Gaslamp Quarter, and Coronado. Many other restaurants are very affordable or offer extra value with fixed-price menus, early-dining specials and early and late happy hours.

WHAT IT COSTS				
	$	**$$**	**$$$**	**$$$$**
Restaurants	under $18	$18–$27	$28–$35	over $35

Prices in the reviews are the average cost of a main course at dinner or, if dinner is not served, at lunch.

DOWNTOWN

GASLAMP QUARTER

$$$ ╳ **Searsucker.** Since opened by celebrity chef Brian Malarkey a few years
AMERICAN ago, this high-energy flagship restaurant has become the Gaslamp's best
for food and energetic atmosphere. Foodies from near and far savor
Malarkey's up-scale down-home fare like small plates of mac and cheese
with fried chicken skins, duck fat fries, and shrimp and grits. He is
masterful with locally caught seafood like opah sauced with chipotle.
The open kitchen serves a full range of poultry and meat dishes, while
specialty cocktails from the bar keep things lively in the sofa-furnished
lounge. If you prefer a quiet place to chat and dine, this isn't for you.
$ *Average main: $30* ⊠ *611 5th Ave., Gaslamp Quarter,* ☎ *619/233–
7327* ⊕ *www.searsucker.com* ⌲ *Reservations essential* ✛ *H2.*

$$ ╳ **Taka.** Pristine fish imported from around the world and presented
JAPANESE creatively attracts crowds nightly to this intimate Gaslamp restaurant.
Take a seat at the bar and watch one of the sushi chefs preparing appetizers, perhaps the monkfish liver with ponzu or some slices of tender
hamachi sashimi. Table service is available inside and outside where
an omakaze (tasting menu) or eight-piece rolls ranging from spicy tuna
to eel and vegetable can be shared and savored. Hot dishes include
salmon teriyaki and an East-meets-West-style New York steak. The
restaurant is a favorite with Japanese visitors and conventioneers. $ *Av-
erage main: $18* ⊠ *555 5th Ave., Gaslamp Quarter,* ☎ *619/338–0555*
⊕ *www.takasushi.com* ☽ *No lunch* ✛ *H2.*

EAST VILLAGE

$$ ╳ **The Blind Burro.** East Village families, baseball fans heading to or from
MODERN PETCO Park, and happy-hour bound singles flock to this airy restau-
MEXICAN rant with Baja-inspired food and drink with an Asian twist. Traditional
FAMILY margaritas get a fresh kick from fruit juices or jalapeño peppers; other
Fodor's Choice libations include sangrias and Mexican beers, all perfect pairings for
★ house-made guacamole, ceviche, or salsas with chips. For variety, try
the grilled yellowtail fish collar glazed with orange-chipotle BBQ sauce.
No enchiladas or burritos are served here, but the taco, torta entrée, and
side choices are extensive and innovative. Don't miss the spicy off-the-
cob corn and save room for warm cinnamon-sugared churros. $ *Aver-
age main: $18* ⊠ *639 J St., East Village,* ☎ *619/795–7880* ⊕ *www.the
blindburro.com* ✛ *H3.*

LITTLE ITALY

$$$ ╳ **Juniper & Ivy.** Celebrity chef Richard Blais's hot new addition to San
MODERN Diego's restaurant scene fills an open-beamed former packing house
AMERICAN with seating for 250 and an open stainless-steel dream kitchen where
diners can watch the chef and team in action. Blais sources local farm
fresh ingredients for his "left coast cookery" with a molecular gastronomy twist. Oysters on the half shell are dotted with liquid nitro-
gen-frozen "pearls" of horseradish cream and a gazpacho is topped
with buttermilk "snow." Even familiar carne asada surprises as spicy
steak tartare on toast. The comfort-food crowd might want to order
from the "secret menu" with its "In & Haute" double-patty burger
served with fries. ■ TIP➔ **Restaurant valet parking is only $5.** $ *Average*

main: $28 ✉ *2228 Kettner Blvd., Little Italy,* ☎ *619/269–9036* 🌐 *www.juniperandivy.com* 🕒 *No lunch* ⊕ *E5.*

$$ MODERN AMERICAN Fodor's Choice ★ 🍴 **Prepkitchen Little Italy.** Urbanites craving a hip casual setting and gourmet menu pack architectural salvage-styled Prepkitchen Little Italy, tucked upstairs above a busy corner in this thriving neighborhood. With first-date cocktails, after-work brews or birthday champagne, diners relish familiar choices like catch-of-the day, chops, and roast chicken paired with seasonal fruits and vegetables with flare and daring. Generously sized dishes like spicy Carlsbad mussels or zesty tagliatelle Bolognese could serve as dinner for two. Farmers' market flatbreads, changed daily, are made for sharing, too, while the hefty WNL Burger topped with bacon and egg is a staple for lunch, brunch, and dinner. **TIP→ For cheap treats, fill up on $5 tapas during the daily happy hour.** [$] *Average main: $24* ✉ *1660 India St., Little Italy,* ☎ *619/398–8383* 🕒 *No lunch weekends* ⊕ *E5.*

BALBOA PARK AND BANKERS HILL

BALBOA PARK

$$ ECLECTIC 🍴 **The Prado at Balboa Park.** Striking Spanish-Moorish details like painted ceilings and wrought-iron chandeliers are only part of the appeal of this lovely restaurant in the historic House of Hospitality. It also makes contemporary fare, friendly service and patio dining available to legions of museum- and theatergoers who come to Balboa Park. The bar is a fashionable destination for creative drinks and light nibbles spiced with Latin, Italian, and Asian flavors. In the dining room, lunch specialties range from fish tacos and panini to risotto and paella; for dinner opt for one of the unusual surf 'n' turf combos. Late evening happy hours are ideal for posttheater snacks and drinks. **TIP→ Parking in Balboa Park can be daunting; take advantage of the valet parking at the entrance of the restaurant.** [$] *Average main: $27* ✉ *1549 El Prado, Balboa Park,* ☎ *619/557–9441* 🌐 *www.pradobalboa.com* 🕒 *No dinner Mon.* ⊕ *E5.*

BANKERS HILL

$$ MODERN AMERICAN Fodor's Choice ★ 🍴 **Bankers Hill bar and grill.** The living wall of succulents, hip warehouse interior, and wine-bottle chandeliers suit this vibrant restaurant where good times and great eats meet. An after-work crowd joins residents of this quiet stretch of Bankers Hill for happy-hour cocktails, craft beers, and well-curated wines served from the zinc bar. Don't be surprised when the sommelier, also a cicerone (beer expert), suggests unusual brews to pair with everything from appetizers to dessert. Dinner standbys—mostly sophisticated comfort food often with Southwest flair—include the crispy BBQ pork tacos, Mexican-style red snapper, a juicy burger, seasonal bruschetta, and truffled french fries. Always save room for the silky butterscotch pudding topped with brittle and whipped cream. [$] *Average main: $21* ✉ *2202 4th Ave., Bankers Hill,* ☎ *619/231–0222* 🌐 *www.bankershillsd.com* 🕒 *No lunch* ⊕ *E5.*

$$ ITALIAN Fodor's Choice ★ 🍴 **Cucina Urbana.** Twentysomethings mingle with boomers in this convivial Bankers Hill dining room and bar, one of the most popular restaurants in town. Country-farmhouse decor that mixes rolling pins with modern art looks and feels festive. The open kitchen turns out innovative

Italian food with a California sensibility to enjoy traditionally or at communal tables. Many dishes are under $20, including crowd-pleasing short-rib pappardelle, fried stuffed squash blossoms, ricotta gnudi and thin-crust pizzas. At the in-house Wine Shop, purchase reasonably priced bottles from "the Americas and Mediterranean," opened tableside for an $8 corkage fee. End the meal with espresso sipped between bites of gelato, tiramisu, or cannoli. [$] *Average main: $21* ✉ *505 Laurel St., Bankers Hill,* ☎ *619/239–2222* 🌐 *www.cucinaurbana.com* ✍ *Reservations essential* ⏲ *No lunch Sat.–Mon.* ✥ *E5.*

OLD TOWN AND UPTOWN

OLD TOWN

$ SEAFOOD FAMILY

🍴 **Blue Water Seafood Market & Grill.** Blame a television segment by Guy Fieri on "Diners, Drive-ins and Dives" for the long lines of fans from around the globe. But it's the fresh seafood cooked to order that keeps them coming back to this no-frills fish market and restaurant. Have the fish, including wild salmon, ahi, halibut, yellowtail, your way—grilled with a choice of marinades and served with a side or on a salad, tortilla, or sandwich bread. Other favorites include fish-and-chips, ahi poke, lobster bisque, and cioppino. Beer lovers will enjoy local craft brews on tap. On the kids' menu is grilled cheddar cheese for seafood-averse little ones. [$] *Average main: $11* ✉ *3667 India St., Old Town,* ☎ *619/497–0914* 🌐 *www.bluewaterseafoodsandiego.com* ✍ *Reservations not accepted* ✥ *D4.*

HILLCREST AND MISSION HILLS

$$ MEXICAN FAMILY Fodor'sChoice ★

🍴 **Ortega's Bistro.** Seafood lovers have long flocked to Puerto Nuevo, the "lobster village" just south of San Diego in Baja California, Mexico. When a family that operates several Puerto Nuevo restaurants opened Ortega's in Hillcrest, it quickly became a top draw for authentic Baja coastal cuisine, minus the long lines to cross the border. The delicious house-made, Mexican fare stars succulent, sweet Baja-style lobster (steamed then grilled) served with beans, rice and made-to-order tortillas. At market price, it can top $35 a serving; but there are plenty of less-pricy menu options, too, including two versions of tortilla soup, melt-in-your-mouth carnitas (slow-cooked pork), made-at-the-table guacamole, and Ensenada-style battered fish tacos. The pomegranate margaritas are a must, as is the special red salsa for authentic spice. [$] *Average main: $19* ✉ *141 University Ave., Hillcrest,* ☎ *619/692–4200* 🌐 *www.ortegasbistro.com* ✥ *E4.*

$$ MODERN AMERICAN Fodor'sChoice ★

🍴 **The Red Door.** Farm-to-table at this cottage-comfy Mission Hills restaurant starts at owners Trish and Tom Watlington's extensive home garden that supplies half the needed produce and herbs. Local organic growers and ranchers add everything else showcased on the constantly changing menu. In the hands of chef Karrie Hills, these ingredients are expertly cooked and creatively paired. Residents from around the county have discovered her fried green tomatoes topped with stuffed squash blossoms and lasagna with chard and kale pasta. Hills also turns out satisfying desserts like crème brûlée "of the moment" and light-as-a-feather sherry poppy-seed cakes. Ask the affable staff for help matching

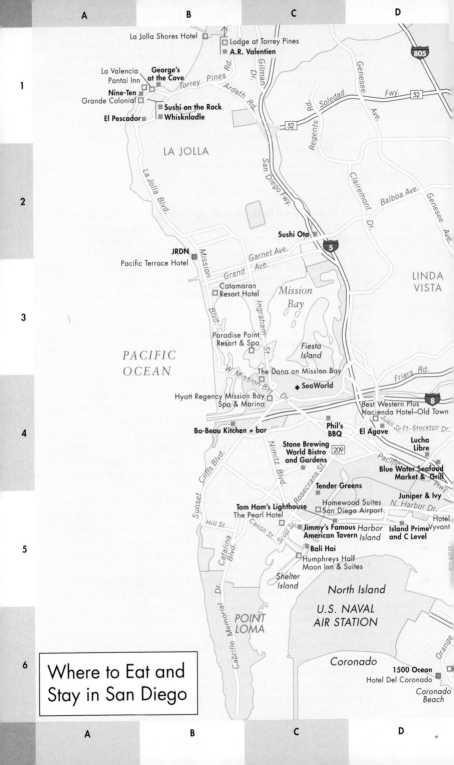

A | B | C | D

1

La Jolla Shores Hotel
Lodge at Torrey Pines
A.R. Valentien

La Valencia
Pantai Inn
George's
at the Cove
Nine-Ten
Grande Colonial
Sushi on the Rock
Whisknladle
El Pescador

Torrey Pines Rd.
Ardath Rd.
Gilman Dr.
Genesee Ave.
Soledad
Fwy.
52
805

LA JOLLA

52
San Diego Fwy.
Regents Rd.
Clairemont Dr.
Balboa Ave.
Genesee Ave.

2

La Jolla Blvd.
Sushi Ota
5
LINDA VISTA

3

JRDN
Pacific Terrace Hotel
Mission Blvd.
Grand Ave.
Garnet Ave.
Catamaran Resort Hotel
Mission Bay
Ingraham St.
Fiesta Island

PACIFIC OCEAN

Paradise Point Resort & Spa
W. Mission Bay Dr.
The Dana on Mission Bay
SeaWorld
Hyatt Regency Mission Bay Spa & Marina
Friars Rd.
8
Best Western Plus Hacienda Hotel–Old Town
Juan St. Ft. Stockton Dr.

4

Bo-Beau Kitchen + bar
Sunset Cliffs Blvd.
Nimitz Blvd.
Phil's BBQ
Stone Brewing World Bistro and Gardens
209
Rosecrans St.
El Agave
Lucha Libre
Pacific Hwy.
Blue Water Seafood Market & Grill
Juniper & Ivy
N. Harbor Dr.
Tender Greens
Homewood Suites
San Diego Airport
Tom Ham's Lighthouse
The Pearl Hotel
Canon St.
Scott St.
Jimmy's Famous American Tavern
Harbor Island
Island Prime and C Level
Hotel Vyvant

5

Hill St.
Catalina Blvd.
Cabrillo Memorial Dr.
Bali Hai
Humphreys Half Moon Inn & Suites
Shelter Island
North Island
U.S. NAVAL AIR STATION

POINT LOMA

Coronado
Orange

6

Where to Eat and Stay in San Diego

1500 Ocean
Hotel Del Coronado
Coronado Beach

A | B | C | D

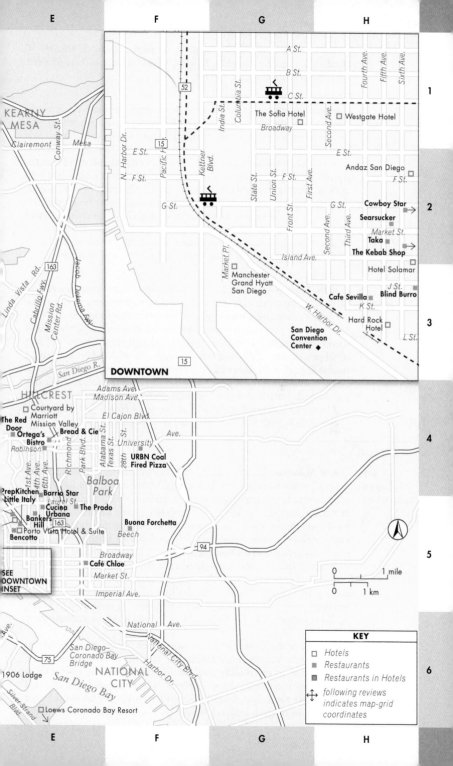

dishes with wines offered by the glass. [$] *Average main: $24* ✉ *741 W. Washington St., Mission Hills,* ☎ *619/295–6000* 🌐 *www.thereddoorsd.com* 🕒 *No lunch weekends* ✥ *E4.*

NORTH PARK

$ ITALIAN FAMILY Fodor's Choice ★ 🍴 **Buona Forchetta.** A golden-domed pizza oven, named Sofia after the owner's daughter, delivers authentic Neapolitan-style pizza to fans who often line up for patio tables at this dog- and kid-friendly Italian café in South Park. Slices of classic margarita or truffle-flavored mozzarella and mushroom pizzas make a meal or can be shared, but don't miss the equally delicious appetizers like the tender calamari or succulent artichokes, heaping fresh salads or fresh pastas, including a hearty lasagna, delicate ravioli, or gnocchi with wild boar sauce. Enjoy house sangrias and wines by the carafe, a craft beer, or a glass of reasonably priced Italian wine. Save room for *dolci,* too—cannoli, gelato, tiramisu, and other Italian desserts. [$] *Average main: $15* ✉ *3001 Beech St., Hillcrest,* 🌐 *www.buonaforchettasd.com* 🕒 *No lunch Mon. and Tues.* ✥ *F5.*

PACIFIC BEACH

$$$$ AMERICAN 🍴 **JRDN.** Seating in this chic ocean-facing restaurant (pronounced Jordan), in the boutique Tower23 Hotel, is divided between a long, narrow outdoor terrace and a series of relatively intimate indoor rooms. Chef Nick Shinton prepares modern steak-house fare including chops and steaks with sauces of the diner's choosing, lightened with lots of seasonal produce and a raw bar menu. Lunch and weekend brunch have a similar appeal, with dishes like eggs Benedict with citrus hollandaise, a blackened mahimahi sandwich, and hamachi sashimi salad. On Friday and Saturday the bar is jammed with under-thirty types eager to see and be seen. [$] *Average main: $37* ✉ *Tower 23 Hotel, 723 Felspar St., Pacific Beach,* ☎ *858/270–5736* 🌐 *www.t23hotel.com* ✥ *B3.*

LA JOLLA

$$$$ AMERICAN Fodor's Choice ★ 🍴 **A. R. Valentien.** Champions of in-season, fresh-today produce and seafood, executive chef Jeff Jackson and Chef de Cuisine Kelli Crosson have made this cozy room in the luxurious, Craftsman-style Lodge at Torrey Pines one of San Diego's top fine dining destinations. Their food combinations are simultaneously simple and delightfully inventive—pork belly with strawberry, kale and quinoa salad; halibut with roasted eggplant and curried cucumbers; or oak fire-cooked pork loin with chard, red walnuts, and roasted apricots. Lunch and dinner tasting menus ($75) are like a walk through a farmers' market. Still there are menu perennials like the silky chicken liver pâté. In good weather, enjoy meals plus ocean views from the terrace. [$] *Average main: $38* ✉ *11480 N. Torrey Pines Rd., La Jolla,* ☎ *858/777–6635* 🌐 *www.arvalentien.com* ✥ *B1.*

$$$$ AMERICAN Fodor's Choice ★ 🍴 **George's at the Cove.** La Jolla's ocean-view destination restaurant includes three dining areas: California Modern on the bottom floor, George's Bar in the middle, and Ocean Terrace on the roof. Hollywood types and other visiting celebrities can be spotted at California Modern, the sleek main dining room with its wall of windows. Elegant preparations of fresh seafood, tender beef, and California lamb reign,

which star-chef Trey Foshee enlivens with amazing local produce. Give special consideration to the legendary "fish tacos." Two levels of tasting menus are available, but the four-course offering generally is perfect for pocketbook and palate. For a more casual and inexpensive experience, go to the indoor/outdoor George's Bar, where you can enjoy pastas and grilled fish while watching a game, or head upstairs to the outdoor-only Ocean Terrace for spectacular views of La Jolla Cove. $ *Average main: $36* ⊠ *1250 Prospect St., La Jolla,* ☎ *858/454–4244* ⊕ *www. georgesatthecove.com* ⌂ *Reservations essential* ✚ *B1.*

$$
SEAFOOD
Fodor's Choice
★

╳ **Whisknladle.** This hip, popular eatery has won national acclaim for its combination of casual comfort and a menu of ever-changing local fare. In nice weather, request a patio table to enjoy the people-watching along with original or classic cocktails like the cucumber honey mimosa or house sangria. Executive chef Ryan Johnston's commitment to farm-fresh, from-scratch cooking shines in the sharable charcuterie board with house-made salumi, pâté, pickles, and condiments served with grilled crusty bread. Ask servers about salads, pastas, flatbreads, and entrées with that day's seasonal ingredients that can range from tree-ripened peaches to radish greens and new potatoes. Desserts change, too, but one timeless favorite is the decadent meringue topped with peanut butter ice cream and fudge sauce. $ *Average main: $26* ⊠ *1044 Wall St., La Jolla,* ☎ *858/551–7575* ⊕ *www.whisknladle.com* ⌂ *Reservations essential* ✚ *B1.*

POINT LOMA, SHELTER ISLAND, AND HARBOR ISLAND

POINT LOMA

$$
BISTRO

╳ **Bo-Beau kitchen + bar.** Ocean Beach is a slightly eccentric beach town, not a place diners would expect to find this warm, romantic bistro that evokes a French farmhouse. Executive chef Katherine Humphus, who refined her skills at French Laundry and New York's wd-50, crafted a satisfying French-inspired menu of soups, woodstone oven flatbreads, mussels, and other bistro classics served in cozy dining rooms and a rustic outdoor patio. Go traditional with boeuf bourguignon or chicken fricassee or spice it up with a flatbread topped with butternut squash, leeks, Italian cheeses, and pumpkin seeds. Don't leave without a side of the popular crispy brussels sprouts. Tuesday's "Cheap Date Night" special offers two entrées and bottle of wine for $39. $ *Average main: $19* ⊠ *4996 W. Point Loma Blvd., Ocean Beach,* ☎ *619/224–2884* ⊕ *www.bobeaukitchen.com* ☾ *No lunch* ✚ *B4.*

$$
ECLECTIC
FAMILY

╳ **Stone Brewing World Bistro and Gardens.** Judging by the lines out the door, this 23,000 square-foot monument to beer and good food in Liberty Station is a crowd-pleaser, especially for fans of San Diego's nationally known craft beer scene. BBQ duck tacos, chicken tikka masala, and other dishes on the global menu are perfect pairings with on-tap and bottled beers from around the world and Stone's own artisan brews like Arrogant Bastard Ale. Dine indoors in high-ceiling rooms guarded by etched-metal gargoyles and lit by beer-bottle chandeliers. Or, relax outdoors where parents often unwind as their kids enjoy the parklike grounds. Before leaving, browse the company store for hip logo-wear like hats, hoodies, and even a onesie for babies. $ *Average main: $20*

✉ *2816 Historic Decatur Rd., Suite 116, Liberty Station,* ☎ *619/269–2100* 🌐 *www.stonelibertystation.com* *Reservations essential* ✣ *C4.*

$ AMERICAN FAMILY 🍴 **Tender Greens.** "Farm-fresh ingredients served up with little fuss" is the ethos behind this casual cafeteria-style spot, now in Liberty Station, La Jolla, and downtown San Diego. All are very popular at lunch but the lines move quickly. Expect big salads like seared tuna Niçoise with quail egg, P. Balistreri salumi with kale, or grilled Thai octopus with green papaya. Naturally raised beef and chicken are roasted or grilled and then tucked into sandwiches or served as a dinner plate with vegetables. Wine and house-made soups and desserts round out the menu. [$] *Average main: $12* ✉ *2400 Historic Decatur Rd., Point Loma,* ☎ *619/226–6254* 🌐 *tendergreens.com* ✣ *C5.*

SHELTER ISLAND

$$ HAWAIIAN 🍴 **Bali Hai.** For more than 50 years, generations of San Diegans and visitors have enjoyed this Polynesian-theme icon with its stunning bay and city skyline views. Much of the kitsch has been replaced by more contemporary decor, but you'll still spot tikis here and there. The menu is a fusion of Hawaiian, Asian, and California cuisines with an emphasis on seafood. Standouts include the Hawaiian tuna poke, Mongolian lamb with pad Thai, and pan-seared barramundi with coconut lobster sauce. Vegetarian and gluten-free menus also are offered. A visit won't be complete without a world-famous Bali Hai Mai Tai topped with a little umbrella. [$] *Average main: $23* ✉ *2230 Shelter Island Dr., Shelter Island,* ☎ *619/222–1181* 🌐 *www.balihairestaurant.com* ✣ *C5.*

HARBOR ISLAND

$$$$ MODERN AMERICAN Fodor's Choice ★ 🍴 **Island Prime and C Level.** Two restaurants in one share this enviable spot on the shore of Harbor Island: the splurge-worthy Island Prime steak house and the relaxed C Level with a choice terrace fanned by sea breezes. Both venues tempt with unrivaled views of downtown San Diego's impressive skyline. Island Prime's surf-and-turf dinner menu offers a trio of fillets topped with blue cheese, wild mushrooms, and blue crab along with Alaskan king crab legs and lobster. At C Level, sharable plates are often Asian fusion-inspired, like the ahi stack with mango salsa and taro chips, or comfort food like the bacon-lobster sandwich. Chef Deborah Scott also offers a tasty "fuel" menu with lighter fare. The not-to-be-missed dessert is a decadent sundae—warm brownie, peanut-butter ice cream, whipped cream, and a maraschino cherry. [$] *Average main: $36* ✉ *880 Harbor Island Dr., Harbor Island,* ☎ *619/298–6802* 🌐 *www.islandprime.com* ✣ *D5.*

$$$ SEAFOOD 🍴 **Tom Ham's Lighthouse.** It's hard to top this longtime Harbor Island restaurant's incredible views across San Diego Bay to the downtown skyline and Coronado Bridge. Now a new alfresco dining deck and a contemporary seafood-focused menu ensure the dining experience doesn't take a back seat to the scenery. Sample the iced shellfish platter before moving on to traditional lobster bouillabaisse and paella or an adventuresome squid-ink risotto. The family-owned institution also serves a popular Sunday brunch that stars crab legs, peel-and-eat shrimp, smoked salmon, and oysters along with bottomless orange or pineapple mimosas. Prefer beer? Choose from a long list of on-tap

and bottled craft brews. $ *Average main: $30* ⊠ *2150 Harbor Island Dr., Harbor Island,* ☎ *619/291–9110* ⊕ *www.tomhamslighthouse.com* ⊙ *No lunch Sun.* ✛ *C5.*

WHERE TO STAY

In San Diego, you could plan a luxurious vacation, staying at a hotel with 350-thread-count sheets, wall-mounted flat screens, and panoramic Pacific views. But with some flexibility—maybe opting for a partial-view room with standard TVs—it's possible to experience the city's beauty at half the price.

Any local will tell you two things about San Diego: No. 1, the weather really is perfect; and No. 2, the area's neighborhoods and beach communities offer great diversity, from lively urban vacations to laid-back beachfront escapes. You'll need a car if you stay outside Downtown, but the coastal communities are rich with lodging options. For families, Uptown, Mission Valley, and Old Town are close to SeaWorld and the San Diego Zoo, offering good-value accommodations with extras like sleeper sofas and video games.

Many hotels promote discounted weekend packages to fill rooms after convention and business customers leave town. You can save on hotels and attractions by visiting the San Diego Convention and Visitors Bureau website (⊕ *www.sandiego.org*) for a free Vacation Planning Kit with a Travel Value Coupon booklet.

Use the coordinate (✛ A1) at the end of each listing to locate a site on the corresponding map.

PRICES

Note that even in the most expensive areas, you can find affordable rooms. High season is summer, and rates are lowest in fall. If an ocean view is important, request it when booking, but it will cost you.

Hotel reviews have been shortened. For full information, visit Fodors.com.

WHAT IT COSTS			
$	**$$**	**$$$**	**$$$$**
Hotels under $150	$150–$225	$226–$300	over $300

Hotel prices are the cost of a standard double room in high season, excluding 10.5% tax.

DOWNTOWN

GASLAMP QUARTER

$$$ **Hard Rock Hotel.** Self-billed as a hip playground for rock stars and people who want to party like them, the Hard Rock is near PETCO Park overlooking glimmering San Diego Bay. **Pros:** central location; energetic scene; luxurious rooms. **Cons:** pricey drinks; some attitude. $ *Rooms from: $276* ⊠ *207 5th Ave., Gaslamp Quarter,* ☎ *619/702–3000,*

HOTEL
Fodor's Choice
★

866/751–7625 ⊕ *www.hardrockhotelsd.com* ⤴ *244 rooms, 176 suites* ⦸ *No meals* ⊹ *H3.*

$$$ 🏨 **Hotel Solamar.** The hip Solamar is best known for its pool-side rooftop
HOTEL bar, LoungeSix, and stylish lobby decor. **Pros:** great restaurant; attentive
FAMILY service; upscale rooms. **Cons:** busy valet parking; bars are crowded and
Fodor's Choice noisy on weekends. $ *Rooms from: $265* ✉ *435 6th Ave., Gaslamp*
★ *Quarter,* ☎ *619/819–9500, 877/230–0300* ⊕ *www.hotelsolamar.com*
⤴ *217 rooms, 16 suites* ⦸ *No meals* ⊹ *H2.*

$$$ 🏨 **The Sofia Hotel.** This stylish and centrally located boutique hotel may
HOTEL have small rooms, but it more than compensates with pampering extras
Fodor's Choice like motion-sensor temperature controls, a Zen-like 24-hour yoga stu-
★ dio, and in-suite spa services. **Pros:** upscale amenities; historic building;
near shops and restaurants. **Cons:** busy area; small rooms. $ *Rooms*
from: $259 ✉ *150 W. Broadway, Gaslamp Quarter,* ☎ *619/234–9200,*
800/826–0009 ⊕ *www.thesofiahotel.com* ⤴ *183 rooms, 28 suites*
⦸ *No meals* ⊹ *G1.*

$$$ 🏨 **Westgate Hotel.** A modern high-rise near Horton Plaza hides San
HOTEL Diego's most opulent old-world-style hotel, featuring a lobby outfitted
Fodor's Choice with bronze sculptures and Baccarat chandeliers. **Pros:** elegant rooms;
★ grand lobby; near shopping. **Cons:** formal atmosphere; mandatory
facility fee. $ *Rooms from: $239* ✉ *1055 2nd Ave., Gaslamp Quarter,*
☎ *619/238–1818, 800/522–1564* ⊕ *www.westgatehotel.com* ⤴ *216*
rooms, 7 suites ⦸ *No meals* ⊹ *H1.*

LITTLE ITALY

$ 🏨 **Hotel Vyvant.** You'll find more amenities at other downtown hotels but
B&B/INN it's hard to beat this property's value and charm. **Pros:** good location;
historic property; welcoming staff. **Cons:** some shared baths; no park-
ing. $ *Rooms from: $139* ✉ *505 W. Grape St., Little Italy,* ☎ *619/230–*
1600, 800/518–9930 ⊕ *www.hotelvyvant.com* ⤴ *21 rooms, 2 suites*
⦸ *Breakfast* ⊹ *E5.*

EMBARCADERO

$$$ 🏨 **Manchester Grand Hyatt San Diego.** Primarily for business travelers, this
HOTEL hotel between Seaport Village and the convention center is San Diego's
FAMILY largest, and its 33- and 40-story towers make it the West Coast's tallest
waterfront hotel. **Pros:** great views; conference facilities; good location;
spacious rooms. **Cons:** very busy; some trolley noise. $ *Rooms from:*
$239 ✉ *1 Market Pl., Embarcadero,* ☎ *619/232–1234, 800/233–1234*
⊕ *www.manchestergrand.hyatt.com* ⤴ *1,552 rooms, 76 suites* ⦸ *No*
meals ⊹ *G3.*

OLD TOWN, MISSION VALLEY

OLD TOWN

$ 🏨 **Best Western Plus Hacienda Hotel–Old Town.** Perched on a hill in the
HOTEL heart of Old Town, this hotel is known for its expansive courtyards,
FAMILY outdoor fountains, and maze of stairs that connect eight buildings of
guest rooms. **Pros:** airport shuttle; well-maintained outdoor areas.
Cons: some rooms need renovating; spotty service; complicated layout.
$ *Rooms from: $129* ✉ *4041 Harney St., Old Town,* ☎ *619/298–4707*

🌐 *www.haciendahotel-oldtown.com* 🛏 *178 rooms, 20 suites* 🍴 *No meals* ✣ *D4.*

MISSION VALLEY

$ HOTEL FAMILY Fodor'sChoice ★ 🏨 **Courtyard by Marriott Mission Valley.** Amenities abound for families seeking a fun and casual base for trips to SeaWorld and the zoo. **Pros:** easy freeway access to area attractions; good value; nice perks for families and business travelers. **Cons:** few stores and restaurants in walking distance; halls can be noisy with kids. [$] *Rooms from: $149* ✉ *595 Hotel Circle S, Mission Valley,* ☎ *619/291–5720, 800/321–2211* 🌐 *www.marriott.com* 🛏 *309 rooms, 8 suites* 🍴 *No meals* ✣ *E4.*

MISSION BAY AND BEACHES

MISSION BAY

$$ RESORT FAMILY 🏨 **The Dana on Mission Bay.** This waterfront resort down the road from SeaWorld has an ideal location for active leisure travelers. **Pros:** water views; many outdoor activities. **Cons:** some rooms need renovation; many children in common areas. [$] *Rooms from: $159* ✉ *1710 W. Mission Bay Dr., Mission Bay,* ☎ *619/222–6440, 800/445–3339* 🌐 *www.thedana.com* 🛏 *259 rooms, 12 suites* 🍴 *No meals* ✣ *C4.*

$$$ RESORT FAMILY 🏨 **Hyatt Regency Mission Bay Spa & Marina.** This modern property has many desirable amenities, including balconies with excellent views of the garden, bay, ocean, or swimming pool courtyard. **Pros:** close proximity to water sports; 120-foot waterslides in pools, plus kiddie slide. **Cons:** slightly hard to navigate surrounding roads; thin walls; not centrally located. [$] *Rooms from: $299* ✉ *1441 Quivira Rd., Mission Bay,* ☎ *619/224–1234, 800/233–1234* 🌐 *www.missionbay.hyatt.com* 🛏 *300 rooms, 129 suites* 🍴 *No meals* ✣ *C4.*

$$$ RESORT FAMILY 🏨 **Paradise Point Resort & Spa.** Minutes from SeaWorld but hidden in a quiet part of Mission Bay, the beautiful landscape of this 44-acre resort offers plenty of space for families to play and relax. **Pros:** water views; pools; good service. **Cons:** not centrally located; motel-thin walls; parking and resort fees. [$] *Rooms from: $279* ✉ *1404 Vacation Rd., Mission Bay,* ☎ *858/274–4630, 800/344–2626* 🌐 *www.paradisepoint.com* 🛏 *462 cottages* 🍴 *No meals* ✣ *C3.*

PACIFIC BEACH

$$$$ RESORT 🏨 **Pacific Terrace Hotel.** Travelers love this terrific beachfront hotel and the ocean views from most rooms; it's a perfect place for watching sunsets over the Pacific. **Pros:** beach views; large rooms; friendly service. **Cons:** busy and sometimes noisy area; lots of traffic. [$] *Rooms from: $428* ✉ *610 Diamond St., Pacific Beach,* ☎ *858/581–3500, 800/344–3370* 🌐 *www.pacificterrace.com* 🛏 *61 rooms, 12 suites* 🍴 *No meals* ✣ *B3.*

LA JOLLA

$$$$ HOTEL Fodor'sChoice ★ 🏨 **Grande Colonial.** This white wedding cake–style hotel in the heart of La Jolla village has ocean views and charming European details that include chandeliers, mahogany railings, and French doors. **Pros:** near shopping; near beach; superb restaurant. **Cons:** somewhat busy street; no fitness center. [$] *Rooms from: $319* ✉ *910 Prospect St., La Jolla,*

☎ *858/454–2181, 877/792–8053* ⊕ *www.thegrandecolonial.com* ⌂ *52 rooms, 41 suites* ⦿ *No meals* ✛ *B1.*

$$$
HOTEL
FAMILY

⌂ **La Jolla Shores Hotel.** One of San Diego's few hotels actually on the beach, this property is part of La Jolla Beach and Tennis Club. **Pros:** on beach; great views; quiet area. **Cons:** not centrally located; pool can be noisy. Ⓢ *Rooms from: $279* ✉ *8110 Camino del Oro, La Jolla,* ☎ *858/459–8271, 877/346–6714* ⊕ *www.ljshoreshotel.com* ⌂ *127 rooms, 1 suite* ⦿ *No meals* ✛ *B1.*

$$$$
HOTEL

⌂ **La Valencia.** This pink Spanish-Mediterranean confection drew Hollywood film stars in the 1930s and '40s with its setting and views of La Jolla Cove; now it draws the Kardashians. **Pros:** upscale rooms; views; near beach. **Cons:** standard rooms are tiny; lots of traffic outside. Ⓢ *Rooms from: $380* ✉ *1132 Prospect St., La Jolla,* ☎ *858/454–0771, 800/451–0772* ⊕ *www.lavalencia.com* ⌂ *82 rooms, 15 villas, 15 suites* ⦿ *No meals* ✛ *B1.*

$$$$
RESORT
Fodor'sChoice
★

⌂ **Lodge at Torrey Pines.** This beautiful Craftsman-style lodge sits on a bluff between La Jolla and Del Mar and commands a coastal view. **Pros:** spacious upscale rooms; good service; adjacent the famed Torrey Pines Golf Course. **Cons:** not centrally located; expensive. Ⓢ *Rooms from: $450* ✉ *11480 N. Torrey Pines Rd., La Jolla,* ☎ *858/453–4420, 888/826–0224* ⊕ *www.lodgetorreypines.com* ⌂ *169 rooms, 8 suites* ⦿ *No meals* ✛ *B1.*

$$$$
HOTEL

⌂ **Pantai Inn.** Located along La Jolla coastline with ocean views from almost every corner, this sophisticated, Bali-inspired inn offers a mix of studios, one- and two-bedroom suites, cottages, and townhomes. **Pros:** spacious rooms; ocean views; free parking. **Cons:** no pool; no fitness center. Ⓢ *Rooms from: $350* ✉ *1003 Coast Blvd., La Jolla,* ☎ *858/224–7600, 855/287–2682* ⊕ *www.pantai.com* ⌂ *7 rooms, 24 suites* ⦿ *Breakfast* ✛ *B1.*

POINT LOMA AND CORONADO WITH HARBOR AND SHELTER ISLANDS

POINT LOMA

$$$
HOTEL
FAMILY
Fodor'sChoice
★

⌂ **Homewood Suites San Diego Airport.** Families and business travelers on long trips will benefit from the space and amenities at this all-suites hotel. **Pros:** complimentary grocery shopping service; free parking; close to paths for joggers and bikers. **Cons:** often crowded dining room; far from nightlife. Ⓢ *Rooms from: $289* ✉ *2576 Laning Rd., Point Loma,* ☎ *619/222–0500* ⊕ *www.homewoodsuites.com* ⌂ *150 suites* ⦿ *Multiple meal plans* ✛ *C5.*

$
HOTEL
Fodor'sChoice
★

⌂ **The Pearl Hotel.** This previously vintage motel received a makeover, turning it into a retro-chic hangout decorated with kitschy lamps and original, in-room art by local children. **Pros:** near marina; hip bar/restaurant on-site (dinner only, except for seasonal specials). **Cons:** not centrally located; one bed in rooms. Ⓢ *Rooms from: $139* ✉ *1410 Rosecrans St., Point Loma,* ☎ *619/226–6100* ⊕ *www.thepearlsd.com* ⌂ *23 rooms* ⦿ *No meals* ✛ *C5.*

SHELTER ISLAND

$$
RESORT

Humphreys Half Moon Inn & Suites. This sprawling South Seas–style resort has grassy open areas with palms and tiki torches; many of the rooms have water views. **Pros:** water views; near marina; free admission to Backstage Live music club. **Cons:** resort fee; vast property; not centrally located. $ *Rooms from: $219* ✉ *2303 Shelter Island Dr., Shelter Island,* ☎ *619/224–3411, 800/542–7400* ⊕ *www.halfmooninn.com* ⇒ *128 rooms, 54 suites* ⊙ *No meals* ✢ *C5.*

CORONADO

$$$$
RESORT
FAMILY
Fodor'sChoice
★

Hotel Del Coronado. As much of a draw today as it was when it opened in 1888, the Victorian-style "Hotel Del" is always alive with activity, as guests—including U.S. presidents and celebrities—and tourists marvel at the fanciful architecture and ocean views. **Pros:** romantic; on the beach; hotel spa. **Cons:** some rooms are small; expensive dining; hectic public areas. $ *Rooms from: $329* ✉ *1500 Orange Ave., Coronado,* ☎ *800/468–3533, 619/435–6611* ⊕ *www.hoteldel.com* ⇒ *679 rooms, 78 cottages and villas* ⊙ *No meals* ✢ *D6.*

$$$
RESORT
FAMILY

Loews Coronado Bay Resort. You can park your boat at the 80-slip marina of this romantic retreat set on a secluded 15-acre peninsula on the Silver Strand. **Pros:** great restaurants; lots of activities; all rooms have furnished balconies with water views. **Cons:** far from anything; confusing layout. $ *Rooms from: $259* ✉ *4000 Coronado Bay Rd., Coronado,* ☎ *619/424–4000, 800/815–6397* ⊕ *www.loewshotels.com/ CoronadoBay* ⇒ *402 rooms, 37 suites* ⊙ *No meals* ✢ *E6.*

$$$$
B&B/INN
Fodor'sChoice
★

1906 Lodge at Coronado Beach. Smaller but no less luxurious than the sprawling beach resorts of Coronado, this lodge welcomes couples for romantic retreats two blocks from the ocean. **Pros:** most suites feature Jacuzzi tubs, fireplaces, and porches; historic property; free underground parking. **Cons:** too quiet for families; no pool. $ *Rooms from: $309* ✉ *1060 Adella Ave., Coronado,* ☎ *619/437–1900, 866/435–1906* ⊕ *www.1906lodge.com* ⇒ *6 rooms, 11 suites* ⊙ *Some meals* ✢ *D6.*

NIGHTLIFE

A couple of decades ago, San Diego scraped by on its superb daytime offerings. Those sleepy-after-dark days are over; San Diego now sizzles when the sun goes down. Of particular interest to beer lovers, the city has become internationally acclaimed for dozens of breweries, beer pubs, and festivals.

The most obvious destination for visitors is the Gaslamp Quarter, a 16-block former red-light district gone glam. The debauchery is slightly more modest these days—or at least legal, anyway. Between the Gaslamp and neighboring East Village, there's truly something for everyone, from secretive speakeasies to big, bangin' dance clubs and chic rooftop lounges to grimy dives. If you're staying in the Gaslamp, it's the perfect place to party. If you're driving from elsewhere, prepare to pay. Your best options: parking lots (prices start at $20) or valet (at some restaurants and clubs).

The epicenter of gay culture is Hillcrest, where you'll find bars and clubs catering primarily to the LGBT crowd—though everyone is welcome. East of Hillcrest is North Park, where hip twenty- and thirtysomethings hang out at edgy scenester hot spots. Nearby South Park and University Heights also have a few cool offerings. A cab from Downtown to any of these 'hoods costs about $15.

Pacific Beach tends to draw college kids who don't know when to say when, while Ocean and Mission beaches pull laid-back surfers and their cohorts. La Jolla, for the most part, is a snooze if you're in the mood to booze late at night.

DOWNTOWN

GASLAMP QUARTER

BARS

Fodor's Choice ★ Rooftop 600 @Andaz. At this rooftop bar and lounge atop the Andaz hotel, a fashionable crowd sips cocktails poolside while gazing at gorgeous views of the city. Thursday through Saturday, the scene heats up with a DJ spinning dance music, while velvet ropes and VIP bottle service please the A-listers (like Prince Harry) in the crowd. ⊠ *600 F St., Gaslamp Quarter,* ☎ *619/849–1234* ⊕ *www.rooftop600.com.*

Fluxx. Arguably the hottest club in the Gaslamp, this Vegas-style, multi-theme space is packed to the gills on weekends with pretty people dancing to house and electro music and dropping major cash at the bar. ■ TIP→ Get here early for a lower cover and to avoid the epic lines that snake around the block. ⊠ *500 4th Ave., Gaslamp Quarter,* ☎ *619/232–8100* ⊕ *www.fluxxsd.com.*

MUSIC CLUBS

House of Blues. The local branch of the renowned music chain is decorated floor to ceiling with colorful folk art and features three different areas to hear music. There's something going on here just about every night of the week, and the gospel brunch on select Sundays is one of the most praiseworthy events in town. Can we get a hallelujah? ⊠ *1055 5th Ave., Gaslamp Quarter,* ☎ *619/299–2583* ⊕ *www.houseofblues.com.*

OFF THE BEATEN PATH
The Casbah. This small club near the airport, the unofficial headquarters of the city's indie music scene, has a national reputation for showcasing up-and-coming acts of all genres. Nirvana, Smashing Pumpkins, and the White Stripes all played here on the way to stardom. ⊠ *2501 Kettner Blvd., Middletown,* ☎ *619/232–4355* ⊕ *www.casbahmusic.com.*

EAST VILLAGE

BARS

Cat Eye Club. Separated from the hectic hustle of East Village by just a short and dimly lit foyer, Cat Eye Club might as well be in an entirely different world. More specifically, it's a trip back to the 1960s, with mid-century modern furnishings, a Wurlitzer jukebox and Rat Pack flicks on regular rotation. Their menu of tiki cocktails ranges from simple sips to punchbowls, or for those who prefer their drinks flashier, the Cradle of Life, garnished with a flaming lime wedge. ⊠ *370 7th Ave., East Village,* ⊕ *cateyeclubsd.com.*

Fodor's Choice ★ **Noble Experiment.** There are a handful of speakeasy-style bars in San Diego, though none deliver so far above and beyond the novelty quite like this cozy-yet-swank cocktail lounge hidden in the back of a burger restaurant. Seek out the hidden door (hint: look for the stack of kegs), tuck into a plush leather booth next to the wall of golden skulls, and sip on the best craft cocktails in the city. ■ TIP→ Reservations are almost always a must, so be sure to call ahead. ⊠ 777 G St., East Village, ☎ 619/888–4713 ⊕ nobleexperimentsd.com.

LITTLE ITALY

3

BARS

Fodor's Choice ★ **The Waterfront Bar & Grill.** It isn't really on the waterfront, but San Diego's oldest bar was once the hangout of Italian fishermen. Most of the collars are now white, and patrons enjoy an excellent selection of beers, along with chili, burgers, fish-and-chips, and other great-tasting grub, including fish tacos. Get here early, as there's almost always a crowd. ⊠ 2044 Kettner Blvd., Little Italy, ☎ 619/232–9656 ⊕ www.waterfront barandgrill.com.

COFFEEHOUSES

Extraordinary Desserts. A delicious visual treat, with a lacy, laser-cut metal facade and elegant teak patio, also satisfies every sort of culinary craving, from savory to sweet and everything in between. The wine, beer, and bubbly list is très chic, too. ⊠ 1430 Union St., Little Italy, ☎ 619/294–7001 ⊕ www.extraordinarydesserts.com.

OLD TOWN AND UPTOWN

HILLCREST

GAY NIGHTLIFE

Fodor's Choice ★ **Baja Betty's.** Although it draws plenty of gay customers, the festive and friendly atmosphere is popular with just about everyone in the Hillcrest area (and their pets are welcome, too). The bar staff stocks more than 100 brands of tequila and mixes plenty of fancy cocktails. ⊠ 1421 University Ave., Hillcrest, ☎ 619/269–8510 ⊕ www.bajabettyssd.com.

Urban Mo's Bar and Grill. Cowboys gather for line dancing and two-stepping on the wooden dance floor—but be forewarned, yee-hawers, it can get pretty wild on Western nights. There are also Latin, hip-hop, and drag revues but the real allure is in the creative drinks ("Gone Fishing"—served in a fishbowl, for example) and the breezy patio where love (or something like it) is usually in the air. ⊠ 308 University Ave., Hillcrest, ☎ 619/491–0400 ⊕ www.urbanmos.com.

MISSION HILLS

PIANO BARS

Fodor's Choice ★ **Starlite.** Bar-goers are dazzled by Starlite's award-winning interior design, which includes rock walls, luxe leather booths, and a massive mirror-mounted chandelier. A hexagonal wood-plank entryway leads to a sunken white bar, where sexy tattooed guys and girls mix creative cocktails, such as the signature Starlite Mule, served in a copper mug. An iPod plays eclectic playlists ranging from old-timey jazz and blues to obscure vintage rock (and DJs are on hand on certain evenings).

CLOSE UP

San Diego On Tap

The secret is out: San Diego is the nation's best beer town. In addition to more than 60 local breweries, San Diego has a stretch of beer-nerd heaven nicknamed the Belgian Corridor (30th Street in North/South Park). You can find all styles of beer in San Diego, from the meek to the mighty, but many local brewers contend that the specialty is the big, bold Double IPA (also called an Imperial IPA). It's an India Pale Ale with attitude—and lots of hops. Nearly every local brewery has its own version.

Bars with the best microbrew selection: Blind Lady Ale House, Hamilton's Tavern, Live Wire, O'Brien's, Toronado.

Best fests: Want one location and a seemingly endless supply of beer? Try the San Diego Festival of Beers (September ⊕ www.sdbeerfest.org), San Diego Beer Week (November ⊕ www.sdbw.org), and the Strong Ale Fest (December). Find more listings at ⊕ www.sandiegobrewersguild.org.

Best way to sample it all: Sign up for Brewery Tours of San Diego (⊕ www.brewerytoursofsandiego.com) to sample the best craft beers without a second thought about directions or designated drivers.

SAN DIEGO'S BEST BREWERIES

You can also head to the source, where beer is brewed. These are outside the city center, but worth the trek for beer aficionados.

Fodor's Choice ★ Alpine Brewing Co. Well worth the mountain drive, this family-owned operation may be itty-bitty, but it's also a big champ: brewmaster Pat McIlhenney, a former fire captain, has won national and international kudos for his hopped-up creations and took the title of the fifth-best brewery in the nation from *Beer Advocate*. Tasters are only a buck each, or fill a growler, which holds a half gallon, for future imbibing. If they're on tap, don't pass up Duet, Pure Hoppiness, or Exponential Hoppiness. Alpine recently opened a pub a few doors down where you can taste flights of their various beers. ⊠ *2351 Alpine Blvd., Alpine,* ☎ *619/445–2337* ⊕ *www.alpinebeerco.com.*

Ballast Point Brewing Co. Until recently, you had to head to the Miramar/Scripps Ranch area for a tasting at Ballast Point, which was worth the drive. But the craft brewery recently opened a local taproom in Little Italy (2215 India Street). There are plenty of opportunities to sample their beers at local pubs, however—the Sculpin IPA is outstanding, and for more adventurous drinkers, the much hotter Habanero sculpin, which is brewed with habanero peppers. ⊠ *10051 Old Grove Rd., Scripps Ranch,* ☎ *858/695–2739* ⊕ *www.ballastpoint.com.*

Stone Brewing World Gardens and Bistro. The Big Daddy of San Diego craft brewing was founded by a couple of basement beer tinkerers in 1996; the company now exports its aggressively hoppy beers—instantly identifiable by their leering gargoyle labels—to bars and stores across the nation. Stone's monumental HQ is off the beaten path, but totally worth a visit for its tours ($3 includes souvenir tasting glass), vast on-tap selection (not just Stone beers), and hard-to-beat bistro eats. ⊠ *1999 Citracado Pkwy., Escondido, California, United States* ☎ *760/294–7866* ⊕ *www.stonebrew.com.*

During warmer months, procuring a spot on the outside wood-decked patio is an art form. ⊠ *3175 India St., Mission Hills,* ☎ *619/358–9766* ⊕ *www.starlitesandiego.com.*

NORTH PARK

BARS

Fodor'sChoice **Seven Grand.** This whiskey lounge is a swanky addition to an already
★ thriving North Park nightlife scene and a welcome alternative to the neighboring dives and dance clubs. Live jazz, a tranquil atmosphere, and a bourbon-loving craft cocktail list keep locals flocking. ⊠ *3054 University Ave., North Park,* ☎ *619/269–8820* ⊕ *www.sevengrandbars. com/sd.*

Toronado. One of San Diego's favorite gathering spots for hop-heads is named in honor of the San Francisco beer bar of the same name. The beer list—both on tap and by the bottle—is hard to beat. The place can get noisy, but the food—a mix of burgers and American-style comfort food—more than makes up for it. ⊠ *4026 30th St., North Park,* ☎ *619/282–0456* ⊕ *www.toronadosd.com.*

MISSION BAY AND THE BEACHES

PACIFIC BEACH

BARS

JRDN. This contemporary lounge (pronounced "Jordan") occupies the ground floor of Pacific Beach's chicest boutique hotel, Tower23, and offers a more sophisticated vibe in what is a very party-happy neighborhood. Sleek walls of windows and an expansive patio overlook the boardwalk. ⊠ *723 Felspar St., Pacific Beach,* ☎ *858/270–5736* ⊕ *www. t23hotel.com.*

PERFORMING ARTS

TICKETS

Arts Tix. You can buy advance tickets, many at half price, to theater, music, and dance events at Arts Tix. ⊠ *28 Horton Plaza, 3rd Ave. and Broadway, Gaslamp Quarter,* ☎ *858/381–5595* ⊕ *www.sdartstix.com.*

DANCE

California Ballet Company. The company performs high-quality contemporary and classical works September through May at the **Civic Theatre.** The *Nutcracker* is staged annually around the holiday season. ⊠ *1100 3rd Ave., Downtown,* ☎ *619/570–1100* ⊕ *www.californiaballet.org*

Balboa Theatre. This historic landmark hosts ballet, music, plays, and even stand-up comedy performances. ⊠ *868 4th Ave., Downtown,* ☎ *619/570–1100* ⊕ *www.sandiegotheatres.org*

MUSIC

Fodor's Choice ★ **Copley Symphony Hall.** The great acoustics here are surpassed only by the incredible Spanish baroque interior. Not just the home of the San Diego Symphony Orchestra, the renovated 2,200-seat 1920s-era theater has also hosted major stars like Elvis Costello, Leonard Cohen, and Sting. ⊠ *750 B St., Downtown,* ☎ *619/235–0804* ⊕ *www.sandiegosymphony. org.*

San Diego Symphony Orchestra. The orchestra's events include classical concerts and summer and winter pops, nearly all of them at Copley Symphony Hall. The outdoor Summer Pops series is held on the Embarcadero, on North Harbor Drive beyond the convention center. ⊠ *Box office, 750 B. St., Downtown,* ☎ *619/235–0804* ⊕ *www. sandiegosymphony.org.*

Spreckels Organ Pavilion. Home of a giant outdoor pipe organ donated to the city, the beautiful Spanish baroque pavilion hosts concerts by civic organist Carol Williams and guest organists on most Sunday afternoons and on Monday evenings in summer. Local military bands, gospel groups, and barbershop quartets also perform here. All shows are free. ⊠ *2211 Pan American Rd. E, Balboa Park,* ☎ *619/702–8138* ⊕ *spreckelsorgan.org.*

THEATER

Fodor's Choice ★ **La Jolla Playhouse.** Under the artistic direction of Christopher Ashley, the playhouse presents exciting and innovative plays and musicals on three stages. Many Broadway shows—among them *Memphis, Tommy,* and *Jersey Boys*—have previewed here before their East Coast premieres. Its Without Walls program also ensures that the productions aren't limited to the playhouse, having put on site-specific shows in places like outdoor art spaces, cars, and even the ocean. ⊠ *University of California at San Diego, 2910 La Jolla Village Dr., La Jolla,* ☎ *858/550–1010* ⊕ *www.lajollaplayhouse.org.*

Fodor's Choice ★ **The Old Globe.** This complex, comprising the Sheryl and Harvey White Theatre, the Lowell Davies Festival Theatre, and the Old Globe Theatre, offers some of the finest theatrical productions in Southern California. Theater hits such as *The Full Monty* and *Dirty Rotten Scoundrels,* both of which went on to Broadway, premiered on these famed stages. The Old Globe presents the family-friendly *How the Grinch Stole Christmas* around the holidays, as well as a renowned summer Shakespeare Festival with three to four plays in repertory. ⊠ *1363 Old Globe Way, Balboa Park,* ☎ *619/234–5623* ⊕ *www.oldglobe.org.*

SPORTS AND THE OUTDOORS

BASEBALL

Long a favorite spectator sport in San Diego, where games are rarely rained out, baseball gained even more popularity in 2004 with the opening of PETCO Park, a stunning 42,000-seat facility in the heart of Downtown.

San Diego Padres. From April into October, the Padres slug it out for bragging rights in the National League West. Home games are played at PETCO Park. Tickets are usually available on game day, but rival matchups against the Los Angeles Dodgers and the San Francisco Giants often sell out quickly. For an inexpensive day at the ballpark, go for "The Park at the Park" tickets ($10 and up, depending on demand; available for purchase at the park only) and have a picnic on the grass while watching the game on one of several giant-screen TVs. You also get access to the full concourse. Head to the fifth floor to find a Stone Brewing outdoor beer garden with sweeping views of downtown and the San Diego Bay. ⊠ *100 Park Blvd., East Village,* ☎ *619/795–5000, 877/374–2784* ⊕ *sandiego.padres.mlb.com.*

BIKING

San Diego offers bountiful opportunities for bikers, from casual board-walk cruises to strenuous rides into the hills. The mild climate makes biking in San Diego a year-round delight. Bike culture is respected here, and visitors are often impressed with the miles of designated bike lanes running alongside city streets and coastal roads throughout the county.

Cheap Rentals Mission Beach. A little over a block off the boardwalk, this place has good daily and weekly prices for surfboards, stand-up pad-dleboards, kayaks, skateboards, ice chests, umbrellas, chairs, and bike rentals, including beach cruisers, tandems, hybrids, and two-wheeled baby carriers. Demand is high during the busy season (May through September), so call to reserve equipment ahead of time. ⊠ *3689 Mission Blvd., Mission Beach,* ☎ *858/488–9070, 800/941–7761* ⊕ *www. cheap-rentals.com.*

Holland's Bicycles. This is a great bike rental source on Coronado Island. It also has another store (**Bikes and Beyond** ☎ *619/435–7180)* located at the ferry landing, so you can jump on your bike as soon as you cross the harbor from downtown San Diego. ⊠ *977 Orange Ave., Coronado,* ☎ *619/435–3153* ⊕ *www.hollandsbicycles.com.*

Route S21. On many summer days, Route S21, aka Old Highway 101, from La Jolla to Oceanside looks like a freeway for cyclists. About 24 miles long, it's easily the most popular and scenic bike route around, never straying far from the beach. Although the terrain is fairly easy, the long, steep Torrey Pines grade is famous for weeding out the weak. Another Darwinian challenge is dodging slow-moving pedestrians and cars pulling over to park in towns like Encinitas and Del Mar. ⊠ *La Jolla, California, United States.*

DIVING

Ocean Enterprises Scuba Diving. Stop in for everything you need to plan a diving adventure, including equipment, advice, and instruction. ✉ *7710 Balboa Ave., Suite 101, Clairemont Mesa,* ☎ *858/565–6054* ⊕ *www. oceanenterprises.com.*

San Diego–La Jolla Underwater Park Ecological Preserve. Diving enthusiasts the world over come to San Diego to snorkel and scuba dive off La Jolla at the underwater preserve. Because all sea life is protected here, this 533-acre preserve (all of La Jolla Cove to La Jolla Shores) is the best place to see large lobsters, sea bass, and sculpin (scorpion fish), as well as numerous golden garibaldi damselfish, the state marine fish. It's common to see hundreds of beautiful (and harmless) leopard sharks schooling at the north end of the cove, near La Jolla Shores, especially in summer. ✉ *La Jolla Shores and Ellen Browning Scripps Park, La Jolla,* .

Scuba San Diego. This center is well regarded for its top-notch instruction and certification programs, as well as for guided dive tours. Trips include dives to kelp reefs in La Jolla Cove, and night diving at La Jolla Canyon. ✉ *San Diego Hilton Hotel, 1775 E. Mission Bay Dr., Mission Bay,* ☎ *619/260–1880* ⊕ *www.scubasandiego.com.*

FISHING

Fisherman's Landing. You can book space on a fleet of luxury vessels from 57 feet to 124 feet long and embark on multiday trips in search of yellowfin tuna, yellowtail, and other deep-water fish. Half-day fishing and whale-watching trips are also available. ✉ *2838 Garrison St., Point Loma,* ☎ *619/221–8500* ⊕ *www.fishermanslanding.com.*

H&M Landing. Join one of the West's oldest sportfishing companies for year-round fishing trips plus whale-watching excursions from December through March. ✉ *2803 Emerson St., Point Loma,* ☎ *619/222–1144* ⊕ *www.hmlanding.com.*

FOOTBALL

San Diego Chargers. Part of the NFL's West division, the offensive-minded San Diego–based Chargers play their home games at Qualcomm Stadium. Particularly intense are the Chargers' games with AFC West rivals the Oakland Raiders. The team began in 1960, with its first season in L.A., but then moved to San Diego since 1961. Its iconic lightning bolt has stayed with the team and uniforms through the decades. ✉ *9449 Friars Rd., Mission Valley,* ☎ *858/874–4500 Charger Park, 877/242–7437 season tickets* ⊕ *www.chargers.com.*

GOLF

Balboa Park Municipal Golf Course. San Diego's oldest public course is five minutes from downtown in the heart of Balboa Park and offers impressive views of the city and the bay. The course includes a 9-hole executive course and a challenging 18-hole course that weaves among the park's canyons with some tricky drop-offs. Finish off your round with biscuits and gravy and a mimosa at Tobey's 19th Hole Cafe, a greasy spoon that's also Balboa Park's best-kept secret. ⊠ *2600 Golf Course Dr., Balboa Park,* ☎ *619/235–1184* ⊕ *www.balboagc.com* 🖼 *9 holes: $18 weekdays, $23 weekends. 18 holes: $40 weekdays, $50 weekends* 🕈 *27 holes, 6281 yards, par 72.*

Fodor's Choice ★ **Coronado Municipal Golf Course.** Spectacular views of downtown San Diego and the Coronado Bridge as well as affordable prices make this public course one of the busiest in the world. Bordered by the bay, the trick is to keep your ball out of the water. Wind can add some difficulty, but otherwise this is a leisurely course and a good one to walk. It's difficult to get on unless you reserve a tee time 3 to 14 days in advance. The course's Bayside Grill restaurant is well-known for its Thursday and Sunday night prime rib dinner. Reservations are recommended. ⊠ *2000 Visalia Row, Coronado,* ☎ *619/435–3121* ⊕ *www.golfcoronado.com* 🖼 *$18 for 9 holes, $35 for 18 holes weekdays, $40 weekends* 🕈 *18 holes, 6590 yards, par 72.*

Omni La Costa Resort and Spa. One of the premier golf resorts in Southern California, La Costa over the years has hosted many of the best professional golfers in the world as well as prominent politicians and Hollywood celebrities. The resort recently remodeled both its courses. The Dick Wilson–designed Champions course has new bent grass greens, Bermuda fairways, and bunkers. The more spacious Legends Course received a complete makeover including a redesign of all 18 greens, as well as new bunkers and turfgrass plantings. After a day on the links you can wind down with a massage, steam bath, and dinner at the resort. ⊠ *2100 Costa del Mar Rd., Carlsbad, California, United States* ☎ *800/854–5000* ⊕ *www.lacosta.com* 🖼 *$210 Mon.–Thurs., $230 Fri.–Sun.* 🕈 *Champions: 18 holes, 6608 yards, par 72; Legends: 18 holes, 6524 yards, par 72.*

Fodor's Choice ★ **Park Hyatt Aviara Golf Club.** This golf course consistently ranks as one of the best in California and is the only course in San Diego designed by Arnold Palmer. The course features gently rolling hills dotted with native wildflowers and views of the protected adjacent Batiquitos Lagoon and the Pacific Ocean. There are plenty of bunkers and water features for those looking for a challenge, and the golf carts, included in the cost, come fitted with GPS systems that tell you the distance to the pin. The two-story Spanish colonial clubhouse has full-size lockers, lounge areas, a bar, and a steak house. ⊠ *7447 Batiquitos Dr., Carlsbad, California, United States* ☎ *760/603–6900* ⊕ *www.golfaviara.com* 🖼 *Members: $130 Mon.–Thurs., $150 Fri.–Sun. Nonmembers: $225 Mon.–Thurs., $245 Fri.–Sun.* 🕈 *18 holes, 7007 yards, par 72.*

Fodor's Choice ★ **Torrey Pines Golf Course.** Due to its cliff-top location overlooking the Pacific and its classic championship holes, Torrey Pines is one of the best public golf courses in the United States. The course was the site of the 2008 U.S. Open and has been the home of the Farmers Insurance Open since 1968. The par-72 South Course, redesigned by Rees Jones in 2001, receives rave reviews from touring pros; it is longer, more challenging, and more expensive than the North Course. Tee times may be booked from 8 to 90 days in advance (☎ *877/581–7171*) and are subject to an advance booking fee ($43). ✉ *11480 N. Torrey Pines Rd., La Jolla,* ☏ *858/452–3226, 800/985–4653* ⊕ *www.torreypinesgolfcourse. com* 🏌️ *South: $183 weekdays, $229 weekends. North: $100 weekdays, $125 weekends; $40 for golf cart* 🏌️ *South: 18 holes, 7227 yards, par 72; North: 18 holes, 6874 yards, par 72.*

HIKING AND NATURE TRAILS

Fodor's Choice
★

Bayside Trail at Cabrillo National Monument. Driving here is a treat in itself, as a vast view of the Pacific unfolds before you. The view is equally enjoyable on Bayside Trail (2 miles round-trip), which is home to the same coastal sagebrush that Juan Rodriguez Cabrillo saw when he first discovered the California coast in the 16th century. After the hike, you can explore nearby tide pools, the monument statue, and the Old Point Loma Lighthouse. Don't worry if you don't see everything on your first visit; your entrance receipt ($5 per car) is good for seven days. ✉ *1800 Cabrillo Memorial Dr., Point Loma,* ✛ *From I–5, take the Rosecrans exit and turn right on Canon St. then left on Catalina Blvd. (also known as Cabrillo Memorial Dr.); follow until the end* ☏ *619/557–5450* ⊕ *www.nps.gov/cabr.*

Torrey Pines State Reserve. Hikers and runners will appreciate this park's many winning features: switch-back trails that descend to the sea, an unparalleled view of the Pacific, and a chance to see the Torrey pine tree, one of the rarest pine breeds in the United States. The reserve hosts guided nature walks as well. All food is prohibited at the reserve, so save the picnic until you reach the beach below. Parking is $12–$15, depending on day and season. ✉ *12600 N. Torrey Pines Rd., La Jolla,* ✛ *Exit I–5 at Carmel Valley Rd. and head west toward Coast Hwy. 101 until you reach N. Torrey Pines Rd.; turn left* ☏ *858/755–2063* ⊕ *www.torreypine.org.*

KAYAKING, SAILING, AND BOATING

Hike Bike Kayak San Diego. This shop offers several kayak tours, from easy excursions in Mission Bay that are well suited to families and beginners to more advanced jaunts. Tours include kayaking the caves off La Jolla coast, whale-watching (from a safe distance) December through March, moonlight and sunset trips, and a cruise into the bay to see SeaWorld's impressive fireworks shows over the water in the summer. Tours last two to three hours and require a minimum of four people. ✉ *2222 Ave. de la Playa, La Jolla,* ☏ *858/551–9510* ⊕ *www. hikebikekayak.com.*

SURFING

If you're a beginner, consider paddling in the waves off Mission Beach, Pacific Beach, Tourmaline Surfing Park, La Jolla Shores, Del Mar, or Oceanside. More experienced surfers usually head for Sunset Cliffs, La Jolla reef breaks, Black's Beach, or Swami's in Encinitas. All necessary equipment is included in the cost of all surfing schools. Beach-area Y's offer surf lessons and surf camp in the summer months and during spring break.

Cheap Rentals Mission Beach. Many local surf shops rent both surf and bodyboards. Cheap Rentals Mission Beach is right off the boardwalk, just steps from the waves. It rents wet suits, bodyboards, and skimboards in addition to soft surfboards and long and short fiberglass rides. It also has good hourly to weekly pricing on paddleboards and accessories. ☒ *3689 Mission Blvd., Mission Beach*, ☎ *858/488–9070, 800/941–7761* ⊕ *www.cheap-rentals.com.*

SHOPPING

San Diego's retail venues are as diverse as the city's vibrant neighborhoods. From La Jolla's tony boutiques to the outlet malls at San Ysidro, you'll find stores that appeal to every taste and budget.

DOWNTOWN

The Gaslamp Quarter, Downtown's trendy hot spot, is where you'll find independent shops selling urban apparel, unique home decor items, and vintage treasures. If you can't find it in the boutiques, head for Westfield Horton Plaza, the Downtown mall with more than 130 stores and 26 eateries.

Just a hop, skip, and a jump from the Gaslamp Quarter, the 130-block East Village neighborhood contains shops catering to local hipsters and visitors looking for edgy street wear, novelty T-shirts, and offbeat accessories. Some of the best shopping can be found from 8th to 10th avenues between Broadway and J Street.

Nearby, Little Italy is the place to find contemporary art, clothing from local designers, and home-decor items. Kettner Boulevard and India Street from Laurel to Date Street are the heart of the Art and Design District.

Into kitschy gifts and souvenirs? Downtown's Seaport Village has an abundance of quirky shops that won't disappoint, plus you'll be able to enjoy the coastal breezes while you shop for that Coronado Bridge snow globe.

Spanning 14 acres and offering more than 50 shops and 18 restaurants, Seaport Village is by far the most popular destination in the waterfront Embarcadero neighborhood.

SHOPPING CENTER

Westfield Horton Plaza. This downtown shopping, dining, and entertainment mecca fronts Broadway and G Street from 1st to 4th avenues and covers more than six city blocks. Designed by Jon Jerde and completed in 1985, Westfield Horton Plaza is a collage of colorful tile work, banners waving in the air, and modern sculptures. The complex rises in uneven, staggered levels to five floors; great views of downtown from the harbor to Balboa Park and beyond can be had here.

Macy's and Nordstrom department stores anchor the plaza housing clothing, sporting-goods, jewelry, and gift shops. Other attractions include a movie complex, restaurants, and the respected San Diego Repertory Theatre below ground level. In 2008 the **Balboa Theater**, contiguous with the shopping center, reopened its doors after a $26.5-million renovation. The historic 1920s theater seats 1,400 and offers live arts and cultural performances throughout the week.

The mall has a multilevel parking garage; even so, lines to find a space can be long. ■TIP➔ **Entering the parking structure on G Street rather than 4th Avenue generally means less traffic and more parking space.** Parking validation is complimentary whether you spend a bundle or just window-shop. Validation machines throughout the center allow for three hours' free parking; after that it's $8 per hour (or $2 per 15-minute increment). If you use this notoriously confusing fruit-and-vegetable–themed garage, be sure to remember at which produce level you've left your car. If you're staying downtown, the Old Town Trolley Tour will drop you directly in front of Westfield Horton Plaza. ✉ *324 Horton Plaza, Gaslamp Quarter,* ☎ *619/239–8180* ⊕ *www.westfield. com/hortonplaza* ⊘ *Weekdays 10–9, Sat. 10–8, Sun. 11–6.*

OLD TOWN AND UPTOWN

OLD TOWN

Tourist-focused Old Town, north of Downtown off I–5, has a festival-like ambience that also makes it a popular destination for locals. At Old Town Historic Park, you'll feel like a time traveler as you visit shops housed in restored adobe buildings. Farther down the street you'll find stores selling Mexican blankets, piñatas, and glassware. Old Town Market offers live entertainment, local artists selling their wares from carts, and a market crammed with unique apparel, home-decor items, toys, jewelry, and food.

MARKET

Fodor's Choice ★ **Bazaar del Mundo Shops.** An arcade with a Mexican villa theme, the Bazaar hosts riotously colorful gift shops such as **Ariana**, for ethnic and artsy women's fashions; **Artes de Mexico,** which sells handmade Latin American crafts and Guatemalan weavings; and **The Gallery,** which carries handmade jewelry, Native American crafts, collectible glass, and original serigraphs by John August Swanson. The **Laurel Burch Gallerita** carries the complete collection of the northern California artist's signature jewelry, accessories, and totes. ✉ *4133 Taylor St., at Juan St., Old Town,* ☎ *619/296–3161* ⊕ *www.bazaardelmundo.com.*

UPTOWN

Hillcrest has a large gay community and boasts many avant-garde apparel shops alongside gift, book, and music stores. South Park's 30th, Juniper, and Fern streets have everything from the hottest new denim lines to baby gear and craft supplies. The shops and art galleries in upscale Mission Hills, west of Hillcrest, have a modern and sophisticated ambience that suits the well-heeled residents.

MISSION VALLEY

Northeast of Downtown near I–8 and Route 163, Mission Valley holds two major shopping centers and a few smaller strip malls.

MALL

Fodor'sChoice ★ **Fashion Valley.** More than 18 million shoppers visit Fashion Valley each year. That's more than the combined attendance of SeaWorld, LEGO-LAND, the San Diego Padres, the San Diego Chargers, and the San Diego Zoo. San Diego's best and most upscale mall has a contemporary Mission theme, lush landscaping, and more than 200 shops and restaurants. Acclaimed retailers like Nordstrom, Neiman Marcus, and Tiffany are here, along with boutiques from fashion darlings like Michael Kors, Jimmy Choo, Tory Burch, and James Perse. H&M is a favorite of fashionistas in search of edgy and affordable styles. Free wireless Internet service is available throughout the mall. Select "Simon WiFi" from any Wi-Fi–enabled device to log onto the network. ■TIP➔ If you show this Fodor's book at Simon Guest Services (lower level, along the walkway between Prada and Banana Republic), you will get a complimentary Style Pass, which can get you savings at more than 70 of Fashion Valley's stores, boutiques, and restaurants. ✉ *7007 Friars Rd., Mission Valley,* ☎ *619/688–9113* ⊕ *www.simon.com/mall/fashion-valley.*

NORTH PARK

North Park, east of Hillcrest, is a retro buff's paradise, with resale shops, trendy boutiques, and stores that sell mostly handcrafted items.

CLOTHING AND ACCESSORIES

Fodor'sChoice ★ **Aloha Sunday Supply Co.** This clean, white boutique with high ceilings and blond-wood accents carries no Billabong or Quicksilver, but make no mistake, this is a surf shop. The store sells only handcrafted pieces like Matuse wet suits, American-made Thorogood leather boots and the store's own brand of tailored men's clothing designed by co-owner and former professional surfer Kahana Kalama. ✉ *3039 University Ave.,* ☎ *619/269–9838* ⊕ *alohasunday.com.*

LA JOLLA

Known as San Diego's answer to Rodeo Drive in Beverly Hills, La Jolla has chic boutiques, art galleries, and gift shops and plenty of celebrity sightings. Prospect Street and Girard Avenue are the primary shopping stretches, and North Prospect is chockablock with art galleries. Parking is tight in the village. Most shops on Prospect Street stay open until 10 pm on weeknights to accommodate evening strollers.

CORONADO

Coronado's resort hotels attract tourists in droves, but somehow the town has managed to avoid being overtaken by chain stores. Friendly shopkeepers make the boutiques lining Orange Avenue, Coronado's main drag, a good place to browse for clothes, home-decor and gift items, and gourmet foods.

SHOPPING CENTER

Fodor'sChoice ★ **Hotel Del Coronado.** At the dozen gift shops within the peninsula's main historic attraction, you can purchase sportswear, designer handbags, jewelry, and antiques. **Babcock & Story Emporium** carries an amazing selection of home decor items, garden accessories, and classy gifts. **Blue**

Octopus is a children's store featuring creative toys, gifts, and apparel. **Spreckels Sweets & Treats** offers old-time candies, freshly made fudge, and decadent truffles. **Kate's** has stylish fashions and accessories, while **Brady's for Men,** with its shirts and jackets, caters to well-dressed men. **Crown Jewels Coronado** features fine jewelry, some inspired by the sea. ⊠ *1500 Orange Ave., Coronado,* ☎ *619/435–6611* ⊕ *hoteldel.com/ activities/coronado-shopping.*

SIDE TRIPS TO NORTH COUNTY

DEL MAR

23 miles north of Downtown San Diego on I–5, 9 miles north of La Jolla on Rte. S21.

Del Mar is best known for its quaint old section west of Interstate 5 marked with a glamorous racetrack, half-timber buildings, chic shops, tony restaurants, celebrity visitors, and wide beaches.

EXPLORING

FAMILY **Del Mar Fairgrounds.** The Spanish Mission–style fairground is the home of the **Del Mar Thoroughbred Club** (☎ *858/755–1141* ⊕ *www.dmtc. com*). Crooner Bing Crosby and his Hollywood buddies—Pat O'Brien, Gary Cooper, and Oliver Hardy, among others—organized the club in the 1930s, and the racing here (usually July through September, Wednesday through Monday, post time 2 pm) remains a fashionable affair. Del Mar Fairgrounds hosts more than 100 different events each year, including the San Diego County Fair, the Del Mar National Horse Show in April and May, and the fall Scream Zone that's popular with local families. ⊠ *2260 Jimmy Durante Blvd., Del Mar, California, United States* ☎ *858/755–1161* ⊕ *www.delmarfairgrounds.com.*

WHERE TO EAT

$$$$ ╳ **Addison.** The sophisticated and stylish dining room and adjacent bar
FRENCH feel Italian and clubby, with intricately carved dark-wood motifs, and
Fodor'sChoice the tables, by contrast, are pure white, adorned with a single flower.
★ Acclaimed chef William Bradley serves up explosive flavors in his 4-, 7-, and 10-course prix-fixe dinners, such as Prince Edward Island mussels with chickpeas, garlic confit, and saffron. Entrées might include red pepper Tart Tatan or salmon with sauce beets, apples, and fennel. Addison delights wine lovers with 160 pages of choices from around the world. Ⓢ *Average main: $98* ⊠ *5200 Grand Del Mar Way, Del Mar, California, United States* ☎ *858/314–1900* ⊕ *www.addisondelmar.com* ⌲ *Reservations essential* ☉ *Closed Sun. and Mon. No lunch.*

$$$ ╳ **Market Restaurant + Bar.** Carl Schroeder, one of California's hottest
AMERICAN young chefs, draws well-heeled foodies to sample his creative and fun
Fodor'sChoice California fare, much of it with an Asian flare. The menu changes
★ regularly depending upon what's fresh. Schroeder's seasonally inspired dishes have a playful spirit, whether it's a blue cheese soufflé with seasonal fruit, a Maine lobster salad with mango, or coriander-spiced red snapper with prawn dumplings. A well-edited wine list offers food-friendly wines by the best and brightest young winemakers around the

world. Desserts are exquisite, such as the salty-sweet "S'Mores Bar" or the chocolate butterscotch trio. $ *Average main: $30* ✉ *3702 Via de la Valle, Del Mar, California, United States* ☎ *858/523–0007* ⊕ *www. marketdelmar.com* ⚐ *Reservations essential* ☉ *No lunch.*

WHERE TO STAY

$$$$ ⊡ **The Grand Del Mar.** Mind-blowing indulgence in serene surround-
RESORT ings, from drop-dead gorgeous guest accommodations to myriad out-
FAMILY door adventures, sets the opulent Mediterranean-style Grand Del Mar
Fodor's Choice apart from any other luxury hotel in San Diego. **Pros:** ultimate lux-
★ ury; secluded, on-site golf course. **Cons:** service can be slow; hotel is not on the beach. $ *Rooms from: $595* ✉ *5200 Grand Del Mar Ct.,* ☎ *858/314–2000, 866/305–1528* ⊕ *www.thegranddelmar.com* ⇆ *218 rooms, 31 suites* ⦿ *No meals.*

CARLSBAD

6 miles north of Encinitas on Rte. S21, 36 miles north of Downtown San Diego on I–5.

Once-sleepy Carlsbad has long been popular with beachgoers and sun seekers. On a clear day in this village, you can take in sweeping ocean views that stretch from La Jolla to Oceanside by walking the 2-mile-long seawalk running between the Encina power plant and Pine Street. En route, you'll find several stairways leading to the beach and quite a few benches. Inland are LEGOLAND California and other attractions in its vicinity.

EXPLORING

FAMILY **Flower Fields at Carlsbad Ranch.** The largest bulb production farm in
Fodor's Choice Southern California has hillsides abloom here each spring, when thou-
★ sands of Giant Tecolote ranunculus produce a stunning 50-acre display of color against the backdrop of the blue Pacific Ocean. Other knock-outs include the rose gardens—with examples of every All-American Rose Selection award-winner since 1940—and a historical display of Paul Ecke poinsettias. Open to the public during this time, the farm offers family activities that include a LEGO Flower Garden and a kids' playground. ✉ *5704 Paseo del Norte, east of I–5, Carlsbad, Califor-nia, United States* ☎ *760/431–0352* ⊕ *www.theflowerfields.com* ⊡ *$12* ☉ *Mar.–May, daily 9–6.*

FAMILY **LEGOLAND California Resort.** The centerpiece of a development that
Fodor's Choice includes resort hotels, a designer discount shopping mall, an aquarium,
★ and a waterpark, LEGOLAND has rides and diversions geared to kids ages 2 to 12. Bring bathing suits; there are lockers at the entrance and at Pirate Shores. The main events are as follows:

Movie Experience: Take a behind-the-scenes view of moviemaking LEGOLAND style.

Lost Kingdom Adventure: Armed with a laser blaster, you'll journey through ancient Egyptian ruins in a desert roadster, scoring points as you hit targets.

A LEGOLAND model worker puts the finishing touches on the San Francisco portion of Miniland U.S.A.

Star Wars Miniland: Follow the exploits of Yoda, Princess Leia, Obi-Wan, Anakin, R2, Luke, and the denizens of the six *Star Wars* films. Some kids loop back several times to take it all in.

Miniland U.S.A.: This miniature, animated, interactive collection of U.S. icons was constructed out of 24 million LEGO bricks!

Soak-N-Sail: Hundreds of gallons of water course through 60 interactive features, including a pirate shipwreck–theme area. You'll need your swimsuit for this one.

Dragon Coaster: Little kids love this popular indoor/outdoor steel roller coaster that goes through a castle. Don't let the name frighten you—the motif is more humorous than scary.

Driving School: Kids ages 6 to 13 can drive speed-controlled cars (not on rails) on a miniature road; driver's licenses are awarded after the course. Volvo Junior is the pint-size version for kids 3 to 5.

■ **TIP→** The best value is one of the Hopper Tickets that give you one admission to LEGOLAND plus Sea Life Aquarium and/or the LEGOLAND Water Park. These can be used on the same day or on different days. Purchase tickets online for discounted pricing. Go midweek to avoid the crowds.

LEGOLAND Hotel: Opened in 2013, this is the place for the family that eats, sleeps, and lives LEGO. Family rooms are themed Pirate, Adventure, and Kingdom, with corresponding LEGO-style decor. Each room has sleeping quarters for up to three kids. The hotel has interactive play areas, a restaurant, bar, and swimming pool, but best of all, guests get early admission to the park.

Be sure to try Granny's Apple Fries, Castle Burgers, and Pizza Mania for pizzas and salads. The Market near the entrance has excellent coffee, fresh fruit, and yogurt. ✉ *1 Legoland Dr., Carlsbad, California, United States* ✣ *Exit I–5 at Cannon Rd. and follow signs east ¼ mile* ☎ *760/918–5346* 🌐 *california.legoland.com* 🎟 *LEGOLAND $83 adults, $73 children; parking $15* ⏲ *Park: late May–early Sept., daily (hrs vary), early Sept.–late May, Thurs.–Sun. Water Park: May–Aug. Aquarium: Daily. Check website or call for specifics* ⏲ *Closed Tues. and Wed. except summer and holiday weeks.*

3

WHERE TO EAT

$$$ MEDITERRANEAN

🍴 **BlueFire Grill.** Fire and water drama defines this signature restaurant that's part of La Costa resort complex. The centerpiece of the resort's entrance plaza, the grill holds an outdoor patio with fire pits, fountains, and a year-round floral display. Inside is a contemporary Mission-style room surrounding a green bottle glass fountain that extends the length of the main dining room. The menu features local seafood and vegetables combined in exciting ways. As a starter, try the Baja ceviche, followed by short-rib bourguignon. [$] *Average main: $34* ✉ *2100 Costa Del Mar Rd., Carlsbad, California, United States* ☎ *760/929–6306* 🌐 *www.lacosta.com* ✍ *Reservations essential* ⏲ *Closed Sun.–Tues. No lunch.*

WHERE TO STAY

$$$$ RESORT FAMILY Fodor's Choice ★

🏨 **Omni La Costa Resort and Spa.** This chic Spanish colonial oasis on 400 tree-shaded acres has ample guest rooms, two golf courses, and is known for being family-friendly, with plenty of kids' activities (including a kids' club, teen lounge, seven swimming pools, three waterslides, and a water play zone). **Pros:** adult-only pool; excellent kids' facilities; spa under the stars. **Cons:** very spread out, making long walks necessary; lots of kids; parking spread all over the property. [$] *Rooms from: $349* ✉ *2100 Costa del Mar Rd., Carlsbad, California, United States* ☎ *760/438–9111, 800/854–5000* 🌐 *www.lacosta.com* 🛏 *607 rooms, 137 villas* 🍽 *No meals.*

$$$ RESORT FAMILY Fodor's Choice ★

🏨 **Park Hyatt Aviara Resort.** The quietly elegant hilltop retreat with a golf course is one of the most luxurious hotels in the San Diego area, where oversized rooms have every possible amenity (including private terraces and deep soaking tubs) and one of the most sublime views in Southern California, overlooking Batiquitos Lagoon and the Pacific. **Pros:** unbeatable location; tram rides; many nature trails. **Cons:** $25 resort fee; $35 parking. [$] *Rooms from: $279* ✉ *7100 Aviara Resort Dr., Carlsbad, California, United States* ☎ *800/233–1234, 760/448–1234* 🌐 *www.parkhyattaviara.com* 🛏 *329 rooms, 44 suites* 🍽 *No meals.*

OCEANSIDE

8 miles north of Carlsbad on Rte. S21, 37 miles north of Downtown San Diego on I–5.

EXPLORING

FAMILY

Fodor's Choice

★

Old Mission San Luis Rey. Known as the King of the Missions, the 18th, the largest, and the most prosperous of California's missions was built in 1798 by Franciscan friars under the direction of Father Fermin Lasuen to help educate and convert local Native Americans. The *sala* (parlor), the kitchen, a friar's bedroom, a weaving room, and a collection of religious art and old Spanish vestments convey much about early mission life. A location for filming Disney's 1950's *Zorro* TV series, the well-preserved mission is still owned by the Franciscans. ✉ *4050 Mission Ave., Oceanside, California, United States* ☎ *760/757–3651* ⊕ *www.sanluisrey.org* ✆ *$5* ☉ *weekdays 9:30–5, weekends 10–5.*

ESCONDIDO

8 miles north of Rancho Bernardo on I–15, 31 miles northeast of Downtown San Diego on I–15.

EXPLORING

FAMILY

Fodor's Choice

★

San Diego Zoo Safari Park. A branch of the San Diego Zoo, 35 miles to the south, the 1,800-acre preserve in the San Pasqual Valley is designed to protect endangered species from around the world. Exhibit areas have been carved out of the dry, dusty canyons and mesas to represent the animals' natural habitats in various parts of Africa and Asia.

✉ *15500 San Pasqual Valley Rd., Escondido, California, United States* ✛ *Take I–15 north to Via Rancho Pkwy. and follow signs, 6 miles* ☎ *760/747–8702* ⊕ *www.sdzsafaripark.org* ✆ *$46 one-day pass including Africa tram ride; multipark and multiday passes are available; special safaris are extra starting at $50 per person; parking $12* ☉ *Daily 9–dusk.*

The best way to see these preserves is to take the 25-minute, 2½-mile Africa tram safari, included with admission. As you pass in front of the large, naturally landscaped enclosures, you can see animals bounding across prairies and mesas as they would in the wild. More than 3,500 animals of more than 400 species roam or fly above the expansive grounds. Predators are separated from prey by deep moats, but only the elephants, tigers, lions, and cheetahs are kept in enclosures. Good viewpoints are at the Elephant Viewing Patio, African Plains Outlook, and Kilmia Point. ■TIP➔ **Prepare for summer heat. Wear a hat, cool clothing, and drink plenty of water; water refills are free. Also walk in the shade whenever possble. In summer, when the park stays open late, the trip is especially enjoyable in the early evening, when the heat has subsided and the animals are active and feeding. When the tram travels through the park after dark, sodium-vapor lamps illuminate the active animals. Photographers with zoom lenses can get spectacular shots of zebras, gazelles, and rhinos.**

For a more focused view of the park, you can take one of several other safaris that are well worth the additional charge. You can choose from several behind-the-scenes safaris, fly above it all via the zip-line safari, or get up close to giraffes and rhinos on a Caravan safari.

The park is as much a botanical garden as a zoo, serving as a "rescue center" for rare and endangered plants. Unique gardens include cacti and succulents from Baja California, a bonsai collection, a fuchsia display, native plants, and protea.

The Lion Camp gives you a close-up view of the king of beasts in a slice of African wilderness complete with sweeping plains and rolling hills. As you walk through this exhibit, you can watch the giant cats lounging around through a 40-foot-long window. The last stop is a research station, where you can see them all around you through glass panels.

The ticket booths at Nairobi Village, the park's center, are designed to resemble the tomb of an ancient king of Uganda. Animals in the Petting Kraal here affectionately tolerate tugs and pats and are quite adept at posing for pictures with toddlers. At the Congo River Village 10,000 gallons of water pour each minute over a huge waterfall into a large lagoon. Hidden Jungle, an 8,800-square-foot greenhouse, is a habitat for creatures that creep, flutter, or just hang out in the tropics. Gigantic cockroaches and bird-eating spiders share the turf with colorful butterflies and hummingbirds and oh-so-slow-moving two-toed sloths. Lorikeet Landing holds 75 of the loud and colorful small parrots—you can buy a cup of nectar at the aviary entrance to induce them to land on your hand. The park's newest project is the Tull Family Tiger Trail, a Sumatran tiger habitat opened in 2014, where you can get face-to-face (with a glass between) with the gorgeous cats. The 5-acre exhibit features a waterfall and swimming hole, and addresses poaching and other environmental threats to the species.

All the park's walk-to exhibits and animal shows (included in admission) are entertainingly educational. The gift shops are well worth a visit for their limited-edition items. There are lots of restaurants, snack bars, and some picnic areas. Rental lockers, strollers, and wheelchairs are available. You can also arrange to stay overnight in the park in summer on a Roar and Snore Sleepover ($140 and up, plus admission).

ORANGE COUNTY AND CATALINA ISLAND

With Disneyland and Knott's Berry Farm

Visit Fodors.com for advice, updates, and bookings

WELCOME TO ORANGE COUNTY AND CATALINA ISLAND

TOP REASONS TO GO

★ **Disney Magic:** Walking down Main Street, U.S.A., with Cinderella's Castle straight ahead, you really will feel that you're in one of the happiest places on Earth.

★ **Beautiful Beaches:** Surf, swim, paddleboard, or just relax on one of the state's most breathtaking stretches of coastline. Keep in mind, the water may be colder than you expect.

★ **Island Getaways:** Just a short high-speed catamaran ride away, Catalina Island feels 1,000 miles from the mainland. Wander around charming Avalon, or explore the unspoiled beauty of the island's wild interior.

★ **The Fine Life:** Some of the state's wealthiest communities are in coastal Orange County, so spend at least part of your stay here experiencing how the other half lives.

★ **Family Fun:** Spend some quality time with the kids riding roller coasters, eating ice cream, fishing off ocean piers, and bodysurfing.

1 Disneyland Resort. Southern California's top family destination has expanded from the humble park of Walt Disney's vision to a megaresort with more attractions spilling over into Disney's California Adventure. But kids (and many adults) still consider it the happiest place on Earth.

2 Knott's Berry Farm. Amusement park lovers should check out this Buena Park attraction, with thrill rides, the *Peanuts* gang, and lots of fried chicken and boysenberry pie.

3 Coastal Orange County. OC's beach communities may not be quite as glamorous as seen on TV, but coastal spots like Huntington Beach, Newport Harbor, and Laguna Beach are perfect for chilling out in a beachfront hotel.

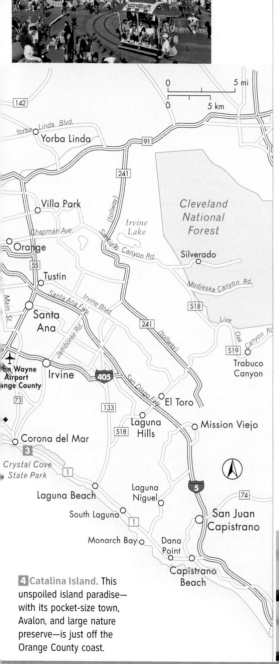

GETTING ORIENTED

Like Los Angeles, Orange County stretches over a large area, lacks a singular focal point, and has limited public transportation. You'll need a car and a sensible game plan to make the most of your visit. Anaheim, home of Disneyland, has every style of hotel imaginable, from family-friendly motels to luxurious high-rises. The coastal cities are more expensive but have cooler weather in summer, and marvelous beaches that you can enjoy throughout the year.

4

4 Catalina Island. This unspoiled island paradise—with its pocket-size town, Avalon, and large nature preserve—is just off the Orange County coast.

Updated
by Kathy A.
McDonald

With its tropical flowers and palm trees, the stretch of coast between Seal Beach and San Clemente is often called the California Riviera. Exclusive Newport Beach, artsy Laguna, and the surf town of Huntington Beach are the stars, but lesser-known gems on the glistening coast—such as Corona del Mar—are also worth visiting. Offshore, meanwhile, lies gorgeous Catalina Island, a terrific spot for diving, snorkeling, and hiking.

Few of the citrus groves that gave Orange County its name remain. This region south and east of Los Angeles is now ruled by tourism and high-tech business instead of farmers. Despite a building boom that began in the 1990s, the area is still a place to find wilderness trails, canyons, greenbelts, and natural environs. And just offshore is a deep-water wilderness that's possible to explore via daily whale-watching excursions.

PLANNING

GETTING HERE AND AROUND
AIR TRAVEL
Orange County's main facility is John Wayne Airport Orange County (SNA), which is served by eight major domestic airlines and a commuter line. Long Beach Airport (LGB) is served by three airlines, including its major player, JetBlue. It's roughly 20 to 30 minutes by car from Anaheim.

Super Shuttle and Prime Time Airport Shuttle provide transportation from John Wayne and LAX to the Disneyland area of Anaheim. Round-trip fares average about $22 per person from John Wayne and $34 from LAX.

BUS TRAVEL

The Orange County Transportation Authority will take you virtually anywhere in the county, but it will take time; OCTA buses go from Knott's Berry Farm and Disneyland to Huntington Beach and Newport Beach. Bus 1 travels along the coast; buses 701 and 721 provide express service to Los Angeles.

Bus Contacts Orange County Transportation Authority ☎ 714/636-7433 ⊕ www.octa.net.

CAR TRAVEL

The San Diego Freeway (Interstate 405), the coastal route, and the Santa Ana Freeway (Interstate 5), the inland route, run north–south through Orange County. South of Laguna, Interstate 405 merges into Interstate 5 (called the San Diego Freeway south from this point). A toll road, Highway 73, runs 15 miles from Newport Beach to San Juan Capistrano; it costs $6.65–$7.35 (lower rates are for weekends and off-peak hours) and is usually less jammed than the regular freeways. Keep in mind, however, there are no toll booths on OC toll roads; payment is required via a FastTrak transponder (available at AAA, Costco, and Albertson's). Some car-rental companies (like Avis) provide them for a daily service fee; Hertz does not. Using California toll roads or express lanes without a transponder in a rental car may result in hefty fees. Do your best to avoid all Orange County freeways during rush hours (6–9 am and 3:30–6:30 pm). Highway 55 leads to Newport Beach. The Pacific Coast Highway (Highway 1) allows easy access to beach communities, and is the most scenic route, but expect it to be crowded, especially on summer weekends.

FERRY TRAVEL

Catalina Express offers two ferry services to Catalina Island, one from Long Beach (about 90 minutes) and one from Newport Beach (about 75 minutes). Reservations are advised for summers and weekends. During the winter months, ferry crossings are not as frequent as in the summer high season.

TRAIN TRAVEL

Amtrak makes daily stops in Orange County at all major towns. Metrolink is a weekday commuter train that runs to and from Los Angeles and Orange County.

Train Contacts Amtrak ☎ 800/872-7245 ⊕ www.amtrak.com. **Metrolink** ☎ 800/371-5465 ⊕ www.metrolinktrains.com.

RESTAURANTS

Much like those of L.A., restaurants in Orange County are generally casual, and you'll rarely see men in jackets and ties. Nevertheless, at top resort hotel dining rooms, many guests choose to dress up.

Of course, there's also a swath of casual places along the beachfronts—seafood takeout, taquerias, burger joints—that won't mind if you wear flip-flops. Reservations are recommended for the nicest restaurants.

Many places don't serve past 11 pm, and locals tend to eat early. Remember that according to California law, smoking is prohibited in all enclosed areas.

HOTELS

Along the coast there are remarkable luxury resorts; if you can't afford a stay, pop in for the view at Laguna Beach's Montage or the always welcoming Ritz-Carlton at Dana Point. For a taste of the OC glam life, have lunch overlooking the yachts of Newport Bay at the Balboa Bay Resort.

As a rule, lodging prices tend to rise the closer the hotels are to the beach. If you're looking for value, consider a hotel that is inland along the Interstate 405 freeway corridor.

In most cases, you can take advantage of some of the facilities of the high-end resorts, such as restaurants and spas, even if you aren't an overnight guest. *Hotel reviews have been shortened. For full information, visit Fodors.com.*

WHAT IT COSTS				
	$	**$$**	**$$$**	**$$$$**
RESTAURANTS	under $16	$16–$22	$23–$30	over $30
HOTELS	under $120	$120–$175	$176–$250	over $250

Restaurant prices are the average cost of a main course at dinner or, if dinner is not served, at lunch, excluding sales tax. Hotel prices are the lowest cost of a standard double room in high season, excluding service charges and tax.

VISITOR INFORMATION

The Anaheim/Orange County Visitor and Convention Bureau is an excellent resource for both leisure and business travelers and can provide materials on many area attractions. It's on the main floor of the Anaheim Convention Center.

The Orange County Tourism Council's website is also a useful source of information.

Information Anaheim/Orange County Visitor & Convention Bureau
✉ *Anaheim Convention Center, 800 W. Katella Ave., Anaheim* ☎ *714/765–8888* ⊕ *www.anaheimoc.org.* **Orange County Visitors Association** ⊕ *www.visittheoc. com.*

DISNEYLAND RESORT

26 miles southeast of Los Angeles, via I-5.

The snowcapped Matterhorn, the centerpiece of the Magic Kingdom, punctuates the skyline of Anaheim. Since 1955, when Walt Disney chose this once-quiet farming community for the site of his first amusement park, Disneyland has attracted more than 616 million visitors and tens of thousands of workers, and Anaheim has been their host.

To understand the symbiotic relationship between Disneyland and Anaheim, you need only look at the resort's dedicated freeway off-ramp and the combined effort by Disney and the city to revitalize Anaheim's tourist center and run-down areas, and to expand and renovate the Disney properties into what is known now as Disneyland Resort.

The resort is a sprawling complex that includes Disney's two amusement parks; three hotels; and Downtown Disney, a shopping, dining, and entertainment promenade. Anaheim's tourist center includes Angel Stadium of Anaheim, home of baseball's 2002 World Series Champions Los Angeles Angels of Anaheim; the Honda Center (formerly the Arrowhead Pond), which hosts concerts and the Anaheim Ducks hockey team; and the enormous Anaheim Convention Center.

GETTING HERE

Disney is about a 30-mile drive from either LAX or Downtown. From LAX, follow Sepulveda Boulevard south to the Interstate 105 freeway and drive east 16 miles to the Interstate 605 north exit. Exit at the Santa Ana Freeway (Interstate 5) and continue south for 12 miles to the Disneyland Drive exit. Follow signs to the resort. From Downtown, follow Interstate 5 south 28 miles and exit at Disneyland Drive. **Disneyland Resort Express** (☎ *800/828–6699* ⊕ *graylineanaheim.com*) offers daily nonstop bus service between LAX, John Wayne Airport, and Anaheim. Reservations are not required. The cost is $30 one-way from LAX, and $20 from John Wayne Airport.

SAVING TIME AND MONEY

If you plan to visit for more than a day, you can save money by buying two- three-, four-, and five-day Park Hopper tickets that grant same-day "hopping" privileges between Disneyland and Disney's California Adventure. You get a discount on the multiple-day passes if you buy online through the Disneyland website.

A one-day Park Hopper pass costs $155 for anyone 10 or older, $149 for kids ages 3–9. Admission to either park (but not both) is $99 or $93 for kids 3–9; kids 2 and under are free.

In addition to tickets, parking is $17–$22 (unless your hotel has a shuttle or is within walking distance), and meals in the parks and at Downtown Disney range from $10 to $30 per person.

DISNEY'S TOP ATTRACTIONS

Finding Nemo: Board a yellow submarine and view a 3-D animated adventure.

Haunted Mansion: A "doombuggy" takes you through a spooky old plantation mansion.

Matterhorn Bobsleds: At the center of the Magic Kingdom, this roller coaster simulates bobsleds.

Pirates of the Caribbean: Watch buccaneers wreak havoc as you float along in a rowboat.

Space Mountain: This scary-but-thrilling roller coaster is indoors—and mostly in the dark.

DISNEYLAND

After celebrating its 60th anniversary in 2015, Disneyland continues to be a favorite destination for locals and visitors alike, making it not only a happy place but also a crowded place. Arrive early or stay late for the most satisfying visit. The nightly fireworks spectacular now includes expanded digital light displays and there's a new nighttime parade, "Paint the Night," that features 1.5 million LED lights.

FAMILY

Fodor'sChoice

★

Disneyland. One of the biggest misconceptions people have about Disneyland is that they've "been there, done that" if they've visited either Florida's mammoth Walt Disney World or one of the Disney parks overseas. But Disneyland, which opened in 1955 and is the only one of the parks to have been overseen by Walt himself, has a genuine historic feel and occupies a unique place in the Disney legend. Expertly run, with polite and helpful staff ("cast members" in the Disney lexicon), the park has plenty that you won't find anywhere else—such as the Indiana Jones Adventure ride and Storybook Land, with its miniature replicas of animated Disney scenes from classics such as *Pinocchio* and *Alice in Wonderland*. Characters appear for autographs and photos throughout the day; times and places are posted at the entrances. Live shows, parades, strolling musicans, nightly fireworks, and endless snack choices add to the carnival atmosphere. You can also meet some of the animated icons at one of the character meals served at the three Disney hotels (open to the public). Belongings can be stored in lockers just off Main Street; stroller rentals at the entrance gate are a convenient option for families with small tykes. ✉ *1313 S. Disneyland Dr., between Ball Rd. and Katella Ave., Anaheim* ☎ *714/781–4636 Guest information* ⊕ *www.disneyland.com* ✆ *$96; parking $17* ☉ *Hrs vary.*

PARK NEIGHBORHOODS
Neighborhoods for Disneyland are arranged in geographic order.

MAIN STREET,
U.S.A.

Walt's hometown of Marceline, Missouri, was the inspiration behind this romanticized image of small-town America, circa 1900. The sidewalks are lined with a penny arcade, an endless supply of sugar confections, shops that sell everything from tradable pins to Disney-theme clothing, and a photo shop that offers souvenirs created via Disney's PhotoPass (on-site photographers capture memorable moments digitally—you can access in person or online). Main Street opens a half hour before the rest of the park, so it's a good place to explore if you're getting an early start to beat the crowds (it's also open an hour after the other attractions close, so you may want to save your shopping for the end of the day). **Main Street Cinema** offers a cool respite from the crowds and six classic Disney animated shorts, including *Steamboat Willie*. There's rarely a wait to enter. Grab a cappuccino and fresh-made pastry at the Jolly Holiday bakery to jump-start your visit. Board the **Disneyland Railroad** here to save on walking; it tours all the lands plus offers unique views of Splash Mountain and the Grand Canyon and Primeval World dioramas.

NEW ORLEANS
SQUARE

This mini–French Quarter, with narrow streets, hidden courtyards, and live street performances, is home to two iconic attractions and the Cajun-inspired Blue Bayou restaurant. **Pirates of the Caribbean** now features Jack Sparrow and the cursed Captain Barbossa, in a nod to the blockbuster movies of the same name, plus enhanced special effects and battle scenes (complete with cannonball explosions). Nearby, the **Haunted Mansion** continues to spook guests with its stretching room and "doombuggy" rides (plus there's now an expanded storyline for the

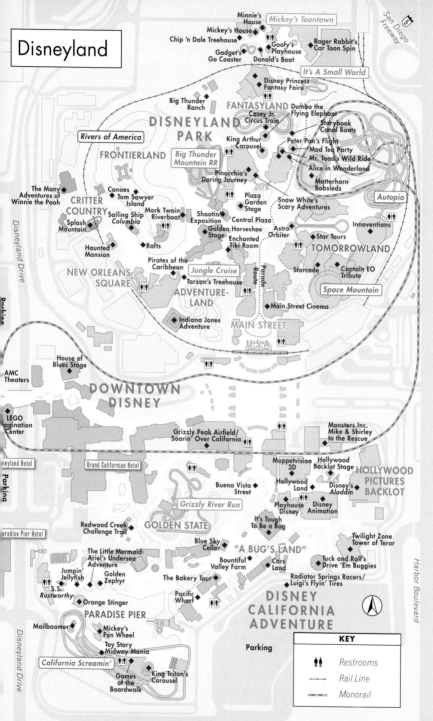

Disneyland

Mickey's Toontown
Minnie's House
Mickey's House
Chip 'n Dale Treehouse
Gadget's Go Coaster
Goofy's Playhouse
Donald's Boat
Roger Rabbit's Car Toon Spin

It's A Small World

DISNEYLAND PARK

Rivers of America

FRONTIERLAND

Big Thunder Ranch

Big Thunder Mountain RR

FANTASYLAND
Disney Princess Fantasy Faire
Casey Jr. Circus Train
King Arthur Carousel
Dumbo the Flying Elephant
Storybook Canal Boats
Peter Pan's Flight
Mad Tea Party
Mr. Toad's Wild Ride
Alice in Wonderland
Matterhorn Bobsleds

Pinocchio's Daring Journey

Autopia

Plaza Garden Stage
Central Plaza
Snow White's Scary Adventures

The Many Adventures of Winnie the Pooh

CRITTER COUNTRY
Canoes
Tom Sawyer Island
Sailing Ship *Columbia*
Mark Twain Riverboat
Shootin' Exposition
Golden Horseshoe Stage
Enchanted Tiki Room
Astro Orbiter
Star Tours
Innoventions

TOMORROWLAND

Splash Mountain
Haunted Mansion
Rafts
Pirates of the Caribbean

NEW ORLEANS SQUARE
Jungle Cruise
Tarzan's Treehouse

Starcade
Captain EO Tribute

Space Mountain

ADVENTURELAND

Main Street Cinema

Indiana Jones Adventure

MAIN STREET, U.S.A.

House of Blues Stage

AMC Theaters

DOWNTOWN DISNEY

LEGO Imagination Center

Grizzly Peak Airfield/ Soarin' Over California

Monsters Inc. Mike & Shirley to the Rescue

Disneyland Drive

Parking

Disneyland Hotel

Grand Californian Hotel

Muppetvision 3D
Hollywood Backlot Stage
Hollywood Land
Disney's *Aladdin*

HOLLYWOOD PICTURES BACKLOT

Parking

Buena Vista Street

Grizzly River Run

Playhouse Disney
Disney Animation

Paradise Pier Hotel

Redwood Creek Challenge Trail

GOLDEN STATE

It's Tough To Be a Bug

Blue Sky Cellar

"A BUG'S LAND"

Twilight Zone Tower of Teror

The Little Mermaid– Ariel's Undersea Adventure
Golden Zephyr
Jumpin' Jellyfish
S.S. *Rustworthy*
Orange Stinger

Bountiful Valley Farm
Cars Land

Tuck and Roll's Drive 'Em Buggies

Radiator Springs Racers/ Luigi's Flyin' Tires

The Bakery Tour

Pacific Wharf

DISNEY CALIFORNIA ADVENTURE

Mailboomer

PARADISE PIER

Mickey's Fun Wheel
Toy Story Midway Mania

California Screamin'

Games of the Boardwalk
King Triton's Carousel

Parking

Disneyland Drive

San Diego Freeway

Harbor Boulevard

Katella Avenue

KEY	
👫	Restrooms
+—+	Rail Line
▭▭	Monorail

beating-heart bride). Its *Nightmare Before Christmas* holiday overlay is an annual tradition. This is a good area to get a casual bite to eat; the clam chowder in sourdough bread bowls, sold at the French Market Restaurant and Royal Street Veranda, is a popular choice. Food carts offer everything from just-popped popcorn to churros, and even fresh fruit.

FRONTIERLAND Between Adventureland and Fantasyland, Frontierland transports you to the Wild, Wild West with its rustic buildings, shooting gallery, mountain range, and foot-stompin' dance hall. The marquee attraction, **Big Thunder Mountain Railroad,** is a relatively tame roller coaster ride (no steep descents) that takes the form of a runaway mine car as it rumbles past desert canyons and an old mining town. Tour the Rivers of America on the **Mark Twain Riverboat,** in the company of a grizzled old river pilot, or circumnavigate the globe on the **Sailing Ship Columbia,** though its operating hours are usually limited to weekends. From here you can raft over to Pirate's Lair on **Tom Sawyer Island,** which now features pirate-theme caves, treasure hunts, and music, along with plenty of caves and hills to climb and explore. If you don't mind tight seating, have a snack at the Golden Horseshoe Restaurant while enjoying the always-entertaining comedy and bluegrass show of Billy Hill and the Hillybillies. Children won't want to miss **Big Thunder Ranch,** a small petting zoo featuring pigs, goats, and cows, beyond Big Thunder Mountain.

CRITTER Down-home country is the theme in this shady corner of the park,
COUNTRY where Winnie the Pooh and Davy Crockett make their homes. Here you can find **Splash Mountain,** a classic flume ride accompanied by music and appearances by Brer Rabbit and other characters from *Song of the South.* Don't forget to check out your photo (the camera snaps close-ups of each car just before it plunges into the water) on the way out. The patio of the popular Hungry Bear Restaurant has great views of Tom Sawyer's Island and Davy Crockett's Explorer Canoes.

ADVEN- Modeled after the lands of Africa, Polynesia, and Arabia, this tiny tropi-
TURELAND cal paradise is worth braving the crowds that flock here for the ambience and better-than-average food. Sing along with the animatronic birds and tiki gods in the **Enchanted Tiki Room,** sail the rivers of the world with joke-cracking skippers on **Jungle Cruise,** and climb the *Disneyodendron semperflorens* (aka always-blooming Disney tree) to **Tarzan's Treehouse,** where you can walk through scenes, some interactive, from the 1999 animated film. Cap off the visit with a wild Jeep ride at **Indiana Jones Adventure,** where the special effects and decipherable hieroglyphics distract you while you're waiting in line. The skewers (some vegetarian options available) at Bengal Barbecue and pineapple whip at Tiki Juice Bar are some of the best fast-food options in the park.

FANTASYLAND Sleeping Beauty Castle marks the entrance to Fantasyland, a visual wonderland of princesses, spinning teacups, flying elephants, and other classic storybook characters. Rides and shops (such as the princess-theme Once Upon a Time and Gepetto's Toys and Gifts) take precedence over restaurants in this area of the park, but outdoor carts sell everything from churros to turkey legs. Tots love the **King Arthur Carousel, Casey**

BEST TIPS FOR DISNEYLAND

Buy entry tickets in advance. Many nearby hotels sell park admission tickets; you can also buy them through the Disney website. If you book a package deal, such as those offered through AAA, tickets are included, too.

The lines at the ticket booths can take more than an hour on busy days, so you'll definitely save time by buying in advance, especially if you're committed to going on a certain day regardless of the weather.

Come midweek. Weekends, especially in summer, are a mob scene. Holidays are crowded, too. A rainy winter weekday is often the least crowded time to visit.

Plan your times to hit the most popular rides. Fodorites recommend getting to the park as early as possible and staying as late as possible. If you're at the park when the gates open, make a beeline for the top rides before the crowds reach a critical mass. Another good time is the late evening, when the hordes thin out somewhat, and during a parade or other show. Save the quieter attractions for midafternoon.

Use FASTPASS. These passes allow you to reserve your place in line at some of the most crowded attractions (only one at a time). Distribution machines are posted near the entrances of each attraction. Feed in your park admission ticket, and you'll receive a pass with a printed time frame (generally up to 1–1½ hours later) during which you can return to wait in a much shorter line.

Plan your meals to avoid peak mealtime crowds. Start the day with a big breakfast, so you won't be too hungry at noon, when restaurants and vendors get swarmed. Wait to have lunch until after 1.

If you want to eat at the **Blue Bayou** in New Orleans Square, you can make a reservation up to six months in advance online. Another (cheaper) option is to bring your own food. There are areas just outside the park gates with picnic tables set up for this. And it's always a good idea to bring water.

Check the daily events schedule online or at the park entrance. During parades, fireworks, and other special events, sections of the parks clog with crowds. This can work for you or against you. An event could make it difficult to get around a park—but if you plan ahead, you can take advantage of the distraction to hit popular rides.

Send the Teens Next Door. Disneyland's newer sister park, California Adventure, features more intense rides suitable for older kids (Park Hopper passes include admission to both parks).

Jr. Circus Train, and **Storybook Land Canal Boats.** This is also home to **Mr. Toad's Wild Ride, Peter Pan's Flight,** and **Pinocchio's Daring Journey,** classic, movie-theater-dark rides that immerse riders in Disney fairy tales and appeal to adults and kids alike. The Abominable Snowman pops up on the **Matterhorn Bobsleds,** a roller coaster that twists and turns up and around on a made-to-scale model of the real Swiss mountain. Anchoring the east end of Fantasyland is **It's a Small World,** a smorgasbord of dancing animatronic dolls, cuckoo clock–covered walls, and variations of the song everyone knows, or soon *will* know, by heart. Beloved Disney characters like Ariel from *Under the Sea* are also part of the mix. Fantasy Faire is a fairy tale–style village that collects all the Disney princesses together. Each has her own reception nook in the Royal Hall. Condensed retellings of *Tangled* and *Beauty and the Beast* take place at the Royal Theatre.

MICKEY'S TOONTOWN Geared toward small fries, this lopsided cartoonlike downtown, complete with cars and trolleys that invite exploring, is where Mickey, Donald, Goofy, and other classic Disney characters hang their hats. One of the most popular attractions is **Roger Rabbit's Car Toon Spin**, a twisting, turning cab ride through the Toontown of *Who Framed Roger Rabbit?* You can also walk through **Mickey's House** to meet and be photographed with the famous mouse, take a low-key ride on **Gadget's Go Coaster**, or bounce around the fenced-in playground in front of **Goofy's House**.

TOMOR-ROWLAND This popular section of the park continues to tinker with its future, adding and enhancing rides regularly. One of the newest attractions, Star Tours, is a 3-D immersive experience in the world of *Star Wars*. **Finding Nemo's Submarine Voyage** updates the old Submarine Voyage ride with the exploits of Nemo, Dory, Marlin, and other characters from the Disney Pixar film. Try to visit this popular ride early in the day if you can and be prepared for a wait. The interactive **Buzz Lightyear Astro Blasters** lets you zap your neighbors with laser beams and compete for the highest score. Hurtle through the cosmos on **Space Mountain** or check out mainstays like the futuristic **Astro Orbiter** rockets, **Innoventions**, a self-guided tour of the latest toys and gadgets of tomorrow. Disneyland Monorail and Disneyland Railroad both have stations here. There's also a video arcade and dancing water fountain that makes a perfect playground for kids on hot summer days. The Jedi Training Academy spotlights future Luke Skywalkers in the *Star Wars*–theme show's crowd.

Besides the eight lands, the daily live-action shows and parades are always crowd-pleasers. *Fantasmic!* is a musical, fireworks, and laser show in which Mickey and friends wage a spellbinding battle against Disneyland's darker characters. Spots are now secured through the FASTPASS system: pick up passes in Frontierland near Big Thunder Trail. If there are two shows scheduled for the day, the second one tends to be less crowded. A fireworks display sparks up most evenings. Brochures with maps, available at the entrance, list show and parade times.

DISNEY CALIFORNIA ADVENTURE

Almost as popular as its sister park across the plaza, Disney California Adventure embraces the Golden State—the way Walt Disney first saw it back in the late 1920s—and features rides and attractions based on hit Pixar films like *Cars* and *A Bug's Life*. Teens and tweens like the edgier thrill rides, while wee ones can tour undersea with Ariel and partake in other age-appropriate adventures. At night, don't miss the

DID YOU KNOW?

Apparently, the plain purple teacup in Disneyland's Mad Tea Party ride spins the fastest—though no one knows why.

World of Color light and water show. Unlike Disneyland, the theme park's restaurants offer beer, wine, and craft cocktails.

FAMILY **Disney California Adventure.** The sprawling Disney California Adventure,
Fodor's Choice adjacent to Disneyland (their entrances face each other), pays tribute to
★ the Golden State with eight theme areas that re-create vintage architectural styles and embrace several hit Pixar films via engaging attractions. In 2012 the front gate was revamped—visitors now enter through the art deco–style Buena Vista Street—and the 12-acre Cars Land and Radiator Springs Racers, an immediate blockbuster hit (FASTPASS tickets for the ride run out early most days) was added. Other popular attractions include World of Color, a nighttime water-effects show, and Toy Story Mania!, an interactive adventure ride hosted by Woody and Buzz Lightyear. At night the park takes on neon-color hues as glowing signs light up Route 66 in Cars Land and Mickey's Fun Wheel, a mega-size Ferris wheel on the Paradise Pier. Unlike at Disneyland, cocktails, beer, and wine are available, and there's even an outdoor dance spot, the Mad T Party. Live nightly entertainment also features a 1930s jazz troupe that arrives in a vintage jalopy. ⊠ *1313 S. Disneyland Dr., between Ball Rd. and Katella Ave., Anaheim* ☎ *714/781–4636* ⊕ *www.disneyland. com* ⊴ *$96; parking $17* ⊗ *Hrs vary.*

PARK NEIGHBORHOODS
Neighborhoods for Disney California Adventure are arranged in geographic order.

BUENA VISTA California Adventure's grand entryway re-creates the lost 1920s of Los
STREET Angeles that Walt Disney encountered when he moved to the Golden State. There's a **Red Car trolley** (modeled after Los Angeles's bygone streetcar line); hop on for the brief ride to Hollywood Land. Buena Vista Street is also home to a Starbucks outlet—within the Fiddler, Fifer & Practical Café—and the upscale Carthay Circle Restaurant and Lounge, which serves modern craft cocktails and beer.

GRIZZLY PEAK A makeover in 2015 transformed the former Condor Flats (an often
AIRFIELD underused corner of the park) into the Grizzly Peak Airfield, an area reminiscent of California's national parks in the 1960s. Dive into California's history and the natural beauty of the High Sierras with nature trails, a winery, and a tortilla factory (with free samples). Gentle and inspiring, **Soarin' Over California** is a spectacular simulated hang-glider ride over California terrain. Test your outdoorsman skills on the **Redwood Creek Challenge Trail,** a challenging trek across net ladders and suspension bridges. **Grizzly River Run** mimics the river rapids of the Sierra Nevadas; be prepared to get soaked.

HOLLYWOOD With a main street modeled after Hollywood Boulevard, a fake blue-
LAND sky backdrop, and real soundstages, this area celebrates California's most famous industry. **Disney Animation** gives you an insider's look at the work of animators and how they create characters. **Turtle Talk with Crush** lets kids have an unrehearsed talk with computer-animated Crush, a sea turtle from *Finding Nemo.* The Hyperion Theater hosts **Aladdin—A Musical Spectacular,** a 45-minute live performance with terrific visual effects. **Plan on getting in line about half an hour in advance: the show is worth the wait.** On the film-inspired ride, **Monsters, Inc.**

Mike & Sulley to the Rescue, you climb into taxis and travel the streets of Monstropolis on a mission to safely return Boo to her bedroom. A major draw for older kids is the looming **Twilight Zone Tower of Terror,** which drops riders 13 floors. Their screams can be heard throughout the park!

A BUG'S LAND Inspired by the 1998 film *A Bug's Life,* this section skews its attractions to an insect's point of view. Kids can spin around in giant takeout Chinese food boxes on **Flik's Flyers,** and hit the bug-shaped bumper cars on **Tuck and Roll's Drive 'Em Buggies.** The short show *It's Tough to Be a Bug!* gives a 3-D look at insect life.

CARS LAND Amble down Route 66, the main thoroughfare of Cars Land, a pitch-perfect re-creation of the vintage highway. Quick eats are found at the Cozy Cone Motel (in a teepee-shape motor court), while Flo's V8 café serves hearty comfort food. Start your day at Radiator Springs Racers, the park's most popular attraction, where waits can be two hours or longer. Strap into a nifty sports car and meet the characters of Pixar's *Cars*; the ride ends in a speedy auto race through the red rocks and desert of Radiator Springs.

PACIFIC WHARF The Wine Country Trattoria is a great place for Italian specialties paired with California wine; relax outside on the restaurant's terrace for a casual bite. Mexican cuisine and potent margaritas are available at the Cocina Cucamonga Mexican Grill and Rita's Baja Blenders.

PARADISE PIER This section re-creates the glory days of California's seaside piers. If you're looking for thrills, the **California Screamin'** roller coaster takes its riders from 0 to 55 mph in about four seconds and proceeds through scream tunnels, steeply angled drops, and a 360-degree loop. **Goofy's Sky School** is a rollicking roller coaster ride that goes up three stories and covers more than 1,200 feet of track. **Mickey's Fun Wheel,** a giant Ferris wheel, provides a good view of the grounds at a more leisurely pace. There are also carnival games, a fish-theme carousel, and Ariel's Grotto, where future princesses can dine with the mermaid and her friends (reservations are a must). Get a close-up look at Ariel's world on the **Little Mermaid—Ariel's Undersea Adventure.** The best views of the nighttime music, water, and light show, *World of Color,* are from the paths along Paradise Bay. Book a prix-fixe three-course dinner at the Wine Country Trattoria that includes a ticket to a viewing area to catch all the show's stunning visuals.

OTHER ATTRACTIONS

FAMILY **Downtown Disney.** Downtown Disney is a 20-acre promenade of dining, shopping, and entertainment that connects the resort's hotels and theme parks. Restaurant-nightclub **House of Blues** spices up its Delta-inspired ribs and seafood with various live music acts on an intimate two-story stage. At **Ralph Brennan's Jazz Kitchen** you can dig into New Orleans–style food and music. Sports fans gravitate to **ESPN Zone,** with American grill food, interactive video games, and 120 HDTVs telecasting worldwide sports events. An **AMC** multiplex movie theater with stadium-style seating plays the latest blockbusters and, naturally, a couple of kid flicks. Shops sell everything from Disney goods to antique jewelry—don't miss **Disney Vault 28,** a hip boutique that sells

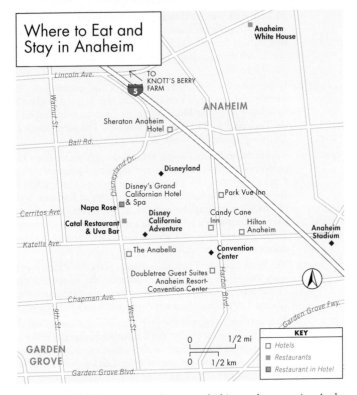

Where to Eat and Stay in Anaheim

■ Anaheim White House

Lincoln Ave.

TO KNOTT'S BERRY FARM

5

ANAHEIM

Sheraton Anaheim Hotel □

Ball Rd.

Walnut St.

Disneyland Dr.

♦ Disneyland

Disney's Grand Californian Hotel & Spa

□ Park Vue Inn

Napa Rose ■

Cerritos Ave.

Catal Restaurant & Uva Bar ■

Disney California Adventure ♦

Candy Cane Inn □

Hilton Anaheim □

Anaheim Stadium ♦

Katella Ave.

The Anabella □

Convention Center ♦

Doubletree Guest Suites □ Anaheim Resort-Convention Center

Harbor Blvd.

Chapman Ave.

9th St.

West St.

Garden Grove Fwy.

0   1/2 mi

0   1/2 km

GARDEN GROVE

Garden Grove Blvd.

KEY
□ Hotels
■ Restaurants
■ Restaurant in Hotel

designer-made Disney wear and couture clothing and accessories. At the mega-sized **Lego Store** there are hands-on demonstrations and space to play with the latest Lego creations. Parking is a deal: the first three hours are free, with two extra hours with validation. ⊠ *1580 Disneyland Dr., Anaheim* ☎ *714/300–7800* ⊕ *disneyland.disney.go.com/downtown-disney* ⊠ *Free* ☉ *Daily 7 am–2 am; hrs at shops and restaurants vary.*

WHERE TO EAT

$$$$
NORTHERN
ITALIAN

✕ **Anaheim White House.** Several small dining rooms are set with crisp linens and candles in this flower-filled 1909 mansion. The northern Italian menu includes steak, rack of lamb, and fresh seafood. Try the signature ravioli *arragosta,* lobster-filled pasta in a ginger-and-citrus sauce. A three-course, prix-fixe express lunch, served weekdays, costs $22. Ⓢ *Average main: $35* ⊠ *887 S. Anaheim Blvd., Anaheim* ☎ *714/772–1381* ⊕ *www.anaheimwhitehouse.com* ☉ *No lunch Sat.*

$$$
MEDITERRANEAN

✕ **Catal Restaurant & Uva Bar.** Famed chef Joachim Splichal and his staff take a relaxed approach at this bi-level Mediterranean spot. People-watch at the colorful, outdoor Uva (Spanish for "grape") bar on the ground floor, where there are specialty cocktails, craft beers, and more than 40 wines by the glass. Burgers here are crowd-pleasers, as are appetizers from corn arepas to lemony hummus. Upstairs, Catal's menu has tapas, a variety of flavorful paellas (lobster is worth the splurge), and charcuterie. ■TIP→ Reserve a table on the outdoor terrace for an awesome view of the Disneyland fireworks. $ *Average main: $30* ✉ *Downtown Disney, 1580 S. Disneyland Dr., Suite 103, Anaheim* ☎ *714/774–4442* ⊕ *www.patinagroup.com.*

$$$$ ✕ **Napa Rose.** Done up in a lovely Craftsman style, this eatery overlooks
AMERICAN a woodsy corner of Disney's California Adventure park. The contemporary cuisine is matched with an extensive wine list, with 1,000 labels and 80 available by the glass. For a look into the open kitchen, sit at the counter and watch the chefs as they whip up such signature dishes as pan-roasted diver scallops in a sauce of lobster, lemon, and vanilla, and grilled lamb porterhouse chop in a sangiovese jus. There's also a list of kid-friendly dishes. A cocktail on the outdoor patio with a fire pit is a pleasant way to end the night. The four-course, $100 prix-fixe menu changes weekly. $ *Average main: $40* ✉ *Disney's Grand Californian Hotel, 1600 S. Disneyland Dr., Anaheim* ☎ *714/300–7170, 714/781–3463 Reservations* ⊕ *disneyland.disney.go.com/grand-californian-hotel/napa-rose* ⚐ *Reservations essential.*

WHERE TO STAY

$$ ⛫ **The Anabella.** At the Anaheim Convention Center, this hotel's Span-
HOTEL ish Mission–style exterior and leafy landscaping set it apart from other budget properties. **Pros:** 15-minute walk to Disneyland and California Adventure entrance; extended happy hour at hotel bar; free Wi-Fi. **Cons:** some complaints about lack of maintenance. $ *Rooms from: $175* ✉ *1030 W. Katella Ave., Anaheim* ☎ *714/905–1050, 800/863–4888* ⊕ *www.anabellahotel.com* ⇥ *234 rooms, 124 suites* ⭘*No meals.*

$$ ⛫ **Candy Cane Inn.** One of the Disneyland area's first hotels, the Candy
HOTEL Cane is one of Anaheim's most relaxing properties, with spacious and understated rooms and an inviting palm-fringed pool. **Pros:** proximity to everything Disney; friendly service; well-lighted property. **Cons:** rooms and lobby are on the small side; all rooms face parking lot. $ *Rooms from: $158* ✉ *1747 S. Harbor Blvd., Anaheim* ☎ *714/774–5284, 800/345–7057* ⊕ *www.candycaneinn.net* ⇥ *171 rooms* ⭘*Breakfast.*

$$$$ ⛫ **Disney's Grand Californian Hotel & Spa.** The most opulent of Disney-
RESORT land's three hotels, the Craftsman-style Grand Californian offers views
FAMILY of Disney California Adventure and Downtown Disney. **Pros:** gorgeous
Fodor's Choice lobby; plenty for families; direct access to California Adventure. **Cons:** the
★ self-parking lot is across the street; standard rooms are on the small side. $ *Rooms from: $534* ✉ *1600 S. Disneyland Dr., Anaheim* ☎ *714/635–2300, 714/956–6425 reservations* ⊕ *disneyland.disney.go.com/grand-californian-hotel* ⇥ *904 rooms, 44 suites, 50 villas* ⭘*No meals.*

$$ ⛫ **Doubletree Guest Suites Anaheim Resort–Convention Center.** This upscale
HOTEL hotel near the Anaheim Convention Center and a 20-minute walk from Disneyland caters to business travelers and vacationers alike. **Pros:** huge suites; elegant lobby; walking distance to a variety of restaurants. **Cons:** a bit far from Disneyland; pool area is small. $ *Rooms from: $169* ✉ *2085 S. Harbor Blvd., Anaheim* ☎ *714/750–3000, 800/215–7316* ⊕ *doubletree3.hilton.com* ⇥ *50 rooms, 202 suites* ⭘*No meals.*

$$ ⛫ **Hilton Anaheim.** Next to the Anaheim Convention Center, this busy
HOTEL Hilton is one of the largest hotels in Southern California, with a restau-
FAMILY rant and food court, cocktail lounges, a full-service gym, and its own

Starbucks. **Pros:** efficient service; great children's programs; some rooms have views of the nightly fireworks. **Cons:** huge size can be daunting; fee to use health club. [$] *Rooms from: $159* ✉ *777 Convention Way, Anaheim* ☎ *714/750–4321, 800/445–8667* 🌐 *www.anaheim.hilton.com* 🛏 *1,479 rooms, 93 suites* 🍴 *No meals.*

$$$ HOTEL 👪 **Park Vue Inn.** Watch the nightly fireworks from the rooftop sundeck at this bougainvillea-covered Spanish-style inn, one of the closest lodgings to Disneyland main gate. **Pros:** easy walk to Disneyland, Downtown Disney, and Disney California Adventure; good value; some rooms have bunk beds. **Cons:** all rooms face the parking lot; rooms near the breakfast room can be noisy. [$] *Rooms from: $179* ✉ *1570 S. Harbor Blvd., Anaheim* ☎ *714/772–3691, 800/334–7021* 🌐 *www.parkvueinn.com* 🛏 *80 rooms, 6 suites* 🍴 *Breakfast.*

SPORTS AND THE OUTDOORS

Anaheim Ducks. The National Hockey League's Anaheim Ducks, winners of the 2007 Stanley Cup, play at Honda Center. ✉ *Honda Center, 2695 E. Katella Ave., Anaheim* ☎ *877/945–3946* 🌐 *ducks.nhl.com.*

Los Angeles Angels of Anaheim. Professional baseball's Los Angeles Angels of Anaheim play at Angel Stadium. An "Outfield Extravaganza" celebrates great plays on the field, with fireworks and a geyser exploding over a model evoking the California coast. ✉ *Angel Stadium, 2000 E. Gene Autry Way, Anaheim* ☎ *714/940–2000* 🌐 *www.angelsbaseball.com* [M] *Metrolink Angels Express.*

KNOTT'S BERRY FARM

25 miles south of Los Angeles, via I-5, in Buena Park.

Knott's Berry Farm welcomes guests with its mix of Americana, zooming roller coasters, *Peanuts* characters, and a touch of the Wild West. The new (in May 2015) 4-D underwater ride, *Voyage to the Iron Reef*, demonstrates the park's commitment to keeping up with the times, but there's plenty of old-fashioned fun. Ride a steam engine–drawn train through Badlands, speed backwards on Boomerang, or just dig into some fabulous fried chicken—Knott's continues to be a crowd-pleaser for all ages.

FAMILY **Knott's Berry Farm.** The land where the boysenberry was invented (by crossing raspberry, blackberry, and loganberry bushes) is now occupied by Knott's Berry Farm. In 1934 Cordelia Knott began serving chicken dinners on her wedding china to supplement her family's income—or so the story goes. The dinners and her boysenberry pies proved more profitable than husband Walter's farm, so the two moved first into the restaurant business and then into the entertainment business. The park is now a 160-acre complex with 40 rides, dozens of restaurants and shops, a brick-by-brick replica of Philadelphia's Independence Hall, and loads of Americana. Although it has plenty to keep small children occupied, the park is best known for its awesome rides.The Boardwalk area was expanded in 2013, adding two coasters—the stomach-churning Rip Tide turns thrill-seekers upside down and around several times—water features to cool things off on hot days, and a lighted promenade. And, yes, you can still get that boysenberry pie (and jam, juice—you name it). ✉ *8039 Beach Blvd.* ✛ *Between La Palma Ave. and Crescent St., 2 blocks south of Hwy. 91* ☎ *714/220–5200* ⊕ *www.knotts.com* ✉ *$65.*

PARK NEIGHBORHOODS

Neighborhoods for Knott's Berry Farm are arranged in geographic order.

CAMP SNOOPY It can be gridlock on weekends, but small fries love this miniature High Sierra wonderland where the *Peanuts* gang hangs out. Tykes can push and pump their own mini–mining cars on **Huff and Puff,** zip around a pint-size racetrack on **Charlie Brown Speedway,** and hop aboard **Woodstock's Airmail,** a kids' version of the park's Supreme Scream ride. Most of the rides here are geared toward kids only, leaving parents to cheer them on from the sidelines. **Sierra Sidewinder,** a roller coaster near the entrance of Camp Snoopy, is aimed at older children, with spinning saucer-type vehicles that go a maximum speed of 37 mph.

FIESTA VILLAGE Over in **Fiesta Village** are two more musts for adrenaline junkies: **Montezooma's Revenge,** a roller coaster that goes from 0 to 55 mph in less than five seconds, and **Jaguar!,** which simulates the motions of a cat stalking its prey, twisting, spiraling, and speeding up and slowing down as it takes you on its stomach-dropping course. There's also **Hat Dance,** a version of the spinning teacups but with sombreros, and a 100-year-old **Dentzel Carousel,** complete with an antique organ and menagerie of hand-carved animals.

THE BOARDWALK Not-for-the-squeamish thrill rides and skill-based games dominate the scene at the **boardwalk.** New roller coasters—Coast Rider, Surfside Glider, and Pacific Scrambler—were added in 2013 and surround a pond that keeps things cooler on hot days. Go head over heels on the **Boomerang** roller coaster, then do it again—backward. The boardwalk is also home to a string of test-your-skill games that are fun to watch whether you're playing or not, and Johnny Rockets, the park's newest restaurant.

GHOST TOWN Clusters of authentic old buildings relocated from their original mining-town sites mark this section of the park. You can stroll down the street, stop and chat with a blacksmith, pan for gold (for a fee), crack open a geode, check out the chalkboard of a circa-1875 schoolhouse, and ride an original Butterfield stagecoach. Looming over it all is **GhostRider,** Orange County's first wooden roller coaster. Traveling up to 56 mph and reaching 118 feet at its highest point, the park's biggest attraction is riddled with sudden dips and curves, subjecting riders to forces up to three times that of gravity. On the Western-theme **Silver Bullet,** riders are sent to a height of 146 feet and then back down 109 feet. Riders spiral, corkscrew, fly into a cobra roll, and experience overbanked curves. The **Calico Mine** ride descends into a replica of a working gold mine. The **Timber Mountain Log Ride** is a visitor favorite—the flume ride underwent a complete renovation in 2013. Also found here is the park's newest thrill ride, the **Pony Express,** a roller coaster that lets riders saddle up on packs of "horses" tethered to platforms that take off on a series of hairpin turns and travel up to 38 mph. Don't miss the **Western Trails Museum,** a dusty old gem full of Old West memorabilia and rural Americana, plus menus from the original chicken restaurant, and an impressive antique button collection. **Calico Railroad** departs regularly from Ghost Town station for a round-trip tour of the park (bandit holdups notwithstanding).

This section is also home to **Big Foot Rapids,** a splash-fest of white-water river rafting over towering cliffs, cascading waterfalls, and wild rapids. Don't miss the visually stunning show at **Mystery Lodge,** which tells the story of Native Americans in the Pacific Northwest with lights, music, and beautiful images.

INDIAN TRAILS Celebrate Native American traditions through interactive exhibits like tepees and daily dance and storytelling performances.

Knott's Soak City Water Park is directly across from the main park on 13 acres next to Independence Hall. It has a dozen major water rides; the latest is **Pacific Spin,** an oversize waterslide that drops riders 75 feet into a catch pool. There's also a children's pool, 750,000-gallon wave pool, and funhouse. Soak City's season runs mid-May to mid-September. It's open daily after Memorial Day, weekends only after Labor Day, and then closes for the season.

WHERE TO EAT AND STAY

$$ AMERICAN FAMILY

🍴 **Mrs. Knott's Chicken Dinner Restaurant.** Cordelia Knott's fried chicken and boysenberry pies drew crowds so big that Knott's Berry Farm was built to keep the hungry customers occupied while they waited. The restaurant's current incarnation (outside the park's entrance) still serves crispy fried chicken, along with fluffy handmade biscuits, mashed potatoes, and Mrs. Knott's signature chilled cherry-rhubarb compote. On a busy day the restaurant will cook up 1,200 chickens. The wait, unfortunately, can be an hour or more on weekends and longer on holidays (Mother's Day is crazy busy!). To beat the lines, order from the adjacent takeout counter and enjoy a picnic at the duck pond. Jump-start a visit to the park with a hearty breakfast here. There's three hours of free parking in the lot across from the restaurant. [$] *Average main: $18* ✉ *Knott's Berry Farm Marketplace, 8039 Beach Blvd.* ☎ *714/220–5080* 🌐 *www.knotts.com/california-marketplace/mrs-knott-s-chicken-dinner-restaurant.*

$ RESORT FAMILY

🏨 **Knott's Berry Farm Hotel.** This convenient high-rise hotel is run by the park and sits right on park grounds surrounded by graceful palm trees. **Pros:** easy access to Knott's Berry Farm; plenty of family activities; basketball court. **Cons:** lobby and hallways can be noisy; public areas show significant wear and tear. [$] *Rooms from: $99* ✉ *7675 Crescent Ave.* ☎ *714/995–1111, 866/752–2444* 🌐 *www.knottshotel.com* 🛏 *320 rooms* 🍽 *No meals.*

COASTAL ORANGE COUNTY

Running along the Orange County coastline is scenic Pacific Coast Highway (Highway 1, known locally as PCH). Older beachfront settlements, with their modest bungalow-style homes, are joined by posh gated communities. The pricey land between Newport Beach and Laguna Beach is where Laker Kobe Bryant, novelist Dean Koontz, and a slew of Internet and finance moguls live.

A mural at Huntington Beach

Though the coastline is rapidly being filled in, there are still a few stretches of beautiful, protected open land. And at many places along the way you can catch an idealized glimpse of the Southern California lifestyle: surfers hitting the beach, boards under their arms.

LONG BEACH AND SAN PEDRO

About 25 miles southeast of Los Angeles, via I-110 south.

The port cities of Long Beach and San Pedro are L.A.'s gateway to the Pacific. From both waterfronts there are ferries to Catalina Island and fishing charters. Long Beach also welcomes cruise ships, offers whale-watching excursions, and is home to the now retired grande dame of trans-Atlantic crossings, *The Queen Mary.*

EXPLORING

FAMILY **Aquarium of the Pacific.** Sea lions, nurse sharks, and penguins, oh my!—this aquarium focuses on creatures of the Pacific Ocean. The main exhibits include large tanks of sharks, sting rays, and ethereal sea dragons, which the aquarium has successfully bred in captivity. The Great Hall features the multimedia attraction *Penguins,* a panoramic film that captures the world of this endangered species. Be sure to say hello to Betty, a rescue at the engaging sea otter exhibit. For a nonaquatic experience, head to Lorikeet Forest, a walk-in aviary full of the friendliest parrots from Australia. Buy a cup of nectar and smile as you become a human bird perch. If you're a true animal lover, book an up-close-and-personal Animal Encounters Tour ($109) to learn about and assist in the care and feeding of the animals; or find out how the aquarium functions with the extensive Behind the Scenes Tour ($42.95, including admission). Certified divers can book a supervised dive in the aquarium's Tropical Reef Habitat ($299). Twice daily whale-watching trips on the *Harbor Breeze* depart from the dock adjacent to the aquarium; summer sightings of blue whales are an unforgettable thrill. ✉ *100 Aquarium Way, Long Beach* ☎ *562/590–3100* 🌐 *www.aquariumofpacific.org* 🎫 *$28.95* 🕒 *Daily 9–6.*

FAMILY **Cabrillo Marine Aquarium.** Dedicated to the marine life that flourishes off the Southern California coast, this Frank Gehry–designed center gives an intimate and instructive look at local sea creatures. Head to the Exploration Center and S. Mark Taper Foundation Courtyard for kid-friendly interactive exhibits and activity stations. Especially fun is the "Crawl In" aquarium, where you can be surrounded by fish without getting wet. From March through July the aquarium organizes a legendary grunion program, when you can see the small, silvery fish as they come ashore at night to spawn on the beach. **TIP→ After visiting the museum, stop for a picnic or beach stroll along Cabrillo Beach.** ✉ *3720 Stephen M. White Dr., San Pedro, Los Angeles* ☎ *310/548–7562* 🌐 *www.cabrillomarineaquarium.org* 🎫 *$5 suggested donation, parking $1 per hr* 🕒 *Tues.–Fri. noon–5, weekends 10–5.*

FAMILY ***Queen Mary.*** This impressive example of 20th-century cruise ship opulence is the last of its kind. And there's a saying among staff members that the more you get to know the *Queen Mary,* the more you realize she has an endearing personality to match her wealth of history. The beautifully preserved art deco–style ocean liner was launched in 1936 and made 1,001 transatlantic crossings before finally berthing in Long Beach in 1967. Today there's a popular Princess Diana exhibit and a daily British-style high tea.

On board you can take one of a dozen tours, such as the informative Behind the Scenes walk or the downright spooky Haunted Encounters tour. (Spirits have reportedly been spotted in the pool and engine room.) You could stay for dinner at one of the ship's restaurants, listen to live jazz in the original first-class lounge, or even spend the night in one of the 346 wood-panel cabins. The ship's neighbor, a geodesic dome originally built to house Howard Hughes's *Spruce Goose* aircraft, now serves as a terminal for Carnival Cruise Lines, making the *Queen Mary* the perfect pit stop before or after a cruise. Anchored next to the *Queen* is the *Scorpion,* a Russian submarine you can tour for a look at Cold War history. ✉ *1126 Queens Hwy., Long Beach* ☎ *877/342–0738* 🌐 *www.queenmary.com* 🎫 *Tours $29–$80, including a self-guided audio tour* 🕒 *Hrs vary for tours.*

WHERE TO STAY

$$$ HOTEL 🏨 **Hotel Maya–a Doubletree Hotel.** Brightly painted, and spread out on 11 acres with its own sandy beach, the Hotel Maya brings a tropical flair to Long Beach's waterfront. **Pros:** low-key vibe; dedicated staff; waterfront location. **Cons:** location is slightly confusing for first-time visitors. [$] *Rooms from: $179* ✉ *700 Queensway Dr., Long Beach* ☎ *562/435–7676* 🌐 *www.hotelmayalongbeach.com* 🛏 *112 rooms, 87 suites* 🍴 *No meals.*

$$ HOTEL FAMILY 🏨 **Hotel Queen Mary.** Experience the golden age of transatlantic travel without the seasickness: a 1936–art deco style reigns on the *Queen Mary,* from the ship's mahogany paneling to its nickel-plated doors to the majestic Grand Salon. **Pros:** a walkable historic Promenade deck; views from Long Beach out to the Pacific; art deco details. **Cons:** spotty service; vintage soundproofing makes for a challenging night's sleep. [$] *Rooms from: $129* ✉ *1126 Queens Hwy., Long Beach* ☎ *562/435–3511, 877/342–0742* 🌐 *www.queenmary.com* 🛏 *346 staterooms, 8 suites* 🍴 *No meals.*

$$ B&B/INN 🏨 **The Varden.** Constructed in 1929 to house Bixby Knolls Sr.'s mistress, Dolly Varden, this small, historic, European-style hotel, on the metro line in downtown Long Beach, now caters to worldly budget travelers. **Pros:** great value for downtown location; discount passes to Gold's Gym across the street; complimentary continental breakfast. **Cons:** no resort services; small rooms. [$] *Rooms from: $129* ✉ *335 Pacific Ave., Long Beach* ☎ *562/432–8950* 🌐 *www.thevardenhotel.com* 🛏 *35 rooms* 🍴 *No meals.*

4

HUNTINGTON BEACH

40 miles southeast of Los Angeles, I-5 south to I-605 south to I-405 south to Beach Blvd.

Once a sleepy residential town with little more than a string of rugged surf shops, Huntington Beach has transformed itself into a resort destination. The town's appeal is its broad white-sand beaches with often towering waves, complemented by a lively pier, shops and restaurants on Main Street, and a growing collection of resort hotels.

A draw for sports fans and partiers of all stripes is the U.S. Open professional surf competition, which brings a festive atmosphere to town annually in late July. There's even a Surfing Walk of Fame, with plaques set in the sidewalk around the intersection of PCH and Main Street.

ESSENTIALS

Visitor Information Visit Huntington Beach ✉ *301 Main St., Suite 212* ☎ *714/969–3492, 800/729–6232* 🌐 *www.surfcityusa.com.*

EXPLORING

FAMILY **Bolsa Chica Ecological Reserve.** Wildlife lovers and bird-watchers flock to Bolsa Chica Ecological Reserve, which has a 1,180-acre salt marsh where 321 of Orange County's 420 bird species—including great blue herons, snowy and great egrets, and brown pelicans—have been spotted in the past decade. Throughout the reserve are trails for bird-watching, including a comfortable 1½-mile loop. Free guided tours depart from the walking bridge on the second Saturday of each month at 10 am. At noon most Saturdays the public can help feed the center's marine and small animals. There are two entrances off the Pacific Coast Highway: one close to the Interpretive Center and a second one 1 mile south on Warner Avenue, opposite Bolsa Chica State Beach. ✉ *Bolsa Chica Wetlands Interpretive Center, 3842 Warner Ave.* ☎ *714/846–1114* 🌐 *www.bolsachica.org* 🎟 *Free* ⏲ *Interpretive Center daily 9–4.*

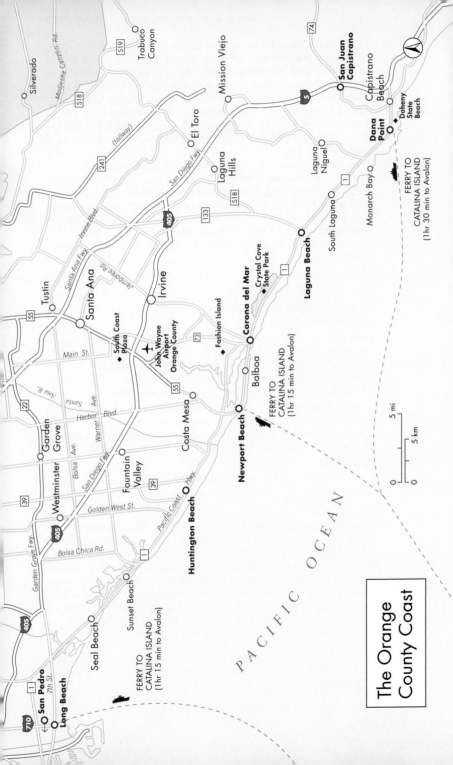

The Orange County Coast

Bolsa Chica State Beach. In the northern section of the city, Bolsa Chica State Beach is usually less crowded than its southern neighbors. The sand is somewhat gritty and not the cleanest, but swells make it a hot surfing spot. Picnic sites and barbecue pits can be reserved in advance. Fire pits attract beachgoers most nights. **Amenities:** food and drink; lifeguards; parking (fee); showers; toilets. **Best for:** sunset; surfing; swimming; walking. ⊠ *Pacific Coast Hwy., between Seapoint St. and Warner Ave.* ☎ *714/846–3460* ⊕ *www.parks.ca.gov/?page_id=642* ☞ *$15 parking.*

Huntington Pier. This pier stretches 1,856 feet out to sea, well past the powerful waves that gave Huntington Beach the title of "Surf City U.S.A." A farmers' market and arts fair is held on Friday afternoons; an informal car show sets up most weekends. ⊠ *Pacific Coast Hwy.* ⊕ *www.huntingtonbeachca.gov.*

4

NEED A BREAK?

Ruby's. At the end of Huntington Pier sits Ruby's, part of a California chain of 1940s-style burger joints. Try the Cobb, with bacon and slices of avocado. Breakfast is served daily until 11:30 am. ⊠ *1 Main St.* ☎ *714/969–7829* ⊕ *www.rubys.com.*

International Surfing Museum. Just up Main Street from Huntington Pier, the International Surfing Museum pays tribute to the sport's greats with an impressive collection of surfboards and related memorabilia. They've even got the Bolex camera used to shoot the 1966 surf documentary *Endless Summer.* ⊠ *411 Olive Ave.* ☎ *714/960–3483* ⊕ *www.surfingmuseum. org* ☞ *$2* ⊗ *Sun. and Wed.–Fri. noon–5, Tues. noon–8, Sat. noon–7.*

BEACHES

Huntington City Beach. Stretching for 3½ miles from Bolsa Chica State Beach to Huntington State Beach, Huntington City Beach is most crowded around the pier; amateur and professional surfers brave the waves daily on its north side. Fire pits, numerous concession stands, an area for dogs, and well-raked white sand make this a popular beach come summertime. **Amenities:** food and drink; lifeguards; parking (fee); showers; toilets. **Best for:** sunset; surfing; swimming; walking. ⊠ *Pacific Coast Hwy., from Beach Blvd. to Seapoint St.* ☎ *714/536–5281, 714/536–9303 Surf report* ⊕ *www.ci.huntington-beach.ca.us* ☞ *Parking $15 weekdays, $17 weekends, $20–$27 holidays.*

Huntington State Beach. This state beach also has 200 fire pits, so it's popular day and night. There are changing rooms, concession stands, lifeguards, Wi-Fi access, and ample parking. A 6-mile bike path connects to the area's other stretches of sand. Picnic areas can be reserved in advance for a $150 fee, otherwise it's first come, first served. On hot days, expect crowds at this broad, soft sandy beach. **Amenities:** food and drink; lifeguards; parking (fee); showers; toilets. **Best for:** sunset; surfing; swimming; walking. ⊠ *Pacific Coast Hwy., from Beach Blvd. south to Santa Ana River* ☎ *714/536–1454* ⊕ *www.parks.ca.gov/?page_id=643* ☞ *$15 parking.*

WHERE TO EAT

$$$$
SEAFOOD
FAMILY

✕ **Duke's.** Freshly caught seafood reigns supreme at this homage to surfing legend Duke Kahanamoku; it's also a prime people-watching spot right at the beginning of Huntington Pier. Choose from several fish-of-the-day selections—many with Hawaiian flavors—prepared in one of five ways.

Or try the crispy coconut shrimp or tuna tacos with Maui onions. Duke's mai tai is not to be missed. $ *Average main: $34* ⊠ *317 Pacific Coast Hwy.* ☎ *714/374–6446* ⊕ *www.dukeshuntington.com.*

$$ ✕**Lou's Red Oak BBQ.** You won't find any frills at Lou's Red Oak BBQ—
AMERICAN just barbecue pork, grilled linguica, rotisserie chicken, and a lot of beef. Try the tri-tip (either as an entrée or on a toasted bun smothered with traditional Santa Maria–style salsa) or the smoked turkey plate for a hearty meal. $ *Average main: $18* ⊠ *21501 Brookhurst St.* ☎ *714/965–5200* ⊕ *www.lousbbq.com.*

$ ✕**Wahoo's Fish Taco.** Proximity to the ocean makes this eatery's
MEXICAN mahimahi-filled tacos taste even better. This healthy fast-food chain—
FAMILY tagged with dozens of surf stickers—brought Baja's fish tacos north of the border to quick success. $ *Average main: $9* ⊠ *120 Main St.* ☎ *714/536–2050* ⊕ *www.wahoos.com.*

WHERE TO STAY

$$$$ 🛏 **Shorebreak Hotel.** Across the street from the beach, this boutique hotel
HOTEL attracts a mix of couples, families, and the hipster-surfer crowd. **Pros:** proximity to beach and shops; free use of beach cruiser bikes; quiet rooms despite central location. **Cons:** steep valet parking fee; courtyard rooms have uninspiring alley views. $ *Rooms from: $289* ⊠ *500 Pacific Coast Hwy.* ☎ *714/861–4470, 877/212–8597* ⊕ *www.shorebreakhotel. com* ⬡ *157 rooms* ⦿*No meals.*

SPORTS AND THE OUTDOORS

SURFING

Corky Carroll's Surf School. This surf school organizes lessons, weeklong workshops, and international surf camps at Bolsa Chica State Beach. Private lessons are available year-round. ☎ *714/969–3959* ⊕ *www. surfschool.net.*

Dwight's. You can rent bikes, wet suits, surfboards, and boogie boards at Dwight's, one block south of Huntington Pier. ⊠ *201 Pacific Coast Hwy.* ☎ *714/536–8083* ⊕ *www.dwightsbeachconcession.com.*

SHOPPING

HSS Pierside. The best surf-gear source is HSS Pierside, across from Huntington Pier. It's staffed by true surf enthusiasts. ⊠ *300 Pacific Coast Hwy.* ☎ *714/841–4000* ⊕ *www.hsssurf.com.*

NEWPORT BEACH

6 miles south of Huntington Beach via the Pacific Coast Highway.

Newport Beach has evolved from a simple seaside village to an icon of chic coastal living. Its ritzy reputation comes from megayachts bobbing in the harbor, boutiques that rival those in Beverly Hills, and spectacular homes overlooking the ocean.

Newport is said to have the highest per-capita number of Mercedes-Benzes in the world; inland Newport Beach's concentration of high-rise office buildings, shopping centers, and luxury hotels drive the economy. But on the city's Balboa Peninsula, you can still catch a glimpse of a more innocent, down-to-earth beach town scattered with taco spots, tackle shops, and sailor bars.

Riding the waves at Newport Beach

Visitor Information Visit Newport Beach ✉ *Atrium Court at Fashion Island, 401 Newport Center Dr.* ☎ *855/563–9767* ⊕ *www.visitnewportbeach.com.*

EXPLORING

Balboa Island. This sliver of terra firma in Newport Harbor boasts quaint streets tightly packed with impossibly charming multimillion-dollar cottages. The island's main drag, Marine Avenue, is lined with equally picturesque cafés and shops.

NEED A BREAK?

Sugar 'N Spice. Stop by ice cream parlor Sugar 'N Spice for a Balboa Bar—a slab of vanilla ice cream dipped first in chocolate and then in a topping of your choice such as hard candy or Oreo crumbs. Other parlors serve the concoction, but Sugar 'N Spice claims to have invented it back in 1945. ✉ *310 Marine Ave., Balboa Island* ☎ *949/673–8907.*

Balboa Peninsula. Newport's best beaches are on Balboa Peninsula, where many jetties pave the way to ideal swimming areas. The most intense bodysurfing place in Orange County and arguably on the West Coast, known as the **Wedge,** is at the south end of the peninsula. It was created by accident in the 1930s when the Federal Works Progress Administration built a jetty to protect Newport Harbor. ■ **TIP→ Rip currents mean it's strictly for the pros—but it sure is fun to watch an experienced local ride it.** ⊕ *www.visitnewportbeach.com/vacations/balboa-peninsula.*

FAMILY **ExplorOcean.** This destination has exhibits on the history of the harbor, ocean explorers, and scientific aspects of the Pacific Ocean. There's a fleet of ship models: some date to 1798, and one is made entirely of gold and silver. Other fun features include a touch tank holding local sea creatures and a lab for kids that encourages innovation. Summer hours vary. ✉ *600 E. Bay Ave.* ☎ *949/675–8915* 🌐 *www.explorocean.org* 🎟 *$5* 🕒 *Wed.–Thurs. noon–4, Fri. and Sun. noon–6, Sat. 11–5.*

Newport Harbor. Sheltering nearly 10,000 small boats, Newport Harbor may seduce even those who don't own a yacht. Spend an afternoon exploring the charming avenues and surrounding alleys. Several grassy areas on the primarily residential Lido Isle have views of the water. ✉ *Pacific Coast Hwy.*

Newport Pier. Jutting out into the ocean near 20th Street, Newport Pier is a popular fishing spot. Street parking is difficult, so grab the first space you find and be prepared to walk. On weekday mornings you're likely to encounter dory fishermen hawking their predawn catches, as they've done for generations. On weekends the area is alive with kids of all ages on in-line skates, skateboards, and bikes dodging pedestrians and whizzing past fast-food joints and classic dive bars. ✉ *72 McFadden Pl.*

Orange County Museum of Art. This museum features a collection of modernist paintings and sculpture by California artists like Richard Diebenkorn, Ed Ruscha, Robert Irwin, and Chris Burden. There are also cutting-edge international works and changing contemporary art exhibitions. ✉ *850 San Clemente Dr.* ☎ *949/759–1122* 🌐 *www.ocma.net* 🎟 *$10; Free admission on Fri.* 🕒 *Wed. and Fri.–Sun. 11–5, Thurs. 11–8.*

WHERE TO EAT

$$$ BRASSERIE
🍴 **Basilic.** This intimate French-Swiss bistro adds a touch of old-world elegance to the island with its white linen and flower-topped tables. Chef Bernard Althaus grows the herbs used in his classic French dishes. Head here for charcuterie, steak au poivre, and a fine Bordeaux. [$] *Average main: $28* ✉ *217 Marine Ave., Balboa Island* ☎ *949/673–0570* 🌐 *www.basilicrestaurant.com* 🕒 *Closed Sun. and Mon. No lunch.*

$ SEAFOOD
🍴 **Bear Flag Fish Co.** Expect long lines in summer at this indoor/outdoor dining spot serving up the freshest local fish (swordfish, sea bass, halibut, and tuna) and a wide range of creative seafood dishes (the Hawaiian-style *poke* salad with ahi tuna is a local favorite). Order at the counter, which doubles as a seafood market, and sit inside the airy dining room or outside on a grand patio. One of the few restaurants in Southern California with its own fishing boat, there's a good chance some line-caught local fish will be on the menu. Oysters are a great choice, and the fish tacos topped with the house-made hot sauce are not to be missed. [$] *Average main: $10* ✉ *Newport Peninsula, 3421 Via Lido* ☎ *949/673–3474* 🌐 *www.bearflagfishco.com.*

$$$$ SEAFOOD
🍴 **The Cannery.** This 1920s cannery building still teems with fish, but now they go into dishes on the eclectic Pacific Rim menu rather than being packed into crates. Settle in at the sushi bar, in the dining room, or on the patio before choosing between sashimi, seafood platters, or the upscale surf-and-turf with bone-in rib-eye steaks and grilled Maine lobsters. The menu includes a selection of steaks, ribs, and seafood from the world's waters. Many diners arrive by boat, as there's a convenient dock off the front entrance. [$] *Average main: $35* ✉ *3010 Lafayette Rd.* ☎ *949/566–0060* 🌐 *www.cannerynewport.com.*

$$$ ✗ **3-Thirty-3.** If there's a nightlife "scene" to be had in Newport Beach,
AMERICAN this is it. This stylish eatery attracts a convivial crowd—both young
and old—for midday, sunset, and late-night dining. A long list of
small, shareable plates heightens the camaraderie. Pair a cocktail with
charred lollipop lamb chops or chicken satay while you check out the
scene, or settle in for a dinner of Kobe flatiron steak or sesame-topped
ahi tuna. Ⓢ *Average main: $26* ⊠ *333 Bayside Dr.* ☎ *949/673–8464*
⊕ *www.3thirty3nb.com.*

WHERE TO STAY

$$$$ Ⓣ **Balboa Bay Resort.** Sharing the same frontage as the private Balboa
RESORT Bay Club that once hosted Humphrey Bogart, Lauren Bacall, and the
FAMILY Reagans, this waterfront resort has one of the best bay views around.
Pros: exquisite bayfront views; comfortable beds; a raked beach for
guests. **Cons:** not much within walking distance; $20 nightly hospital-
ity fee. Ⓢ *Rooms from: $309* ⊠ *1221 W. Coast Hwy.* ☎ *949/645–5000*
⊕ *www.balboabayresort.com* ⤴ *149 rooms, 10 suites* ⦿ *No meals.*

$$$$ Ⓣ **The Island Hotel.** Across the street from stylish Fashion Island, this
HOTEL 20-story tower caters to business types during the week and luxury seek-
ers on weekends. **Pros:** lively lounge scene; first-class spa; great location.
Cons: steep valet parking prices; some rooms have views of mall; pricey.
Ⓢ *Rooms from: $259* ⊠ *690 Newport Center Dr.* ☎ *949/759–0808,*
866/554–4620 ⊕ *www.theislandhotel.com* ⤴ *295 rooms, 83 suites*
⦿ *No meals.*

SPORTS AND THE OUTDOORS

BOAT RENTALS
Balboa Boat Rentals. You can tour Lido and Balboa isles with kayaks
($18 an hour), stand-up paddleboards ($25 an hour), small motor-
boats ($70 an hour), and electric boats ($80 to $95 an hour) at Bal-
boa Boat Rentals. ⊠ *510 E. Edgewater Ave.* ☎ *949/673–7200* ⊕ *www.*
boats4rent.com.

BOAT TOURS
Catalina Flyer. At Balboa Pavilion, the Catalina Flyer operates a 90-min-
ute daily round-trip passage to Catalina Island for $70. Reservations are
required; check the schedule in January and February, as crossings may
be cancelled due to annual maintenance. ⊠ *400 Main St.* ☎ *800/830–*
7744, 949/673–5245 ⊕ *www.catalinainfo.com.*

Hornblower Cruises & Events. This operator books three-hour weekend
dinner cruises with dancing for $85. The two-hour Sunday brunch
cruise starts at $63. Cruises traverse the mostly placid and scenic
waters of Newport Harbor. ⊠ *2431 West Coast Hwy.* ☎ *888/467–6256*
⊕ *www.hornblower.com.*

FISHING
Davey's Locker. In addition to a complete tackle shop, Davey's Locker
offers half-day sportfishing trips starting at $41.50. Whale-watching
excursions begin at $32 for weekdays. ⊠ *Balboa Pavilion, 400 Main*
St. ☎ *949/673–1434* ⊕ *www.daveyslocker.com.*

Newport Beach Golf Course. An 18-hole executive course, Newport
Beach Golf Course is also lighted for night play. Rates start at $23

A whimbrel hunts for mussels at Crystal Cove State Park.

(Mon.–Thurs.). Reservations are accepted up to one week in advance, but walk-ins are accommodated when possible. ⊠ *3100 Irvine Ave.* ☎ *949/852–8681* ⊕ *www.npbgolf.com* ⅄ *18 holes, 3180 yards, par 59.* ⊠ *$23* Mon.–Thurs., *$27* Fri.–Sun.

SHOPPING

Balboa Pavilion. On the bay side of the peninsula, Balboa Pavilion was built in 1905. Today it is home to a restaurant and shops and serves as a departure point for Catalina Island ferries and whale-watching cruises. In the blocks around the pavilion you can find restaurants, shops, and the small Balboa Fun Zone, a local kiddie hangout with a Ferris wheel. On the other side of the narrow peninsula is Balboa Pier. ⊠ *400 Main St.* ⊕ *www.balboapavilion.com.*

Fashion Island. Shake the sand out of your shoes to head inland to the ritzy Fashion Island outdoor mall, a cluster of arcades and courtyards complete with koi pond, fountains, and a family-friendly trolley—plus some awesome ocean views. It has the luxe department stores Neiman Marcus and Bloomingdale's, plus expensive spots like Jonathan Adler, Kate Spade, and Michael Stars. ⊠ *401 Newport Center Dr., between Jamboree and MacArthur Blvds., off PCH* ☎ *949/721–2000, 855/658–8527* ⊕ *www.shopfashionisland.com.*

CORONA DEL MAR

2 miles south of Newport Beach, via PCH.

A small jewel on the Pacific Coast, Corona del Mar (known by locals as "CDM") has exceptional beaches that some say resemble their majestic

Northern California counterparts. South of CDM is an area referred to as the Newport Coast or Crystal Cove—whatever you call it, it's another dazzling spot on the California Riviera.

EXPLORING

FAMILY

Fodor'sChoice

★

Crystal Cove State Park. Midway between Corona del Mar and Laguna, Crystal Cove State Park is a favorite of local beachgoers and wilderness trekkers. It encompasses a 3.2-mile stretch of unspoiled beach and has some of the best tide-pooling in Southern California. Here you can see starfish, crabs, and other sea life on the rocks. The park's 2,400 acres of backcountry are ideal for hiking, horseback riding, and mountain biking, but stay on the trails to preserve the beauty. **Crystal Cove Historic District** holds a collection of 46 handmade historic cottages (16 of which are available for overnight rental), decorated and furnished to reflect the 1935 to 1955 beach culture that flourished here. On the sand above the high tide line and on a bluff above the beach, the cottages offer a funky look at beach life 50 years ago. ⊠ *8471 N. Coast Hwy., Laguna Beach* 🕾 *949/494–3539* ⊕ *www.crystalcovestatepark. com* 🚗 *$15 parking* ⊙ *Daily 6–dusk*

Reserve America. Cottages, which average $180 per night for four people, can be reserved up to six months in advance from Reserve America. 🕾 *800/444–7275* ⊕ *www.reserveamerica.com.*

Store. The Store carries fine-art photography works by local plein air artists, as well as jewelry, children's toys, and beach apparel. 🕾 *949/376–8762.*

NEED A
BREAK?

Beachcomber at Crystal Cove Café. Beach culture flourishes in the Crystal Cove Historic District's restaurant, the Beachcomber at Crystal Cove Café. The umbrella-laden deck is just a few steps above the white sand. The wait on weekends and holidays can be quite long. ⊠ *Crystal Cove, 15 Crystal Cove, Newport Coast* 🕾 *949/376–6900* ⊕ *www.thebeachcombercafe.com.*

Sherman Library and Gardens. This 2½-acre botanical garden and library specializes in the history of the Pacific Southwest. You can wander among cactus gardens, rose gardens, a wheelchair-height touch-and-smell garden, and a tropical conservatory. There's a good gift shop, too. Café Jardin serves lunch on weekdays and Sunday brunch. ⊠ *2647 E. Pacific Coast Hwy.* 🕾 *949/673–2261* ⊕ *www.slgardens.org* 🚗 *$5* ⊙ *Daily 10:30–4.*

BEACHES

FAMILY

Corona del Mar State Beach. This beach is actually made up of two beaches, Little Corona and Big Corona, separated by a cliff. Both have soft, golden-hue sand. Facilities include fire pits and volleyball courts. Two colorful reefs (and the fact that it's off-limits to boats) make Corona del Mar great for snorkelers and beachcombers. Parking in the lot is a steep $15 daily and $20 on holidays, but you can often find a spot on the street on weekdays. **Amenities:** lifeguards; parking (fee); showers; toilets. **Best for:** snorkeling; sunset; swimming. ⊠ *3100 Ocean Blvd., Newport Beach* 🕾 *949/644–3151* ⊕ *www.parks.ca.gov.*

WHERE TO EAT AND STAY

$ ✕ **Pacific Whey Cafe.** The ovens rarely get a break here; everything is
AMERICAN   made from scratch daily. Pick up a BLTA (a BLT with avocado) for a picnic across the street at Crystal Cove State Park. Or stay—at a communal
table inside or in the courtyard, which has an ocean view—for organic
buckwheat pancakes or grilled salmon with citrus sauce. $ *Average
main: $10* ⊠ *Crystal Cove Promenade, 7962 E. Coast Hwy., Newport
Coast* ☎ *949/715–2200* ⊕ *www.pacificwhey.com.*

$$$$ ⊡ **The Resort at Pelican Hill.** Adjacent to Crystal Cove State Park, this
RESORT   Mediterranean-style resort has spacious bungalow suites, each with Ital-
FAMILY   ian limestone fireplaces and marble baths, built into terraced hillsides
overlooking the Pacific. **Pros:** paradise for golfers; gracious, attentive
staff. **Cons:** sky-high prices; common areas can feel cold. $ *Rooms
from: $595* ⊠ *22701 Pelican Hill Rd. S, Newport Coast* ☎ *949/612–
0332, 855/315–8214* ⊕ *www.pelicanhill.com* ↩ *204 suites, 128 villas*
|○| *No meals.*

SHOPPING

Crystal Cove Promenade. Adding to Orange County's overwhelming supply of high-end shopping and dining is Crystal Cove Promenade, which
might be described as the toniest strip mall in America. The storefronts and restaurants of this Mediterranean–inspired center are lined
up across the street from Crystal Cove State Park, with the shimmering
Pacific waters in plain view. ⊠ *7772–8112 E. Coast Hwy., Newport
Beach* ☎ *949/494–1239* ⊕ *www.crystalcove.com/beach-living/shopping*

LAGUNA BEACH

*10 miles south of Newport Beach on PCH, 60 miles south of Los Ange-
les on I-5 south to Hwy. 133, which turns into Laguna Canyon Rd.*

Fodor'sChoice   Even the approach tells you that Laguna Beach is exceptional. Driv-
★   ing in along Laguna Canyon Road from the Interstate 405 freeway
gives you the chance to cruise through a gorgeous coastal canyon, large
stretches of which remain undeveloped. You'll arrive at a glistening
wedge of ocean.

Laguna's welcome mat is legendary. On the corner of Forest and Park
avenues is a gate proclaiming, "This gate hangs well and hinders none,
refresh and rest, then travel on." A gay community has long been established here. Art galleries dot the village streets, and there's usually someone daubing up in Heisler Park. Along the Pacific Coast Highway you'll
find dozens of clothing boutiques, jewelry shops, and cafés.

ESSENTIALS

Visitor Information Laguna Beach Visitors Center ⊠ *381 Forest Ave.*
☎ *949/497–9229, 800/877–1115* ⊕ *www.lagunabeachinfo.com.*

EXPLORING

Laguna Art Museum. This museum displays American art, with an emphasis on California artists from all periods. Special exhibits change quar-
terly. ⊠ *307 Cliff Dr.* ☎ *949/494–8971* ⊕ *www.lagunaartmuseum.org*
⊡ *$7* ⊙ *Fri.–Tues. 11–5, Thurs. 11–9.*

Looking for shells on Laguna Beach, one of the nicest stretches of sand in Southern California

Laguna Coast Wilderness Park. The Laguna Coast Wilderness Park is spread over 7,000 acres of fragile coastal territory, including the canyon. The 40 miles of trails are great for hiking and mountain biking, and are open daily, weather permitting. Docent-led hikes are given Saturday mornings. No dogs are allowed in the park. ⊠ *18751 Laguna Canyon Rd.* ☎ *949/923–2235* ⊕ *www.ocparks.com/parks/lagunac* 🖃 *$3 parking.*

BEACHES

1,000 Steps Beach. Off South Coast Highway at 9th Street, 1,000 Steps Beach is a hard-to-find spot tucked away in a neighborhood with great waves and hard-packed, white sand. There aren't really 1,000 steps down (but when you hike back up, it'll certainly feel like it). **Amenities:** parking. **Best for:** sunset; surfing; swimming. ⊠ *South Coast Hwy., at 9th St.*

FAMILY **Main Beach Park.** A stocky 1920s lifeguard tower marks Main Beach Park, where a wooden boardwalk separates the sand from a strip of lawn. Walk along this soft-sand beach, or grab a bench and watch people bodysurfing, playing volleyball, or scrambling around two half-basketball courts. The beach also has children's play equipment. Most of Laguna's hotels are within a short (but hilly) walk. **Amenities:** lifeguards; parking; showers; toilets. **Best for:** sunset; swimming; walking. ⊠ *Broadway at S. Coast Hwy.*

Wood's Cove. Off South Coast Highway, Wood's Cove is especially quiet during the week. Big rock formations hide lurking crabs. This is a prime scuba-diving spot, and at high tide much of the beach is underwater. Climbing the steps to leave, you can see a Tudor-style mansion that was once home to Bette Davis. Street parking is limited. **Amenities:** none. **Best for:** snorkeling; scuba diving; sunset. ✉ *Diamond St. and Ocean Way.*

WHERE TO EAT

$$$ INTERNATIONAL 🍴 **Sapphire Laguna.** This Laguna Beach establishment is part gourmet pantry (a must-stop for your every picnic need) and part global dining adventure. Iranian-born chef Azmin Ghahreman takes you on a journey through Europe and Asia with dishes ranging from a pork shank cassoulet to Jamaican curried black cod. More than a dozen beers from around the world and a fittingly eclectic wine list round out the experience. The dining room is intimate and earthy, but infused with local style. Brunch is a favorite with locals, as well—enjoy it on the patio in good weather. [$] *Average main: $27* ✉ *The Old Pottery Place, 1200 S. Coast Hwy.* ☎ *949/715–9888* 🌐 *www.sapphirellc.com.*

$$$$ MODERN AMERICAN Fodor's Choice ★ 🍴 **Studio.** In a nod to Laguna's art history, Studio has house-made specialties that entice the eye as well as the palate. You can't beat the location, atop a 50-foot bluff overlooking the Pacific Ocean. And because the restaurant occupies its own Craftsman-style bungalow, it doesn't feel like a hotel dining room. Under the deft direction of Executive Chef Craig Strong, the menu changes seasonally and features the finest seafood and the freshest locally grown produce (some herbs come from a small garden just outside the kitchen). You might begin with paper-thin charred shrimp carpaccio or black pepper–seared hamachi before moving on to perfectly cooked King salmon in subtle coriander sauce or lamb chops on a bed of polenta. The wine list here is bursting with nearly 2,500 labels. Service is crisp and attentive. [$] *Average main: $55* ✉ *Montage Laguna Beach, 30801 S. Coast Hwy.* ☎ *949/715–6420* 🌐 *www.studiolagunabeach.com* ✍ *Reservations essential* 🕒 *Closed Mon. No lunch.*

$ VEGETARIAN 🍴 **Zinc Café & Market.** Families flock to this small Laguna Beach institution for reasonably priced breakfast and lunch options. Try the signature quiches or poached egg dishes in the morning, or swing by later in the day for healthy salads, house-made soups, quesadillas, or pizzettes. The café also has great artisanal cheeses and gourmet goodies you can take with you or savor on the outdoor patio. All the sweets are house-made, including the mega-size brownies. [$] *Average main: $12* ✉ *350 Ocean Ave.* ☎ *949/494–6302* 🌐 *www.zinccafe.com* 🕒 *No dinner Nov.–Apr.*

WHERE TO STAY

$$$ HOTEL 🏨 **La Casa del Camino.** This historic Spanish-style hotel opened in 1929 and was once a favorite of Hollywood stars. **Pros:** breathtaking views from rooftop lounge; personable service; close to beach. **Cons:** some rooms face the highway; frequent events can make hotel noisy; some rooms are very small. [$] *Rooms from: $229* ✉ *1289 S. Coast Hwy.* ☎ *949/497–2446, 855/634–5736* 🌐 *www.lacasadelcamino.com* 🛏 *26 rooms, 10 suites* 🍽 *No meals.*

$$$$ RESORT FAMILY Fodor's Choice ★ 🏨 **Montage Laguna Beach.** Laguna's connection to the Californian plein-air artists is mined for inspiration at this head-turning, lavish hotel. **Pros:** top-notch, enthusiastic service; idyllic coastal location; special programs cover everything from art to marine biology. **Cons:** multinight stays required on weekends and holidays; $36 valet parking. [$] *Rooms*

from: $595 ✉ *30801 S. Coast Hwy.* ☎ *949/715–6000, 866/271–6953* 🌐 *www.montagelagunabeach.com* 🛏 *188 rooms, 60 suites* 🍴 *No meals.*

$$$$ RESORT 🏨 **Surf & Sand Resort.** One mile south of downtown, this Laguna Beach property is even more wonderful than longtime fans remember. **Pros:** easy beach access; intimate property; slightly removed from Main Street crowds. **Cons:** pricey valet parking; surf can be quite loud. [$] *Rooms from: $575* ✉ *1555 S. Coast Hwy.* ☎ *949/497–4477, 877/741–5908* 🌐 *www.surfandsandresort.com* 🛏 *154 rooms, 13 suites* 🍴 *No meals.*

NIGHTLIFE AND PERFORMING ARTS

Laguna Playhouse. Dating back to the 1920s, the Laguna Playhouse mounts a variety of productions, from classics to youth-oriented plays. ✉ *606 Laguna Canyon Rd.* ☎ *949/497–2787* 🌐 *www.lagunaplayhouse.com.*

SPORTS AND THE OUTDOORS

WATER SPORTS

Hobie Sports. In summer, rent bodyboards at Hobie Sports. ✉ *294 Forest Ave.* ☎ *949/497–3304* 🌐 *www.hobiesurfshop.com.*

SHOPPING

Coast Highway, Forest and Ocean avenues, and Glenneyre Street are full of art galleries, fine jewelry stores, and clothing boutiques.

Candy Baron. Get your sugar fix at the time-warped Candy Baron, filled with old-fashioned goodies like gumdrops, bull's-eyes, and more than a dozen barrels of saltwater taffy. ✉ *231 Forest Ave.* ☎ *949/497–7508* 🌐 *www.thecandybaron.com.*

DANA POINT

10 miles south of Laguna Beach, via the Pacific Coast Highway.

Dana Point's claim to fame is its small-boat marina tucked into a dramatic natural harbor and surrounded by high bluffs. The early-March Dana Point Festival of the Whales celebrates the passing gray-whale migration with two weekends full of activities.

EXPLORING

Dana Point Harbor. This harbor was first described more than 100 years ago by its namesake, Richard Henry Dana, in his book *Two Years Before the Mast.* At the marina are docks for private boats and yachts, shops, restaurants, and boat, kayak, stand-up paddleboard, and bike rentals. The harbor is also the departure point for whale-watching expeditions. ✉ *Dana Point Harbor Dr.* ☎ *949/923–2255* 🌐 *www.danapointharbor.com*

Doheny State Beach. At the south end of Dana Point, Doheny State Beach is one of Southern California's top surfing destinations, but there's a lot more to do within this 61-acre area. There are five indoor tanks and an interpretive center devoted to the wildlife of the Doheny Marine Refuge, as well as food stands, picnic facilities, and volleyball courts. Divers and anglers hang out at the beach's western end, and during low tide the tide pools beckon both young and old. The water quality occasionally falls below state standards—signs are posted if that's the case. **Amenities:** food and drink; lifeguards; parking (fee); showers; toilets. **Best for:** partiers; sunset; surfing; swimming; walking. ✉ *25300 Dana Point Harbor Dr.* ☎ *949/496–6171* 🌐 *www.dohenystatebeach.org* 🎫 *$15 parking.*

FAMILY **Ocean Institute.** Marine science and history are the focus at the Ocean Institute, where you'll find indoor tanks with touchable sea creatures, an accessible man-made tide pool, and the complete skeleton of a gray whale. Anchored outside is *The Pilgrim,* a full-size replica of the square-rigged vessel on which Richard Henry Dana sailed. You can tour the boat on Sunday from 10 to 2. Weekend whale-watching cruises are available year-round. ✉ *24200 Dana Point Harbor Dr.* ☎ *949/496–2274* 🌐 *www.ocean-institute.org* 🎫 *$6.50* 🕒 *Weekends 10–3.*

WHERE TO EAT

$$$ SEAFOOD 🍴 **Wind & Sea.** Unobstructed marina views make this a particularly appealing place for lunch or a sunset dinner. On warm days, patio tables beckon you outside, and looking out on the Pacific might put you in the mood for a retro cocktail like a mai tai. Among the entrées, the macadamia-crusted mahimahi and the grilled teriyaki shrimp stand out. The Sunday breakfast buffet is good value at $16 per person. [$] *Average main: $28* ✉ *Dana Point Harbor, 34699 Golden Lantern St.* ☎ *949/496–6500* 🌐 *www.windandsearestaurants.com.*

WHERE TO STAY

$$$ B&B/INN 🏨 **Blue Lantern Inn.** Combining New England–style architecture with a Southern California setting, this grey-clapboard B&B rests on a bluff overlooking the harbor and ocean. **Pros:** bikes to borrow; one room welcomes pets; free Wi-Fi and parking. **Cons:** nearby restaurant can be noisy. [$] *Rooms from: $250* ✉ *34343 St. of the Blue Lantern* ☎ *949/661–1304, 800/950–1236* 🌐 *www.bluelanterninn.com* 🛏 *29 rooms* 🍽 *Breakfast.*

$$$$ RESORT FAMILY Fodor's Choice ★ 🏨 **Ritz-Carlton, Laguna Niguel.** Combine the Ritz-Carlton's top-tier level of service with an unparalleled view of the Pacific, and you're in the lap of luxury at this resort. **Pros:** beautiful grounds and views; luxurious bedding; seamless service. **Cons:** some rooms are small for the price; in-house dining prices are high. [$] *Rooms from: $475* ✉ *1 Ritz-Carlton Dr.* ☎ *949/240–2000, 800/542–8680* 🌐 *www.ritzcarlton.com/lagunaniguel* 🛏 *367 rooms, 29 suites* 🍽 *No meals.*

$$$$ RESORT 🏨 **St. Regis Monarch Beach.** Grand and sprawling, the St. Regis can satisfy your every whim with its 172 acres of grounds, private beach club, 18-hole Robert Trent Jones Jr.–designed golf course, three swimming pools, and tennis courts.**Pros:** immaculate rooms; big bathrooms with deep tubs; beautiful spa. **Cons:** hotel layout is somewhat confusing; high parking fees. [$] *Rooms from: $495* ✉ *1 Monarch Beach Resort, off Niguel Rd.* ☎ *949/234–3200, 888/627–7219* 🌐 *www.stregismb.com* 🛏 *325 rooms, 75 suites.*

SPORTS AND THE OUTDOORS

Capt. Dave's Dolphin & Whale Watching Safari. You have a good chance of getting a water's-eye view of resident dolphin pods and migrating humpback and gray whales if you take one of these tours via a solid and steady catamaran. Dave Anderson, a marine naturalist and filmmaker, and his wife run the safaris year-round. The endangered blue whale is reliably spotted in summer. Reservations are required for the safaris, which last 2½ hours and cost $59 ($39 ages 2–12). ✉ *24440 Dana Point Harbor Dr.* ☎ *949/488-2828* ⊕ *www.dolphinsafari.com.*

Dana Wharf Sportfishing & Whale Watching. Whale-watching excursions are offered by Dana Wharf Sportfishing & Whale Watching from early November to late April. Tickets cost $45 and reservations are required. ✉ *34675 Golden Lantern St.* ☎ *888/224–0603* ⊕ *www.danawharf.com.*

SAN JUAN CAPISTRANO

5 miles north of Dana Point via Hwy. 74, 60 miles north of San Diego via I-5.

4

San Juan Capistrano is best known for its historic mission, where the swallows traditionally return each year, migrating from their winter haven in Argentina (though these days they are more likely to choose other local sites for nesting). St. Joseph's Day, March 19, launches a week of fowl festivities. Charming antiques stores, which range from pricey to cheap, line Camino Capistrano.

GETTING HERE AND AROUND

If you arrive by train, which is far more romantic and restful than battling freeway traffic, you'll be dropped off across from the mission at the San Juan Capistrano depot. With its appealing brick café and preserved Santa Fe cars, the depot retains much of the magic of early American railroads. If driving, park near Ortega and Camino Capistrano, the city's main streets.

EXPLORING

FAMILY **Mission San Juan Capistrano.** Founded in 1776 by Father Junípero Serra, Fodor'sChoice Mission San Juan Capistrano was one of two Roman Catholic outposts ★ between Los Angeles and San Diego. The Great Stone Church, begun in 1797, is the largest structure created by the Spanish in California. Many of the mission's adobe buildings have been preserved to illustrate mission life, with exhibits of an olive millstone, tallow ovens, tanning vats, metalworking furnaces, and the padres' living quarters. The gardens, with their fountains, are a lovely spot in which to wander. The bougainvillea-covered Serra Chapel is believed to be the oldest church still standing in California, and is the only building remaining in which Fr. Serra actually led Mass. Mass takes place weekdays at 7 am in the chapel. Enter via a small gift shop in the gatehouse. ✉ *Camino Capistrano and Ortega Hwy.* ☎ *949/234–1300* ⊕ *www.missionsjc.com* ✉ *$9* ☉ *Daily 9–5.*

WHERE TO EAT

$$ ✕ **The Ramos House Cafe.** It may be worth hopping the Amtrak to San AMERICAN Juan Capistrano just for the chance to have breakfast or lunch at one of Orange County's most beloved restaurants. Here's your chance to visit one of Los Rios Historic District's board-and-batten homes dating back to 1881. This café sits practically on the railroad tracks across from the depot—nab a table on the patio and dig into a hearty breakfast, such as the smoked bacon scramble. The weekend brunch ($40

Mission San Juan Capistrano

per person) includes champagne, memorable mac-and-cheese with wild mushrooms, and chocolate bacon coffee cake. Every item on the menu illustrates chef-owner John Q. Humphreys's creative hand. $ *Average main: $18* ⊠ *31752 Los Rios St.* ☎ *949/443–1342* ⊕ *www.ramoshouse. com* ⊘ *Closed Mon. No dinner.*

NIGHTLIFE

Swallow's Inn. Across the way from Mission San Juan Capistrano you'll spot a line of Harleys in front of the Swallow's Inn. Despite a somewhat tough look, it attracts all kinds—bikers, surfers, modern-day cowboys, grandparents—for a drink, a casual bite, karaoke nights, and some rowdy live music. ⊠ *31786 Camino Capistrano* ☎ *949/493–3188* ⊕ *www.swallowsinn.com.*

CATALINA ISLAND

Fodor's Choice
★

Just 22 miles out from the L.A. coastline, across from Newport Beach and Long Beach, Catalina has virtually unspoiled mountains, canyons, coves, and beaches; best of all, it gives you a glimpse of what undeveloped Southern California once looked like.

Water sports are a big draw, as divers and snorkelers come for the exceptionally clear water surrounding the island. Kayakers are attracted to the calm cove waters and thrill seekers have made the eco-themed zip line so popular that there are nighttime tours via flashlight in summer. The main town, Avalon, is a charming, old-fashioned beach community, where yachts and pleasure boats bob in the crescent bay. Wander beyond the main drag and find brightly painted little bungalows fronting the sidewalks; golf carts are the preferred mode of transport.

In 1919 William Wrigley Jr., the chewing-gum magnate, purchased a controlling interest in the company developing Catalina Island, whose most famous landmark, the Casino, was built in 1929 under his orders. Because he owned the Chicago Cubs baseball team, Wrigley made Catalina the team's spring training site, an arrangement that lasted until 1951.

In 1975 the Catalina Island Conservancy, a nonprofit foundation, acquired about 88% of the island to help preserve the area's natural flora and fauna, including the bald eagle and the Catalina Island fox. These days the conservancy is restoring the rugged interior country with plantings of native grasses and trees. Along the coast you might spot oddities like electric perch, saltwater goldfish, and flying fish.

GETTING HERE AND AROUND

BUS TRAVEL

Catalina Safari Shuttle Bus has regular bus service (in season) between Avalon, Two Harbors, and several campgrounds. The trip between Avalon and Two Harbors takes two hours and costs $54 one-way.

Bus Contacts Catalina Safari Shuttle Bus ☎ *310/510–4205, 877/778–8322.*

FERRY TRAVEL

Two companies offer ferry service to Catalina Island. The boats have both indoor and outdoor seating and snack bars. Excessive baggage is not allowed, and there are extra fees for bicycles and surfboards. The waters around Santa Catalina can get rough, so if you're prone to seasickness, come prepared. Winter, holiday, and weekend schedules vary, so reservations are recommended.

Catalina Express makes an hour-long run from Long Beach or San Pedro to Avalon and a 90-minute run from Dana Point to Avalon with some stops at Two Harbors. Round-trip fares begin at $74.50, with discounts for seniors and kids. On busy days a $15 upgrade to the Commodore Lounge, when available, is worth it. Service from Newport Beach to Avalon is available through the Catalina Flyer. Boats leave from Balboa Pavilion at 9 am (in season), take 75 minutes to reach the island, and cost $70 round-trip. Return boats leave Catalina at 4:30 pm. Reservations are required for the Catalina Flyer and recommended for all weekend and summer trips. ■TIP→ **Keep an eye out for dolphins, which sometimes swim alongside the ferries.**

Ferry Contacts Catalina Express ☎ *800/481–3470, 562/485–3300* ⊕ *www.catalinaexpress.com.* **Catalina Flyer** ☎ *949/673–5245* ⊕ *www.catalinainfo.com.*

GOLF CARTS

Golf carts constitute the island's main form of transportation for sightseeing in the area, however some parts of town are off limits, as is the island's interior. You can rent them along Avalon's Crescent Avenue and Pebbly Beach Road for about $40 per hour with a $40 deposit, payable via cash or traveler's check only.

Golf Cart Rentals Island Rentals ⊠ *125 Pebbly Beach Rd., Avalon* ☎ *310/510–1456* ⊕ *www.catalinagolfcartrentals.com.*

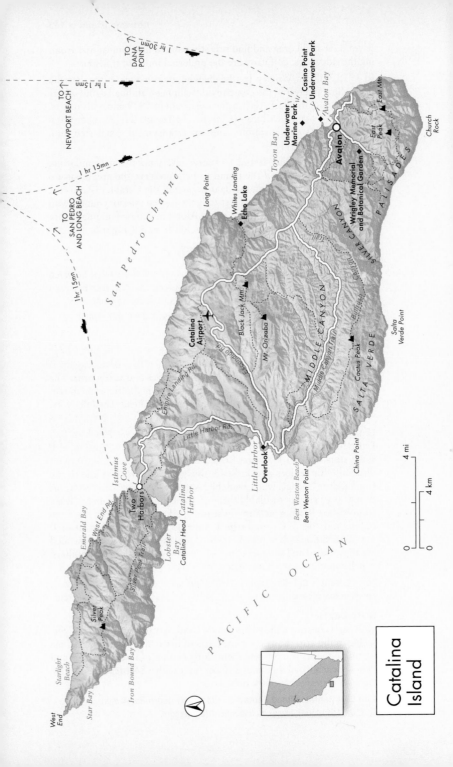

Catalina Island

HELICOPTER TRAVEL

Island Express helicopters depart hourly from San Pedro, Santa Ana, and Long Beach next to the Queen Mary (8 am–dusk). The trip from Long Beach takes about 15 minutes and costs $125 one-way, $250 round-trip (plus tax). Winter rates are lower. Reservations a week in advance are recommended.

Helicopter Contacts Island Express ☎ *800/228-2566* ⊕ *www.islandexpress. com.*

TIMING

Although Catalina can be seen in one very hectic day, several inviting hotels make it worth extending your stay for one or more nights. A short itinerary might include breakfast on the pier, a tour of the interior, a snorkeling excursion at Casino Point, or beach day at the Descanso Beach Club and a romantic waterfront dinner in Avalon.

After late October, rooms are much easier to find on short notice, rates drop dramatically, and many hotels offer packages that include transportation from the mainland and/or sightseeing tours. January to March you have a good chance of spotting migrating gray whales on the ferry crossing.

TOURS

Catalina Adventure Tours. Catalina Adventure Tours, which has booths at the boat landing and on the pier, arranges hikes and tours inland as well as on the water. ☎ *877/510–2888* ⊕ *www.catalinaadventuretours.com.*

Catalina Island Conservancy. The Catalina Island Conservancy organizes custom ecotours and hikes of the interior. Naturalist guides drive open Jeeps through some gorgeously untrammeled parts of the island. Tours start at $70 per person for a two-hour trip (two-person minimum); you can also book half- and full-day tours. The tours run year-round. ⊠ *125 Claressa Ave., Avalon* ☎ *310/510–2595* ⊕ *www.catalinaconservancy. org.*

Santa Catalina Island Company. Santa Catalina Island Company runs 16 Discovery Tours, including the *Flying Fish* boat trip (summer evenings only); a comprehensive inland motor tour; a tour of Skyline Drive; several Casino tours; a scenic tour of Avalon; a glass-bottom-boat tour; an undersea tour on a semisubmersible vessel; an eco-themed zip-line tour that traverses a scenic canyon; a speedy Dolphin Quest that searches for all manner of sea creatures. Reservations are highly recommended for the inland tours. Tours cost $12 to $178. There are ticket booths on the Green Pleasure Pier, at the Casino, in the plaza, and at the boat landing. ☎ *877/778–8322* ⊕ *www.visitcatalinaisland.com.*

VISITOR INFORMATION

Visitor Contacts Catalina Island Chamber of Commerce & Visitors Bureau ⊠ *#1 Green Pleasure Pier, Avalon* ☎ *310/510–1520* ⊕ *www.catalinachamber. com.*

AVALON

A 1- to 2-hour ferry ride from Long Beach, Newport Beach, or San Pedro; a 15-minute helicopter ride from Long Beach or San Pedro, slightly longer from Santa Ana.

Avalon, Catalina's only real town, extends from the shore of its natural harbor to the surrounding hillsides. Its resident population is about 3,800, but it swells with tourists on summer weekends. Most of the city's activity, however, is centered on the pedestrian mall on Crescent Avenue, and most sights are easily reached on foot. Private cars are restricted, and rental cars aren't allowed, but taxis, trams, and shuttles can take you anywhere you need to go. Bicycles, electric bikes, and golf carts can be rented from shops along Crescent Avenue.

EXPLORING

Fodor's Choice
★

Casino. This circular white structure is one of the finest examples of art deco architecture anywhere. Its Spanish-inspired floors and murals gleam with brilliant blue and green Catalina tiles. In this case, *casino,* the Italian word for "gathering place," has nothing to do with gambling. To the right of the theater's grand entrance is the quaint Catalina Island Museum, which examines chronicle 7,000 years of island history. First-run movies are screened nightly at the Avalon Theatre, noteworthy for its classic 1929 theater pipe organ and art deco wall murals.

The Santa Catalina Island Company leads two tours of the Casino—the 30-minute basic tour ($12) and the 90-minute behind-the-scenes tour ($26), which leads visitors through the green room and into the Wrigleys' private lounge. ⊠ *1 Casino Way* ☎ *310/510–2414 museum, 310/510–0179 theater* ⊕ *www.catalinamuseum.org* ✉ *Museum $5* ⊘ *Daily 10–5.*

New Year's Eve dance. The same big-band dances that made the Casino famous in the 1930s and '40s still take place several times a year. The New Year's Eve dance is hugely popular and sells out well in advance. ☎ *310/510–1520.*

Casino Point Dive Park. In front of the Casino are the crystal-clear waters of the Casino Point Dive Park, a protected marine preserve where moray eels, bat rays, spiny lobsters, harbor seals, and other sea creatures cruise around kelp forests and along the sandy bottom. It's a terrific site for scuba diving, with some shallow areas suitable for snorkeling. Equipment can be rented on and near the pier. The shallow waters of Lover's Cove, east of the boat landing, are also good for snorkeling.

Green Pleasure Pier. Head to the Green Pleasure Pier for a good vantage point of Avalon. On the pier you can find the visitor information, snack stands, and scads of squawking seagulls. It's also the landing where visiting cruise-ship passengers catch tenders back out to their ship. ⊠ *End of Catalina Ave.*

Wrigley Memorial and Botanic Garden. Two miles south of the bay is Wrigley Memorial and Botanic Garden, home to plants native to Southern California. Several grow only on Catalina Island—Catalina ironwood, wild tomato, and rare Catalina mahogany. The Wrigley family commissioned the garden as well as the monument, which has a grand staircase and a Spanish-style mausoleum inlaid with colorful Catalina tile. Wrigley Jr. was once buried here but his remains were moved to Pasadena during the Second World War. ✉ *Avalon Canyon Rd.* ☎ *310/510–2897* 🌐 *www.catalinaconservancy.org* 🎫 *$7* 🕒 *Daily 8–5.*

WHERE TO EAT

$$$ SEAFOOD 🍴 **Bluewater Avalon.** Overlooking the ferry landing and the entire harbor, the open-to-the-salt-air Bluewater Avalon offers freshly caught fish, savory chowders, and all manner of shellfish. If they're on the menu, don't miss the swordfish steak or the sand dabs. The dining room has an understated nautical vibe. Fishing rods serve as room dividers, and plank floors lend a casual feel inside and out. Vintage black-and-white photos acknowledge the island's famed sports fishing legacy. The wraparound patio is the preferred spot to dine, but beware of aggressive seagulls that may try to snatch your food. Happy hour attracts a crowd for the craft beers, potent cocktails, and tasty bites like popcorn shrimp and oyster shooters. [$] *Average main: $25* ✉ *306 Crescent Ave.* ☎ *310/510–3474* 🌐 *www.bluewateravalon.com.*

$ AMERICAN FAMILY 🍴 **Descanso Beach Club.** Set on an expansive deck overlooking the water, Descanso Beach Club serves a wide range of favorites: peel-and-eat shrimp, hamburgers, salads, nachos, and wraps are all part of the selection. Watch the harbor seals frolic just offshore while sipping the island's super-sweet signature cocktail, the Buffalo Milk, a mix of fruit liqueurs, vodka, and whipped cream. Fire pits and chic beach cabanas add to the scene, as does the sound of happy and terrified screams from the zip-liners in the canyon above the beach. [$] *Average main: $15* ✉ *Descanso Beach, 1 Descanso Ave.* ☎ *310/510–7410.*

$$$ SEAFOOD 🍴 **The Lobster Trap.** Seafood rules at the Lobster Trap—the restaurant's owner has his own boat and fishes for the catch of the day and, in season, spiny lobster. Ceviche is a great starter, always fresh and brightly flavored. Locals (you'll see many at the small counter) come for the relaxed atmosphere, large portions, draft beer, and live music on weekend nights. [$] *Average main: $24* ✉ *128 Catalina St.* ☎ *310/510–8585* 🌐 *catalinalobstertrap.com.*

WHERE TO STAY

$$$ HOTEL 🏨 **Aurora Hotel & Spa.** In a town dominated by historic properties, the Aurora is refreshingly contemporary, with a hip attitude and sleek furnishings. **Pros:** trendy design; quiet location off main drag; close to restaurants. **Cons:** standard rooms are small, even by Catalina standards; no elevator. [$] *Rooms from: $249* ✉ *137 Marilla Ave., Avalon* ☎ *310/510–0454, 800/422–6836* 🌐 *www.auroracatalina.com* 🛏 *15 rooms, 3 suites* 🍽 *Breakfast.*

$$$ HOTEL 🏨 **Hotel Metropole and Market Place.** Set over a bustling maze of shops, this hotel has plenty of modern amenities. **Pros:** family-friendly vibe; outdoor hot tub and sundeck; convenient location. **Cons:** some rooms on small side. [$] *Rooms from: $229* ✉ *205 Crescent Ave.* ☎ *310/510–1884, 800/541–8528* 🌐 *www.hotel-metropole.com* 🛏 *44 rooms, 8 suites, 1 villa* 🍽 *Breakfast.*

$$$ HOTEL 🏨 **Hotel Villa Portofino.** Steps from the Green Pleasure Pier, this European-style hotel creates an intimate feel with brick courtyards and walkways

and suites named after Italian cities. **Pros:** romantic; close to beach; incredible sun deck. **Cons:** ground floor rooms can be noisy; some rooms are on small side; no elevator. [$] *Rooms from: $235* ✉ *111 Crescent Ave.* ☎ *310/510–0555, 888/510–0555* 🌐 *www.hotelvillaportofino.com* 🛏 *35 rooms* 🍴 *Breakfast.*

$$$ HOTEL — 🏨 **Hotel Vista del Mar.** On the bay-facing Crescent Avenue, this third-floor property is steps from the beach, where complimentary towels, chairs, and umbrellas await guests. **Pros:** comfortable beds; central location; modern decor. **Cons:** no restaurant or spa facilities; few rooms with ocean views; no elevator. [$] *Rooms from: $250* ✉ *417 Crescent Ave.* ☎ *310/510–1452, 800/601–3836* 🌐 *www.hotel-vistadelmar.com* 🛏 *12 rooms, 2 suites* 🍴 *Breakfast.*

$$$$ B&B/INN — 🏨 **The Inn on Mt. Ada.** If you stay in the mansion where Wrigley Jr. once lived, you can enjoy all the comforts of a millionaire's home—at a millionaire's prices. **Pros:** timeless charm; shuttle from heliport and dock; incredible views. **Cons:** smallish rooms and bathrooms; expensive. [$] *Rooms from: $390* ✉ *398 Wrigley Rd.* ☎ *310/510–2030, 877/778–9395* 🌐 *www.visitcatalinaisland.com* 🛏 *6 rooms* 🕒 *Closed Jan.* 🍴 *Some meals.*

$$$$ HOTEL — 🏨 **Pavilion Hotel.** This mid-century-modern style hotel is Avalon's most citified spot, though just a few steps from the sand. **Pros:** centrally located, steps from the beach and harbor; friendly staff; plush bedding. **Cons:** no pool. [$] *Rooms from: $265* ✉ *513 Crescent Ave.* ☎ *310/510–1788, 877/778–8322* 🌐 *www.visitcatalinaisland.com* 🛏 *69 rooms, 2 suites* 🍴 *Breakfast.*

SPORTS AND THE OUTDOORS

BICYCLING

Brown's Bikes. Look for rentals on Crescent Avenue and Pebbly Beach Road, where Brown's Bikes is located. Beach cruisers and mountain bikes start at $20 per day. Electric bikes are also on offer. ✉ *107 Pebbly Beach Rd.* ☎ *310/510–0986* 🌐 *www.catalinabiking.com.*

DIVING AND SNORKELING

The Casino Point Underwater Park, with its handful of wrecks, is best suited for diving. Lover's Cove is better for snorkeling (but you'll share the area with glass-bottom boats). Both are protected marine preserves.

Catalina Divers Supply. Head to Catalina Divers Supply to rent equipment, sign up for guided scuba and snorkel tours, and attend certification classes. It also has an outpost at the Dive Park at Casino Point. ✉ *7 Green Pleasure Pier* ☎ *310/510–0330* 🌐 *www.catalinadiverssupply.com.*

HIKING

Catalina Island Conservancy. The conservancy has maps of the island's east-end hikes, such as Hermit's Gulch Trail. **TIP→ For a pleasant 4-mile hike out of Avalon, take Avalon Canyon Road to the Wrigley Botanical Garden and follow the trail to Lone Pine. At the top there's an amazing view of the Palisades cliffs and, beyond them, the sea.** ✉ *125 Claressa Ave.* ☎ *310/510–2595* 🌐 *www.catalinaconservancy.org.*

5

LOS ANGELES

WELCOME TO LOS ANGELES

TOP REASONS TO GO

★ **People-watching:** Celeb spotting in Beverly Hills, trying to get past the velvet rope at hip clubs, hanging out on the Venice Boardwalk . . . there's always something (or someone) interesting to see.

★ **Trendy restaurants:** Celebrity is big business here, so it's no accident that the concept of the celebrity chef is a key part of the city's dining scene.

★ **Hollywood magic:** A massive chunk of the world's entertainment is developed, written, filmed, edited, distributed, and sold here; you'll hear people discussing "the Industry" wherever you go.

★ **The beach:** Getting some beach time is practically a requirement—spending an afternoon (or three) on the sand is an integral part of the SoCal lifestyle.

★ **Chic shopping:** From Beverly Hills's Rodeo Drive and Downtown's Fashion District to the funky boutiques of Los Feliz, Silver Lake, and Echo Park, L.A. is a shopper's paradise.

1 Downtown. Downtown L.A. shows off spectacular modern architecture with the swooping Walt Disney Concert Hall and the stark Cathedral of Our Lady of the Angels. The Music Center and the Museum of Contemporary Art anchor a world-class arts scene, while Olvera Street, Chinatown, and Little Tokyo reflect the city's history and diversity.

2 Hollywood and the Studios. Glitzy and tarnished, good and bad— Hollywood is just like the entertainment business itself. The Walk of Fame, TCL Chinese Theatre, Paramount Pictures, and the Hollywood Bowl keep the glamorous past alive. Universal Studios Hollywood, Warner Bros., and NBC Television Studios are in the San Fernando Valley.

3 Beverly Hills and the Westside. Go for the glamour, the restaurants, and the scene. Rodeo Drive is particularly good for a look at wretched or ravishing excess. But don't forget the Westside's cultural attractions—especially the dazzling Getty Center. West Hollywood's an area for urban indulgences— shopping, restaurants, nightspots—rather than sightseeing. Its main arteries

are the Sunset Strip and Melrose Avenue, lined with shops ranging from punk to postmodern.

4 Santa Monica and the Beaches. These desirable beach communities move from ultrarich, ultracasual Malibu to bohemian/transitioning Venice, with liberal, Mediterranean-style Santa Monica in between.

5 Pasadena. Its own separate city, Pasadena is a quiet area with outstanding Arts and Crafts homes, good dining, and a pair of exceptional museums: Huntington Library and Norton Simon Museum.

GETTING ORIENTED

Looking at a map of sprawling Los Angeles, first-time visitors are sometimes overwhelmed. Where to begin? What to see first? And what about all those freeways? Here's some advice: relax. Begin by setting your priorities—movie and television buffs should first head to Hollywood, Universal Studios, and a taping of a television show. Beach lovers and nature types might start out in Santa Monica, Venice, or Malibu, or spend an afternoon in Griffith Park, one of the country's largest city parks. Culture vultures should make a beeline for the twin Gettys (the center in Brentwood and the villa near Malibu), the Los Angeles County Museum of Art (LACMA), or Downtown's MOCA trio of museums. And urban explorers might begin with Downtown L.A.

5

SOUTH-OF-THE-BORDER FLAVOR

From Cal-Mex burritos to Mexico City–style tacos, Southern California is a top stateside destination for experiencing Mexico's myriad culinary styles.

Many Americans are surprised to learn that the Mexican menu goes far beyond Tex-Mex (or Cal-Mex) favorites like burritos, chimichangas, enchiladas, fajitas, and nachos—many of which were created or popularized stateside. Indeed, Mexico has rich, regional food styles, like the complex *mole* sauces of Puebla and Oaxaca and the fresh *ceviches* of Veracruz, as well as the trademark snack of Mexico City: tacos.

In Southern California tacos are an obsession, with numerous blogs and websites dedicated to the quest for the perfect taco. They're everywhere—in ramshackle taco stands, roving trucks, and strip-mall taquerias. Whether you're looking for a cheap snack or a lunch on-the-go, SoCal's taco selection can't be beat. But be forewarned: there may not be an English menu. Here we've noted unfamiliar taco terms, along with other potentially new-to-you items from the Mexican menu.

THIRST QUENCHERS

Spanish for "fresh water," *agua fresca* is a nonalcoholic Mexican drink made from fruit, rice, or seeds that are blended with sugar and water. Fruit flavors like lemon, lime, and watermelon are common. Other varieties include *agua de Jamaica*, flavored with red hibiscus petals; *agua de horchata*, a cinnamon-scented rice milk; and *agua de tamarindo*, a bittersweet variety flavored with tamarind. For something with more of a kick, try a *Michelada*, a beer with a mixture of lime juice, chili sauce, and other savory ingredients. It's typically served in a salt-rimmed glass with ice.

DECODING THE MENU

Ceviche—Citrus-marinated raw seafood appetizer from the Gulf shores of Veracruz. Often eaten with tortilla chips.

Chile relleno—Roasted poblano pepper that is stuffed with ingredients like ground meat or cheese, then dipped in egg batter, fried, and served in tomato sauce.

Clayuda—A Oaxacan dish similar to pizza. Large corn tortillas are baked until hard, then topped with ingredients like refried beans, cheese, and salsa.

Fish taco—A specialty in Southern California, the fish taco is a soft corn tortilla stuffed with grilled or fried white fish (mahimahi, tilapia, or wahoo), pico de gallo, *crema*, and shredded cabbage.

Gordita—"Little fat one" in Spanish, this dish is like a taco, but the cornmeal shell is thicker, similar to pita bread.

Mole—A complex, sweet sauce with Aztec roots made from more than 20 ingredients, including chilies, cinnamon, cumin, anise, black pepper, sesame seeds, and Mexican chocolate. There are many types of mole using various chilies and ingredient combinations, but the most common is *mole poblano* from the Puebla region.

Quesadilla—A snack made from a fresh tortilla that is folded over and stuffed with simple fillings like cheese, then toasted on a griddle. Elevated versions

of the quesadilla may be stuffed with sautéed *flor de calabaza* (squash blossoms) or *huitlacoche* (corn mushrooms).

Salsa—A class of cooked or raw sauces made from chilies, tomatoes, and other ingredients. Popular salsas include *pico de gallo*, a fresh sauce made from chopped tomatoes, onions, chilies, cilantro, and lime; *salsa verde*, made with tomatillos instead of tomatoes; and *salsa roja*, a cooked sauce made with chilies, tomatoes, onion, garlic, and cilantro.

Sopes—A small, fried corn cake topped with ingredients like refried beans, shredded chicken, and salsa.

Taco—In Southern California, as in Mexico, tacos are made from soft, palm-sized corn tortillas folded over and filled with meat, chopped onion, cilantro, and salsa. Common taco fillings include *al pastor* (spiced pork), *barbacoa* (braised beef), *carnitas* (roasted pork), *cecina* (chili-coated pork), *carne asada* (roasted, chopped beef), *chorizo* (spicy sausage), *lengua* (beef tongue), *sesos* (cow brain), and *tasajo* (spiced, grilled beef).

Tamales—Sweet or savory corn cakes that are steamed, and may be filled with cheese, roasted chilies, shredded meat, or other fillings.

Torta—A Mexican sandwich served on a crusty sandwich roll. Fillings often include meat, refried beans, and cheese.

5

Updated by
Michele Bigley

Los Angeles is as much a fantasy as it is a physical city. A mecca for face-lifts, film noir, shopping starlets, beach bodies, and mind-numbing traffic, it is a true urban mash-up, equal parts glamour and grit.

Yes, you'll encounter traffic-clogged freeways, but there are also palm tree–lined, walkable pockets like Venice's Abbot Kinney. You'll drive past Beverly Hills mansions and spy palaces perched atop hills, but you'll also see the roots of midcentury modern architecture in Silver Lake. You'll soak up the sun in Santa Monica and then find yourself barhopping in the city's revitalized Downtown while chomping on scrumptious fish tacos along the way.

You might think that you'll have to spend most of your visit in a car, but that's not the case. In fact, getting out of your car is the only way to really get to know the various entertainment-industry-centered financial, beachfront, wealthy, and fringe neighborhoods and mini-cities that make up the vast L.A. area. But remember, no single locale—whether it be Malibu, Downtown, Beverly Hills, or Burbank—fully embodies Los Angeles. It's in the mix that you'll discover the city's character.

PLANNING

WHEN TO GO

Almost any time of the year is the right time to go to Los Angeles; the climate is mild and pleasant year-round. Winter brings crisp, sunny, unusually smogless days from about November to May (expect brief rains from December to April). Los Angeles summers, which are virtually rainless, can lead to air-quality alerts. Prices skyrocket and reservations are a must when tourism peaks from July through early October.

GETTING HERE AND AROUND

AIR TRAVEL

It's generally easier to navigate the secondary airports than to get through sprawling LAX, the city's major gateway. Bob Hope Airport in Burbank is closest to Downtown, and domestic flights to it can be cheaper than those to LAX—it's definitely worth checking out. From

Long Beach Airport it's equally convenient to go north to central Los Angeles or south to Orange County. Flights to Orange County's John Wayne Airport are often more expensive than those to the other secondary airports. Parking at the smaller airports is cheaper than at LAX.

At LAX, SuperShuttle allows walk-on shuttle passengers without prior reservations. FlyAway buses travel between LAX and Van Nuys, Westwood, La Brea, and Union Station in Downtown.

Airports Bob Hope Airport (BUR) ✉ 2627 N. Hollywood Way, near I–5 and U.S. 101, Burbank ☎ 818/840–8840 ⊕ www.burbankairport.com. **John Wayne Airport** (SNA) ✉ 18601 Airport Way, Santa Ana ☎ 949/252–5200 ⊕ www.ocair. com. **LA/Ontario International Airport** (ONT) ✉ E. Airport Dr., off I–10, Ontario ☎ 909/937–2700 ⊕ www.lawa.org/welcomeont.aspx. **Long Beach Airport** (LGB) ✉ 4100 Donald Douglas Dr., Long Beach ☎ 562/570–2600 ⊕ www.lgb.org. **Los Angeles International Airport** (LAX) ✉ 1 World Way, off Hwy. 1 ☎ 310/646– 5252 ⊕ www.lawa.org.

Shuttles FlyAway ☎ 866/435–9529 ⊕ www.lawa.org. **SuperShuttle** ☎ 323/775–6600, 800/258–3826 ⊕ www.supershuttle.com.

BUS TRAVEL

Inadequate public transportation has plagued L.A. for decades. That said, many local trips can be made, with time and patience, by buses run by the Los Angeles County Metropolitan Transit Authority. In certain cases—visiting the Getty Center, for instance, or Universal Studios—buses may be your best option. There's a special Dodger Stadium Express that shuttles passengers between Union Station and the ballpark for home games. It's free if you have a ticket in hand, and saves you parking-related stress.

Metro Buses cost $1.75, plus 50¢ for each transfer to another bus or to the subway. A one-day pass costs $7, and a weekly pass is $25 for unlimited travel on all buses and trains. Passes are valid from Sunday through Saturday. For the fastest service, look for the red-and-white Metro Rapid buses; these stop less frequently and are able to extend green lights. There are 25 Metro Rapid routes, including along Wilshire and Vermont boulevards.

Other bus services make it possible to explore the entire metropolitan area. DASH minibuses cover six different circular routes in Hollywood, Mid-Wilshire, and Downtown. You pay 50¢ every time you get on. The Santa Monica Municipal Bus Line, also known as the Big Blue Bus, is a pleasant and inexpensive way to move around the Westside. Trips cost $1, and transfers are free. An express bus to and from Downtown L.A., run by Culver CityBus, costs $1.

Bus Information Culver CityBus ☎ 310/253–6510 ⊕ www.culvercity.org. **DASH** ☎ 310/808–2273 ⊕ www.ladottransit.com/dash. **Los Angeles County Metropolitan Transit Authority** ☎ 323/466–3876 ⊕ www.metro.net. **Santa Monica Municipal Bus Line** ☎ 310/451–5444 ⊕ www.bigbluebus.com.

CAR TRAVEL

If you're used to driving in a congested urban area, you shouldn't have too much trouble navigating the streets of Los Angeles. If not, L.A. can be unnerving. Nevertheless, the city evolved with drivers in mind.

Streets are wide and parking garages abound, so it's more car-friendly than many older big cities.

Remember that most freeways are known by a name and a number; for example, the San Diego Freeway is Interstate 405 (or just The 405), the Hollywood Freeway is U.S. 101, the Ventura Freeway is a different stretch of U.S. 101, the Santa Monica Freeway is Interstate 10, and the Harbor Freeway is Interstate 110. It helps, too, to know which direction you're traveling; say, west toward Santa Monica or east toward Downtown Los Angeles. Distance in miles doesn't mean much, depending on the time of day you're traveling: the short 10-mile drive between the San Fernando Valley and Downtown Los Angeles might take an hour to travel during rush hour but only 20 minutes at other times.

There are plenty of identical or similarly named streets in L.A. (Beverly Boulevard and Beverly Drive, for example), so be as specific as you can when asking directions. Expect sudden changes in addresses as streets pass through neighborhoods, then incorporated cities, then back into neighborhoods. This can be most bewildering on Robertson Boulevard, an otherwise useful north–south artery that, by crossing through L.A., West Hollywood, and Beverly Hills, dips in and out of several such numbering shifts in a matter of miles.

Information California Highway Patrol ☎ *800/427–7623 for road conditions* ⊕ *www.chp.ca.gov.*

Emergency Services Metro Freeway Service Patrol ☎ *323/982–4900 for breakdowns* ⊕ *www.metro.net.*

METRO RAIL TRAVEL

Metro Rail covers only a small part of L.A.'s vast expanse, but it's convenient, frequent, and inexpensive. Most popular with visitors is the underground Red Line, which runs from Downtown's Union Station through Mid-Wilshire, Hollywood, and Universal City on its way to North Hollywood, stopping at the most popular tourist destinations along the way.

The light-rail Green Line stretches from Redondo Beach to Norwalk, while the partially underground Blue Line travels from Downtown to the South Bay. The monorail-like Gold Line extends from Union Station to Pasadena and Sierra Madre. The Orange Line, a 14-mile bus corridor, connects the North Hollywood subway station with the western San Fernando Valley.

Most recently unveiled was the Expo Line, which connects Downtown to Culver City. When completed, it will reach nearly to the Pacific Ocean.

There's daily service from about 4:30 am to 12:30 am, with departures every 5 to 15 minutes. On weekends trains run until 2 am. Buy tickets from station vending machines; fares are $1.75, or $7 for an all-day pass.

Metro Rail Information Los Angeles County Metropolitan Transit Authority ☎ *323/466–3876* ⊕ *www.metro.net.*

TAXI AND LIMOUSINE TRAVEL

Instead of trying to hail a taxi on the street, phone one of the many taxi companies. The metered rate is $2.70 per mile, plus a $2.85 per-fare charge. Taxi rides from LAX have an additional $4 surcharge. Be aware that distances are greater than they might appear on the map, so fares add up quickly.

On the other end of the price spectrum, limousines come equipped with everything from full bars to nightclub-style sound-and-light systems. Most charge by the hour, with a three-hour minimum.

Limo Companies ABC Limo ☎ *818/637–2277* ⊕ *www.abclimola.com.* **American Executive** ☎ *800/927–2020* ⊕ *www.americanexecutiveairportlimo.com.* **Dav El Chauffeured Transportation Network** ☎ *800/922–0343* ⊕ *www.davel.com.* **First Class Limousine Service** ☎ *800/400–9771* ⊕ *www.first-classlimo.com.* **ITS** ☎ *800/487–4255* ⊕ *www.itslimo.com.*

Taxi Companies Beverly Hills Cab Co. ☎ *800/273–6611* ⊕ *www.beverlyhillscabco.com.* **Checker Cab** ☎ *800/300–5007* ⊕ *www.ineedtaxi.com.* **United Independent Taxi** ☎ *800/822–8294* ⊕ *www.unitedtaxi.com.* **Yellow Cab Los Angeles** ☎ *800/200–1085, 877/733–3305* ⊕ *www.layellowcab.com.* **Independent Cab Co.** ☎ *800/521–8294* ⊕ *www.taxi4u.com.*

TRAIN TRAVEL

Downtown's Union Station is one of the great American railroad terminals. The interior includes comfortable seating, a restaurant, and several snack bars. As the city's rail hub, it's the place to catch an Amtrak or Metrolink commuter train. Among Amtrak's Southern California routes are 22 daily trips to San Diego and five to Santa Barbara. Amtrak's luxury *Coast Starlight* travels along the spectacular coastline from Seattle to Los Angeles in just a day and a half (though it's often a little late). The *Sunset Limited* arrives from New Orleans, and the *Southwest Chief* comes from Chicago.

Information Amtrak ☎ *800/872–7245* ⊕ *www.amtrak.com.* **Metrolink** ☎ *800/371–5465* ⊕ *www.metrolinktrains.com.* **Union Station** ✉ *800 N. Alameda St.* ☎ *213/683–6979* ⊕ *www.amtrak.com.*

VISITOR INFORMATION

Discover Los Angeles publishes an annually updated general information packet with suggestions for entertainment, lodging, and dining, as well as a list of special events. There are two visitor information centers, both accessible to Metro stops: the Hollywood & Highland entertainment complex and Union Station.

Contacts Beverly Hills Conference and Visitors Bureau ☎ *310/248–1000, 800/345–2210* ⊕ *www.lovebeverlyhills.com.* **Discover Los Angeles** ☎ *213/624–7300, 800/228–2452* ⊕ *www.discoverlosangeles.com.* **Hollywood Chamber of Commerce** ☎ *323/469–8311* ⊕ *www.hollywoodchamber.net.* **Long Beach Area Convention and Visitors Bureau** ☎ *562/436–3645* ⊕ *www.visitlongbeach.com.* **Pasadena Convention and Visitors Bureau** ☎ *626/795–9311* ⊕ *www.pasadenacal.com.* **Santa Monica Convention & Visitors Bureau** ☎ *310/393–7593, 800/544–5319* ⊕ *www.santamonica.com.* **Visit California** ☎ *916/444–4429, 800/862–2543* ⊕ *www.visitcalifornia.com.* **Visit West Hollywood** ☎ *310/289–2525, 800/368–6020* ⊕ *www.visitwesthollywood.com.*

EXPLORING LOS ANGELES

Star-struck . . . excessive . . . smoggy . . . superficial. There's a modicum of truth to each of the adjectives regularly applied to L.A. But Angelenos—and most objective visitors—dismiss their prevalence as signs of envy from people who hail from places less blessed with fun and sun.

Pop culture, for instance, *does* permeate life in LaLaLand: a massive economy employing millions of Southern Californians is built around it. Nevertheless, this city also boasts highbrow appeal, having amassed an impressive array of world-class museums and arts venues. America's second-largest city has more depth than paparazzi shutters can ever capture.

DOWNTOWN

If there's one thing Angelenos love, it's a makeover, and city planners have put the wheels in motion for a dramatic revitalization. Downtown is both glamorous and gritty and is an example of Los Angeles's complexity as a whole. There's a dizzying variety of experiences not to be missed here if you're curious about the artistic, historic, ethnic, or sports-loving sides of L.A.

Downtown Los Angeles isn't just one neighborhood: it's a cluster of pedestrian-friendly enclaves where you can sample an eclectic mix of flavors, wander through world-class museums, and enjoy great live performances or sports events.

TOP ATTRACTIONS

FAMILY **California Science Center.** You're bound to see excited kids running up to the dozens of interactive exhibits here that illustrate the relevance of science to everyday life. Clustered in different "worlds," the center keeps young guests busy for hours. They can design their own buildings and learn how to make them earthquake-proof; watch Tess, the dramatic, 50-foot animatronic star of the exhibit "Body Works," demonstrate how the body's organs work together; and ride a bike across a trapeze wire three stories high in the air. One of the exhibits in the Air & Space section shows how astronauts Pete Conrad and Dick Gordon made it to outer space in the Gemini 11 capsule in 1966; also here is NASA's massive space shuttle *Endeavor*, for which a timed ticket is needed to visit. The IMAX theater screens science-related large-format films. ⊠ *700 Exposition Park Dr., Exposition Park* ☎ *213/744–7400, 323/724–3623* ⊕ *www.californiasciencecenter.org* 🖃 *Permanent exhibitions, free; fees for some attractions, special exhibitions, and IMAX screenings vary* ⊙ *Daily 10–5.*

Fodor'sChoice **Cathedral of Our Lady of the Angels.** A half-block from Frank Gehry's
★ curvaceous Walt Disney Concert Hall sits the austere Cathedral of Our Lady of the Angels—a spiritual draw as well as an architectural attraction. Controversy surrounded Spanish architect José Rafael Moneo's unconventional design for the seat of the Archdiocese of Los Angeles. But judging from the swarms of visitors and the standing-room-only holiday masses, the church has carved out a niche for itself in Downtown L.A.

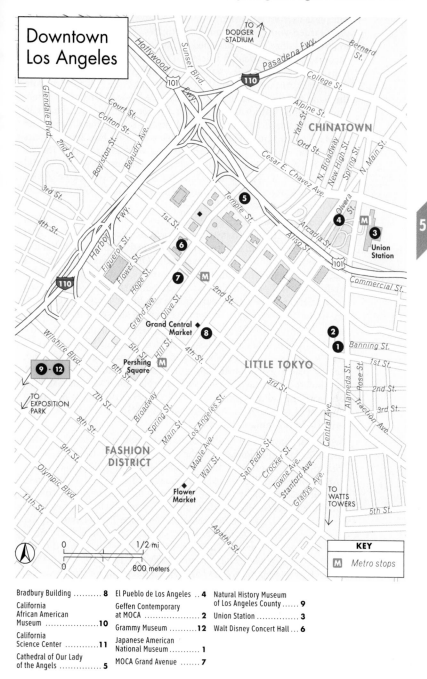

Downtown Los Angeles

The plaza in front is glaringly bright on sunny days, though a children's play garden with bronze animals mitigates the starkness somewhat. Imposing bronze doors, designed by local artist Robert Graham, are decorated with multicultural icons. The canyonlike interior is spare, polished, and airy. By day, sunlight illuminates the sanctuary through translucent curtain walls of thin Spanish alabaster, a departure from the usual stained glass. Artist John Nava used residents from his hometown of Ojai, California, as models for some of the 135 figures in the tapestries that line the nave walls. Head underground to wander the mausoleum's mazelike white-marble corridors. Free guided tours start at the entrance fountain at 1 pm on weekdays. ■TIP➔ **There's plenty of underground visitors parking; the vehicle entrance is on Hill Street.** ⊠ *555 W. Temple St., Downtown* ☎ *213/680–5200* ⊕ *www. olacathedral.org* ⊠ *Free, parking $4 every 15 min, $18 maximum* ⊙ *Weekdays 6–6, Sat. 9–6, Sun. 7–6.*

El Pueblo de Los Angeles. The oldest section of the city, known as El Pueblo de Los Angeles, represents the rich Mexican heritage of L.A. It had a close shave with disintegration in the early 20th century, but key buildings were preserved, and eventually **Olvera Street,** the district's heart, was transformed into a Mexican-American marketplace. Today vendors still sell puppets, leather goods, sandals, and woolen shawls from stalls lining the narrow street. You can find everything from donkey-shape salt and pepper shakers to gorgeous glassware and pottery.

At the beginning of Olvera Street is the Plaza, a Mexican-style park with plenty of benches and walkways shaded by a huge Moreton Bay fig tree. On weekends, mariachi bands and folkloric dance groups perform. Nearby places worth investigating include the historic Avila Adobe, the Chinese American Museum, Plaza the Firehouse Museum, and the America Tropical Interpretive Center. Exhibits at the Italian American Museum of Los Angeles, which debuted in 2015, chronicle the area's formerly heavy Italian presence.

Two major annual events, the Blessing of the Animals and Las Posadas, take place at El Pueblo. On the Saturday before Easter, Angelenos bring their pets—not just dogs and cats, but also horses, pigs, cows, birds, hamsters—to be blessed by a priest. For Las Posadas, every night between December 16th and 24th merchants and visitors parade up and down the street, led by children dressed as angels, to commemorate Mary and Joseph's search for shelter on Christmas Eve. ⊠ *Avila Adobe/ Olvera Street Visitors Center, E-10 Olvera St., Downtown* ☎ *213/628– 1274* ⊕ *elpueblo.lacity.org* ⊠ *Free for Olvera Street and guided tours, fees at some museums* ⊙ *Visitor center daily 9–4, vendor hrs vary; tours (departing from tour office next to Plaza Firehouse Museum) Tues.–Sat. at 10, 11, and noon.*

Geffen Contemporary at MOCA. The Geffen Contemporary is one of architect Frank Gehry's boldest creations. The location, with 40,000 square feet of exhibition space the largest of the three MOCA branches, used to be a police car warehouse. Works from the museum's permanent collection on display here include the artists Willem de Kooning, Franz Kline, Jackson Pollock, Mark Rothko, and Cindy Sherman. ⊠ *152 N. Central*

Ave., Downtown ☎ 213/626–6222 ⊕ www.moca.org/museum/moca_geffen.php ☞ $12; free on Thurs. evenings ☉ Mon. and Fri. 11–5, Thurs. 11–8, weekends 11–6.

Grammy Museum. The interactive Grammy Museum brings the music industry's history to life. The museum, which has 30,000 square feet of space, has four floors of films and interactive exhibits on the craft of music-making and the stories of stars, divas, and other performers from before and since recorded music began. Past temporary exhibitions have included the letters of Tupac Shakur, the "Taylor Swift Experience," and the "Comedy of Rodney Dangerfield." ✉ 800 W. Olympic Blvd., Downtown ☎ 213/765–6800 ⊕ www.grammymuseum.org ☞ $12.95 ☉ Weekdays 11:30–7:30, weekends 10–7:30.

MOCA Grand Avenue. The main branch of the Museum of Contemporary Art, designed by Arata Isozaki, contains underground galleries and presents elegant exhibitions. A huge Nancy Rubins sculpture fashioned from used airplane parts graces the museum's front plaza. ■TIP➔ **Take advantage of the free audio tour.** ✉ 250 S. Grand Ave., Downtown ☎ 213/626–6222 ⊕ www.moca.org/museum/moca_grandave.php ☞ $12; free Thurs. evening ☉ Mon. and Fri. 11–5, Thurs. 11–8, weekends 11–6.

Fodor's Choice ★ **Walt Disney Concert Hall.** One of the architectural wonders of Los Angeles, the 2,265-seat hall is a sculptural monument of gleaming, curved steel designed by Frank Gehry. It's part of a complex that includes a public park, gardens, shops, and two outdoor amphitheaters, one of them atop the concert hall. The acoustically superlative venue is the home of the city's premier orchestra, the Los Angeles Philharmonic, whose music director, Gustavo Dudamel, is an international celebrity in his own right. The orchestra's season runs from late September to early June. The highly praised Los Angeles Master Chorale (⊕ www.lamc.org) also performs here. Big-name acts such as Pink Martini and local favorite Ozomatli fill the house during the off-season. ■TIP➔ **Free 60-minute guided tours are offered on most days, and there are self-guided audio tours.** ✉ 111 S. Grand Ave., Downtown ☎ 323/850–2000 ⊕ www.laphil.org ☞ Tours free ☉ Tours most days between 10 and 2, departing from the Grand Lobby.

WORTH NOTING

Bradbury Building. Stunning wrought-iron railings, ornate plaster moldings, pink marble staircases, a birdcage elevator, and a skylighted atrium that rises almost 50 feet: it's easy to see why the Bradbury Building leaves visitors awestruck. Designed in 1893 by a novice architect who drew his inspiration from a science-fiction story and a conversation with his dead brother via a Ouija board, the office building was originally the site of turn-of-the-20th-century sweatshops, but now houses a variety of businesses that try to keep normal working conditions despite the

Frank Gehry's Walt Disney Concert Hall was an instant L.A. icon.

barrage of picture-snappers. Scenes from *Blade Runner* and *China-town* were filmed here. Visits are limited to the lobby and the first-floor landing. ⊠ *304 S. Broadway, at 3rd St., Downtown* ☎ *213/626–1893* ⊙ *Weekdays 9–5.*

California African American Museum. With more than 3,500 historical arti-facts, this museum showcases contemporary art of the African diaspora. Artists represented here include Betye Saar, Charles Haywood, and June Edmonds. The museum has a research library with more than 20,000 books available for public use. ■ TIP➔ **If possible, visit on a Sunday, when there's almost always a diverse lineup of speakers and perfor-mances.** ⊠ *600 State Dr., Exposition Park* ☎ *213/744–7432* ⊕ *www. caamuseum.org* ⊠ *Free* ⊙ *Tues.–Sat. 10–5, Sun. 11–5.*

Japanese American National Museum. What was it like to grow up on a sugar plantation in Hawaii? How difficult was life for Japanese Ameri-cans interned in concentration camps during World War II? These ques-tions are addressed by changing exhibitions at this museum in Little Tokyo that also include fun tributes to anime and Hello Kitty. Volun-teer docents are on hand to share their own stories and experiences. The museum occupies its original site in a renovated 1925 Buddhist temple and an 85,000-square-foot adjacent pavilion. ⊠ *100 North Cen-tral Ave., off E. 1st St., Downtown* ☎ *213/625–0414* ⊕ *www.janm.org* ⊠ *$9* ⊙ *Tues., Wed., and Fri.–Sun. 11–5, Thurs. noon–8.*

FAMILY **Natural History Museum of Los Angeles County.** The hot ticket at this beaux arts–style museum completed in 1913 is the Dinosaur Hall, whose more than 300 fossils include adult, juvenile, and baby skeletons of the fearsome Tyrannosaurus rex. The Discovery Center lets kids and curious grown-ups touch real animal pelts, and the Insect Zoo gets everyone up close and personal with the white-eyed assassin bug and other creepy crawlers. A massive hall displays dioramas of animals in their natural habitats. Also look for pre-Columbian artifacts and crafts from the South Pacific, as well as the informative "Collapse" exhibit, inspired by author Jared Diamond's research into why some societies succeed and others fail. Outdoors, the 3½-acre Nature Gardens shelter native plant and insect species and contain an expansive edible garden. ⊠ *900 Exposition Blvd., off I–110, near Vermont Ave., Exposition Park* ☎ *213/763–3466* ⊕ *www.nhm.org* ⊠ *$12* ☉ *Daily 9:30–5.*

Union Station. Even if you don't plan on traveling by train anywhere, head here to soak up the ambience of a great rail station. Envisioned by John and Donald Parkinson, the architects who also designed the grand City Hall, the 1939 masterpiece combines Spanish Colonial Revival and art deco elements that have retained their classic warmth and quality. The waiting hall's commanding scale and enormous chandeliers have provided the backdrop for countless scenes in films, TV shows, and music videos. ⊠ *800 N. Alameda St., Downtown.*

HOLLYWOOD AND THE STUDIOS

The Tinseltown mythology of Los Angeles was born in Hollywood. Daytime attractions can be found on foot around the home of the Academy Awards at the Dolby Theatre, part of the Hollywood & Highland entertainment complex. The adjacent TCL Chinese Theatre delivers silver screen magic with its cinematic facade and ornate interiors from a bygone era. Walk the renowned Hollywood Walk of Stars to find your favorite celebrities' hand- and footprints. In summer, visit the crown jewel of Hollywood, the Hollywood Bowl, which features shows by the Los Angeles Philharmonic.

To the north there's Studio City, a thriving commercial strip at the base of the Hollywood Hills that's home to many smaller film companies and lunching studio execs; Universal City, where you'll find Universal Studios Hollywood; and bustling Burbank, home of several of the major studios. In Los Feliz, to the east, Griffith Park connects L.A.'s largest greenbelt with the oh-so hip Vermont Avenue area. Beyond that you'll find Silver Lake and Echo Park.

TOP ATTRACTIONS

Dolby Theatre. The interior design of the theater that hosts the Academy Awards was inspired by European opera houses, but underneath all the trimmings the space has one of the finest technical systems in the world. A tour of the Dolby, which debuted in 2001 as the Kodak Theatre, is a worthwhile expense for movie buffs who just can't get enough insider information. Tour guides share plenty of behind-the-scenes tidbits about Oscar ceremonies as they escort you through the theater. You'll get to step into the VIP lounge where celebrities mingle on the big night and get a bird's-eye view from the balcony seating. ■ **TIP→ If you have the Go Los Angeles Card, the tour is included.** ⊠ *6801 Hollywood Blvd., Hollywood* ☎ *323/308–6300* ⊕ *www.dolbytheatre.com* ⊠ *Tour $19* ☉ *Daily 10:30–4.*

Fodor's Choice
★

Griffith Observatory. High on a hillside overlooking the city, Griffith Observatory is one of the area's most celebrated landmarks. Its interior is just as impressive as its exterior, thanks to a massive expansion and cosmic makeover completed a decade ago. Highlights of the building include the Foucault's pendulum hanging in the main lobby, the planet exhibitions on the lower level, and the playful wall display of galaxy-themed jewelry along the twisty indoor ramp.

In true L.A. style, the Leonard Nimoy Event Horizon Theater presents guest speakers and shows on space-related topics and discoveries. The Samuel Oschin Planetarium features an impressive dome, digital projection system, theatrical lighting, and a stellar sound system. Shows are $7.

Grab a meal at the Café at the End of the Universe, which serves up dishes created by celebrity chef Wolfgang Puck. ■TIP→ **For a fantastic view, come at sunset to watch the sky turn fiery shades of red with the city's skyline silhouetted.** ⊠ *2800 E. Observatory Ave., Griffith Park* ☎ *213/473–0800* ⊕ *www.griffithobservatory.org* ☉ *Tues.–Fri. noon–10, weekends 10–10.*

Griffith Park. The country's largest municipal park, the 4,210-acre Griffith Park is a must for nature lovers, the perfect spot for respite from the hustle and bustle of the surrounding urban areas. Plants and animals native to Southern California can be found within the park's borders, including deer, coyotes, and even a reclusive mountain lion. Bronson Canyon (where the Batcave from the 1960s *Batman* TV series is located) and Crystal Springs are favorite picnic spots.

The park is named after Colonel Griffith J. Griffith, a mining tycoon who donated 3,000 acres to the city in 1896. As you might expect, the park has been used as a film and television location for at least a century. Here you'll find the Griffith Observatory, the Los Angeles Zoo, the Greek Theater, two golf courses, hiking and bridle trails, a swimming pool, a merry-go-round, and an outdoor train museum. ⊠ *4730 Crystal Springs Dr., Griffith Park* ☎ *323/913–4688* ⊕ *www.laparks. org/dos/parks/griffithpk* ☑ *Free; attractions inside park have separate admission fees* ☉ *Daily 5 am–10:30 pm. Mountain roads close at sunset.*

Fodor's Choice
★

Hollywood Museum. Lovers of Tinseltown's glamorous past may find themselves humming "Hooray for Hollywood" as they tour this gem of cinema history inside the Max Factor Building. For years, Factor's famous makeup was manufactured on the top floors, and on the ground floor was a salon. After an extensive renovation, this art deco landmark that Factor purchased in 1928 now holds this museum with more than 10,000 bits of film memorabilia.

Exhibits include sections dedicated to Marilyn Monroe, Michael Jackson, and Bob Hope, and to costumes and props from such films as *Moulin Rouge, The Silence of the Lambs,* and *Planet of the Apes.* There's also an impressive gallery of photos showing movie stars frolicking at the Brown Derby, Ciro's, the Trocadero, the Mocambo, and other fabled venues.

Hallway walls are covered with the autograph collection of ultimate fan Joe Ackerman; aspiring filmmakers may want to check out the early film equipment. The museum's showpiece is the Max Factor exhibit, where

5

Hollywood

The Music Box @ Fonda Theatre

Capitol Records Tower

Pantages Theatre

Hollywood/Vine

Avalon Theatre

Hollywood Blvd.

Egyptian Theatre

Hollywood Wax Museum

Guiness World of Records

Ripley's Believe It Or Not

Hollywood/Highland

1/4 mi

1/4 km

separate dressing rooms are dedicated to Factor's "color harmony," which created distinct looks for "brownettes" (Factor's term), redheads, and, of course, bombshell blonds. You can practically smell the peroxide of Marilyn Monroe getting her trademark platinum look here. Also worth a peek are makeup cases owned by Lucille Ball, Lana Turner, Ginger Rogers, Bette Davis, Rita Hayworth, and others who made Max Factor makeup popular. ⊠ *1660 N. Highland Ave., at Hollywood Blvd., Hollywood* ☏ *323/464–7776* ⊕ *www.thehollywoodmuseum.com* 🖅 *$15* ☉ *Wed.–Sun. 10–5.*

Hollywood Walk of Fame. Along Hollywood Boulevard (and part of Vine Street) runs a trail of affirmations for entertainment-industry overachievers. On this mile-long stretch of sidewalk, inspired by the concrete handprints in front of TCL Chinese Theatre, names are embossed in brass, each at the center of a pink star embedded in dark-gray terrazzo. They're not all screen deities; many stars commemorate people who worked in a technical field, such as sound or lighting. The first eight stars were unveiled in 1960 at the northwest corner of Highland Avenue and Hollywood Boulevard: Olive Borden, Ronald Colman, Louise Fazenda, Preston Foster, Burt Lancaster, Edward Sedgwick, Ernest Torrence, and Joanne Woodward (some of these names have stood the test of time better than others). Since then, more than 2,000 others have been immortalized, though that honor doesn't come cheap—upon selection by a special committee, the personality in question (or more likely his or her movie studio or record company) pays about $30,000 for the privilege. To aid you in spotting celebrities you're looking for, stars are identified by one of five icons: a motion-picture camera, a radio microphone, a television set, a record, or a theatrical mask. ⊠ *Hollywood Blvd. and Vine St., Hollywood* ☏ *323/469–8311* ⊕ *www.walkoffame.com.*

Fodor's Choice ★ **Paramount Pictures.** With a history dating to the early 1920s, the Paramount lot was home to some of Hollywood's most luminous stars, including Mary Pickford, Rudolph Valentino, Mae West, Marlene Dietrich, and Bing Crosby. For decades director Cecil B. DeMille's base of operations, Paramount offers probably the most authentic studio tour, giving you a real sense of the film industry's history. This is the only major studio from film's golden age left in Hollywood—all the others are in Burbank, Universal City, or Culver City.

Memorable movies and TV shows with scenes shot here include *Sunset Boulevard, Forrest Gump,* and *Titanic.* Many of the *Star Trek* movies and TV series were shot entirely or in part here, and several seasons of *I Love Lucy* were shot on the portion of the lot Paramount acquired in 1967 from Lucille Ball. You can take a two-hour studio tour or a 4½-hour VIP tour, led by guides who walk and trolley you around the back lots. As well as gleaning some gossipy history, you'll spot the sets of TV and film shoots in progress. Reserve ahead for tours, which are for those ages 10 and up. ■**TIP**➜ You can be part of the audience for live TV tapings (tickets are free), but you must book ahead. ⊠ *5555 Melrose Ave., Hollywood* ☏ *323/956–1777* ⊕ *www.paramountstudiotour. com* 🖅 *$53 regular tour, $178 VIP tour* ☉ *Tours daily 9:30–2.*

TCL Chinese Theatre. The stylized Chinese pagodas and temples of the former Grauman's Chinese Theatre have become a shrine both to stardom and the combination of glamour and flamboyance that inspire the phrase "only in Hollywood." Although you have to buy a movie ticket to appreciate the interior trappings, the courtyard is open to the public. The main theater itself is worth visiting, if only to see a film in the same setting as hundreds of celebrities who have attended big premieres here.

And then, of course, outside in front are the oh-so-famous cement hand- and footprints. This tradition is said to have begun at the theater's opening in 1927, with the premiere of Cecil B. DeMille's *King of Kings*, when actress Norma Talmadge just happened to step in wet cement. Now more than 160 celebrities have contributed imprints for posterity, including some oddball specimens, such as casts of Whoopi Goldberg's dreadlocks. ⊠ *6925 Hollywood Blvd., Hollywood* ☎ *323/461–3331* ⊕ *www.tclchinesetheatres.com.*

FAMILY **Universal Studios Hollywood.** Universal is more a theme park with lots of roller coasters and thrill rides than a backstage pass, though its tour provides a good firsthand look at familiar TV and movie sets. Despite the amusement park clichés, many first-timers consider this studio a must-see. The favorite attraction is the tram tour, during which you can experience the parting of the Red Sea; duck from dinosaurs in Jurassic Park; visit Dr. Seuss's Whoville; see the airplane wreckage of *War of the Worlds* and the still-creepy house from *Psycho;* and be attacked by the killer shark of *Jaws* fame. ■TIP→ The tram ride is usually the best place to begin your visit, because the lines become longer as the day wears on.

Most attractions are designed to give you a thrill in one form or another, including the spine-tingling Transformers: The Ride 3-D ride or the bone-rattling roller coaster Revenge of the Mummy. The House of Horrors is guaranteed to provide screams, while the Animal Actors show offers milder entertainment courtesy of some talented furry friends. The Simpsons Ride takes you on a hair-raising animated journey through the clan's hometown of Springfield. If you're looking for something for grown-ups, CityWalk is a separate venue run by Universal Studios, where you'll find shops, restaurants, nightclubs, and movie theaters. ⊠ *100 Universal City Pl., Universal City* ☎ *818/622–3801* ⊕ *www. universalstudioshollywood.com* ⊒ *$84, parking $15 ($10 after 3)* ⊘ *Contact park for seasonal hrs.*

Warner Bros. Studios. If you're looking for an authentic behind-the-scenes look at how films and TV shows are made, head to this major studio center, one of the world's busiest. After a short film on the studio's movies and TV shows, hop aboard a tram for a ride through the sets and soundstages of such favorites as *Casablanca* and *Rebel Without A Cause.* You'll see the bungalows where Marlon Brando, Bette Davis, and other icons relaxed between shots, and the current production offices for Clint Eastwood and George Clooney. You might even spot a celeb or see a shoot in action—tours change from day to day depending on the productions taking place on the lot.

Tours are given at least every hour, more frequently from May to September, and last 2 hours and 25 minutes. Reservations are required, and advance notice is needed for people with mobility issues. Children under eight are not admitted. A five-hour deluxe tour costing $250 includes lunch and lets you spend more time on the sets, with more opportunities for behind-the-scenes peeks and star-spotting. ⊠ *3400 W. Riverside Dr., Burbank* ☎ *877/492–8687* ⊕ *wbstudiotour.com* ✉ *$52, $250 for deluxe tour* ☉ *Mon.–Sat. 8:15–5:30; hrs vary on Sun.*

WORTH NOTING

Hollywood and Vine. The mere mention of this intersection inspires images of a street corner bustling with movie stars, hopefuls, and moguls arriving on foot or in Duesenbergs and Rolls-Royces. In the old days this was the hub of the radio and movie industry: film stars like Gable and Garbo hustled in and out of their agents' office buildings (some now converted to luxury condos) at these fabled cross streets. Even the Red Line Metro station here keeps up the Hollywood theme, with a *Wizard of Oz*–style yellow brick road, vintage movie projectors, and old film reels on permanent display. Sights visible from this intersection include the Capitol Records Building, the Avalon Theater, the Pantages Theater, and the W Hollywood Hotel. ⊠ *Hollywood Ave. and Vine St.*

Pantages Theatre. Just steps from the fabled intersection of Hollywood and Vine, this Hollywood Boulevard landmark is an art deco palace originally built as a vaudeville showcase in 1930. Once host of the Academy Awards, it's now home to such Broadway shows as *The Lion King, Hairspray, Wicked,* and *The Book of Mormon.* ⊠ *6233 Hollywood Blvd., Hollywood* ☎ *323/468–1770* ⊕ *www.hollywood pantages.com.*

Hollywood Sign. With letters 50 feet tall, Hollywood's trademark sign can be spotted from miles away. The icon, which originally read "Hollywoodland," was erected in the Hollywood Hills in 1923 to promote a real-estate development. In 1949 the "land" portion of the sign was taken down. By 1973 the sign had earned landmark status, but since the letters were made of wood, its longevity came into question. A makeover project was launched and the letters were auctioned off (rocker Alice Cooper bought the "o" and singing cowboy Gene Autry sponsored an "l") to make way for a new sign made of sheet metal. Inevitably, the sign has drawn pranksters who have altered it over the years, albeit temporarily, to spell out "Hollyweed" (in the 1970s, to push for more lenient marijuana laws), "Go Navy" (before a Rose Bowl game), and "Perotwood" (during businessman Ross Perot's 1992 presidential bid). A fence and surveillance equipment have since been installed to deter intruders. ■TIP➔ Use caution if driving up to the sign on residential streets, because many cars speed around the blind corners. ⊠ *Griffith Park, Mt. Lee Dr., Hollywood* ⊕ *www.hollywoodsign.org.*

BEVERLY HILLS AND THE WESTSIDE

Beverly Hills delivers wealth and excess on a dramatic, cinematic scale. West Hollywood is not a place to see things (like museums or movie studios) as much as it is a place to *do* things—like go to a nightclub, eat at a world-famous restaurant, or attend an art gallery opening.

The three-block stretch of Wilshire Boulevard known as Museum Row, east of Fairfax Avenue, features intriguing museums and a prehistoric tar pit to boot. Wilshire Boulevard itself is something of a cultural monument—it begins its grand 16-mile sweep to the sea in Downtown L.A.

For some privileged Angelenos, the city begins west of La Cienega Boulevard, where keeping up with the Joneses becomes an epic pursuit. Chic, attractive neighborhoods with coveted postal codes—Bel Air, Brentwood, Westwood, West Los Angeles, and Pacific Palisades—are home to power couples pushing power kids in power strollers. Still, the Westside is rich in culture—and not just entertainment-industry culture. It's home to the monumental Getty Center and the engrossing Museum of Tolerance.

TOP ATTRACTIONS

FAMILY **The Getty Center.** With its curving walls and isolated hilltop perch, the
Fodor's Choice Getty Center resembles a pristine fortified city of its own. You may have
★ been lured here by the beautiful views of Los Angeles—on a clear day stretching all the way to the Pacific Ocean—but the amazing architecture, uncommon gardens, and fascinating art collections will be more than enough to capture and hold your attention. When the sun is out, the complex's rough-cut travertine marble skin seems to soak up the light.

Getting to the center involves a bit of anticipatory lead-up. At the base of the hill, a pavilion disguises the underground parking structure. From there you either walk or take a smooth, computer-driven tram up the steep slope, checking out the Bel Air estates across the humming 405 freeway. The five pavilions that house the museum surround a central courtyard and are bridged by walkways. From the courtyard, plazas, and walkways, you can survey the city from the San Gabriel Mountains to the ocean.

In a ravine separating the museum and the Getty Research Institute, conceptual artist Robert Irwin created the playful Central Garden in stark contrast to Meier's mathematical architectural geometry. The garden's design is what Hollywood feuds are made of: Meier couldn't control Irwin's vision, and the two men sniped at each other during construction, with Irwin stirring the pot with every loose twist his garden path took. The result is a refreshing garden walk whose focal point is an azalea maze (some insist the Mickey Mouse shape is on purpose) in a reflecting pool.

Inside the pavilions are the galleries for the permanent collections of European paintings, drawings, sculpture, illuminated manuscripts, and decorative arts, as well as American and European photographs. The Getty's collection of French furniture and decorative arts, especially from the early years of Louis XIV (1643–1715) to the end of the reign

A mural depicting Hollywood's legends (John Wayne, Elvis Presley, and Marilyn Monroe) adorns a wall of West Hollywood's Stella Adler Academy on Highland Avenue.

of Louis XVI (1774–92), is renowned for its quality and condition; you can see a pair of completely reconstructed salons. In the paintings galleries, a computerized system of louvered skylights allows natural light to filter in, creating a closer approximation of the conditions in which the artists painted. Notable among the paintings are Rembrandt's *The Abduction of Europa*, Van Gogh's *Irises*, Monet's *Wheatstack, Snow Effects,* and *Morning,* and James Ensor's *Christ's Entry into Brussels.*

If you want to start with a quick overview, pick up the brochure in the entrance hall that guides you to 15 highlights of the collection. There's also an instructive audio tour (free, but you have to leave ID) with commentaries by art historians. Art information rooms with multimedia computer stations contain more details about the collections. The Getty also presents lectures, films, concerts, and special programs for kids, families, and all-around culture lovers. The complex includes an upscale restaurant and downstairs cafeteria with panoramic window views. There are also outdoor coffee bar cafés. ■ TIP→ On-site parking is subject to availability and can fill up by late afternoon on holidays and summer weekends, so try to come early in the day. Public buses (Metro Rapid Line 734) also serve the center. ⌧ *1200 Getty Center Dr., Brentwood* ☎ *310/440–7300* ⊕ *www.getty.edu* ⌧ *Free; parking $15* ☉ *Tues.–Fri. and Sun. 10–5:30, Sat. 10–9.*

Fodor's Choice
★

Los Angeles County Museum of Art (LACMA). Without a doubt, this is the focal point of the museum district that runs along Wilshire Boulevard. Chris Burden's *Urban Light* sculpture, composed of more than 220 restored cast-iron antique street lamps, elegantly marks the location. Inside you'll find one of the country's most comprehensive art

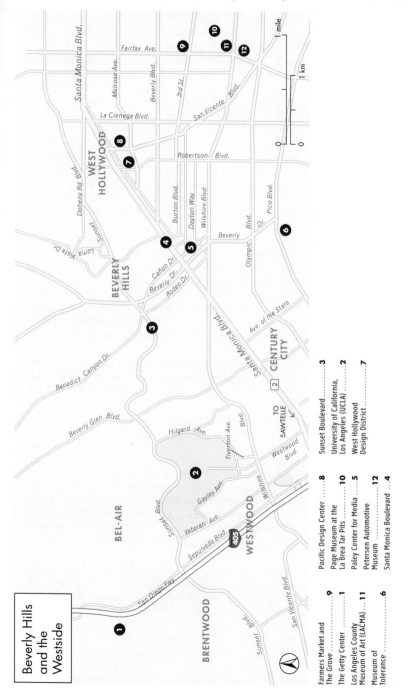

Beverly Hills and the Westside

5

collections, with more than 120,000 objects dating from ancient times to the present. The museum, which opened in 1965, now includes numerous buildings that cover more than 20 acres.

The permanent collection's strengths include works by prominent Southern California artists; Latin American artists such as Diego Rivera and Frida Kahlo; Islamic and European art; paintings by Henri Matisse, Rene Magritte, Paul Klee, and Wassily Kandinsky; art representing the ancient civilizations of Egypt, the Near East, Greece, and Rome; and costumes and textiles dating back to the 16th century.

The Broad Contemporary Art Museum, designed by Renzo Piano, opened in 2008 and impresses with three vast floors. BCAM presents contemporary art from LACMA's collection in addition to temporary exhibitions that explore the interplay between the present and the past. In 2010 the Lynda and Stewart Resnick Exhibition Pavilion, a stunning, light-filled space also designed by Renzo Piano, added more gallery space.

LACMA's other spaces include the Ahmanson Building, a showcase for Art of the Pacific, European, Middle Eastern, South and Southeast Asian collections; the Robert Gore Rifkind Center for German Expressionist Studies; the Art of the Americas Building; the Pavilion for Japanese Art, featuring scrolls, screens, drawings, paintings, textiles, and decorative arts from Japan; the Bing Center, a research library, resource center, and theater; and the Boone's Children's Gallery, located in the Hammer Building, where story time and art lessons are among the activities offered.

■TIP→ Temporary exhibits sometimes require tickets purchased in advance. ✉ *5905 Wilshire Blvd., Miracle Mile* ☎ *323/857–6000* ⊕ *www.lacma.org* 🏷 *$15* ☽ *Mon., Tues., and Thurs. 11–5, Fri. 11–8, weekends 10–7.*

FAMILY **Museum of Tolerance.** This museum unflinchingly confronts bigotry and racism. One of the most affecting sections covers the Holocaust, with film footage of deportations and concentration camps. As you enter, you're issued a "passport" bearing the name of a child whose life was dramatically changed by the Nazis; as you go through the exhibit, you learn the fate of that child. An exhibit called "Anne: The Life and Legacy of Anne Frank," brings her story to life through immersive environments, multimedia presentations, and interesting artifacts. Simon Wiesenthal's Vienna office is set exactly as the famous "Nazi hunter" had it while performing his research that brought more than 1,000 war criminals to justice.

Interactive exhibits include the Millennium Machine, which engages visitors in finding solutions to human rights abuses around the world; Globalhate.com, which examines hate on the Internet by exposing problematic sites via touch-screen computer terminals; and the Point of View Diner, a re-creation of a 1950s diner that "serves" a menu of controversial topics on video jukeboxes.

Although every exhibit may not be appropriate for children, school tours regularly visit the museum. ■TIP→ Plan to spend at least three hours touring the museum; making a reservation, wise at all times, is especially recommended for Friday, Sunday, and holiday visits. ✉ *9786 W. Pico Blvd., south of Beverly Hills* ☎ *310/553–8403* ⊕ *www. museumoftolerance.com* 🖅 *$15.50* ⊗ *Apr.–Oct., weekdays 10–5, Sun. 11–5; Nov.–Mar., weekdays 10–3, Sun. 11–5.*

Pacific Design Center. World-renowned architect Cesar Pelli's original vision for the Pacific Design Center was three buildings that together housed designer showrooms, office buildings, parking, and more—a virtual multibuilding shrine to design. These architecturally intriguing buildings were built years apart: the building sheathed in blue glass (known as the Blue Whale) opened in 1975; the green building opened in 1988. The final "Red" building opened in 2013, completing Pelli's grand vision all of these many years later. All together the 1.2 million-square-foot vast complex covers more than 14 acres, housing more than 120 design showrooms as well as 2,100 interior product lines. You'll also find restaurants such as Red Seven by Wolfgang Puck, the Silver-screen movie theater, and an outpost of the Museum of Contemporary Art. ✉ *8687 Melrose Ave., West Hollywood* ☎ *310/657–0800* ⊕ *www. pacificdesigncenter.com* ⊗ *Weekdays 9–5.*

FAMILY **Page Museum at the La Brea Tar Pits.** If your children have prehistoric animals on the brain, show them where Ice Age fossils come from by taking them to the stickiest park in town. The area formed when deposits of oil rose to the earth's surface, collected in shallow pools, and coagulated into asphalt. In the early 20th century geologists discovered that all that goo contained the largest collection of Pleistocene, or Ice Age, fossils ever found at one location: more than 600 species of birds, mammals, plants, reptiles, and insects. Roughly 100 tons of fossil bones have been removed in excavations during the last 100 years, making this one of the world's most famous fossil sites. You can see most of the pits through chain-link fences, and the new Excavator Tour gets you as close as possible to the action. (The pits can be a little smelly, but your kids may well love this, too.)

Pit 91 and Project 23 are ongoing excavation projects; tours are given, and you can volunteer to help with the excavations in the summer. Several pits are scattered around Hancock Park and the surrounding neighborhood; construction in the area has often had to accommodate them, and in nearby streets and along sidewalks, little bits of tar occasionally ooze up. The museum displays fossils from the tar pits and has a glass-walled laboratory that allows visitors to view paleontologists and volunteers as they work on specimens. ✉ *5801 Wilshire Blvd., Miracle Mile* ☎ *323/857–6300* ⊕ *www.tarpits.org* 🖅 *$12* ⊗ *Daily 9:30–5.*

Santa Monica Boulevard. From La Cienega Boulevard in the east to Doheny Drive in the west, Santa Monica Boulevard is the commercial core of West Hollywood's gay community, with restaurants and cafés, bars and clubs, bookstores and galleries, and other establishments catering largely to gays and lesbians. Twice a year—during June's L.A. Pride and on Halloween, in October—the boulevard becomes an open-air festival. ✉ *Santa Monica Blvd., between La Cienega Blvd. and Doheny Dr.* ⊕ *weho.org.*

Sunset Boulevard. One of the most fabled avenues in the world, Sunset Boulevard began humbly enough in the 18th century as a route from El Pueblo de Los Angeles to the Pacific Ocean. Today, as it passes through West Hollywood it becomes the sexy and seductive Sunset Strip, where rock and roll had its heyday and cocktail bars charge a premium for the views. It slips quietly into the tony environs of Beverly Hills and Bel Air, twisting and winding past gated estates and undulating vistas. ⊠ *Sunset Blvd., West Hollywood.*

WORTH NOTING

Paley Center for Media. Architect Richard Meier, also responsible for the Getty Center, designed this sleek stone-and-glass building that holds a world-class collection of television and radio programs. You can search for more than 150,000 of them, spanning eight decades, on an easy-to-use computer, then settle into comfortable seating and watch them on monitors. A visit here is a blissful way to while away the hours. Craving a disco-infused, late-1970s episode of *Sesame Street?* It's here, along with award shows, radio serials, and hundreds of TV sitcoms. The library plays snippets of a variety of programs from a roast of Dean Martin to an interview with John Lennon. ■ TIP➔ **Free parking is available in the lot off Santa Monica Boulevard.** ⊠ *465 N. Beverly Dr., Beverly Hills* 🕾 *310/786–1000* ⊕ *www.paleycenter.org* ☉ *Wed.–Sun. noon–5.*

FAMILY **Petersen Automotive Museum.** L.A. is a mecca for car lovers, which explains the popularity of this museum with a collection of more than 300 automobiles and other motorized vehicles. But you don't have to be a gearhead to appreciate the Petersen. There's a lot of interesting history here. You can learn how Los Angeles grew up around its freeways, how cars evolve from the design phase to the production line, and how automobiles have influenced film and television. To see how the vehicles, many of them quite rare, are preserved and maintained, take the 90-minute tour of the basement-level Vault. Young kids aren't allowed in the Vault, but they can (and likely will) enjoy the rest of the museum. Except for the Vault, still open for tours, the museum closed for most of 2015 for a major redesign and renovation. ⊠ *6060 Wilshire Blvd., Miracle Mile* 🕾 *323/930–2277* ⊕ *www.petersen.org* ☉ *Museum closed until late 2015 except for Vault tours. Call or check website for hrs and prices.*

University of California, Los Angeles (UCLA). With spectacular buildings such as a Romanesque library, the parklike campus of UCLA makes for a fine stroll through one of California's most prestigious universities. In the heart of the north campus, the **Franklin Murphy Sculpture Garden** contains more than 70 works by artists such as Henry Moore and Gaston Lachaise. The 7-acre **Mildred E. Mathias Botanic Garden,** home to some 5,000 species of plants from all over the world, is in the southeast section of the campus, accessible from Tiverton Avenue. West of the main-campus bookstore, the **J.D. Morgan Center and Athletic Hall of Fame** displays the sports memorabilia and trophies of the university's athletic departments and championship teams.

Campus maps and information are available at kiosks at major entrances, and free two-hour walking tours of the campus are given on most weekdays at 10:15 and 2:15 and on Saturday at 10:15. The main entrance gate is on Westwood Boulevard. Campus parking costs $12, but there's also a lot at UCLA Parking Structure 4 off Sunset Boulevard that only charges you according to the time you stay—starting at as little as $1 for about 20 minutes. ⊠ *Bordered by Le Conte, Hilgard, and Gayley Aves. and Sunset Blvd., Westwood* ☎ *310/825–8764* ⊕ *www.ucla.edu.*

West Hollywood Design District. More than 200 businesses—art galleries, antiques shops, fashion outlets (including Rag & Bone and Christian Louboutin), and interior design stores—are found in the design district. There are also about 40 restaurants, including the famous paparazzi magnet, the Ivy. All are clustered within walking distance of each other—a rare L.A. treat. ⊠ *Melrose Ave. and Robertson and Beverly Blvds.* ☎ *310/289–2534* ⊕ *wehodesigndistrict.com.*

SANTA MONICA AND THE BEACHES

Hugging the Santa Monica Bay in an arch, the desirable communities of Malibu, Santa Monica, and Venice move from ultrarich, ultracasual Malibu to bohemian, borderline seedy Venice. What they have in common is cleaner air, mild temperatures, horrific traffic, and an emphasis on the beach-focused lifestyle that many people consider the hallmark of Southern California.

Fodor's Choice **Getty Villa Malibu.** Feeding off the cultures of ancient Rome, Greece, and
★ Etruria, the villa exhibits astounding antiquities, though on a first visit even they take a backseat to their environment. This megamansion sits on some of the most valuable coastal property in the world. Modeled after an Italian country home, the Villa dei Papiri in Herculaneum, the Getty Villa includes beautifully manicured gardens, reflecting pools, and statuary. The largest and loveliest garden, the Outer Peristyle, gives you glorious views over a rectangular reflecting pool and geometric hedges to the Pacific. The new structures blend thoughtfully into the rolling terrain and significantly improve the public spaces, such as the new outdoor amphitheater, gift store, café, and entry arcade. Talks and educational programs are offered at an indoor theater. ■ TIP→ An advance timed entry ticket is required for admission. Tickets are free and may be ordered from the museum's website or by phone. ⊠ *17985 Pacific Coast Hwy., Pacific Palisades* ☎ *310/440–7300* ⊕ *www.getty. edu* ⌦ *Free, tickets required; parking $15* ⊗ *Wed.–Mon. 10–5.*

FAMILY **Santa Monica Pier.** Souvenir shops, carnival games, arcades, eateries, an outdoor trapeze school, the **Pacific Park** amusement park, a small aquarium, and other attractions contribute to the festive atmosphere of this truncated pier at the foot of Colorado Boulevard below Palisades Park. The pier's trademark 46-horse Looff Carousel, built in 1922, has appeared in several films, including *The Sting.* The Soda Jerks ice cream fountain inside the carousel building brings smiles to children's faces. Free concerts are held on the pier in the summer. ⊠ *Colorado Ave. and the ocean, Santa Monica* ☎ *310/458–8900* ⊕ *www.santamonicapier.org* ⊗ *Hrs. vary by season; check website before visiting.*

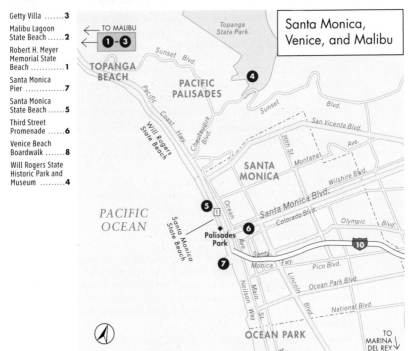

Third Street Promenade. Stretch your legs along this pedestrians-only three-block stretch of 3rd Street, just a whiff away from the Pacific, lined with jacaranda trees, ivy-topiary dinosaur fountains, strings of lights, and branches of nearly every major U.S. retail chain. Outdoor cafés, street vendors, movie theaters, and a rich nightlife make this a main gathering spot for locals, visitors, street musicians, and performance artists. Plan a night just to take it all in or take an afternoon for a long people-watching stroll. There's plenty of parking in city structures on the streets flanking the promenade. **Santa Monica Place,** at the south end of the promenade, is a sleek outdoor mall and foodie haven. Its three stories are home to Bloomingdale's, Burberry, Coach, and other upscale retailers. Don't miss the ocean views from the rooftop food court. ⊠ *Third St., between Colorado and Wilshire Blvds., Santa Monica* ⊕ *www.downtownsm.com.*

Venice Beach Boardwalk. The surf and sand of Venice are fine, but the main attraction here is the boardwalk scene, which is a cosmos all its own. Go on weekend afternoons for the best people-watching experience. You can also swim, fish, surf, skateboard, and play racquetball, handball, shuffleboard, and basketball (the boardwalk is the site of hotly contested pickup games). You can rent a bike or in-line skates and hit the Strand bike path, then pull up a seat at a sidewalk café and watch the action unfold. ⊠ *1800 Ocean Front Walk, west of Pacific Ave., Venice* ☎ *310/392–4687* ⊕ *www.westland.net/venice.*

Will Rogers State Historic Park and Museum. A humorist, actor, and rambling cowboy, Will Rogers lived on this site in the 1920s and 1930s. His ranch house, a folksy blend of Navajo rugs and Mission-style furniture, has become a museum featuring Rogers memorabilia. A short film presented in the visitor center highlights Rogers' roping technique and homey words of wisdom. Open for docent-led tours, the ranch house features Rogers' stuffed practice calf and the high ceiling he raised so he could practice his famed roping style indoors.

Rogers was a polo enthusiast, and in the 1930s his front-yard polo field attracted such friends as Douglas Fairbanks Sr. for weekend games. Today the park's broad lawns are excellent for picnicking, and there are miles of eucalyptus-lined trails for hiking. Free weekend games are scheduled from April through October, weather permitting.

Also part of the park is **Inspiration Point Trail.** Who knows how many of Will Rogers' famed witticisms came to him while he and his wife hiked or rode horses along this trail from their ranch. The point is on a detour off the lovely 2-mile loop, which you can join near the riding stables beyond the parking lot. On a clear (or merely semiclear) day, the panorama is one of L.A.'s widest and most "wow"-inducing, from the peaks of the San Gabriel Mountains in the distant east to the Oz-like cluster of downtown skyscrapers to Catalina Island looming off the coast to the southwest. If you're looking for a longer trip, the top of the loop meets up with the 65-mile Backbone Trail, which connects to Topanga State Park. ⊠ *1501 Will Rogers State Park Rd., Pacific Palisades* ☎ *310/454–8212* ⊠ *Free; parking $12* ⊙ *Parking daily 8–dusk; house tours Thurs. and Fri., hourly 11–3, weekends, hourly 10–4.*

BEACHES

Malibu Lagoon State Beach. Bird-watchers, take note: in this 5-acre marshy area near Malibu Beach Inn you can spot egrets, blue herons, avocets, and gulls. (You need to stay on the boardwalks so as not to disturb their habitats.) The path leads out to a rocky stretch of Surfrider Beach, and makes for a pleasant stroll. The sand is soft, clean, and white, and you're also likely to spot a variety of marine life. Look for the signs to help identify these sometimes exotic-looking creatures. The lagoon is particularly enjoyable in the early morning and at sunset—and even more so now, thanks to a restoration effort that improved the lagoon's smell. The parking lot has limited hours, but street-side parking is usually available at off-peak times. It's near shops and a theater. **Amenities:** lifeguards; parking (fee); showers; toilets. **Best for:** sunset; walking. ⊠ *23200 Pacific Coast Hwy., Malibu* ☎ *310/457–8143* ⊕ *www.parks. ca.gov* ⊠ *$12 parking.*

Fodor'sChoice ★ **Robert H. Meyer Memorial State Beach.** Part of Malibu's most beautiful coastal area, this beach is made up of three minibeaches—El Pescador, La Piedra, and El Matador—each with the same spectacular view. Scramble down the steps to the rocky coves via steep, steep stairways; all food and water needs to be toted in, as there are no services. Portable toilets at the trailhead are the only restrooms. "El Mat" has a series

DID YOU KNOW?

Venice Beach is part of skateboarding's Dogtown, where
the Zephyr Team (or Z-Boys)
created the modern version
of the sport.

of caves, Piedra some nifty rock formations, and Pescador a secluded feel, but they're all picturesque and fairly private. ⚠ **Keep track of the incoming tide, so you don't get trapped between those otherwise scenic boulders. Amenities:** parking (fee); toilets. **Best for:** solitude; sunset; surfing; walking. ⊠ *32350, 32700, and 32900 Pacific Coast Hwy., Malibu* ☎ *818/880–0363* ⊕ *www.parks.ca.gov* ⊡ *Parking $8.*

Santa Monica State Beach. The first beach you'll hit after the Santa Monica Freeway (I–10) runs into the Pacific Coast Highway, wide and sandy Santa Monica is *the* place for sunning and socializing. Be prepared for a mob scene on summer weekends, when parking becomes an expensive ordeal. Swimming is fine (with the usual post-storm pollution caveat); for surfing, go elsewhere. For a memorable view, climb up the stairway over the PCH to Palisades Park, at the top of the bluffs. Free summer-evening concerts are held on the pier on Thursday nights. **Amenities:** food and drink; lifeguards; parking (fee); showers; toilets; water sports. **Best for:** sunset; surfing; swimming; walking. ⊠ *1642 Promenade, Pacific Coast Hwy. at California Incline, Santa Monica* ☎ *310/458–8573* ⊕ *www.smgov.net/portals/beach* ⊡ *$10 parking.*

PASADENA AREA

Although seemingly absorbed into the general Los Angeles sprawl, Pasadena is a separate and distinct city. Noted for its Tournament of Roses, seen around the world each New Year's Day, the city brims with noteworthy spots, from its gorgeous Craftsman homes to its exceptional museums, particularly the Norton Simon and the Huntington Library, Art Collections, and Botanical Gardens. Where else can you see a Chaucer manuscript and rare cacti in one place?

TOP ATTRACTIONS

Gamble House. Built by Charles and Henry Greene in 1908, this American Arts and Crafts bungalow illustrates the incredible craftsmanship that went into early L.A. architecture. The term *bungalow* can be misleading, since the Gamble House is a huge three-story home. To wealthy Easterners such as the Gambles (as in Procter & Gamble), this type of vacation home seemed informal compared with their mansions back home. Admirers swoon over the teak staircase and cabinetry, the Greene and Greene–designed furniture, and an Emil Lange glass door. The dark exterior has broad eaves, with sleeping porches on the second floor. An hour-long, docent-led tour of the Gamble's interior will draw your eye to the exquisite details. If you want to see more Greene and Greene homes, buy a self-guided tour map of the neighborhood in the bookstore. ⊠ *4 Westmoreland Pl., Pasadena* ☎ *626/793–3334* ⊕ *www.gamblehouse.org* ⊡ *$15* ⊙ *Thurs.–Sun. noon–3; tickets go on sale Thurs.–Sat. at 10, Sun. at 11:30. 1-hr tour every 20–30 min.*

Fodor'sChoice **Huntington Library, Art Collections, and Botanical Gardens.** If you have time ★ for just one stop in the Pasadena area, be sure to see this sprawling estate built for railroad tycoon Henry E. Huntington in the early 1900s. Henry and his wife, Arabella (who was also his aunt by marriage), voraciously collected rare books and manuscripts, botanical specimens, and 18th-century British art. The institution they established became

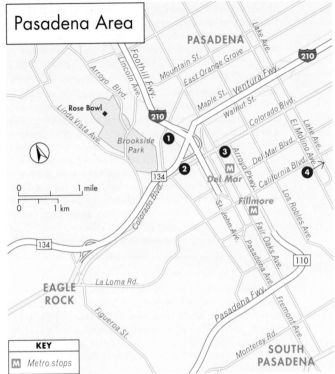

Pasadena Area

one of the most extraordinary cultural complexes in the world. Among the highlights are John Constable's intimate *View on the Stour near Dedham* and the monumental *Sarah Siddons as the Tragic Muse* by Joshua Reynolds.

The Virginia Steele Scott Gallery of American Art, added in 2014, includes paintings by Mary Cassatt, Frederic Remington, and others from colonial times to the 20th century. The library contains more than 700,000 books and 4 million manuscripts, including one of the world's biggest history of science collections. The recently renovated Library Main Hall combines early-20th-century opulence with digital-age panache. The thoughtful permanent exhibit is organized around 12 focal points, among them a Gutenberg Bible and Shakespeare's early editions, illuminating connections between events, images and texts from the 14th into the 20th century.

Don't resist being lured outside into the Botanical Gardens, which extend out from the main building. The 10-acre Desert Garden has one of the world's largest groups of mature cacti and other succulents (visit on a cool morning or late afternoon). The Shakespeare Garden, meanwhile, blooms with plants mentioned in Shakespeare's works. The Japanese Garden features an authentic ceremonial teahouse built in Kyoto in the 1960s. A waterfall flows from the teahouse to the ponds below. In the Rose Garden Tea Room, afternoon tea is served (reserve in advance). The Chinese Garden sinews around waveless pools.

The Rose Hills Foundation Conservatory for Botanical Science, a massive greenhouse-style center, has dozens of hands-on exhibits perfect for the whole family. And the Bing Children's Garden lets tiny tots explore the ancient elements of water, fire, air, and earth. A 1¼-hour guided tour of the botanical gardens is led by docents at posted times, and a free brochure with map and highlights is available in the entrance pavilion. ⊠ *1151 Oxford Rd., San Marino* ☎ *626/405–2100* ⊕ *www.huntington.org* ☞ *$20 weekdays, $23 weekends* ☉ *Mon. and Wed.–Fri. noon–4:30, weekends 10:30–4:30.*

Fodor's Choice
★

Norton Simon Museum. Long familiar to TV viewers of the New Year's Day Tournament of Roses Parade, this low-profile brown building is more than just a background for the passing floats. It's one of the finest midsize museums anywhere, with a collection that spans more than 2,000 years of Western and Asian art. It all began in the 1950s when Norton Simon (Hunt-Wesson Foods, McCalls Corporation, and Canada Dry) started collecting works by Degas, Renoir, Gauguin, and Cézanne. His collection grew to include old masters, impressionists, and modern works from Europe, as well as Indian and Southeast Asian art.

Today the Norton Simon Museum is richest in works by Rembrandt, Picasso, and, most of all, Degas—this is one of the only two U.S. institutions (the other is New York's Metropolitan Museum of Art) to hold nearly all of the artist's model bronzes; the museum also has the casts he used to make the collection. Renaissance, baroque, and rococo masterpieces include Raphael's *Madonna with Child with Book* (1503), Rembrandt's *Portrait of a Bearded Man in a Wide-Brimmed Hat* (1633), and a magical Tiepolo ceiling, *The Triumph of Virtue and Nobility Over Ignorance* (1740–50). The museum's impressionist and post-impressionist (Van Gogh, Matisse, Cézanne, Monet, Renoir) and cubist (Braque, Gris) works are extensive.

Several Rodin sculptures grace the front garden. Head down to the bottom floor to see temporary exhibits and phenomenal Southeast Asian and Indian sculptures and artifacts, where pieces like a Ban Chiang blackware vessel date to well before 1000 BC. Don't miss a living artwork outdoors: the garden, conceived by noted southern California landscape designer Nancy Goslee Power. The tranquil pond was inspired by Monet's gardens at Giverny. ⊠ *411 W. Colorado Blvd., Pasadena* ☎ *626/449–6840* ⊕ *www.nortonsimon.org* ☞ *$12, free 1st Fri. of month 6–9 pm* ☉ *Wed., Thurs., and Sat.–Mon. noon–6, Fri. noon–9.*

WORTH NOTING

Old Town Pasadena. This 22-block historic district contains a vibrant mix of restored 19th-century brick buildings interspersed with contemporary architecture. Chain stores have muscled in, but there are still some homegrown shops, plenty of tempting cafés and restaurants, and a bustling beer scene. In the evening and on weekends, the streets are packed with people. Old Town's main action takes place on Colorado Boulevard between Pasadena Avenue and Arroyo Parkway. ⊠ *Pasadena.*

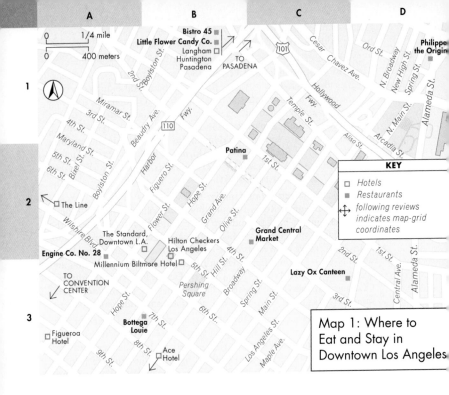

Map 1: Where to Eat and Stay in Downtown Los Angeles

KEY

□	Hotels
■	Restaurants
✛	following reviews indicates map-grid coordinates

WHERE TO EAT

Dining out in Los Angeles tends to be a casual affair, and even at some of the most expensive restaurants you're likely to see customers in jeans (although this is not necessarily considered in good taste). Despite its veneer of decadence, L.A. is not a particularly late-night city for eating (the reenergized Hollywood dining scene is emerging as a notable exception). The peak dinner times are from 7 to 9, and most restaurants won't take reservations after 10 pm. Generally speaking, restaurants are closed either on Sunday or Monday; a few are shuttered both days. Most places—even the upscale spots—are open for lunch on weekdays, when Hollywood megadeals are conceived.

Use the coordinate (✛ 1:A1) at the end of each listing to locate a site on the corresponding map.

WHAT IT COSTS				
	$	$$	$$$	$$$$
Restaurants	under $18	$18–$24	$25–$35	over $35

Prices are the average cost of a main course at dinner or, if dinner is not served, at lunch, excluding 9.75% tax.

DOWNTOWN

$$$ ITALIAN Fodor's Choice ★ 🍴 **Bottega Louie.** Inside a former Brooks Brother's store, this lively Italian restaurant and gourmet market sits high atop the list of downtown culinary darlings. Vast open spaces, stark white walls, and windows that stretch from floor to ceiling lend it a grand and majestic aura. Stylish servers weave in and out of the dining room carrying bowls of pasta, trays of thin-crust pizzas, and entrées that range from shrimp scampi to a hearty New York strip steak. For a lighter meal, simply order from the small-plates menu, which might include crab beignets, burrata and roasted vine tomatoes, and asparagus with a poached egg. Don't let the crowd waiting for a table deter you: order a glass of Prosecco from the bar and nibble on a brightly colored macaron while you ogle the beautiful Angelenos in attendance. [$] *Average main: $25* ✉ *700 S. Grand Ave., Downtown* ☎ *213/802–1470* 🌐 *www.bottegalouie.com* ✍ *Reservations not accepted* ✥ *1:A3.*

$$ INTERNATIONAL 🍴 **Lazy Ox Canteen.** A neighborhood favorite in artsy Little Tokyo, the dimly lit Lazy Ox is often filled with downtown dwellers lured in by the restaurant's flavorful food, great wine, and moderate prices. The diverse culinary background of chef Josef Centeno has resulted in seasonal eats that range from caramelized onion soup to porcini rosemary ragout. Try the chicharrones, the crispy cast-iron chicken, or the burger with white cheddar and whole-grain mustard. The restaurant has a lively weekend brunch; there's an outdoor patio for enjoying L.A.'s great weather. Parking can be difficult here. [$] *Average main: $22* ✉ *241 S. San Pedro St., Downtown* ☎ *213/626–5299* 🌐 *www.lazyoxcanteen.com* ✥ *1:D3.*

$$$$ FRENCH 🍴 **Patina.** Opened by chef Joachim Splichal, Patina occupies a coveted location inside the Frank Gehry–designed Walt Disney Concert Hall. The contemporary space, surrounded by a rippled "curtain" of rich walnut, is an elegant, dramatic stage for the acclaimed restaurant's contemporary French cuisine. Patina offers three- to eight-course tasting menus. The seasonally changing specialties might include langoustine and bone marrow, a variation of suckling pig served six ways, and the 63°C Duck Egg, with duck bacon, soubise, and a rosemary smoked-potato mousseline Kataifi nest. Finish with a hard-to-match cheese tray—orchestrated by a genuine *maître fromager* (cheese master), no less—and the fromage blanc soufflé served with house-made bourbon ice cream. [$] *Average main: $79* ✉ *Walt Disney Concert Hall, 141 S. Grand Ave., Downtown* ☎ *213/972–3331* 🌐 *www.patinagroup.com* ✍ *Reservations essential* ⏲ *Closed Mon.* ✥ *1:B2.*

$ AMERICAN FAMILY Fodor's Choice ★ 🍴 **Philippe the Original.** Dating from 1908, L.A.'s oldest restaurant claims that the French dip sandwich originated here. You can get one made with beef, pork, ham, lamb, or turkey on a freshly baked roll; the house hot mustard is as famous as the sandwiches. Philippe earns its reputation by maintaining traditions, from sawdust on the floor to long communal tables where customers debate the Dodgers or local politics. The home cooking—orders are taken at the counter where some of the motherly servers have managed their long lines for decades—includes huge breakfasts, chili, pickled eggs, and a generous pie selection. The best bargain: a cup of java for 49¢. [$] *Average main: $7* ✉ *1001 N.*

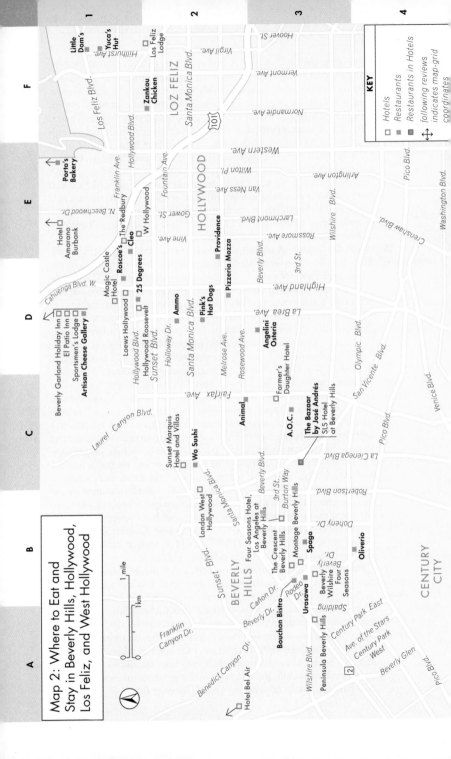

Map 2: Where to Eat and Stay in Beverly Hills, Hollywood, Los Feliz, and West Hollywood

KEY

□ Hotels
■ Restaurants
■ Restaurants in Hotels
↔ following reviews indicates map-grid coordinates

Beverly Garland Holiday Inn
El Patio Inn
Sportsmen's Lodge
Artisan Cheese Gallery

Hotel Amarano Burbank

Porto's Bakery

Little Dom's
Yuca's Hut
Los Feliz Lodge

Zankou Chicken

LOZ FELIZ

Magic Castle Hotel
Loews Hollywood
Hollywood Roosevelt

Roscoe's
The Redbury
Cleo
25 Degrees
W Hollywood

Ammo
Pink's Hot Dogs

Providence
Pizzeria Mozza

HOLLYWOOD

Angelini Osteria

Sunset Marquis Hotel and Villas
Wa Sushi

Animal

Farmer's Daughter Hotel

A.O.C.

The Bazaar by José Andrés
SLS Hotel at Beverly Hills

London West Hollywood

Four Seasons Hotel, Los Angeles at Beverly Hills
The Crescent Beverly Hills
Montage Beverly Hills
Spago

Oliverio

BEVERLY HILLS

Bouchon Bistro
Urasawa
Beverly Wilshire Four Seasons

CENTURY CITY

Peninsula Beverly Hills

Hotel Bel Air

1 mile
1 km

Alameda St., Downtown ☎ *213/628–3781* 🌐 *www.philippes.com* ✍ *Reservations not accepted* ✥ *1:D1.*

HOLLYWOOD AND THE STUDIOS

BURBANK

$ CUBAN FAMILY 🍴 **Porto's Bakery.** Waiting in line at Porto's is as much a part of the experience as is indulging in a roasted pork sandwich or a chocolate-dipped croissant. Just minutes away from Griffith Park, this bakery and café has been an L.A. staple for more than 50 years. Porto's bustles with an ambitious lunch crowd, but counter service is quick and efficient. Go for one of the tasty sandwiches like the *pan con lechon* (roasted pork), or try the filling plate of *ropa vieja* (shredded beef). Skipping dessert here would just be wrong. [$] *Average main: $10* ✉ *3614 W. Magnolia Blvd., Burbank* ☎ *818/846–9100* 🌐 *www.portosbakery.com* ✥ *2:E1.*

HOLLYWOOD

$$ AMERICAN 🍴 **Ammo.** This hip canteen proves that designers and photographers, regulars here, have good taste in food as well as fashion. The ever-evolving menu changes with the seasons: lunch might be French lentil salad, a perfectly cooked burger, or a prosciutto, mozzarella, and arugula sandwich. Start dinner with one of the kitchen's market-fresh salads, then follow up with a baby-artichoke pizza or a grilled hanger steak. The crisp, minimal setting is cool but not chilly. [$] *Average main: $23* ✉ *1155 N. Highland Ave., Hollywood* ☎ *323/871–2666* 🌐 *www.ammocafe.com* ✥ *2:D2.*

$$$ AMERICAN 🍴 **Animal.** When foodies in Los Angeles need a culinary thrill, they come to this Fairfax District restaurant that's light on the flash but heavy on serious food. The James Beard award–winning restaurant is owned by Jon Shook and Vinny Dotolo, who shot to fame with a stint on *Iron Chef* and later with their own show called *Two Dudes Catering.* With a closing time of midnight, the small restaurant is one of L.A.'s few late-night spots for a sophisticated bite. Sample the barbecue pork belly sandwiches, poutine with oxtail gravy, foie gras *loco moco* (a hamburger topped with foie gras, quail egg, and Spam), and grilled quail served with plum *char-siu* (barbecued pork). For dessert, the house specialty is a multilayer bacon-chocolate crunch bar. [$] *Average main: $25* ✉ *435 N. Fairfax Ave., Hollywood* ☎ *323/782–9225* 🌐 *www.animalrestaurant.com* ✍ *Reservations essential* 🕒 *No lunch* ✥ *2:C2.*

$$$ MEDITERRANEAN 🍴 **Cleo.** Tucked away in the Redbury Hotel and frequented by rockers and DJs, Cleo buzzes with energy in both its ambience and its fresh approach to Mediterranean cuisine. Start with a trio of dips that include hummus with tahini, thick yogurt with feta, and a *muhammara* (walnut garlic spread), served with fresh-from-the-oven flatbread. Chicken and lamb kebabs are an ideal segue into the main courses. Also good here are the perfectly roasted lamb shank and the moussaka made with eggplant, beef ragout, feta, and pine nuts. The thoughtful cocktail menu, decent wine list, and enthusiastic staff make Cleo a great place to spend the evening—Hollywood style. [$] *Average main: $25* ✉ *Redbury Hotel, 1717 Vine St., Hollywood* ☎ *323/962–1711* 🌐 *www.cleorestaurant.com* 🕒 *No lunch* ✥ *2:E1.*

5

$ AMERICAN FAMILY 🍴 **Pink's Hot Dogs.** Orson Welles ate 18 of these hot dogs in one sitting, and you, too, will be tempted to order more than one. The chili dogs are the main draw, but the menu has expanded to include a Martha Stewart Dog (a 10-inch frank topped with mustard, relish, onions, tomatoes, sauerkraut, bacon, and sour cream). Since 1939, Angelenos and tourists alike have been lining up to plunk down some modest change for one of the greatest guilty pleasures in L.A. Pink's is open until 3 am on weekends. [$] *Average main: $4* ✉ *709 N. La Brea Ave., Hollywood* ☎ *323/931–4223* 🌐 *www.pinkshollywood.com* ✍ *Reservations not accepted* 💳 *No credit cards* ✥ *2:D2.*

$$ ITALIAN Fodor's Choice ★ 🍴 **Pizzeria Mozza.** This casual venue elevates the humble "pizza joint." With traditional Mediterranean items like white anchovies, squash blossoms, and Gorgonzola, the pies—thin-crusted delights with golden, blistered edges—are more Campania than California, and virtually every one is a winner. Antipasti include simple salads, roasted bone marrow, and platters of *salumi* (cured meats). All sing with vibrant flavors thanks to superb market-fresh ingredients, and daily specials may include favorites like lasagna. Like the dishes on the menu, the wines on the Italian-only list are both interesting and affordable. Walk-ins are welcome at the bar. [$] *Average main: $19* ✉ *641 N. Highland Ave., Hollywood* ☎ *323/297–0101* 🌐 *www.pizzeriamozza.com* ✍ *Reservations essential* ✥ *2:D2.*

$$$$ SEAFOOD Fodor's Choice ★ 🍴 **Providence.** Chef-owner Michael Cimarusti has elevated Providence to the ranks of America's finest seafood restaurants. Co-owner Donato Poto smoothly oversees the elegant dining room, which is outfitted with subtle nautical accents. Obsessed with quality and freshness, the meticulous Cimarusti maintains a network of specialty purveyors, some of whom tip him off to their catches before they even hit the dock. This exquisite seafood then receives the chef's application of French technique, traditional American themes, and Asian accents in dishes on elaborate tasting menus. On Friday, Providence serves à la carte items; the rest of the week, delight in the chef's whims. Pastry chef David Rodriguez's exquisite desserts are not to be missed. TIP→ **For a splurge, consider the six-course dessert tasting menu.** [$] *Average main: $100* ✉ *5955 Melrose Ave., Hollywood* ☎ *323/460–4170* 🌐 *www.providencela.com* ✍ *Reservations essential* 🕓 *No lunch Mon.–Thurs. and weekends* ✥ *2:E2.*

$ SOUTHERN FAMILY 🍴 **Roscoe's House of Chicken and Waffles.** Don't be put off by the name of this casual eatery, which honors a late-night combo popularized in Harlem jazz clubs. Roscoe's is *the* place for down-home Southern cooking. Just ask the patrons, who drive from all over L.A. for Roscoe's bargain-price fried chicken, wonderful waffles (which indeed turn out to be a great partner for fried chicken), buttery chicken livers, and toothsome grits. Although Roscoe's has the intimate feel of a smoky jazz club, those musicians hanging out here are just taking five. [$] *Average main: $10* ✉ *1514 N. Gower St., Hollywood* ☎ *323/466–7453* 🌐 *www.roscoeschickenandwaffles.com* ✍ *Reservations not accepted* ✥ *2:D1.*

$ MIDDLE EASTERN FAMILY 🍴 **Zankou Chicken.** This aromatic, Armenian-style rotisserie chicken with crisp, golden skin is one of L.A.'s truly great budget meals. It's served with pita bread, veggies, hummus, and unforgettable garlic sauce. If this doesn't do it for you, try the kebabs, falafel, or sensational *shawarma* (spit-roasted lamb or chicken) plates. $ *Average main: $9* ✉ *5065 W. Sunset Blvd., Hollywood* ☎ *323/665–7845* ⚐ *Reservations not accepted* ✛ *2:F2.*

LOS FELIZ

$$ ✕ **Little Dom's.** With a vintage bar and dapper barkeep who mixes up
ITALIAN seasonally inspired retro cocktails, an attached Italian deli where you
Fodor's Choice can pick up a pork-cheek sub, and a $15 Monday-night supper, it's not
★ surprising that Little Dom's is a neighborhood gem. Cozy and inviting, with big leather booths you can sink into for the night, the restaurant puts a modern spin on classic Italian dishes such as wild-boar meatballs, almond-milk ricotta agnolotti, and grilled steak slathered in Parmesan. This is a terrific spot for weekend brunch. For an L.A. experience, order a bottle of the well-priced house wine and take a seat on the sidewalk patio. $ *Average main: $20* ✉ *2128 Hillhurst Ave., Los Feliz* ☎ *323/661–0055* ⊕ *www.littledoms.com* ⚐ *Reservations essential* ✛ *2:F1.*

$ ✕ **Yuca's Hut.** Blink, and you could miss this place, whose reputation far
MEXICAN exceeds its size. Quite possibly the tiniest restaurant to have received
FAMILY a James Beard award, Yuca's is known for *carne asada* (marinated
Fodor's Choice beef), *cochinita pibil* (Yucatán-style roasted pork) tacos, burritos, and
★ banana leaf–wrapped tamales. This is a fast-food restaurant in the finest tradition—independent, family-owned, and sticking to what it does best. The liquor store next door sells plenty of Coronas to Yuca's customers soaking up the sun on the makeshift parking-lot patio. There's no chance of satisfying a late-night craving, though: the restaurant closes at 6 pm. $ *Average main: $9* ✉ *2056 N. Hillhurst Ave., Los Feliz* ☎ *323/662–1214* ⊕ *www.yucasla.com* ⚐ *Reservations not accepted* ▭ *No credit cards* ⊙ *Closed Sun. No dinner* ✛ *2:F1.*

STUDIO CITY

$ ✕ **Artisan Cheese Gallery.** Taste your way through triple cream, goat's
DELI milk, blues, and other aromatic cheeses at this charming locale that
FAMILY serves up cheese and charcuterie plates, super sandwiches, and oversize salads. Sampling the cheeses and meats is encouraged, so don't be shy to ask. Grab a table on the small outdoor patio and enjoy the people-watching. $ *Average main: $12* ✉ *12023 Ventura Blvd., Studio City* ☎ *818/505–0207* ⊕ *www.artisancheesegallery.com* ⚐ *Reservations not accepted* ✛ *2:D1.*

BEVERLY HILLS AND THE WESTSIDE

BEVERLY HILLS

$$$$ ✕ **The Bazaar by José Andrés.** Celebrity Spanish chef José Andrés has
SPANISH conquered L.A. with a multifaceted concept restaurant that includes two dining rooms (one classic, one modern), a cocktail bar stocked with liquid nitrogen, and a flashy patisserie. Half of the menu is dedicated to traditional Spanish tapas: *bacalao* (salt cod) fritters with honey aioli, creamy chicken croquetas, and plates of chorizo or prized jamón Ibérico. The other half involves wild inventions of molecular gastronomy, including "liquid" olives (created through a technique called spherification) and an ethereal version of the traditional tortilla

Española in which an egg is cooked slowly at 63°C, just short of what would produce coagulation. Splendid Spanish vintages grace the wine list. For dessert, the patisserie serves up playful items such as beet meringue with pistachios, foie gras cotton candy, and chocolate lollipops. [$] *Average main: $61* ✉ *SLS Hotel at Beverly Hills, 465 S. La Cienega Blvd., Beverly Hills* ☎ *310/246–5555* 🌐 *sbe.com/restaurants/brands/thebazaar* ✍ *Reservations essential* ⏲ *No lunch* ✥ *2:C3.*

$$$ FRENCH Fodor's Choice ★ 🍴 **Bouchon Bistro.** Chef Thomas Keller of New York City's Per Se and the Napa Valley's The French Laundry established this grand and majestic bistro in Beverly Hills. Everything about Bouchon makes you feel pampered. Look for filtered Norwegian water served at every table, twig-shape baguettes made fresh in the kitchen, and an expansive wine list celebrating California and French wines. This foodie scene embraces celebrities and high-profile chefs and locals. Start with the classic onion soup that arrives with a bubbling lid of cheese, or the salmon rillettes, which are big enough to share. For dinner, there's steak and frites, roasted chicken, steamed Maine mussels, and a delicious grilled *croque madame.* For a sweet bite, order an espresso and the profiteroles or the bite-size brownies served with homemade vanilla ice cream. [$] *Average main: $35* ✉ *235 N. Cañon Dr., Beverly Hills* ☎ *310/271–9910* 🌐 *www.thomaskeller.com* ✍ *Reservations essential* ✥ *2:B3.*

$$ ITALIAN 🍴 **Oliverio.** This restaurant feels straight out of the movie *Valley of the Dolls.* Midcentury modern design lends a touch of vintage authenticity that blends seamlessly with the restaurant's Californian sensibility and chef Mirko Paderno's fresh, updated Italian cuisine. Enjoy a starter of fritto misto or a cauliflower soufflé; for dinner try the chicken diavolo, beef short ribs, or risotto Milanese. The private poolside cabanas are popular for celebrations. [$] *Average main: $23* ✉ *Avalon Hotel, 9400 W. Olympic Ave., Beverly Hills* ☎ *310/277–5221* 🌐 *www.avalonbeverlyhills.com* ✥ *2:B4.*

$$$ MODERN AMERICAN Fodor's Choice ★ 🍴 **Spago Beverly Hills.** The flagship restaurant of Wolfgang Puck is a modern L.A. classic. Spago centers on a buzzing outdoor courtyard shaded by 100-year-old olive trees. From an elegantly appointed table inside, you can glimpse the exhibition kitchen and, on rare occasions, the affable owner greeting his famous friends (these days, compliments to the chef go to Lee Hefter). The people-watching here is worth the price of admission, but the clientele is surprisingly inclusive, from the biggest Hollywood stars to Midwestern tourists to foodies more preoccupied with vintages of Burgundy than with faces from the cover of *People.* The daily-changing menu might offer Cantonese-style duck, some traditional Austrian specialties, or a pizza with wild mushrooms, baby asparagus, and sun-dried tomatoes. Dessert is magical, with everything from an ethereal apricot soufflé to Austrian *Kaiserschmarrn* (crème fraîche pancakes with fruit). [$] *Average main: $32* ✉ *176 N. Cañon Dr., Beverly Hills* ☎ *310/385–0880* 🌐 *www.wolfgangpuck.com* ✍ *Reservations essential* ⏲ *No lunch Sun.* ✥ *2:B3.*

$$$$ JAPANESE Fodor's Choice ★ 🍴 **Urasawa.** This understated sushi bar has precious few seats, resulting in incredibly personalized service. At a minimum of $375 per person for a strictly *omakase* (chef's choice) meal, Urasawa remains the priciest restaurant in town, but the endless parade of masterfully crafted,

exquisitely presented dishes renders few regrets. The maple sushi bar, sanded daily to a satinlike finish, is where most of the action takes place. You might be served velvety bluefin toro paired with beluga caviar, slivers of foie gras to self-cook *shabu shabu* style, or egg custard layered with *uni* (sea urchin), glittering with gold leaf. This is also the place to come during *fugu* season, when the legendary, potentially deadly blowfish is artfully served to adventurous diners. $ *Average main: $375* ⊠ *218 N. Rodeo Dr., Beverly Hills* ☎ *310/247–8939* ⌖ *Reservations essential* ☉ *Closed Sun. and Mon. No lunch* ✛ *2:B3.*

WEST HOLLYWOOD

$$$$ ✗ **Angelini Osteria.** You might not guess it from the modest, rather
ITALIAN congested dining room, but this is one of L.A.'s most celebrated Ital-
Fodor'sChoice ian restaurants. The key is chef-owner Gino Angelini's thoughtful use
★ of superb ingredients, evident in dishes such as a chopped salad with white beans, cucumbers, pistachios, and avocado, and cavatelli with mussels, clams, shrimp, peas, and saffron. Whole branzino, liberally crusted in sea salt, and boldly flavored rustic specials like tender veal kidneys or rich oxtail stew, as well as pastas heaping with white truffles (for a whopping $85) consistently impress. An intelligent selection of mostly Italian wines complements the menu. $ *Average main: $40* ⊠ *7313 Beverly Blvd., West Hollywood* ☎ *323/297–0070* ⊕ *www. angeliniosteria.com* ⌖ *Reservations essential* ☉ *Closed Mon. No lunch weekends* ✛ *2:D3.*

$$$$ ✗ **A.O.C.** This restaurant and wine bar revolutionized L.A.'s dining
MEDITERRANEAN scene, pioneering the small-plate format that swept the city. The space
Fodor'sChoice is dominated by a long, candle-laden bar serving more than 50 wines by
★ the glass. There's also a charcuterie bar. The tapaslike menu is perfectly calibrated to the wine list; you could pick duck confit, lamb roulade with mint pistou, an indulgent slice of ricotta tartine, or just plunge into one of the city's best cheese selections. Named for the acronym for Appellation d'Origine Contrôlée, the regulatory system that ensures the quality of local wines and cheeses in France, A.O.C. upholds the standard of excellence. $ *Average main: $36* ⊠ *8700 W. 3rd St., West Hollywood* ☎ *323/653–6359* ⊕ *www.aocwinebar.com* ⌖ *Reservations essential* ☉ *No lunch weekdays* ✛ *2:C3.*

$$$ ✗ **Wa Sushi & Bistro.** Founded by three alums of trendsetting Matsuhisa,
JAPANESE Wa offers a more personalized experience with high-quality ingredients and intriguing Japanese cooking. Particularly enticing are dishes enhanced with French-inspired sauces. For instance, the Chilean sea bass is layered with foie gras and bathed in a port reduction, while the Santa Barbara prawns are dosed with a perfect *beurre blanc* prepared on a rickety range behind the sushi bar. Wa's hillside location allows for seductive city views from a small handful of tables dressed up with linen and candles. $ *Average main: $31* ⊠ *1106 N. La Cienega Blvd., West Hollywood* ☎ *310/854–7285* ⌖ *Reservations essential* ☉ *Closed Mon. No lunch* ✛ *2:C2.*

5

CLOSE UP

Local Chains Worth Stopping For

It's said that the drive-in burger joint was invented in L.A., probably to meet the demands of an ever-mobile car culture. Burger aficionados line up at all hours outside **In-N-Out Burger** (🌐 *www.in-n-out.com*, multiple locations), still a family-owned operation whose terrific made-to-order burgers are revered by Angelenos. Locals often get their burger fix off the "not-so-secret" menu, with variations like "Animal Style" (mustard-grilled patty with grilled onions and extra spread), a "4 x 4" (four burger patties and four cheese slices, for big eaters) or the bun-less "Protein Style" that comes wrapped in lettuce. The company's website lists explanations for other popular secret menu items.

Tommy's sells a delightfully sloppy chili burger; the original location (✉ *2575 Beverly Blvd., Downtown* ☎ *213/389–9060*) is a no-frills culinary landmark. For rotisserie chicken that will make you forget the Colonel forever, head to **Zankou Chicken** (✉ *5065 Sunset Blvd., Hollywood* ☎ *323/665–7845* 🌐 *www.zankouchicken.com*), a small chain noted for its golden crispy-skinned birds, potent garlic sauce, and Armenian specialties. Homesick New Yorkers will appreciate **Jerry's Famous Deli** (✉ *10925 Weyburn Ave., Westwood* ☎ *310/208–3354* 🌐 *www.jerrysfamousdeli.com*), where the massive menu includes all the classic deli favorites. With a lively bar scene, good barbecued ribs, and contemporary takes on old favorites, the more upscale **Houston's** (✉ *202 Wilshire Blvd., Santa Monica* ☎ *310/576–7558* 🌐 *www.hillstone.com*) is a popular local hangout. And **Señor Fish** (✉ *422 E. 1st St., Downtown* ☎ *213/625–0566* 🌐 *www.senorfish.net*) is known for its healthy Mexican seafood specialties, such as scallop burritos and ceviche tostadas.

WEST LOS ANGELES

$ AMERICAN Fodor's Choice ★ 🍴 **The Apple Pan.** A favorite since 1947, this unassuming joint with a horseshoe-shape counter—no tables here—turns out one heck of a good burger. Try the cheeseburger with Tillamook cheddar, or perhaps the hickory burger topped with barbecue sauce. You can also find great fries and, of course, an apple pie indulgent enough to christen the restaurant (although many regulars argue that the banana cream deserves the honor). Be prepared to wait, but the veteran countermen turn the stools at a quick pace. In the meantime, grab a cup of Sanka and enjoy a little vintage Los Angeles. [$] *Average main: $7* ✉ *10801 W. Pico Blvd., West L.A.* ☎ *310/475–3585* ✍ *Reservations not accepted* ▭ *No credit cards* ⏲ *Closed Mon.* ✥ *3:D2.*

SANTA MONICA AND VENICE

SANTA MONICA

$$ AMERICAN 🍴 **Farmshop.** Southern California native Jeffrey Cerciello brought a little Napa Valley to this classic spot that pays attention to the details but also keeps things refreshingly simple. Order the buttermilk biscuits served with quince preserves, French toast with pear marmalade and raisins, and baked eggs with wild greens, fennel cream, and flavorful sourdough

toast. Lunch is an assortment of farm-fresh salads, savory soups, and sandwiches. Try the warm Dungeness crab salad made with butter lettuce, sunchokes, and curly mustard greens, or the smoked salmon tartine dressed with caper berries and pickled vegetables on rye bread. ⓢ *Average main: $23* ✉ *Brentwood Country Mart, 225 26th St., Santa Monica* ☎ *310/566–2400* ⊕ *www.farmshopla.com* ✛ *3:B2.*

$ ✕ **Father's Office.** With a facade distinguished by a vintage neon sign, this
AMERICAN   pub is famous for handcrafted beers and a brilliant signature burger. Topped with Gruyère and Maytag blue cheeses, caramelized onions, and applewood-smoked bacon compote, the "Office Burger" is a guilty pleasure worth waiting in line for, which is usually required. Get a side order of the addictive sweet-potato fries served in a miniature shopping cart with aioli—don't even think of asking for ketchup, because FO enforces a strict no-substitutions policy. Other options include steak frites and Spanish-style tapas. ■TIP→ **Because Father's Office is a bar, it's strictly for diners 21 and older.** ⓢ *Average main: $12* ✉ *1018 Montana Ave., Santa Monica* ☎ *310/393–2337* ⊕ *www.fathersoffice.com* ⌧ *Reservations not accepted* ⊘ *No lunch weekdays* ✛ *3:B2.*

$$$$ ✕ **Mélisse.** In a city where informality reigns, this is one of the dressier,
FRENCH   but not stuffy, establishments. The dining room is contemporary yet ele-
Fodor'sChoice   gant, with well-spaced tables topped with flowers and fine china. Chef-
★   owner Josiah Citrin enhances his modern French cooking with seasonal California produce. The tasting menu might feature a white-corn ravioli in brown butter–truffle froth, lobster Bolognese, and elegant tableside presentations of Dover sole and stuffed rotisserie chicken. The cheese cart is packed with domestic and European selections. ■TIP→ **The tasting menu can be tailored to please vegetarians.** ⓢ *Average main: $135* ✉ *1104 Wilshire Blvd., Santa Monica* ☎ *310/395–0881* ⊕ *www. melisse.com* ⌧ *Reservations essential* ⊘ *Closed Sun. and Mon. No lunch* ✛ *3:B2.*

$$ ✕ **Santa Monica Seafood.** The Cigliano family began its modest sea-
SEAFOOD   food business on Santa Monica Pier in the early 1930s. The restaurant
FAMILY   remains a Southern California favorite, even in its swankier digs along Wilshire Boulevard. It expanded the retail market and made room for a café where you can enjoy oysters and champagne while wearing jeans and flip-flops. The simple menu includes Italian flavors in such dishes as the rainbow trout drizzled with olive oil and spices. There are also sandwiches, soups, and plates for kids. Take time to stroll around the market, read up on the history, and enjoy free tastings of the specials. ⓢ *Average main: $20* ✉ *1000 Wilshire Blvd., Santa Monica* ☎ *310/393–5244* ⊕ *www.santamonicaseafood.com* ✛ *3:B2.*

$$$$ ✕ **Valentino.** With an awe-inspiring wine list—nearly 2,800 labels con-
ITALIAN   suming 130 pages, cataloguing the contents of a cellar overflowing with more than 80,000 bottles—this restaurant is nothing short of heaven for oenophiles. The newly expanded wine bar allows wine lovers to familiarize themselves with that list in a casual setting while enjoying carpaccio and similar nibbles. In the 1970s suave owner Piero Selvaggio introduced L.A. to his exquisite modern Italian cuisine, and he continues to impress with dishes such as a *timballo* of wild mushrooms with rich Parmigiano-Reggiano saffron *fonduta*, a fresh risotto with market

5

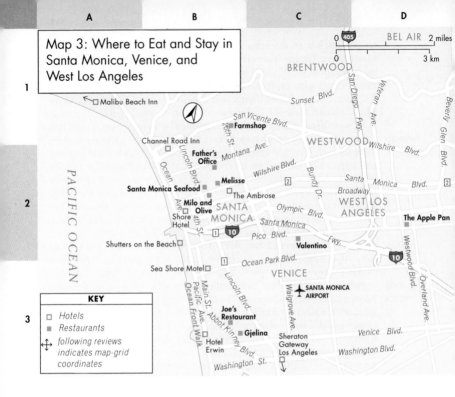

Map 3: Where to Eat and Stay in
Santa Monica, Venice, and
West Los Angeles

vegetables, a memorable osso buco, and sautéed branzino with lemon emulsion. $ *Average main: $44* ⊠ *3115 Pico Blvd., Santa Monica* ☎ *310/829–4313* ⊕ *www.valentinosantamonica.com* ⌛ *Reservations essential* ☉ *Closed Sun. and Mon. No lunch Sat. and Mon.–Thurs.* ⊕ *3:C2.*

VENICE

$$ ✕ **Gjelina.** This handsome restaurant comes alive the minute you walk
AMERICAN   through the rustic wooden door and into a softly lit dining room with long communal tables. The menu is smart and seasonal, with small plates, cheese and charcuterie, pastas, and pizza. Begin with a wild nettle pizza, heirloom lettuce and hemp-seed salad, or grilled squid with lentils and salsa verde. For the main course, there's the crispy duck leg confit and pan-seared Niman Ranch rib eye. Typically crowded and noisy, the outdoor patio is a great spot to hang out. The late-night menu lures an enthusiastic post-pub crowd. $ *Average main: $20* ⊠ *1429 Abbot Kinney Blvd., Venice* ☎ *310/450–1429* ⊕ *www.gjelina. com* ⌛ *Reservations essential* ⊕ *3:B3.*

$$$ ✕ **Joe's Restaurant.** In a century-old beach house, Joe Miller has cre-
AMERICAN   ated the definitive neighborhood restaurant with a citywide reputa-tion. His imaginative French-influenced California cooking focuses on fresh ingredients. Start with tuna tartare or porcini ravioli in a

mushroom-Parmesan broth, and continue with Berkshire pork *crépi-nette* (a type of sausage) or potato-crusted red snapper in Port sauce. For dessert, try the chocolate crunch cake with hazelnuts and house-made coffee ice cream. Lunch is a terrific value—all entrées cost $18 or less and come with soup or salad. Sunday suppers cost $25, and the four-course farmers' market food and cocktail pairings, nightly for dinner, run $48. $ *Average main: $25* ✉ *1023 Abbott Kinney Blvd., Venice* ☎ *310/399–5811* ⊕ *www.joesrestaurant.com* ☽ *Closed Mon.* ✛ *3:B3*

PASADENA

$$$
FRENCH

✕ **Bistro 45.** One of Pasadena's most stylish and sophisticated dining spots, Bistro 45 blends traditional French themes with modern concepts to create fanciful California hybrids that delight locals and visitors alike. Seared ahi tuna with a black-and-white-sesame crust, and duck with a tamari-ginger sauce incorporate Pacific Rim accents. The art-deco bungalow has been tailored into a sleek environment. Oenophiles, take note: in addition to maintaining one of the best wine lists in town, owner Robert Simon regularly hosts lavish wine dinners. $ *Average main: $25* ✉ *45 S. Mentor Ave., Pasadena* ☎ *626/795–2478* ⊕ *www. bistro45.com* ⌂ *Reservations essential* ☽ *Closed Mon. No lunch week-ends* ✛ *1:B1.*

$
CAFÉ
FAMILY

✕ **Little Flower Candy Co.** This quaint café charms the hearts and taste buds of locals with its seasonally driven menu of sandwiches, salads, soups, and incredible baked goods. The owner, Christine Moore, made a name for herself in the candy world with sea-salt caramels and pil-lowy marshmallows. The café is nestled against sloping hills for an away-from-it-all feel, even though downtown is but a few miles away. This is a terrific place to grab a coffee, a fresh berry pastry, or a light meal before heading out for an afternoon of shopping. $ *Average main: $12* ✉ *1424 W. Colorado Blvd., Pasadena* ☎ *626/304–4800* ⊕ *www. littleflowercandyco.com* ☽ *Closed Sun.* ✛ *1:B1.*

WHERE TO STAY

Updated by
Michele Bigley

When looking for a hotel, don't write off the pricier establishments immediately. Price categories are determined by "rack rates"—the list price of a hotel room, which is usually discounted. Specials abound, particularly Downtown on the weekends. Many hotels have packages that include breakfast, theater tickets, spa services, or exotic rental cars. Pricing is very competitive, so always check out the hotel website in advance for current special offers. When making reservations, particu-larly last-minute ones, check the hotel's website for exclusive Internet specials or call the property directly.

Use the coordinate (✛ 1:B2) at the end of each listing to locate a site on the corresponding map. Hotel reviews have been shortened. For full information, visit Fodors.com.

WHAT IT COSTS				
	$	$$	$$$	$$$$
Hotels	under $200	$200–$300	$301–$400	over $400

Hotel prices are the lowest cost of a standard double room in high season, excluding taxes (as high as 14%, depending on the region).

DOWNTOWN

$$ **Ace Hotel.** A hipster haven, the Ace wears multiple hats as a hotel,
HOTEL   theater, neighborhood diner/coffee shop, and series of lounges, where you can barhop by elevator. **Pros:** lively public areas; great room rates; free Wi-Fi. **Cons:** expensive parking rates compared to nightly rates ($36); some kinks in the service; compact and somewhat awkwardly designed rooms. $ *Rooms from: $239* ✉ *929 S. Broadway, Downtown* ☎ *213/623–3233* ⊕ *www.acehotel.com/losangeles* ⤴ *182 rooms, 1 suite* ⦿ *No meals* ✛ *1:B3.*

$$ **Hilton Checkers Los Angeles.** Opened as the Mayflower Hotel in 1927,
HOTEL   Checkers retains much of its original character and period detail, but it also has contemporary luxuries such as pillow-top mattresses and plasma TVs. **Pros:** historic charm; 24-hour room service; business-friendly; rooftop pool and spa. **Cons:** no on-street parking and valet is over $40; some rooms are compact; urban setting. $ *Rooms from: $259* ✉ *535 S. Grand Ave., Downtown* ☎ *213/624–0000, 800/445–8667* ⊕ *www.hiltoncheckers.com* ⤴ *188 rooms, 5 suites* ⦿ *No meals* ✛ *1:B2.*

$$ **The Line.** This boutique hotel pays homage to its Koreatown address
HOTEL   with a dynamic dining concept by superstar Roy Choi, artsy interiors, and a hidden karaoke speakeasy, aptly named Speek. **Pros:** free bikes to explore the area; cheery staff; celebratory atmosphere. **Cons:** design might feel cold and too ambitious for some; expensive parking ($32). $ *Rooms from: $269* ✉ *3515 Wilshire Blvd., Hollywood* ☎ *213/381–7411* ⊕ *www.thelinehotel.com* ⤴ *362 rooms, 26 suites* ⦿ *No meals* ✛ *1:A2.*

$$ **Millennium Biltmore Hotel.** A downtown treasure, this gilded 1923
HOTEL   beaux-arts masterpiece exudes ambience and history. **Pros:** historic character; famed filming location; many extras in club-level rooms. **Cons:** pricey valet parking; standard rooms are compact. $ *Rooms from: $239* ✉ *506 S. Grand Ave., Downtown* ☎ *213/624–1011, 866/866–8086* ⊕ *www.millenniumhotels.com* ⤴ *635 rooms, 48 suites* ⦿ *No meals* ✛ *1:B3.*

$$ **The Standard, Downtown L.A.** Though this hotel was built in 1955 as the
HOTEL   headquarters of Standard Oil, you might not know it, because the building was completely revamped in 2002 under the sharp eye of owner André Balazs, who ordered up a sleek, cutting-edge feel. **Pros:** on-site Rudy's barbershop for grooming; 24/7 coffee shop for dining; rooftop pool and lounge for fun. **Cons:** disruptive party scene on weekends and holidays; street noise; pricey valet parking. $ *Rooms from: $240* ✉ *550 S. Flower St., Downtown* ☎ *213/892–8080* ⊕ *www.standardhotels.com* ⤴ *171 rooms, 36 suites* ⦿ *No meals* ✛ *1:B2.*

HOLLYWOOD AND THE STUDIOS

BURBANK

$$ **Hotel Amarano Burbank.** Close to Burbank's TV and movie studios,
HOTEL the smartly designed Amarano feels like a Beverly Hills boutique hotel,
complete with 24-hour room service, a homey on-site restaurant and
lounge, and spiffy rooms. **Pros:** boutique style; pleasant breakfast room.
Cons: street noise. $ *Rooms from: $269* ✉ *322 N. Pass Ave., Burbank*
☎ *818/842–8887, 888/956–1900* ⊕ *www.hotelamarano.com* ⟿ *98
rooms, 34 suites* ‖*No meals* ✛ *2:E1.*

HOLLYWOOD

$$$ **Hollywood Roosevelt Hotel.** Think hip bachelor pad when considering
HOTEL the Roosevelt, known for its party-centric, heart-of-Hollywood vibe
Fodor'sChoice and for hosting the first Academy Awards ceremony. **Pros:** in the heart
★ of Hollywood's action and a block from the Metro; lively social scene;
great burgers at the on-site 25 Degrees restaurant. **Cons:** reports of noise
and staff attitude; stiff parking fees. $ *Rooms from: $319* ✉ *7000 Hollywood Blvd., Hollywood* ☎ *323/466–7000, 800/950–7667* ⊕ *www.
hollywoodroosevelt.com* ⟿ *305 rooms, 48 suites* ‖*No meals* ✛ *2:D2.*

$$ **Loews Hollywood.** Part of the massive Hollywood & Highland shop-
HOTEL ping and entertainment complex, the 20-story Loews is at the center
FAMILY of Hollywood's action but manages to deliver a quiet night's sleep.
Pros: large rooms with contemporary-styled furniture; free Wi-Fi; Red
Line Metro–station adjacent; attached to a mall with plentiful dining
options. **Cons:** corporate feeling; very touristy; pricy parking. $ *Rooms
from: $239* ✉ *1755 N. Highland Ave., Hollywood* ☎ *323/856–1200,
800/769–4774* ⊕ *www.loewshotels.com/en/Hollywood-Hotel* ⟿ *604
rooms, 33 suites* ‖*No meals* ✛ *2:D1.*

$ **Magic Castle Hotel.** Close to the action (and traffic) of Hollywood,
HOTEL this former apartment building faces busy Franklin Avenue and is a
FAMILY quick walk to the Metro Red Line stop at Hollywood & Highland.
Fodor'sChoice **Pros:** friendly and able staff; free Wi-Fi; good value. **Cons:** traffic-heavy
★ locale; no elevator; small bathrooms. $ *Rooms from: $184* ✉ *7025
Franklin Ave., Hollywood* ☎ *323/851–0800, 800/741–4915* ⊕ *www.
magiccastlehotel.com* ⟿ *7 rooms, 36 suites* ‖*Breakfast* ✛ *2:D1.*

$$$ **The Redbury.** In the heart of Hollywood's nightlife, near the inter-
HOTEL section of Hollywood and Vine, the Redbury is designed to appeal to
Fodor'sChoice guests' inner bohemian. **Pros:** kitchenettes, washer-dryers and spacious
★ suites are ideal for those staying a while; excellent dining. **Cons:** no
pool or on-site gym; noisy on lower floors; some guests may find the
Hollywood scene too hyperactive. $ *Rooms from: $369* ✉ *1717 Vine
St., Hollywood* ☎ *323/962–1717, 977/962–1717* ⊕ *www.theredbury.
com* ⟿ *57 suites* ‖*No meals* ✛ *2:E1.*

$$$$ **W Hollywood.** Just off the historic intersection of Hollywood and
HOTEL Vine and above a busy Metro station, the W Hollywood is ultramodern and outfitted for the wired traveler. **Pros:** metro stop outside the
front door; all the necessities for an in-room party, from ice to cocktail
glasses. **Cons:** small pool; pricy dining and valet parking; soundproof-
ing issues. $ *Rooms from: $659* ✉ *6250 Hollywood Blvd., Hollywood*

☎ 323/798–1300, 888/625–4955 🌐 *www.whotels.com/hollywood* 🛏 *265 rooms, 40 suites* 🍴 *No meals* ✣ *2:E1.*

LOS FELIZ

$ RENTAL 🏨 **Los Feliz Lodge.** Checking into this bungalow-style lodge is like crashing at an eco-minded and artsy friend's place: you let yourself into an apartment that has a fully stocked kitchen, a washer and dryer, and a communal patio. **Pros:** homey feel; within walking distance to restaurants; ideal for longer stays. **Cons:** no on-site restaurant or pool. [$] *Rooms from: $155* ✉ *1507 N. Hoover St., Los Feliz* ☎ *323/660–4150* 🌐 *www.losfelizlodge.com* 🛏 *5 rooms* 🍴 *No meals* ✣ *2:F2.*

STUDIO CITY

$ HOTEL FAMILY 🏨 **Sportsmen's Lodge.** The sprawling five-story hotel, a San Fernando Valley landmark, has an updated contemporary look. **Pros:** close to Ventura Boulevard restaurants; free shuttle and discounted tickets to Universal Hollywood; quiet garden-view rooms worth asking for. **Cons:** pricey daily self-parking fee; a distance from the city. [$] *Rooms from: $184* ✉ *12825 Ventura Blvd., Studio City* ☎ *818/769–4700, 800/821–8511* 🌐 *www.sportsmenslodge.com* 🛏 *177 rooms, 13 suites* 🍴 *No meals* ✣ *2:D1.*

BEVERLY HILLS AND THE WESTSIDE

BEL AIR

$$$$ HOTEL Fodor's Choice ★ 🏨 **Hotel Bel-Air.** This Spanish Mission-style icon has been a discreet hillside retreat for celebrities and society types since 1946; and now courtesy of star designers Alexandra Champalimaud and David Rockwell, the rooms and suites, many of which feature fireplaces and private patios, are decidedly more modern. **Pros:** full of history (and stories); lovely pool; spacious rooms. **Cons:** attracts society crowd; hefty price tag; a car is essential. [$] *Rooms from: $895* ✉ *701 Stone Canyon Rd., Bel Air* ☎ *310/472–1211, 800/648–4097* 🌐 *www.hotelbelair.com* 🛏 *52 rooms, 39 suites* 🍴 *No meals* ✣ *2:A2.*

BEVERLY HILLS

$$$$ HOTEL 🏨 **Beverly Wilshire, a Four Seasons Hotel.** Built in 1928, the Italian Renaissance–style Wilshire wing of this fabled hotel is replete with elegant details: crystal chandeliers, oak paneling, walnut doors, crown moldings, and marble. **Pros:** chic location; top-notch service; refined vibe. **Cons:** small lobby; valet parking backs up at peak times; expensive dining options. [$] *Rooms from: $635* ✉ *9500 Wilshire Blvd., Beverly Hills* ☎ *310/275–5200, 800/427–4354* 🌐 *www.fourseasons.com/beverlywilshire* 🛏 *258 rooms, 137 suites* 🍴 *No meals* ✣ *2:B3.*

$$ HOTEL Fodor's Choice ★ 🏨 **The Crescent Beverly Hills.** Built in 1926 as a dorm for silent-film actors, the Crescent is now a sleek boutique hotel with a great location—within the Beverly Hills shopping triangle—and with an even better price. **Pros:** upscale service at Beverly Hills's lowest price; on-site restaurant CBH's cuisine and happy hour; restaurant is fashionista central. **Cons:** dorm-size rooms; gym an additional fee and only accessible from outside hotel; no elevator. [$] *Rooms from: $231* ✉ *403 N. Crescent Dr.,*

Beverly Hills ☎ *310/247–0505* 🌐 *www.crescentbh.com* 🛏 *35 rooms* 🍴 *No meals* ⊕ *2:B3.*

$$$$ HOTEL **Four Seasons Hotel, Los Angeles at Beverly Hills.** High hedges and patio gardens make this hotel a secluded retreat that even the hum of traffic can't permeate, one reason it's a favorite of Hollywood's elite. **Pros:** expert concierge; deferential service; celebrity magnet. **Cons:** Hollywood scene in bar and restaurant means rarefied prices. [$] *Rooms from: $605* ✉ *300 S. Doheny Dr., Beverly Hills* ☎ *310/273–2222, 800/332–3442* 🌐 *www.fourseasons.com/losangeles* 🛏 *185 rooms, 100 suites* 🍴 *No meals* ⊕ *2:B3.*

$$$$ HOTEL Fodor's Choice ★ **Montage Beverly Hills.** The nine-story, Mediterranean-style palazzo is dedicated to welcoming those who relish luxury, providing classic style and exemplary service. **Pros:** a feast for the senses; intricate architectural details; obliging, highly trained staff. **Cons:** the hefty tab for all this finery. [$] *Rooms from: $655* ✉ *225 N. Cañon Dr., Beverly Hills* ☎ *310/860–7800, 888/860–0788* 🌐 *www.montagebeverlyhills.com* 🛏 *146 rooms, 55 suites* 🍴 *No meals* ⊕ *2:B3.*

$$$$ HOTEL Fodor's Choice ★ **Peninsula Beverly Hills.** This French Riviera–style palace is a favorite of Hollywood bold-face names, but visitors consistently describe a stay here as near perfect. **Pros:** central, walkable Beverly Hills location; stunning flower arrangements; one of the city's best concierges. **Cons:** very expensive; room decor might be too ornate for some. [$] *Rooms from: $795* ✉ *9882 S. Santa Monica Blvd., Beverly Hills* ☎ *310/551–2888, 800/462–7899* 🌐 *www.beverlyhills.peninsula.com* 🛏 *142 rooms, 37 suites, 16 villas* 🍴 *No meals* ⊕ *2:A3.*

$$$ HOTEL **SLS Hotel at Beverly Hills.** Imagine dropping into Alice in Wonderland's rabbit hole: this is what design maestro Philippe Starck's sleek, textured, and tchotchke-filled SLS lobby feels like. **Pros:** a vibrant destination with lofty ambitions; excellent design and cuisine; great for celebrity spotting. **Cons:** standard rooms are compact; pricey dining and parking; design might seem cold to some. [$] *Rooms from: $399* ✉ *465 S. La Cienega Blvd., Beverly Hills* ☎ *310/247–0400* 🌐 *www.slshotels.com* 🛏 *236 rooms, 61 suites* 🍴 *No meals* ⊕ *2:C3.*

WEST HOLLYWOOD

$ HOTEL Fodor's Choice ★ **Farmer's Daughter Hotel.** A favorite of *The Price Is Right* and *American Idol* hopefuls (both TV shows tape at the CBS studios nearby) as well as local hipsters, this motel has a tongue-in-cheek country style with farm tools as art, a hopping Sunday brunch, and a little pool accented by giant rubber duckies and bean bags. **Pros:** great central city location; across from the cheap eats of the Farmers Market and The Grove's shopping and entertainment mix. **Cons:** shaded pool; no bathtubs. [$] *Rooms from: $160* ✉ *115 S. Fairfax Ave., Farmers Market* ☎ *323/937–3930, 800/334–1658* 🌐 *www.farmersdaughterhotel.com* 🛏 *63 rooms, 2 suites* 🍴 *No meals* ⊕ *2:C3.*

$$$ HOTEL **The London West Hollywood.** Just off the Sunset Strip, cosmopolitan and chic in design, the London West Hollywood is known for its large suites, rooftop pool with citywide views, and luxury touches throughout. **Pros:** perfectly designed interiors; hillside and city views from generous-size suites; steps from the Strip. **Cons:** too refined for kids to be comfortable; lower floors have mundane views. [$] *Rooms from: $349* ✉ *1020*

5

N. San Vicente Blvd., West Hollywood ☎ *310/854–1111, 866/282–4560* 🌐 *www.thelondonwesthollywood.com* 🛏 *225 suites* 🍴 *No meals* ✥ *2:B2.*

$$$ HOTEL Fodor's Choice ★ 🏨 **Sunset Marquis Hotel & Villas.** If you're in town to cut your new hit single, you'll appreciate this near-the-Strip spot with two on-site recording studios; or if you're in the market to rock out with celebs, you, too, will appreciate this hidden retreat in the heart of West Hollywood. **Pros:** superior service; discreet setting just off the Strip; clublike atmosphere; free passes to Equinox nearby. **Cons:** rooms can feel dark; small balconies. [$] *Rooms from: $350* ✉ *1200 N. Alta Loma Rd., West Hollywood* ☎ *310/657–1333, 800/858–9758* 🌐 *www.sunsetmarquis.com* 🛏 *102 suites, 52 villas* 🍴 *No meals* ✥ *2:C2.*

SANTA MONICA AND THE BEACHES

LOS ANGELES INTERNATIONAL AIRPORT

$ HOTEL 🏨 **Sheraton Gateway Los Angeles.** LAX's swanky hotel just had some serious work done to her already sleek look, yet her appeal runs deeper than her style, with in-transit visitors loving the 24-hour room service, fitness center, and airport shuttle. **Pros:** significantly lower weekend rates; free LAX shuttle. **Cons:** convenient to airport but not much else. [$] *Rooms from: $149* ✉ *6101 W. Century Blvd., Los Angeles International Airport* ☎ *310/642–1111, 800/325–3535* 🌐 *www.sheratonlosangeles.com* 🛏 *714 rooms, 88 suites* 🍴 *No meals* ✥ *3:C3.*

MALIBU

$$$$ B&B/INN 🏨 **Malibu Beach Inn.** Set right on exclusive and private Carbon Beach, the hotel is home to all manner of the super-rich: the location doesn't get any better than this. **Pros:** live like a billionaire in designer-perfect interiors right on the beach. **Cons:** billionaire's travel budget also required; noise of PCH; no pool, gym, or hot tub. [$] *Rooms from: $675* ✉ *22878 Pacific Coast Hwy., Malibu* ☎ *310/456–6444* 🌐 *www.malibubeachinn.com* 🛏 *41 rooms, 6 suites* 🍴 *No meals* ✥ *3:A1.*

SANTA MONICA

$$ HOTEL 🏨 **The Ambrose.** An air of tranquillity pervades the four-story Ambrose, which blends right into its mostly residential Santa Monica neighborhood. **Pros:** recycling bins in each room; nontoxic housekeeping products used; food service a plus for weary travelers; free Wi-Fi and parking. **Cons:** quiet, residential area of Santa Monica. [$] *Rooms from: $249* ✉ *1255 20th St., Santa Monica* ☎ *310/315–1555, 877/262–7673* 🌐 *www.ambrosehotel.com* 🛏 *77 rooms* 🍴 *Breakfast* ✥ *3:B2.*

$ B&B/INN Fodor's Choice ★ 🏨 **Channel Road Inn.** A quaint surprise in Southern California, the Channel Road Inn is every bit the country retreat bed-and-breakfast lovers adore, with four-poster beds with fluffy duvets and a cozy living room with fireplace. **Pros:** quiet residential neighborhood close to beach; free Wi-Fi and evening wine and hors d'oeuvres. **Cons:** no pool. [$] *Rooms from: $195* ✉ *219 W. Channel Rd., Santa Monica* ☎ *310/459–1920* 🌐 *www.channelroadinn.com* 🛏 *13 rooms, 2 suites* 🍴 *Breakfast* ✥ *3:B2.*

$ HOTEL 🏨 **Sea Shore Motel.** On Santa Monica's busy Main Street, the Sea Shore is a throwback to Route 66 and to '60s-style, family-run roadside motels.

Pros: close to beach and restaurants; free Wi-Fi and parking; great value for the location. **Cons:** street noise; motel-style decor and beds. *Rooms from: $150 ✉ 2637 Main St., Santa Monica ☎ 310/392–2787 ⊕ www.seashoremotel.com ⇆ 19 rooms, 5 suites ǀ◎ǀ No meals ✢ 3:B3.*

$$$$ HOTEL Fodor's Choice ★ **Shore Hotel.** With views of the Santa Monica Pier, this hotel with a friendly staff offers eco-minded travelers stylish rooms with a modern design and scenic views steps from the sand and sea. **Pros:** excellent location near beach and Third Street Promenade; low carbon footprint hotel; free Wi-Fi. **Cons:** expensive rooms and parking fees; fronting busy Ocean Avenue. *Rooms from: $459 ✉ 1515 Ocean Ave., Santa Monica ☎ 310/458–1515 ⊕ shorehotel.com ⇆ 144 rooms, 20 suites ǀ◎ǀ No meals ✢ 3:B2.*

$$$$ HOTEL FAMILY Fodor's Choice ★ **Shutters on the Beach.** Set right on the sand, this gray-shingle inn has become synonymous with in-town escapism, and while the hotel's service gets mixed reviews from some readers, the beachfront location and show-house decor make this one of SoCal's most popular luxury hotels. **Pros:** romantic; discreet; residential vibe; steps to the sand. **Cons:** service not as good as it should be; very expensive. *Rooms from: $800 ✉ 1 Pico Blvd., Santa Monica ☎ 310/458–0030, 800/334–9000 ⊕ www.shuttersonthebeach.com ⇆ 186 rooms, 12 suites ǀ◎ǀ No meals ✢ 3:B2.*

VENICE

$$ HOTEL **Hotel Erwin.** A boutique hotel a block off the Venice Beach Boardwalk, the Erwin has spacious, airy rooms and a happening and newly expanded rooftop bar and lounge. **Pros:** close to Santa Monica without hefty prices; staff is friendly and helpful; great food. **Cons:** some rooms face a noisy alley; no pool. *Rooms from: $279 ✉ 1697 Pacific Ave., Venice ☎ 310/452–1111, 800/786–7789 ⊕ www.hotelerwin.com ⇆ 119 rooms ǀ◎ǀ No meals ✢ 3:B3.*

PASADENA

$$$ HOTEL FAMILY Fodor's Choice ★ **The Langham Huntington, Pasadena.** An azalea-filled Japanese garden and the unusual Picture Bridge, with murals celebrating California's history, are just two of the scenic attributes of this grande dame that opened in 1907 and has been a mainstay of Pasadena's social history pretty much ever since. **Pros:** great for a romantic escape; excellent restaurant; top-notch spa. **Cons:** in a suburban neighborhood far from local shopping and dining. *Rooms from: $379 ✉ 1401 S. Oak Knoll Ave., Pasadena ☎ 626/568–3900 ⊕ www.pasadena.langhamhotels.com ⇆ 342 rooms, 38 suites ǀ◎ǀ No meals ✢ 1:B1.*

NIGHTLIFE AND PERFORMING ARTS

Local publications *Los Angeles* magazine (⊕ *www.la.com*) and *LA Weekly* (⊕ *www.laweekly.com*) are great places to discover what's happening in Los Angeles. Lifestyle websites UrbanDaddy (⊕ *www.urbandaddy.com/home/la*) and Flavorpill (⊕ *www.flavorpill.com/losangeles*) do a good job of keeping track of the latest nightlife events and recently opened bars and clubs.

5

NIGHTLIFE

The focus of nightlife once centered on the Sunset Strip, with its multitude of bars, rock clubs, and dance spots, but more neighborhoods are competing with each other and forcing the nightlife scene to evolve. Although the Strip can be a worthwhile trip, other areas of the city are catching people's attention. Downtown Los Angeles, for instance, is becoming a destination in its own right, drawing cocktail connoisseurs at Seven Grand and rooftop revelers at the Standard.

Parking can be a pain if you're the type who insists on circling the block until you find a space. Most neighborhoods near party-heavy areas like West Hollywood require residential parking permits, so sometimes you're better off with a garage or valet parking. Either option costs from $5 to $20.

DOWNTOWN

BARS

Fodor'sChoice
★
The Standard, Downtown L.A. With a backdrop of city skyline, the rooftop bar of The Standard, Downtown L.A. is a longtime favorite. Where else can you find drinks, dancing, a tempting swimming pool, and waterbeds (yes, waterbeds)? It's easy to spend the whole evening here—which is probably a good idea, considering the lengthy weekend lines. The west side of the roof is an enclosed *Biergarten* where you can order food. You can play a game of Ping-Pong at SPiN Standard on the mezzanine. Expect to pay a $20 cover charge on Friday and Saturday after 7 pm. ✉ *550 S. Flower St., at 6th St., Downtown* ☎ *213/892–8080* ⊕ *www.standardhotels.com.*

HOLLYWOOD

BARS

Fodor'sChoice
★
Musso & Frank Grill. The prim and proper vibe of this old-school steak house won't appeal to those looking for a raucous night out, but its appeal lies more in its history and sturdy drinks. Established in 1919, its dark wood decor, red tuxedo–clad waiters, and bartenders of great skill can easily shuttle you back to its Hollywood heyday when Marilyn Monroe, F. Scott Fitzgerald, and Greta Garbo used to hang around sipping martinis. ✉ *6667 Hollywood Blvd., Hollywood* ☎ *323/467–7788* ⊕ *mussoandfrank.com.*

Three Clubs. Whether its claim of being the area's first martini bar lounge is true or not, this bar that's been around since the 1940s takes its martinis and other cocktails seriously. The focus is on fresh and local ingredients for all the cocktails. There's a small cover charge to watch the comedy and burlesque shows presented on the stage in the back, but if you just want to drink in the front room, it's free. Don't be surprised by all the well-coiffed young people hanging about. ✉ *1123 Vine St., Hollywood* ☎ *323/462–6441* ⊕ *www.threeclubs.com.*

Yamashiro Hollywood. Modeled after a mansion in Kyoto, this Japanese place with a hillside perch has spectacular koi ponds and gardens, as well as sweeping views of Hollywood's twinkling lights. Additional lures here include the tasty, if pricey, food and delicious drinks. ■ TIP→ **The**

mandatory valet parking costs $9. ⊠ *1999 N. Sycamore Ave., Hollywood* ☎ *323/466–5125* ⊕ *www.yamashirohollywood.com.*

CLUBS

Boardner's. This neighborhood bar has been around for decades, and its dim lighting and leather booths give it a well-worn feel. Thanks to its location a half-block off Hollywood Boulevard, there aren't many tourists here—Boardner's draws a local crowd and the occasional celeb. The adjoining dance floor now has its own entrance and cover charge. Even after more than a decade and a half in this space, the Saturday Goth night remains popular. ⊠ *1652 N. Cherokee Ave., Hollywood* ☎ *323/462–9621* ⊕ *www.boardners.com.*

COMEDY

Groundlings Theatre. The improv and sketch comedy troupe the Groundlings has been entertaining audiences for 40 years, with famous alums often turning up in films and on television. *Saturday Night Live* snagged Will Ferrell, Will Forte, and Kristin Wiig from here, to name a few. Shows often sell out from Wednesday to Sunday; cover charges run from $10 to $20. ⊠ *7307 Melrose Ave., Hollywood* ☎ *323/934–4747* ⊕ *www.groundlings.com.*

Upright Citizens Brigade. The L.A. offshoot of New York's famous troupe continues its tradition of sketch comedy and improv with weekly shows like "Facebook" (where the audience's online profiles are mined for material). UCB's shows attract celebrity guest stars from time to time, along with a rotating cast of regulars that includes *30 Rock*'s Jack McBrayer and *The League*'s Paul Scheer. The crew has another theater on Sunset. ⊠ *5919 Franklin Ave., Hollywood* ☎ *323/908–8702* ⊕ *www. ucbtheatre.com.*

LIVE MUSIC

Avalon. This multitasking art deco venue offers both live music and club nights because, well, why not? The killer sound system, cavernous space, and multiple bars make it a perfect venue for both. The club is best-known for its DJs, who often spin well past the 2 am cutoff for drinks. The crowd can be a mixed bag, depending on the night, but if you're looking to dance, you likely won't be disappointed. Upstairs is **Bardot**, a loungier version of Avalon with its own musical offerings. ⊠ *1735 N. Vine St., Hollywood* ☎ *323/462–8900* ⊕ *www. avalonhollywood.com.*

Fodor's Choice ★ **El Floridita.** Although the exterior might not look like much, El Floridita is a popular live salsa music spot on Monday, Friday, and Saturday, with dancers ranging from enthusiasts to those just trying to keep up. There's a $10 cover to listen to the band, although admission is free with dinner. Reservations are recommended to guarantee a table. ⊠ *1253 N. Vine St., Hollywood* ☎ *323/871–8612* ⊕ *www.elfloridita.com.*

Largo. The welcoming vibe of this venue attracts big-name performers who treat its stage as their home base in Los Angeles. Standouts include the musician and music producer Jon Brion, who often appears here with special drop-in guests (Fiona Apple and Andrew Bird, to name two). Comedians Sarah Silverman and Patton Oswalt each host a monthly comedy show. Bring cash for drinks in the Little Room before the show. ✉ *366 N. La Cienega Blvd., Hollywood* ☎ *310/855–0350* ⊕ *www.largo-la.com.*

BARS

The Abbey. Don't let the church theme scare you off: this club's fun atmosphere makes it a central gathering point for West Hollywood. Most folks partying in the area often wind up here at one point or another, whether for drinking or dancing (or even a champagne brunch the next morning). The patio, with its new retractable roof, is perfection both day and night, with music keeping everyone in an upbeat mood. ✉ *692 N. Robertson Blvd., West Hollywood* ☎ *310/289–8410* ⊕ *www. abbeyfoodandbar.com.*

Rainbow Bar & Grill. Its location next door to a long-running music venue, the Roxy, helped cement this bar and restaurant's status as a legendary watering hole for musicians (as well as their entourages and groupies). The Who, Guns N' Roses, Poison, Kiss—and many others—have all passed through the doors. Expect a $5 to $10 cover, but you'll get the money back in drink tickets or a food discount. ✉ *9015 Sunset Blvd., West Hollywood* ☎ *310/278–4232* ⊕ *www.rainbowbarandgrill.com.*

The Standard. Summer weekend pool parties are downright notorious at the Standard Hollywood. A cushy spot among the party places on Sunset Boulevard, the Pool Deck has DJs at the ready to welcome the masses. Wednesday brings live acoustic music—a definite contrast to the weekend scene. ✉ *The Standard Hollywood, 8300 Sunset Blvd., West Hollywood* ☎ *323/650–9090* ⊕ *www.standardhotels.com.*

CLUBS

Rage. The various events at this gay bar and dance club draw different crowds—show queens for Broadway musical sing-alongs, drag queens (and more show queens) for the Dreamgirls Revue, half-nude chiseled-bodied men for Fetch Tuesdays and Thursday Night College Night. There's lots of eye candy, even more so on weekends. ✉ *8911 Santa Monica Blvd., West Hollywood* ☎ *310/652–7055* .

COMEDY

Comedy Store. Three stages give seasoned and unseasoned comedians a place to perform and try out new material, with performers such as Louis C.K. and Sarah Silverman dropping by just for fun. The front bar along Sunset Boulevard is a popular hangout after or between shows, oftentimes with that night's comedians mingling with fans. ✉ *8433 Sunset Blvd., West Hollywood* ☎ *323/650–6268* ⊕ *www.thecomedy store.com.*

Improv. Standup comics have been making audiences at the Improv laugh for years. Wednesday's ComedyJuice is popular with locals, while weekend shows draw out-of-towners to see better-known comedians. The cover charge runs from $10 to $30. ✉ *8162 Melrose Ave., West Hollywood* ☎ *323/651–2583* ⊕ *www.improv.com.*

Laugh Factory. Top standup comics appear at this Sunset Boulevard mainstay, often working out the kinks in new material in advance of national tours. Stars such as Kevin Hart and Tim Allen sometimes drop by unannounced, and Kevin Nealon puts on a monthly show. Midnight Madness on the weekends is extremely popular, with comics performing more daring sets. ⊠ *8001 Sunset Blvd., West Hollywood* ☎ *323/656–1336* ⊕ *www.laughfactory.com* 🎫 *$20.*

LIVE MUSIC

The Troubadour. The intimate vibe of the Troubadour helps make this club a favorite with music fans. This music venue has been open since 1957, and has a storied past. These days, the eclectic lineup is still attracting the crowds, with the focus mostly on rock, indie, and folk music. Those looking for drinks can imbibe at the adjacent bar. ⊠ *9081 Santa Monica Blvd., West Hollywood* ⊕ *www.troubadour.com.*

Viper Room. This club's been around for more than 20 years, and its rock and alternative shows still attract a crowd. The cover charge usually runs around $15 but can go higher, depending on the act. ⊠ *8852 W. Sunset Blvd., West Hollywood* ☎ *310/358–1881* ⊕ *www.viperroom.com.*

Whisky A Go-Go. The hardcore metal and rock scene is alive and well at the legendary Whisky A Go-Go, where Janis Joplin, Led Zeppelin, Alice Cooper, Van Halen, the Doors (briefly the house band), and Frank Zappa all played. On the Strip for more than five decades, the Whisky still favors underground acts. ⊠ *8901 Sunset Blvd., West Hollywood* ☎ *310/652–4202* ⊕ *www.whiskyagogo.com.*

ECHO PARK AND SILVER LAKE

BARS

Cha Cha Lounge. This place's decor—part tiki hut, part tacky party palace—shouldn't work, but it does. An import from Seattle, its cheap drinks, foosball tables, and jovial atmosphere make it a natural party scene. It draws a hipster crowd, which can be good or bad, depending on whom you ask. ⊠ *2375 Glendale Blvd., Silver Lake* ☎ *323/660–7595* ⊕ *www.chachalounge.com.*

Tiki-Ti. The cozy feel of this Polynesian-theme bar is due in part to its small size—12 seats at the bar, plus a few tables along one side. Open since 1961, it serves strong rum drinks that draw crowds on the weekend. Don't be surprised to find a line outside. ⊠ *4427 Sunset Blvd., Silver Lake* ☎ *323/669–9381* ⊕ *www.tiki-ti.com.*

LIVE MUSIC

The Echo. This favorite spot in Echo Park showcases up-and-coming bands, with soul or reggae dance nights and DJ mash-up sessions rounding out the calendar. The basement level Echoplex has twice the space, so it can book bigger names. ⊠ *1154 Glendale Blvd., Echo Park* ☎ *213/413–8200* ⊕ *www.attheecho.com*

the **Echoplex.** the Echoplex books bigger national tours and events. ⊠ *1822 Sunset Blvd., Echo Park* ☎ *213/413–8200* ⊕ *www.attheecho.com.*

The Satellite. This venue hosts a variety of bands, mostly indie rockers. Monday nights are free, and feature exciting up-and-coming acts. Cover charges on other days range from $8 to $15. ⊠ *1717 Silver Lake Blvd., Silver Lake* ☎ *323/661–4380* ⊕ *www.thesatellitela.com.*

Silverlake Lounge. The lounge presents indie, rock, and classical (yep) performers. It's not really the space to see bands you might have heard of, but if you're patient you might discover one that could hit the big time. The cover charge can reach $8. ⊠ *2906 Sunset Blvd., Silver Lake* ☎ *323/663–9636* ⊕ *www.thesilverlakelounge.com.*

SANTA MONICA
LIVE MUSIC
McCabe's Guitar Shop. This famous guitar shop is known for its weekend concerts. You may not recognize all the musicians who perform here, but the shows sell out quickly. Don't expect food or drinks (it's a music shop, after all). ⊠ *3101 Pico Blvd., Santa Monica* ☎ *310/828–4497* ⊕ *www.mccabes.com.*

PERFORMING ARTS

CONCERT HALLS

Fodor's Choice ★ **Dorothy Chandler Pavilion.** Opera and ballet fans flock to the Dorothy Chandler Pavilion, and with good reason: the performers here are always top-notch, and there's a good balance between new and classical works. L.A. Opera continues as the long-running resident company, and touring ballet troupes perform here as well. Now more than a half-century old, the hall looks as elegant as ever, from the requisite theater curtain to the large-scale crystal chandeliers and the art collection. Ticket holders can attend free talks that take place an hour before opera performances. Music Director James Conlon generally hosts the talks, although other scholars sometimes speak. ■TIP➜ **Reservations for the talks aren't required, but it's wise to arrive early because space is limited.** ⊠ *135 N. Grand Ave., Downtown* ☎ *213/972–7211* ⊕ *www. musiccenter.org.*

Greek Theatre. Outstanding musical acts of all styles perform at the outdoor Greek Theatre. Taking advantage of the pleasant Los Angeles weather from May through November, acts such as Beck, the Flaming Lips, and Chicago have all graced the stage. The 5,800-seat amphitheater is in Griffith Park. You may encounter slow preshow traffic on the way to the venue, but you'll also venture past beautiful Hollywood Hills homes and park foliage. Pay lots are available for parking, but wear comfortable shoes and expect to do some walking, as some of the lots require a fairly long trek. ⊠ *2700 N. Vermont Ave., Los Feliz* ☎ *323/665–5857* ⊕ *www.greektheatrela.com.*

Fodor's Choice ★ **Hollywood Bowl.** For those seeking a quintessential Los Angeles experience, a concert on a summer night at the Bowl, the city's iconic outdoor venue, is unsurpassed. The Bowl has presented world-class performers since it opened in 1920. The L.A. Philharmonic plays here from June to September; its performances and other events draw large crowds. Parking is limited near the venue, but there are additional remote parking locations served by shuttles. You can bring food and drink to any event, which Angelenos often do, though you can only bring alcohol when the LA Phil, as the orchestra is known, is performing. (Bars sell alcohol at all events, and there are dining options.) It's wise to bring a jacket even if daytime temperatures have been warm—the Bowl can get quite chilly at night. ■ TIP→ Visitors can sometimes watch the LA Phil practice for free, usually on a weekday; call ahead for times. ⊠ *2301 Highland Ave., Hollywood* ☎ *323/850–2000* ⊕ *www.hollywoodbowl.com.*

Microsoft Theater. Hosting a variety of concerts and big-name awards shows—the Emmys, American Music Awards, and the BET Awards—this theater and the surrounding L.A. Live complex are a draw for those looking for a fun night out. The emphasis the building places on acoustics and versatile seating arrangements means that all seats are good, whether you're at an intimate John Legend concert or the People's Choice Awards. Outside, the L.A. Live complex hosts restaurants and attractions, including the Grammy Museum, to keep patrons entertained before, after, and even when not attending a concert. ⊠ *777 Chick Hearn Ct., Downtown* ☎ *213/763–6030* ⊕ *www. microsofttheater.com.*

Shrine Auditorium. Since opening in 1926, the auditorium has hosted nearly every major awards show—including the Oscars, Emmys, and Grammys—at one point or another. These days the venue and adjacent Expo Hall present everything from concerts to cheerleading competitions. The Shrine's Moorish Revival–style architecture is an event in itself. ⊠ *665 W. Jefferson Blvd., Downtown* ☎ *213/748–5116* ⊕ *www. shrineauditorium.com.*

FILM

Watching movies here isn't merely an efficient way to kill time, but it's an *event*. With theaters this close to the movie studios, it's not unusual for major directors or actors to participate in a post-film discussion. Whether it's a first-run film or a revival, the show will likely be worth the trip out.

The American Cinemathèque at the Aero and Egyptian Theatres. Film enthusiasts will enjoy the roster of movies put on by the American Cinemathèque, with classic and independent films screening at two theaters, the Aero and the Egyptian. Expect everything from Hitchcock thrillers to anime from Hayao Miyazaki, along with occasional question-and-answer sessions with directors and actors following film screenings. The Egyptian Theatre, in Hollywood, has the distinction of hosting the first-ever movie premiere, back in 1922 when it opened. Its Egyptian-theme courtyard and columns have been restored to preserve its history. The Aero Theatre, in Santa Monica, opened in 1940. ⊠ *6712 Hollywood Blvd., Hollywood* ☎ *323/466–3456* ⊕ *www.americancinema theque.com.*

Aero Theatre. This Santa Monica–based American Cinematheque theater first opened in 1940 and shows movies on a big screen. ⊠ *1328 Montana Ave., Santa Monica* ☎ *323/466–3456* ⊕ *www. americancinematheque.com.*

Fodor's Choice
★
ArcLight. This big multiplex's screens include the historically important Cinerama Dome, that impossible-to-miss golf ball–looking structure built in 1963 to showcase widescreen Cinerama films. The ArcLight attempts to problem-solve the issues associated with going to the movies, and with assigned seating for movies, space for parking, a shopping area, a restaurant, and a bar, the complex has a lot going for

it. The events calendar is worth paying attention to, as directors and actors often drop by to chat with audiences. Leonardo DiCaprio, for example, stopped in for a Q&A about his role in *The Wolf of Wall Street*. ■TIP➔ Evening shows on the weekend feature "21+" shows, at which moviegoers can bring alcoholic beverages into the screening rooms. ⊠ *6360 Sunset Blvd., Hollywood* ☎ *323/464–4226* ⊕ *www. arclightcinemas.com.*

Cinefamily at The Silent Movie Theatre. Although the name may imply that only silent movies show here, this theater has bloomed beyond that with its schedule of quirky indie films and other happenings. Regular events include podcast recordings by comedians Doug Benson and Greg Proops and Friday-night Heavy Midnites movie screenings of offbeat films. Silent films run on the first Wednesday of every month, though that's subject to change. ⊠ *611 N. Fairfax Ave., Fairfax District* ☎ *323/655–2510* ⊕ *www.cinefamily.org.*

THEATER

Center Theatre Group. Each of the three venues that comprise the Center Theatre Group—the Ahmanson, the Taper, and the Douglas—has its own style of shows, from premieres of plays written by notables like Culture Clash to touring productions of Broadway sell-outs like *Matilda: The Musical.* ⊠ *135 N. Grand Ave., Downtown* ☎ *213/972–7211* ⊕ *www.centertheatregroup.org*

Ahmanson Theatre. The largest of L.A.'s Center Group's three theaters is Ahmanson Theatre in Downtown Los Angeles with a varying audience capacity of 1,600 to 2,000, and a number of larger-scale classic revivals, dramas, musicals, and comedies happen here. Recent musical *Leap of Faith* had its world premiere at Ahmanson Theatre and went on to earn a Tony Award nomination in 2012. ⊠ *135 N. Grand Ave., Downtown* ☎ *213/628–2772* ⊕ *www.centertheatregroup.org.*

Mark Taper Forum. The focus at Mark Taper Forum, next door to the Ahmanson Theater in Downtown, is on dramas and comedies. Plenty of shows that premiere here go on to Broadway and off-Broadway theaters (a number of Pulitzer Prize–winning plays have also been developed here). ⊠ *135 N. Grand Ave., Downtown* ☎ *213/628–2772* ⊕ *www. centertheatregroup.org.*

Kirk Douglas Theatre. This Culver City theater, which stages new, modern works, is the smallest venue of the group at 317 seats. It uses its small size to its advantage by hosting more intimate workshops and readings. ⊠ *9820 W. Washington Blvd., Culver City* ☎ *213/628–2772* ⊕ *www.centertheatregroup.org.*

Geffen Playhouse. Well-known actors are sometimes on the bill at the Geffen, and plays launched here have wound up on Broadway. Hershey Felder, the city's favorite musical-theater performer, often debuts new work at the playhouse, and with two stages hosting world premieres and critically acclaimed works, there's nearly always something compelling to watch. ■TIP➔ Free events are frequently put on for ticket holders, including Wine Down Sundays, featuring music and wine sampling before Sunday evening shows. ⊠ *10886 Le Conte Ave., Westwood* ☎ *310/208–5454* ⊕ *www.geffenplayhouse.com.*

Ricardo Montalbán Theatre. Plays, musicals, and concerts all happen at this midsize theater, mostly focusing on Latin culture. The Montalbán collaborates with local arts groups and, having a rooftop basketball court, hosts the occasional sports-themed event. ⊠ *1615 N. Vine St., Hollywood* ☎ *323/871–2420* ⊕ *www.themontalban.com.*

Pantages Theatre. For the grand-scale theatrics of a Broadway show, such as *The Lion King* and *The Book of Mormon,* the 2,703-seat Pantages is one of the first places to check out. ⊠ *6233 Hollywood Blvd., Hollywood* ☎ *800/982–2787* ⊕ *www.hollywoodpantages.com.*

SPORTS AND THE OUTDOORS

BASEBALL

Dodgers. The Dodgers take on their National League rivals at one of major league baseball's most comfortable ballparks, Dodger Stadium. ⊠ *Dodger Stadium, 1000 Elysian Park Ave., exit off I–110, Downtown* ☎ *323/224–1507* ⊕ *www.dodgers.com.*

Los Angeles Angels of Anaheim. The Angels often contend for the top slot in the Western Division of pro baseball's American League. ⊠ *Angel Stadium of Anaheim, 2000 E. Gene Autry Way, Anaheim* ☎ *714/940–2000* ⊕ *www.angelsbaseball.com.*

BASKETBALL

L.A.'s pro basketball teams play at the Staples Center.

Los Angeles Clippers. L.A.'s "other" pro basketball team, the Clippers, was formerly an easy ticket, but these days the club routinely sells out its home games. ⊠ *Staples Center, 1111 S. Figueroa St., Downtown* ☎ *213/742–7100* ⊕ *www.nba.com/clippers.*

Los Angeles Lakers. The team of pro-basketball champions Magic and Kareem is gone, and Shaq and Kobe have slipped in recent years, but games are still intense, especially if the Lakers are playing their NBA rivals, the Celtics, Clippers, or Spurs. ⊠ *Staples Center, 1111 S. Figueroa St., Downtown* ☎ *310/426–6000* ⊕ *www.nba.com/lakers.*

Los Angeles Sparks. The women's pro basketball team has made it to the WNBA playoffs a dozen times in the past two decades. ⊠ *Staples Center, 1111 S. Figueroa St., Downtown* ☎ *310/426–6031* ⊕ *www. sparks.wnba.com.*

SHOPPING

DOWNTOWN

Downtown L.A. is dotted with ethnic neighborhoods (Olvera Street, Chinatown, Koreatown, Little Tokyo) and several large, open-air shopping venues (the Fashion District, the Flower Market, and the Jewelry District).

The Santa Monica Pier is packed with fun diversions and hosts free concerts in summer.

SHOPPING STREETS AND DISTRICTS

Fashion District. Although this 100-block hub of the West Coast fashion industry is mainly a wholesale market, more than 1,000 independent stores sell to the general public. The massive **Flower District,** featuring the country's largest wholesale flower market, and the **Fabric District** are also here. Bargaining is expected, but note that most sales are cash-only. Dressing rooms are scarce, as are parking spaces on weekends. ⊠ *Roughly between I–10 and 7th St., and S. San Pedro and S. Main Sts., Downtown* ⊕ *www.fashiondistrict.org.*

Santee Alley. Situated in the Fashion District, Santee Alley is known for back-alley deals on knock-offs of designer sunglasses, jewelry, handbags, shoes, and clothing. Be prepared to haggle, and don't lose sight of your wallet. Weekend crowds can be overwhelming, but there's plenty of street food to keep your energy up. ⊠ *Santee St. and Maple Ave. from Olympic Blvd. to 11th St., Downtown* ⊕ *www.thesanteealley.com.*

Jewelry District. Filled with bargain hunters, these crowded sidewalks resemble a slice of Manhattan. Expect to save big on everything from wedding bands to sparkling belt buckles. The more upscale stores are along Hill Street between 6th and 7th streets. There's a parking garage next door on Broadway. ⊠ *Between Olive St. and Broadway from 5th to 8th St., Downtown.*

Fodor'sChoice
★

Olvera Street. Historic buildings line this redbrick walkway overhung with grape vines. At dozens of clapboard stalls you can browse south-of-the-border goods—leather sandals, woven blankets, and devotional candles, as well as cheap toys and souvenirs—and sample outstanding tacos. With the musicians and cafés providing the soundtrack, the area is constantly lively. ⊠ *Between Cesar Chavez Ave. and Arcadia St., Downtown* ⊕ *www.olvera-street.com.*

HOLLYWOOD AND THE STUDIOS

From records to lingerie to movie memorabilia, this area is a mixed bag when it comes to shopping.

BOOKS AND MUSIC

Fodor's Choice ★ **Amoeba Records.** Touted as the "World's Largest Independent Record Store," Amoeba is a playground for music-lovers, with a knowledgeable staff and a focus on local artists. Catch in-store appearances by artists and bands that play sold-out shows at venues down the road. There's a rich stock of new and used CDs and DVDs, LPs, and 45s, an impressive cache of collectibles, and walls filled with concert posters. ⊠ *6400 W. Sunset Blvd., at Cahuenga Blvd., Hollywood* ☎ *323/245–6400* ⊕ *www. amoeba.com.*

CLOTHING

Lost & Found. The owner of this place describes it as "Alice in Wonderland meets Jimi Hendrix." It's actually six storefronts selling clothing for men, women, and children; brass jewelry from France; African silk batiks; and other goodies from around the world. There's also a Santa Monica location. ⊠ *6320 Yucca St., Hollywood* ☎ *323/856–5872.*

Hollywood & Highland. Full of designer shops (BCBGMaxAzria, Louis Vuitton) and chain stores (Victoria's Secret, Fossil, and Sephora), this entertainment complex is a huge tourist magnet. The design pays tribute to the city's film legacy, with a grand staircase leading up to a pair of three-story-tall stucco elephants, a nod to the 1916 movie *Intolerance.* Pause at the entrance arch, called Babylon Court, which frames a picture-perfect view of the Hollywood Sign. On the second level, next to the Dolby Theatre, is a visitor information center with maps, brochures, and a multilingual staff. The streets nearby provide the setting for Sunday's Hollywood Farmers Market, where you're likely to spot a celebrity or two picking up fresh produce or stopping to pick up breakfast from the food vendors. ⊠ *Hollywood Blvd. and Highland Ave., Hollywood* ☎ *323/817–0220* ⊕ *www.hollywoodandhighland.com.*

BEVERLY HILLS AND THE WESTSIDE

BEVERLY HILLS

The shops of Beverly Hills, particularly Rodeo Drive, are a big draw for window-shopping, and leave visitors awestruck by L.A.'s glitz and excess. It's easy to stroll this area on foot, stopping into big-name luxury jewelers and department stores such as Cartier and Barneys New York.

BEAUTY

MAC. This beauty emporium is what's called a "professional" store, with lines of products not available at the chain's regular outlets. This is also a place to arrange for makeup lessons or all-out makeovers, or even to prepare for red carpet or other special events. The artists here are fashion show and award-season veterans. ⊠ *133 N. Robertson Blvd., West Hollywood* ☎ *310/271–9137* ⊕ *www.maccosmetics.com.*

BOOKS

Taschen. Philippe Starck designed the Taschen space to evoke a cool 1920s Parisian salon—a perfect showcase for the publisher's coffee-table books about architecture, travel, culture, and (often racy) photography. A suspended glass-cube gallery in back hosts art exhibits and has limited edition books. ⊠ *354 N. Beverly Dr., Beverly Hills* ☎ *310/274-4300* ⊕ *www.taschen.com.*

CLOTHING

Theodore. One of the area's few indie clothing stores, Theodore is a haven for the young and perhaps rebellious to pick up James Perse T-shirts, jeans of all labels, and hoodies. Upstairs, browse the avant-garde designer duds from names like Ann Demeulemeester and Jean Paul Gaultier. Next door, Theodore Man has faux-scruffy leather jackets and other items for the guys. ⊠ *336 N. Camden Dr., Beverly Hills* ☎ *310/276-0663* ⊕ *www.theodorebh.com.*

Tory Burch. Preppy, stylish, and colorful clothes appropriate for a road trip to Palm Springs or a flight to Palm Beach fill this flagship boutique. ⊠ *142 S. Robertson Blvd., Beverly Hills* ☎ *310/248-2612* ⊕ *www.tory burch.com.*

DEPARTMENT STORES

Barneys New York. This is truly an impressive one-stop shop for high fashion. Deal hunters will appreciate the Co-op section, which introduces indie designers before they make it big. Shop for beauty products, shoes, and accessories on the first floor, then wind your way up the staircase for couture. Keep your eyes peeled for fabulous and/or famous folks spearing salads at Fred's on the top floor. ⊠ *9570 Wilshire Blvd., Beverly Hills* ☎ *310/276-4400* ⊕ *www.barneys.com.*

MALLS AND SHOPPING CENTERS

Beverly Center. This is one of the more traditional malls you can find in L.A., with eight levels of stores, including Macy's, Bloomingdale's, and the luxury retailer Henri Bendel. Fashion is the biggest draw, and there's a little something for everyone, from D&G to H&M, and many shops in the midrange, including Banana Republic, Club Monaco, and Coach. Look for inexpensive accessories at Aldo or edgy dresses at Maje; there's even a destination for the race-car obsessed at the Ferrari Store. Inside there are casual dining choices at the top-floor food court, and several popular chain restaurants are outside on the ground floor. ⊠ *8500 Beverly Blvd., West Hollywood* ☎ *310/854-0071* ⊕ *www. beverlycenter.com.*

SHOPPING NEIGHBORHOODS

Rodeo Drive. One of L.A.'s biggest tourist attractions, Rodeo Drive (pronounced Ro-DAY-o) is lined with shops featuring the biggest names in fashion. Along this pie slice of luxury bordered by Santa Monica and Wilshire boulevards and Beverly Drive, you'll see well-coiffed, well-heeled ladies toting multiple packages to their Mercedeses and paparazzi staking out street corners. Steep price tags on designer labels make it a "just looking" experience for many residents and tourists alike. ⊠ *Beverly Hills* ⊕ *www.rodeodrive-bh.com.*

WEST HOLLYWOOD

This is prime shopping real estate, with everything from bridal couture design shops to furnishing stores sharing sidewalk space along posh streets like Melrose Place and Robertson Boulevard. It's also worth strolling West 3rd Street, which is lined with independent but affordable boutiques and several of the city's hottest restaurants and cafés.

CLOTHING

Fodor's Choice ★ **American Rag Cie.** Half the store features new clothing from established and emerging labels, and the other side is stocked with well-preserved vintage clothing organized by color and style. You'll also find plenty of shoes and accessories being picked over by the hippest of Angelenos. ⊠ *150 S. La Brea Ave., Beverly–La Brea* ☎ *323/935–3154* ⊕ *www. amrag.com*

Fodor's Choice ★ **Fred Segal.** The ivy-covered building and security guards in the parking lot might tip you off that this is *the* place to be. Visit during the lunch hour to stargaze at the super-trendy café. This L.A. landmark is subdivided into small boutiques purveying everything from couture clothing to skateboard wear. The entertainment industry's fashion fiends are addicted to these exclusive creations, many from cult designers just beginning to dazzle the masses. ⊠ *8118 Melrose Ave., near West Hollywood* ☎ *323/651–4129* ⊕ *www.fredsegal.com.*

James Perse. These soft cotton T-shirts (and sweaters and fleece pullovers) are quintessentially L.A. Find them here in an immaculate, gallerylike space with sleek furnishings. ⊠ *8914 Melrose Ave., West Hollywood* ☎ *310/276–7277* ⊕ *www.jamesperse.com.*

Fodor's Choice ★ **Maxfield.** A modern concrete structure holds one of L.A.'s too-cool-for-school high-fashion sources, with sleek-as-can-be offerings from Chanel, Saint Laurent, Balmain, and Rick Owen. It's for serious shoppers (or gawkers) only. ⊠ *8825 Melrose Ave., at Robertson Blvd., West Hollywood* ☎ *310/274–8800* ⊕ *www.maxfieldla.com.*

Stacey Todd. All wood, white, and natural light, chic Stacy Todd has a denim bar stocked with Rag & Bone, DSquared, and other brands. Classic, menswear-inspired clothing by luxe labels, including Helmut Lang and Band of Outsiders, pair with bohemian-tough accessories like Isabel Marant boots. Candles, coffee-table books, and bath and body products are among the lifestyle items. A second store is in Studio City. ⊠ *454 N. Robertson Blvd., West Hollywood* ☎ *310/659–8633* ⊕ *www. staceytoddboutique.com.*

MALLS AND SHOPPING CENTERS

Fodor's Choice ★ **Farmers Market.** The granddaddy of L.A. markets dates back to 1935, and the amazing array of clapboard stalls (selling everything from candy to hot sauce, just-picked fruit to fresh lamb), wacky regulars, and a United Nations of food choices must be experienced to be appreciated. Employees from the nearby CBS studios mingle with hungover clubbers and elderly locals at dozens of eateries, movie theaters, and shops under one huge roof. The green trolley shuttles visitors between the Farmers Market and the nearby Grove. ⊠ *6333 W. 3rd St., at Fairfax Ave., Fairfax District* ☎ *323/933–9211 Farmers Market* ⊕ *www.farmers marketla.com.*

5

SANTA MONICA AND THE BEACHES

The breezy beachside communities of Santa Monica and Venice are ideal for leisurely shopping. Scads of tourists (and some locals) gravitate to Santa Monica Place and the Third Street Promenade, a popular pedestrians-only shopping area that is within walking distance of the beach and historic Santa Monica Pier. ■TIP➔ Parking in Santa Monica is next to impossible on Wednesday, when some streets are blocked off for the farmers' market, but there are several parking structures with free parking for an hour or two.

BEAUTY

Strange Invisible Perfumes. A custom-made fragrance by perfumer Alexandra Balahoutis might run you thousands of dollars, but you can pick up ready-made scents, such as citrusy Fair Verona and sultry Black Rosette, for much less. Her exquisitely designed shop is both modern and romantic. ⊠ *1138 Abbot Kinney Blvd., Venice* ☏ *310/314–1505* ⊕ *www.siperfumes.com.*

BOOKS AND MUSIC

Arcana. The store, a treasure for art lovers, stocks new, rare, and out-of-print books on architecture, design, and fashion—with an especially impressive selection on photography. ⊠ *8675 W. Washington Blvd., Santa Monica* ☏ *310/458–1499* ⊕ *www.arcanabooks.com.*

CLOTHING

Heist. Owner Nilou Ghodsi sends thank-you notes to customers and employs a sales staff that is friendly and helpful but not overbearing. The focus at this airy boutique is on elegantly edgy separates from American designers like Nili Lotan and Gary Graham, as well as hard-to-find French and Italian designers. ⊠ *1100 Abbot Kinney Blvd., Venice* ☏ *310/450–6531* ⊕ *shopheist.com.*

MALLS AND SHOPPING CENTERS

Malibu Lumberyard. This shopping complex is your entrée into California beachfront living. Emblematic Malibu lifestyle stores include James Perse, Maxfield, and a too-chic J. Crew outpost. The playground and alfresco dining area make this a hub for beautiful starlets and their little ones. ⊠ *3939 Cross Creek Rd., Malibu* ⊕ *www.themalibulumberyard.com.*

PASADENA

BOOKS

Fodor's Choice ★

Vroman's Bookstore. Southern California's oldest and largest independent bookseller is justly famous for its great service. A newsstand, a café, and a stationery store add to the appeal. Some 400 author events annually, plus a kids' zone complete with play area, make this a truly outstanding destination. ⊠ *695 E. Colorado Blvd., Pasadena* ☏ *626/449–5320* ⊕ *www.vromansbookstore.com.*

THE CENTRAL COAST

From Ventura to Big Sur with
Channel Islands National Park

WELCOME TO THE CENTRAL COAST

TOP REASONS TO GO

★ **Incredible nature:** The wild and wonderful Central Coast is home to Channel Islands National Park, two national marine sanctuaries, state parks and beaches, and the rugged Los Padres National Forest.

★ **Edible bounty:** Land and sea provide enough fresh regional foods to satisfy the most sophisticated foodies—grapes, strawberries, seafood, olive oil, and much more. Get your fill at countless farmers' markets, wineries, and restaurants.

★ **Outdoor activities:** Kick back and revel in the California lifestyle. Surf, golf, kayak, hike, play tennis—or just hang out and enjoy the gorgeous scenery.

★ **Small-town charm, big-city culture:** With all the amazing cultural opportunities—museums, theater, music, and festivals—you might start thinking you're in L.A. or San Francisco.

★ **Wine tasting:** Central Coast wines earn high critical praise. Sample them in urban tasting rooms, dusty crossroads towns, and at high- and low-tech rural wineries.

1 Ventura County. Ventura is a classic California city with a thriving arts community, miles of beaches, and a vibrant harbor—the gateway to Channel Islands National Park. Home to 145 species of plants and animals found nowhere else on Earth, Channel Islands National Park encompasses five islands and a mile of surrounding ocean. Inland, tiny, artsy Ojai plays host to folks who want to golf, meditate, and commune with tony peers in an idyllic mountain setting.

Pacific Grove
Salinas
Monterey
SALINAS VALLEY
101
Carmel-by-the-Sea
Gonzales
SANTA LUCIA RANGE
Carmel Valley
G16
Soledad
1
Greenfield
Point Sur
Big Sur
Pfeiffer Point
King City
5
San Lucas
Lopez Point
Lucia
101
G18
PACIFIC COAST HWY
San Miguel
Point Piedras Blancas
San Simeon
Paso Robles
Cambria
46
Templeton
Atascadero
Harmony
Cayucos
4
58
PACIFIC OCEAN
Estero Bay
Morro Bay
1
Los Osos
San Luis Obispo
Pismo Beach
Avila Beach
Arroyo Grande
Grover Beach
Oceano
Guadalupe
Point Sal
1
Purisima Point
Lompoc
Point Arguello
Point Conception

2 Santa Barbara. Down-home surfers rub elbows with Hollywood celebrities in sunny, well-scrubbed Santa Barbara, 95 miles north of Los Angeles. Its Spanish-Mexican heritage is reflected in the architectural style of its mission, court-house, and many homes and public buildings.

3 Northern Santa Barbara County. Wineries, ranches, and small villages dominate the quintessen-tially Californian landscape here. The quaint Danish town of Solvang is worth a stop for its half-timber buildings, galleries, and bakeries.

4 San Luis Obispo County. Friendly college town San Luis Obispo serves as the hub of a burgeoning wine region that stretches nearly 100 miles from Pismo Beach north to Paso Robles; the 230-plus wineries here have earned reputations for high-quality vintages that rival those of Northern California.

5 Big Sur Coastline. Rugged cliffs meet the Pacific for more than 60 miles—one of the most scenic and dramatic drives in the world.

GETTING ORIENTED

The Central Coast region begins about 60 miles north of Los Angeles, near the seaside city of Ventura. North along the sinuous coastline from here lie the cities of Santa Barbara and San Luis Obispo, and beyond them the smaller towns of Morro Bay, Cambria, and Big Sur. The nearly 300-mile drive through this region, especially the sec-tion of Highway 1 from San Simeon to Big Sur, is one of the most scenic in the state.

6

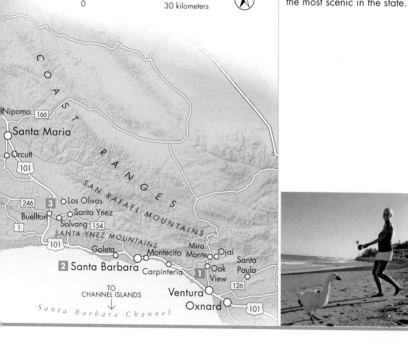

Updated by Cheryl Crabtree

Balmy weather, glorious beaches, crystal clear air, and serene landscapes have lured people to the Central Coast since prehistoric times. Today it's also known for its farm-fresh bounty, from grapes vintners craft into world-class wines to strawberries and other produce chefs incorporate into distinctive cuisine. The scenic variety along the Pacific coast is equally impressive—you'll see everything from dramatic cliffs and grass-tufted bluffs to wildlife estuaries and miles of dunes. It's an ideal place to relax, slow down, and appreciate the abundant natural beauty.

Offshore, a pristine national park and a vast marine sanctuary protect the wild, wonderful underwater resources of this incredible corner of the planet. But not all of the Central Coast's top attractions are natural: Ventura, Santa Barbara, and San Luis Obispo are filled with sparkling examples of Spanish-Mediterranean architecture, bustling shopping districts, and first-rate restaurants showcasing regional foods and wines.

PLANNING

WHEN TO GO

The Central Coast climate is mild year-round. If you like to swim in warmer (if still nippy) ocean waters, July and August are the best months to visit. Be aware that this is also high season. Fog often rolls in along the coastal areas in early summer; you'll need a jacket, especially after sunset, close to the shore. It usually rains from December through March. From April to early June and in early fall the weather is almost as fine as in high season, and the pace is less hectic.

GETTING HERE AND AROUND

AIR TRAVEL

Alaska Air, American/US Airways, and United fly to Santa Barbara Airport (SBA), 9 miles from downtown. United and US Airways provide service to San Luis Obispo County Regional Airport (SBP), 3 miles from downtown San Luis Obispo.

Santa Barbara Airbus shuttles travelers between Santa Barbara and Los Angeles for $50 one-way and $95 round-trip. The Santa Barbara Metropolitan Transit District Bus 11 ($1.75) runs every 30 minutes from the airport to the downtown transit center. A taxi between the airport and the hotel districts costs between $22 and $40.

Airport Contacts San Luis Obispo County Regional Airport ⊠ *903 Airport Dr., off Hwy. 227, San Luis Obispo* ☎ *805/781–5205* ⊕ *sloairport.com.* **Santa Barbara Airport** ⊠ *500 Fowler Rd., off U.S. 101 Exit 104B, Santa Barbara* ☎ *805/683–4011* ⊕ *flysba.com.* **Santa Barbara Airbus** ☎ *805/964–7759, 800/423–1618* ⊕ *www.sbairbus.com.* **Santa Barbara Metropolitan Transit District** ☎ *805/963–3366* ⊕ *sbmtd.gov.*

BUS TRAVEL

Greyhound provides service from Los Angeles and San Francisco to San Luis Obispo, Ventura, and Santa Barbara. Local transit companies serve these three cities and several smaller towns. Buses can be useful for visiting some urban sights, particularly in Santa Barbara; they're less so for rural ones.

Bus Contacts Greyhound ☎ *800/231–2222* ⊕ *www.greyhound.com.*

CAR TRAVEL

Driving is the easiest way to experience the Central Coast. U.S. 101 and Highway 1, which run north–south, are the main routes to and through the Central Coast from Los Angeles and San Francisco. Highly scenic Highway 1 hugs the coast, and U.S. 101 runs inland. Between Ventura County and northern Santa Barbara County, the two highways are the same road. Highway 1 again separates from U.S. 101 north of Gaviota, then rejoins the highway at Pismo Beach. Along any stretch where these two highways are separate, U.S. 101 is the quicker route.

The most dramatic section of the Central Coast is the 70 miles between San Simeon and Big Sur. The road is narrow and twisting, with a single lane in each direction. In fog or rain the drive can be downright nerve-racking; in wet seasons mudslides can close portions of the road.

Other routes into the Central Coast include Highway 46 and Highway 33, which head, respectively, west and south from Interstate 5 near Bakersfield.

Road Conditions Caltrans ☎ *800/427–7623, 888/836–0866 Hwy. 1 visitor hotline (Cambria north to Carmel)* ⊕ *www.dot.ca.gov.*

TRAIN TRAVEL

The Amtrak *Coast Starlight,* which runs between Los Angeles and Seattle via Oakland, stops in Paso Robles, San Luis Obispo, Santa Barbara, and Oxnard. Amtrak runs several *Pacific Surfliner* trains and buses daily between San Luis Obispo, Santa Barbara, Los Angeles, and San Diego.

Metrolink Regional Rail Service trains connect Ventura and Oxnard with Los Angeles and points between.

Train Contacts Amtrak ☎ *800/872–7245* ⊕ *www.amtrak.com or www.amtrak california.com.* **Metrolink** ☎ *800/371–5465* ⊕ *metrolinktrains.com.*

RESTAURANTS

The cuisine in Ventura and Santa Barbara is every bit as eclectic as it is in California's bigger cities; fresh seafood is a standout. A foodie renaissance has overtaken the entire region from Ventura to Paso Robles, spawning dozens of restaurants touting locavore cuisine made with fresh organic produce and meats. Dining attire on the Central Coast is generally casual, though slightly dressy casual wear is the custom at pricier restaurants.

HOTELS

Expect to pay top dollar for rooms along the shore, especially in summer. Moderately priced hotels and motels do exist—most just a short drive inland from their higher-price counterparts. Make your reservations as early as possible, and take advantage of midweek specials to get the best rates. It's common for lodgings to require two-day minimum stays on holidays and some weekends, especially in summer, and to double rates during festivals and other events. *Hotel reviews have been shortened. For full information, visit Fodors.com.*

WHAT IT COSTS				
	$	**$$**	**$$$**	**$$$$**
Restaurants	under $16	$16–$22	$23–$30	over $30
Hotels	under $120	$120–$175	$176–$250	over $250

Restaurant prices are the average cost of a main course at dinner or, if dinner is not served, at lunch, excluding sales tax of 8%–8.25% (depending on location). Hotel prices are the lowest cost of a standard double room in high season, excluding service charges and 9%–12% occupancy tax.

TOURS

Many tour companies will pick you up at your hotel or central locations; ask about this when booking.

Cloud Climbers Jeep and Wine Tours. This outfit conducts trips in open-air, six-passenger jeeps to the Santa Barbara/Santa Ynez mountains and Wine Country. Tour options include wine tasting, mountain, sunset, and a discovery adventure for families. The company also offers a four-hour All Around Ojai Tour and arranges horseback riding and trap-shooting tours. ☎ *805/646–3200* ⊕ *ccjeeps.com* ✉ *From $89.*

Grapeline Wine Tours. Wine and vineyard picnic tours in Paso Robles and the Santa Ynez Valley are Grapeline's specialty. ☎ *888/894–6379* ⊕ *gogrape.com* ✉ *From $109.*

Santa Barbara Wine Country Cycling Tours. The company leads half- and full-day tours of the Santa Ynez wine region, conducts hiking and cycling tours, and rents bicycles. ☎ *888/557–8687, 805/686–9490* ⊕ *winecountrycycling.com* ✉ *From $80.*

Stagecoach Wine Tours. Locally owned and operated, Stagecoach runs daily wine-tasting excursions through the Santa Ynez Valley in vans, minicoaches, and SUVs. ✉ *Solvang* ☏ *805/686–8347* ⊕ *winetours santaynez.com* ✉ *From $155.*

Sustainable Vine Wine Tours. This green-minded company specializes in eco-friendly Santa Ynez Valley wine tours in nine-passenger Mercedes Sprinter vans. Trips include tastings at limited-production wineries committed to sustainable practices. An organic picnic lunch is served. ☏ *805/698–3911* ⊕ *sustainablevine.com* ✉ *$150.*

VISITOR INFORMATION

Contacts Central Coast Tourism Council ⊕ *centralcoast-tourism.com.*

VENTURA COUNTY

Ventura County was first settled by the Chumash Indians. Spanish missionaries were the first Europeans to arrive, followed by Americans and other Europeans, who established towns, transportation networks, and highly productive farms. Since the 1920s, agriculture has been steadily replaced as the area's main industry—first by the oil business and more recently by tourism.

Accessible via boat or plane from Ventura and Santa Barbara, Channel Islands National Park is a series of five protected islands just 11 miles offshore where hiking, kayaking, and wildlife viewing abound.

VENTURA

60 miles north of Los Angeles.

Like Los Angeles, the city of Ventura enjoys gorgeous weather and sun-kissed beaches—but without the smog and congestion. The miles of beautiful beaches attract athletes—bodysurfers and boogie boarders, runners and bikers—and those who'd rather doze beneath an umbrella all day. Ventura Harbor is home to myriad fishing boats, restaurants, and water-activity centers where you can rent boats and take harbor cruises. Foodies can get their fix all over Ventura—dozens of upscale cafés and wine and tapas bars have opened in recent years. Arts and antiques buffs have long trekked downtown to browse the galleries and shops there.

GETTING HERE AND AROUND

Amtrak and Metrolink trains serve the area from Los Angeles. Greyhound buses stop in Ventura; Gold Coast Transit serves the city and the rest of Ventura County.

U.S. 101 is the north–south main route into town, but for a scenic drive, take Highway 1 north from Santa Monica. The highway merges with U.S. 101 just south of Ventura. ■ TIP➜ Traveling north to Ventura from Los Angeles on weekdays, it's best to depart before 6 am, between 10 and 2, or after 7, or you'll get caught in the extended rush-hour traffic. Coming south from Santa Barbara, depart before 1 or after 6. On weekends, traffic is generally fine except southbound on U.S. 101 between Santa Barbara and Ventura on Sunday late afternoon and early evening.

ESSENTIALS

Bus Contact **Gold Coast Transit** ☎ *805/643–3158* 🌐 *www.goldcoasttransit.org.*

Visitor Information **Ventura Visitors and Convention Bureau** ✉ *Downtown Visitor Center, 101 S. California St.* ☎ *805/648–2075, 800/483–6214* 🌐 *visitventuraca.com.*

EXPLORING

Mission San Buenaventura. The ninth of the 21 California missions, Mission San Buenaventura was established in 1782 but burned to the ground in the 1790s. It was rebuilt and rededicated in 1809. A self-guided tour takes you through a small museum, a quiet courtyard, and a chapel with 250-year-old paintings. ✉ *211 E. Main St., at Figueroa St.* ☎ *805/643–4318* 🌐 *www.sanbuenaventuramission.org* 🎟 *$4* 🕒 *Sun.–Fri. 10–5, Sat. 9–5.*

Museum of Ventura County. Exhibits in a contemporary complex of galleries and a sunny courtyard plaza tell the story of Ventura County from prehistoric times to the present. A highlight is the gallery that contains Ojai artist George Stuart's historical figures, dressed in exceptionally detailed, custom-made clothing reflecting their particular eras. In the courtyard, eight panels made with 45,000 pieces of cut glass form a history timeline. ✉ *100 E. Main St., at S. Ventura Ave.* ☎ *805/653–0323* 🌐 *venturamuseum.org* 🎟 *$5, free 1st Sun. of month* 🕒 *Tues.–Sun. 11–5.*

Fodor's Choice ★ **Ventura Oceanfront.** Four miles of gorgeous coastline stretch from the county fairgrounds at the northern border of the city of San Buenaventura, through San Buenaventura State Beach, down to Ventura Harbor in the south. The main attraction here is the San Buenaventura City Pier, a landmark built in 1872 and restored in 1993. Surfers rip the waves just north of the pier, and sunbathers relax on white-sand beaches on either side. The mile-long promenade and the Omer Rains Bike Trail north of the pier attract scores of joggers, surrey cyclers, and bikers throughout the year. ✉ *California St., at ocean's edge.*

WHERE TO EAT

$$ SEAFOOD 🍴 **Brophy Bros.** The Ventura outpost of the wildly popular Santa Barbara restaurant provides the same fresh seafood-oriented meals in a spacious second-story setting overlooking the harbor. Feast on everything from fish-and-chips and crab cakes to chowder and delectable fish—often straight from the boats moored below. [$] *Average main: $22* ✉ *1559 Spinnaker Dr., in Ventura Harbor Village* ☎ *805/639–0865* 🌐 *brophybros.com* ✍ *Reservations not accepted.*

$$$ AMERICAN Fodor's Choice ★ 🍴 **Café Zack.** A local favorite for anniversary and other celebratory occasions, Zack's serves classic European dishes in an intimate, two-room 1930s cottage adorned with local art. One standout appetizer is the lobster and sweet corn in a curry cream sauce. Entrées of note include seafood curry and filet mignon, the latter typically crusted in peppercorns or topped with porcini mushrooms. The crowd-pleaser for dessert is Zack's pie, with chocolate ganache poured into a pecan-cinnamon crust and topped with whipped cream and caramel sauce. [$] *Average main: $25* ✉ *1095 E. Thompson Blvd., at S. Ann St.* ☎ *805/643–9445* 🌐 *cafezack.com* 🕒 *Closed Sun. No lunch Sat.*

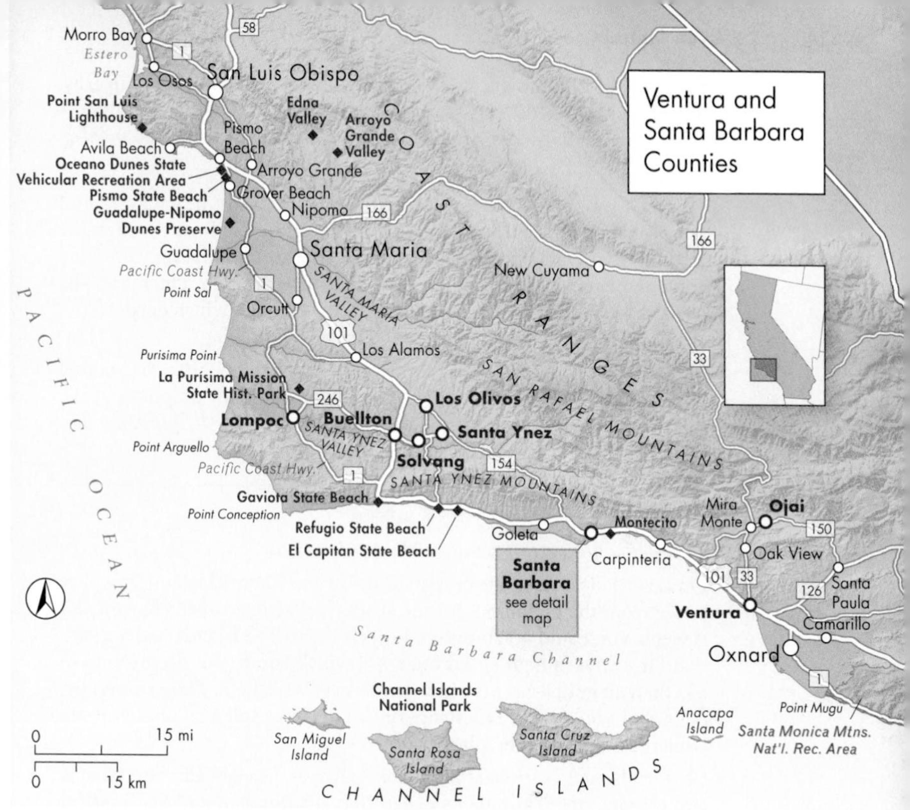
Ventura and Santa Barbara Counties
Morro Bay
Estero Bay
Los Osos
San Luis Obispo
Point San Luis Lighthouse
Edna Valley
Arroyo Grande Valley
Avila Beach
Pismo Beach
Arroyo Grande
Oceano Dunes State Vehicular Recreation Area
Grover Beach
Pismo State Beach
Nipomo
Guadalupe-Nipomo Dunes Preserve
Guadalupe
Santa Maria
Pacific Coast Hwy.
Point Sal
Orcutt
Santa Maria Valley
Coast Ranges
New Cuyama
Los Alamos
Purisima Point
La Purísima Mission State Hist. Park
San Rafael Mountains
Los Olivos
Lompoc
Buellton
Santa Ynez
Santa Ynez Valley
Solvang
Point Arguello
Santa Ynez Mountains
Gaviota State Beach
Point Conception
Refugio State Beach
El Capitan State Beach
Goleta
Montecito
Mira Monte
Ojai
Oak View
Carpinteria
Santa Barbara see detail map
Santa Paula
Ventura
Camarillo
Oxnard
Pacific Ocean
Santa Barbara Channel
Channel Islands National Park
San Miguel Island
Santa Rosa Island
Santa Cruz Island
Anacapa Island
Point Mugu
Santa Monica Mtns. Nat'l. Rec. Area
Channel Islands
0 15 mi
0 15 km
58
1
166
101
246
154
33
150
126

$$ SEAFOOD 🍴 **Lure Fish House.** Fresh, sustainably caught seafood charbroiled over a mesquite grill, a well-stocked oyster bar, specialty cocktails, and a wine list heavy on local vintages lure diners into this slick, nautical-theme space downtown. The menu centers on the mostly local catch and organic vegetables, and includes tacos, sandwiches, and salads. Regulars rave about the shrimp-and-chips, cioppino, and citrus crab-cake salad. [$] *Average main: $19* ✉ *60 S. California St.* ☎ *805/567–4400* 🌐 *www.lurefishhouse.com.*

WHERE TO STAY

$$ HOTEL 🏨 **Crowne Plaza Ventura Beach.** A 12-story hotel with an enviable location on the beach and next to a historic pier, the Crowne Plaza is within walking distance of downtown restaurants and nightlife. **Pros:** on the beach; near downtown; steps from waterfront. **Cons:** early-morning train noise; waterfront crowded in summer; most rooms on the small side. [$] *Rooms from: $169* ✉ *450 E. Harbor Blvd.* ☎ *800/842–0800, 805/648–2100* 🌐 *cpventura.com* 🛏 *254 rooms, 4 suites* 🍽 *No meals.*

$$ RESORT 🏨 **Four Points by Sheraton Ventura Harbor Resort.** An on-site restaurant, spacious rooms, and a slew of amenities make this 17-acre property—which includes sister hotel Holiday Inn Express—a popular and practical choice for Channel Islands visitors. **Pros:** close to island transportation; mostly quiet; short drive to historic downtown. **Cons:** not in

the heart of downtown; noisy seagulls sometimes congregate nearby. [$] *Rooms from: $160* ✉ *1050 Schooner Dr.* ☎ *805/658–1212, 800/368–7764* 🌐 *fourpoints.com/ventura* 🛏 *102 rooms, 4 suites* 🍴 *No meals.*

SPORTS AND THE OUTDOORS

The most popular outdoor activities in Ventura are beachgoing and whale-watching. California gray whales migrate offshore through the Santa Barbara Channel from late December through March; giant blue and humpback whales feed here from mid-June through September. The channel teems with marine life year-round, so tours, which depart from Ventura Harbor, include more than just whale sightings.

Island Packers Cruises. A cruise through the Santa Barbara Channel with Island Packers will give you the chance to spot dolphins, seals, and sometimes even whales. ✉ *Ventura Harbor, 1691 Spinnaker Dr.* ☎ *805/642–1393* 🌐 *islandpackers.com.*

CHANNEL ISLANDS NATIONAL PARK

11 miles southwest of Ventura Harbor via boat.

On crystal clear days the craggy peaks of the Channel Islands are easy to see from the mainland, jutting from the Pacific in such sharp detail it seems you could reach out and touch them. The islands really aren't that far away—a high-speed boat will whisk you to the closest ones in less than an hour—yet very few people ever visit them. Those adventurous types who do will experience one of the most splendid land-and-sea wilderness areas on the planet.

Channel Islands National Park includes five of the eight Channel Islands and the one nautical mile of ocean that surrounds them. Six nautical miles of surrounding channel waters are designated a National Marine Sanctuary, and are teeming with life, including giant kelp forests, 345 fish species, dolphins, whales, seals, sea lions, and seabirds. To maintain the integrity of their habitats, pets are not allowed in the park.

GETTING HERE AND AROUND

Most visitors access the Channel Islands via an Island Packers boat from Ventura Harbor. To reach the harbor by car, exit U.S. 101 in Ventura at Seaward Boulevard or Victoria Avenue and follow the signs to Ventura Harbor/Spinnaker Drive. An Island Packers boat heads to Anacapa Island from Oxnard's Channel Islands Harbor, which you can reach from Ventura Harbor by following Harbor Boulevard south about 6 miles and continuing south on Victoria Avenue. Private vehicles are not permitted on the islands.

BOAT TOURS

Island Packers. Sailing on high-speed catamarans from Ventura or a mono-hull vessel from Oxnard, Island Packers goes to Santa Cruz Island daily most of the year, weather permitting. The boats also go to Anacapa several days a week, and to the outer islands from April through November. They also cruise along Anacapa's north shore on three-hour wildlife tours (no disembarking) several times a week. ✉ *3550 Harbor Blvd., Oxnard* ☎ *805/642–1393* 🌐 *www.islandpackers.com* 🎟 *$36–$147.*

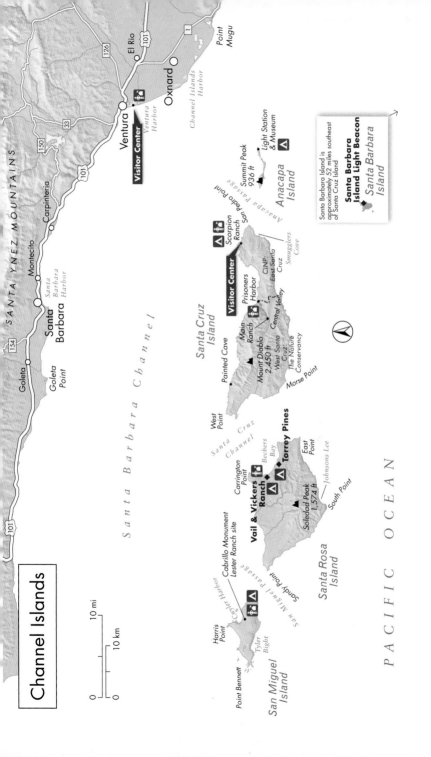

Channel Islands

Point Mugu

El Rio

Oxnard

Channel Islands Harbor

Ventura

Ventura Harbor

Visitor Center

Carpinteria

Montecito

Santa Barbara Harbor

Santa Barbara

S A N T A   Y N E Z   M O U N T A I N S

Goleta

Goleta Point

S a n t a   B a r b a r a   C h a n n e l

Anacapa Passage

San Pedro Point

Summit Peak 936 ft

Light Station & Museum

Anacapa Island

Scorpion Ranch

Smugglers Cove

Prisoners Harbor

Visitor Center

CINP: East Santa Cruz

Central Valley

Santa Cruz Island

Painted Cave

Main Ranch

Mount Diablo 2,450 ft

West Santa Cruz: The Nature Conservancy

Morse Point

West Point

Santa Cruz Channel

Bechers Bay

Carrington Point

Vail & Vickers Ranch

Torrey Pines

East Point

Johnsons Lee

Soledad Peak 1,574 ft

South Point

Santa Rosa Island

Cabrillo Monument Lester Ranch site

Cuyler Harbor

San Miguel Passage

Sandy Point

Harris Point

Tyler Bight

San Miguel Island

Point Bennett

P A C I F I C   O C E A N

Santa Barbara Island is approximately 52 miles southeast of Santa Cruz Island

Santa Barbara Island Light Beacon

Santa Barbara Island

0   10 mi
0   10 km

EXPLORING
TOP ATTRACTIONS
Channel Islands National Park Visitor Center. The park's Robert J. Lago-marsino Visitor Center has a museum, a bookstore, and a three-story observation tower with telescopes. The museum's exhibits and a 24-minute film, *Treasure in the Sea,* provide an engaging overview of the islands. In the marine life exhibit, sea stars cling to rocks, anemones wave their colorful, spiny tentacles, and a brilliant orange Garibaldi darts around. Also on display are full-size reproductions of a male northern elephant seal and the pygmy mammoth skeleton unearthed on Santa Rosa Island in 1994.

On weekends and holidays at 11 and 3, rangers lead various free public programs describing park resources, and from Wednesday through Saturday in summer the center screens live ranger broadcasts of hikes (at 11) and dives (at 2) on Anacapa Island. Webcam images of bald eagles and other land and sea creatures are shown at the center and on the park's website. ✉ *1901 Spinnaker Dr., Ventura* ☎ *805/658–5730* ⊕ *www.nps.gov/chis* ⊙ *Daily 8:30–5.*

Santa Cruz Island. Five miles west of Anacapa, 96-square-mile Santa Cruz Island is the largest of the Channel Islands. The National Park Service manages the easternmost 24% of the island; the rest is owned by the Nature Conservancy, which requires a permit to land. When your boat drops you off on a portion of the 70 miles of craggy coastline, you see two rugged mountain ranges with peaks soaring to 2,500 feet and deep canyons traversed by streams. This landscape is the habitat of a remarkable variety of flora and fauna—more than 600 types of plants, 140 kinds of land birds, 11 mammal species, five varieties of reptiles, and three amphibian species live here. Bird-watchers may want to look for the endemic island scrub jay, which is found nowhere else in the world.

One of the largest and deepest sea caves in the world, **Painted Cave,** lies along the northwest coast of Santa Cruz. Named for the colorful lichen and algae that cover its walls, Painted Cave is nearly ¼ mile long and 100 feet wide. In spring a waterfall cascades over the entrance. Kayakers may encounter seals or sea lions cruising alongside their boats inside the cave. The Channel Islands hold some of the richest archaeological resources in North America; all artifacts are protected within the park. Remnants of a dozen Chumash villages can be seen on the island. The largest of these villages, at the eastern end, occupied the area now called **Scorpion Ranch.** The Chumash mined extensive chert deposits on the island for tools to produce shell-bead money, which they traded with people on the mainland. You can learn about Chumash history and view artifacts, tools, and exhibits on native plant and wildlife at the interpretive visitor center near the landing dock. Visitors can also explore remnants of the early-1900s ranching era in the restored historic adobe and outbuildings. ✉ *Channel Islands National Park.*

WORTH NOTING
Anacapa Island. Most people think of Anacapa as an island, but it's actually comprised of three narrow islets. The tips of these volcanic formations nearly touch, the islets are inaccessible from one another

except by boat. All three have towering cliffs, isolated sea caves, and natural bridges; Arch Rock, on East Anacapa, is one of the best-known symbols of Channel Islands National Park.

Wildlife viewing is the main activity on East Anacapa, particularly in summer when seagull chicks are newly hatched and sea lions and seals lounge on the beaches. Exhibits at East Anacapa's compact **museum** include the original lead-crystal Fresnel lens from the 1932 lighthouse.

Over on West Anacapa, depending on the season and the number of desirable species lurking about there, boats travel to **Frenchy's Cove.** On a voyage here you might see anemones, limpets, barnacles, mussel beds, and colorful marine algae in the pristine tide pools. The rest of West Anacapa is closed to protect nesting brown pelicans. ⊠ *Channel Islands National Park.*

San Miguel Island. The westernmost of the Channel Islands, San Miguel Island is frequently battered by storms sweeping across the North Pacific. The 15-square-mile island's wild, windswept landscape is lush with vegetation. Point Bennett, at the western tip, offers one of the world's most spectacular wildlife displays when more than 100,000 pinnipeds hit its beach. Explorer Juan Rodríguez Cabrillo was the first European to visit this island; he claimed it for Spain in 1542. Legend holds that Cabrillo died on one of the Channel Islands—no one knows where he's buried, but there's a memorial to him on a bluff above Cuyler Harbor. ⊠ *Channel Islands National Park.*

Santa Barbara Island. At about 1 square mile, Santa Barbara Island is the smallest of the Channel Islands and nearly 35 miles south of the others. Triangular in shape, Santa Barbara's steep cliffs—which offer a perfect nesting spot for the Scripps's murrelet, a rare seabird—are topped by twin peaks. In spring you can enjoy a brilliant display of yellow coreopsis. Learn about the wildlife on and around the islands at the island's small museum. ⊠ *Channel Islands National Park.*

Santa Rosa Island. Between Santa Cruz and San Miguel, Santa Rosa is the second largest of the Channel Islands. The terrain along the coast varies from broad, sandy beaches to sheer cliffs—a central mountain range, rising to 1,589 feet, breaks the island's relatively low profile. Santa Rosa is home to about 500 species of plants, including the rare Torrey pine, and three unusual mammals, the island fox, the spotted skunk, and the deer mouse. They hardly compare, though, to their predecessors: a nearly complete skeleton of a 6-foot-tall pygmy mammoth was unearthed in 1994.

From 1901 to 1998, cattle were raised at the island's **Vail & Vickers Ranch.** The route from Santa Rosa's landing dock to the campground passes by the historic ranch buildings, barns, equipment, and the wooden pier where cattle were brought onto the island. ⊠ *Channel Islands National Park.*

SPORTS AND THE OUTDOORS

Channel Islands Outfitters *(⇨ see Santa Barbara Sports and the Outdoors)* arranges paddling, kayaking, and other Channel Islands excursions out of Ventura and Santa Barbara, and various concessionaires at

Ventura Harbor Village (☎ *805/477–0470* ⊕ *www.venturaharborvillage. com*) arrange diving, kayaking, and other rentals and tours. Island Packers conducts whale-watching cruises.

DIVING

Some of the best snorkeling and diving in the world can be found in the cool waters surrounding the Channel Islands. In the relatively warm water around Anacapa and eastern Santa Cruz, photographers can get great shots of rarely seen giant black bass swimming among the kelp forests. Here you also find a reef covered with red brittle starfish. If you're an experienced diver, you might swim among five species of seals and sea lions, or try your hand at spearing rockfish or halibut near San Miguel and Santa Rosa. The best time to scuba dive is in summer and fall, when the water is often clear up to a 100-foot depth.

KAYAKING

The most remote parts of the Channel Islands are accessible only by a sea kayak. Some of the best kayaking in the park can be found on Anacapa, Santa Barbara, and the eastern tip of Santa Cruz. It's too far to kayak from the mainland out to the islands, but outfitters have tours that take you to the islands. Tours are offered year-round, but high seas may cause trip cancellations between December and March. ⚠ **Channel waters can be unpredictable and challenging. Guided trips are highly recommended.**

WHALE-WATCHING

About a third of the world's cetacean species (27 to be exact) can be seen in the Santa Barbara Channel. In July and August, humpback and blue whales feed off the north shore of Santa Rosa. From late December through March, up to 10,000 gray whales pass through the Santa Barbara Channel on their way from Alaska to Mexico and back again, and on a whale-watching trip during this time frame you should see one or more of them. Other types of whales, but fewer in number, swim the channel from June through August.

OJAI

15 miles north of Ventura.

The Ojai Valley, which director Frank Capra used as a backdrop for his 1936 film *Lost Horizon,* sizzles in the summer when temperatures routinely reach 90°F. The acres of orange and avocado groves here evoke postcard images of long-ago agricultural Southern California. Many artists and celebrities have sought refuge from life in the fast lane in lush Ojai.

GETTING HERE AND AROUND

From northern Ventura, Highway 33 veers east from U.S. 101 and climbs inland to Ojai. From Santa Barbara, exit U.S. 101 at Highway 150 in Carpinteria, then travel east 20 miles on a twisting, two-lane road that is not recommended at night or during poor weather. You can also access Ojai by heading west from Interstate 5 on Highway 126. Exit at Santa Paula and follow Highway 150 north for 16 miles to Ojai. Gold Coast Transit provides service to Ojai from Ventura.

Ojai can be easily explored on foot; you can also hop on the Ojai Trolley ($1, or $2 day pass), which until about 5 pm follows two routes around Ojai and neighboring Miramonte on weekdays and one route on weekends. Tell the driver you're visiting and you'll get an informal guided tour.

ESSENTIALS

Bus Contacts Gold Coast Transit ☎ *805/643–3158* 🌐 *www.goldcoasttransit.org.* **Ojai Trolley** ☎ *805/646–5581* 🌐 *www.ojaitrolley.com.*

Visitor Information Ojai Visitors Bureau ✉ *206 N. Signal St., Ste. P, at E. Ojai Ave.* ☎ *888/652–4669* 🌐 *ojaivisitors.com* 🕒 *Weekdays 8–5.*

EXPLORING

Ojai Avenue. The work of local artists is displayed in the Spanish-style shopping arcade along the avenue downtown. On Sunday between 9 and 1, organic and specialty growers sell their produce at the outdoor market behind the arcade.

Ojai Valley Museum. The museum collects, preserves, and presents exhibits about the art, history, and culture of Ojai and Ojai Valley. Walking tours of Ojai depart from here. ✉ *130 W. Ojai Ave.* ☎ *805/640–1390* 🌐 *ojaivalleymuseum.org* 🎟 *Museum $5, walking tour $7 ($15 family)* 🕒 *Tues.–Sat. 10–4, Sun. noon–4; tours Oct.–July, Sat. 10:30.*

Ojai Valley Trail. The 18-mile trail is open to pedestrians, joggers, equestrians, bikers, and others on nonmotorized vehicles. You can access it anywhere along its route. ✉ *Parallel to Hwy. 33 from Soule Park in Ojai to ocean in Ventura* ☎ *888/652–4669* 🌐 *ojaivisitors.com.*

WHERE TO EAT

$$$ MEDITERRANEAN 🍴 **Azu.** Slick furnishings, piped-in jazz, craft cocktails, and local beers and wines draw diners to this artsy Mediterranean bistro known for tapas made from organic ingredients. You can also order soups, salads, and bistro fare such as steak frites and paella. Save room for the homemade gelato. [$] *Average main: $25* ✉ *457 E. Ojai Ave.* ☎ *805/640–7987* 🌐 *azuojai.com.*

$ ITALIAN 🍴 **Boccali's.** Edging a ranch, citrus groves, and a seasonal garden that provides produce for menu items, the modest but cheery Boccali's attracts many loyal fans. When it's warm, you can dine alfresco in the oak-shaded patio and lawn area and sometimes listen to live music. The family-run operation, best known for hand-rolled pizzas and home-style pastas (don't miss the eggplant lasagna), also serves a popular seasonal strawberry shortcake. [$] *Average main: $15* ✉ *3277 Ojai Ave., about 2 miles east of downtown* ☎ *805/646–6116* 🌐 *boccalis.com* 💳 *No credit cards* 🕒 *No lunch Mon. and Tues.*

$$$ EUROPEAN 🍴 **Suzanne's Cuisine.** Peppered filet mignon, linguine with steamed clams, and pan-roasted salmon with a roasted mango sauce are among the offerings at this European-style restaurant. Seafood, roasted meats and poultry, and vegetarian dishes dominate the dinner menu, and salads and soups star at lunchtime. All the desserts are made on the premises. [$] *Average main: $28* ✉ *502 W. Ojai Ave.* ☎ *805/640–1961* 🌐 *suzannescuisine.com* 🕒 *Closed Tues.*

WHERE TO STAY

$$
B&B/INN

The Blue Iguana Inn & Suites. Artists run this Southwestern-style hotel, and their works and those of other local artists decorate the rooms. **Pros:** colorful art everywhere; secluded. **Cons:** 2 miles from downtown; on a highway; small. $ *Rooms from: $129* ✉ *11794 N. Ventura Ave.* ☎ *805/646–5277* ⊕ *iguanainnsofojai.com* ➔ *4 rooms, 8 suites, 8 cottages* ⦿ *Breakfast.*

$$$
RESORT

Oaks at Ojai. Rejuvenation is the name of the game at this destination spa where you can work out all day or just lounge by the pool. **Pros:** great place to get fit; peaceful retreat; healthful meals. **Cons:** some rooms are basic; on main road through town. $ *Rooms from: $250* ✉ *122 E. Ojai Ave.* ☎ *805/646–5573, 800/753–6257* ⊕ *oaksspa.com* ➔ *44 rooms, 2 suites* ⦿ *All meals* ➱ *2-night minimum stay.*

$$$$
RESORT
Fodor's Choice
★

Ojai Valley Inn & Spa. This outdoorsy, golf-oriented resort and spa is set on beautifully landscaped grounds, with hillside views in nearly all directions. **Pros:** gorgeous grounds; exceptional outdoor activities; romantic yet kid-friendly. **Cons:** expensive; areas near restaurants can be noisy. $ *Rooms from: $400* ✉ *905 Country Club Rd.* ☎ *805/646–1111, 855/697–8780* ⊕ *ojairesort.com* ➔ *231 rooms, 77 suites* ⦿ *No meals.*

SANTA BARBARA

27 miles northwest of Ventura and 29 miles west of Ojai.

Santa Barbara has long been an oasis for Los Angelenos seeking respite from big-city life. The attractions begin at the ocean and end in the foothills of the Santa Ynez Mountains. A few miles up the coast east and west—but still very much a part of Santa Barbara—are the exclusive residential districts of Montecito and Hope Ranch. Santa Barbara is on a jog in the coastline, so the ocean is actually to the south, instead of the west; for this reason, directions can be confusing. "Up" the coast toward San Francisco is west, "down" toward Los Angeles is east, and the mountains are north.

GETTING HERE AND AROUND

U.S. 101 is the main route into Santa Barbara. If you're staying in town, a car is handy but not essential; the beaches and downtown are easily explored by bicycle or on foot. Visit the Santa Barbara Car Free website for bike-route and walking-tour maps, suggestions for car-free vacations, and transportation discounts.

Santa Barbara Metropolitan Transit District's Line 22 bus serves major tourist sights. Several bus lines connect with the very convenient electric shuttles that cruise the downtown and waterfront every 10 to 15 minutes (50¢ each way).

Santa Barbara Trolley Co. operates a motorized San Francisco–style cable car that loops past major hotels, shopping areas, and attractions from 10 to 4. Get off whenever you like, and pick up another trolley (they come every hour) when you're ready to move on. The fare is $22 for the day.

TOURS

Land and Sea Tours. This outfit conducts 90-minute narrated tours in an amphibious 49-passenger vehicle nicknamed the Land Shark. The adventure begins with a drive through the city, followed by a plunge into the harbor for a cruise along the coast. ⊠ *10 E. Cabrillo Blvd., at Stearns Wharf* ☎ *805/683–7600* ⊕ *out2seesb.com* ⊠ *From $30* ⊗ *Tours May–Oct., daily noon, 2, and 4; Nov.–Apr., daily noon and 2.*

ESSENTIALS

Transportation Contacts Santa Barbara Car Free ☎ *805/696–1100* ⊕ *santabarbaracarfree.org.* **Santa Barbara Metropolitan Transit District** ☎ *805/963–3366* ⊕ *sbmtd.gov.* **Santa Barbara Trolley Co.** ☎ *805/965–0353* ⊕ *www.sbtrolley.com.*

Visitor Information Santa Barbara Visitor Center ⊠ *1 Garden St., at Cabrillo Blvd.* ☎ *805/965–3021, 805/568–1811* ⊕ *www.sbchamber.org* ⊗ *Feb.–Oct., Mon.–Sat. 9–5, Sun. 10–5; Nov.–Jan., Mon.–Sat. 9–4, Sun. 10–4.* **Visit Santa Barbara** ⊠ *500 E. Montecito St.* ☎ *805/966–9222* ⊕ *www.santabarbaraca.com.*

EXPLORING

6

Santa Barbara's waterfront is beautiful, with palm-studded promenades and plenty of sand. In the few miles between the beaches and the hills are downtown, Mission Santa Barbara, and the Santa Barbara Botanic Garden.

TOP ATTRACTIONS

El Presidio State Historic Park. Founded in 1782, El Presidio was one of four military strongholds established by the Spanish along the coast of California. The park encompasses much of the original site in the heart of downtown. El Cuartel, the adobe guardhouse, is the oldest building in Santa Barbara and the second oldest in California. ■ TIP➔ **Admission is free for children 16 and under.** ⊠ *123 E. Canon Perdido St., at Anacapa St.* ☎ *805/965–0093* ⊕ *www.sbthp.org* ⊠ *$5* ⊗ *Daily 10:30–4:30.*

FAMILY **Lotusland.** The 37-acre estate called Lotusland once belonged to the Fodor'sChoice Polish opera singer Ganna Walska, who purchased it in the late 1940s ★ and lived here until her death in 1984. Many of the exotic trees and other subtropical flora were planted in 1882 by horticulturist R. Kinton Stevens. On the two-hour guided tour—the only option for visiting unless you're a member (reserve well ahead in summer)—you'll see an outdoor theater, a topiary garden, a lotus pond, and a huge collection of rare cycads, an unusual plant genus that has been around since the time of the dinosaurs. ■ TIP➔ **Child-friendly family tours are available for groups with children under the age of 10; contact Lotusland for scheduling.** ⊠ *695 Ashley Rd., off Sycamore Canyon Rd. (Hwy. 192), Montecito* ☎ *805/969–9990* ⊕ *lotusland.org* ⊠ *$45* ⊗ *Mid-Feb.–mid-Nov., Wed.–Sat. at 10 and 1:30 by appointment only.*

Fodor'sChoice **Mission Santa Barbara.** Widely referred to as the "Queen of Missions," ★ this is one of the most beautiful and frequently photographed buildings in coastal California. Dating to 1786, the architecture evolved from adobe-brick buildings with thatch roofs to more permanent edifices as the mission's population burgeoned. An earthquake in 1812

Continued on page 248

DID YOU KNOW?

The mission fathers followed in the footsteps of explorer and navigator Juan Rodriguez Cabrillo, who in 1542 had claimed most of the California coast for Spain.

CALIFORNIA'S MISSIONS

Their soul may belong to Spain, their heart to the New World, but the historic missions of California, with their lovely churches, beckon the traveler on a soulful journey back to the very founding of the American West.

by Cheryl Crabtree and Robert I.C. Fisher

California history changed forever in the 18th century when Spanish explorers founded a series of missions along the Pacific coast. Believing they were following God's will, they wanted to spread the gospel and convert as many natives as possible. The process produced a collision between the Hispanic and California Indian cultures, resulting in one of the most striking legacies of Old California: the Spanish mission churches. Rising like mirages in the middle of desert plains and rolling hills, these historic sites transport you back to the days of the Spanish colonial period.

GOD AND MAN IN CALIFORNIA

The Alta California territory came under pressure in the 1760s when Spain feared foreign advances into the territory explorer Juan Rodríguez Cabrillo had claimed for the Spanish crown back in 1542. But how could Spain create a visible and viable presence halfway around the world? They decided to build on the model that had already worked well in Spain's Mexico colony. The plan involved establishing a series of missions, to be operated by the Catholic Church and protected by four of Spain's *presidios* (military outposts). The native Indians—after quick conversion to Christianity—would provide the labor force necessary to build mission towns.

FATHER OF THE MISSIONS

Father Junípero Serra is an icon of the Spanish colonial period. At the behest of the Spanish government, the diminutive padre—then well into his fifties, and despite a chronic leg infection— started out on foot from Baja California to search for suitable mission sites, with a goal of reaching Monterey. In 1769 he helped establish Alta California's first mission in San Diego and continued his travels until his death, in 1784, by which time he had founded eight more missions.

The system ended about a decade after the Mexican government took control of Alta California in the early 1820s and began to secularize the missions. The church lost horses and cattle, as well as vast tracts of land, which the Mexican government in turn granted to private individuals. They also lost laborers, as the Indians were for the most part free to find work and a life beyond the missions. In 1848, the Americans assumed control of the territory, and California became part of the United States. Today, these missions stand as extraordinary monuments to their colorful past.

Mission Santa Barbara Museum

MISSION ACCOMPLISHED

California's Mission Trail is the best way to follow in the fathers' footsteps. Here, below, are its 21 settlements, north to south.

Amazingly, all 21 Spanish missions in California are still visible—some in their pristine historic state, others with modifications made over the centuries. Many are found on or near the "King's Road"—El Camino Real—which linked these mission outposts. At the height of the mission system the trail was approximately 600 miles long, eventually extending from San Diego to Sonoma. Today the road is commemorated on portions of routes 101 and 82 in the form of roadside bell markers erected by CalTrans every one to two miles between San Diego and San Francisco.

San Francisco Solano, Sonoma (1823; this was the final California mission constructed.)

San Rafael, San Rafael (1817)

San Francisco de Asís (aka Mission Dolores), San Francisco (1776). Situated in the heart of San Francisco,

Mission Santa Clara de Asís

these mission grounds and nearby Arroyo de los Dolores (Creek of Sorrows) are home to the oldest intact building in the city.

Santa Clara de Asís, Santa Clara (1777). On the campus of Santa Clara University, this beautifully restored mission contains original paintings, statues, a bell, and hundreds of artifacts, as well as a spectacular rose garden.

San José, Fremont (1797)

Santa Cruz, Santa Cruz (1791)

San Juan Bautista, San Juan Bautista (1797). Immortalized in Hitchcock's *Vertigo*, this remarkably preserved pueblo contains the largest church of all the California missions, as well as 18th- and 19th-century buildings and a sprawling plaza.

San Carlos Borromeo del Río Carmelo, Carmel (1770). Carmel Mission was head-

quarters for the California mission system under Father Serra and the Father Presidents who succeeded him; the on-site museum includes Serra's tiny sleeping quarters (where he died in 1784).

Nuestra Señora de la Soledad, Soledad (1791)

San Antonio de Padua, Jolon (1771)

San Miguel Arcángel, San Miguel (1797). San Miguel boasts the only intact original interior wall painting in any of the missions, painted in 1821 by Native American converts under the direction of Spanish artist Esteban Muras.

Painting from 1818, San Juan Bautista.

Clear Lake   Yuba City   Auburn
Woodland
San Francisco Solano
Napa   SACRAMENTO
Sonoma   Fairfield
Lodi
San Rafael   San Francisco de Asís
Berkeley
SAN FRANCISCO   Santa Clara de Asís
82   San José
San Jose   101
Santa Cruz   San Juan Bautista
Castroville   San Carlos Borromeo del Río Carmelo
Monterey   Carmel
Big Sur   Soledad
Nuestra Señora de la Soledad
San Antonio de Padua

Mission Santa Inés

San Luis Obispo de Tolosa, San Luis Obispo (1772). Bear meat from grizzlies captured here saved the Spaniards from starving, which helped convince Father Serra to establish a mission.

La Purísima Concepción, Lompoc (1787). La Purísima is the nation's most completely restored mission complex. It is now a living-history museum with a church and nearly forty craft and residence rooms.

Santa Inés, Solvang (1804). Home to one of the most significant pieces of religious art created by a California mission Indian.

Santa Bárbara, Santa Barbara (1786). The "Queen of the Missions" has twin bell towers, gorgeous gardens with heirloom plant varietals, a massive collection of rare artworks and artifacts, and lovely stonework.

San Buenaventura, Ventura (1782). This was the last mission founded by Father Serra; it is still an active parish in the Archdiocese of Los Angeles.

Mission San Fernando Rey de España

San Fernando Rey de España, Mission Hills (1797)

San Gabriel Arcángel, San Gabriel (1771)

San Luis Rey de Francia, Oceanside (1798)

San Juan Capistrano, San Juan Capistrano (1776). This mission is famed for its Saint Joseph's Day (March 19) celebration of the return of swallows in the springtime. The mission's adobe walls enclose acres of lush gardens and historic buildings.

San Diego de Alcalá, San Diego (1769). This was the first California missions constructed, although the original was destroyed in 1775 and rebuilt over a number of years.

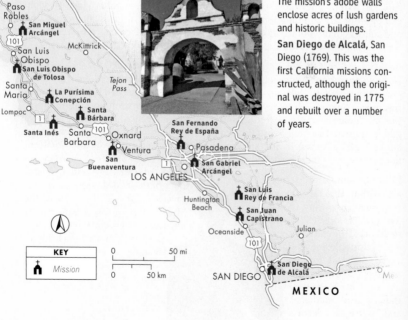

6

IN FOCUS CALIFORNIA'S MISSIONS

SPANISH MISSION STYLE

(left) Mission San Luis Rey de Francia; (right) Mission San Antonio de Padua

The Spanish mission churches derive much of their strength and enduring power from their extraordinary admixture of styles. They are spectacular examples of the combination of races and cultures that bloomed along Father Serra's road through Alta California.

SPIRIT OF THE PLACE

In building the missions, the Franciscan padres had to rely on available resources. Spanish churches back in Europe boasted marble floors and gilded statues. But here, whitewashed adobe walls gleamed in the sun and floors were often merely packed earth.

However simple the structures, the art within the mission confines continued to glorify the Church. The padres imported much finery to decorate the churches and perform the mass— silver, silk and lovely paintings to teach the life of Christ to the Indians and soldiers and settlers. Serra himself commissioned

fine artists in Mexico to produce custom works using the best materials and according to exact specifications. Sculptures of angels, Mary, Joseph, Jesus and the Franciscan heroes and saints—and of course the Stations of the Cross—adorned all the missions.

AN ENDURING LEGACY

Mission architecture reflects a gorgeous blend of European and New World influences. While naves followed the simple forms of Franciscan Gothic, cloisters (with beautiful arcades) adopted aspects of the Romanesque style, and ornamental touches of the Spanish Renaissance— including red-tiled roofs and wrought-iron grilles—added even more elegance. In the 20th century, the Mission Revival Style had a huge impact on architecture and design in California, as seen in examples ranging from San Diego's Union Station to Stanford University's main quadrangle.

Father Junípero Serra statue at Mission San Gabriel

FOR WHOM THE BELLS TOLLED

Perhaps the most famous architectural motif of the Spanish Mission churches was the belltower. These took the form of either a campanile—a single tower called a campanario—or, more spectacularly, of an open-work espedaña, a perforated adobe wall housing a series of bells (notable examples of this form are at San Juan Capistrano and San Diego de Alcalá). Bells were essential to maintaining the routines of daily life at the missions.

MISSION LIFE
Morning bells summoned residents to chapel for services; noontime bells introduced the main meal, while the evening bells sounded the alert to gather around 5 pm for mass and dinner. Many of the natives were happy with their new faith, and even enjoyed putting in numerous hours a week working as farmers, soapmakers, weavers, and masons.

Others were less willing to abandon their traditional culture, but were coerced to abide by the new Spanish laws and mission rules. Natives were sometimes mistreated by the friars, who used a system of punishments typical of the times to enforce submission to the new culture.

NATIVE TRAGEDY
In the end, mission life proved extremely destructive to the Native Californian population. European diseases and contaminated water caused the death of nearly a third, with some tribes—notably the Chumash—suffering disproportionately.

Despite these losses, small numbers did survive. After the Mexican government secularized the missions in 1833, a majority of the native population was reduced to poverty. Some stayed at the missions, while others went to live in the pueblos, ranchos, and countryside.

Many Native Californian people today still work and live near the missions that are monuments to their artistry skills.

FOR MORE INFORMATION

California Missions Foundation

☎ 805/963-1633

⊕ www.california
missionsfoundation.org

Top, Mission San Gabriel Arcángel
Bottom, Mission San Miguel Arcángel

destroyed the third church built on the site. Its replacement, the present structure, is still a functioning Catholic church. Mission Santa Barbara has a splendid Spanish/ Mexican colonial art collection, as well as Chumash sculptures and the only Native American–made altar and tabernacle left in the California missions. Docents lead 60-minute

> **BEST VIEWS**
>
> Drive along Alameda Padre Serra, a hillside road that begins near the mission and continues to Montecito, to feast your eyes on spectacular views of the city and the Santa Barbara Channel.

tours ($9 adult) Thursday and Friday at 11 and Saturday at 10:30. ⊠ *2201 Laguna St., at E. Los Olivos St.* ☎ *805/682–4149 gift shop, 805/682–4713* ⊕ *www.santabarbaramission.org* ⊠ *$7* ⊙ *Daily 9–4:15 (4:30 in summer).*

Santa Barbara Botanic Garden. Five miles of scenic trails meander through the garden's 78 acres of native plants. The Mission Dam, built in 1806, stands just beyond the redwood grove and above the restored aqueduct that once carried water to Mission Santa Barbara. More than a thousand plant species thrive in various themed sections, including mountains, deserts, meadows, redwoods, and Channel Islands. ■ TIP→ **A conservation center dedicated to rare and endangered plant species opens in 2016.** ⊠ *1212 Mission Canyon Rd., north of Foothill Rd. (Hwy. 192)* ☎ *805/682–4726* ⊕ *www.sbbg.org* ⊠ *$10* ⊙ *Mar.–Oct., daily 9–6; Nov.–Feb., daily 9–5. Guided tours weekends at 11 and 2, Mon. at 2.*

Fodor's Choice
★

Santa Barbara County Courthouse. Hand-painted tiles and a spiral staircase infuse the courthouse, a national historic landmark, with the grandeur of a Moorish palace. This magnificent building was completed in 1929. An elevator rises to an arched observation area in the tower that provides a panoramic view of the city. Before or after you take in the view, you can (if it's open) visit an engaging gallery devoted to the workings of the tower's original, still operational Seth Thomas clock. The murals in the ceremonial chambers on the courthouse's second floor were painted by an artist who did backdrops for some of Cecil B. DeMille's films. ⊠ *1100 Anacapa St., at E. Anapamu St.* ☎ *805/962–6464* ⊕ *www.santabarbaracourthouse.org* ⊙ *Weekdays 8–4:45, weekends 10–4:45. Free guided tours weekdays at 10:30, daily at 2.*

QUICK
BITES

Jeannine's. Take a break from State Street shopping at Jeannine's, revered locally for its wholesome sandwiches, salads, and baked goods, made from scratch with organic and natural ingredients. Pick up a turkey cranberry or chicken pesto sandwich to go, and picnic in the courthouse gardens a block away. ⊠ *La Arcada, 15 E. Figueroa St., at State St.* ☎ *805/966–1717* ⊕ *jeannines.com/restaurants* ⊙ *Daily 6:30–3.*

Santa Barbara Museum of Art. The highlights of this museum's permanent collection include ancient sculpture, Asian art, impressionist paintings, contemporary art, photography, and American works in several mediums. ⊠ *1130 State St., at E. Anapamu St.* ☎ *805/963–4364* ⊕ *sbma.*

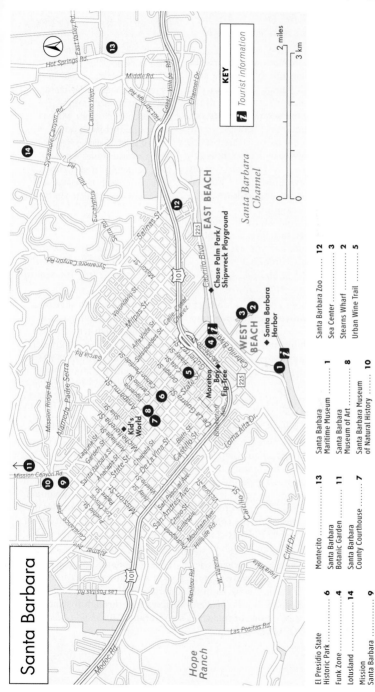

Santa Barbara

KEY

🛈 *Tourist Information*

EAST BEACH

Santa Barbara Channel

Chase Palm Park/
Shipwreck Playground

WEST
BEACH

♦ Santa Barbara
Harbor

🛈

0 ───── 2 miles

0 ───── 3 km

El Presidio State
Historic Park **6**

Funk Zone **4**

Lotusland **14**

Mission
Santa Barbara **9**

Montecito **13**

Santa Barbara
Botanic Garden **11**

Santa Barbara
County Courthouse **7**

Santa Barbara
Maritime Museum **1**

Santa Barbara
Museum of Art **8**

Santa Barbara Museum
of Natural History **10**

Santa Barbara Zoo **12**

Sea Center **3**

Stearns Wharf **2**

Urban Wine Trail **5**

6

net ✉ *$10, free Thurs. 5–8* ☉ *Tues., Wed., Fri., and weekends 11–5, Thurs. 11–8.*

FAMILY **Santa Barbara Museum of Natural History.** The gigantic blue whale skeleton greets you at the entrance to this complex whose major draws include its planetarium, space lab, and gem and mineral display. Startlingly alive-looking stuffed specimens, complete with nests and eggs, roost in the bird hall, and a room of dioramas illustrates Chumash Indian history and culture. Outdoors, nature trails wind through the serene oak-studded grounds.
■ TIP➔ A Nature Pass, available at the museum and the associated Sea Center, is good for discounted admission to both facilities. ✉ *2559 Puesta del Sol Rd., off Mission Canyon Rd.* ☎ *805/682–4711* ⊕ *sbnature.org* ✉ *$12; free 3rd Sun. of month Sept.–Apr.* ☉ *Daily 10–5.*

SANTA BARBARA STYLE

After a 1925 earthquake demolished many buildings, the city seized a golden opportunity to assume a Spanish-Mediterranean style. It established an architectural board of review, which, along with city commissions, created strict building codes for the downtown district: red-tile roofs, earth-tone facades, arches, wrought-iron embellishments, and height restrictions (about four stories).

FAMILY **Santa Barbara Zoo.** This compact zoo's gorgeous grounds shelter elephants, gorillas, exotic birds, and big cats. For small children, there's a scenic railroad and barnyard petting zoo. Three high-tech dinosaurs perform in live stage shows (free with admission), daily in summer and on weekends the rest of the year. ■ TIP➔ The palm-studded lawns on a hilltop overlooking the beach are perfect spots for family picnics. ✉ *500 Niños Dr., off El Cabrillo Blvd.* ☎ *805/962–5339 main line, 805/962–6310 information* ⊕ *santabarbarazoo.org* ✉ *Zoo $15, parking $6* ☉ *Daily 10–5.*

FAMILY **Sea Center.** A branch of the Santa Barbara Museum of Natural History, the center specializes in Santa Barbara Channel marine life and conservation. Though small compared to aquariums in Monterey and Long Beach, this is a fascinating, hands-on marine science laboratory that lets you participate in experiments, projects, and exhibits, including touch pools. The two-story glass walls here open to stunning ocean, mountain, and city views. ■ TIP➔ Purchase a Nature Pass, available here, for discounted admission to the center and the natural history museum. ✉ *211 Stearns Wharf* ☎ *805/962–2526* ⊕ *sbnature.org* ✉ *$8* ☉ *Daily 10–5.*

Stearns Wharf. Built in 1872, Stearns Wharf is Santa Barbara's most visited landmark. Expansive views of the mountains, cityscape, and harbor unfold from every vantage point on the three-block-long pier. Although it's a nice walk from the Cabrillo Boulevard parking areas, you can also park on the pier and then wander through the shops or stop for a meal at one of the wharf's restaurants. ✉ *Cabrillo Blvd. and State St.* ⊕ *stearnswharf.org.*

WORTH NOTING

Funk Zone. A formerly run-down industrial neighborhood near the waterfront and train station, the Funk Zone has evolved into a hip hangout filled with wine-tasting rooms, arts-and-crafts studios, murals, breweries, restaurants, and small shops. It's fun to poke around the three-square-block district. ■TIP➔ Street parking is limited, so leave your car in a nearby city lot and cruise up and down the alleys on foot. ✉ *Between State and Garden Sts. and Cabrillo Blvd. and U.S. 101* ⊕ *funkzone.net.*

Montecito. Since the late 1800s the tree-studded hills and valleys of this town have attracted the rich and famous: Hollywood icons, business tycoons, tech moguls, and old-money families who installed themselves years ago. Shady roads wind through the community, which consists mostly of gated estates. Swank boutiques line **Coast Village Road,** where well-heeled residents such as Oprah Winfrey sometimes browse for truffle oil, picture frames, and designer jeans. Residents also hang out in the Upper Village, a chic shopping area with restaurants and cafés at the intersection of San Ysidro and East Valley roads.

FAMILY **Santa Barbara Maritime Museum.** California's seafaring history is the focus here. High-tech, hands-on exhibits, such as a sportfishing activity that lets participants haul in a "big one" and a local surfing history retrospective, make this a fun stop for families. The museum's shining star is a rare, 17-foot-tall Fresnel lens from the historic Point Conception Lighthouse. ■TIP➔ Ride the elevator to the fourth-floor observation area for great harbor views. ✉ *113 Harbor Way, off Shoreline Dr.* ☎ *805/962–8404* ⊕ *www.sbmm.org* ✉ *$7* ☉ *June–Aug., Thurs.–Tues. 10–6; Sept.–May, Thurs.–Tues. 10–5.*

Urban Wine Trail. Nearly two-dozen winery tasting rooms form the Urban Wine Trail; most are within walking distance of the waterfront and the lower State Street shopping and restaurant district. **Santa Barbara Winery,** at 202 Anacapa Street, and **Au Bon Climat,** at 813 Anacapa Street, are good places to start your oenological trek. ⊕ *urbanwinetrailsb.com.*

BEACHES

FAMILY
Fodor'sChoice
★
East Beach. The wide swath of sand at the east end of Cabrillo Boulevard is a great spot for people-watching. East Beach has sand volleyball courts, summertime lifeguard and sports competitions, and arts-and-crafts shows on Sunday and holidays. You can use showers, a weight room, and lockers (bring your own towel) and rent umbrellas and boogie boards at the Cabrillo Bathhouse. Next door, there's an elaborate jungle-gym play area for kids. Hotels line the boulevard across from the beach. **Amenities:** food and drink; lifeguards in summer; parking (fee); showers; toilets; water sports. **Best for:** walking; swimming; surfing. ✉ *1118 Cabrillo Blvd., at Ninos Dr.* ☎ *805/897–2680.*

Santa Barbara's downtown is attractive, but be sure to also visit its beautiful—and usually uncrowded—beaches.

WHERE TO EAT

$$$ JAPANESE 🍴 **Arigato Sushi.** You might have to wait for a table at this two-story restaurant and sushi bar—locals line up early for the wildly creative combination rolls and other delectables. Fans of authentic Japanese food sometimes disagree about the quality of the seafood, but all dishes are fresh and artfully presented. The menu includes traditional dishes as well as innovative creations such as jalapeño yellowtail sashimi and ahi carpaccio. [$] *Average main: $30* ✉ *1225 State St., near W. Victoria St.* ☎ *805/965–6074* 🌐 *www.arigatosb.com* ✍ *Reservations not accepted* ⏲ *No lunch.*

$$ SEAFOOD 🍴 **Brophy Bros.** The outdoor tables at this casual harborside restaurant have perfect views of the marina and mountains. Staffers serve enormous, exceptionally fresh fish dishes—don't miss the seafood salad and chowder—and provide guests with a pager if there's a long wait for a table. Stroll along the waterfront until the beep lets you know your table's ready. Hugely popular, Brophy Bros. can be crowded and loud, especially on weekend evenings. [$] *Average main: $22* ✉ *119 Harbor Way, off Shoreline Dr.* ☎ *805/966–4418* 🌐 *brophybros.com.*

$$$ MODERN AMERICAN Fodor's Choice ★ 🍴 **The Lark.** Shared dining—small plates and larger—and a seasonal menu showcasing local ingredients are the focus at this urban-chic restaurant named for an overnight all-Pullman train that chugged into the nearby railroad station for six decades. Sit at the 24-seat communal table set atop vintage radiators, or at tables and booths crafted from antique Spanish church pews and other repurposed or recycled materials. Drink options range from classic and handcrafted locavore

cocktails to wines curated by the master sommelier at the adjacent Les Marchands wine bar. $ *Average main: $23 ⊠ 131 Anacapa St., at E. Yanonali St.* ☎ *805/284–0370* ⊕ *www.thelarksb.com* ⊗ *Closed Mon. No lunch.*

$$$$
ITALIAN
✕ **Olio e Limone.** Sophisticated Italian cuisine (with an emphasis on Sicily) is served at this restaurant near the Arlington Center. The juicy veal chop is popular, but surprises abound here; be sure to try unusual dishes such as ribbon pasta with quail and sausage in a mushroom ragout, or the duck ravioli. Tables are placed close together, so this may not be the best spot for inti-

mate conversations. Next door are the more casual Olio Pizzeria, a combination pizzeria and wine bar, and Olio Crudo, a raw bar. $ *Average main: $31 ⊠ 17 W. Victoria St., at State St.* ☎ *805/899–2699* ⊕ *www.olioelimone.com* ⊗ *No lunch Sun.*

$$$
SOUTHERN
✕ **Palace Grill.** Mardi Gras energy, team-style service, lively music, and great food have made the Palace a Santa Barbara icon. Acclaimed for its Cajun and creole dishes such as blackened redfish and jambalaya with dirty rice, the Palace also serves Caribbean fare, including a delicious coconut-shrimp dish. Be prepared to wait for a table on Friday and Saturday nights (when reservations are taken for a 5:30 seating only), though the live entertainment and free appetizers, sent out front when the line is long, will whet your appetite for the feast to come. $ *Average main: $29 ⊠ 8 E. Cota St., at State St.* ☎ *805/963–5000* ⊕ *palacegrill.com.*

$$$$
AMERICAN
Fodor'sChoice
★
✕ **The Stonehouse.** The elegant Stonehouse is inside a century-old granite former farmhouse at the San Ysidro Ranch resort. Executive chef Matt Johnson creates outstanding regional cuisine centered on top-quality local ingredients complemented by herbs and vegetables from the on-site garden. The menu changes constantly, but might include pan-seared abalone or classic steak Diane flambéed tableside. Dine on the radiant-heated oceanview deck, next to a fountain under a canopy of loquat trees, or in the romantic, candlelit dining room overlooking a creek. ■ TIP→ **The Plow & Angel pub, downstairs, serves casual bistro fare.** $ *Average main: $49 ⊠ 900 San Ysidro La., off San Ysidro Rd., Montecito* ☎ *805/565–1700* ⊕ *www.sanysidroranch.com* ⌖ *Reservations essential* ⊗ *No lunch Mon. and Tues.*

$$$
ITALIAN
Fodor'sChoice
★
✕ **Toma.** Seasonal, locally sourced ingredients and softly lit muted-yellow walls evoke the flavors and charms of Tuscany and the Mediterranean at this rustic-romantic restaurant across from the harbor and West Beach. Ahi sashimi tucked in a crisp sesame cone is a popular appetizer, after which you can proceed to a house-made pasta dish or rock shrimp gnocchi. Mains of note include the tender braised beef

short ribs and savory cioppino. Central Coast and Italian wines figure prominently on the carefully selected wine list. $ *Average main: $26* ✉ *324 W. Cabrillo Blvd., near Castillo St.* ☎ *805/962–0777* ⊕ *www. tomarestaurant.com* ⊘ *No lunch.*

$$$ ✕ **Wine Cask.** A reinvention of a same-named local favorite that closed
AMERICAN a few years back, the Wine Cask serves bistro-style meals in a comfortable and classy dining room. The dishes are paired with wines from Santa Barbara's most extensive wine list. The more casual bar-café, Intermezzo, across the courtyard, serves pizzas, salads, small plates, wines, and cocktails and is open late. $ *Average main: $29* ✉ *El Paseo, 813 Anacapa St., at E. De La Guerra St.* ☎ *805/966–9463* ⊕ *winecask. com* ⚑ *Reservations essential.*

WHERE TO STAY

$$$$ 🏨 **Bacara Resort & Spa.** A luxury resort with four restaurants and a
RESORT 42,000-square-foot spa and fitness center with 36 treatment rooms, the
Fodor'sChoice Bacara provides a gorgeous setting for relaxing retreats. **Pros:** serene
★ natural setting; nature trails; first-rate spa; three zero-edge pools; in-room iPads for quick service orders and lighting and climate control. **Cons:** pricey; not close to downtown; sand on beach not pristine enough for some. $ *Rooms from: $450* ✉ *8301 Hollister Ave., Goleta* ☎ *805/968–0100, 855/817–9782* ⊕ *www.bacararesort.com* ⇶ *313 rooms, 45 suites* ¶◯| *No meals.*

$$$$ 🏨 **Belmond El Encanto.** Following years of extensive renovations by Ori-
HOTEL ent-Express, this Santa Barbara icon lives on to thrill a new generation
Fodor'sChoice of guests with its relaxed-luxe bungalow rooms, lush gardens, and per-
★ sonalized service. **Pros:** revitalized historic landmark; stellar spa facility; drinks and dining with stunning views; friendly and personal service; free use of electric bikes. **Cons:** long walk to downtown; pricey; guests staying for more than a few days may find the restaurant menus limited. $ *Rooms from: $650* ✉ *800 Alvarado Pl.* ☎ *805/845–5800, 800/393–5315* ⊕ *belmond.com/elencanto* ⇶ *70 rooms, 22 suites* ¶◯| *No meals.*

$$$$ 🏨 **Canary Hotel.** The only full-service hotel in the heart of downtown,
HOTEL this Kimpton property blends a casual, beach-getaway feel with urban sophistication. **Pros:** easy stroll to museums, shopping, dining; friendly, attentive service; adjacent fitness center. **Cons:** across from transit center; a mile from the beach. $ *Rooms from: $400* ✉ *31 W. Carrillo St.* ☎ *805/884–0300, 877/468–3515* ⊕ *www.canarysantabarbara.com* ⇶ *77 rooms, 20 suites* ¶◯| *No meals.*

$$$$ 🏨 **Four Seasons Resort The Biltmore Santa Barbara.** Surrounded by lush,
RESORT perfectly manicured gardens and across from the beach, Santa Barbara's
Fodor'sChoice grande dame has long been a favorite for quiet, California-style luxury.
★ **Pros:** first-class resort; historic Santa Barbara character; personal service; steps from the beach. **Cons:** back rooms are close to train tracks; expensive. $ *Rooms from: $545* ✉ *1260 Channel Dr.* ☎ *805/969–2261, 805/332–3442 reservations* ⊕ *www.fourseasons.com/santabarbara* ⇶ *181 rooms, 26 suites* ¶◯| *No meals.*

$$ 🏨 **Franciscan Inn.** A block from the harbor and West Beach, the family-
HOTEL owned Franciscan has spacious, beach-theme rooms. **Pros:** near water-front and harbor; friendly staff; good value; family-friendly. **Cons:** busy

lobby; pool can be crowded. $ *Rooms from: $175* ⊠ *109 Bath St.* ☎ *805/963–8845* ⊕ *www.franciscaninn.com* ↪ *33 rooms, 20 suites* ⦿ *Breakfast.*

$$$ 🏨 **Hotel Indigo.** The closest hotel to the train station, artsy Hotel Indigo
HOTEL is a fine choice for travelers who appreciate contemporary art and want easy access to dining, nightlife, and the beach. **Pros:** multilingual staff; a block from Stearns Wharf; great value for location. **Cons:** showers only (no bathtubs); train whistles early morning; rooms on small side. $ *Rooms from: $189* ⊠ *121 State St.* ☎ *805/966–6586, 877/270–1392 toll-free* ⊕ *www.indigosantabarbara.com* ↪ *41 rooms* ⦿ *No meals.*

$ 🏨 **Motel 6 Santa Barbara Beach.** A half block from East Beach amid fan-
HOTEL cier hotels sits this basic but comfortable motel—the first Motel 6 in existence, and the first in the chain to transform into a contemporary Euro-style abode. **Pros:** very close to zoo and beach; friendly staff; clean. **Cons:** no frills; motel-style rooms; no breakfast. $ *Rooms from: $119* ⊠ *443 Corona Del Mar Dr.* ☎ *805/564–1392, 800/466–8356* ⊕ *motel6. com* ↪ *51 rooms* ⦿ *No meals.*

$$$$ 🏨 **San Ysidro Ranch.** At this romantic hideaway on a historic property
RESORT in the Montecito foothills—where John and Jackie Kennedy spent their
Fodor's Choice honeymoon and Oprah sends her out-of-town visitors—guest cottages
★ are scattered among groves of orange trees and flower beds. **Pros:** ultimate privacy; surrounded by nature; celebrity hangout; pet-friendly. **Cons:** very expensive; too remote for some. $ *Rooms from: $695* ⊠ *900 San Ysidro La., Montecito* ☎ *805/565–1700, 800/368–6788* ⊕ *www. sanysidroranch.com* ↪ *23 rooms, 4 suites, 14 cottages* ⦿ *No meals* ↻ *2-day minimum stay on weekends, 3 days on holiday weekends.*

$$$$ 🏨 **Simpson House Inn.** If you're a fan of traditional bed-and-breakfast
B&B/INN inns, this property, with its beautifully appointed Victorian main house
Fodor's Choice and acre of lush gardens, is for you. **Pros:** elegant; impeccable landscap-
★ ing; within walking distance of downtown. **Cons:** some rooms in main building are small; two-night minimum stay on weekends. $ *Rooms from: $255* ⊠ *121 E. Arrellaga St.* ☎ *805/963–7067, 800/676–1280* ⊕ *www.simpsonhouseinn.com* ↪ *11 rooms, 4 cottages* ⦿ *Breakfast.*

$$$$ 🏨 **The Upham.** Built in 1871, this downtown Victorian in the arts and
B&B/INN culture district has been restored as a full-service hotel. **Pros:** 1-acre garden; easy walk to theaters; on-site restaurant; many room choices. **Cons:** some rooms are small; not near beach or waterfront. $ *Rooms from: $275* ⊠ *1404 De la Vina St.* ☎ *805/962–0058, 800/727–0876* ⊕ *www.uphamhotel.com* ↪ *46 rooms, 4 suites* ⦿ *Breakfast* ↻ *2-night minimum stay on weekends.*

NIGHTLIFE AND PERFORMING ARTS

The bar, club, and live-music scene centers on lower State Street, between the 300 and 800 blocks. The arts district, with theaters, restaurants, and cafés, starts around the 900 block of State and continues north to the 1300 block. To see what's scheduled around town, pick up the free weekly *Santa Barbara Independent* newspaper or visit its website, ⊕ *www.independent.com.*

NIGHTLIFE

James Joyce. A good place to have a few beers and while away an evening, the James Joyce sometimes hosts folk and rock performers. ⊠ *513 State St., at W. Haley St.* ☎ *805/962–2688* ⊕ *sbjamesjoyce.com.*

Joe's Cafe. Steins of beer and stiff cocktails accompany hearty bar food at Joe's. It's a fun, if occasionally rowdy, collegiate scene. ⊠ *536 State St., at E. Cota St.* ☎ *805/966–4638* ⊕ *joescafesb.com.*

Les Marchands. Brian McClintic, one of four real-life candidates trying to achieve master sommelier status in the 2013 film *Somm* (he succeeded), co-owns and operates this combination wine bar, store, and eatery in the Funk Zone. ■ **TIP→ From Friday through Sunday, you can combine your wine tasting with ramen slurping.** ⊠ *131 Anacapa St., at Yananoli St.* ☎ *805/284–0380* ⊕ *www.lesmarchandswine.com.*

SOhO. A hip restaurant, bar, and music club, SOhO books bands, from jazz to blues to rock. ⊠ *1221 State St., at W. Victoria St.* ☎ *805/962–7776* ⊕ *www.sohosb.com.*

PERFORMING ARTS

Arlington Theatre. This Moorish-style auditorium presents touring performers and films throughout the year. ⊠ *1317 State St., at Arlington Ave.* ☎ *805/963–4408* ⊕ *thearlingtontheatre.com.*

The Granada Theatre. A restored, modernized landmark that dates from 1924, the Granada hosts Broadway touring shows and dance, music, and other cultural events. ⊠ *1214 State St., at E. Anapamu St.* ☎ *805/899–2222* ⊕ *granadasb.org.*

Lobero Theatre. A state landmark, the Lobero hosts community theater groups and touring professionals. ⊠ *33 E. Canon Perdido St., at Anacapa St.* ☎ *805/963–0761* ⊕ *www.lobero.com.*

Fodor's Choice ★ **Old Spanish Days Fiesta.** The city celebrates its Spanish, Mexican, and Chumash heritage in early August with events that include music, dancing, an all-equestrian parade, a carnival, and a rodeo. ⊕ *oldspanishdaysfiesta.org.*

Fodor's Choice ★ **Santa Barbara International Film Festival.** The 12-day festival in late January and early February attracts film enthusiasts and major stars to downtown venues for screenings, panels, and tributes. ⊕ *sbiff.org.*

SPORTS AND THE OUTDOORS

BIKING

Cabrillo Bike Lane. The level, two-lane, 3-mile Cabrillo Bike Lane passes the Santa Barbara Zoo, the Andree Clark Bird Refuge, beaches, and the harbor. There are restaurants along the way, and you can stop for a picnic along the palm-lined path looking out on the Pacific.

Wheel Fun Rentals. You can rent bikes, quadricycles, and skates here. ⊠ *23 E. Cabrillo Blvd.* ☎ *805/966–2282* ⊕ *wheelfunrentalssb.com.*

BOATS AND CHARTERS

Channel Islands Outfitters. A full-service paddle-sports center in the harbor, this outfit rents kayaks, stand-up paddleboards, surfboards, boogie boards, and water-sports gear, and conducts guided tours and excursions. ✉ *117 B Harbor Way, off Shoreline Dr.* ☎ *805/899–4925 tours, 805/617–3425 rentals* ⊕ *www.channelislandso.com.*

Fodor's Choice ★ **Condor Express.** From SEA Landing, the *Condor Express*, a 75-foot high-speed catamaran, whisks up to 149 passengers toward the Channel Islands on whale-watching excursions and sunset and dinner cruises. ✉ *301 W. Cabrillo Blvd.* ☎ *805/882–0088, 888/779–4253* ⊕ *condorexpress.com.*

Santa Barbara Sailing Center. The center offers sailing instruction; rents and charters sailboats, kayaks, and stand-up paddleboards; and organizes dinner and sunset champagne cruises, island excursions, and whale-watching trips. ✉ *Santa Barbara Harbor launching ramp* ☎ *805/962–2826* ⊕ *www.sbsail.com.*

Truth Aquatics. Truth runs kayaking, paddleboarding, hiking, and scuba excursions to the National Marine Sanctuary and Channel Islands National Park. ✉ *Departures from SEA Landing, Santa Barbara Harbor* ☎ *805/962–1127* ⊕ *truthaquatics.com.*

> ### EARTH DAY
>
> In 1969, 200,000 gallons of crude oil spilled into the Santa Barbara Channel, causing an immediate outcry from residents. The day after the spill, Get Oil Out (GOO) was established; the group helped lead the successful fight for legislation to limit and regulate offshore drilling in California. The Santa Barbara spill also spawned Earth Day, which is still celebrated across the nation today.

6

SHOPPING

CLOTHING

Diani. This upscale, European-style women's boutique dresses clients in designer clothing from around the world. Sibling shoe and home-and-garden shops are nearby. ✉ *1324 State St., at Arlington Ave.* ☎ *805/966–3114, 805/966–7175 shoe shop* ⊕ *dianiboutique.com.*

Surf N Wear's Beach House. This shop carries surf clothing, gear, and collectibles; it's also the home of Santa Barbara Surf Shop and the exclusive local dealer of Surfboards by Yater. ✉ *10 State St., at Cabrillo Blvd.* ☎ *805/963–1281* ⊕ *surfnwear.com.*

Wendy Foster. This store sells casual-chic women's fashions. ✉ *833 State St., at W. Canon Perdido St.* ☎ *805/966–2276* ⊕ *wendyfoster.com.*

FOOD AND WINE

Santa Barbara Public Market. A dozen food and beverage vendors occupy this spacious arts district galleria that opened in 2014. Stock up on fresh seafood, meats, pastas, and other gourmet goodies; sip on handcrafted wines and beers; and nosh on locally made noodles, ice cream, and baked goods. ✉ *38 W. Victoria St., at Chapala St.* ☎ *805/770–7702* ⊕ *sbpublicmarket.com.*

SHOPPING AREAS

Fodor's Choice ★ **El Paseo.** Wine tasting rooms, shops, art galleries, and studios share the courtyard and gardens of El Paseo, a historic arcade. ✉ *Canon Perdido St., between State and Anacapa Sts.*

Fodors Choice **State Street.** Between Cabrillo Boulevard and Sola Street, State Street is
★ a shopper's paradise. Chic malls, quirky storefronts, antiques empo-
ria, elegant boutiques, and funky thrift shops abound. You can shop
on foot or ride a battery-powered trolley (50¢) that runs between the
waterfront and the 1300 block. Nordstrom and Macy's anchor **Paseo
Nuevo,** an open-air mall in the 700 block. Shops, restaurants, galleries,
and fountains line the tiled walkways of **La Arcada,** a small complex of
landscaped courtyards in the 1100 block designed by architect Myron
Hunt in 1926.

NORTHERN SANTA BARBARA COUNTY

The Santa Ynez Mountains divide Santa Barbara County geographically; U.S. 101 passes through a mountain tunnel leading inland. Northern Santa Barbara County used to be known for sprawling ranches and
strawberry and broccoli fields. Today its 200-plus wineries and 22,000
acres of vineyards dominate the landscape from the Santa Ynez Valley
in the south to Santa Maria in the north. Though more than 50 grape
varietals are grown in the county, more than half the vineyards are
planted to Chardonnay, Pinot Noir, and Syrah.

GETTING HERE AND AROUND

Two-lane Highway 154 over San Marcos Pass is the shortest and most
scenic route from Santa Barbara into the Santa Ynez Valley. You can
also drive along U.S. 101 north 43 miles to Buellton, then 7 miles east
through Solvang to Santa Ynez. Santa Ynez Valley Transit shuttle buses
serve Santa Ynez, Los Olivos, Ballard, Solvang, and Buellton. COLT
Wine Country Express buses connect Lompoc, Buellton, and Solvang
on weekdays except holidays.

ESSENTIALS

Bus Contacts COLT Wine Country Express ✉ *Lompoc* ☎ *805/736–7666*
⊕ *cityoflompoc.com/transit.* **Santa Ynez Valley Transit** ☎ *805/688–5452*
⊕ *syvt.com.*

Visitor Information Santa Barbara Vintners ☎ *805/688–0881* ⊕ *www.
sbcountywines.com.* **Visit Santa Barbara** ⊕ *www.santabarbaraca.com.* **Visit the
Santa Ynez Valley** ⊕ *www.visitsyv.com.*

SANTA YNEZ

31 miles north of Goleta.

Founded in 1882, the tiny town of Santa Ynez still has many of its original frontier buildings. You can walk through the three-block downtown
area in a few minutes, shop for antiques, and hang around the old-time
saloon. At some of the Santa Ynez Valley's best restaurants, you just
might bump into one of the celebrities who own nearby ranches.

GETTING HERE AND AROUND

Take Highway 154 over San Marcos Pass or U.S. 101 north 43 miles
to Buellton, then 7 miles east.

6

EXPLORING

Gainey Vineyard. The 1,800-acre Gainey Ranch, straddling the banks of the Santa Ynez River, includes about 100 acres of organic vineyards: Sauvignon Blanc, Merlot, Cabernet Sauvignon, and Cabernet Franc. The winery also makes wines from Chardonnay, Pinot Noir, and Syrah grapes from the Santa Rita Hills. You can taste the latest releases—the estate Pinot Noir is especially good—in a Spanish-style hacienda overlooking the ranch. ⊠ *3950 E. Hwy. 246* ☎ *805/688–0558* ⊕ *www. gaineyvineyard.com* 🍷 *Tasting $15* ⊙ *Daily 10–5.*

WHERE TO EAT AND STAY

$$$ ✕ **Santa Ynez Kitchen.** The owners of Toscana, a popular eatery in L.A.'s
ITALIAN   Brentwood neighborhood, run this rustic-chic restaurant with an Italy-meets-California Wine Country vibe. Chef and co-owner Luca Crestanelli, a native of Verona, Italy, typically offers about 10 seasonal daily specials. Menu regulars include Spanish-octopus salad, nettle ricotta gnocchi, wood-fired pizzas, and oak-grilled entrées such as salmon puttanesca and organic chicken. Save room for the gelatos or the "not-so-classic" tiramisu, served in small Mason jars. A big draw is the full bar, where resident mixologist Alberto Battaglini crafts creative cocktails using fresh local ingredients. $ *Average main: $23* ⊠ *1110 Faraday St., at Sagunto St.* ☎ *805/691–9794* ⊕ *www.sykitchen.com* ⊙ *No lunch Mon. and Tues.*

$$ ✕ **Trattoria Grappolo.** Authentic Italian fare, an open kitchen, and festive,
ITALIAN   family-style seating make this trattoria equally popular with celebrities from Hollywood and ranchers from the Santa Ynez Valley. Thin-crust pizza, homemade ravioli, risottos, and seafood linguine are among the menu favorites. The noise level tends to rise in the evening, so this isn't the best spot for a romantic getaway. $ *Average main: $22* ⊠ *3687-C Sagunto St.* ☎ *805/688–6899* ⊕ *trattoriagrappolo.com* ⊙ *No lunch Mon.*

$$$$ 🏠 **ForFriends Inn.** Four close friends—Jim and Debbie Campbell and
B&B/INN   Dave and Katie Pollock—own and operate this luxury bed-and-breakfast, designed as a social place where friends gather to enjoy good wine, food, and music in a casual backyard setting. **Pros:** relaxed, intimate setting; walk to restaurants; friendly innkeepers; "Friendship Pass" provides perks and savings at restaurants and wineries. **Cons:** not suitable for children; no pets allowed. $ *Rooms from: $295* ⊠ *1121 Edison St.* ☎ *805/693–0303* ⊕ *www.forfriendsinn.com* 🛏 *5 rooms, 2 cottages* ❙❊❙ *Breakfast.*

SPORTS AND THE OUTDOORS

Santa Barbara Soaring. The outfit's scenic glider rides last from 10 to 50 minutes. Tour options include the Santa Ynez Valley, coastal mountains and the Channel Islands, and celebrity homes. ⊠ *Santa Ynez Airport, 900 Airport Rd.* ☎ *805/688–2517* ⊕ *www.sbsoaring.com* 🎫 *$157–$419.*

LOS OLIVOS

4 miles north of Santa Ynez.

This pretty village was once on Spanish-built El Camino Real (Royal Road) and later a stop on major stagecoach and rail routes. Tasting rooms, art galleries, antiques stores, and country markets line Grand Avenue and intersecting streets for several blocks.

GETTING HERE AND AROUND

From U.S. 101 north or south, exit at Highway 154 and drive east about 8 miles. From Santa Barbara, travel 30 miles northwest on Highway 154.

EXPLORING

Blair Fox Cellars. Blair Fox, a Santa Barbara native, crafts small-lot Rhône-style wines made from organic grapes. The bar in his rustic Los Olivos tasting room, where you can sample exceptional vineyard-designated Syrahs and other wines, was hewn from Australian white oak reclaimed from an old Tasmanian schoolhouse. ✉ *2902–B San Marcos Ave.* ☎ *805/691–1678* 🌐 *www.blairfoxcellars.com* 🎫 *Tasting $12* 🕒 *Sept.–May, Thurs.–Sun. noon–5; June–Aug., Thurs.–Mon. noon–5.*

Daniel Gehrs Tasting Room. Heather Cottage, built in the early 1900s as a doctor's office, houses winemaker Gehrs's tasting room, where you can sample Port, Chardonnay, Gewürztraminer, Riesling, and other small-lot wines. ✉ *2939 Grand Ave.* ☎ *805/693–9686* 🌐 *danielgehrswines.com* 🎫 *Tastings $5–$10* 🕒 *Sun.–Fri. 11–5, Sat. 11–6.*

Firestone Vineyard. Heirs to the Firestone tire fortune developed (but no longer own) this winery known for Chardonnay, Gewürztraminer, Merlot, Riesling, and Syrah—and for the fantastic valley views from its tasting room and picnic area. The tour here is highly informative. ✉ *5017 Zaca Station Rd., off U.S. 101* ☎ *805/688–3940* 🌐 *www.firestonewine.com* 🎫 *Tastings $10–$15* 🕒 *Daily 10–5; tours 11:15, 1:15, and 3:15.*

WHERE TO EAT AND STAY

$$ AMERICAN 🍴 **Los Olivos Cafe.** Part wine store and part social hub, this café focuses on wine-friendly fish, pasta, and meat dishes, plus salads, pizzas, and burgers. Don't miss the homemade muffuletta and olive tapenade spreads. [$] *Average main: $21* ✉ *2879 Grand Ave.* ☎ *805/688–7265* 🌐 *www.losolivoscafe.com.*

$$$ AMERICAN 🍴 **Sides Hardware & Shoes: A Brothers Restaurant.** Inside a historic storefront they renovated, brothers Matt and Jeff Nichols serve comfort food prepared with panache. The Kobe-style burgers, especially the one with bacon and white cheddar, make a great lunch, and the dinner favorites include fried chicken, Scottish salmon, and lamb sirloin with goat cheese gnocchi. [$] *Average main: $28* ✉ *2375 Alamo Pintado Ave.* ☎ *805/688–4820* 🌐 *brothersrestaurant.com.*

$$$$ B&B/INN Fodor's Choice ★ 🏨 **The Ballard Inn & Restaurant.** Set among orchards and vineyards in the tiny town of Ballard, 2 miles south of Los Olivos, this inn makes an elegant wine-country escape. **Pros:** exceptional food; attentive staff; secluded. **Cons:** some baths could use updating. [$] *Rooms from: $265* ✉ *2436 Baseline Ave., Ballard* ☎ *805/688–7770, 800/638–2466* 🌐 *ballardinn.com* 🛏 *15 rooms* 🍽 *Breakfast.*

$$$$
B&B/INN

Fess Parker's Wine Country Inn and Spa. This luxury inn includes an elegant, tree-shaded French country–style main building and an equally attractive annex across the street with a pool and day spa. **Pros:** convenient wine-touring base; walking distance from restaurants and galleries; well-appointed rooms. **Cons:** pricey; not pet-friendly. $ *Rooms from: $395* ✉ *2860 Grand Ave.* ☎ *805/688–7788, 800/446–2455* ⊕ *www.fessparkerinn.com* ⤳ *15 rooms, 4 suites* ⏃ *Breakfast.*

SOLVANG

5 miles south of Los Olivos.

You'll know you've reached the town of Solvang when the architecture suddenly changes to half-timber buildings and windmills. Danish educators settled the town in 1911—the flatlands and rolling green hills reminded them of home. Solvang has attracted tourists for decades, but it's lately become more sophisticated, with smorgasbords giving way to galleries, upscale restaurants, and wine-tasting rooms by day and wine bars by night. The visitor center, on Copenhagen Drive, has walking-tour maps (also available online). The Sweet Treats tour covers the town's Danish bakeries, confectionary stores, and ice-cream parlors. The Olsen's and Solvang bakeries and Ingeborg's Danish Chocolates are worth investigating.

GETTING HERE AND AROUND

Highway 246 West (Mission Drive) traverses Solvang, connecting with U.S. 101 to the west and Highway 154 to the east. Alamo Pintado Road connects Solvang with Ballard and Los Olivos to the north. Park your car in one of the free public lots and stroll the town. Or take the bus: Santa Ynez Valley Transit shuttles run between Solvang and nearby towns.

ESSENTIALS

Visitor Information Solvang Conference & Visitors Bureau ✉ *1639 Copenhagen Dr., at 2nd St.* ☎ *805/688-6144* ⊕ *www.solvangusa.com.*

EXPLORING

Mission Santa Inés. The mission holds an impressive collection of paintings, statuary, vestments, and Chumash and Spanish artifacts in a serene bluff-top setting. You can tour the museum, sanctuary, and gardens. ✉ *1760 Mission Dr., at Alisal Rd.* ☎ *805/688–4815* ⊕ *missionsantaines. org* 🎟 *$5* ⏱ *Daily 9–4:30.*

Rideau Vineyard. This winery celebrates its locale's rich history—the King of Spain himself once owned this land, and the tasting room occupies a former guest ranch inn—but fully embraces the area's wine-making present. Wines made from the Rhône varietals Grenache, Mourvèdre, Roussanne, Syrah, and Viognier are the specialty here. ✉ *1562 Alamo Pintado Rd., 2 miles north of Hwy. 246* ☎ *805/688–0717* ⊕ *rideauvineyard.com* 🎟 *Tastings $12–$15* ⏱ *Daily 11–5.*

Sevtap. Winemaker Art Sevtap, an Istanbul native, is often on hand to pour samples of his limited-production wines—mostly from Bordeaux varietals but also Chardonnay, Sangiovese, and Syrah—in this artsy wine bar that's decked out with Tibetan prayer flags and chalkboard walls and has a stage where guests can pick up a guitar and strum away. ✉ *1576 Copenhagen Dr., Ste. 1, near Atterdag Rd.* ☎ *805/693–9200* 🌐 *www.sevtapwinery.com* 🎫 *Tasting $15* 🕒 *Sun., Mon., and Thurs. 11–8, Fri. and Sat. 11–9.*

WHERE TO EAT

$$$ AMERICAN Fodor's Choice ★ 🍴 **Root 246.** This chic restaurant's chefs tap local purveyors and shop for organic ingredients at farmers' markets before deciding on the day's menu. Depending on the season, you might feast on Dungeness crab, a savory cassoulet, Santa Maria–style tri-tip grilled over an oak fire, or seaweed-crusted steelhead trout in a smoky red wine broth. The 1,800-bottle wine selection includes many regional offerings. Root 246's gorgeous design incorporates wood, stone, tempered glass, and leather elements. [$] *Average main: $30* ✉ *Hotel Corque, 420 Alisal Rd., at Molle Way* ☎ *805/686–8681* 🌐 *www.root-246.com* 🕒 *Closed Mon. No lunch Tues.–Sat.*

$$$ AMERICAN 🍴 **Succulent Café.** Locals flock to this cozy café for its comfort cuisine and regional wines and craft beers. Order at the counter, and staffers will deliver your meal to the interior dining areas or the sunny outdoor patio. For breakfast—on weekends and holiday Mondays only—try the cinnamon-cumin pulled pork. Served on homemade biscuits, it's topped with bacon gravy and pineapple chutney. Buttermilk fried-chicken salad and the house-roasted turkey sandwich, both succulent indeed, are two top lunch choices; dinnertime favorites include artisanal cheese and charcuterie plates, and rack of lamb crusted with pumpkin seeds. [$] *Average main: $23* ✉ *1555 Mission Dr., at 4th Pl.* ☎ *805/691–9444* 🌐 *succulentcafe.com* 🕒 *Closed Tues. No breakfast weekdays except holiday Mon.*

WHERE TO STAY

$$$$ RESORT 🏨 **Alisal Guest Ranch and Resort.** Since 1946 this 10,000-acre ranch has been popular with celebrities and plain folk alike. **Pros:** Old West atmosphere; many activities; ultraprivate. **Cons:** isolated; not close to downtown. [$] *Rooms from: $525* ✉ *1054 Alisal Rd.* ☎ *805/688–6411, 800/425–4725* 🌐 *alisal.com* 🛏 *36 rooms, 37 suites* 🍽 *Some meals.*

$$$ HOTEL Fodor's Choice ★ 🏨 **Hotel Corque.** Owned by the Santa Ynez Band of Chumash Indians, the stunning three-story "Corque" provides a full slate of upscale amenities. **Pros:** front desk staff are trained concierges; short walk to shops, tasting rooms and restaurants; free Wi-Fi. **Cons:** no kitchenettes or laundry facilities; pricey. [$] *Rooms from: $239* ✉ *400 Alisal Rd.* ☎ *805/688–8000, 800/624–5572* 🌐 *hotelcorque.com* 🛏 *122 rooms, 10 suites* 🍽 *No meals.*

$$ B&B/INN 🏨 **Solvang Gardens Lodge.** The lush gardens with fountains and waterfalls and the cheery English-country-theme rooms make for a peaceful retreat just a few blocks—but worlds away—from Solvang's main tourist area. **Pros:** homey; family-friendly; colorful gardens. **Cons:** some rooms tiny; some need upgrades. [$] *Rooms from: $125* ✉ *293 Alisal Rd.* ☎ *805/688–4404, 888/688–4404* 🌐 *www.solvanggardens.com* 🛏 *16 rooms, 8 suites* 🍽 *Breakfast.*

PERFORMING ARTS

Solvang Festival Theater. Pacific Conservatory of the Performing Arts presents crowd-pleasing musicals *(My Fair Lady, Man of La Mancha)* and classic *(Cyrano de Bergerac)* and contemporary plays at this 700-seat outdoor amphitheater. ✉ *420 2nd St., at Molle Way* ☎ *805/922–8313* ⊕ *pcpa.org* ☉ *June–Oct.*

BUELLTON

3 miles west of Solvang.

A crossroads town at the intersection of U.S. 101 and Highway 246, Buellton has evolved from a sleepy gas and coffee stop into an enclave of wine-tasting rooms, beer gardens, and restaurants. It's also a gateway to Lompoc and the Santa Rita Hills Wine Trail to the west, and to Solvang, Santa Ynez, and Los Olivos to the east.

GETTING HERE AND AROUND

Driving is the easiest way to get to Buellton. From Santa Barbara, follow U.S. 101 north to the Highway 246 exit. Santa Ynez Valley Transit serves Buellton with shuttle buses from Solvang and nearby towns.

ESSENTIALS

Visitor Information Buellton Visitors Bureau ✉ *597 Avenue of the Flags, No. 101* ☎ *805/688–7829, 800/324–3800* ⊕ *visitbuellton.com.* **Santa Rita Hills Wine Trail** ⊕ *santaritahillswinetrail.com.*

EXPLORING

Alma Rosa Winery. Winemaker Richard Sanford helped put Santa Barbara County on the international wine map with a 1989 Pinot Noir. For Alma Rosa, started in 2005, he crafts wines from grapes grown on 100-plus acres of certified organic vineyards in the Santa Rita Hills. The Pinot Noirs and Chardonnays are exceptional. ✉ *181-C Industrial Way, off Hwy. 246, west of U.S. 101* ☎ *805/688–9090* ⊕ *almarosawinery.com* 🍷 *Tastings $10–$15* ☉ *Sun.–Thurs. 11–4:30; Fri. and Sat. 11–6:30.*

Industrial Way. A half-mile west of U.S. 101, head south from Highway 246 on Industrial Way to explore a hip and happening collection of food and drink destinations. Top stops include **Industrial Eats** (a craft butcher shop and restaurant), **Figueroa Mountain Brewing Co.**, the **Alma Rosa Winery** tasting room *(⇨ see above)*, **Avant Tapas and Wine**, and the **Ascendant Spirits Distillery.** ✉ *Industrial Way, off Hwy. 246.*

Lafond Winery and Vineyards. A rich, concentrated Pinot Noir is the main attention-getter at this winery that also produces noteworthy Chardonnays and Syrahs. Bottles with Lafond's SRH (Santa Rita Hills) label are an especially good value. The winery also has a tasting room at 111 East Yanonali Street in Santa Barbara's Funk Zone. ✉ *6855 Santa Rosa Rd., west off U.S. 101 Exit 139* ☎ *805/688–7921* ⊕ *lafondwinery.com* 🍷 *Tasting $10 (includes logo glass)* ☉ *Daily 10–5.*

WHERE TO EAT

$$$ AMERICAN 🍴 **The Hitching Post II.** You'll find everything from grilled artichokes to quail at this casual eatery, but most people come for the smoky Santa Maria–style barbecue. Be sure to try a glass of owner-chef-winemaker Frank Ostini's signature Highliner Pinot Noir, a star in the film *Sideways.* [$] *Average main: $30* ✉ *406 E. Hwy. 246, off U.S. 101* ☎ *805/688–0676* 🌐 *hitchingpost2.com* 🕒 *No lunch.*

LOMPOC

20 miles west of Solvang.

Known as the flower-seed capital of the world, Lompoc is blanketed with vast fields of brightly colored flowers that bloom from May through August. Also home to a starkly beautiful mission, Lompoc has emerged as a major Pinot Noir and Chardonnay grape-growing region. Overlapping the Santa Rita Hills Wine Trail in parts, the Lompoc Wine Trail includes wineries in the Wine Ghetto, a downtown industrial park, and along Highway 246 and (to the south) Santa Rosa Road, which form a loop between Lompoc and Buellton.

GETTING HERE AND AROUND

Driving is the easiest way to get to Lompoc. From Santa Barbara, follow U.S. 101 north to Highway 1 exit off Gaviota Pass, or Highway 246 west at Buellton.

ESSENTIALS

Visitor Information Lompoc Valley Chamber of Commerce & Visitors Bureau ✉ *111 S. I St., at Hwy. 246* ☎ *805/736–4567, 800/240–0999* 🌐 *lompoc.com.*

EXPLORING

FAMILY **La Purísima Mission State Historic Park.** The state's most fully restored mission, founded in 1787, stands in a stark and still remote location that powerfully evokes the lives and isolation of California's Spanish settlers. Docents lead tours every afternoon, and vivid displays illustrate the secular and religious activities that formed mission life. ✉ *2295 Purisima Rd., off Hwy. 246* ☎ *805/733–3713* 🌐 *www.lapurisimamission.org* 🎫 *$6 per vehicle* 🕒 *Daily 9–5; tour daily at 1.*

Lompoc Wine Ghetto. Laid-back tasting rooms can be found in a downtown industrial park. Taste of Sta. Rita Hills, Fiddlehead Cellars, and Flying Goat are three rooms worth checking out here. ✉ *200 N. 9th St.* 🌐 *lompoctrail.com* 🎫 *Tasting fees vary, some free* 🕒 *Most tasting rooms open Thurs.–Sun., 11 or noon until 4 or 5; some also Mon. and by appointment.*

SAN LUIS OBISPO COUNTY

San Luis Obispo County's pristine landscapes and abundant wildlife areas, especially those around Morro Bay, have long attracted nature lovers. In the south, Pismo Beach and other coastal towns have great sand and surf; inland, a booming wine region stretches from the Edna,

Arroyo Grande, and Avila valleys and Nipomo in the south to Paso Robles in the north.

GETTING HERE AND AROUND

San Luis Obispo Regional Transit Authority operates buses in San Luis Obispo and serves Paso Robles as well as Pismo Beach and other coastal towns.

ESSENTIALS

Transportation Contact San Luis Obispo Regional Transit Authority ☎ 805/541–2228 ⊕ www.slorta.org.

> **VOLCANOES?**
>
> Those funny-looking, sawed-off peaks along the drive from Pismo Beach to Morro Bay are the Nine Sisters—a series of ancient volcanic plugs. Morro Rock, the northernmost sibling and a state historic monument, is the most famous and photographed of the clan.

Visitor Information Highway 1 Discovery Route ⊠ San Luis Obispo ⊕ highway1discoveryroute.com. **SLO Wine Country** ☎ 805/541–5868 ⊕ www.slowine.com. **Visit San Luis Obispo County** ⊠ 835 12th St., Ste. 204, Paso Robles ☎ 805/541–8000 ⊕ www.visitsanluisobispocounty.com.

PISMO BEACH

40 miles north of Lompoc.

About 20 miles of sandy shoreline—nicknamed the Bakersfield Riviera for the throngs of vacationers who come here from the Central Valley—begins at the town of Pismo Beach. The southern end of town runs along sand dunes, some of which are open to cars and off-road vehicles. Sheltered by the dunes, a grove of eucalyptus trees attracts thousands of migrating monarch butterflies from November through February. A long, broad beach fronts the center of town, where a municipal pier extends into the sea at the foot of shop-lined Pomeroy Street. To the north, hotels and homes perch atop chalky oceanfront cliffs. Fewer than 10,000 people live in this quintessential surfer haven, but Pismo Beach has a slew of hotels and restaurants with great views of the Pacific Ocean.

GETTING HERE AND AROUND

Pismo Beach straddles both sides of U.S. 101. If you're coming from the south and have time for a scenic drive, exit U.S. 101 in Santa Maria and take Highway 166 west for 8 miles to Guadalupe and follow Highway 1 north 16 miles to Pismo Beach. South County Area Transit (*SCAT;* ⊕ *www.slorta.org*) buses run throughout San Luis Obispo and connect the city with nearby towns. On summer weekends, the free Avila Trolley extends service to Pismo Beach.

ESSENTIALS

Visitor Information California Welcome Center ⊠ 333 Five Cities Dr. ☎ 805/773–7924. **Pismo Beach Visitors Information Center** ⊠ Dolliver St./Hwy. 1, at Hinds Ave. ☎ 800/443–7778, 805/773–4382 ⊕ classiccalifornia.com ⊙ Weekdays 9–5, Sat. 11–4, Sun. 10–2.

BEACHES

Fodor's Choice ★ **Oceano Dunes State Vehicular Recreation Area.** Part of the spectacular Guadalupe-Nipomo Dunes, this 3,600-acre coastal playground is one of the few places in California where you can drive or ride off-highway vehicles on the beach and sand dunes. Hike, ride horses, kiteboard, join a Hummer tour, or rent an ATV or a dune buggy and cruise up the white-sand peaks for spectacular views. At **Oso Flaco Lake Nature Area**—3 miles west of Highway 1 on Oso Flaco Road—a 1½-mile boardwalk over the lake leads to a platform with views up and down the coast. Leashed dogs are allowed in much of the park except Oso Flaco and Pismo Dunes Natural Reserve. **Amenities:** food and drink; lifeguards (seasonal); parking (fee); showers; toilets; water sports. **Best for:** sunset; surfing; swimming; walking. ✉ *West end of Pier Ave., off Hwy. 1, Oceano* ☎ *805/473–7220* 🌐 *www.parks.ca.gov* 🎟 *$5 per vehicle* 🕒 *Daily 6 am–11 pm; Oso Flaco Lake sunrise–sunset.*

Pismo State Beach. Hike, surf, ride horses, swim, fish in a lagoon or off the pier, and dig for Pismo clams at this busy state beach. One of the day-use parking areas is off Highway 1 near the **Monarch Butterfly Grove,** where from November through February monarch butterflies nest in eucalyptus and Monterey pines. The other parking area is about 1½ miles south at Pier Avenue. **Amenities:** food and drink; lifeguards (seasonal); parking (fee); showers; toilets; water sports. **Best for:** sunset; surfing; swimming; walking. ✉ *555 Pier Ave., off Hwy. 1, 3 miles south of downtown Pismo Beach, Oceano* ☎ *805/489–1869* 🌐 *www.parks.ca.gov* 🎟 *Day use $5 per vehicle if parking at the beach* 🕒 *Day use 6 am–11 pm.*

WHERE TO EAT

$$$ SEAFOOD 🍴 **Cracked Crab.** This traditional New England–style crab shack imports fresh seafood daily from Australia, Alaska, and the East Coast. Fish is line-caught, much of the produce is organic, and everything is made from scratch. For a real treat, don a bib and sample a bucket of steamed shellfish with Cajun sausage, potatoes, and corn on the cob, all dumped right onto your table. [$] *Average main: $26* ✉ *751 Price St., near Main St.* ☎ *805/773–2722* 🌐 *www.crackedcrab.com* ✍ *Reservations not accepted.*

$ AMERICAN FAMILY 🍴 **Doc Burnstein's Ice Cream Lab.** The delectable ice creams are churned onsite at this beloved old-fashioned parlor east of Pismo Beach. Top-selling flavors include the Elvis Special (banana and peanut butter) and Motor Oil, a blend of dark chocolate and Kahlúa with a fudge swirl. Slip into a wooden booth and watch an antique model train chug around a circular ceiling track. **TIP→ There's a second Lab in downtown San Luis Obispo at 860 Higuera Street.** [$] *Average main: $6* ✉ *114 W. Branch St., at Nevada St., east off U.S. 101, Arroyo Grande* ☎ *805/474–4068* 🌐 *docburnsteins.com.*

$$ MODERN AMERICAN Fodor's Choice ★ 🍴 **Ember.** A barn-style restaurant with high ceilings and an open kitchen, Ember enjoys a red-hot reputation for Italian-inflected dishes prepared in an authentic Tuscan fireplace or a wood-burning oven. Chef-owner Brian Collins, a native of Arroyo Grande, the town bordering Pismo Beach, honed his culinary skills at Berkeley's legendary Chez Panisse Restaurant. His seasonal menu changes monthly, but nearly always

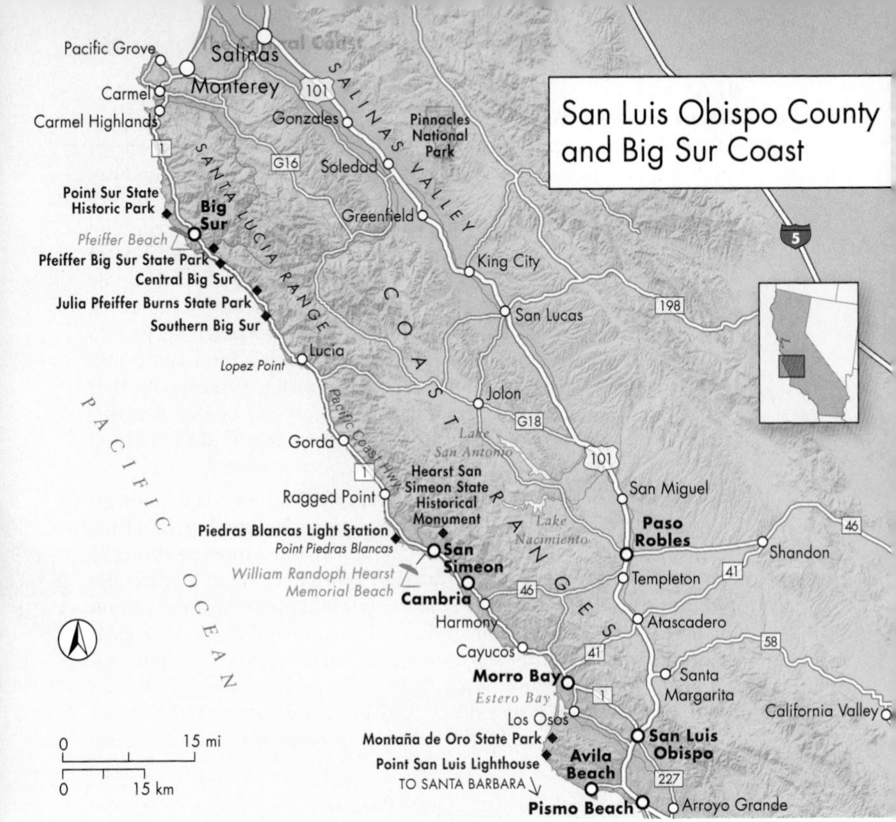

includes a starter of local abalone and crispy pork belly, several flatbread pizzas, grilled rib-eye steak, and chicken cooked under a brick on the hearth. **■TIP→ Ember doesn't accept reservations, so come before 6 or after 8 to avoid a wait.** [$] *Average main: $22* ✉ *1200 E. Grand Ave., at Brisco Rd., Arroyo Grande* ☎ *805/474–7700* 🌐 *www.emberwoodfire.com* ✍ *Reservations not accepted* 🕒 *Closed Mon. and Tues. No lunch.*

$$$ ITALIAN 🍴 **Giuseppe's Cucina Italiana.** The classic flavors of southern Italy are highlighted at this lively downtown spot. Most recipes originate from Bari, a seaport on the Adriatic; the menu includes breads and pizzas baked in the wood-burning oven, hearty dishes such as osso buco and lamb, and homemade pastas. The wait for a table can be long, but sometimes an accordion player gets the crowd singing. [$] *Average main: $24* ✉ *891 Price St., at Pismo Ave.* ☎ *805/773–2870* 🌐 *giuseppesrestaurant.com* ✍ *Reservations not accepted.*

WHERE TO STAY

$$$$ RESORT 🏨 **Dolphin Bay Resort & Spa.** On grass-covered bluffs overlooking Shell Beach, this luxury resort looks and feels like an exclusive community of villas. **Pros:** lavish apartment units; killer views; walking distance from the beach. **Cons:** hefty price tag; vibe too upper-crust for some. [$] *Rooms from: $405* ✉ *2727 Shell Beach Rd.* ☎ *805/773–4300,*

800/516–0112 reservations, 805/773–8900 restaurant 🌐 *thedolphinbay.com* 🛏 *60 suites* 🍴 *No meals.*

$$$$ HOTEL 🏨 **Pismo Lighthouse Suites.** Each of the well-appointed two-room, two-bath suites at this oceanfront resort has a private balcony or patio. **Pros:** lots of space for families and groups; nice pool area. **Cons:** not easy to walk to main attractions; some units are next to busy road. [$] *Rooms from: $259* ✉ *2411 Price St.* ☎ *805/773–2411, 800/245–2411* 🌐 *www.pismolighthousesuites.com* 🛏 *70 suites* 🍴 *Breakfast.*

AVILA BEACH

4 miles north of Pismo Beach.

FAMILY Because the village of Avila Beach and the sandy, cove-front shoreline for which it's named face south into the Pacific Ocean, they get more sun and less fog than any other stretch of coast in the area. With its fortuitous climate and protected waters, Avila's public beach draws sunbathers and families; summer weekends are very busy. Downtown Avila Beach has a lively seaside promenade and some shops and hotels, but for real local color, head to the far end of the cove and watch the commercial fishers offload their catch on the old Port San Luis wharf. On Friday from mid-April through mid-September, a fish and farmers' market livens up the beach area with music, fresh local produce and seafood, and children's activities.

6

GETTING HERE AND AROUND

Exit U.S. 101 at Avila Beach Drive and head 3 miles west to reach the beach. The free Avila Trolley operates weekends year-round, plus Friday afternoon and evening from April to September. The minibuses connect Avila Beach and Port San Luis to Shell Beach, with multiple stops along the way. Service extends to Pismo Beach in summer.

ESSENTIALS

Visitor Information Avila Beach Tourism Alliance 🌐 *visitavilabeach.com.*

EXPLORING

FAMILY **Avila Valley Barn.** An old-fashioned, family-friendly country store jam-packed with local fruits and vegetables, prepared foods, and gift items, Avila Valley Barn also gives visitors a chance to experience rural American traditions. You can pet farm animals and savor homemade ice cream and pies daily, and on weekends ride a hay wagon out to the fields to pick your own produce. ✉ *560 Avila Beach Dr., San Luis Obispo* ☎ *805/595–2816* 🌐 *avilavalleybarn.com* 🕒 *Daily 9–5* 🕒 *Closed Tues. and Wed. Jan.–Mar.*

Central Coast Aquarium. You'll learn all about local marine plants and animals from the hands-on exhibits at this science center next to the main beach. ✉ *50 San Juan St., at 1st St., off Avila Beach Dr.* ☎ *805/595–7280* 🌐 *www.centralcoastaquarium.com* 🎟 *$8* 🕒 *June–Aug., Tues.–Sun. 10–5; Sept.–May, weekends 10–4 and holiday breaks.*

FAMILY **Point San Luis Lighthouse.** Docents lead hikes along scenic Pecho Coast Trail (3½ miles round-trip) to see the historic 1890 lighthouse and its rare Fresnel lens. ■ TIP→ **If you'd prefer a lift out to the lighthouse, join a trolley tour. Hikes and tours require reservations.** ✉ *Point San*

Luis, 1¾ miles west of Harford Pier, Port San Luis ☎ 855/533–7843, 805/528–8758 hikes reservations ⊕ sanluislighthouse.org ☜ Trolley tours $20; hikes free ($5 to enter lighthouse) ☉ Trolley tours Wed. at noon, Sat. at noon, 1, and 2; hikes Wed. and Sat. at 9.

BEACHES

FAMILY **Avila State Beach.** At the edge of a sunny cove next to downtown shops and restaurants, Avila's ½-mile stretch of white sand is especially family-friendly, with a playground, barbecue and picnic tables, volleyball and basketball courts, and lifeguards on watch in summer and on many holiday weekends. The free beachfront parking fills up fast, but there's a nearby pay lot ($5 for the day, $1 after 4 pm). Dogs aren't allowed on the beach from 10 to 5. **Amenities:** food and drink; lifeguards (seasonal); parking (free); showers; toilets; water sports. **Best for:** sunset; surfing; swimming; walking. ⊠ *Avila Beach Dr., at 1st St.* ⊕ *visitavilabeach.com* ☜ *Free* ☉ *Daily 6 am–10 pm.*

WHERE TO EAT AND STAY

$$$ ✕ **Ocean Grill.** Across from the promenade, beach, and pier, Ocean Grill
SEAFOOD serves up fresh seafood to diners who typically arrive before sunset to enjoy the views. Boats anchored in the bay provide much of the seafood, which pairs well with the mostly regional wines on the list. Southern California craft beers are also well represented. Along with fish and shellfish, the chefs prepare wood-fired pizzas and land-based entrées such as steaks and chops, and there are gluten-free and vegetarian options. $ *Average main: $28* ⊠ *268 Front St.* ☎ *805/595–4050* ⊕ *www.oceangrillavila.com* ☉ *No lunch Mon.–Thurs.*

$$$$ ⚏ **Avila La Fonda.** Modeled after a village in early California's Mexican
HOTEL period, Avila La Fonda surrounds guests with rich jewel tones, fountains, and upscale comfort. **Pros:** one-of-a-kind theme and artwork; flexible room combinations; a block from the beach. **Cons:** pricey; most rooms don't have an ocean view. $ *Rooms from: $329* ⊠ *101 San Miguel St.* ☎ *805/595–1700* ⊕ *avilalafondahotel.com* ⇌ *28 rooms, 1 suite* ⫶○⫶ *No meals.*

$$$ ⚏ **Avila Lighthouse Suites.** Families, honeymooners, and business travelers
HOTEL all find respite at this two-story, all-suites luxury hotel. **Pros:** directly across from sand; easy walk to restaurants and shops; free underground parking. **Cons:** noise from passersby can be heard in room; some ocean-view rooms have limited vistas. $ *Rooms from: $229* ⊠ *550 Front St.* ☎ *805/627–1900, 800/372–8452* ⊕ *www.avilalighthousesuites.com* ⇌ *54 suites* ⫶○⫶ *Breakfast.*

$$ ⚏ **Sycamore Mineral Springs Resort.** This wellness resort's hot mineral
RESORT springs bubble up into private outdoor tubs on an oak-and-sycamore-forest hillside. **Pros:** great place to rejuvenate; nice hiking; incredible spa services. **Cons:** rooms vary in quality; 2½ miles from the beach. $ *Rooms from: $169* ⊠ *1215 Avila Beach Dr., San Luis Obispo* ☎ *805/595–7302* ⊕ *www.sycamoresprings.com* ⇌ *26 rooms, 46 suites* ⫶○⫶ *No meals.*

6

SAN LUIS OBISPO

8 miles north of Avila Beach.

About halfway between San Francisco and Los Angeles, San Luis Obispo spreads out below gentle hills and rocky extinct volcanoes. Its main appeal lies in its architecturally diverse, pedestrian-friendly downtown, which bustles with shoppers, restaurant goers, and students from California Polytechnic State University, known as Cal Poly.

> **DEEP ROOTS**
>
> Way back in the 1700s, the Spanish padres who accompanied Father Junípero Serra planted grapevines from Mexico along California's Central Coast, and began using European wine-making techniques to turn the grapes into delectable vintages.

GETTING HERE AND AROUND

U.S. 101/Highway 1 traverses the city for several miles. From the north, Highway 1 merges with U.S. 101 when it reaches the city limits. The wineries of the Edna Valley and Arroyo Grande Valley wine regions lie south of town off Highway 227, the parallel (to the east) Orcutt Road, and connecting roads.

SLO City Transit buses operate daily; Regional Transit Authority (SLORTA) buses connect with north county towns. The Downtown Trolley provides evening service to the city's hub every Thursday, on Friday from June to early September, and on Saturday from April through October.

ESSENTIALS

Visitor Information San Luis Obispo Chamber of Commerce ⊠ *895 Monterey St.* ☎ *805/781-2777* ⊕ *www.visitslo.com.* **San Luis Obispo City Visitor Information** ⊕ *www.sanluisobispovacations.com.*

EXPLORING

TOP ATTRACTIONS

Mission San Luis Obispo de Tolosa. Sun-dappled Mission Plaza fronts the fifth mission established in 1772 by Franciscan friars. A small museum exhibits artifacts of the Chumash Indians and early Spanish settlers. ⊠ *751 Palm St., at Chorro St.* ☎ *805/543-6850* ⊕ *www.missionsanluisobispo.org* ⊠ *$3* ⊙ *Early Mar.–early Nov., daily 9–5; early Nov.–early Mar., daily 9–4.*

Fodor's Choice ★ **Talley Vineyards.** Acres of Chardonnay and Pinot Noir, plus smaller parcels of Sauvignon Blanc, Syrah, and other varietals blanket Talley's mountain-ringed dell in the Arroyo Grande Valley. The estate tour ($40), worth a splurge, includes wine and cheese, a visit to an 1860s adobe, and barrel-room tastings of upcoming releases. ⊠ *3031 Lopez Dr., off Orcutt Rd., Arroyo Grande* ☎ *805/489-0446* ⊕ *talleyvineyards.com* ⊠ *Tastings $8–$15; tours $15–$40* ⊙ *Daily 10:30–4:30; tours by appointment.*

WORTH NOTING

Edna Valley Vineyard. For sweeping valley views and crisp Sauvignon Blancs and Chardonnays, head to the modern tasting bar here. ■ TIP→ **The reserve tasting ($15) is the best option here.** ⊠ *2585 Biddle*

Ranch Rd., off Edna Rd. ☎ *805/544–5855* 🌐 *www.ednavalleyvineyard.com* 🎫 *Tastings $10–$15* 🕑 *Daily 10–5.*

Niven Family Wine Estates. A refurbished 1909 schoolhouse serves as tasting room for six Niven Family wineries: Baileyana, Cadre, Tangent, Trenza, True Myth, and Zocker. The winemaker for all these labels is Christian Roguenant, whose Cadre Pinot Noirs are worth checking out. ✉ *5828 Orcutt Rd., at Righetti Rd.* ☎ *805/269–8200* 🌐 *www.nivenfamilywines.com* 🎫 *Tasting $12* 🕑 *Daily 10–5.*

Old Edna. This peaceful, 2-acre site once *was* the town of Edna. Nowadays you can peek at the vintage 1897 and 1908 farmhouse cottages, taste Sextant wines, pick up sandwiches at the gourmet deli, and stroll along Old Edna Lane. ✉ *1655 Old Price Canyon Rd., at Hwy. 227* ☎ *805/710–3701 Old Edna Townsite, 805/542–0133 tasting room and deli* 🌐 *oldedna.com.*

FAMILY **San Luis Obispo Children's Museum.** Activities at this facility geared to kids under age eight include an "imagination-powered" elevator that transports visitors to a series of underground caverns. Elsewhere, simulated lava and steam sputter from an active volcano. Kids can pick rubber fruit at a farmers' market and race in a fire engine to fight a fire. ✉ *1010 Nipomo St., at Monterey St.* ☎ *805/544–5437* 🌐 *www.slocm.org* 🎫 *$8* 🕑 *May–Aug., Mon.–Wed. 10–3, Thurs.–Sat. 10–5, Sun. and some holidays 1–5; Sept.–Apr., Tues. and Wed. 10–3, Thurs.–Sat. 10–5, Sun. and some holidays 1–5.*

6

Wolff Vineyards. Syrah, Petite Sirah, and Riesling join the expected Pinot Noir and Chardonnay as the stars at this family-run winery 6 miles south of downtown. The pourers are super-friendly, and you'll often meet one of the owners or their children in the tasting room. With its hillside views, the outdoor patio is a great place to enjoy an afternoon picnic. ✉ *6238 Orcutt Rd., near Biddle Ranch Rd.* ☎ *805/781–0448* 🌐 *www.wolffvineyards.com* 🎫 *Tasting $10* 🕑 *Daily 11–5.*

WHERE TO EAT

$$ ECLECTIC 🍴 **Big Sky Café.** Family-friendly Big Sky turns local and organically grown ingredients into global dishes, starting with breakfast. Just pick your continent: Brazilian churrasco chicken breast, Thai catfish, North African vegetable stew, Maryland crab cakes. Vegetarians have ample choices. [$] *Average main: $17* ✉ *1121 Broad St., at Higuera St.* ☎ *805/545–5401* 🌐 *bigskycafe.com* ✍ *Reservations not accepted.*

$$ NORTHERN ITALIAN 🍴 **Café Roma.** At this Railroad Square restaurant you can dine on authentic northern Italian cuisine in the warmly lit dining room or out on the covered patio. Menu favorites include ricotta-filled squash blossoms, and beef tenderloin glistening with porcini butter and a Pinot Noir reduction. [$] *Average main: $20* ✉ *1020 Railroad Ave., at Osos St.* ☎ *805/541–6800* 🌐 *www.caferomaslo.com* 🕑 *No lunch weekends.*

$$$ MODERN AMERICAN 🍴 **Foremost Wine Company.** A hip combination restaurant, wine bar, lounge, and wineshop in the Creamery building, a former dairy, Foremost focuses on community-linked food and wine and sustainable practices. The bar, dining areas, and wine store occupy a huge interior space with copper-topped tables and other furnishings made with repurposed materials. Native Parisienne chef Julie Simon oversees a seasonal menu

that typically includes small plates and dishes to share: grilled octopus, lamb tartare, roast duck crostini, and pappardelle in a duck-pork Bolognese sauce. Vegan and vegetarian options are plentiful. $ *Average main: $28* ✉ *570 Higuera St., near Nipomo St.* ☎ *805/439–3410* ⊕ *foremostwineco.com* ⚑ *Reservations not accepted* ⊙ *Closed Mon.*

$$$
INTERNATIONAL

✕ **Luna Red.** A spacious, contemporary space with a festive outdoor patio, this restaurant near Mission Plaza serves creative tapas and cocktails. The small plates include lamb sausage flatbread, avocado-tuna ceviche, and *piquillo* peppers stuffed with goat cheese. Turkey confit in mole sauce and coconut milk-braised pork shoulder are two large plates of note. $ *Average main: $25* ✉ *1023 Chorro St., at Monterey St.* ☎ *805/540–5243* ⊕ *www.lunaredslo.com.*

$$
ECLECTIC

✕ **Novo Restaurant & Lounge.** In the colorful dining room or on the large creek-side deck, this animated downtown eatery will take you on a culinary world tour. The salads, small plates, and entrées come from nearly every continent. The wine and beer list also covers the globe and includes local favorites. $ *Average main: $20* ✉ *726 Higuera St., at Broad St.* ☎ *805/543–3986* ⊕ *www.novorestaurant.com.*

WHERE TO STAY

$$$
HOTEL

🏨 **Apple Farm.** Decorated to the hilt with floral bedspreads and watercolors by local artists, this Wine Country–theme hotel is highly popular. **Pros:** flowers everywhere; convenient to Cal Poly and U.S. 101; creekside setting. **Cons:** hordes of tourists during the day; some rooms too floral for some people's tastes. $ *Rooms from: $219* ✉ *2015 Monterey St.* ☎ *800/255–2040, 805/544-2040* ⊕ *www.applefarm.com* ⮑ *104 rooms* ⦿ *No meals.*

$$$
HOTEL

🏨 **Granada Hotel & Bistro.** Built in 1922 and sparkling again after renovations completed in 2012, the Granada is the only full-service hotel in the heart of downtown. **Pros:** free parking; easy walk to downtown; luxurious rooms and amenities. **Cons:** some rooms are tiny; sometimes noisy near restaurant kitchen. $ *Rooms from: $249* ✉ *1126 Morro St.* ☎ *805/544–9100* ⊕ *granadahotelandbistro.com* ⮑ *17 rooms* ⦿ *No meals.*

$$$
HOTEL

🏨 **Madonna Inn.** From its rococo bathrooms to its pink-on-pink froufrou steak house, the Madonna Inn is fabulous or tacky, depending on your taste. **Pros:** fun, one-of-a-kind experience; on-site horseback riding for all levels. **Cons:** rooms vary widely; must appreciate kitsch. $ *Rooms from: $189* ✉ *100 Madonna Rd.* ☎ *805/543–3000, 800/543–9666* ⊕ *www.madonnainn.com* ⮑ *106 rooms, 4 suites* ⦿ *No meals.*

$$$
B&B/INN

🏨 **Petit Soleil.** A cobblestone courtyard, country-French custom furnishings, and Gallic music piped through the halls evoke a Provençal mood at this cheery inn. **Pros:** French details throughout; scrumptious breakfasts; cozy rooms. **Cons:** sits on a busy avenue; cramped parking. $ *Rooms from: $179* ✉ *1473 Monterey St.* ☎ *805/549–0321, 800/676–1588* ⊕ *psslo.com* ⮑ *15 rooms, 1 suite* ⦿ *Breakfast.*

NIGHTLIFE AND PERFORMING ARTS

SLO's club scene is centered on Higuera Street, off Monterey Street.

Koberl at Blue. A trendy crowd hangs out at this upscale restaurant's slick bar to sip on exotic martinis and the many local and imported beers and wines. ⊠ *998 Monterey St., at Osos St.* ☏ *805/783–1135* ⊕ *epkoberl.com.*

Linnaea's. A mellow java joint, Linnaea's sometimes hosts poetry readings, as well as blues, jazz, and folk music performances. ⊠ *1110 Garden St., at Higuera St.* ☏ *805/541–5888* ⊕ *linnaeas.com.*

Mother's Tavern. Chicago-style MoTav draws crowds with good pub food and live entertainment in a turn-of-the-20th-century setting, complete with antique U.S. flags and a wall-mounted moose head. ⊠ *725 Higuera St., at Broad St.* ☏ *805/541–8733* ⊕ *www.motherstavern.com.*

SLO Brew. Handcrafted microbrews and live music most nights make for a winning combination at this downtown watering hole and restaurant that opened in new digs in 2015. ⊠ *1119 Garden St.* ☏ *805/543–1843* ⊕ *slobrewingco.com.*

Performing Arts Center, San Luis Obispo. A truly great performance space, the center hosts live theater, dance, and music. ⊠ *Cal Poly, 1 Grand Ave., off U.S. 101* ☏ *805/756–4849* ⊕ *www.pacslo.org.*

MORRO BAY

14 miles north of San Luis Obispo.

Commercial fishermen slog around Morro Bay in galoshes, and beat-up fishing boats bob in the bay's protected waters. Nature-oriented activities take center stage here: kayaking, hiking, biking, fishing, and wildlife-watching around the bay and national marine estuary and along the state beach.

GETTING HERE AND AROUND

From U.S. 101 south or north, exit at Highway 1 in San Luis Obispo and head west. Scenic Highway 1 passes through the eastern edge of town. From Atascadero, two-lane Highway 41 West treks over the mountains to Morro Bay. San Luis Obispo RTA Route 12 buses travel year-round between Morro Bay, San Luis Obispo, Cayucos, Cambria, San Simeon, and Hearst Castle. The Morro Bay Shuttle picks up riders throughout the town from Friday through Monday in summer ($1.25 one-way, $3 day pass).

ESSENTIALS

Visitor Information Morro Bay Visitors Center ⊠ *255 Morro Bay Blvd., at Morro Ave.* ☏ *805/225–1633, 800/231–0592* ⊕ *www.morrobay.org* ☉ *Daily 9–5.*

EXPLORING

Embarcadero. The center of Morro Bay action on land is the Embarcadero, where vacationers pour in and out of souvenir shops and seafood restaurants and stroll or bike along the scenic half-mile Harborwalk to Morro Rock. From here, you can get out on the bay in a kayak or tour boat. ⊠ *On waterfront from Beach St. to Tidelands Park.*

FAMILY **Morro Bay State Park Museum of Natural History.** The museum's entertaining interactive exhibits explain the natural environment and how to preserve it—in the bay and estuary and on the rest of the planet. ■TIP→ **Kids age 16 and under are admitted free.** ⊠ *State Park Rd.,* *south of downtown* ☎ *805/772–2694* 🌐 *www.ccnha.org/morrobay* 🎫 *$3* 🕓 *Daily 10–5.*

Morro Rock. At the mouth of Morro Bay stands 576-foot-high Morro Rock, one of nine small volcanic peaks, or morros, in the area. A short walk leads to a breakwater, with the harbor on one side and crashing ocean waves on the other. You may not climb the rock, where endangered falcons and other birds nest. Sea lions and otters often play in the water below the rock. ✉ *Northern end of Embarcadero.*

WHERE TO EAT

$$ SEAFOOD 🍴 **Dorn's Original Breakers Cafe.** This restaurant overlooking the harbor has satisfied local appetites since 1942. In addition to straight-ahead dishes such as cod or shrimp fish-and-chips or calamari tubes sautéed in butter and wine, Dorn's serves breakfast. [$] *Average main: $22* ✉ *801 Market Ave., at Morro Bay Blvd.* ☎ *805/772–4415* 🌐 *dornscafe.com.*

$ SOUTHWESTERN 🍴 **Taco Temple.** This family-run diner serves some of the freshest food around. The seafood-heavy menu includes salmon burritos, superb fish tacos with mango salsa, and other dishes hailing from somewhere between California and Mexico. [$] *Average main: $15* ✉ *2680 Main St., at Elena St., just north of Hwy. 1/Hwy. 41 junction* ☎ *805/772–4965* ✍ *Reservations not accepted* 💳 *No credit cards* 🕓 *Closed Tues.*

$$$ SEAFOOD 🍴 **Windows on the Water.** Diners at this second-floor restaurant view the sunset through giant picture windows. Meanwhile, fresh fish and other dishes based on local ingredients emerge from the wood-fired oven in the open kitchen, and oysters on the half shell beckon from the raw bar. The California-centric wine list includes about 20 selections poured by the glass. [$] *Average main: $30* ✉ *699 Embarcadero, at Pacific St.* ☎ *805/772–0677* 🌐 *www.windowsmb.com* 🕓 *No lunch.*

WHERE TO STAY

$$$ B&B/INN Fodor's Choice ★ 🏨 **Anderson Inn.** Friendly, personalized service and an oceanfront setting keep loyal patrons returning to this Embarcadero inn. **Pros:** walk to restaurants and sights; spacious rooms; attentive service. **Cons:** not low-budget; waterfront area can get crowded. [$] *Rooms from: $249* ✉ *897 Embarcadero* ☎ *805/772–3434, 866/950–3434 toll-free reservations* 🌐 *andersoninnmorrobay.com* 🛏 *8 rooms* 🍽 *No meals.*

$$$$ B&B/INN 🏨 **Cass House.** In tiny Cayucos, 4 miles north of Morro Bay, a shipping pioneer's 1867 home is now a luxurious bed-and-breakfast surrounded by rose and other gardens. **Pros:** historic property; some ocean views; excellent meals. **Cons:** away from nightlife and attractions; not good for families. [$] *Rooms from: $265* ✉ *222 N. Ocean Ave., Cayucos* ☎ *805/995–3669* 🌐 *casshouseinn.com* 🛏 *4 rooms* 🍽 *Breakfast.*

$$$ HOTEL 🏨 **Embarcadero Inn.** The rooms at this waterfront hotel are cheery and welcoming, and many have fireplaces. **Pros:** across from waterfront. **Cons:** tiny lobby; no pool. [$] *Rooms from: $185* ✉ *456 Embarcadero* ☎ *805/772–2700, 800/292–7625* 🌐 *www.embarcaderoinn.com* 🛏 *29 rooms, 4 suites* 🍽 *Breakfast.*

SPORTS AND THE OUTDOORS

Kayak Horizons. This outfit rents kayaks and paddleboards and gives lessons and guided tours. ✉ *551 Embarcadero, near Marina St.* ☎ *805/772–6444* ⊕ *kayakhorizons.com.*

Sub-Sea Tours & Kayaks. You can view sea life aboard this outfit's glass-bottom boat, watch whales from its catamaran, or rent a kayak or canoe. ✉ *699 Embarcadero* ☎ *805/772–9463* ⊕ *subseatours.com.*

Virg's Landing. Virg's conducts deep-sea-fishing and whale-watching trips. ✉ *1169 Market Ave.* ☎ *805/772–1222* ⊕ *virgslanding.com.*

PASO ROBLES

30 miles north of San Luis Obispo; 25 miles northwest of Morro Bay.

In the 1860s, tourists began flocking to this ranching outpost to "take the cure" in a bathhouse fed by underground mineral hot springs. An Old West town emerged, and grand Victorian homes went up, followed in the 20th century by Craftsman bungalows. These days, the wooded hills of Paso Robles west of U.S. 101 and the flatter, more open land to the freeway's east hold more than 250 wineries, many with tasting rooms. Hot summer days, cool nights, and varied soils and microclimates allow growers to cultivate an impressive array of Bordeaux, Rhône, and other grape types. Cabernet Sauvignon grows well in the Paso Robles AVA—32,000 of its 600,000-plus acres are planted to grapes—as do Petit Verdot, Grenache, Syrah, Viognier, and Zinfandel. In recognition of the diverse growing conditions, the AVA was divided into 11 subappellations in 2014. Pick up a wine-touring map at lodgings, wineries, and attractions around town. The fee at most tasting rooms is between $5 and $15; many lodgings pass out discount coupons.

Upmarket restaurants, bars, antiques stores, and little shops fill the streets around oak-shaded City Park, where special events of all kinds—custom car shows, an olive festival, Friday-night summer concerts—take place on many weekends. Despite its increasing sophistication, Paso (as the locals call it) retains a small-town vibe. The city celebrates its cowboy roots in late July and early August with the two-week California Mid-State Fair, complete with livestock auctions, carnival rides, and corn dogs.

GETTING HERE AND AROUND

U.S. 101 runs north–south through Paso Robles. Highway 46 West links Paso Robles to Highway 1 and Cambria on the coast. Highway 46 East connects Paso Robles with Interstate 5 and the San Joaquin Valley. Public transit is not convenient for wine touring and sightseeing.

Visitor Information Paso Robles CAB Collective ☎ *888/963–9934* ⊕ *pasoroblescab.com.* **Paso Robles Wine Country Alliance** ☎ *805/239–8463, 800/549–9463* ⊕ *www.pasowine.com.* **Rhone Rangers/Paso Robles** ⊕ *rhonerangers.org/pasorobles.* **Paso Robles Visitor Center** ✉ *1225 Park St., near 12th St.* ☎ *805/238–0506* ⊕ *travelpaso.com.*

EXPLORING
TOP ATTRACTIONS

Fodor'sChoice ★ **Calcareous Vineyard.** Elegant wines, a stylish tasting room, and knockout hilltop views make for a winning experience at this winery along winding Peachy Canyon Road. Cabernet Sauvignon, Syrah, and Zinfandel grapes thrive in the summer heat and limestone soils of the two vineyards near the tasting room, and a third vineyard on cooler York Mountain produces Pinot Noir, Chardonnay, and a Cabernet with a completely different character from the Peachy Canyon edition. ■ **TIP→ The picnic area's expansive eastward views invite lingering.** ⊠ *3430 Peachy Canyon Rd.* ☎ *805/239–0289* ⊕ *calcareous.com* ☞ *Tasting $10; tour and tasting (reservations required) $35* ⊙ *Daily 11–5.*

FAMILY **Estrella Warbirds Museum.** An entertaining homage to fighter planes, flyboys, and flygirls, this museum maintains indoor exhibits about wartime aviation and displays retired specimens (of planes) outdoors and in repair shops. Bonus attraction: a huge building with spruced-up autos, drag racers, and "funny cars." ⊠ *4251 Dry Creek Rd., off Airport Rd., north off Hwy. 46E* ☎ *805/227–0440* ⊕ *ewarbirds.org* ☞ *$10* ⊙ *Thurs.–Sun. and Mon. legal holidays 10–4.*

Firestone Walker Brewing Company. At this working craft brewery you can sample medal-winners such as the Double Barrel Ale and learn about the beer-making process on 30-minute guided tours of the brew house and cellar. ⊠ *1400 Ramada Dr., east side of U.S. 101; exit at Hwy. 46 W/Cambria, but head east* ☎ *805/225–5911* ⊕ *www.firestonebeer.com* ☞ *Tastings $1.50–$3 per sample, tour free* ⊙ *Daily 10–5; tours on the half hr Fri.–Sun. 10:30–4:30, Mon.–Thurs. by appointment.*

Halter Ranch Vineyard. A good place to learn about contemporary Paso Robles wine making, this ultramodern operation produces high-quality wines from estate-grown Bordeaux and Rhône grapes grown in sustainably farmed vineyards. The gravity-flow winery, which you can view on tours, is a marvel of efficiency. Ancestor, the flagship wine, a potent Bordeaux-style blend of Cabernet Sauvignon, Petit Verdot, and Malbec, is named for the ranch's huge centuries-old coast oak tree. ⊠ *8910 Adelaida Rd., at Vineyard Dr.* ☎ *888/367–9977* ⊕ *www.halterranch.com* ☞ *Tasting $10* ⊙ *Daily 11–5; winery/cave tour weekends at 11, noon, and 1 (reservations required), weekdays by appointment.*

Fodor'sChoice ★ **HammerSky Vineyards.** Owner Doug Hauck bucks a few trends by focusing on Merlot and Zinfandel, two varietals of variable popularity in recent years. Hauck makes excellent small lots of each, along with a Merlot-heavy Bordeaux-style blend; on the lighter side are Sauvignon Blanc and a Rosé of Zinfandel. Set amid rolling hills of vineyards punctuated by a huge oak, HammerSky's bright-white contemporary structure houses both the tasting and barrel-aging rooms; an outdoor patio has views of the estate vines. ⊠ *7725 Vineyard Dr., at Jensen Rd.* ☎ *805/239–0930* ⊕ *www.hammersky.com* ☞ *Tasting $10* ⊙ *Thurs.–Sun. 11–5 (closes on some summer days at 3:30 for weddings).*

Fodor'sChoice ★ **Jada Vineyard & Winery.** Winemaker David Galzignato, formerly of the Napa Valley's Charles Krug Winery, crafts Jada's nuanced, highly structured wines. Two worth checking out are Jack of Hearts, starring Petit

Verdot, and Passing By, a Cabernet-heavy blend. Galzignato also shines with Tannat and with Rhône-style wines, particularly Grenache. At tastings, the wines are paired with gourmet cheeses or organic chocolates. ⊠ *5620 Vineyard Dr., north of Hwy. 46 W* ☎ *805/226–4200* ⊕ *jadavineyard.com* 🍷 *Tastings $10–$15* ⊙ *Daily 11–5.*

Fodor's Choice **Justin Vineyards & Winery.** Suave Justin built its reputation—and, claim some, the Paso Robles wine region's ★ as well—on Isosceles, a hearty Bordeaux blend, usually of Cabernet Sauvignon, Cabernet Franc, and Merlot. Justin's Cabernet Sauvignon is also well regarded, as is the Right Angle blend of Cab and three other varietals. Tastings here take place in an expansive room whose equally expansive windows provide views of Justin's hillside vineyards. ⊠ *11680 Chimney Rock Rd., 15 miles west of U.S. 101's Hwy 46 E exit; take 24th St. west and follow road (name changes along the way) to Chimney Rock Rd.* ☎ *805/238–6932, 800/726–0049* ⊕ *justinwine. com* 🍷 *Tasting $15, tour and tasting $20* ⊙ *Daily 10–4:30; tours 10 and 2:30 (reservations recommended).*

Fodor's Choice **Pasolivo.** While touring the idyllic west side of Paso Robles, take a break ★ from wine tasting by stopping at Pasolivo. Find out how the artisans here make their Tuscan-style olive oils on a high-tech Italian press, and test the acclaimed results. ⊠ *8530 Vineyard Dr., west off U.S. 101 (Exit 224) or Hwy. 46 W (Exit 228)* ☎ *805/227–0186* ⊕ *www.pasolivo.com* 🍷 *Free* ⊙ *Daily 11–5.*

Tablas Creek Vineyard. Tucked in the western hills of Paso Robles, Tablas Creek is known for its blends of organically grown, hand-harvested Rhône varietals. Roussanne and Viognier are the standout whites; the Mourvèdre-heavy blend called Panoplie (it also includes Grenache and Syrah) has received high praise in recent years. ■ TIP→ **There's a fine picnic area here.** ⊠ *9339 Adelaida Rd., west of Vineyard Dr.* ☎ *805/237–1231* ⊕ *www.tablascreek.com* 🍷 *Tasting $10 (reserve $40 by appointment), tour free* ⊙ *Daily 10–5; tour 10:30 and 2 by appointment.*

WORTH NOTING

Paso Robles Pioneer Museum. The delightful museum's one-room schoolhouse and its displays of ranching paraphernalia, horse-drawn vehicles, hot-springs artifacts, and photos evoke Paso's rural heritage. ⊠ *2010 Riverside Ave., at 21st St.* ☎ *805/239–4556* ⊕ *www.pasoroblespioneer museum.org* 🍷 *Free* ⊙ *Thurs.–Sun. 1–4.*

Villa San-Juliette Vineyard & Winery. Two *American Idol* producers established this winery northeast of Paso Robles. With a cast that includes Petit Verdot, a fine Grenache, and a perky Albariño (a Spanish white

---

SIP CERTIFICATION

Many wineries in Paso Robles take pride in being SIP (Sustainability in Practice) Certified, for which they undergo a rigorous third-party audit of their entire operations. Water and energy conservation practices are reviewed, along with pest management and other aspects of farming. Also considered are the wages, benefits, and working conditions of the employees, and the steps taken to mitigate the impact of grape growing and wine production on area habitats.

6

varietal), their stylish operation is no flash in the pan. From 11 to 4 you can order snacks, panini, pizzas, soup and salad, and cheese and charcuterie plates to enjoy with your wine in the tasting room or on the view-filled outdoor terrace. ⊠ *6385 Cross Canyons Rd., at Ranchita Canyon Rd., San Miguel* ☎ *805/467–0014* ⊕ *www.villasanjuliette.com* ⊡ *Tasting $10* ⊙ *Daily 11–5.*

WHERE TO EAT

$$$
AMERICAN

✕ **Artisan.** Innovative variations on traditional American comfort cuisine and an urban vibe have made this bistro a hit with winemakers, locals, and tourists. Chef Chris Kobayashi uses regional, organic, wild-caught ingredients to put a fresh spin on dishes such as rabbit Stroganoff, boar tenderloin with fennel risotto, and wild king salmon with succotash and bacon. There's often a fine wood-fired pizza with duck confit, kale, and charred onions. ■TIP➡ **Save room for home-style desserts that include sundaes, puddings, cakes, and cookies.** $ *Average main: $30* ⊠ *843 12th St., at Pine St.* ☎ *805/237–8084* ⊕ *artisanpasorobles.com.*

$$$
FRENCH

✕ **Bistro Laurent.** Owner-chef Laurent Grangien's handsome, welcoming French bistro occupies an 1890s brick building across from City Park. He focuses on traditional dishes such as duck confit, rack of lamb, and onion soup, but always prepares a few au courant daily specials as well. The wines, sourced from the adjacent wineshop, come from around the world. $ *Average main: $28* ⊠ *1202 Pine St., at 12th St.* ☎ *805/226–8191* ⊕ *www.bistrolaurent.com* ⊙ *Closed Sun. and Mon.*

$$$
MODERN ITALIAN
Fodor'sChoice
★

✕ **Il Cortile.** One of two Paso establishments owned by chef Santos MacDonal and his wife, Carole, this Italian restaurant entices diners with complex flavors and a contemporary space with art-deco overtones. Consistent crowd-pleasers often on the menu include beef carpaccio with white truffle cream sauce and shaved black truffles; pork osso buco, perhaps served with Parmesan herb risotto; and braised beef cheeks over white polenta. ■TIP➡ **Carole selected the Central Coast and Italian wines here specifically to pair with Santos's dishes; it's worth asking her or your waiter for suggestions.** $ *Average main: $26* ⊠ *608 12th St., near Spring St.* ☎ *805/226–0300* ⊕ *ilcortileristorante. com* ⊙ *Closed Tues. No lunch.*

$$$
SOUTH
AMERICAN
Fodor'sChoice
★

✕ **La Cosecha.** At barlike, tin-ceilinged La Cosecha (Spanish for "the harvest"), Honduran-born chef Santos MacDonal faithfully re-creates dishes from Spain and South America that pair well with the restaurant's craft beers, cocktails, and white-wine sangria and other wines. Noteworthy starters include *pastelitos catracho*, Honduran-style empanadas in a light tomato sauce served with *queso fresco* (fresh cheese) and micro cilantro. If it's on the menu, consider trying the *moqueca*, a Brazilian seafood stew in a piquant coconut-milk base. $ *Average main: $29* ⊠ *835 12th St., near Pine St.* ☎ *805/237–0019* ⊕ *lacosechabr.com* ⊙ *Closed Mon.*

$$$
AMERICAN

✕ **McPhee's Grill.** Just south of Paso Robles in tiny Templeton, this casual chophouse in an 1860s wood-frame storefront serves sophisticated, contemporary versions of traditional Western fare such as oak-grilled filet mignon and fresh seafood tostadas. The house-label wines, made especially for the restaurant, are quite good. $ *Average main: $25* ⊠ *416 S. Main St., at 5th St., Templeton* ☎ *805/434–3204* ⊕ *mcphees grill.com* ⊙ *No lunch Sun.*

$$ ✕**Panolivo Family Bistro.** Affordable French fare draws patrons to this
FRENCH café north of the town square. For breakfast, try a fresh pastry or quiche, or build your own omelet. Lunch and dinner choices include sandwiches, salads, and fresh pastas—including cannelloni stuffed with vegetables or stewed beef—along with traditional dishes such as snails baked in garlic-butter sauce and beef bourguignon. ■TIP→ At $30, the three-course prix-fixe dinner option is a good value. $ *Average main: $20 ✉ 1344 Park St., at 14th St. ☎ 805/239–3366 ⊕ www. panolivo.com.*

$$ ✕**Thomas Hill Organics Market Bistro & Wine Bar.** Chef Christopher Man-
MODERN ning, whose previous stops include the Napa Valley restaurant of spar-
AMERICAN kling-wine maker Domaine Chandon, brings French flair and finesse to
Fodor's Choice this brick-walled downtown favorite. The menu might include seared
★ scallops flavorfully matched with pork belly and served on creamy polenta; tender pan-roasted duck with braised fennel, pomegranate, and persimmon; and beef tenderloin with a Cabernet Sauvignon bordelaise. The wine list celebrates local wines. With many by the half-glass, you can sample a good cross-section. $ *Average main: $17 ✉ 1313 Park St., at 13th St. ☎ 805/226–5888 ⊕ thomashillorganics.com.*

WHERE TO STAY

$$$$ 🏨**Hotel Cheval.** Equestrian themes surface throughout this intimate,
HOTEL European-style boutique hotel a half-block from the main square and
Fodor's Choice near some of Paso's best restaurants. **Pros:** near downtown restaurants;
★ sophisticated; personal service. **Cons:** views aren't great; no pool or hot tub. $ *Rooms from: $330 ✉ 1021 Pine St. ☎ 805/226–9995, 866/522– 6999 ⊕ www.hotelcheval.com ⤳ 16 rooms *|O|* Breakfast.*

$$$ 🏨**La Bellasera Hotel & Suites.** The swankest full-service hotel for miles
HOTEL around, La Bellasera caters to those looking for high-tech amenities and easy access to major Central Coast roadways. **Pros:** convenient to highways; tons of amenities. **Cons:** far from downtown; at a major intersection. $ *Rooms from: $199 ✉ 206 Alexa Ct. ☎ 805/238–2834, 866/782–9669 ⊕ labellasera.com ⤳ 35 rooms, 25 suites *|O|* No meals.*

$$ 🏨**La Quinta Inn & Suites.** A good value for Paso Robles, this three-story
HOTEL chain property attracts heavy repeat business with its upbeat staff and slew of perks. **Pros:** quiet; well maintained; upbeat staff; good for leisure or business travelers; pet-friendly; free weekday wine-tasting sessions. **Cons:** conventional decor. $ *Rooms from: $155 ✉ 2615 Buena Vista Dr. ☎ 805/239–3004, 800/753–3757 ⊕ www.laquintapasorobles.com ⤳ 101 rooms and suites *|O|* Breakfast.*

$$ 🏨**Paso Robles Inn.** On the site of an old spa hotel of the same name,
HOTEL the inn is built around a lush, shaded garden with a pool. **Pros:** private spring-fed hot tubs; historic property; across from town square. **Cons:** fronts a busy street; rooms vary in size and amenities. $ *Rooms from: $139 ✉ 1103 Spring St. ☎ 805/238–2660, 800/676–1713 ⊕ pasoroblesinn.com ⤳ 92 rooms, 6 suites *|O|* No meals.*

$$$$ 🏨**SummerWood Inn.** Easygoing hospitality, vineyard-view rooms, and
B&B/INN elaborate breakfasts make this inn a mile west of U.S. 101 worth seeking
Fodor's Choice out. **Pros:** convenient wine-touring base; accommodating staff; elabo-
★ rate breakfasts; complimentary tastings at associated winery. **Cons:**

6

some noise from nearby highway during the day. $ *Rooms from: $275* ✉ *2130 Arbor Rd., 1 mile west of U.S. 101, at Hwy. 46 W* ☎ *805/227–1111* ⊕ *www.summerwoodwine.com/inn* ⤿ *9 rooms* ⚭ *Breakfast.*

PERFORMING ARTS
Vina Robles Amphitheatre. At this 3,300-seat, Mission-style venue with good food, wine, and sight lines, you can enjoy acclaimed musicians in concert. ✉ *Vina Robles winery, 3800 Mill Rd., off Hwy. 46* ☎ *805/227–4812* ⊕ *vinarobles.com* ⊙ *May–Nov.*

CAMBRIA

28 miles west of Paso Robles; 20 miles north of Morro Bay.

Cambria, set on piney hills above the sea, was settled by Welsh miners in the 1890s. In the 1970s the isolated setting attracted artists and other independent types; the town now caters to tourists, but it still bears the imprint of its bohemian past. Both of Cambria's downtowns, the original East Village and the newer West Village, are packed with art and crafts galleries, antiques shops, cafés, restaurants, and bed-and-breakfasts.

Two diverting detours lie between Morro Bay and Cambria. In the laid-back beach town of **Cayucos,** 4 miles north of Morro Bay, you can stroll the long pier, feast on chowder (at Duckie's), and sample the namesake delicacies of the Brown Butter Cookie Co. Over in **Harmony,** a cute former dairy town 7 miles south of Cambria, you can take in the glassworks, pottery, and other artsy enterprises.

GETTING HERE AND AROUND
Highway 1 leads to Cambria from the north and south. Highway 246 West curves from U.S. 101 through the mountains to Cambria. San Luis Obispo RTA Route 12 buses stop in Cambria (and Hearst Castle).

ESSENTIALS
Visitor Information Cambria Chamber of Commerce ☎ *805/927–3624* ⊕ *cambriachamber.org.*

EXPLORING
Fiscalini Ranch Preserve. Walk along a mile-long coastal bluff trail to spot migrating whales, otters, and shore birds at this 450-acre public open space. Miles of additional scenic trails crisscross the protected habitats of rare and endangered species of flora and fauna, including a Monterey pine forest, western pond turtles, monarch butterflies, and burrowing owls. Dogs are permitted on-leash everywhere and off-leash on all trails except the bluff. ✉ *Hwy. 1, between Cambria Rd. and Main St. to the north, and Burton Dr. and Warren Rd. to the south; access either end of bluff trail off Windsor Blvd.* ☎ *805/927–2856* ⊕ *ffrpcambria.org.*

Leffingwell Landing. A state picnic ground, the landing is a good place for examining tidal pools and watching otters as they frolic in the surf. ✉ *North end of Moonstone Beach Dr., Cambria* ☎ *805/927–2070.*

Moonstone Beach Drive. The drive runs along a bluff above the ocean, paralleled by a 3-mile boardwalk that winds along the beach. On this photogenic walk you might glimpse sea lions and sea otters, and perhaps a gray whale during winter and spring. Year-round, birds fly about, and tiny creatures scurry amid the tidepools. ✉ *Off Hwy. 1.*

WHERE TO EAT

$$ MODERN AMERICAN 🍴 **Centrally Grown.** A collection of sustainably conscious spaces fashioned from repurposed materials, Centrally Grown encompasses a deli and market, exotic gardens, and a second-floor restaurant with fantastic views of San Simeon Bay and the Big Sur Coast. At the market and deli (open daily from 8 to 7), you can pick up organic and natural food to go or to enjoy in the gardens. The restaurant, decorated in a "planet-friendly chic" style that includes a driftwood archway, serves classic California cuisine with global influences. The colorful gardens, dense with native and water-wise plants and exotic varietals, are well worth a stroll. [$] *Average main: $18* ✉ *7432 Exotic Garden Dr., off Hwy. 1, Cambria* ☎ *800/717–4379* 🌐 *centrallygrown.com.*

$$ AMERICAN FAMILY 🍴 **Linn's Restaurant.** Homemade olallieberry pies, soups, potpies, and other farmhouse comfort foods share the menu at this spacious East Village restaurant with fancier farm-to-table dishes such as organic, free-range chicken topped with raspberry-orange-cranberry sauce. Also on-site are a bakery, a café serving more casual fare (take-out available), and a gift shop that sells gourmet foods. [$] *Average main: $21* ✉ *2277 Main St., at Wall St., Cambria* ☎ *805/927–0371* 🌐 *www.linnsfruitbin.com.*

$$ ECLECTIC 🍴 **Robin's.** A multiethnic, vegetarian-friendly dining experience awaits you at this cozy East Village cottage. Dinner choices include wild prawn enchiladas, Moroccan-spiced grilled salmon, Japanese scallops, and short ribs. Lunchtime's extensive salad and sandwich menu embraces burgers and tofu alike. **■ TIP→ Unless it's raining, ask for a table on the secluded (heated) garden patio.** [$] *Average main: $22* ✉ *4095 Burton Dr., at Center St., Cambria* ☎ *805/927–5007* 🌐 *robinsrestaurant.com.*

$$$ SEAFOOD Fodor's Choice ★ 🍴 **Sea Chest Oyster Bar and Restaurant.** Cambria's best place for seafood fills up soon after it opens at 5:30. Those in the know grab seats at the oyster bar and take in spectacular sunsets while watching the chefs broil fresh halibut, steam garlicky clams, and fry crispy calamari steaks. If you arrive to a wait, play cribbage or checkers in the game room. [$] *Average main: $28* ✉ *6216 Moonstone Beach Dr., near Weymouth St., Cambria* ☎ *805/927–4514* 🌐 *www.seachestrestaurant.com* ✍ *Reservations not accepted* 💳 *No credit cards* ⏲ *Closed Tues. mid-Sept.–May. No lunch.*

WHERE TO STAY

$ HOTEL 🏨 **Bluebird Inn.** This sweet motel in Cambria's East Village sits amid beautiful gardens along Santa Rosa Creek. **Pros:** excellent value; well-kept gardens; friendly staff. **Cons:** few frills; basic rooms; on Cambria's main drag; not on beach. [$] *Rooms from: $90* ✉ *1880 Main St., Cambria* ☎ *805/927–4634, 800/552–5434* 🌐 *bluebirdmotel.com* 🛏 *37 rooms* 🍽 *No meals.*

$$ RESORT 🏨 **Cambria Pines Lodge.** This 25-acre retreat up the hill from the East Village is a good choice for families. **Pros:** short walk from downtown; many recreational facilities; verdant gardens; spacious grounds. **Cons:** service and housekeeping not always top-quality; some units need updating. [$] *Rooms from: $149* ✉ *2905 Burton Dr., Cambria*

☎ *805/927–4200, 800/966–6490* ⊕ *www.cambriapineslodge.com* ⤵ *77 rooms, 75 suites* ⦿⟨ *Breakfast.*

$$$
B&B/INN

⟨⟩ **J. Patrick House.** Monterey pines and flower gardens surround this Irish-theme inn, which sits on a hilltop above Cambria's East Village. **Pros:** fantastic breakfasts; friendly innkeepers; quiet neighborhood. **Cons:** few rooms; fills up quickly. ⟨$⟩ *Rooms from: $185* ⊠ *2990 Burton Dr., Cambria* ☎ *805/927–3812, 800/341–5258* ⊕ *jpatrickhouse.com* ⤵ *8 rooms* ⦿⟨ *Breakfast.*

$$
HOTEL

⟨⟩ **Moonstone Landing.** This up-to-date motel's amenities, reasonable rates, and accommodating staff make it a Moonstone Beach winner. **Pros:** sleek furnishings; across from the beach; cheery lounge. **Cons:** narrow property; some rooms overlook a parking lot. ⟨$⟩ *Rooms from: $125* ⊠ *6240 Moonstone Beach Dr., Cambria* ☎ *805/927–0012, 800/830–4540* ⊕ *www.moonstonelanding.com* ⤵ *29 rooms* ⦿⟨ *Breakfast.*

SAN SIMEON

9 miles north of Cambria; 65 miles south of Big Sur.

Whalers founded San Simeon in the 1850s, but had virtually abandoned it by 1865, when Senator George Hearst began purchasing most of the surrounding ranch land. Hearst turned San Simeon into a bustling port, and his son, William Randolph Hearst, further developed the area while erecting Hearst Castle. Today San Simeon is basically a strip of unremarkable gift shops and so-so motels that straddle Highway 1 about 4 miles south of the castle's entrance, but **Old San Simeon**, right across from the entrance, is worth a peek. Julia Morgan, William Randolph Hearst's architect, designed some of the village's Mission Revival–style buildings.

GETTING HERE AND AROUND

Highway 1 is the only way to reach San Simeon. Connect with the highway off U.S. 101 directly or via rural routes such as Highway 41 West (Atascadero to Morro Bay) and Highway 46 West (Paso Robles to Cambria).

EXPLORING

TOP ATTRACTIONS

Fodor's Choice ★

Hearst Castle. Officially known as "Hearst San Simeon State Historical Monument," Hearst Castle sits in solitary splendor atop La Cuesta Encantada (the Enchanted Hill). Its buildings and gardens spread over 127 acres that were the heart of newspaper magnate William Randolph Hearst's 250,000-acre ranch. Hearst commissioned renowned California architect Julia Morgan to design the estate, but he was very much involved with the final product, a blend of Italian, Spanish, and Moorish styles. The 115-room main structure and three huge "cottages" are connected by terraces and staircases and surrounded by pools, gardens, and statuary. In its heyday the castle, whose buildings hold about 22,000 works of fine and decorative art, was a playground for Hearst and his guests—Hollywood celebrities, political leaders, scientists, and other well-known figures. Construction began in 1919 and was never officially completed. Work was halted in 1947 when Hearst had to leave San Simeon because of failing health. The Hearst Corporation donated the property to the State of California in 1958., and it is now part of the state park system.

Access to the castle is through the visitor center at the foot of the hill, where you can view educational exhibits and a 40-minute film about Hearst's life and the castle's construction. Buses from the center zigzag up to the hilltop estate, where guides conduct four daytime tours, each with a different focus: Grand Rooms, Upstairs Suites, Designing the Dream, and Cottages and Kitchen. These tours take about three hours and include the movie and time at the end to explore the castle's exterior and gardens. In spring and fall, docents in period costume portray Hearst's guests and staff for the Evening Tour, which begins around sunset. Reservations are recommended for all tours, which include a ½-mile walk and between 150 and 400 stairs. ✉ *San Simeon State Park, 750 Hearst Castle Rd.* ☎ *800/444–4445* ⊕ *www.hearstcastle.org* 🎟 *Daytime tours $25, evening tours $36* ⊗ *Tours daily 9–3:20, later in summer; additional tours take place most Fri. and Sat. evenings Mar.–May and Sept.–Dec.*

FAMILY **Piedras Blancas Elephant Seal Rookery.** A large colony of elephant seals (at last count 17,000 members) gathers every year at Piedras Blancas Elephant Seal Rookery, on the beaches near Piedras Blancas Lighthouse. The huge males with their pendulous, trunklike noses typically start appearing on shore in late November, and the females begin to arrive in December to give birth—most babies are born in the last two weeks of January. The newborn pups spend about four weeks nursing before their mothers head out to sea, leaving them on their own; the "weaners" leave the rookery when they are about 3½ months old. The seals return in the spring and summer months to molt or rest, but not en masse as in winter. You can watch them from a boardwalk along the bluffs just a few feet above the beach; do not attempt to approach them, as they are wild animals. The nonprofit Friends of the Elephant Seal runs a small visitor center and gift shop at 250 San Simeon Avenue in San Simeon. ✉ *Off Hwy. 1, 4½ miles north of Hearst Castle, just south of Piedras Blancas Lighthouse* ☎ *805/924–1628* ⊕ *elephantseal.org.*

Piedras Blancas Light Station. If you think traversing craggy, twisting Highway 1 is tough, imagine trying to navigate a boat up the rocky coastline (*piedras blancas* means "white rocks" in Spanish) near San Simeon before lighthouses were built. Captains must have cheered wildly when the beam began to shine here in 1875. Try to time a visit to include a morning tour (reservations not required). ■ TIP➔ **Do not meet at the gate to the lighthouse—you'll miss the tour. Meet your guide instead at the former Piedras Blancas Motel, a mile and a half north of the light station.** ☎ *805/927–7361* ⊕ *piedrasblancas.org* 🎟 *$10* ⊗ *Tour at 9:45, mid-June–Aug. Mon.–Sat.; Sept.–mid-June Tues., Thurs., and Sat.; no tour on national holidays* ⌁ *No pets allowed.*

WORTH NOTING

Hearst Ranch Winery. Old whaling equipment and Hearst Ranch and Hearst Castle memorabilia decorate this winery's casual Old San Simeon outpost. The tasting room occupies part of Sebastian's, a former whaling store built in 1852 and moved by oxen to its present location in 1878. The flagship wines include a Bordeaux-style red blend with Petite Sirah added to round out the flavor, and Rhône-style white and red blends. Malbec and Tempranillo are two other strong suits. **■ TIP→ Templeton chef Ian McPhee serves burgers and other lunch items at the adjacent deli, whose outdoor patio is a delight in good weather.** ✉ *442 SLO San Simeon Rd., off Hwy. 1* ☎ *805/467–2241* 🌐 *www.hearstranchwinery.com* 🎟 *Tasting $10* 🕒 *Daily 11–5.*

BEACHES

William Randolph Hearst Memorial Beach. This wide, sandy beach edges a protected cove on both sides of San Simeon Pier. Fish from the pier or from a charter boat, picnic and barbecue on the bluffs, or boogie board or bodysurf the relatively gentle waves. In summer you can rent a kayak and paddle out into the bay for close encounters with marine life and sea caves. The NOAA Coastal Discovery Center, next to the parking lot, has interactive exhibits and hosts educational activities and events. **Amenities:** food and drink; parking; toilets; water sports. **Best for:** sunset; swimming; walking. ✉ *750 Hearst Castle Rd., off Hwy. 1, west of Hearst Castle entrance* ☎ *805/927–2020, 805/927–6575 Coastal Discovery Center* 🌐 *www.parks.ca.gov* 🎟 *Free* 🕒 *Beach daily sunrise–sunset; Discovery Center Fri.–Sun. and holidays 11–5.*

WHERE TO STAY

$$$ HOTEL 🏨 **Best Western Cavalier Oceanfront Resort.** Reasonable rates, an oceanfront location, evening bonfires, and well-equipped rooms—some with wood-burning fireplaces and private patios—make this motel a great choice. **Pros:** on the bluffs; fantastic views; close to Hearst Castle. **Cons:** room amenities and sizes vary; pools are small and sometimes crowded. [$] *Rooms from: $189* ✉ *9415 Hearst Dr.* ☎ *805/927–4688, 800/826–8168* 🌐 *www.cavalierresort.com* 🛏 *90 rooms* 🍴 *No meals.*

BIG SUR COASTLINE

Long a retreat of artists and writers, Big Sur is a place of ancient forests and rugged shoreline, stretching 90 miles from San Simeon to Carmel. Residents have protected it from overdevelopment, and much of the region lies within several state parks and the more than 165,000-acre Ventana Wilderness, itself part of the Los Padres National Forest.

ESSENTIALS

Visitor Information **Big Sur Chamber of Commerce** ☎ *831/667–2100* 🌐 *bigsurcalifornia.org.*

SOUTHERN BIG SUR

Hwy. 1 from San Simeon to Julia Pfeiffer Burns State Park.

This especially rugged stretch of oceanfront is a rocky world of mountains, cliffs, and beaches.

GETTING HERE AND AROUND

Highway 1 is the only major access route from north or south. From the south, access Highway 1 from U.S. 101 in San Luis Obispo. From the north, take rural route Highway 46 West (Paso Robles to Cambria) or

Highway 41 West (Atascadero to Morro Bay). Nacimiento-Fergusson Road snakes through mountains and forest from U.S. 101 at Jolon about 25 miles to Highway 1 at Kirk Creek, about 4 miles south of Lucia; this curving, at times precipitous road is a motorcyclist favorite, not recommended for the faint of heart or during inclement weather.

EXPLORING

Fodor's Choice ★ **Highway 1.** One of California's most spectacular drives, Highway 1 snakes up the coast north of San Simeon. Numerous pullouts along the way offer tremendous views and photo ops. On some of the beaches huge elephant seals lounge nonchalantly, seemingly oblivious to the attention of rubberneckers. Heavy rain sometimes causes mudslides that block the highway north and south of Big Sur. 🌐 *www.dot.ca.gov.*

Fodor's Choice ★ **Julia Pfeiffer Burns State Park.** The park provides fine hiking, from an easy ½-mile stroll with marvelous coastal views to a strenuous 6-mile trek through redwoods. The big draw here, an 80-foot waterfall that drops into the ocean, gets crowded in summer; still, it's an astounding place to contemplate nature. Migrating whales, harbor seals, and sea lions can sometimes be spotted just offshore. ✉ *Hwy. 1, 15 miles north of Lucia* ☎ *831/667–2315* 🌐 *www.parks.ca.gov* 🎟 *$10* 🕒 *Daily sunrise–sunset.*

WHERE TO STAY

$$ HOTEL 🏨 **Ragged Point Inn.** At this cliff-top resort—the only inn and restaurant for miles around—glass walls in most rooms open to awesome ocean views. **Pros:** on the cliffs; good food; idyllic views. **Cons:** busy road stop during the day; often booked for weekend weddings. [$] *Rooms from: $169* ✉ *19019 Hwy. 1, 20 miles north of San Simeon, Ragged Point* ☎ *805/927–4502, 805/927–5708 restaurant* 🌐 *raggedpointinn.com* 🛏 *39 rooms* 🍴 *No meals.*

$$$ RESORT 🏨 **Treebones Resort.** Perched on a hilltop, surrounded by national forest and stunning, unobstructed ocean views, this yurt resort provides a stellar back-to-nature experience along with creature comforts. **Pros:** 360-degree views; spacious pool area; comfortable beds. **Cons:** steep paths; no private bathrooms; not good for families with young children. [$] *Rooms from: $225* ✉ *71895 Hwy. 1, Willow Creek Rd., 32 miles north of San Simeon, 1 mile north of Gorda* ☎ *805/927–2390, 877/424–4787* 🌐 *www.treebonesresort.com* 🛏 *16 yurts, 5 campsites, 1 human nest w/campsite* 🍴 *Breakfast* ☞ *2-night minimum.*

CENTRAL BIG SUR

Hwy. 1, from Partington Cove to Bixby Bridge.

The countercultural spirit of Big Sur—which instead of a conventional town is a loose string of coast-hugging properties along Highway 1—is alive and well today. Its few residents include the very wealthy, the enthusiastically outdoorsy, and the thoroughly evolved: since the 1960s the Esalen Institute, a center for alternative education and East–West philosophical study, has attracted seekers of higher consciousness and devotees of the property's hot springs. Today posh and rustic resorts hidden among the redwoods cater to visitors drawn from near and far by the extraordinary scenery and serene isolation.

WORD OF MOUTH

"The Central Coast in all its glory: I proposed to my fiancé 10 minutes after I took this photo in Julia Pfeiffer Burns State Park." —photo by Valhalla, Fodors.com member

GETTING HERE AND AROUND

From the north, follow Highway 1 south from Carmel. From the south, continue the drive north from Julia Pfeiffer Burns State Park *(above)* on Highway 1. Monterey-Salinas Transit operates the Line 22 Big Sur bus from Monterey and Carmel to Central Big Sur (the last stop is Nepenthe), daily from late May to early September and weekends only the rest of the year.

Bus Contact Monterey-Salinas Transit ☎ *888/678–2871* ⊕ *mst.org.*

EXPLORING

Bixby Creek Bridge. The graceful arc of Bixby Creek Bridge is a photographer's dream. Built in 1932, the bridge spans a deep canyon, more than 100 feet wide at the bottom. From the north-side parking area you can admire the view or walk the 550-foot structure. ⊠ *Hwy. 1, 6 miles north of Point Sur State Historic Park, 13 miles south of Carmel.*

Pfeiffer Big Sur State Park. Among the many hiking trails at Pfeiffer Big Sur, a short route through a redwood-filled valley leads to a waterfall. You can double back or continue on the more difficult trail along the valley wall for views over miles of treetops to the sea. ⊠ *47225 Hwy. 1* ☎ *831/667–2315* ⊕ *www.parks.ca.gov* ☉ *$10 per vehicle* ⊙ *Daily sunrise–sunset.*

Point Sur State Historic Park. An 1889 lighthouse at this state park still stands watch from atop a large volcanic rock. Four lighthouse keepers lived here with their families until 1974, when the light station became automated. Their homes and working spaces are open to the public only on 2½- to 3-hour ranger-led tours. Considerable walking, including up two stairways, is involved. Strollers are not allowed. ⊠ *Hwy. 1, 7 miles north of Pfeiffer Big Sur State Park* ☎ *831/625–4419* ⊕ *www.pointsur. org* ☉ *$12* ⊙ *Tours generally Nov.–Mar., weekends at 10, Wed. at 1; Apr.–Oct., Sat. and Wed. at 10 and 2, Sun. at 10; July–Aug. additional tour at 10; call to confirm.*

BEACHES

Pfeiffer Beach. Through a hole in one of the gigantic boulders at secluded Pfeiffer Beach, you can watch the waves break first on the sea side and then on the beach side. Keep a sharp eye out for the unsigned, ungated road to the beach: it branches west of Highway 1 between the post office and Pfeiffer Big Sur State Park. The 2-mile, one-lane road descends sharply. **Amenities:** parking (fee); toilets. **Best for:** solitude; sunset. ⊠ *Off Hwy. 1, 1 mile south of Pfeiffer Big Sur State Park* ☉ *$10 per vehicle* ⊙ *Daily 9–8.*

WHERE TO EAT

$$$ ✕ **Big Sur Roadhouse.** The chef at this colorful bistro perks up Califor-
ECLECTIC nia favorites with seasonal Big Sur ingredients such as lemons, grapefruit, chanterelles, and locally sourced meats. Popular dishes include duck confit, vegetarian pastas, Dungeness crab salad on brioche toast, and breaded pork loin with wild mushroom spaetzle, caramelized fennel, and sauerkraut. The roadhouse serves breakfast, lunch, and dinner. ■ **TIP→ Save room for house-made ice cream or a sorbet float.**

$ *Average main: $27* ⊠ *Hwy. 1, 1 mile north of Pfeiffer Big Sur State Park* ☎ *831/667–2370* ⊕ *bigsurroadhouse.com.*

$$$ ✕ **Deetjen's Big Sur Inn.** The candle-lighted, creaky-floor restaurant in the
AMERICAN main house at the historic inn of the same name is a Big Sur institution.
Fodor's Choice It serves spicy seafood paella, grass-fed filet mignon, and rack of lamb
★ for dinner and flavorful eggs Benedict for breakfast. The chef sources
most ingredients from purveyors known for sustainable practices. $ *Average main: $30* ⊠ *Hwy. 1, 3½ miles south of Pfeiffer Big Sur State Park*
☎ *831/667–2378* ⊕ *deetjens.com* ☉ *No lunch.*

$$$ ✕ **Nepenthe.** It may be that no other restaurant between San Francisco
AMERICAN and Los Angeles has a better coastal view than Nepenthe. The food
and drink are overpriced but good; there are burgers, sandwiches, and
salads for lunch, and fresh fish and hormone-free steaks for dinner. For
the real show, settle on the terraced deck in the late afternoon, order
a glass from the extensive wine list, and watch the sun slip into the
Pacific Ocean. The less expensive, outdoor Café Kevah serves brunch
and lunch. $ *Average main: $30* ⊠ *48510 Hwy. 1, 2½ miles south of
Big Sur Station* ☎ *831/667–2345* ⊕ *nepenthebigsur.com.*

$$$$ ✕ **The Restaurant at Ventana.** The Ventana Inn's restaurant sits high on
AMERICAN a ridge, and a magnificent terrace offers stunning ocean views. The
Fodor's Choice redwood, copper, and cedar elements indoors complement the natural
★ setting outside, but the design flourishes and gleaming fixtures place
the facility firmly in the 21st century. So, too, does chef Paul Corsentino's menu, which might include creative dishes such as quail tempura,
grilled octopus, or a New York strip steak served with barley and wild
mushrooms. Regional and international wines on a comprehensive list
pair well with these dishes, many of whose ingredients are sourced
from local purveyors, and the bar serves seasonal specialty cocktails
and California craft beers. The restaurant is open for breakfast, lunch,
and dinner. $ *Average main: $36* ⊠ *48123 Hwy. 1, 1½ miles south of
Pfeiffer Big Sur State Park* ☎ *831/667–4242* ⊕ *www.ventanainn.com*
⌂ *Reservations essential.*

$$$$ ✕ **Sierra Mar.** Ocean-view dining doesn't get much better than this. At
AMERICAN cliff's edge 1,200 feet above the Pacific at the ultra-chic Post Ranch
Fodor's Choice Inn, Sierra Mar serves cutting-edge American cuisine made from mostly
★ organic, seasonal ingredients, some from the on-site chef's garden. The
four-course prix-fixe option always shines. The nine-course Taste of Big
Sur menu centers on ingredients grown or foraged on the property or
sourced locally. The restaurant's wine list is among the nation's most
extensive. ■TIP→ **If you're unable to reserve a table for dinner, you can
sit at the bar, which opens at 5:30 (first-come, first-served), or opt for
the abbreviated prix-fixe ($55 and $95) lunch.** $ *Average main: $125*
⊠ *Hwy. 1, 1½ miles south of Pfeiffer Big Sur State Park* ☎ *831/667–
2800* ⊕ *postranchinn.com/dining* ⌂ *Reservations essential.*

WHERE TO STAY

$$$ ⊤ **Big Sur Lodge.** The lodge's modern, motel-style cottages with Mission-
HOTEL style furnishings and vaulted ceilings sit in a meadow, surrounded by
redwood trees and flowering shrubbery. **Pros:** secluded setting near
trailheads; good camping alternative; rates include state parks pass.
Cons: basic rooms; walk to main lodge. $ *Rooms from: $204* ⊠ *Pfeiffer*

6

Big Sur State Park, 47225 Hwy. 1 ☎ 831/667–3100, 800/424–4787 🌐 www.bigsurlodge.com ⇨ 61 rooms 🍴 No meals.

$$$ B&B/INN 🏨 **Big Sur River Inn.** The main draws of this rustic property are the lawns and wooded grounds fronting the Big Sur River. **Pros:** riverside setting; next to a restaurant and small market; outdoor pool. **Cons:** thin walls in some rooms; no phone in rooms. [$] *Rooms from: $200* ✉ *Hwy. 1, 2 miles north of Pfeiffer Big Sur State Park* ☎ *831/667–2700, 800/548–3610* 🌐 *bigsurriverinn.com* ⇨ *14 rooms, 6 suites* 🍴 *No meals.*

$$ B&B/INN 🏨 **Deetjen's Big Sur Inn.** This historic 1930s Norwegian-style property is endearingly rustic, especially if you're willing to go with a camplike flow. **Pros:** tons of character; wooded grounds. **Cons:** thin walls; some rooms don't have private baths; no TVs or Wi-Fi; limited cell phone access. [$] *Rooms from: $170* ✉ *Hwy. 1, 3½ miles south of Pfeiffer Big Sur State Park* ☎ *831/667–2377* 🌐 *deetjens.com* ⇨ *20 rooms, 15 with bath* 🍴 *No meals* ☞ *2-night minimum stay on weekends.*

$$$ HOTEL 🏨 **Glen Oaks Big Sur.** At this rustic-modern cluster of adobe-and-redwood buildings, you can choose between motel-style rooms, cabins, and cottages in the woods. **Pros:** in the heart of town; walking distance of restaurants. **Cons:** near busy road and parking lot; no TVs. [$] *Rooms from: $225* ✉ *Hwy. 1, 1 mile north of Pfeiffer Big Sur State Park* ☎ *831/667–2105* 🌐 *www.glenoaksbigsur.com* ⇨ *16 rooms, 2 cottages, 7 cabins* 🍴 *No meals.*

$$$$ RESORT Fodor's Choice ★ 🏨 **Post Ranch Inn.** This luxurious retreat, designed exclusively for adult getaways, has remarkably environmentally conscious architecture. **Pros:** world-class resort; spectacular views; gorgeous property with hiking trails. **Cons:** expensive; austere design; not a good choice if heights scare you. [$] *Rooms from: $675* ✉ *Hwy. 1, 1½ miles south of Pfeiffer Big Sur State Park* ☎ *831/667–2200, 800/527–2200* 🌐 *www.postranchinn.com* ⇨ *39 rooms, 1 house* 🍴 *Breakfast.*

$$$$ HOTEL Fodor's Choice ★ 🏨 **Ventana.** Hundreds of celebrities, from Oprah Winfrey to Sir Anthony Hopkins, have escaped to Ventana, a romantic resort on 243 tranquil acres 1,200 feet above the Pacific. **Pros:** secluded; nature trails everywhere; rates include daily guided hike, yoga, wine and cheese hour. **Cons:** expensive; some rooms lack an ocean view. [$] *Rooms from: $650* ✉ *Hwy. 1, almost 1 mile south of Pfeiffer Big Sur State Park* ☎ *831/667–2331, 800/628–6500* 🌐 *www.ventanainn.com* ⇨ *28 rooms, 31 suites* 🍴 *Breakfast.*

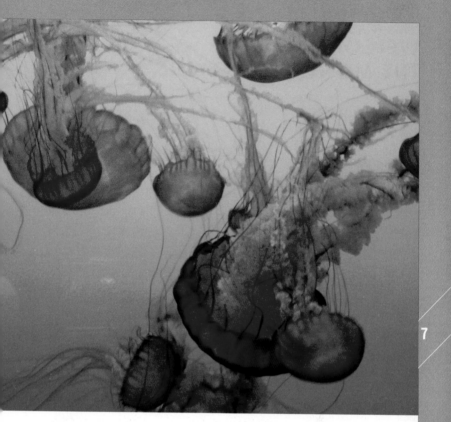

THE MONTEREY BAY AREA

From Carmel to Santa Cruz

Visit Fodors.com for advice, updates, and bookings

WELCOME TO
THE MONTEREY BAY AREA

TOP REASONS
TO GO

★ **Marine life:** Monterey Bay is the location of the world's third-largest marine sanctuary, home to whales, otters, and other underwater creatures.

★ **Getaway central:** For more than a century, urbanites have come to the Monterey Bay area to unwind, relax, and have fun. It's a great place to browse unique shops and galleries, ride a giant roller coaster, or play a round of golf on a world-class course.

★ **Nature preserves:** More than the sea is protected here: the region boasts nearly 30 state parks, beaches, and preserves—fantastic places for walking, jogging, hiking, and biking.

★ **Wine and dine:** The area's rich agricultural bounty translates into abundant fresh produce, great wines, and fabulous dining. It's no wonder more than 300 culinary events take place here every year.

★ **Small-town vibes:** Even the cities here are friendly, walkable places where you'll feel like a local.

```
0          5 mi
0     5 km
```

Santa Cruz

1 Carmel and Pacific Grove. Exclusive Carmel-by-the-Sea and Carmel Valley Village burst with historic charm, fine dining, and unusual boutiques that cater to celebrity residents and well-heeled visitors. Nearby 17-Mile Drive—quite possibly the prettiest stretch of road you'll ever travel—runs between Carmel-by-the-Sea and Victorian-studded Pacific Grove, home to thousands of migrating monarch butterflies between October and February.

2 Monterey. A former Spanish military outpost, Monterey's well-preserved historic district is a hands-on history lesson. Cannery Row, the center of Monterey's once-thriving sardine industry, has been reborn as a tourist attraction with shops, restaurants, hotels, and the Monterey Bay Aquarium.

3 Around Monterey Bay. Much of California's lettuce, berries, artichokes, and brussels sprouts is grown in Salinas and other towns. Salinas is also home to the National Steinbeck Center, and Moss Landing encompasses pristine wildlife wetlands. Aptos, Capitola, and Soquel are former lumber towns that became popular seaside resorts more than a century ago. Today they're filled with antiques shops, restaurants, and wine-tasting rooms; you'll also find some of the bay's best beaches along the shore here.

4 Santa Cruz. Santa Cruz shows its colors along an old-time beach boardwalk and municipal wharf. A University of California campus imbues the town with arts and culture and a liberal mind-set.

GETTING ORIENTED

North of Big Sur the coastline softens into lower bluffs, windswept dunes, pristine estuaries, and long, sandy beaches, bordering one of the world's most amazing marine environments—Monterey Bay. On the Monterey Peninsula, at the southern end of the bay, are Carmel-by-the-Sea, Pacific Grove, and Monterey; Santa Cruz sits at the northern tip of the crescent. In between, Highway 1 cruises along the coastline, passing windswept beaches piled high with sand dunes. Along the route are wetlands and artichoke and strawberry fields.

7

Updated by Cheryl Crabtree

Natural beauty is at the heart of the Monterey Bay area's enormous appeal—it's everywhere, from the redwood-studded hillsides to the pristine shoreline with miles of walking paths and bluff-top vistas. Nature even takes center stage indoors at the world-famous Monterey Bay Aquarium, but history also draws visitors, most notably to Monterey's well-preserved waterfront district. Quaint, walkable towns and villages such as Carmel-by-the-Sea and Carmel Valley Village lure with smart restaurants and galleries, while sunny Aptos, Capitola, Soquel, and Santa Cruz, with miles of sand and surf, attract surfers and beach lovers.

Monterey Bay life centers on the ocean. The bay itself is protected by the Monterey Bay National Marine Sanctuary, the nation's largest undersea canyon—bigger and deeper than the Grand Canyon. On-the-water activities abound, from whale-watching and kayaking to sailing and surfing. Bay cruises from Monterey and Moss Landing almost always encounter other enchanting sea creatures, among them sea otters, sea lions, and porpoises.

Land-based activities include hiking, zip-lining in the redwood canopy, and wine tasting along urban and rural trails. Golf has been an integral part of the Monterey Peninsula's social and recreational scene since the Del Monte Golf Course opened in 1897. Pebble Beach's championship courses host prestigious tournaments, and though the green fees at these courses can run up to $500, elsewhere on the peninsula you'll find less expensive options. And, of course, whatever activity you pursue, natural splendor appears at every turn.

PLANNING

WHEN TO GO

Summer is peak season; mild weather brings in big crowds. In this coastal region a cool breeze generally blows and fog often rolls in from offshore; you will frequently need a sweater or windbreaker. Off-season, from November through April, fewer people visit and the mood is mellower. Rainfall is heaviest in January and February. Fall and spring days are often clearer than those in summer.

GETTING HERE AND AROUND

AIR TRAVEL

Monterey Regional Airport, 3 miles east of downtown Monterey off Highway 68, is served by Alaska, Allegiant, American, United, and US Airways. Taxi service costs from $18 to $20 to downtown, and from $26 to $35 to Carmel. Monterey Airbus service between the region and the San Jose and San Francisco airports starts at $40; the Early Bird Airport Shuttle costs from $80 to $190 ($195 from Oakland).

Airport Contacts Monterey Regional Airport (MRY) ✉ 200 Fred Kane Dr., at Olmsted Rd., off Hwy. 68, Monterey ☎ 831/648–7000 ⊕ www.montereyairport. com.

Ground Transportation Central Coast Cab Company ☎ 831/626–3333. **Early Bird Airport Shuttle** ☎ 831/462–3933 ⊕ www.earlybirdairportshuttle. com. **Monterey Airbus** ☎ 831/373–7777 ⊕ www.montereyairbus.com. **Yellow Cab** ☎ 831/333–1234.

BUS TRAVEL

Greyhound serves Santa Cruz and Salinas from San Francisco and San Jose. The trips take about 3 and 4½ hours, respectively. Monterey-Salinas Transit (MST) provides frequent service in Monterey County (from $1.50 to $3.50; day pass $10), and Santa Cruz METRO ($2; day pass from $6 to $10) buses operate throughout Santa Cruz County. You can switch between the lines in Watsonville.

Bus Contacts Greyhound ☎ 800/231–2222 ⊕ www.greyhound.com. **Monterey-Salinas Transit** ☎ 888/678–2871 ⊕ mst.org. **Santa Cruz METRO** ☎ 831/425–8600 ⊕ scmtd.com.

CAR TRAVEL

Highway 1 runs south–north along the coast, linking the towns of Carmel-by-the-Sea, Monterey, and Santa Cruz; some sections have only two lanes. The freeway, U.S. 101, lies to the east, roughly parallel to Highway 1. The two roads are connected by Highway 68 from Pacific Grove to Salinas; Highway 156 from Castroville to Prunedale; Highway 152 from Watsonville to Gilroy; and Highway 17 from Santa Cruz to San Jose. ⚠ **Traffic near Santa Cruz can crawl to a standstill during commuter hours. In the morning, avoid traveling between 7 and 9; in the afternoon avoid traveling between 4 and 7.**

The drive south from San Francisco to Monterey can be made comfortably in three hours or less. The most scenic way is to follow Highway 1 down the coast. A generally faster route is Interstate 280 south to Highway 85 to Highway 17 to Highway 1. The drive from the Los

Angeles area takes five or six hours. Take U.S. 101 to Salinas and head west on Highway 68. You can also follow Highway 1 up the coast.

TRAIN TRAVEL

Amtrak's *Coast Starlight* runs between Los Angeles, Oakland, and Seattle. From the train station in Salinas you can connect with buses serving Carmel and Monterey, and from the train station in San Jose with buses to Santa Cruz.

Train Contacts Amtrak ☎ *800/872–7245* 🌐 *amtrak.com.*

RESTAURANTS

The Monterey Bay area is a culinary paradise. The surrounding waters are full of fish, wild game roams the foothills, and the inland valleys are some of the most fertile in the country—local chefs draw on this bounty for their fresh, truly Californian cuisine. Except at beachside stands and inexpensive eateries, where anything goes, casual but neat dress is the norm.

HOTELS

Accommodations in the Monterey area range from no-frills motels to luxurious hotels. Pacific Grove, amply endowed with ornate Victorian houses, is the region's bed-and-breakfast capital; Carmel also has charming inns. Lavish resorts cluster in exclusive Pebble Beach and pastoral Carmel Valley.

High season runs from May through October. Rates in winter, especially at the larger hotels, may drop by 50% or more, and smaller inns often offer midweek specials. Whatever the month, some properties require a two-night stay on weekends. *Hotel reviews have been shortened. For full information, visit Fodors.com.* ⚠ **Many of the fancier accommodations aren't suitable for children; if you're traveling with kids, ask before you book.**

WHAT IT COSTS

	$	$$	$$$	$$$$
Restaurants	under $16	$16–$22	$23–$30	over $30
Hotels	under $120	$120–$175	$176–$250	over $250

Restaurant prices are the average cost of a main course at dinner or, if dinner is not served, at lunch, excluding sales tax of 8¼%–9½% (depending on location). Hotel prices are the lowest cost of a standard double room in high season, excluding service charges and 10%–10½% tax.

TOUR OPTIONS

Ag Venture Tours & Consulting. Crowd-pleasing half- and full-day wine-tasting, sightseeing, and agricultural tours are Ag Venture's specialty. Tastings are at Monterey and Santa Cruz Mountains wineries; sightseeing opportunities include the Monterey Peninsula, Big Sur, and Santa Cruz; and the agricultural forays take in the Salinas and Pajaro valleys. Customized itineraries can be arranged. ☎ *831/761–8463* 🌐 *agventuretours.com* 🎫 *From $75.*

California Parlor Car Tours. This outfit operates motor-coach tours from San Francisco that include one or two days in Monterey and Carmel. The company's three-day San Francisco–Los Angeles tours include stops in Monterey and Carmel. ☎ *415/474–7500, 800/227–4250* ⊕ *www. calpartours.com* ✉ *From $80 (day) and $267 (overnight).*

Monterey Guided Wine Tours. The company's guides lead customized wine tours in Monterey, Carmel, and Carmel Valley, along with the Santa Lucia Highlands, the Santa Cruz Mountains, and the Paso Robles area. Tours, which typically last from four to six hours, take place in a town car, a stretch limo, or a party bus. ☎ *831/920–2792* ⊕ *montereyguidedwinetours.com* ✉ *From $85.*

VISITOR INFORMATION

Contacts Monterey County Convention & Visitors Bureau ☎ *888/221–1010* ⊕ *www.seemonterey.com.* **Monterey Wine Country** ☎ *831/375–9400* ⊕ *www. montereywines.org.* **Santa Cruz County Conference & Visitors Council** ✉ *303 Water St., No. 100, Santa Cruz* ☎ *831/425–1234, 800/833–3494* ⊕ *santacruz. org.* **Santa Cruz Mountain Winegrowers Association** ✉ *725 Front St., No. 112, Santa Cruz* ☎ *831/685–8463* ⊕ *www.scmwa.com.*

CARMEL AND PACIFIC GROVE

As Highway 1 swings inland about 30 miles north of Big Sur, historic Carmel-by-the Sea anchors the southern entry to the Monterey Peninsula—a gorgeous promontory at the southern tip of Monterey Bay. Just north of Carmel along the coast, the legendary 17-Mile Drive wends its way through private Pebble Beach and the town of Pacific Grove. Highway 1 skirts the peninsula to the east with more direct access to Pebble Beach and Pacific Grove.

CARMEL-BY-THE-SEA

26 miles north of Big Sur.

Even when its population quadruples with tourists on weekends and in summer, Carmel-by-the-Sea, commonly referred to as Carmel, retains its identity as a quaint village. Self-consciously charming, the town is populated by many celebrities, major and minor, and has its share of quirky ordinances. For instance, women wearing high heels do not have the right to pursue legal action if they trip and fall on the cobblestone streets, and drivers who hit a tree and leave the scene are charged with hit-and-run.

Buildings have no street numbers—street names are written on discreet white posts—and consequently no mail delivery. One way to commune with the locals: head to the post office. Artists started this community, and their legacy is evident in the numerous galleries.

GETTING HERE AND AROUND

From north or south follow Highway 1 to Carmel. Head west at Ocean Avenue to reach the main village hub. In summer the MST Carmel-by-the-Sea Trolley loops around town to the beach and mission every 30 minutes or so.

Monterey Bay Area

Santa Cruz · Soquel · Aptos · Capitola · Rio del Mar · Corralitos · Gilroy

SANTA CRUZ MOUNTAINS

The Forest of Nisene Marks State Park

Natural Bridges State Beach · Twin Lakes State Beach · Soquel Cove · La Selva Beach · Freedom · Watsonville

New Brighton State Beach · Seacliff State Beach · Pajaro · Las Lomas

Pajaro River

Elkhorn Slough National Estuarine Research Reserve

Moss Landing · San Juan Bautista

GABILAN RANGE

Dolan Rd. · Prunedale

Castroville

Asilomar State Beach · Point Pinos

MONTEREY BAY

Monterey see detail map · Marina · Salinas

Pacific Grove · Seaside · Sand City

Spanish Bay · Spreckels

17-Mile Drive · Del Rey Oaks

Carmel Beach · Cypress Point

Pebble Beach

SALINAS VALLEY

Salinas River

Carmel-by-the-Sea

Carmel River State Beach

Carmel Bay · Point Lobos State Natural Reserve · Carmel Highlands · Yankee Point

Refuge · Earthbound Farm · Carmel Valley Rd.

Garland Ranch Regional Park

Carmel Valley Village

SIERRA DE SALINAS

TO PINNACLES NATIONAL PARK

0   5 mi
0   5 km

TOURS

Carmel Walks. For insight into Carmel's history and culture, join one of these guided two-hour ambles through hidden courtyards, gardens, and pathways. Tours depart from the Pine Inn courtyard, on Lincoln Street. Call to reserve a spot. ⊠ *Lincoln St. at 6th Ave.* ☎ *831/223–4399* ⊕ *carmelwalks.com* ☚ *From $25* ⊘ *Tues.–Fri. 10, Sat. 10 and 2.*

ESSENTIALS

Visitor Information Carmel Chamber of Commerce ⊠ *Visitor Center, San Carlos, between 5th and 6th* ☎ *831/624–2522, 800/550–4333* ⊕ *carmelcalifornia.org* ⊘ *Daily 10–5.*

EXPLORING

TOP ATTRACTIONS

Carmel Mission. Long before it became a shopping and browsing destination, Carmel was an important religious center during the establishment of Spanish California. That heritage is preserved in the Mission San Carlos Borroméo del Rio Carmelo, more commonly known as the Carmel Mission. Founded in 1771, it served as headquarters for the mission system in California under Father Junípero Serra. Adjoining the stone church is a tranquil garden planted with California poppies. Museum rooms at the mission include an early kitchen, Serra's spartan sleeping quarters and burial shrine, and the first college library in California. ✉ *3080 Rio Rd., at Lasuen Dr.* ☎ *831/624–1271* ⊕ *carmelmission.org* ☞ *$6.50* ⊙ *May–Aug., daily 9:30–6:45; Sept.–Apr., daily 9:30–4:45.*

Fodors Choice **Ocean Avenue.** Downtown Carmel's chief lure is shopping, especially along its main street, Ocean Avenue, between Junipero Avenue and Camino Real. The architecture here is a mishmash of ersatz Tudor, Mediterranean, and other styles.

Fodors Choice **Point Lobos State Natural Reserve.** A 350-acre headland harboring a wealth of marine life, the reserve lies a few miles south of Carmel. The best way to explore here is to walk along one of the many trails. The Cypress Grove Trail leads through a forest of Monterey cypress (one of only two natural groves remaining) that clings to the rocks above an emerald-green cove. Sea Lion Point Trail is a good place to view sea lions. From those and other trails, you might also spot otters, harbor seals, and (in winter and spring) migrating whales. An additional 750 acres of the reserve is an undersea marine park open to qualified scuba divers. No pets are allowed. ■TIP→ **Arrive early (or in late afternoon) to avoid crowds; the parking lots fill up.** ✉ *Hwy. 1* ☎ *831/624–4909, 831/624–8413 water sports reservations* ⊕ *www.pointlobos.org* ☞ *$10 per vehicle* ⊙ *Daily 8 am–½ hr after sunset.*

WORTH NOTING

Carmel Wine Walk By-the-Sea. If you purchase a Wine Walk Passport, you can park the car and sample local wines at any nine of 14 tasting rooms, all within a few blocks of each other in downtown Carmel. Individual passports be used by two or more people at the same tasting room, and they entitle holders to free corkage at some local restaurants. ✉ *Carmel Chamber of Commerce Visitor Center, San Carlos St., between 5th and 6th Aves.* ☎ *831/624–2522, 800/550–4333* ⊕ *carmelcalifornia. org* ☞ *$65.*

Dawson Cole Fine Art. Amazing images of dancers, athletes, and other humans in motion come to life in this gallery that is devoted to the artworks of Monterey Bay resident Richard MacDonald, one of the most famed figurative sculptors of our time. ✉ *Lincoln St., at 6th Ave.* ☎ *800/972–5528* ⊕ *dawsoncolefineart.com* ☞ *Free* ⊙ *Mon.–Sat. 10–6, Sun. 10–5:30.*

Tor House. Scattered throughout the pines of Carmel-by-the-Sea are houses and cottages originally built for the writers, artists, and photographers who discovered the area decades ago. Among the most impressive dwellings is Tor House, a stone cottage built in 1919 by poet Robinson Jeffers on a craggy knoll overlooking the sea. Portraits, books, and unusual art objects fill the low-ceilinged rooms. The highlight of the small estate is Hawk Tower, a detached edifice set with stones from the Carmel coastline—as well as one from the Great Wall of China. The docents who lead tours (six people maximum) are well informed about the poet's work and life. ■**TIP**➔ **To reserve a tour, which is recommended, email** *thf@torhouse.org.* ✉ *26304 Ocean View Ave.* ☎ *831/624–1813, 831/624–1840 direct docent office line, Fri. and Sat. only* ⊕ *www.torhouse.org* ✉ *$10* ☽ *Hourly tours Fri. and Sat. 10–3* ☞ *No children under 12.*

BEACHES

Carmel Beach. Carmel-by-the-Sea's greatest attraction is its rugged coastline, with pine and cypress forests and countless inlets. Carmel Beach, an easy walk from downtown shops, has sparkling white sands and magnificent sunsets. ■**TIP**➔ **Dogs are allowed to romp off-leash here.** **Amenities:** parking (no fee); toilets. **Best For:** sunset; surfing; walking. ✉ *End of Ocean Ave.*

Carmel River State Beach. This sugar-white beach, stretching 106 acres along Carmel Bay, is adjacent to a bird sanctuary, where you might spot pelicans, kingfishers, hawks, and sandpipers. Dogs are allowed on leash. **Amenities:** parking (no fee); toilets. **Best For:** sunrise; sunset; walking. ✉ *Off Scenic Rd., south of Carmel Beach* ☎ *831/649–2836* ⊕ *www.parks.ca.gov* ✉ *Free* ☽ *Spring–fall, daily 8–7; winter, daily 8 am–½ hr after sunset.*

WHERE TO EAT

$$$$
EUROPEAN

✕ **Anton and Michel.** Carefully prepared European cuisine is the draw at this airy restaurant. The rack of lamb is carved at the table, the grilled halloumi cheese and tomatoes are meticulously stacked and served with basil and Kalamata olive tapenade, and the desserts are set aflame before your eyes. ■**TIP**➔ **For lighter fare with a worldwide flair, head to the bar, where small plates such as Dungeness crab ravioli and brochette of filet mignon with chimichurri sauce are served.** Ⓢ *Average main: $32* ✉ *Mission St. and 7th Ave.* ☎ *831/624–2406* ⊕ *antonandmichel.com* ⟀ *Reservations essential.*

$$$$
AMERICAN
Fodor'sChoice
★

✕ **Aubergine.** To eat and sleep at luxe L'Auberge Carmel is an experience in itself, but even those staying elsewhere can splurge at the inn's intimate restaurant. Chef Justin Cogley's prix-fixe regular menu ($110) includes four or five courses—perhaps chilled Dungeness crab with pumpkin seeds and spaghetti squash, yellowtail with seaweed and hibiscus, dry-aged rib eye grilled over *binchotan* (white charcoal), milk chocolate tart with pear and walnut, and an optional artisanal cheese plate. You can also choose the tasting menu ($145), for which the chefs assemble surprise courses. The well-informed sommelier helps diners navigate the wine list—Aubergine's cellar holds 2,500 bottles—and offers wine pairings for your courses (from $75 to $175). Ⓢ *Average main: $110* ✉ *Monte Verde, at 7th Ave.* ☎ *831/624–8578* ⊕ *auberginecarmel.com* ⟀ *Reservations essential* ☽ *No lunch.*

$$$
MODERN
AMERICAN
Fodor'sChoice
★

✕ **Basil.** Eco-friendly Basil was Monterey County's first restaurant to achieve a green dining certification, recognition of chef-owner Soerke Peters's commitment to using organic, sustainably cultivated ingredients in his cuisine. Peters grows many of his own herbs, which find their way into creative dishes such as black squid linguine with sea urchin sauce, creamy duck liver–pear pâté, and smoked venison and other house-made charcuterie. The grass-fed burger is a good lunch choice, as are, in season, the crab sliders. French toast with poached eggs and truffled mushrooms is a Sunday brunch staple. You can dine in the eight-table interior or on the outdoor covered patio, where heaters and blankets provide warmth year-round. [$] *Average main: $23* ✉ *Paseo Square, San Carlos St., between Ocean Ave. and 7th Ave.* ☎ *831/636–8226* 🌐 *basilcarmel.com* ✍ *Reservations essential.*

$$$$ MEDITERRANEAN 🍴 **Casanova.** This restaurant inspires European-style celebration and romance: accordions hang from the walls, and tiny party lights flicker along the low ceilings. Dishes from southern France and northern Italy—game hen, osso buco, Wagyu beef tartare—predominate. Private dining and a special tasting menu are offered at Van Gogh's Table, a relic from France's Auberge Ravoux, the artist's final residence. [$] *Average main: $32* ✉ *5th Ave., between San Carlos and Mission Sts.* ☎ *831/625–0501* 🌐 *www.casanovarestaurant.com* ✍ *Reservations essential.*

$ AMERICAN 🍴 **The Cottage Restaurant.** This family-friendly spot serves sandwiches, pizzas, and homemade soups at lunch, but the best meal is breakfast (good thing it's served all day). The menu offers six variations on eggs Benedict, and all kinds of sweet and savory crepes. [$] *Average main: $15* ✉ *Lincoln St., between Ocean and 7th Aves.* ☎ *831/625–6260* 🌐 *cottagerestaurant.com* ⏲ *No dinner.*

$$$$ AMERICAN 🍴 **Grasing's Coastal Cuisine.** Chef Kurt Grasing draws from fresh Carmel Coast and Central Valley ingredients to whip up contemporary adaptations of European-provincial and American cooking. Longtime menu favorites include artichoke lasagna in a roasted tomato sauce, duck with fresh cherries in a red wine sauce, a savory paella, and grilled steaks and chops. [$] *Average main: $34* ✉ *6th Ave. and Mission St.* ☎ *831/624–6562* 🌐 *grasings.com* ✍ *Reservations essential.*

$$ TAPAS 🍴 **Mundaka.** The traditional Spanish-style tapas, made with fresh local ingredients, and the full bar attract legions of locals to this downtown spot. Longtime favorites include the chorizo slider with truffle fries, the authentic Valencian paella, and a charcuterie platter made in-house. At the adjacent Mundaka Cafe, the breakfast menu includes Spanish tortillas, Belgian waffles, and homemade baked goods; among the lunchtime choices are sandwiches, soups, and salads. Leashed dogs are welcome at the patio tables. [$] *Average main: $21* ✉ *San Carlos St., between Ocean and 7th Aves.* ☎ *831/624–7400* 🌐 *www.mundakacarmel.com.*

$$$ ITALIAN 🍴 **Vesuvio.** Chef and restaurateur Rich Pèpe heats up the night with this lively trattoria downstairs and swinging rooftop terrace, the Starlight Lounge 65°. Pèpe's elegant take on traditional Italian cuisine yields dishes such as wild-boar Bolognese pappardelle, lobster ravioli, and velvety limoncello mousse cake. Pizzas and small plates are served in the restaurant and two bars. Upstairs, relax in comfy chairs by fire pits and enjoy bird's-eye views of the village. On most nights in summer there's live music. [$] *Average main: $26* ✉ *6th and Junipero Aves.* ☎ *831/625–1766* 🌐 *vesuviocarmel.com* ⏲ *No lunch.*

WHERE TO STAY

$$$ B&B/INN 🏨 **Cypress Inn.** This luxurious inn has a fresh Mediterranean ambience with Moroccan touches. **Pros:** luxury without snobbery; popular lounge and restaurant; British-style afternoon tea on weekends. **Cons:**

Point Lobos Reserve State Park is home to one of the only two natural stands of Monterey cypress in the world.

not for the pet-phobic. $ *Rooms from: $250* ✉ *Lincoln St. and 7th Ave.* ☎ *831/624–3871, 800/443–7443* ⊕ *cypress-inn.com* ↻ *39 rooms, 5 suites* ⦿ *Breakfast.*

$$$$
HOTEL
🍴 **Hyatt Carmel Highlands.** High on a hill overlooking the Pacific, this place has superb views; accommodations include king rooms with fireplaces, suites with personal Jacuzzis, and full town houses with many perks. **Pros:** killer views; romantic getaway; great food. **Cons:** thin walls; must drive to Carmel. $ *Rooms from: $399* ✉ *120 Highlands Dr.* ☎ *831/620–1234, 800/233–1234* ⊕ *highlandsinn.hyatt.com* ↻ *46 rooms, 2 suites.*

$$$$
B&B/INN
Fodor's Choice
★
🍴 **L'Auberge Carmel.** Stepping through the doors of this elegant inn is like being transported to a little European village. **Pros:** in town but off the main drag; four blocks from the beach; full-service luxury. **Cons:** touristy area; not a good choice for families. $ *Rooms from: $435* ✉ *Monte Verde at 7th Ave.* ☎ *831/624–8578* ⊕ *www.laubergecarmel. com* ↻ *20 rooms* ⦿ *Breakfast.*

$$$$
HOTEL
🍴 **La Playa Carmel.** A historic complex of lush gardens and Mediterranean-style buildings, La Playa has light and airy interiors done in Carmel Bay beach-cottage style. **Pros:** residential neighborhood; manicured gardens; two blocks from the beach. **Cons:** four stories (no elevator); busy lobby; some rooms are on the small side. $ *Rooms from: $458* ✉ *Camino Real, at 8th Ave.* ☎ *831/293–6100, 800/582–8900* ⊕ *laplayahotel.com* ↻ *75 rooms* ⦿ *Breakfast.*

$$
HOTEL
🍴 **Mission Ranch.** Movie star Clint Eastwood owns this sprawling property whose accommodations include rooms in a converted barn, and several cottages, some with fireplaces. **Pros:** farm setting; pastoral views;

great for tennis buffs. **Cons:** busy parking lot; must drive to the heart of town. $ *Rooms from: $140* ✉ *26270 Dolores St.* ☎ *831/624–6436, 800/538–8221, 831/625–9040 restaurant* ⊕ *www.missionranchcarmel. com* ☞ *31 rooms* ⦿ *Breakfast.*

$$$$
B&B/INN

⊞ **Tickle Pink Inn.** Atop a towering cliff, this inn has views of the Big Sur coastline, which you can contemplate from your private balcony. **Pros:** close to great hiking; intimate; dramatic views. **Cons:** close to a big hotel; lots of traffic during the day. $ *Rooms from: $309* ✉ *155 Highland Dr.* ☎ *831/624–1244, 800/635–4774* ⊕ *ticklepink.com* ☞ *23 rooms, 10 suites, 1 cottage* ⦿ *Breakfast.*

$$$
B&B/INN

⊞ **Tradewinds Carmel.** This converted motel with sleek decor inspired by the South Seas encircles a courtyard with waterfalls, a meditation garden, and a fire pit. **Pros:** serene; within walking distance of restaurants; friendly service. **Cons:** no pool; long walk to the beach. $ *Rooms from: $250* ✉ *Mission St., at 3rd Ave.* ☎ *831/624–2776* ⊕ *tradewindscarmel. com* ☞ *26 rooms, 2 suites* ⦿ *Breakfast.*

NIGHTLIFE

BARS AND PUBS

Barmel. Al Capone and other Prohibition-era legends once sidled up to this hip nightspot's carved wooden bar. Rock to DJ music and sit indoors, or head out to the pet-friendly patio. Some menu items pay homage to California's early days, and you can order Spanish tapas and wines from the adjacent Mundaka restaurant, which is under the same ownership. ✉ *San Carlos St., between Ocean and 7th Aves.* ☎ *831/626–3400* ⊕ *www.mundakacarmel.com* ▭ *No credit cards.*

Jack London's. Among the few Carmel restaurants that serve food late, this publike hangout, also open for lunch, is a good stop for a beer or cocktail or to watch sports on TV. On most weekends Jack London's hosts live music. The weekday happy hour (from 4 to 6) is a bargain. ✉ *Su Vecino Court, Dolores St., between 5th and 6th Aves.* ☎ *831/624–2336* ⊕ *jacklondonscarmel.com.*

SHOPPING

ART GALLERIES

Carmel Art Association. Carmel's oldest gallery, established in 1927, exhibits original paintings and sculptures by local artists. ✉ *Dolores St., between 5th and 6th Aves.* ☎ *831/624–6176* ⊕ *carmelart.org.*

Galerie Plein Aire. The gallery showcases the oil paintings of a group of local artists. ✉ *Dolores St., between 5th and 6th Aves.* ☎ *831/625–5686* ⊕ *galeriepleinaire.com.*

Gallery Sur. Fine art photography of the Big Sur Coast and the Monterey Peninsula, including scenic shots and golf images, is the focus here. ✉ *6th Ave., between Dolores and Lincoln Sts.* ☎ *831/626–2615* ⊕ *gallerysur.com.*

Weston Gallery. Run by the family of the late Edward Weston, this is hands down the best photography gallery around, with contemporary color photography and classic black-and-whites. ✉ *6th Ave., between Dolores and Lincoln Sts.* ☎ *831/624–4453* ⊕ *westongallery.com.*

CARMEL VALLEY

10 miles east of Carmel.

Carmel Valley Road, which heads inland from Highway 1 south of Carmel, is the main thoroughfare through this valley, a secluded enclave of horse ranchers and other well-heeled residents who prefer the area's sunny climate to coastal fog and wind. Once thick with dairy farms, the valley has evolved into an esteemed wine appellation. Carmel Valley Village has crafts shops, art galleries, and the tasting rooms of numerous local wineries.

GETTING HERE AND AROUND

From U.S. 101 north or south, exit at Highway 68 and head west toward the coast. Scenic, two-lane Laureles Grade winds west over the mountains to Carmel Valley Road north of the village.

TOURS

Carmel Valley Grapevine Express. An incredible bargain, the express—aka MST's Bus 24—travels between downtown Monterey and Carmel Valley Village, with stops near wineries, restaurants, and shopping centers. ☎ *888/678–2871* ⊕ *mst.org* ✉ *$10 all-day pass.*

EXPLORING

TOP ATTRACTIONS

Bernardus Tasting Room. At the tasting room of Bernardus, known for its Bordeaux-style red blend, called Marinus, and Chardonnays, you can sample current releases and library and reserve wines. ⊠ *5 W. Carmel Valley Rd., at El Caminito Rd.* ☎ *831/298–8021, 800/223–2533* ⊕ *bernardus.com* ✉ *Tastings $12–$20* ⊗ *Daily 11–5.*

Château Julien. The expansive winery, best known for its Chardonnays and Merlots, offers daily public tours and a range of private tours and tastings, available by appointment. Tours take in some of the 16-acre estate and its traditional French-style buildings, gardens, and vineyards. ⊠ *8940 Carmel Valley Rd., at Schetter Rd., Carmel* ☎ *831/624–2600* ⊕ *chateaujulien.com* ✉ *Tasting $15 (includes tour), private tours $20–$100* ⊗ *Winery weekdays 8–5, weekends 11–5; public tour (reservations encouraged) daily at 12:30 and 2:30.*

Cowgirl Winery. Cowgirl chic prevails in the main tasting building here, and it's just plain rustic at the outdoor tables, set amid chickens, a tractor, and a flatbed truck. The wines include Chardonnay, Cabernet Sauvignon, Rosé, and some blends. You can order a wood-fired pizza from sister business Corkscrew Café, and play boccie ball, horseshoes, or corn hole until your food arrives. ⊠ *25 Pilot Rd., off W. Carmel Valley Rd.* ☎ *831/298–7030* ⊕ *cowgirlwinery.com* ✉ *Tasting $13* ⊗ *Sun.–Fri. 11:30–5, Sat. until 6 (until 7 Apr.–Oct.).*

Holman Ranch Vineyards Tasting Room. Estate-grown Pinot Gris and Pinot Noir are among the standout wines made by Holman Ranch, which operates a tasting room in Carmel Valley village. If the Heather's Hill Pinot is being poured, be sure to try it. The ranch itself occupies rolling hills once part of the Carmel mission's land grant. You can book winery and vineyard tours by appointment, and the ranch welcomes overnight guests at its 10-room hacienda. ⊠ *19 E. Carmel Valley Rd., Suite C* ☎ *831/659–2640*

🌐 holmanranch.com 🎟 Tastings $8–$12 ⏱ Late May–early Sept., Mon.–Thurs. 11–6, Fri.–Sun. noon–7; early Sept.–late May, daily 11–6.

WORTH NOTING

Earthbound Farm. Pick up fresh vegetables, ready-to-eat meals, gourmet groceries, flowers, and gifts at Earthbound Farm, the world's largest grower of organic produce. You can also take a romp in the kid's garden, cut your own herbs, and stroll through the chamomile aromatherapy labyrinth. Special events, on Saturday from April through December, include bug walks and garlic-braiding workshops. *✉ 7250 Carmel Valley Rd., Carmel ☎ 831/625–6219 🌐 www.ebfarm.com 🎟 Free ⏱ Mon.–Sat. 8–6:30, Sun. 9–6.*

WHERE TO EAT

$$ EUROPEAN

🍴 **Café Rustica.** European country cooking is the focus at this lively roadhouse. Specialties include roasted meats, seafood, pastas, and thin-crust pizzas from the wood-fired oven. It can get noisy inside; for a quieter meal, request a table outside. *[$] Average main: $21 ✉ 10 Delfino Pl., at Pilot Rd., off Carmel Valley Rd. ☎ 831/659–4444 🌐 caferusticavillage.com ✍ Reservations essential ⏱ Closed Mon.*

$$ MODERN AMERICAN

🍴 **Corkscrew Café.** Farm-fresh food is the specialty of this casual, Old Monterey–style bistro. Herbs and seasonal produce come from the Corkscrew's own organic gardens, the catch of the day comes from local waters, and the meats are hormone-free. Popular dishes include the fish tacos, chicken salad, and wood-fired pizzas, which come with classic toppings and unusual ones such as Meyer lemon and prosciutto. You can dine indoors near the open kitchen, or outside in the garden patio. ■ **TIP→ Don't miss the collection of corkscrews from the 17th century to the present.** *[$] Average main: $22 ✉ 55 W. Carmel Valley Rd., at Pilot Rd. ☎ 831/659–8888 🌐 corkscrewcafe.com.*

$$$ AMERICAN

🍴 **Will's Fargo.** Around since the 1920s, this restaurant calls itself a "dressed-up saloon." Steer horns and gilt-frame paintings adorn the walls of the Victorian-style dining room; you can also eat on the patios. The menu, for years mainly seafood and steaks, including a 20-ounce porterhouse, is evolving under new owners, the proprietors of Holman Ranch Vineyards. Their wines, along with those of other local vintners, dominate the extensive list. *[$] Average main: $28 ✉ 16 E. Carmel Valley Rd., at Via Contenta ☎ 831/659–2774 🌐 wfrestaurant.com ⏱ No lunch Sept.–mid-May, no lunch weekdays mid-May.–Aug.*

WHERE TO STAY

$$$$ RESORT Fodor's Choice ★

🏨 **Bernardus Lodge.** The spacious guest rooms at this luxury spa resort, which was completely remodeled before reopening in spring 2015, have vaulted ceilings, French oak floors, featherbeds, fireplaces, patios, and bathrooms with heated-tile floors and soaking tubs for two. **Pros:** exceptional personal service; outstanding food and wine. **Cons:** pricey; some guests can seem snooty. *[$] Rooms from: $475 ✉ 415 W. Carmel Valley Rd. ☎ 831/658–3400 🌐 bernarduslodge.com 🛏 56 rooms, 1 suite.*

$$$$ RESORT Fodor's Choice ★

🏨 **Carmel Valley Ranch.** The activity options at this luxury ranch are so varied that the resort provides a program director to guide you through them. **Pros:** stunning natural setting; tons of activities; state-of-the-art amenities. **Cons:** must drive several miles to shops and nightlife; pricey.

[$] *Rooms from: $335* ✉ *1 Old Ranch Rd., Carmel* ☎ *831/625–9500* 🌐 *carmelvalleyranch.com* 🛏 *181 suites* 🍴 *No meals.*

$$$ HOTEL FAMILY 🏨 **Quail Lodge & Golf Club.** A sprawling collection of ranch-style buildings on 850 acres of meadows, fairways, and lakes, Quail Lodge offers luxury rooms and outdoor activities at surprisingly affordable rates. **Pros:** on the golf course; on-site restaurant. **Cons:** extra fees for athletic passes and some services; 5 miles from the beach and Carmel Valley Village. [$] *Rooms from: $195* ✉ *8205 Valley Greens Dr., Carmel* ☎ *831/624–2888, 866/675–1101 reservations* 🌐 *www.quaillodge.com* 🛏 *77 rooms, 16 suites* 🍴 *Breakfast.*

$$$$ RESORT Fodor's Choice ★ 🏨 **Stonepine Estate Resort.** Set on 330 pastoral acres, the former estate of the Crocker banking family has been converted to a luxurious inn. **Pros:** supremely exclusive. **Cons:** difficult to get a reservation; far from the coast. [$] *Rooms from: $300* ✉ *150 E. Carmel Valley Rd.* ☎ *831/659–2245* 🌐 *www.stonepineestate.com* 🛏 *10 rooms, 2 suites, 3 cottages* 🍴 *No meals.*

SPORTS AND THE OUTDOORS

GOLF

Quail Lodge & Golf Club. Robert Muir Graves designed this championship semiprivate 18-hole course next to Quail Lodge that provides challenging play for golfers of all skill levels. The course, which incorporates five lakes, edges the Carmel River. For the most part flat, the walkable course is well maintained, with stunning views, lush fairways, and ultrasmooth greens. ✉ *8000 Valley Greens Dr., Carmel* ☎ *831/620–8808 golf shop, 831/620–8866 club concierge* 🌐 *www.quaillodge.com* 🎟 *$175 Apr.–Oct., $150 Nov.–Mar.* 🏌 *18 holes, 6500 yards, par 71.*

Rancho Cañada Golf Club. With two 18-hole courses at reasonable rates, this public facility is a local favorite. The gently rolling fairways crisscross the Carmel River, and views of the tree-studded Santa Lucia Mountains appear from nearly every vantage point. ✉ *4860 Carmel Valley Rd., 1 mile east of Hwy. 1, Carmel* ☎ *831/624–0111, 800/536–9459* 🌐 *ranchocanada.com* 🎟 *$70* 🏌 *East Course: 18 holes, 6125 yards, par 71; West Course: 18 holes, 6357 yards, par 71.*

SPA

Fodor's Choice ★ **Refuge.** At this co-ed, European-style center on 2 serene acres you can recharge without breaking the bank. Heat up in the eucalyptus steam room or cedar sauna, plunge into cold pools, and relax indoors in zero-gravity chairs or outdoors in Adirondack chairs around fire pits. Repeat the cycle a few times, then lounge around the thermal waterfall pools. Talk is not allowed, and bathing suits are required. ✉ *27300 Rancho San Carlos Rd., south off Carmel Valley Rd., Carmel* ☎ *831/620–7360* 🌐 *refuge.com* 🎟 *$44* 🕒 *Daily 10–10* ☞ *$109 50-min massage (includes Refuge admission), $12 robe rental, hot tubs (outdoor), sauna, steam room. Services: Aromatherapy, hydrotherapy, massage.*

PEBBLE BEACH

Off North San Antonio Avenue in Carmel-by-the-Sea or off Sunset Drive in Pacific Grove.

Fodor's Choice ★ In 1919 the Pacific Improvement Company acquired 18,000 acres of prime land on the Monterey Peninsula, including the entire Pebble Beach coastal region and much of Pacific Grove. Pebble Beach Golf Links and The Lodge at Pebble Beach opened the same year, and the private enclave evolved into a world-class golf destination with three posh lodges, five golf courses, and some of the West Coast's ritziest homes.

GETTING HERE AND AROUND

If you drive south from Monterey on Highway 1, exit at 17-Mile Drive/Sunset Drive in Pacific Grove to find the northern entrance gate. Coming from Carmel, exit at Ocean Avenue and follow the road almost to the beach; turn right on North San Antonio Avenue to the Carmel Gate. You can also enter through the Highway 1 Gate off Highway 68. Monterey–Salinas Transit buses provide regular service in and around Pebble Beach.

EXPLORING

Fodor's Choice ★ **17-Mile Drive.** Primordial nature resides in quiet harmony with palatial, mostly Spanish Mission–style estates along 17-Mile Drive, which winds through an 8,400-acre microcosm of the Pebble Beach coastal landscape. Dotting the drive are rare Monterey cypresses, trees so gnarled and twisted that Robert Louis Stevenson described them as "ghosts fleeing before the wind." The most famous of these is the **Lone Cypress** (⇨ *see below*). Other highlights include **Bird Rock** and **Seal Rock,** home to harbor seals, sea lions, cormorants, and pelicans and other sea creatures and birds, and the **Crocker Marble Palace,** inspired by a Byzantine castle and easily identifiable by its dozens of marble arches.

Enter 17-Mile Drive at the Highway 1 Gate, at Highway 68; the Carmel Gate, off North San Antonio Avenue; the Pacific Grove Gate, off Sunset Drive; S.F.B. Morse Gate, Morse Drive off Highway 68; and Country Club Gate, at Congress Avenue and Forest Lodge Road. **■ TIP→ If you spend $30 or more on dining or shopping in Pebble Beach and show a receipt upon exiting, you'll receive a refund off the drive's $10 per car fee.** ✉ *Highway 1 Gate, 17-Mile Dr., west of Hwy. 1 and Hwy. 68 intersection* 🎟 *$10 per car, free for bicyclists.*

The Lone Cypress. The most-photographed tree along 17-Mile Drive is the weather-sculpted Lone Cypress, which grows out of a precipitous outcropping above the waves about 1½ miles up the road from Pebble Beach Golf Links. You can't walk out to the tree, but you can stop for a view of it at a small parking area off the road.

WHERE TO STAY

$$$$ RESORT Fodor's Choice ★ 🏨 **Casa Palmero.** This exclusive boutique hotel evokes a stately Mediterranean villa. **Pros:** ultimate in pampering; sumptuous decor; more private than sister resorts; right on the golf course. **Cons:** pricey; may be *too* posh for some. [$] *Rooms from: $910* ✉ *1518 Cypress Dr.* ☎ *831/622–6650, 800/654–9300* 🌐 *www.pebblebeach.com* 🛏 *20 rooms, 4 suites* 🍴 *Breakfast.*

$$$$ RESORT 🏨 **The Inn at Spanish Bay.** This resort sprawls across a breathtaking stretch of shoreline, and has lush, 600-square-foot rooms. **Pros:** attentive service; many amenities; spectacular views. **Cons:** huge hotel; 4 miles from other Pebble Beach Resorts facilities. [$] *Rooms from: $650* ✉ *2700 17-Mile Dr.* ☎ *831/647–7500, 800/654–9300* 🌐 *www.pebblebeach.com* 🛏 *252 rooms, 17 suites.*

$$$$ RESORT 🏨 **The Lodge at Pebble Beach.** Most rooms have wood-burning fireplaces and many have wonderful ocean views at this circa-1919 resort. **Pros:** world-class golf; borders the ocean and fairways; fabulous facilities. **Cons:** some rooms are on the small side; very pricey. [$] *Rooms from: $765* ✉ *1700 17-Mile Dr.* ☎ *831/624–3811, 800/654–9300* 🌐 *www.pebblebeach.com* 🛏 *142 rooms, 19 suites* 🍴 *No meals.*

SPORTS AND THE OUTDOORS

GOLF

Links at Spanish Bay. This course, which hugs a choice stretch of shoreline, was designed by Robert Trent Jones Jr., Tom Watson, and Sandy Tatum in the rugged manner of traditional Scottish links, with sand dunes and coastal marshes interspersed among the greens. A bagpiper signals the course's closing each day. ■ TIP→ **Nonguests of the Pebble Beach Resorts can reserve tee times up to two months in advance.** ✉ *17-Mile Dr., north end* ☎ *800/654–9300* 🌐 *www.pebblebeach.com* 🎟 *$270* ⛳ *18 holes, 6821 yards, par 72.*

Fodor's Choice ★ **Pebble Beach Golf Links.** Each February, show-business celebrities and golf pros team up at this course, the main site of the glamorous AT&T Pebble Beach National Pro-Am tournament. On most days the rest of the year, tee times are available to guests of the Pebble Beach Resorts who book a minimum two-night stay. Nonguests can reserve a tee time only one day in advance on a space-available basis; resort guests can reserve up to 18 months in advance. ✉ *17-Mile Dr., near The Lodge at Pebble Beach* ☎ *800/654–9300* 🌐 *www.pebblebeach.com* 🎟 *$495* ⛳ *18 holes, 6828 yards, par 72.*

Peter Hay. The only 9-hole, par-3 course on the Monterey Peninsula open to the public, Peter Hay attracts golfers of all skill levels. It's an ideal place for warm-ups, practicing short games, and for those who don't have time to play 18 holes. ✉ *17-Mile Dr. and Portola Rd.* ☎ *831/622–8723* 🌐 *www.pebblebeach.com* 🎟 *$30* ⛳ *9 holes, 725 yards, par 27.*

Poppy Hills. An 18-hole course designed in 1986 by Robert Trent Jones Jr., Poppy Hills reopened in 2014 after a yearlong renovation that Jones supervised. Each hole has been restored to its natural elevation along the forest floor, and all 18 greens have been rebuilt with bent grass. Individuals may reserve up to a month in advance. Chef Johnny De Vivo grows and sources organic ingredients that inspire the menus at the course's restaurant. ■ TIP→ **Poppy Hills, owned by a golfing nonprofit, represents good value for this area.** ✉ *3200 Lopez Rd., at 17-Mile Dr.* ☎ *831/622–8239* 🌐 *poppyhillsgolf.com* 🎟 *$210* ⛳ *18 holes, 7002 yards, par 73.5.*

Spyglass Hill. With three holes rated among the toughest on the PGA tour, Spyglass Hill, designed by Robert Trent Jones Sr. and Jr., challenges golfers with its varied terrain but rewards them with glorious views.

DID YOU KNOW?

The Lone Cypress has stood on this rock for more than 250 years. The tree is the official symbol of the Pebble Beach Company.

The first five holes border the Pacific, and the other 13 reach deep into the Del Monte Forest. Reservations are essential and may be made up to one month in advance (18 months for resort guests). ⊠ *Stevenson Dr. and Spyglass Hill Rd.* ☎ *800/654–9300* ⊕ *www.pebblebeach.com* ☞ *$385* ⚑ *18 holes, 6960 yards, par 72.*

PACIFIC GROVE

3 miles north of Carmel-by-the-Sea.

This picturesque town, which began as a summer retreat for church groups more than a century ago, recalls its prim and proper Victorian heritage in its host of tiny board-and-batten cottages and stately mansions. However, long before the church groups flocked here the area received thousands of annual pilgrims—in the form of bright orange-and-black monarch butterflies. They still come, migrating south from Canada and the Pacific Northwest to take residence in pine and eucalyptus groves from October through March. In Butterfly Town USA, as Pacific Grove is known, the sight of a mass of butterflies hanging from the branches like a long, fluttering veil is unforgettable.

A prime way to enjoy Pacific Grove is to walk or bicycle the 3 miles of city-owned shoreline along Ocean View Boulevard, a cliff-top area landscaped with native plants and dotted with benches meant for sitting and gazing at the sea. You can spot many types of birds here, including the web-footed cormorants that crowd the massive rocks rising out of the surf. Two Victorians of note along Ocean View are the Queen Anne–style Green Gables, at No. 301—erected in 1888, it's now an inn—and the 1909 Pryor House, at No. 429, a massive, shingled, private residence with a leaded- and beveled-glass doorway.

GETTING HERE AND AROUND

Reach Pacific Grove via Highway 68 off Highway 1, just south of Monterey. From Cannery Row in Monterey, head north until the road merges with Ocean Boulevard and follow it along the coast. MST buses travel within Pacific Grove and surrounding towns.

EXPLORING

FAMILY **Lovers Point Park.** The coastal views are gorgeous from this waterfront park whose sheltered beach has a children's pool and a picnic area. The main lawn has a volleyball court and a snack bar. ⊠ *Ocean View Blvd. northwest of Forest Ave.* ☎ *831/648–5730.*

FAMILY **Monarch Grove Sanctuary.** The sanctuary is a reliable spot for viewing monarch butterflies between October and March. ■TIP➔ **The best time to visit is between noon and 3 pm.** ⊠ *250 Ridge Rd., off Lighthouse Ave.* ⊕ *www.pgmuseum.org/monarch-viewing.*

Pacific Grove Museum of Natural History. The museum, a good source for the latest information about monarch butterflies, has permanent exhibitions about the butterflies, birds of Monterey County, biodiversity, and plants. There's a native plant garden, and a display documents life in Pacific Grove's 19th-century Chinese fishing village. ⊠ *165 Forest Ave., at Central Ave.* ☎ *831/648–5716* ⊕ *pgmuseum.org* ☞ *$9, free last Sat. of the month* ⊘ *Tues.–Sun. 10–5.*

FAMILY **Point Pinos Lighthouse.** At this 1855 structure, the West Coast's oldest continuously operating lighthouse, you can learn about the lighting and foghorn operations and wander through a small museum containing U.S. Coast Guard memorabilia. ✉ *Asilomar Ave., between Lighthouse Ave. and Del Monte Blvd.* ☎ *831/648–3176* 🌐 *pointpinoslighthouse.org* 🎟 *$2* 🕒 *Thurs.–Mon. 1–4.*

BEACHES

Asilomar State Beach. A beautiful coastal area, Asilomar State Beach stretches between Point Pinos and the Del Monte Forest. The 100 acres of dunes, tidal pools, and pocket-size beaches form one of the region's richest areas for marine life—including surfers, who migrate here most winter mornings. Leashed dogs are allowed on the beach. **Amenities:** none. **Best For:** sunrise; sunset; surfing; walking. ✉ *Sunset Dr. and Asilomar Ave.* ☎ *831/646–6440* 🌐 *www.parks.ca.gov.*

WHERE TO EAT

$$ MODERN AMERICAN 🍴 **Beach House.** Patrons of this blufftop perch sip classic cocktails, sample California fare, and watch the otters frolic on Lovers Point Beach below. Standouts among the appetizers include the crispy shrimp—tossed in a creamy, spicy sauce—and oysters Rockefeller on ciabatta crostini. Among the entrées worth a try are pan-roasted duck breast with brandy-persimmon wild rice, bacon-wrapped meat loaf, and crab-stuffed sole topped with saffron cream. The sunset discounts between 4 and 6 (reservations recommended) are a great value. ■ **TIP→ For the best views of the beach and bay, sit on the heated outdoor patio.** [$] *Average main: $21* ✉ *620 Ocean View Blvd.* ☎ *831/375–2345* 🌐 *beachhousepg.com* 🕒 *No lunch.*

$$$ MEDITERRANEAN Fodor's Choice ★ 🍴 **Fandango.** The menu here is mostly Mediterranean and southern French, with such dishes as osso buco and paella. The decor follows suit: stone walls and country furniture lend the restaurant the earthy feel of a European farmhouse. This is where locals come when they want to have a big dinner with friends, drink wine, have fun, and generally feel at home. [$] *Average main: $28* ✉ *223 17th St., south of Lighthouse Ave.* ☎ *831/372–3456* 🌐 *fandangorestaurant.com.*

$$$ ITALIAN 🍴 **Joe Rombi's La Mia Cucina.** Pasta, fish, steaks, and chops are the specialties at this modern trattoria, the best in town for Italian food. The look is spare and clean, with colorful antique wine posters decorating the white walls. Next door, the affiliated **La Piccola Casa** serves breakfast (baked goods) and lunch daily, plus early dinner from Wednesday through Sunday. [$] *Average main: $23* ✉ *208 17th St., at Lighthouse Ave.* ☎ *831/373–2416* 🌐 *lamiacucinaristorante.com* 🕒 *Closed Mon. and Tues. No lunch.*

$$$ MODERN AMERICAN Fodor's Choice ★ 🍴 **Passionfish.** South American artwork and artifacts decorate Passionfish, and Latin and Asian flavors infuse the dishes. Chef Ted Walter shops at local farmers' markets several times a week to find the best produce, fish, and meat available, then pairs it with creative sauces. The menu might include sea scallops with a caper, raisin, and walnut relish, or banana walnut–bread pudding with honey-ginger ice cream. [$] *Average main: $24* ✉ *701 Lighthouse Ave., at Congress Ave.* ☎ *831/655–3311* 🌐 *passionfish.net* 🕒 *No lunch.*

$$ ✕ **Red House Café.** When it's nice out, sun pours through the big windows
AMERICAN of this cozy restaurant and across tables on the porch; when fog rolls in, the fireplace is lit. The American menu changes with the seasons but grilled lamb chops atop mashed potatoes are often on offer for dinner, and a grilled calamari steak might be served for lunch, either in a salad or as part of a sandwich. Breakfast on weekends is a local favorite. Ⓢ *Average main: $21* ✉ *662 Lighthouse Ave., at 19th St.* ☎ *831/643–1060* ⊕ *redhousecafe.com* ☻ *No dinner Mon.*

$$ ✕ **Taste Café and Bistro.** Grilled marinated rabbit, roasted half chicken,
AMERICAN filet mignon, and other meats are the focus at Taste, which serves hearty European-inspired food in a casual, open-kitchen setting. Ⓢ *Average main: $21* ✉ *1199 Forest Ave., at Prescott La.* ☎ *831/655–0324* ⊕ *taste-cafebistro.com* ☻ *Closed Sun. and Mon.*

WHERE TO STAY

$$ ▦ **Green Gables Inn.** Stained-glass windows and ornate interior details
B&B/INN compete with spectacular ocean views at this Queen Anne–style
Fodor'sChoice mansion. **Pros:** exceptional views; impeccable attention to historic
★ detail. **Cons:** some rooms are small; thin walls. Ⓢ *Rooms from: $155* ✉ *301 Ocean View Blvd.* ☎ *831/375–2095, 800/722–1774* ⊕ *www. greengablesinnpg.com* ⤳ *10 rooms, 7 with bath; 1 suite* ⦿ *Breakfast.*

$$$ ▦ **Martine Inn.** The glassed-in parlor and many guest rooms at this 1899
B&B/INN Mediterranean-style villa have stunning ocean views. **Pros:** romantic; exquisite antiques; fancy breakfast; ocean views. **Cons:** not child-friendly; sits on a busy thoroughfare. Ⓢ *Rooms from: $209* ✉ *255 Ocean View Blvd.* ☎ *831/373–3388, 800/852–5588* ⊕ *martineinn.com* ⤳ *25 rooms* ⦿ *Breakfast.*

MONTEREY

2 miles southeast of Pacific Grove; 2 miles north of Carmel.

Early in the 20th century Carmel Martin, the first mayor of the city of Monterey, saw a bright future for his town: "Monterey Bay is the one place where people can live without being disturbed by manufacturing and big factories. I am certain that the day is coming when this will be the most desirable place in the whole state of California." His Honor was not far off the mark. Monterey is a scenic city filled with early California history: adobe buildings from the 1700s, Colton Hall, where California's first constitution was drafted in 1849, and Cannery Row, made famous by author John Steinbeck. Thousands of visitors come each year to mingle with otters and other sea creatures at the world-famous Monterey Bay Aquarium and in the protected waters of the national marine sanctuary that hugs the shoreline.

GETTING HERE AND AROUND

From San Jose or San Francisco, take U.S. 101 south to Highway 156 West at Prunedale. Head west about 8 miles to Highway 1 and follow it about 15 miles south. From San Luis Obispo, take U.S. 101 north to Salinas and drive west on Highway 68 about 20 miles.

Many MST bus lines connect at the Monterey Transit Center, at Pearl Street and Munras Avenue. In summer (daily from 10 until at least 7), the free MST Monterey Trolley travels from downtown Monterey along Cannery Row to the Aquarium and back.

TOURS

Monterey Movie Tours. Board a customized motor coach and relax while a film-savvy local takes you on a scenic tour of the Monterey Peninsula enhanced by film clips from the more than 200 movies shot in the area. The three-hour adventure travels a 32-mile loop through Monterey, Pacific Grove, and Carmel. ⊠ *Departs from Monterey Conference Center, 1 Portola Plaza* ☎ *831/240–0191, 866/846–0488* ⊕ *montereymovietours.com* ⊠ *$55* ⊙ *Daily at 1.*

Old Monterey Walking Tour. Learn all about Monterey's storied past by joining a guided walking tour through the historic district. Tours begin at Custom House Plaza, across from Fisherman's Wharf. ⊠ *$5, includes admission to Custom House and Pacific House* ⊙ *Fri.–Sun. and Mon. holidays at 10:30, 12:30, and 2.*

ESSENTIALS

Visitor Information Monterey County Convention & Visitors Bureau ☎ *888/221–1010* ⊕ *seemonterey.com.*

EXPLORING

TOP ATTRACTIONS

Cannery Row. When John Steinbeck published the novel *Cannery Row* in 1945, he immortalized a place of rough-edged working people. The waterfront street, edging a mile of gorgeous coastline, once was crowded with sardine canneries processing, at their peak, nearly 200,000 tons of the smelly silver fish a year. During the mid-1940s, however, the sardines disappeared from the bay, causing the canneries to close. Through the years the old tin-roof canneries have been converted into restaurants, art galleries, and malls with shops selling T-shirts, fudge, and plastic sea otters. Recent tourist development along the row has been more tasteful, however, and includes stylish inns and hotels, wine tasting rooms, and upscale specialty shops. ⊠ *Cannery Row, between Reeside and David Aves.* ⊕ *www.canneryrow.com.*

Colton Hall. A convention of delegates met here in 1849 to draft the first state constitution. The stone building, which has served as a school, a courthouse, and the county seat, is a city-run museum furnished as it was during the constitutional convention. The extensive grounds outside the hall surround the Old Monterey Jail. ⊠ *570 Pacific St., between Madison and Jefferson Sts.* ☎ *831/646–5640* ⊕ *www.monterey.org/museums* ⊠ *Free* ⊙ *Daily 10–4 (Sun. and Tues. noon–3 in winter).*

FAMILY **Fisherman's Wharf.** The mournful barking of sea lions provides a steady soundtrack all along Monterey's waterfront, but the best way to actually view the whiskered marine mammals is to walk along one of the two piers across from Custom House Plaza. Lined with souvenir shops, the wharf is undeniably touristy, but it's lively and entertaining. At Wharf No. 2, a working municipal pier, you can see the day's catch being unloaded from fishing boats on one side and fishermen casting their lines into the water on the other. The pier has a couple of low-key

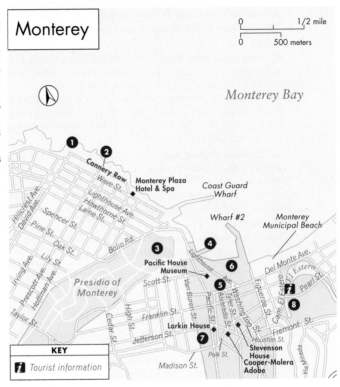

restaurants, from whose seats lucky customers might spot otters and harbor seals. ⌂ *At end of Calle Principal* ⊕ *www.montereywharf.com.*

FAMILY

Fodor'sChoice

★

Monterey Bay Aquarium. Sea creatures surround you the minute you hand over your ticket at this extraordinary facility: right at the entrance dozens of them swim in a three-story-tall, sunlit kelp-forest tank. All the exhibits here provide a sense of what it's like to be in the water with the animals—sardines swim around your head in a circular tank, and jellyfish drift in and out of view in dramatically lighted spaces that suggest the ocean depths. A petting pool puts you literally in touch with bat rays, and the million-gallon Open Seas tank illustrates the variety of creatures, from sharks to placid-looking turtles, that live in the eastern Pacific. At the Splash Zone, which has 45 interactive bilingual exhibits, kids can commune with African black-footed penguins, potbellied seahorses, and other creatures. The only drawback to the aquarium experience is that it must be shared with the throngs that congregate daily, but most visitors think it's worth it. ■TIP➜ **Through 2016, don't miss Tentacles: The Astounding Lives of Octopuses, Squid, and Cuttlefishes, a huge and fascinating exhibit of marine mollusks.** ⌂ *886 Cannery Row, at David Ave.* ☎ *831/648–4800 info, 866/963–9645 for advance tickets* ⊕ *montereybayaquarium.org* ⌑ *$40* ⊙ *Mar.–June, daily 10–6; July–Aug., weekdays, 9:30–6, weekends 9:30–8; Nov.–Feb., daily 10–5.*

Fodor's Choice ★ **Monterey State Historic Park.** You can glimpse Monterey's early history in several well-preserved adobe buildings downtown. Some of the structures have gardens that are themselves worthy sights, and they're visitable even if the buildings, among them **Casa Soberanes,** the **Cooper-Molera Adobe,** the **Larkin House,** and the **Stevenson House,** are closed.

A good place to start is the **Pacific House Museum.** Once a hotel and saloon, this facility, also a visitor center, commemorates life in pioneer-era California with gold-rush relics and photographs of old Monterey. On the upper floor are Native American artifacts, including gorgeous baskets and pottery. In the same plaza is the **Custom House.** Built by the Mexican government in 1827, it's California's oldest standing public building.

> ## JOHN STEINBECK'S CANNERY ROW
>
> "Cannery Row in Monterey in California is a poem, a stink, a grating noise, a quality of light, a tone, a habit, a nostalgia, a dream. Cannery Row is the gathered and scattered, tin and iron and rust and splintered wood, chipped pavement and weedy lots and junk heaps, sardine canneries of corrugated iron, honky tonks, restaurants and whore houses, and little crowded groceries, and laboratories and flophouses."
>
> —John Steinbeck, *Cannery Row*

■TIP→ Because of state budget cuts, some buildings may be closed when you visit, but 24/7 you can access a cell phone tour at ☎ 831/998–9498. ⊠ *Pacific House Museum visitor center, 10 Custom House Plaza* ☎ *831/649–7118* ⊕ *www.parks.ca.gov/mshp* ✉ *Free–$5* ☉ *Call or check website for hrs.*

Museum of Monterey—Stanton Center. The museum displays maritime artifacts, art, photography, and costumes from Monterey's earliest days to the present. The collection's jewel is the enormous Fresnel lens from the Point Sur Light Station. ⊠ *Stanton Center, 5 Custom House Plaza* ☎ *831/372–2608* ⊕ *www.museumofmonterey.org* ✉ *Free* ☉ *May–Aug., Tues.–Sat. 10–7, Sun. noon–5; Sept.–Apr., Wed.–Sat. 11–5, Sun. noon–5.*

WORTH NOTING

A Taste of Monterey. Without driving the back roads, you can taste the wines of nearly 100 area vintners (craft beers, too) while taking in fantastic bay views. Bottles are available for purchase, and food is served from noon until closing. ⊠ *700 Cannery Row, Suite KK* ☎ *831/646–5446, 888/646–5446* ⊕ *atasteofmonterey.com* ✉ *Tastings $10–$20* ☉ *Sun.–Wed. 11–7, Thurs.–Sat. 11–8.*

FAMILY **Dennis the Menace Playground.** The late cartoonist Hank Ketcham designed this play area. Its equipment is on a grand scale and made for Dennis-like daredevils: kid favorites include the roller slide, rock-climbing area, and clanking suspension bridge. You can rent a rowboat or a paddleboat for cruising around U-shaped Lake El Estero, populated with an assortment of ducks, mud hens, and geese. ⊠ *El Estero Park, Pearl St. and Camino El Estero* ☎ *831/646–3866* ⊕ *www.monterey.org/parks* ☉ *Closed Tues., Sept.–May.*

7

Trained "seals" that perform in circuses are actually California sea lions—intelligent, social animals that live (and sleep) close together in groups.

Presidio of Monterey Museum. This spot has been significant for centuries. Its first incarnation was as a Native American village for the Rumsien tribe. The Spanish explorer Sebastián Vizcaíno landed here in 1602, and Father Junípero Serra arrived in 1770. Notable battles fought here include the 1818 skirmish in which the corsair Hipólito Bruchard conquered the Spanish garrison that stood on this site and claimed part of California for Argentina. The indoor museum tells the stories; plaques mark the outdoor sites. ✉ *Presidio of Monterey, Corporal Ewing Rd., off Lighthouse Ave.* ☎ *831/646–3456* 🌐 *www.monterey.org/museums* 🎟 *Free* 🕒 *Mon. 10–1, Thurs.–Sat. 10–4, Sun. 1–4.*

WHERE TO EAT

$$ SEAFOOD — 🍴 **Monterey Fish House.** Casual yet stylish and always packed, this seafood restaurant is removed from the hubbub of the wharf. If the dining room is full, you can wait at the bar and savor plump oysters on the half shell. The bartenders and waitstaff will gladly advise you on the perfect wine to go with your poached, blackened, or oak-grilled seafood. [$] *Average main: $22* ✉ *2114 Del Monte Ave., at Dela Vina Ave.* ☎ *831/373–4647* ✍ *Reservations essential* 🕒 *No lunch weekends.*

$$$ AMERICAN — Fodor's Choice ★ — 🍴 **Montrio Bistro.** This quirky converted firehouse, with its rawhide walls and iron indoor trellises, has a wonderfully sophisticated menu. Chef Tony Baker uses organic produce and meats and sustainably sourced seafood to create imaginative dishes that reflect the area's agriculture—fire-roasted artichokes with Mediterranean relish, for instance, and pesto-rubbed sirloin prepared with brussels sprouts, dates, and smoked bacon. Monterey wineries are well represented on the wine list, and

the signature cocktails are infused with local fruits, herbs, and vegetables. $ *Average main: $25* ✉ *414 Calle Principal, at W. Franklin St.* ☎ *831/648–8880* ⊕ *montrio.com* ⌕ *Reservations essential* ⊘ *No lunch.*

$$$ SEAFOOD ✕ **Old Fisherman's Grotto.** Otters and seals frolic in the water just below this nautical-theme Fisherman's Wharf restaurant famous for its creamy clam chowder. Seafood paella, sand dabs, filet mignon, teriyaki chicken, and several pastas are among the many entrée options. ■TIP→ Reserve a window-side table for the best views. $ *Average main: $26* ✉ *39 Fisherman's Wharf* ☎ *831/375–4604* ⊕ *oldfishermansgrotto.com.*

$ AMERICAN ✕ **Old Monterey Café.** Breakfast here gets constant local raves. The café's fame rests on familiar favorites: a dozen kinds of omelets, and pancakes from blueberry to cinnamon-raisin-pecan. For lunch are good soups, salads, and sandwiches. $ *Average main: $13* ✉ *489 Alvarado St., at Munras Ave.* ☎ *831/646–1021* ⌕ *Reservations not accepted* ⊘ *No dinner.*

$$$$ MODERN AMERICAN Fodor'sChoice ★ ✕ **Restaurant 1833.** Inside the two-story Stokes Adobe, built in 1833, this popular restaurant and bar showcases the region's colorful history and local bounty. Each of the seven dining rooms honors an era and characters from the adobe's past, which includes an early stint as an apothecary. Sit in a leather booth on the Founder's Balcony for a bird's-eye view of the bustling bar scene below, or outdoors by the courtyard fire pits near giant oak, redwood, palm, and magnolia trees. Menu stars include whole roasted truffle chicken, pan-roasted sturgeon, and grilled prime château sirloin with duck-fat potatoes, cipollini onions, and bordelaise sauce. The extensive wine selection will appeal to connoisseurs. $ *Average main: $32* ✉ *500 Hartnell St., at Polk St.* ☎ *831/643–1833* ⊕ *www.restaurant1833.com* ⊘ *No lunch.*

$$$ AMERICAN ✕ **Tarpy's Roadhouse.** Fun, dressed-up American favorites—a little something for everyone—are served in this renovated early-1900s stone farmhouse several miles east of town. The kitchen cranks out everything from Cajun-spiced prawns to meat loaf with marsala-mushroom gravy to grilled ribs and steaks. Eat indoors by a fireplace or outdoors in the courtyard. $ *Average main: $24* ✉ *2999 Monterey–Salinas Hwy., Hwy. 68* ☎ *831/647–1444* ⊕ *tarpys.com.*

> ### FORMER CAPITAL OF CALIFORNIA
>
> In 1602 Spanish explorer Sebastián Vizcaíno stepped ashore on a remote California peninsula. He named it after the viceroy of New Spain—Count de Monte Rey. Soon the Spanish built a military outpost, and the site was the capital of California until the state came under American rule.

WHERE TO STAY

$$$ HOTEL ⬚ **InterContinental The Clement Monterey.** Spectacular bay views, upscale amenities, assiduous service, and a superb location next to the aquarium propelled this luxury hotel to immediate stardom. **Pros:** a block from the aquarium; fantastic waterfront views from some rooms; great for families. **Cons:** a tad formal; pricey. $ *Rooms from: $229* ✉ *750*

7

CLOSE UP

The Monterey Bay National Marine Sanctuary

Although Monterey's coastal landscapes are stunning, their beauty is more than equaled by the wonders that lie offshore. The Monterey Bay National Marine Sanctuary—which stretches 276 miles, from north of San Francisco almost down to Santa Barbara—teems with abundant life, and has topography as diverse as that aboveground.

The preserve's 5,322 square miles include vast submarine canyons, which reach down 10,663 feet at their deepest point. They also encompass dense forests of giant kelp—a kind of seaweed that can grow more than a hundred feet from its roots on the ocean floor. These kelp forests are especially robust off Monterey.

The sanctuary was established in 1992 to protect the habitat of the many species that thrive in the bay. Some animals can be seen quite easily from land. In summer and winter you might glimpse the offshore spray of gray whales as they migrate between their summer feeding grounds in Alaska and their breeding grounds in Baja. Clouds of marine birds—including white-faced ibis, three types of albatross, and more than 15 types of gull—skim the waves, or roost in the rock islands along 17-Mile Drive. Sea otters dart and gambol in the calmer waters of the bay; and of course, you can watch the sea lions—and hear their round-the-clock barking—on the wharves in Santa Cruz and Monterey.

The sanctuary supports many other creatures, however, that remain unseen by most on-land visitors. Some of these are enormous, such as the giant blue whales that arrive to feed on plankton in summer; others, like the more than 22 species of red algae in these waters, are microscopic. So whether you choose to visit the Monterey Bay Aquarium, take a whale-watch trip, or look out to sea with your binoculars, remember you're seeing just a small part of a vibrant underwater kingdom.

Cannery Row ☎ *831/375–4500, 866/781–2406 toll free* 🌐 *www.ictheclementmonterey.com* 🛏 *192 rooms, 16 suites* 🍴 *No meals.*

$$ HOTEL 🏨 **Monterey Bay Lodge.** Its superior amenities and location bordering El Estero Park give this cheerful facility the edge over other area motels. **Pros:** within walking distance of the beach and a playground; quiet at night; good family choice. **Cons:** near a busy boulevard. [$] *Rooms from: $140* ✉ *55 Camino Aguajito* ☎ *831/372–8057, 800/558–1900* 🌐 *montereybaylodge.com* 🛏 *43 rooms, 3 suites* 🍴 *No meals.*

$$$ RESORT 🏨 **Monterey Beach Resort.** One of the area's best values, this hotel has a great waterfront location—2 miles north of Monterey, with views of the bay and the city skyline—and offers a surprising array of amenities. **Pros:** on the beach; great value; family-friendly. **Cons:** several miles from major attractions; big-box mall neighborhood. [$] *Rooms from: $199* ✉ *2600 Sand Dunes Dr.* ☎ *831/394–3321, 800/242–8627* 🌐 *montereybeachresort.com* 🛏 *196 rooms* 🍴 *No meals.*

$$$$ HOTEL 🏨 **Monterey Plaza Hotel & Spa.** Guests at this waterfront Cannery Row hotel can see frolicking sea otters from its wide outdoor patio and many room balconies. **Pros:** on the ocean; many amenities; attentive service.

Cons: touristy area; heavy traffic. $ *Rooms from: $269* ✉ *400 Cannery Row* ☎ *831/646–1700, 800/334–3999* ⊕ *www.montereyplazahotel.com* ⇗ *280 rooms, 10 suites* ⦿ *Multiple meal plans.*

$$$$
B&B/INN
Fodor's Choice
★

🏨 **Old Monterey Inn.** This three-story manor house was the home of Monterey's first mayor, and today it remains a private enclave within walking distance of downtown, set off by lush gardens shaded by huge old trees and bordered by a creek. **Pros:** gorgeous gardens; refined luxury; serene. **Cons:** must drive to attractions and sights; fills quickly. $ *Rooms from: $289* ✉ *500 Martin St.* ☎ *831/375–8284, 800/350–2344* ⊕ *www.oldmontereyinn.com* ⇗ *6 rooms, 3 suites, 1 cottage* ⦿ *Breakfast.*

$$$
HOTEL

🏨 **Spindrift Inn.** This boutique hotel on Cannery Row has beach access and a rooftop garden that overlooks the water. **Pros:** close to aquarium; steps from the beach; friendly staff. **Cons:** throngs of visitors outside; can be noisy; not good for families. $ *Rooms from: $209* ✉ *652 Cannery Row* ☎ *831/646–8900, 800/841–1879* ⊕ *spindriftinn.com* ⇗ *45 rooms* ⦿ *Breakfast.*

NIGHTLIFE AND PERFORMING ARTS

BARS

Turn 12 Bar & Grill. The motorcycles and vintage photographs at this downtown watering hole pay homage to nearby 11-turn Laguna Seca Raceway. The large-screen TVs, heated outdoor patio, happy-hour specials, and live entertainment keep the place jumpin' into the wee hours. ✉ *400 Tyler St., at E. Franklin St.* ☎ *831/372–8876* ⊕ *turn12barandgrill.com.*

Peter B's Brewpub. Housemade beers, 15 HDTVs, a decent pub menu, and a pet-friendly patio ensure lively crowds at this craft brewery in back of the Portola Plaza Hotel. ✉ *2 Portola Plaza* ☎ *831/649–2699* ⊕ *www.peterbsbrewpub.com.*

MUSIC FESTIVALS

Monterey Jazz Festival. The world's oldest jazz festival attracts top-name performers to the Monterey Fairgrounds on the third full weekend of September. ☎ *888/248–6499 ticket office, 831/373–3366* ⊕ *montereyjazzfestival.org.*

THEATER

Bruce Ariss Wharf Theater (*The New Wharf Theatre*). American musicals past and present are the focus here, with dramas and comedies also in the mix. ✉ *One Fisherman's Wharf* ☎ *831/649–2332.*

SPORTS AND THE OUTDOORS

Monterey Bay waters never warm to the temperatures of their Southern California counterparts—the warmest they get is the low 60s. That's one reason why the marine life here is so diverse, which in turn brings out the fishers, kayakers, and whale-watchers. During the rainy winter, the waves grow larger, and surfers flock to the water. On land pretty much year-round, bikers find opportunities to ride, and walkers have plenty of waterfront to stroll.

BIKING

Adventures by the Sea. You can rent surreys plus tandem, standard, and electric bicycles from this outfit that also conducts bike and kayak tours and rents kayaks and standup paddleboards. ⊠ *299 Cannery Row* ☏ *831/372–1807, 800/979–3370 reservations* ⊕ *adventuresbythesea. com* ⊠ *Breakwater Cove, 32 Cannery Row* ⊠ *685 Cannery Row* ⊠ *Beach at Lovers Point, Pacific Grove* ⊠ *Stillwater Cove, 17-Mile Drive, Pebble Beach* ⊠ *210 Alvarado Mall.*

Bay Bikes. For bicycle and surrey rentals, visit Bay Bikes at one of its two Monterey shops. ■ **TIP**➜ **You can rent a bike on Cannery Row and drop it off at the company's Carmel location.** ⊠ *585 Cannery Row* ☏ *831/655–2453* ⊕ *www.baybikes.com* ⊠ *486 Washington St.* ⊠ *3600 The Barnyard, Carmel.*

FISHING

Randy's Fishing and Whale Watching Trips. In business since 1949, Randy's takes beginning and experienced fishers out to sea. ⊠ *66 Fisherman's Wharf* ☏ *831/372–7440, 800/251–7440* ⊕ *randysfishingtrips.com.*

KAYAKING

Fodor'sChoice ★ **Monterey Bay Kayaks.** For many visitors the best way to see the bay is by kayak. This company rents equipment and conducts classes and natural-history tours. ⊠ *693 Del Monte Ave.* ☏ *831/373–5357, 800/649–5357* ⊕ *www.montereybaykayaks.com.*

WALKING

Monterey Bay Coastal Recreation Trail. From Custom House Plaza, you can walk along the coast in either direction on this 29-mile-long trail and take in spectacular views of the sea. The trail runs from north of Monterey in Castroville south to Pacific Grove, with sections continuing around Pebble Beach. Much of the path follows an old Southern Pacific Railroad route. ☏ *888/221–1010* ⊕ *seemonterey.com/things-to-do/parks/coastal-trail.*

WHALE-WATCHING

Thousands of gray whales pass close by the Monterey Coast on their annual migration between the Bering Sea and Baja California, and a whale-watching cruise is the best way to see these magnificent mammals close up. The migration south takes place from December through March; January is prime viewing time. The whales migrate north from March through June. Blue whales and humpbacks also pass the coast; they're most easily spotted in late summer and early fall.

Fast Raft Ocean Safaris. Naturalists lead whale-watching and sightseeing tours of Monterey Bay aboard the 33-foot *Ranger,* a six-passenger, rigid-hull inflatable boat. The speedy craft slips into coves inaccessible to larger vessels; its quiet engines enable intimate marine experiences without disturbing wildlife. Children ages 12 and older are welcome to participate. ⊠ *32 Cannery Row, Suite F2* ☏ *800/979–3370* ⊕ *www. fastraft.com* ⌨ *$140.*

Monterey Bay Whale Watch. The marine biologists here lead three- to five-hour whale-watching tours. ⊠ *84 Fisherman's Wharf* ☏ *831/375–4658* ⊕ *montereybaywhalewatch.com.*

Princess Monterey Whale Watching. Tours are offered daily on a 150-passenger high-speed cruiser and a large 75-foot boat. ⊠ *96 Fisherman's Wharf* ☎ *831/372–2203, 831/205–2370 reservations, 888/223–9153 international reservations* ⊕ *montereywhalewatching.com.*

SHOPPING

Alvarado and nearby downtown streets are good places to start a Monterey shopping spree, especially if you're interested in antiques and collectibles.

Cannery Row Antique Mall. Bargain hunters can sometimes find little treasures at the mall, which houses more than 100 local vendors under one roof. ⊠ *471 Wave St.* ☎ *831/655–0264* ⊕ *canneryrowantiquemall.com* ⊗ *Weekdays 10–5:30, Sat. 10–6, Sun. 10–5.*

Old Monterey Book Co. Antiquarian books and prints are this shop's specialties. ⊠ *136 Bonifacio Pl., off Alvarado St.* ☎ *831/372–3111* ⊗ *Tues. 3–7, Wed.–Sat. 1–5.*

AROUND MONTEREY BAY

As Highway 1 follows the curve of the bay between Monterey and Santa Cruz, it passes through a rich agricultural zone. Opening right onto the bay, where the Salinas and Pajaro rivers drain into the Pacific, a broad valley brings together fertile soil, an ideal climate, and a good water supply to create optimum growing conditions for crops such as strawberries, artichokes, brussels sprouts, and broccoli. Several beautiful beaches line this part of the coast. Salinas and Moss Landing are in Monterey County; the other cities and towns covered here are in Santa Cruz County.

GETTING HERE AND AROUND

All the towns in this area are on or just off Highway 1. MST buses serve Monterey County destinations, connecting in Watsonville with Santa Cruz METRO buses, which operate throughout Santa Cruz County.

SALINAS

17 miles east of Monterey on Hwy. 68.

Salinas, a hard-working city surrounded by vineyards and fruit and vegetable fields, honors the memory and literary legacy of John Steinbeck, its most famous native, with the National Steinbeck Center. The facility is in Old Town Salinas, where renovated turn-of-the-20th-century stone buildings house shops and restaurants.

ESSENTIALS

Train Information Salinas Amtrak Station ⊠ *11 Station Pl., at W. Market St., Salinas* ☎ *800/872–7245* ⊕ *www.amtrak.com.*

Visitor Information California Welcome Center ⊠ *1213 N. Davis Rd., west of U.S. 101, exit 330, Salinas* ☎ *831/757–8687* ⊕ *visitcalifornia.com/attraction/ california-welcome-center-salinas* ⊗ *Open daily 9–5.*

EXPLORING

FAMILY **Monterey Zoo.** Exotic animals, many of them retired from film, television, and live production work or rescued from less than ideal environments, find sanctuary here. For an in-depth experience, stay in a safari bunga-low at Vision Quest Safari B&B, where breakfast is delivered in a basket by an elephant. ⊠ *400 River Rd., off Hwy. 68, Salinas* ☎ *831/455–1901, 800/228–7382* ⊕ *www.montereyzoo.com* ✉ *Tours $10; optional post-tour elephant feeding $5* ☉ *Tours daily at 1, June–Aug. also at 3.*

National Steinbeck Center. The center's exhibits document the life of Pulitzer- and Nobel-prize winner John Steinbeck and the history of the nearby communities that inspired novels such as *East of Eden.* High-lights include reproductions of the green pickup-camper from *Travels with Charley* and the bunkroom from *Of Mice and Men.* **Steinbeck House,** the author's Victorian birthplace, at 132 Central Avenue, is two blocks from the center in a so-so neighborhood. Now a decent lunch spot, it displays memorabilia. ⊠ *1 Main St., at Central Ave., Salinas* ☎ *831/775–4721* ⊕ *steinbeck.org* ✉ *$15* ☉ *Daily 10–5.*

PINNACLES NATIONAL PARK

38 miles southeast of Salinas.

Pinnacles may be the nation's newest national park, but Teddy Roo-sevelt recognized the uniqueness of this ancient volcano—its jagged spires and monoliths thrusting upward from chaparral-covered moun-tains—when he made it a national monument in 1908. Though only about two hours from the bustling Bay Area, the outside world seems to recede even before you reach the park's gates.

GETTING HERE AND AROUND

One of the first things you need to decide when visiting Pinnacles is which entrance—east or west—you'll use, because there's no road con-necting the two rugged peaks separating them. Entering from Highway 25 on the east is straightforward. The gate is only a mile or so from the turnoff. From the west, once you head east out of Soledad on High-way 146, the road quickly becomes narrow and hilly, with many blind curves. Drive slowly and cautiously along the 10 miles or so before you reach the west entrance.

ESSENTIALS

Pinnacles Visitor Center. At the park's main visitor center, located at the eastern entrance, you can purchase admission passes, get maps, browse books, and buy gifts. The adjacent campground store sells snacks and drinks. ⊠ *Hwy. 146, 2 miles west of Hwy. 25, Paicines* ☎ *831/389–4485* ⊕ *www.nps.gov/pinn.*

West Pinnacles Visitor Center. This station is just past the park's western entrance, about 10 miles east of Soledad. Here you can get maps and information, watch a 13-minute film about Pinnacles, and view some displays. ■TIP→ Food and drink aren't available here, so come pre-pared. ⊠ *Hwy. 146, off U.S. 101, Soledad* ☎ *831/389–4427* ⊕ *www.nps.gov/pinn* ☉ *Daily 9–4:30, call or check website to confirm hrs.*

EXPLORING

FAMILY **Pinnacles National Park.** The many attractions at Pinnacles include talus caves, 30 miles of hiking trails, and hundreds of rock climbing routes. A mosaic of diverse habitats supports an amazing variety of wildlife species: 185 birds, 49 mammals, 70 butterflies, and nearly 400 bees. The park is also home to some of the world's remaining few hundred condors in captivity and release areas. Fourteen of California's 25 bat species live in caves and other habitats in the park. President Theodore Roosevelt declared this remarkable 26,000-acre geologic and wildlife preserve a national monument in 1908. President Barack Obama officially designated it a national park in 2013.

The pinnacles are believed to have been created when two major tectonic plates collided and pushed a smaller plate down beneath the earth's crust, spawning volcanoes in what's now called the Gabilan Mountains, southeast of Salinas and Monterey. After the eruptions ceased, the San Andreas Fault split the volcanic field in two, carrying part of it northward to what is now Pinnacles National Park. Millions of years of erosion left a rugged landscape of rocky spires and crags, or pinnacles. Boulders fell into canyons and valleys, creating talus caves and a paradise for modern-day rock climbers. Spring is the most popular time to visit, when colorful wildflowers blanket the meadows, and the light and scenery can be striking in fall and winter; the summer heat is often brutal. The park has two entrances—east and west—but they are not connected. The Pinnacles Visitor Center, Bear Gulch Nature Center, Park Headquarters, the Pinnacles Campground, and the Bear Gulch Cave and Reservoir are on the east side. The Chaparral Parking Area is on the west side, where you can feast on fantastic views of the Pinnacles High Peaks from the parking area. Dogs are not allowed on hiking trails. ■TIP➔ The east entrance is 32 miles southeast of Hollister via Highway 25. The west entrance is about 12 miles east of Soledad via Highway 146. ✉ *5000 Hwy. 146, Paicines* ☎ *831/389–4486, 831/389–4427 Westside* ⊕ *www.nps.gov/pinn* 🌐 *$10 per vehicle, $5 per visitor if biking or walking* ☉ *West entrance, daily 7:30 am–8 pm; West Pinnacles Visitor Center, daily 9–4:30 depending on season (check website or Facebook page to confirm hrs). East entrance, daily 24 hrs; Pinnacles Visitor Center, daily 9:30–5.*

SPORTS AND THE OUTDOORS

HIKING

Hiking is the most popular activity at Pinnacles, with more than 30 miles of trails for every interest and level of fitness. Because there isn't a road through the park, hiking is also the only way to experience its interior, including the High Peaks, the talus caves, and the reservoir.

Balconies Cliffs-Cave Loop. Grab your flashlight before heading out from the Chaparral Trailhead parking lot for this 2.4-mile loop that takes you through the Balconies Caves. This trail is especially beautiful in spring, when an abundance of wildflowers carpets the canyon floor. About 0.6 mile from the start of the trail, turn left to begin ascending the Balconies Cliffs Trail, where you'll be rewarded with close-up views of Machete Ridge and other steep, vertical formations; you'll probably run across a few rock climbers testing their skills. *Easy.* ✉ *Pinnacles National Park*

7

✢ *From West Pinnacles Visitor Contact Station, drive about 2 miles to Chaparral Trailhead parking lot. Trail picks up on west side of lot.*

FAMILY **Moses Spring-Rim Trail Loop.** This is perhaps the most popular hike at Pinnacles, as it's relatively short (2.2 miles) and fun for kids and adults. It takes you to the Bear Gulch cave system, and if your timing is right, you'll pass by several seasonal waterfalls inside the caves (if it's been raining, check with a ranger, as the caves could be flooded). ⚠ **The upper side of the cave is usually closed in spring and early summer to protect the Townsend's big-ear bats and their pups.** *Easy.* ✢ *Trail begins just past Bear Gulch Nature Center, on the south side of overflow parking lot.*

SAN JUAN BAUTISTA

20 miles northeast of Salinas.

Much of the small town that grew up around Mission San Juan Bautista, still a working church, has been protected from development since 1933, when a state park was established here. Small antiques shops and restaurants occupy the Old West and art deco buildings that line 3rd Street.

GETTING HERE AND AROUND

From Highway 1 north or south, exit east onto Highway 156. MST buses do not serve San Juan Bautista.

EXPLORING

San Juan Bautista State Historic Park. With the low-slung, colonnaded **Mission San Juan Bautista** as its drawing card, this park 20 miles northeast of Salinas is about as close to early-19th-century California as you can get. Historic buildings ring the wide green plaza, among them an adobe home furnished with Spanish-colonial antiques, a hotel frozen in the 1860s, a blacksmith shop, a pioneer cabin, and a jailhouse. The mission's cemetery contains the unmarked graves of more than 4,300 Native American converts. ■ **TIP ➔ On the first Saturday of the month, costumed volunteers engage in quilting bees, tortilla making, and other frontier activities, and sarsaparilla and other nonalcoholic drinks are served in the saloon.** ✉ *19 Franklin St., off Hwy. 156, east of U.S. 101* ☎ *831/623–4881* ⊕ *www.parks.ca.gov* 🗓 *$3 park, $4 mission* ☉ *Daily 10–4:30.*

MOSS LANDING

17 miles north of Monterey; 12 miles north of Salinas.

Moss Landing is not much more than a couple of blocks of cafés and restaurants, art galleries, and studios, plus a busy fishing port, but therein lies its charm. It's a fine place to overnight or stop for a meal and get a dose of nature.

GETTING HERE AND AROUND

From Highway 1 north or south, exit at Moss Landing Road on the ocean side. MST buses serve Moss Landing.

TOURS

Elkhorn Slough Safari Nature Boat Tours. This outfit's naturalists lead two-hour tours of Elkhorn Sough aboard a 27-foot pontoon boat. Reservations are required. ⊠ *Moss Landing Harbor* ☎ *831/633–5555* ⊕ *elk hornslough.com* ☐ *$38.*

ESSENTIALS
Visitor Information

Moss Landing Chamber of Commerce ☎ *831/633–4501* ⊕ *mosslanding-chamber.com.*

EXPLORING

Elkhorn Slough National Estuarine Research Reserve. The reserve's 1,400 acres of tidal flats and salt marshes form a complex environment that supports some 300 species of birds. A walk along the meandering waterways and wetlands can reveal hawks, white-tailed kites, owls, herons, and egrets. Also living or visiting here are sea otters, sharks, rays, and many other animals. ■ TIP→ **On weekends, guided walks from the visitor center begin at 10 and 1. On the first Saturday of the month, an early-bird tour departs at 8:30.** ⊠ *1700 Elkhorn Rd., Watsonville* ☎ *831/728–2822* ⊕ *elkhornslough.org* ☐ *$4 day use fee (credit card only)* ◷ *Wed.–Sun. 9–5.*

WHERE TO EAT AND STAY

$$
SOUTH AMERICAN
✕ **Haute Enchilada.** Part of a complex that includes art galleries and an events venue, the Haute (pronounced "hot") adds bohemian character to the seafaring village of Moss Landing. The inventive Latin American–inspired dishes include crab and black corn enchiladas topped with a citrus cilantro cream sauce, and roasted *pasilla* chilies stuffed with mashed plantains and caramelized onions. Gluten-free and vegan options are also on the menu. $ *Average main: $22* ⊠ *7902 Moss Landing Rd.* ☎ *831/633–5843* ⊕ *hauteenchilada.com.*

$$
SEAFOOD
✕ **Phil's Fish Market & Eatery.** Exquisitely fresh, simply prepared seafood (try the cioppino) is on the menu at this warehouselike restaurant on the harbor; all kinds of glistening fish are for sale at the market in the front. ■ TIP→ **Phil's Snack Shack, a tiny sandwich-and-smoothie joint, serves quicker meals at the north end of town.** $ *Average main: $19* ⊠ *7600 Sandholdt Rd.* ☎ *831/633–2152* ⊕ *philsfishmarket.com.*

$$
B&B/INN
⌂ **Captain's Inn.** Commune with nature and pamper yourself with upscale creature comforts at this green-certified complex in the heart of town. **Pros:** walk to restaurants and shops; tranquil natural setting; free Wi-Fi and parking. **Cons:** rooms in historic building don't have water views; far from urban amenities; not appropriate for young children. $ *Rooms from: $155* ⊠ *8122 Moss Landing Rd.* ☎ *831/633–5550* ⊕ *www.captainsinn.com* ⤵ *10 rooms, 1 apartment* ⦿ *Breakfast.*

SPORTS AND THE OUTDOORS
KAYAKING

Monterey Bay Kayaks. Rent a kayak to paddle out into Elkhorn Slough for up-close wildlife encounters. ⊠ *2390 Hwy. 1, at North Harbor* ☎ *831/373–5357, 800/649–5357 toll free* ⊕ *montereybaykayaks.com.*

APTOS

17 miles north of Moss Landing.

Backed by a redwood forest and facing the sea, downtown Aptos—known as Aptos Village—is a place of wooden walkways and false-fronted shops. Antiques dealers cluster along Trout Gulch Road, off Soquel Drive east of Highway 1.

GETTING HERE AND AROUND

Use Highway 1 to reach Aptos from Santa Cruz or Monterey. Exit at State Park Drive to reach the main shopping hub and Aptos Village. You can also exit at Freedom Boulevard or Rio del Mar. Soquel Drive is the main artery through town.

ESSENTIALS

Visitor Information Aptos Chamber of Commerce ✉ *7605-A Old Dominion Ct.* ☎ *831/688–1467* 🌐 *aptoschamber.com.*

BEACHES

FAMILY Fodor's Choice ★ **Seacliff State Beach.** Sandstone bluffs tower above popular Seacliff State Beach. You can fish off the pier, which leads out to a sunken World War I tanker ship built of concrete. Leashed dogs are allowed on the beach. **Amenities:** food and drink; lifeguards; parking (fee); showers; toilets. **Best For:** sunset; swimming; walking. ✉ *201 State Park Dr., off Hwy. 1* ☎ *831/685–6442* 🌐 *www.parks.ca.gov* 🎟 *$10 per vehicle* ⏲ *Daily 8 am–sunset.*

WHERE TO EAT AND STAY

$$$ MEDITERRANEAN 🍴 **Bittersweet Bistro.** A large old tavern with cathedral ceilings houses this popular bistro, where chef-owner Thomas Vinolus draws culinary inspiration from the Mediterranean. The menu changes seasonally, but regular highlights include paella, seafood puttanesca, and pepper-crusted rib-eye steak with Cabernet demi-glace. The chocolate desserts are not to be missed. Breakfast and lunch are available in the casual Bittersweet Café. Leashed dogs are welcome on the outdoor patio, where you can order meaty meals for them. [$] *Average main: $27* ✉ *787 Rio Del Mar Blvd., off Hwy. 1* ☎ *831/662–9799* 🌐 *www.bittersweetbistro.com.*

$$$ HOTEL FAMILY 🏨 **Best Western Seacliff Inn.** Families and business travelers like this 6-acre property near Seacliff State Beach that's more resort than hotel. **Pros:** walking distance to the beach; family-friendly; hot breakfast buffet. **Cons:** close to freeway; occasional nighttime bar noise. [$] *Rooms from: $180* ✉ *7500 Old Dominion Ct.* ☎ *831/688–7300, 800/367–2003* 🌐 *seacliffinn.com* 🛏 *139 rooms, 10 suites* 🍽 *Breakfast.*

$$$ B&B/INN 🏨 **Flora Vista.** Multicolor fields of flowers, strawberries, and veggies unfold in every direction at this luxury neo-Georgian inn on 2 acres south of Aptos. **Pros:** private; near Sand Dollar Beach; flowers everywhere. **Cons:** no restaurants or nightlife within walking distance; not a good place for kids. [$] *Rooms from: $195* ✉ *1258 San Andreas Rd., La Selva Beach* ☎ *831/724–8663, 877/753–5672* 🌐 *floravistainn.com* 🛏 *5 rooms* 🍽 *Breakfast.*

$$$ HOTEL 🏨 **Rio Sands Hotel.** A property-wide makeover completed in 2015 has made this casual two-building complex near the beach an even more exceptional value. **Pros:** two-minute walk to Rio Del Mar Beach

(Seacliff State Beach is also nearby); free parking and Wi-Fi; close to a deli and restaurants. **Cons:** some rooms and suites are small; neighborhood becomes congested in summer. $ *Rooms from: $179* ⊠ *116 Aptos Beach Dr.* ☎ *831/688–3207, 800/826–2077* ⊕ *riosands.com* ⊃ *25 rooms, 25 suites* ⊚ *Breakfast.*

$$$$
RESORT
FAMILY

Seascape Beach Resort. It's easy to unwind at this full-fledged resort on a bluff overlooking Monterey Bay. **Pros:** time share–style apartments; access to miles of beachfront; superb views. **Cons:** far from city life; most bathrooms are small. $ *Rooms from: $300* ⊠ *1 Seascape Resort Dr.* ☎ *831/688–6800, 800/929–7727* ⊕ *seascaperesort.com* ⊃ *285 suites* ⊚ *No meals.*

CAPITOLA AND SOQUEL

4 miles northwest of Aptos.

On the National Register of Historic places as California's first seaside resort town, the village of Capitola has been in a holiday mood since the late 1800s. Casual eateries, surf shops, and ice cream parlors pack its walkable downtown. Inland, across Highway 1, antiques shops line Soquel Drive in the town of Soquel. Wineries dot the Santa Cruz Mountains beyond.

GETTING HERE AND AROUND

From Santa Cruz or Monterey, follow Highway 1 to the Capitola/Soquel (Bay Avenue) exit about 7 miles south of Santa Cruz and head west to reach Capitola and east to access Soquel Village. On summer weekends, park for free in the lot behind the Crossroads Center, a block west of the freeway, and hop aboard the free Capitola Shuttle to the village.

ESSENTIALS

Visitor Information Capitola-Soquel Chamber of Commerce ⊠ *716-G Capitola Ave., Capitola* ☎ *831/475–6522* ⊕ *capitolachamber.com.*

BEACHES

FAMILY
Fodor's Choice
★

New Brighton State Beach. Once the site of a Chinese fishing village, New Brighton is now a popular surfing and camping spot. Its Pacific Migrations Visitor Center traces the history of the Chinese and other peoples who settled around Monterey Bay and documents the migratory patterns of the area's wildlife, such as monarch butterflies and gray whales. Leashed dogs are allowed in the park. New Brighton connects with Seacliff Beach, and at low tide you can walk or run along this scenic stretch of sand for nearly 16 miles south (though you might have to wade through a few creeks). ■ TIP➜ **The 1½-mile stroll from New Brighton to Seacliff's concrete ship is a local favorite. Amenities:** parking (fee); showers; toilets. **Best for:** sunset; swimming; walking. ⊠ *1500 State Park Dr., off Hwy. 1, Capitola* ☎ *831/464–6330* ⊕ *www.parks. ca.gov* ⊠ *$10 per vehicle* ☉ *Day use daily 8 am–sunset.*

WHERE TO EAT

$
SEAFOOD
FAMILY

✕ **Carpo's.** Locals love this casual counter where seafood predominates, but you can also order burgers, salads, and steaks. Baskets of battered snapper are among the favorites, along with calamari, prawns, seafood kebabs, fish-and-chips, and homemade olallieberry pie. Many items cost less than $10. ■ **TIP→ Come early for lunch or dinner to beat the crowds.** [$] *Average main: $11* ✉ *2400 Porter St., at Hwy. 1, Soquel* ☎ *831/476–6260* 🌐 *carpos-restaurant.com.*

CALIFORNIA'S OLDEST RESORT TOWN

As far as anyone knows for certain, Capitola is the oldest seaside resort town on the Pacific Coast. In 1856 a pioneer acquired Soquel Landing, the picturesque lagoon and beach where Soquel Creek empties into the bay, and built a wharf. Another man opened a campground along the shore, and his daughter named it Capitola after a heroine in a novel series. After the train came to town in the 1870s, thousands of vacationers began arriving to bask in the sun on the glorious beach.

$ CAFÉ FAMILY 🍴 **Gayle's Bakery & Rosticceria.** Whether you're in the mood for an orange-olallieberry muffin, a wild rice and chicken salad, or tri-tip on garlic toast, this bakery-deli's varied menu is likely to satisfy. Munch on your lemon meringue tartlet or chocolate brownie on the shady patio, or dig into the daily blue-plate dinner—Southwestern skirt steak with corn pudding, perhaps, or roast turkey breast with Chardonnay gravy—amid the whirl of activity inside. [$] *Average main: $14* ✉ *504 Bay Ave., at Capitola Ave., Capitola* ☎ *831/462–1200* 🌐 *gaylesbakery.com.*

$$$ AMERICAN 🍴 **Michael's on Main.** Creative variations on classic comfort food draw lively crowds to this upscale but casual creekside eatery. Chef Michael Clark's menu changes seasonally, but might include pork osso buco in red-wine tomato-citrus sauce or pistachio-crusted salmon with mint vinaigrette. For a quiet conversation spot, ask for a table on the romantic patio overlooking the creek. The busy bar area hosts live music from Tuesday through Saturday. [$] *Average main: $24* ✉ *2591 Main St., at Porter St., Soquel* ☎ *831/479–9777* 🌐 *michaelsonmain.net* 🕒 *Closed Mon.*

$$$$ EUROPEAN 🍴 **Shadowbrook.** To get to this romantic spot overlooking Soquel Creek, you can take a cable car or walk the stairs down a steep, fern-lined bank beside a running waterfall. Dining room options include the rooftop Redwood Room, the wood-paneled Wine Cellar, the creekside, glass-enclosed Greenhouse, the Fireplace Room, and the airy Garden Room. Prime rib and grilled seafood are the simple menu's stars. Lighter, less expensive entrées are served in the lounge. [$] *Average main: $32* ✉ *1750 Wharf Rd., at Lincoln Ave., Capitola* ☎ *831/475–1511* 🌐 *www.shadowbrook-capitola.com* 🕒 *No lunch.*

WHERE TO STAY

$$$$ B&B/INN 🏨 **Inn at Depot Hill.** This inventively designed bed-and-breakfast in a former rail depot views itself as a link to the era of luxury train travel. **Pros:** short walk to beach and village; historic charm; excellent service. **Cons:** fills quickly; hot-tub conversation audible in some rooms. [$] *Rooms from: $299* ✉ *250 Monterey Ave., Capitola* ☎ *831/462–3376, 800/572–2632* 🌐 *www.innatdepothill.com* 🛏 *12 rooms* 🍽 *Breakfast.*

SANTA CRUZ

5 miles west of Capitola; 48 miles north of Monterey.

The big city on this stretch of the California coast, Santa Cruz (pop. 62,684) is less manicured than Carmel or Monterey. Long known for its surfing and its amusement-filled beach boardwalk, the town is a mix of grand Victorian-era homes and rinky-dink motels. The opening of the University of California campus in the 1960s swung the town sharply to the left politically, and the counterculture more or less lives on here. At the same time, the revitalized downtown and an insane real-estate market reflect the city's proximity to Silicon Valley and to a growing wine country in the surrounding mountains.

GETTING HERE AND AROUND

From the San Francisco Bay Area, take Highway 17 south over the mountains to Santa Cruz, where it merges with Highway 1. Use Highway 1 to get around the area. The Santa Cruz Transit Center is at 920 Pacific Avenue, at Front Street, a short walk from the Wharf and Boardwalk, with connections to public transit throughout the Monterey Bay and San Francisco Bay areas. You can purchase day passes for Santa Cruz METRO buses (⇨ *Bus Travel, in Planner*) here.

ESSENTIALS

Visitor Information Visit Santa Cruz County ⊠ *303 Water St., No. 100* ☎ *831/425–1234, 800/833–3494* ⊕ *www.santacruz.org/regions/santa-cruz.php.*

EXPLORING

TOP ATTRACTIONS

Pacific Avenue. When you've had your fill of the city's beaches and waters, take a stroll in downtown Santa Cruz, especially on Pacific Avenue between Laurel and Water streets. Vintage boutiques and mountain-sports stores, sushi bars, and Mexican restaurants, day spas, and nightclubs keep the main drag and the surrounding streets hopping from mid-morning until late evening.

FAMILY
Fodor'sChoice
★

Santa Cruz Beach Boardwalk. Santa Cruz has been a seaside resort since the mid-19th century. Along one end of the broad, south-facing beach, the Boardwalk has entertained holidaymakers for more than a century. Its Looff carousel and classic wooden Giant Dipper roller coaster, both dating from the early 1900s, are surrounded by high-tech thrill rides and easygoing kiddie rides with ocean views. Video and arcade games, a mini-golf course, and a laser-tag arena pack one gigantic building, which is open daily even if the rides aren't running. You have to pay to play, but you can wander the entire boardwalk for free while sampling delicacies such as corn dogs and garlic fries. ⊠ *Along Beach St.* ☎ *831/423–5590 info line* ⊕ *beachboardwalk.com* ⊠ *$33 day pass for unlimited rides, or pay per ride* ⊗ *Apr.–early Sept., daily; early Sept.–Mar., some rides open weekends and holidays, weather permitting; call for hrs.*

FAMILY
Santa Cruz Municipal Wharf. Jutting half a mile into the ocean near one end of the boardwalk, the century-old Municipal Wharf is lined with

seafood restaurants, a wine bar, souvenir shops, and outfitters offering bay cruises, fishing trips, and boat rentals. A salty soundtrack drifts up from under the wharf, where barking sea lions lounge in heaps on the crossbeams. Docents from the Seymour Marine Discovery Center lead free 30-minute tours on spring and summer weekends at 1 and 3; meet at the stage on the west side of the wharf between Olitas Cantina and Marini's Candies. ⊠ *Beach St. and Pacific Ave.* ☎ *831/459–3800 tour information* ⊕ *santacruzwharf.com.*

Santa Cruz Surfing Museum. This museum inside the Mark Abbott Memorial Lighthouse chronicles local surfing history. Photographs show old-time surfers, and a display of boards includes rarities such as a heavy redwood plank predating the fiberglass era and the remains of a modern board chomped by a great white shark. Surfer docents reminisce about the good old days. ⊠ *Lighthouse Point Park, 701 W. Cliff Dr., near Pelton Ave.* ☎ *831/420–6289* ⊕ *santacruzsurfingmuseum.org* 💲 *$2* ⊘ *Sept.–June, Thurs.–Mon. noon–4; July–Aug., Wed.–Mon. 10–5.*

Fodor'sChoice ★ **West Cliff Drive.** The road that winds along an oceanfront bluff from the municipal wharf to Natural Bridges State Beach makes for a spectacular drive, but it's even more fun to walk or bike the paved path that parallels the road. Surfers bob and swoosh in Monterey Bay at several points near the foot of the bluff, especially at a break known as **Steamer Lane.** Named for a surfer who died here in 1965, the nearby Mark Abbott Memorial Lighthouse stands at Point Santa Cruz, the cliff's major promontory. From here you can watch pinnipeds hang out, sunbathe, and frolic on Seal Rock.

WORTH NOTING

FAMILY **Monterey Bay National Marine Sanctuary Exploration Center.** The interactive and multimedia exhibits at this fascinating interpretive center reveal and explain the treasures of the nation's largest marine sanctuary. The two-story building, across from the main beach and municipal wharf, has films and exhibits about migratory species, watersheds, underwater canyons, kelp forests, and intertidal zones. The second-floor deck has stellar ocean views and an interactive station that provides real-time weather, surf, and buoy reports. ⊠ *35 Pacific Ave., near Beach St.* ☎ *831/421–9993* ⊕ *montereybay.noaa.gov/vc/sec* 💲 *Free* ⊘ *Wed.–Sun. 10–5.*

Mystery Spot. Hokey tourist trap or genuine scientific enigma? Since 1940, curious throngs baffled by the Mystery Spot have made it one of the most visited attractions in Santa Cruz. The laws of gravity and physics don't appear to apply in this tiny patch of redwood forest, where balls roll uphill and people stand on a slant. ■TIP→ **On weekends and holidays, it's wise to purchase tickets online in advance.** ⊠ *465 Mystery Spot Rd., off Branciforte Dr. (north off Hwy. 1)* ☎ *831/423–8897* ⊕ *mysteryspot.com* 💲 *$6, parking $5* ⊘ *Late May–early Sept., daily 10–6; early Sept.–late May, weekdays 10–4, weekends 10–5.*

OFF THE BEATEN PATH **Surf City Vintners.** A dozen tasting rooms of limited-production wineries occupy renovated warehouse spaces west of the beach. MJA, Storrs, and Equinox are good places to start. Also here are the Santa Cruz Mountain Brewing Company and El Salchicheroa, popular for its homemade sausages, jams, and pickled and candied vegetables. ✉ *Swift Street Courtyard, 334 Ingalls St., at Swift St., off Hwy. 1 (Mission St.)* 🌐 *surfcityvintners.com.*

UC Santa Cruz. The 2,000-acre University of California Santa Cruz campus nestles in the forested hills above town. Its sylvan setting, ocean vistas, and redwood architecture make the university worth a visit, as does its **arboretum** ($5, open daily from 9 to 5), whose walking path leads through areas dedicated to the plants of California, Australia, New Zealand, and South Africa. **■ TIP→ Free shuttles help students and visitors get around campus, and you can join a guided tour (online reservation required).** ✉ *Main entrance at Bay and High Sts. (turn left on High for arboretum)* ☎ *831/459–0111* 🌐 *www.ucsc.edu/visit.*

BEACHES

FAMILY **Natural Bridges State Beach.** At the end of West Cliff Drive lies this stretch of soft sand edged with tide pools and sea-sculpted rock bridges. **■ TIP→ From October to early March a colony of monarch butterflies roosts in a eucalyptus grove. Amenities:** lifeguards; parking (fee); toilets. **Best for:** sunrise; sunset; surfing; swimming. ✉ *2531 W. Cliff Dr.* ☎ *831/423–4609* 🌐 *www.parks.ca.gov* 🎟 *Beach free, parking $10* 🕒 *Beach: daily 8 am–sunset. Visitor center: Oct.–Jan., daily 10–4; Feb.–Sept., Fri.–Sun. 10–4.*

Twin Lakes State Beach. Stretching a half-mile along the coast on both sides of the small-craft jetties, Twin Lakes is one of Monterey Bay's sunniest beaches. It encompasses Seabright State Beach (with access in a residential neighborhood on the upcoast side) and Black's Beach on the downcoast side. Families often come here to sunbathe, picnic, and hike the nature trail around adjacent Schwann Lake. Parking is tricky on weekends from April through September, but you can park all day in the harbor pay lot and walk here. Leashed dogs are allowed. **Amenities:** food and drink; lifeguards (seasonal); parking; showers; toilets; water sports (seasonal). **Best for:** sunset; surfing; swimming; walking. ✉ *7th Ave., at East Cliff Dr.* ☎ *831/427–4868* 🌐 *www.parks.ca.gov.*

WHERE TO EAT

$$ MODERN AMERICAN 🍴 **Assembly.** Seasonal, sustainably farmed local ingredients inspire this downtown eatery's rustic California cuisine. The menu changes constantly, but you might find swordfish with preserved-lemon risotto, braised fennel, spinach, and avocado; potato gnocchi with braised chicken, black trumpets, and ricotta cheese; or a burger on a house-made brioche bun. An adjacent pop-up space hosts rising chefs who for two months or so create dishes with ingredients sourced from local purveyors before moving on. [$] *Average main: $19* ✉ *1108 Pacific Ave., at Cathcart St.* ☎ *831/824–6100* 🌐 *assembleforfood.com* 🕒 *Closed Mon. and Tues. during off-season; call to verify hrs.*

$$ SEAFOOD 🍴 **Crow's Nest.** A classic California beachside restaurant, the Crow's Nest sits right on the water in Santa Cruz Harbor. Vintage surfboards and local surf photography line the walls in the main dining room, and

nearly every table overlooks sand and surf. Breakfast favorites include crab-cake eggs Benedict and olallieberry pancakes. Seafood and steaks, served with locally grown vegetables, dominate the lunch and dinner menus; favorite appetizers include fried calamari and the chilled shrimp-stuffed artichoke. For sweeping ocean views and fish tacos, burgers, and other casual fare, head upstairs to the Breakwater Bar & Grill. ■TIP→ **If you're in a hurry, pick up pizzas, sandwiches, soups, and salads at the on-site market.** Ⓢ *Average main: $21* ⊠ *2218 E. Cliff Dr., west of 7th Ave.* ☎ *831/476–4560* ⊕ *crowsnest-santacruz.com.*

$$
MEDITERRANEAN
Fodor'sChoice
★

✕ **Laili Restaurant.** Exotic Mediterranean flavors with an Afghan twist take center stage at this artsy, stylish space with soaring ceilings. Traditional dishes range from Moroccan beet salad and apricot chicken flatbread to pomegranate eggplant and *maush-awa*, a soup with lentils, split peas, and lamb, topped with yogurt. The menus also include housemade pastas and numerous vegetarian options; fresh *naan* and delectable chutneys and dips accompany every meal. Evenings are especially lively, when locals come to relax over wine and soft jazz at the blue-concrete bar, the heated patio with twinkly lights, or at a communal table near the open kitchen. Ⓢ *Average main: $20* ⊠ *101–B Cooper St., near Pacific Ave.* ☎ *831/423–4545* ⊕ *lailirestaurant.com* ⊗ *Closed Mon.*

$$$
ITALIAN

✕ **La Posta.** Authentic Italian fare made with fresh local produce lures diners into cozy, modern-rustic La Posta. Nearly everything is made in-house, from the pizzas and breads baked in the brick oven to the pasta and the vanilla-bean gelato. The seasonal menu includes flavorful dishes such as wild-nettle lasagna, braised lamb shank with saffron-infused vegetables, and sautéed fish from local waters. Ⓢ *Average main: $24* ⊠ *538 Seabright Ave., at Logan St.* ☎ *831/457–2782* ⊕ *lapostarestaurant.com* ⊗ *Closed Mon. No lunch.*

$$$
EUROPEAN

✕ **Oswald.** Sophisticated yet unpretentious European-inspired California cooking is the order of the day at this intimate and stylish bistro. The menu changes seasonally, but might include such items as seafood risotto or crispy duck breast in a pomegranate reduction sauce. The creative concoctions poured at the slick marble bar include whiskey mixed with apple and lemon juice, and tequila with celery juice and lime. ■TIP→ **On Wednesday, a three-course prix-fixe menu (at $29 a good value) is offered in lieu of the regular fare.** Ⓢ *Average main: $26* ⊠ *121 Soquel Ave., at Front St.* ☎ *831/423–7427* ⊕ *oswaldrestaurant.com* ⊗ *Closed Mon. No lunch Tues.–Thurs. and weekends.*

$$
MEDITERRANEAN
Fodor'sChoice
★

✕ **Soif.** Wine reigns at this sleek bistro and wineshop that takes its name from the French word for thirst. The selections come from near and far, and you can order many of them by the taste or glass. Mediterranean-inspired small plates and entrées are served at the copper-top bar, the big communal table, and private tables. A jazz combo or solo pianist plays on some evenings. Ⓢ *Average main: $22* ⊠ *105 Walnut Ave., at Pacific Ave.* ☎ *831/423–2020* ⊕ *soifwine.com* ⊗ *No lunch.*

WHERE TO STAY

$$$ **Babbling Brook Inn.** Though it's in the middle of Santa Cruz, this bed-
B&B/INN and-breakfast has lush gardens, a running stream, and tall trees that make you feel like you're in a secluded wood. **Pros:** close to UCSC; within walking distance of downtown shops; woodsy feel. **Cons:** near a high school; some rooms close to a busy street. $ *Rooms from:* $229 ⊠ *1025 Laurel St.* ☎ 831/427–2437, 800/866–1131 ⊕ *babbling brookinn.com* ⤳ *13 rooms* ⧉ *Breakfast.*

$$ **Carousel Beach Inn.** Remodeled in 2014 in bold, retro seaside style,
HOTEL this basic but comfy motel across the street from the boardwalk is ideal for travelers who want easy access to the sand and the amusement park rides without spending a fortune. **Pros:** steps from Santa Cruz Main Beach; affordable lodging rates and ride packages; free parking and Wi-Fi. **Cons:** no pool or spa; no exercise room; not pet-friendly. $ *Rooms from:* $159 ⊠ *110 Riverside Ave.* ☎ 831/425–7090 ⊕ *santa cruzmotels.com/carousel.html* ⤳ *34 rooms* ⧉ *Breakfast.*

$$$$ **Chaminade Resort & Spa.** Secluded on 300 hilltop acres of redwood and
RESORT eucalyptus forest with hiking trails, this Mission-style complex commands expansive views of Monterey Bay. **Pros:** far from city life; spectacular property; ideal spot for romance and rejuvenation. **Cons:** must drive to attractions and sights; near a major hospital. $ *Rooms from:* $269 ⊠ *1 Chaminade La.* ☎ 800/283–6569 *reservations,* 831/475–5600 ⊕ *www.chaminade.com* ⤳ *112 rooms, 44 suites* ⧉ *No meals.*

$$$ **Hotel Paradox.** About a mile from the ocean and two blocks from
HOTEL Pacific Avenue, this stylish, forest-theme complex is among the few full-service hotels in town. **Pros:** close to downtown and main beach; alternative to beach-oriented lodgings; contemporary feel. **Cons:** pool area can get crowded on warm-weather days; some rooms on the small side. $ *Rooms from:* $200 ⊠ *611 Ocean St.* ☎ 831/425–7100, 855/425–7200 ⊕ *www.thehotelparadox.com* ⤳ *164 rooms, 6 suites* ⧉ *No meals.*

$$$ **Pacific Blue Inn.** Green themes predominate in this three-story, eco-
B&B/INN friendly bed-and-breakfast, completed in 2009 on a sliver of prime downtown property. **Pros:** free parking; free bicycles; downtown location. **Cons:** tiny property; not suitable for children. $ *Rooms from:* $189 ⊠ *636 Pacific Ave.* ☎ 831/600–8880 ⊕ *pacificblueinn.com* ⤳ *9 rooms* ⧉ *No meals.*

$$$$ **Santa Cruz Dream Inn.** A short stroll from the boardwalk and wharf,
HOTEL this full-service luxury hotel is the only lodging in Santa Cruz directly
Fodor'sChoice on the beach. **Pros:** directly on the beach; easy parking; walk to board-
★ walk and downtown. **Cons:** expensive; area gets congested on summer weekends. $ *Rooms from:* $369 ⊠ *175 W. Cliff Dr.* ☎ 831/426–4330, 866/774–7735 *reservations* ⊕ *dreaminnsantacruz.com* ⤳ *149 rooms, 16 suites* ⧉ *No meals.*

$$$ **West Cliff Inn.** With views of the boardwalk and Monterey Bay, the
B&B/INN West Cliff perches on the bluffs across from Cowell Beach. **Pros:** killer
Fodor'sChoice views; walking distance to the beach; close to downtown. **Cons:** board-
★ walk noise; street traffic. $ *Rooms from:* $195 ⊠ *174 West Cliff Dr.* ☎ 800/979–0910 *toll free,* 831/457–2200 ⊕ *www.westcliffinn.com* ⤳ *7 rooms, 2 suites, 1 cottage* ⧉ *Breakfast.*

7

O'Neill: A Santa Cruz Icon

O'Neill wet suits and beachwear weren't exactly born in Santa Cruz, but as far as most of the world is concerned, the O'Neill brand is synonymous with Santa Cruz and surfing legend.

The O'Neill wet-suit story began in 1952, when Jack O'Neill and his brother Robert opened their first Surf Shop in a garage across from San Francisco's Ocean Beach. While shaping balsa surfboards and selling accessories, the O'Neills experimented with solutions to a common surfer problem: frigid waters. Tired of being forced back to shore, blue-lipped and shivering, after just 20 or 30 minutes riding the waves, they played with

various materials and eventually designed a neoprene vest.

In 1959 Jack moved his Surf Shop 90 miles south to Cowell's Beach in Santa Cruz. It quickly became a popular surf hangout, and O'Neill's new wet suits began to sell like hotcakes. In the early 1960s, the company opened a warehouse for manufacturing on a larger scale. Santa Cruz soon became a major surf city, attracting wave riders to prime breaks at Steamer Lane, Pleasure Point, and the Hook. In 1965 O'Neill pioneered the first wet-suit boots, and in 1971 Jack's son invented the surf leash. By 1980, O'Neill stood at the top of the world wet-suit market.

NIGHTLIFE AND PERFORMING ARTS

NIGHTLIFE

Catalyst. This huge, grimy, and fun club books rock, indie rock, punk, death-metal, reggae, and other acts. ⊠ *1011 Pacific Ave.* ☎ *877/987–6487 tickets* ⊕ *catalystclub.com.*

Kuumbwa Jazz Center. The center draws top performers such as the Brubeck Brothers Quartet, Ladysmith Black Mambazo, and Chick Corea; the café serves meals an hour before most shows. ⊠ *320–2 Cedar St.* ☎ *831/427–2227* ⊕ *kuumbwajazz.org.*

PERFORMING ARTS

Tannery Arts Center. The former Salz Tannery now contains studios and live-work spaces for artists whose disciplines range from ceramics and glass to film and digital media. The social center is the **Artbar & Cafe,** which in the late afternoons and evenings hosts poets (Monday), all types of performers (Wednesday), and live music (from Thursday to Saturday). The center also hosts assorted arts events on weekends and occasionally on weekdays. ⊠ *1060 River St., at intersection of Hwys. 1 and 9* ☎ *831/428–8989* ⊕ *scartbar.com.*

SPORTS AND THE OUTDOORS

ADVENTURE TOURS

Mount Hermon Adventures. Zip-line through the redwoods at this adventure center in the Santa Cruz Mountains. On some summer weekends there's an aerial adventure course with obstacles and challenges in the redwoods. ■TIP→ To join a tour (reservations essential), you must be at least 10 years old and weigh between 75 and 250 pounds. ⊠ *17 Conference Dr., 9 miles north of downtown Santa Cruz near Felton, Mount Hermon* ☎ *831/430–4357* ⊕ *mounthermonadventures.com* 🏷 *From $50.*

BICYCLING

Another Bike Shop. Mountain bikers should head here for tips on the best area trails and to browse cutting-edge gear made and tested locally. ⊠ *2361 Mission St., at King St.* ☎ *831/427–2232* ⊕ *www. anotherbikeshop.com.*

BOATS AND CHARTERS

Chardonnay II Sailing Charters. The 70-foot *Chardonnay II* departs year-round from Santa Cruz yacht harbor on whale-watching, sunset, and other cruises around Monterey Bay. Most regularly scheduled excursions cost $64; food and drink are served on many of them. Reservations are essential. ⊠ *Santa Cruz West Harbor, 790 Mariner Park Way* ☎ *831/423–1213* ⊕ *chardonnay.com.*

Stagnaro Sport Fishing, Charters, & Whale Watching Cruises. Stagnaro operates salmon, albacore, and rock-cod fishing expeditions; the fees include bait. The company (aka Santa Cruz Whale Watching) also runs whale-watching, dolphin, and sea-life cruises year-round. ⊠ *1718 Brommer St., near Santa Cruz Harbor* ☎ *831/427–0230, 888/237–7084 tickets, 831/205–2380 international tickets* ⊕ *stagnaros.com* 🏷 *From $48.*

GOLF

Pasatiempo Golf Club. Designed by famed golf architect Dr. Alister Mac-Kenzie in 1929, this semiprivate course, set amid undulating hills just above the city, is among the nation's top championship courses. Golfers rave about the spectacular views and challenging terrain. According to the club, MacKenzie, who designed Pebble Beach's exclusive Cypress Point course and Augusta National in Georgia, the home of the Masters Golf Tournament, declared this his favorite layout. ⊠ *20 Clubhouse Rd.* ☎ *831/459–9155* ⊕ *www.pasatiempo.com* 🏷 *From $260* ⛳ *18 holes, 6125 yards, par 72.*

KAYAKING

Kayak Connection. From March through May, participants in this outfit's tours mingle with gray whales and their calves on their northward journey to Alaska. Throughout the year, the company rents kayaks and paddleboards and conducts tours of Natural Bridges State Beach, Capitola, and Elkhorn Slough. ⊠ *Santa Cruz Harbor, 413 Lake Ave., No. 3* ☎ *831/479–1121* ⊕ *kayakconnection.com* 🏷 *From $60 for scheduled tours.*

Venture Quest Kayaking. Explore hidden coves and kelp forests on guided two-hour kayak tours that depart from Santa Cruz Wharf. The tours include a kayaking lesson. Venture Quest also rents kayaks (and wet suits and gear), and arranges tours at other Monterey Bay destinations, including Elkhorn Slough. ⊠ *2 Santa Cruz Wharf* ☎ *831/427–2267 kayak hotline, 831/425–8445 rental office* ⊕ *kayaksantacruz.com* 🏷 *From $30 for rentals, $58 for tours.*

7

SURFING
EQUIPMENT AND LESSONS
Club-Ed Surf School and Camps. Find out what all the fun is about at Club-Ed. Your first private or group lesson ($90 and up) includes all equipment. ⊠ *Cowell's Beach, at Santa Cruz Dream Inn* ☎ *831/464–0177* ⊕ *club-ed.com.*

Cowell's Beach Surf Shop. This shop sells gear, clothing, and swimwear; rents surfboards, standup paddle boards, and wet suits; and offers lessons. ⊠ *30 Front St.* ☎ *831/427–2355* ⊕ *cowellssurfshop.com.*

SHOPPING

Bookshop Santa Cruz. In 2016 the town's best and most beloved independent bookstore celebrates its 50th anniversary of selling new, used, and remaindered titles. The children's section is especially comprehensive, and the shop's special events calendar is packed with readings, social mixers, book signings, and discussions. ⊠ *1520 Pacific Ave.* ☎ *831/423–0900* ⊕ *bookshopsantacruz.com.*

O'Neill Surf Shop. Local surfers get their wetties (wet suits) and other gear at this O'Neill store or the one in Capitola, at 1115 41st Avenue. There's also a satellite shop on the Santa Cruz Boardwalk. ⊠ *110 Cooper St.* ☎ *831/469–4377* ⊕ *www.oneill.com.*

The True Olive Connection. Taste your way through boutique extra-virgin olive oils and balsamic vinegars from around the world at this family-run shop. You can also pick up gourmet food products and olive-oil-based gift items. There's another location in Aptos. ⊠ *106 Lincoln St., at Pacific Ave.* ☎ *831/458–6457* ⊕ *trueoliveconnection.com* ⊠ *7960 Soquel Dr., Aptos* ☎ *831/612–6932.*

THE INLAND EMPIRE

East of Los Angeles to the
San Jacinto Mountains

WELCOME TO THE INLAND EMPIRE

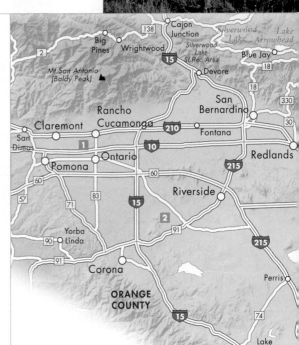

TOP REASONS TO GO

★ **Wine Country:** The idyllic, ever-expanding Temecula Valley is home to family-owned and resort-style wineries cooled by faint ocean breezes.

★ **The Mission Inn:** One of the most unusual hotels in America, Riverside's rambling, eclectic Mission Inn feels like an urban Hearst Castle.

★ **Apple country:** In the Oak Glen apple-growing region, you can attend an old-fashioned hoedown, take a wagon ride, and sample apple pies and homemade ciders.

★ **Soothing spas:** The lushly landscaped grounds, bubbling hot springs, and playful mud baths of Glen Ivy are ideal spots to unwind; Kelly's Spa at the historic Mission Inn provides a cozy Tuscan-style retreat.

★ **Alpine escapes:** Breathe in the clean mountain air or cozy up in a bed-and-breakfast at one of the Inland Empire's great mountain hideaways: Lake Arrowhead, Big Bear, and Idyllwild.

1 The Western Inland Empire. At the foot of 10,064-foot-high Mt. Baldy in the San Gabriel Mountains, the tree-lined communities of Pomona and Claremont are known for their prestigious colleges: California State Polytechnic University–Pomona and the seven-school Claremont Colleges complex. Pomona is urban and industrial, but Claremont is a classic tree-shaded, lively, sophisticated college town that more resembles trendy sections of Los Angeles than the laid-back Inland Empire.

2 Riverside Area. In the late 1700s, Mexican settlers called this now-suburban region Valle de Paraiso. Citrus-growing here began in 1873, when homesteader Eliza Tibbets planted two navel-orange trees in her yard. The area's biggest draws are the majestic Mission Inn, with its fine restaurants and unique history and architecture, and Glen Ivy Hot Springs in nearby Corona.

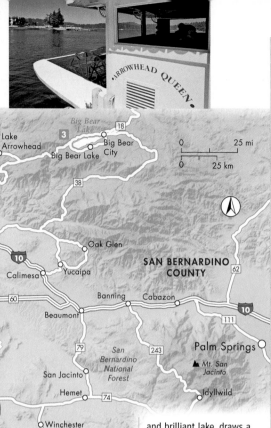

GETTING ORIENTED

Several freeways provide access to the Inland Empire from Los Angeles and San Diego. Ontario and Temecula line up along Interstates 10 and 215; and Corona, Riverside, and San Bernardino lie along Highway 91. As a Los Angeles bedroom community, the area sees nasty freeway congestion on Highway 60 and Interstates 10 and 15, so try to avoid driving during rush hour, usually from 6 to 9 am and 4 to 7 pm.

8

3 San Bernardino Mountains. Lake Arrowhead and always-sunny Big Bear are the recreational centers of this area. Though the two are geographically close, they're distinct in appeal. Lake Arrowhead, with its cool mountain air, trail-threaded woods,

and brilliant lake, draws a summertime crowd—a well-heeled one, if the prices in its shops and restaurants are any indication. Big Bear's ski and snowboarding slopes, cross-country trails, and cheerful lodges come alive in winter and provide a quiet retreat in summer. Even if you're not interested in visiting the resorts themselves, the Rim of the World Scenic Byway (Highway 18), which connects Big Bear Lake and Lake Arrowhead at an elevation up to 8,000 feet, is a magnificent drive. On a clear day, you'll feel that you can see forever.

4 The Southern Inland Empire. Life is quieter in the southern portion of the Inland Empire than it is to the north. In this corner of Riverside County, towns such as Idyllwild and Temecula are oases of the good life for locals and visitors alike.

Updated
by Sarah
Amandolare

Threaded with rolling vineyards, homey agricultural towns, and mountain retreats, the Inland Empire has a humble allure. Often bypassed because of its freeway maze and suburban sprawl, this historically rich region offers visitors a quiet and quirky alternative to metropolitan Los Angeles and San Diego. You can hurtle down a 7,000-foot ski slope perched above a clear blue lake, hike or snowshoe in serene forests, and taste wines wrought by Temecula's misty mornings and subtle ocean breezes. For fresh California flavors, explore apple country in Oak Glen, and trace the roots of the state's navel orange industry in Riverside.

The San Bernardino Mountains offer Big Bear Lake, Lake Arrowhead, and plentiful recreational opportunities, while Idyllwild in the San Jacinto Mountains is a year-round getaway with log cabins galore, an impressive arts scene, and cozy restaurants.

PLANNING

WHEN TO GO

The climate varies greatly, depending on what part of the Inland Empire you're visiting. Summer temperatures in the mountains and in Temecula, 20 miles from the coast, usually hover around 80°F, though it's not uncommon for Riverside to reach temperatures of 100°F or higher. From September to March this area is subject to increasingly high Santa Ana winds, sometimes strong enough to overturn trucks on the freeway. In winter, temperatures in the mountains and in Temecula usually range from 30°F to 55°F, and in the Riverside area from 40°F to 60°F. Most of the ski areas open when the first natural snow falls (usually in November) and close in mid-March.

GETTING HERE AND AROUND

AIR TRAVEL

L.A./Ontario International Airport (ONT) is the local airport. Aeromexico, Alaska, American, Delta, Southwest, and United fly here.

Airport Contacts L.A./Ontario International Airport ✉ *2500 East Airport Dr., Archibald Ave. exit off I-10, Ontario* ☎ *909/937-2700* ⊕ *www.lawa.org.*

CAR TRAVEL

Avoid Highway 91 if possible; it's almost always backed up from Corona through Orange County. Check with Caltrans for information about highway conditions, or dial 511 or log on to the IE511 website, which also has bus-train trip planners.

Contacts Caltrans ☎ *800/427-7623* ⊕ *www.dot.ca.gov.* **IE511** ☎ *877/694-3511* ⊕ *www.ie511.org.*

TRAIN TRAVEL

■TIP➔ **Many locals get around on Metrolink, which is clean and quick, and generally a much nicer way to travel than by bus.** Metrolink trains stop at several stations on the Inter-County, San Bernardino, and Riverside lines. You can buy tickets and passes at station vending machines, or by telephone. The IE511 website *(➪ Car Travel, above)* has bus-train trip planners; dial 511 for recorded train-schedule information.

Train Contacts Metrolink ☎ *800/371-5465* ⊕ *www.metrolinktrains.com.*

RESTAURANTS

Downtown Riverside is home to a few ambitious restaurants, along with the familiar chains. The college town of Claremont has creative contemporary and ethnic fare. Innovative cuisine has become the norm in Temecula, especially at winery restaurants, some of whose chefs specialize in farm-to-table cuisine. The options are more limited in the smaller mountain communities; typically, each town supports a single upscale restaurant, along with fast-food outlets, steak-and-potatoes family spots, and perhaps an Italian or Mexican eatery. Universally, dining out is casual.

HOTELS

In the San Bernardino Mountains many accommodations are bed-and-breakfasts or rustic cabins, though Lake Arrowhead and Big Bear offer more luxurious resort lodging. Rates for Big Bear lodgings fluctuate widely, depending on the season. When winter snow brings droves of Angelenos to the mountains for skiing, expect to pay sky-high prices for any kind of room. Most establishments require a two-night stay on weekends. In Riverside the landmark Mission Inn is the marquee accommodation. In the Wine Country, lodgings can be found at wineries, golf resorts, and chain hotels. *Hotel reviews have been shortened. For full information, visit Fodors.com.*

WHAT IT COSTS			
$	**$$**	**$$$**	**$$$$**
Restaurants	under $16	$16–$22	$23–$30	over $30
Hotels	under $120	$120–$175	$176–$250	over $250

Restaurant prices are the average cost of a main course at dinner or, if dinner is not served, at lunch, excluding sales tax of 8%–9%. Hotel prices are the lowest cost of a standard double room in high season, excluding service charges and 8%–13% tax.

THE WESTERN INLAND EMPIRE

Straddling the line between Los Angeles and San Bernardino counties, the western section of the Inland Empire is home to some of California's oldest vineyards and original citrus orchards. Now a busy suburban community, it holds the closest ski slopes to metro Los Angeles. Fairplex, where the L.A. County Fair is held each year, is here, as is Claremont, home to a collection of high-ranking colleges.

GETTING HERE AND AROUND

To reach this area from Los Angeles, take Interstate 10, which bisects the Western Inland Empire west to east; from Pasadena, take Interstate 210, which runs parallel to the north. Take Highway 57 from Anaheim. Some areas are quite walkable, especially the Claremont Colleges, where you can stroll through parks from one school building to another.

The Foothill Transit Bus Line serves Pomona, Claremont, and Montclair, with stops at Cal Poly and the Fairplex. Metrolink serves the area from Los Angeles and elsewhere.

ESSENTIALS

Bus Contacts Foothill Transit ☎ 800/743–3463 ⊕ www.foothilltransit.org.

POMONA

23 miles north of Anaheim, 27 miles east of Pasadena.

The green hills of Pomona, dotted with horses and houses, are perhaps best known as the site of the Los Angeles County Fair and of California State Polytechnic University–Pomona. Named for the Roman goddess of fruit, the city has a rich citrus-growing heritage.

GETTING HERE AND AROUND

The most direct routes from Los Angeles to Pomona are the Pomona Freeway (Highway 60) and Interstate 10. It pays to check traffic reports before starting out. Mission Boulevard (west–east) and Garey Avenue (north–south) are the main surface streets through downtown.

ESSENTIALS

Visitor Information Pomona Chamber of Commerce ⊠ 101 W. Mission Blvd. ☎ 909/622–8484 ⊕ www.pomonachamber.org.

EXPLORING

California Polytechnic University at Pomona. The university occupies 1,438 rolling acres of the Kellogg Ranch, originally the winter home of cereal magnate W.K. Kellogg. Cal Poly specializes in teaching agriculture, and you can find rose gardens, avocado groves, many farm animals, and a working Arabian horse ranch. The Farm Store (✉ *4102 University Dr. S.* ☎ *909/869–4906*) sells deli and gourmet foods, meat and produce from campus farms, and plants grown in the university nursery. ✉ *3801 W. Temple Ave., at S. University Dr.* ☎ *909/869–7659* ⊕ *www. csupomona.edu* ⊙ *Store daily 10–6.*

Fairplex. The site of the Los Angeles County Fair, North America's largest county fair, the Fairplex exposition center hosts open-air markets, antiques shows, roadster shows, historical train and model train exhibits, horse shows and racing, dog shows, and the annual International Wine and Spirits competition. Also here is the **Wally Parks NHRA Motorsports Museum** (⊕ *www.museum.nhra.com*), which pays tribute to the history of American motor sports with exhibits of vintage racing vehicles and an amusing collection of tricked-out drag-racing cars. ✉ *1101 W. McKinley Ave., off Fairplex Dr.* ☎ *909/623–3111, 909/622–2133 museum* ⊕ *www.fairplex.com* 🎫 *Museum $10* ⊙ *Museum Wed.–Sun. 10–5.*

W.K. Kellogg Arabian Horse Shows. The classic shows, started by cereal maker Kellogg in 1926, remain a tradition on the CSU–Pomona campus. Many purebreds live at the ranch, and the university presents exhibitions of the equines in English and Western tack on the first Sunday of the month at 2 pm from October through May. Stable visits and pony rides ($5) take place after the show. ✉ *3801 W. Temple Ave.* ☎ *909/869–4988* ⊕ *www.csupomona.edu/~equine* 🎫 *$4.*

8

WHERE TO EAT AND STAY

$$$
AMERICAN

× **Pomona Valley Mining Company.** Atop a hill near an old mining site, this rustic steak-and-seafood restaurant provides great city views at night. Though somewhat dated, the decor reflects the regional mining heritage. Authentic gold-rush pieces and 1800s memorabilia hang on the walls, and old lanterns adorn the tables. The food—heavy on steak and prime rib—is well prepared; save space for dessert that includes mud pie or bourbon bread pudding. $ *Average main: $26* ✉ *1777 Gillette Rd.* ☎ *909/623–3515* ⊕ *www.pomonavalleyminingco.com* ⧖ *Reservations essential* ⊙ *Closed Mon. No lunch Tues.–Sat.*

$$
HOTEL

Sheraton Fairplex Hotel & Conference Center. County-fair murals and whimsical carousel animals welcome you to this all-suites hotel at the entrance to Pomona's Fairplex. **Pros:** adjacent to convention center; clean rooms; two flat-screen TVs per room. **Cons:** parts feel dated; not close to many restaurants. $ *Rooms from: $149* ✉ *601 W. McKinley Ave.* ☎ *800/325–3535, 909/622–2220* ⊕ *www.sheratonfairplex.com* ↰ *247 suites* ⦿ *No meals.*

CLAREMONT

4 miles north of Pomona.

The seven Claremont Colleges are among the most prestigious in the nation, lending the town an ambitious and creative energy. The campuses are all laid out cheek-by-jowl; as you wander from one leafy street to the next, you won't be able to tell where one college ends and the next begins.

Claremont was originally the home of the Sunkist citrus growers cooperative movement. Today Claremont Village, home to descendants of those early farmers, is bright and lively—a beautifully restored lemon-packing house, built in 1922, now hosts numerous shops and cafés in College Heights. The business district village, with streets named for prestigious eastern colleges, is walkable and appealing with a collection of boutiques, fancy food emporiums, cafés, and lounges. The downtown district is a beautiful place to visit, with Victorian, Craftsman, and Spanish Colonial buildings.

GETTING HERE AND AROUND

If you're driving, exit Interstate 10 at Indian Hill Boulevard, and drive north to Claremont. Parking can be difficult, although there are metered spots. Overnight parking is prohibited within the village; however there is a parking structure adjacent to the College Heights Packing House that is also north of the freeway; exit Garey and drive toward the mountains. You can reach this area by public transportation, but you'll need a car to get around unless you plan to spend all your time in the Claremont Village.

ESSENTIALS

Visitor Information Claremont Chamber of Commerce ⊠ *205 Yale Ave.* ☎ *909/624–1681* ⊕ *www.claremontchamber.org.*

EXPLORING

Claremont Heritage. College walking tours, historic home tours, and nature tours are conducted throughout the year by Claremont Heritage. On the first Saturday of each month the organization gives guided walking tours ($5) of the village. Self-guided tour maps can be found on the group's website. ⊠ *840 N. Indian Hill Blvd.* ☎ *909/621–0848* ⊕ *www.claremontheritage.org* ⊴ *$5.*

Pomona College Museum of Art. This small campus museum exhibits contemporary art, works by old masters, and Native American art and artifacts. Highlights include a mural by Mexican artist Jose Clemente Orozco, first-edition Goya etchings, and 15th- and 16th-century Italian panel paintings. Thursday-night Art After Hours events often include music by local bands. *Skyspace: Dividing the Light,* a stunning light installation by alumnus James Turrell, is best experienced before sunrise or sunset. ⊠ *333 N. College Ave.* ⊹ *Skyscape: Draper Courtyard, 6th St. and College Way* ☎ *909/621–8283* ⊕ *www.pomona.edu/museum*

[ticket] Free ⏲ Museum: Tues., Wed., and Fri.–Sun., noon–5, Thurs. noon–11. Skyspace: June–Aug., daily 25 minutes before sunset or 100 minutes before sunrise; Sept.–May, Sat.–Mon. only.

QUICK BITES **Bert & Rocky's Cream Company. The sinfully innovative concoctions at this local ice cream store include mint Oreo, blueberry-cheesecake, and the Elvis special with bananas and peanut butter. The vanilla's delightful, too.** ✉ *242 Yale Ave.* ☎ *909/625–1852.*

Fodor's Choice ★ **Rancho Santa Ana Botanic Garden.** Founded in 1927 by Susanna Bixby Bryant, a wealthy landowner and conservationist, the garden is dedicated to the preservation of native California plant species. You can meander here for hours enjoying the shade of an oak tree canopy or take a guided tour of the grounds, whose 86 acres of ponds and greenery shelter California wild lilacs, big berry manzanitas, four-needled piñons, and other specimens. Countless bird species also live here. **TIP→ Guided tram tours are offered the third Sunday of the month on a first come, first served basis.** ✉ *1500 N. College Ave.* ☎ *909/625–8767* 🌐 *www.rsabg.org* [ticket] *$8, tram tour $5 additional* ⏲ *Daily 8–5.*

WHERE TO EAT

$$ ITALIAN 🍴 **La Parolaccia.** Locals line up on weekends for a table at this busy spot where waiters zip through small rooms to deliver fresh and beautifully seasoned fare from an extensive Italian menu. Popular dishes include pasta with salmon and capers and seafood risotto with white wine, garlic, and tomatoes. Topping the dessert list is bread pudding made with ciabatta and crème anglaise. [$] *Average main: $19* ✉ *201 N. Indian Hill Blvd.* ☎ *909/624–1516* 🌐 *www.laparolacciausa.com.*

$$ ECLECTIC 🍴 **Packing House Wines.** This combination wine shop, bar, and restaurant occupies one of Claremont's last four original orange-packing houses built in 1916. Owners Sal and EV Medina sell 1,400 different wines from around the world, and bottles can be purchased and enjoyed on the premises. They also pour many wines by the glass and serve seasonal small plates and specialty cheeses throughout the day. Dinner entrées include diver scallops with risotto and a lamb burger with date-chutney sauce. A delicate chocolate crème brûlée is among the desserts. [$] *Average main: $17* ✉ *540 W. 1st St.* ☎ *909/445–9463* 🌐 *www.packinghousewines.com* ⏲ *Closed Mon.*

$$$$ ITALIAN 🍴 **Tutti Mangia Italian Grill.** A favorite of college students and their visiting parents, this storefront dining room has a warm and cozy feel and menu choices that include roasted double pork chops, osso buco, and pan-roasted salmon with blood-orange sauce. The small plates always entice. [$] *Average main: $40* ✉ *102 Harvard Ave.* ☎ *909/625–4669* 🌐 *www.tuttimangia.com* ✍ *Reservations essential* ⏲ *No lunch weekends.*

$$ ECLECTIC 🍴 **Walter's Restaurant.** With a menu that samples cuisines from western Europe to Afghanistan, Walter's is where locals gather to dine, sip wine, and chat. You can eat outside on the sidewalk, on the lively patio, or in a cozy setting inside. Try the puffy Afghan fries with hot sauce, tabouleh salad, or lamb stew or lamb pilaf. Breakfast possibilities include

omelets, sausage and eggs, and burritos; for lunch are salads, soups, pastas, kebabs, and vegetarian items. $ *Average main: $21* ⊠ *310 N. Yale Ave.* ☎ *909/624–4914* ⊕ *www.waltersrestaurant.com* ⟋ *Reservations essential.*

WHERE TO STAY

$$$
B&B/INN
Fodor'sChoice
★

Casa 425. This boutique inn on a corner opposite the College Heights Lemon Packing House entertainment and shopping complex is the most attractive lodging option in Claremont Village. **Pros:** walking distance to attractions and restaurants; bicycles available; most rooms have soaking tubs. **Cons:** occasional noise. $ *Rooms from: $195* ⊠ *425 W. 1st St.* ☎ *866/450–0425* ⊕ *www.foursisters.com* ⤵ *28 rooms* ⦿ *Some meals.*

$$
HOTEL
FAMILY

DoubleTree by Hilton Hotel Claremont. The hotel of choice for parents visiting children attending local colleges has spacious rooms clustered in three Spanish-style buildings that surround a flower-decked central courtyard. **Pros:** convenient to colleges; swimming pool; chocolate chip cookies. **Cons:** small bathrooms. $ *Rooms from: $169* ⊠ *555 W. Foothill Blvd.* ☎ *909/626–2411* ⊕ *www.doubletreeclaremont.com* ⤵ *190 rooms* ⦿ *No meals.*

NIGHTLIFE

Being a college town, Claremont has many bars and cafés, some of which showcase bands.

Flappers Comedy Club. A typical stand-up venue, Flappers is a branch of a Burbank club. Headliners such as Hal Sparks and Titus perform, as do up-and-coming comedians and occasional celebrity guests such as Maria Bamford and Dana Carvey. Snacks, wine, and beverages are available. ⊠ *532 W. 1st St., at N. Oberlin Ave.* ☎ *818/845–9721* ⊕ *www.flapperscomedy.com* ⊒ *$10–$22, some shows free* ☾ *Closed Mon.–Wed.*

SPORTS AND THE OUTDOORS

SKIING

Mt. Baldy Ski Resort. The 10,064-foot mountain's real name is Mt. San Antonio, but Mt. Baldy Ski Resort—the oldest ski area in Southern California—takes its name from the treeless slopes. The Mt. Baldy base lies at 6,500 feet, and four chairlifts ascend to 8,600 feet. The resort is known for its steep triple-diamond runs; the longest of the 26 runs here is 2,100 vertical feet. Backcountry skiing is available via shuttle in the spring, and there's a school on weekends for kids ages 5 to 12. ■TIP→ **Winter or summer, you can take a scenic chairlift ride ($25) to the Top of the Notch restaurant and hiking and mountain-biking trails.** ⊠ *8401 Mt. Baldy Rd., Mt. Baldy* ☎ *909/982–0800* ⊕ *www. mtbaldyskilifts.com* ⊒ *$69 full-day lift ticket* ☾ *Snow season Nov.– Apr., daily 8–4:30; summer season May–Oct., weekends 7–sunset (days and hrs may vary yr-round, so check to confirm).*

RIVERSIDE AREA

Historic Riverside lies at the heart of the Inland Empire. Major highways linking it to other regional destinations spoke out from this city to the north, south, and east.

GETTING HERE AND AROUND

The most direct route from Los Angeles to Riverside is by Highway 60 (Pomona Freeway). From San Diego take Interstate 15 northeast to the junction with Highway 60. From North Orange County, Highway 91 is the best route.

ESSENTIALS

Bus Contacts Omnitrans ☎ 800/966-6428 ⊕ www.omnitrans.org. **Riverside Transit Authority** ☎ 951/565-5000 ⊕ www.riversidetransit.com.

CORONA

25 miles southeast of Claremont.

Corona's Temescal Canyon is named for the dome-shaped mud saunas that the Luiseño Indians built around the area's artesian hot springs in the early 19th century. Starting in 1860, weary Butterfield Overland Stage Company passengers stopped here to relax in the soothing mineral springs. In 1890 Mr. and Mrs. W.G. Steers turned the springs into Glen Ivy Hot Springs, whose popularity has yet to fade.

GETTING HERE AND AROUND

Primarily a bedroom community, Corona lies at the intersection of Interstate 15 and Highway 91. The many roadside malls make it a convenient stop for food or gas.

EXPLORING

FAMILY **Tom's Farms.** Opened as a produce stand along Interstate 15 in 1974, Tom's Farms has grown to include a locally popular hamburger stand, a furniture showroom, and a sweets shop. You can still buy produce here, but the big draws are various weekend attractions for children: tractor driving, Tom's mining company, a petting zoo, a children's train, a pony ride, free magic shows, face painting, and an old-style carousel. Most cost a modest fee. Of interest for adults is the wine-and-cheese shop, which has more than 600 varieties of wine, including some from the nearby Temecula Valley. ⊠ *23900 Temescal Canyon Rd.* ☎ *951/277-4422* ⊕ *www.tomsfarms.com* ✉ *Free, attraction fees vary; wine tasting $5* ⊙ *Daily 8–8, wine tasting 11–5.*

SPAS

Glen Ivy Hot Springs Spa. Presidents Herbert Hoover and Ronald Reagan are among the guests who have soaked their toes at this beautiful, relaxing spa. Colorful bougainvillea and birds-of-paradise surround the secluded Glen Ivy, which offers a full range of facials, manicures, pedicures, body wraps, and massages. Some treatments are performed in underground granite chambers (highly recommended by readers) known collectively as the Grotto. The Under the Oaks treatment center holds eight open-air massage rooms surrounded by waterfalls and

8

It's okay to get a little dirty at Glen Ivy Hot Springs, which offers a wide variety of treatments at its famous spa—including the red clay pool at Club Mud.

ancient oak trees. Don't bring your best bikini if you plan to dive into the red clay (brought in daily from a local mine) of Club Mud. Paying the admission fee entitles you to lounge here all day. Make reservations for treatments, which cost extra. ✉ *25000 Glen Ivy Rd.* ☎ *888/453-6489* ⊕ *www.glenivy.com* ✉ *Admission Tues.–Thurs. $46, Fri.–Mon. $64; treatments $25–$175* ☽ *Daily 9–4, closes later in warm weather.*

RIVERSIDE

14 miles northeast of Corona, 34 miles northeast of Anaheim.

By 1882 Riverside was home to more than half of California's citrus groves, making it the state's wealthiest city per capita in 1895. The prosperity produced a downtown area of opulent architecture, which is well preserved today. Main Street's pedestrian strip is lined with antiques and gift stores, art galleries, salons, and the UCR/California Museum of Photography.

GETTING HERE AND AROUND

Downtown Riverside lies north of Highway 91 at the University Avenue exit. The Mission Inn is at the corner of Mission Inn Avenue and Orange Street, and key museums, shops, and restaurants are nearby. You can park around here and walk to them.

EXPLORING

Mission Inn Museum. The crown jewel of Riverside is the Mission Inn, a Spanish-Revival hotel whose elaborate turrets, clock tower, mission bells, and flying buttresses rise above downtown. Docents of the

CLOSE UP

Navel Oranges in California: Good as Gold

In 1873 a woman named Eliza Tibbets changed the course of California history when she planted two Brazilian navel-orange trees in her Riverside garden.

The trees flourished in the area's warm climate and rich soil—and before long Tibbett's garden was producing the sweetest seedless oranges anyone had ever tasted. After winning awards at several major exhibitions, Tibbets realized she could make a profit from her trees. She sold buds to the increasing droves of citrus farmers flocking to the Inland Empire, and by 1882, almost 250,000 citrus trees had been planted in Riverside alone. California's citrus industry had been born.

Today Riverside still celebrates its citrus-growing heritage. The downtown Marketplace district contains several restored packing houses, and the Riverside Metropolitan Museum is home to a permanent exhibit of historic tools and machinery once used in the industry. The University of California at Riverside still remains at the forefront of citrus research; its Citrus Variety Collection includes specimens of 1,000 different fruit trees from around the world.

Mission Inn Foundation, whose museum contains displays depicting the building's illustrious history, lead guided tours. Taking his cues from the Spanish missions in San Gabriel and Carmel, architect Arthur B. Benton designed the initial wing, which opened in 1903. Locals G. Stanley Wilson and Peter Weber are credited with the grand fourth section, the Rotunda Wing, completed in 1931. You can climb to the top of its five-story spiral stairway, or linger in the Courtyard of the Birds, where a tinkling fountain and shady trees invite meditation. You can also peek inside the St. Francis Chapel, where celebrities such as Bette Davis, Humphrey Bogart, and Richard and Pat Nixon tied the knot before the Mexican cedar altar. Eight U.S. presidents have patronized the Presidential Lounge, a bright, wood-panel bar. ⊠ *3696 Main St.* ☎ *951/788–9556* ⊕ *www.missioninnmuseum.org* ⊠ *Admission $2, tour $13* ⊙ *Daily 9:30–4:30.*

Riverside Art Museum. Hearst Castle architect Julia Morgan designed this museum that houses a significant collection of paintings by Southern California landscape artists, including William Keith, Robert Wood, and Ralph Love. Major temporary exhibitions are mounted year-round. ⊠ *3425 Mission Inn Ave., at Lime St.* ☎ *951/684–7111* ⊕ *www. riversideartmuseum.org* ⊠ *$5; free 1st Thurs. of month 6–9* ⊙ *Tues.– Sat. 10–4, Sun. 1–4; first Thurs. of month also open 6–9.*

Fodor'sChoice ★ **UCR/California Museum of Photography.** With an impressive collection that includes thousands of Kodak Brownie and Zeiss Ikon cameras, this museum—the centerpiece of UCR ARTSblock—surveys the history of photography *and* the devices that produced it. Exhibitions, some of contemporary images, others historically oriented, are always top-notch and often incorporate photographs from the permanent collection.

8

■ **TIP→ When not on display, works by Ansel Adams, Olindo Ceccarini, and other greats can be viewed by appointment.** ✉ *3824 Main St.* ☎ *951/827–4787* 🌐 *artsblock.ucr.edu/Exhibition* 🎟 *$3* 🕒 *Tues.–Sat. noon–5.*

WHERE TO EAT AND STAY

$$$$ ITALIAN 🍴 **Mario's Place.** The clientele is as beautiful as the food at this intimate jazz and supper club across the street from the Mission Inn. The northern Italian cuisine is first-rate, as are the jazz bands that perform Friday and Saturday at 10 pm. Try the pear-and-Gorgonzola wood-fired pizza, followed by the star-anise panna cotta for dessert. Jazz groups play on weekend nights in the restaurant's lounge. [$] *Average main: $36* ✉ *3646 Mission Inn Ave.* ☎ *951/684–7755* 🌐 *www.mariosplace.com* ✍ *Reservations essential* 🕒 *Closed Sun.*

$ AMERICAN 🍴 **Simple Simon's.** Expect to wait in line at this popular little sandwich shop on the pedestrian-only shopping strip outside the Mission Inn. It's a good place to grab a breakfast sandwich or some French toast. At lunchtime, salads, soups, and sandwiches on house-baked breads are served; standouts include the chicken-apple sausage sandwich and the roast lamb sandwich topped with grilled eggplant, red peppers, and tomato-fennel-olive sauce. [$] *Average main: $10* ✉ *3639 Main St., near 6th St.* ☎ *951/369–6030* ✍ *Reservations not accepted* 🕒 *Closed Sun. No dinner.*

$ HOTEL FAMILY Fodor's Choice ★ 🏨 **Mission Inn and Spa.** One of California's most historic hotels, the inn grew from a modest adobe lodge in 1876 to the grand Spanish-Revival structure it is today. **Pros:** fascinating historical site; luxurious rooms; great restaurants; family friendly. **Cons:** train noise can be deafening at night. [$] *Rooms from: $119* ✉ *3649 Mission Inn Ave.* ☎ *951/784–0300, 800/843–7755* 🌐 *www.missioninn.com* 🛏 *238 rooms, 27 suites* 🍽 *No meals.*

OAK GLEN

33 miles northeast of Riverside.

More than 60 varieties of apples are grown in Oak Glen. This rustic village in the foothills above Yucaipa is home to acres of farms, produce stands, country shops, and homey cafés. The town really comes alive during the fall harvest (from September through December), which is celebrated with piglet races, live entertainment, and other events. Many farms also grow berries and stone fruit, which are available in summer. Most of the apple farms lie along Oak Glen Road.

GETTING HERE AND AROUND

Oak Glen is tucked into a mountainside about halfway up the San Bernardinos. Exit Interstate 10 at Yucaipa Boulevard, heading east to the intersection with Oak Glen Road, a 5-mile loop along which you'll find most of the shops, cafés, and apple orchards.

ESSENTIALS

Visitor Information Oak Glen Apple Growers Association 🌐 *www.oakglen.net.*

EXPLORING

Mom's Country Orchards. Oak Glen's informal information center is at Mom's, where you can belly up to the bar and learn about the nuances of apple tasting, or warm up with a hot cider heated on an antique stove. Organic produce, local honey, apple butter, and salsa are also specialties here. ⊠ *38695 Oak Glen Rd.* ☎ *909/797–4249* ⊕ *momsoakglen.com* ⊗ *Weekdays 10–5, weekends 10–6.*

> ### BEFORE YOU GO PICKING
>
> Be sure to call before visiting the farms, most of which are family run. Unpasteurized cider—sold at some farms—should not be consumed by children, the elderly, or those with weakened immune systems.

FAMILY **Oak Tree Village.** This 14-acre children's park has miniature train rides, trout fishing, gold panning, exotic animal exhibits, shops, and a petting zoo and several eateries. Some activities don't take place year-round. ⊠ *38480 Oak Glen Rd.* ☎ *909/797–4420* ⊕ *www. oaktreevillageoakglen.net* ⊒ *$5* ⊗ *Daily 10–5.*

Rileys at Los Rios Rancho. The fantastic country store at this 100-acre apple farm sells jams, syrups, and candied apples. Drop by the bakery for a hot tri-tip sandwich before heading outside to the picnic grounds for lunch. During the fall you can pick your own apples and pumpkins, take a hayride, or enjoy live bluegrass music. On the rancho grounds, the **Wildlands Conservancy** preserves 400 acres of nature trails, open daily 8–4:30. From April through December, guided night walks take place on the third Saturday of the month. ⊠ *39611 Oak Glen Rd.* ☎ *909/797–1005* ⊕ *www.losriosrancho.com* ⊗ *Oct.–Nov., daily 9–5; Dec.–Sept., Wed.–Sun. 10–5.*

FAMILY **Riley's Farm.** Employees dress in period costumes at this interactive, kid-friendly ranch. Riley's hosts school groups from September to June, and individuals can join the groups by reservation. You can hop on a hayride, take part in a barn dance, pick your own apples, press some cider, or throw a tomahawk while enjoying living-history performances. The farm is also home to Colonial Chesterfield, a replica New England–style estate where costumed 18th-century reenactors offer lessons in cider pressing, candle dipping, colonial games, and etiquette. ⊠ *12261 S. Oak Glen Rd.* ☎ *909/797–7534* ⊕ *www.rileysfarm.com* ⊒ *Free to visit ranch, fees vary for activities* ⊗ *Tues.–Sat. 10–4.*

WHERE TO EAT

$ ╳ **Apple Annie's Restaurant and Bakery.** You won't leave hungry from AMERICAN this country-western diner, known for its five-pound apple pies and family-style seven-course dinners. The decor is comfortable and rustic; old guns and handcuffs hang on the walls alongside pictures of cowboys, trail wagons, and outlaws. Standout dishes include the Annie deluxe burger and the beefeater melt. $ *Average main: $12* ⊠ *38480 Oak Glen Rd.* ☎ *909/797–2311* ⊗ *Mon.–Thurs. 9–6, Fri. and Sat. 8–7, Sun. 8–6.*

8

$ ✕ **Law's Oak Glen Coffee Shop.** Since 1953, this old-fashioned coffee

AMERICAN shop has been serving up hot java, hearty breakfasts and lunches, and famous apple pies. Menu stalwarts include meat loaf, country-fried steak, and Reuben sandwiches. Law's stays open until 7 pm on Friday and closes at 3 the rest of the week. $ *Average main: $8* ✉ *38392 Oak Glen Rd.* ☎ *909/797–1642* ⊕ *www.lawsoakglen.com* ⊗ *No dinner Sat.–Thurs.*

SAN BERNARDINO MOUNTAINS

One of three transverse mountain ranges that lie in the Inland Empire, the San Bernardino range holds the tallest peak in Southern California, San Gorgonio Mountain, at 11,503 feet. It's frequently snowcapped in winter, providing the region's only challenging ski slopes. In summer the forested hillsides and lakes provide a cool retreat from the city for many locals.

LAKE ARROWHEAD

37 miles northeast of Riverside.

Lake Arrowhead Village is an alpine community with lodgings, shops, outlet stores, and eateries that descend a hill to the lake. Outside the village, access to the lake and its beaches is limited to area residents and their guests.

GETTING HERE AND AROUND

Access Lake Arrowhead by driving north from Interstate 10 at Redlands on Highway 210 and continuing north on Highway 330 to the town of Running Springs, where you'll turn west onto Highway 18. Also called the Rim of the World, Highway 18 straddles a mountainside ledge at elevation 5,000 feet, revealing fabulous views. At the Lake Arrowhead turnoff, you'll descend into a wooded bowl surrounding the lake. The village itself is walkable, but hilly. Scenic Highway 173 winding along the east side of the lake offers scenic blue water views through the forest. In winter, check for chain control along this route.

ESSENTIALS

Visitor Information Lake Arrowhead Communities Chamber of Commerce ✉ *28200 Hwy. 189, Lake Arrowhead* ☎ *909/337–3715* ⊕ *lakearrowhead.net.*

EXPLORING

Lake Arrowhead Queen. One of the few ways visitors can access Lake Arrowhead is on a 50-minute *Lake Arrowhead Queen* cruise, operated daily from the Lake Arrowhead Village marina. ✉ *28200 Hwy. 189, Building C-100, Lake Arrowhead* ☎ *909/336–6992* ⊕ *lakearrowhead-queen.com* ✉ *$16.*

WHERE TO EAT AND STAY

$ ✕ **Belgian Waffle Works.** This dockside eatery steps from the *Lake Arrow-*

CAFÉ *head Queen* is quaint and homey, with country decor and beautiful

FAMILY lake views. Dive into a mud-pie Belgian waffle with chocolate fudge sauce or try a Belgian s'more with a marshmallow-and-chocolate sauce. For lunch are burgers, pulled pork sandwiches, tuna melts, chili, meat loaf, chicken dishes, and salads. All go well with the Inland Empire microbrews and Belgian beers poured here. ■TIP→ **Dinner is served in summer only, and even then only until 8 pm.** Ⓢ *Average main: $9* ✉ *28200 Hwy. 189, Suite #150* ☎ *909/337–5222* ⊕ *belgian waffle.com* ♨ *Reservations not accepted* ⊗ *No dinner from early Sept.–late May.*

$$$
RESORT
FAMILY
Fodor's Choice
★

🏨 **Lake Arrowhead Resort and Spa.** This lakeside lodge offers water or forest views from private patios or balconies, and there's a warm and comfy atmosphere throughout thanks to the many fireplaces. **Pros:** beautiful views from most rooms; on-site spa; delicious dining. **Cons:** some rooms have thin walls; daily resort amenity fee ($20). Ⓢ *Rooms from: $215* ✉ *27984 Hwy. 189* ☎ *909/336–1511* ⊕ *www.lakearrowheadresort.com* 🛏 *162 rooms, 11 suites* ⦿ *No meals.*

SPORTS AND THE OUTDOORS

WATERSKIING

McKenzie Waterski School. Summer ski-boat rides and waterskiing and wakeboarding lessons are available through this school in summer. ✉ *28200 Hwy. 189* ☎ *909/337–3814* ⊕ *www.mckenziewaterskischool. com.*

BIG BEAR LAKE

24 miles east of Lake Arrowhead.

When Angelenos say they're going to the mountains, they usually mean Big Bear, where alpine-style villages surround the 7-mile-long lake. The south shore has ski slopes, the Big Bear Alpine Zoo, water-sports opportunities, restaurants, and lodgings that include Apples Bed & Breakfast Inn. The more serene north shore offers easy to moderate hiking and biking trails, splendid alpine scenery, a fascinating nature center, and the gorgeous Windy Point Inn.

8

GETTING HERE AND AROUND

Driving is the best way to get to and explore the Big Bear area. But there are alternatives. The Mountain Area Regional Transit Authority (MARTA) provides bus service to and in San Bernardino Mountain communities and connects with Metrolink and Omnitrans.

ESSENTIALS

Bus Contacts Mountain Transit ☎ 909/878–5200 ⊕ www.mountaintransit.org.

Visitor Information Big Bear Lake Visitors Bureau ✉ 630 Bartlett Rd., near Big Bear Blvd. ☎ 800/424–4232 ⊕ www.bigbearinfo.com.

EXPLORING

FAMILY **Alpine Slide at Magic Mountain.** Take a ride down a twisting Olympic-style bobsled course in winter, or beat the summer heat on a dual waterslide at Alpine Slide, which also has an 18-hole miniature golf course and go-carts. ✉ *800 Wildrose La., at Big Bear Blvd.* ☎ *909/866–4626* ⊕ *www. alpineslidebigbear.com* 🎟 *$6 single rides, $25 5-ride pass, $30 all-day snow-play pass* ⊗ *Weekdays 10–4, weekends 10–dusk.*

FAMILY **Big Bear Alpine Zoo.** This rescue and rehabilitation center specializes in animals native to the San Bernardino Mountains. Among its residents are black and (nonnative) grizzly bears, bald eagles, coyotes, beavers, mountain lions, grey wolves, and bobcats. An animal presentation takes place daily at noon and a feeding tour daily (except Wednesday) at 3. ✉ *43285 Goldmine Dr., at Moonridge Rd.* ☎ *909/584–1299* 🌐 *www.bigbearzoo.com* 🎟 *$12* ⏲ *June–early Sept., daily 10–5; early Sept.–May, weekdays 10–4, weekends 10–5.*

FAMILY Fodor's Choice ★ **Big Bear Discovery Center.** At this nature center you can sign up for canoe and kayak tours of Big Bear Lake, a naturalist-led tour of the Baldwin Lake Ecological Reserve in the spring and summer, and winter snowshoe tours. Exhibits here explain the area's flora and fauna, and staffers provide maps and camping and hiking information. ✉ *40971 N. Shore Dr. (Hwy. 38), 2½ miles east of Fawnskin, Fawnskin* ☎ *909/382–2790* 🌐 *www.mountainsfoundation.org/big-bear-discovery-center* 🎟 *Free* ⏲ *Thurs.–Mon. 8:30–4:30.*

Big Bear Marina. The paddle wheeler *Big Bear Queen* departs from the marina for 90-minute lake tours. The marina also rents fishing boats, jet skis, kayaks, and canoes. ✉ *500 Paine Ct.* ☎ *909/866–3218* 🌐 *www.bigbearmarina.com* 🎟 *$19* ⏲ *Tours May–early Sept., daily noon, 2, and 4; call to confirm.*

FAMILY **Time Bandit Pirate Ship.** Featured in the 1981 movie *Time Bandits*, this small-scale replica of a 17th-century English galleon cruises Big Bear Lake daily from roughly April through October. The ship travels along the southern lakeshore to 6743-foot-high Big Bear Dam; along the way you'll pass big bayfront mansions, some owned by celebrities. A sightseeing excursion with the crew dressed up like pirates, the cruise is popular with kids and adults. There's a bar, but no dining, onboard. ✉ *Holloway's Marina and RV Park, 398 Edgemoor Rd.* ☎ *909/878–4040* 🌐 *www.bigbearboating.com/pirate_ship* 🎟 *$22* ⏲ *Confirmed tours daily at 2 in warm weather; call for additional times.*

WHERE TO EAT

$ NEPALESE FAMILY 🍴 **Himalayan Restaurant.** It's best to order family style at this no-frills storefront restaurant so that everyone gets a taste of the many Nepalese and Indian delicacies offered. Customer favorites include the spicy *mo-mo* (pot stickers), *daal* (green lentils), lamb and shrimp-curry vindaloo, fish and chicken masala, and clay-oven-roasted tandoori meats and seafood. The aromatic teas and lemonades provide a perky contrast to your meal's savory flavors. [$] *Average main: $15* ✉ *672 Pine Knot Ave., Ste. 2* ☎ *909/878–3068* 🌐 *www.himalayanbigbear.com* ✍ *Reservations essential* ⏲ *Closed Wed.*

$$$$ FRENCH 🍴 **Madlon's Restaurant.** A triple threat that also serves breakfast (waffles, eggs Benedict) and lunch (burgers and other standards), this restaurant in a cozy, gingerbread-style cottage shines brightest at dinner with sophisticated French-inspired dishes. As might be expected, escargots, rack of lamb, and dry-aged filet mignon are on the menu, along with diversions like the chicken breast served with dried cherries and a Gorgonzola-sherry sauce or the 18-ounce porterhouse steak. **■ TIP→ Midweek prix-fixe three-course specials include wine.**

$ *Average main: $42* ✉ *829 W. Big Bear Blvd., at Pine View Dr., Big Bear City* ☎ *909/585–3762* ⊕ *www.madlonsrestaurant.com* ⚐ *Reservations essential* ⊗ *Closed Tues.–Thurs.*

WHERE TO STAY

$$$
B&B/INN

🏠 **Apples Bed & Breakfast Inn.** Despite its location on a busy road to the ski lifts, the inn feels remote and peaceful, thanks to the surrounding pines. **Pros:** large rooms; clean; free snacks and movies; delicious big breakfast. **Cons:** some traffic noise; fussy decor; sometimes feels busy. $ *Rooms from: $198* ✉ *42430 Moonridge Rd.* ☎ *909/866–0903* ⊕ *www.applesbigbear.com* ⤴ *19 rooms* ⦿ *Some meals.*

$$$
B&B/INN
Fodor's Choice
★

🏠 **Gold Mountain Manor.** Each room at this restored 1928 log mansion has its own theme based on a rich Hollywood history: the Clark Gable room, for example, contains the Franklin stove that once warmed the honeymoon suite Gable and actress Carole Lombard shared. **Pros:** gracious hosts; snowshoes and kayaks available. **Cons:** somewhat thin walls; 10-minute drive to the village; many stairs; narrow corridors. $ *Rooms from: $179* ✉ *1117 Anita Ave., Big Bear City* ☎ *909/585–6997, 800/509–2604* ⊕ *www.goldmountainmanor.com* ⤴ *4 rooms, 3 suites* ⦿ *Multiple meal plans.*

$
HOTEL

🏠 **Northwoods Resort.** A giant log cabin with the amenities of a resort, Northwoods has a lobby that resembles a 1930s hunting lodge: canoes, antlers, and fishing poles decorate the walls, and there's a grand stone fireplace. **Pros:** pool heated in winter; ski packages available; beautiful grounds. **Cons:** hotel showing its age in places; noise at night in some rooms; rate increases when it snows. $ *Rooms from: $109* ✉ *40650 Village Dr.* ☎ *909/866–3121, 800/866–3121* ⊕ *www.northwoodsresort.com* ⤴ *140 rooms, 7 suites* ⦿ *No meals.*

$$
B&B/INN

🏠 **Windy Point Inn.** Surrounded on three sides by water, Windy Point offers the best views and the most luxurious accommodations in the Big Bear area. **Pros:** secure parking; gracious hosts; privacy; views. **Cons:** remote from lake activities; windy at times. $ *Rooms from: $145* ✉ *31094 North Shore Dr., Fawnskin* ☎ *909/866–2746* ⊕ *windypointinn.com* ⤴ *5 rooms* ⦿ *Breakfast.*

SPORTS AND THE OUTDOORS

BOATS AND CHARTERS

Pine Knot Landing Marina. This full-service marina rents fishing boats, pontoon boats, and kayaks and sells bait, ice, and snacks. You can take water-ski lessons here or pick up some Jet Skis and parasailing equipment. On weekends from late April through September, the paddle wheeler *Miss Liberty* leaves from the landing for a 90-minute tour ($20) of Big Bear Lake. Refreshments are available on board. ✉ *439 Pine Knot Blvd.* ☎ *909/866–7766* ⊕ *pineknotmarina.com.*

HORSEBACK RIDING

Baldwin Lake Stables. Explore the forested mountain on horseback on a group or private guided trail ride (one hour to a half day) arranged by this outfit. The facility has a petting zoo for kids in summer and offers pony rides on weekends. Reservations are required for private rides and suggested for all rides. ✉ *46475 Pioneertown Rd., Big Bear City* ☎ *909/585–6482* ⊕ *www.baldwinlakestables.com* ✍ *From $45 per hr.*

SKIING

Big Bear Mountain Resorts. Two distinct resorts, Bear Mountain and Snow Summit, comprise Southern California's largest winter playground, one of the few that challenge skilled skiers. The complex offers 438 skiable acres, 55 runs, and 26 chairlifts, including four high-speed quads. The vibe is youthful at Bear, which has beginner slopes (training available) and the after-ski hangout The Scene. Snow Summit holds challenging runs and is open for night skiing. On weekends and holidays it's best to reserve tickets for either mountain. Bear rents skis and boards.

The resorts are open in summer for mountain biking, hiking, golfing, and some special events. The Snow Summit Scenic Sky Chair zips to the mountain's 8,200-foot peak, where View Haus ($), a casual outdoor restaurant, has breathtaking views of the lake and San Gorgonio Mountain. ✉ *Big Bear, 880 Summit Blvd., off Moonridge Rd.* ☎ *909/866–5766* ⊕ *www.bigbearmountainresorts.com* ✍ *$64–$79.*

THE SOUTHERN INLAND EMPIRE

The southern end of the Inland Empire is devoted to the good life. Mile-high Idyllwild atop Mt. San Jacinto holds a renowned arts academy, charming restaurants, and galleries. It's also a good place to hike, mountain climb, and test high-altitude biking skills. Temecula, lying at the base of the mountain, is a popular wine region, where you'll find vineyards, tasting rooms, fine dining, and cozy lodgings.

IDYLLWILD

44 miles east of Riverside.

Set in a valley halfway up Mt. San Jacinto, Idyllwild has been a serene forested getaway for San Diegans and Angelenos for nearly a century. The town's simple, quiet lifestyle attracts artists and performers as well as outdoor types who enjoy hiking, biking, and serious rock climbing.

GETTING HERE AND AROUND

Two routes from the interstates lead to Idyllwild; both are slow and winding but provide memorable mountain views. From Interstate 10 in Banning, take scenic Highway 243 south to Idyllwild. From Interstate 15 near Lake Elsinore, drive east on Highway 74 to Highway 243 and turn north. Once in Idyllwild, you can walk nearly everywhere in the village, though you'll need to drive to trailheads, fishing holes, and rock-climbing locations.

ESSENTIALS

Visitor Information Idyllwild Town Crier and Visitor Center ✉ *54325 N. Circle Dr.* ⊕ *www.idyllwildchamber.com* ☉ *Weekdays 9–5, Sat. 10–4, Sun. 10–2.*

EXPLORING

FAMILY **Idyllwild Nature Center.** At the center you can learn about the area's Native American history and listen to traditional storytellers. Outside are 3 miles of hiking trails, plus biking and equestrian trails and picnic areas. The park is pet-friendly. ✉ *25225 Hwy. 243* ☎ *951/659–3850* 🌐 *www.rivcoparks.org/parks* 🎟 *$3* 🕒 *Tues.–Sun. 9–4* 🕒 *Closed Mon.*

WHERE TO EAT

$$$$ FRENCH 🍴 **Restaurant Gastrognome.** Elegant and dimly lighted, with wood paneling, lace curtains, and an oft-glowing fireplace, "The Gnome" is where locals go for a romantic dinner. The overall feel is French, but the menu goes beyond the Gallic, with entrées such as calamari almandine, sausage pasta, and lobster tacos. The French onion soup always satisfies, and the roast duck with orange sauce and barbecued beef ribs are excellent as well. The crème brûlée makes for a sweet finale. For lighter dinner fare, check out the café menu. [$] *Average main: $39* ✉ *54381 Ridgeview Dr.* ☎ *951/659–5055* 🌐 *www.gastrognome.com* ✍ *Reservations essential.*

PERFORMING ARTS

Idyllwild Arts Academy. The academy provides professional training for gifted arts students and presents more than 95 summer workshops in dance, music, Native American arts, theater, visual arts, and writing. Free summer concerts and theater productions feature students and professional performers. ✉ *52500 Temecula Rd.* ☎ *951/659–2171* 🌐 *www.idyllwildarts.org.*

SPORTS AND THE OUTDOORS

FISHING

Lake Fulmor. The lake is stocked with rainbow trout, largemouth bass, catfish, and bluegill. To fish, you'll need a California fishing license and a National Forest Adventure Pass ($5 per vehicle per day). ✉ *Hwy. 243, 10 miles north of Idyllwild* ☎ *951/659–2117* 🌐 *www.fs.usda.gov/sbnf.*

HIKING

Humber Park Trailhead. Two great hikes begin at this site, the 2.5-mile Devils Slide Trail and the 2.6-mile Ernie Maxwell Scenic Trail. Adventure permits ($5) are needed for both; wilderness permits are also needed for Devils Slide. ✉ *At top of Fern Valley Rd.* ☎ *951/659–2117* 🌐 *www.fs.usda.gov/recarea/sbnf/recarea/?recid=26483.*

Pacific Crest Trail. Access the trail at Highway 74, 1 mile east of Highway 371; or via the Fuller Ridge Trail at Black Mountain Road, 15 miles north of Idyllwild. Permits ($5 per day), required for camping and day hikes in the San Jacinto Wilderness, are available at the Idyllwild Ranger Station or online. ✉ *Ranger Station, Pine Crest Ave., off Hwy. 243* ☎ *951/659–2117 ranger* 🌐 *www.fs.usda.gov/sbnf.*

TEMECULA

43 miles south of Riverside, 60 miles north of San Diego, 90 miles southeast of Los Angeles.

Fodor's Choice ★ Temecula, with its rolling green vineyards, country inns, and first-rate restaurants, bills itself as "Southern California Wine Country." The region, on the verge of a development explosion, is home to three-dozen wineries, several of which offer spas, fine dining, or luxury lodging and shopping. Not to be missed are the small, family-run vineyards whose devotion to showcasing Temecula's unique combination of climates and soils—the terroir, as the French call it, results in some impressive wines.

The name Temecula comes from a Luiseño Indian word meaning "where the sun shines through the mist"—ideal conditions for growing wine grapes. Intense afternoon sun and cool nighttime temperatures, complemented by ocean breezes that flow through the Rainbow and Santa Margarita gaps in the coastal range, help grapevines flourish in the area's granite soil. Once best known for Chardonnay, Temecula Valley winemakers are moving in new directions, producing Viognier, Syrah, and other Rhône-style blended whites and reds.

The oldest wineries are strung out along Rancho California Road, east of Interstate 15; a few newer ones lie along the eastern portion of De Portola Road. Most wineries charge a small fee (usually from $10 to $15) for a tasting that includes several wines. On its website the Temecula Valley Winegrowers Association offers suggestions for self-guided winery tours and has coupons good for tasting discounts.

GETTING HERE AND AROUND

Interstate 15 cuts right through Temecula. The wineries lie on the east side of the freeway along Rancho California Road. Old Town Temecula lies west of the freeway along Front Street.

TOURS

Destination Temecula. Full-day winery tours run by Destination Temecula include stops at three wineries, a picnic lunch, and time to explore Old Town Temecula. The company picks up participants in Old Town Temecula and at San Diego hotels. ☎ 951/695–1232 ⊕ www.destem. com ✉ From $89 round-trip.

Grapeline Wine Country Shuttle. Enthusiastic local experts lead tours of Temecula Valley wineries, including excursions that incorporate cheese tastings, insider visits with vintners, and catered picnic lunches. Tours are lively, with plenty of banter and insights courtesy of the Grapeline staff, whose familiarity with the Temecula wine-making scene enriches the experience. Full- and half-day tours are offered, with private or shared transportation by luxury SUV, limousine, or coach bus. Participants are picked up at area hotels, in Old Town Temecula, and elsewhere in Southern California. ☎ 951/693–5755, 888/894–6379 ⊕ www.gogrape.com ✉ From $69.

VISITOR INFORMATION

Temecula Valley Convention and Visitors Bureau ✉ 28690 Mercedes St. ☎ 951/491–6085, 888/363–2852 ⊕ www.temeculacvb.com.

Temecula Valley Winegrowers Association ✉ 34567 Rancho California Rd. ☎ 951/699–3626 ⊕ www.temeculawines.org.

EXPLORING

TOP ATTRACTIONS

Fodor'sChoice ★ **Hart Family Winery.** A perennial crowd-pleaser, this winery specializes in well-crafted red wines made by father-son winemakers Joe and Jim Hart. Joe, who started the winery in the 1970s with his wife, Nancy, focuses on growing grapes suited to the Temecula region's singular climate and soils—Zinfandel, Cabernet Sauvignon, and Sangiovese as might be expected, but also little known varietals such as Aleatico, used in the winery's marvelous dessert wine. The reds are the stars, though, along with the amiable Hart family members themselves. ⊠ *41300 Avenida Biona* ☎ *951/676–6300* ⊕ *www.hartfamilywinery.com* ✉ *Tasting $10* ⊙ *Daily 9–4:30.*

Old Town Temecula. For a bit of old-fashioned fun, head to Old Town Temecula, where turn-of-the-20th-century-style storefronts and boardwalks extend for 12 blocks. Along with more than 60 restaurants and boutiques, there are antiques stores, a performing arts center and jazz club, and art galleries. A crop of upstarts, including a gourmet cheese shop and hip brewpubs, is lending youthful energy to the scene. ⊠ *Front St., between Rancho California Rd. and Hwy. 79* ☎ *888/363–2852* ⊕ *www.visittemeculavalley.com.*

FAMILY **Pennypickle's Workshop—Temecula Children's Museum.** If you have the kids along, check out the fictional 7,500-square-foot workshop of Professor Phineas T. Pennypickle, PhD. This elaborately decorated children's museum is filled with secret passageways, machines, wacky contraptions, and time-travel inventions. ■TIP→ **Take one of the two-hour tours offered daily to get the most out of your visit.** ⊠ *42081 Main St.* ☎ *951/308–6376* ⊕ *www.pennypickles.org* ✉ *$5* ⊙ *Tues.–Sat. 10–5, Sun. 12:30–5.*

Ponte Family Estates. Lush gardens and more than 300 acres of vineyards provide a rustic, elegant setting at Ponte, whose small-lot wines range from sparklers and light whites to potent Super Tuscan–style offerings. In the airy, light-filled tasting room you can sample the aptly named Super T, a blend of Cabernet Sauvignon and Sangiovese grapes, and other vintages crafted by winemaker Mark Schabel; ceramics, specialty foods, and gift baskets are for sale at the adjacent marketplace. The shaded outdoor Restaurant at Ponte serves salads, wood-fired pizzas, and seafood daily for lunch and on weekends for dinner. ⊠ *35053 Rancho California Rd.* ☎ *951/694–8855* ⊕ *www.pontewinery.com* ✉ *Tasting $15 weekdays, $20 weekends* ⊙ *Winery daily 10–5; restaurant Mon.–Thurs. 11–4, Fri. and Sat. 11–8, Sun. 11–5.*

WORTH NOTING

Callaway Vineyard and Winery. One of Temecula's oldest wineries is centered on a stunning steel-and-glass cube with vineyard views all around. You can draw your own wine from tap stations placed around the room. Callaway made its reputation with Chardonnay, but these days also does well with Roussanne, Sangiovese, Mourvèdre, Dolcetto, and other varietals. The winery's Meritage Restaurant specializes in tapas,

8

salads, and sandwiches. ✉ *32720 Rancho California Rd.* ☎ *951/676–4001* ⊕ *www.callawaywinery.com* ▣ *Tasting $10–$15; tour $5* ⊙ *Daily 10–5; tours weekdays 11, 1, 3; weekends 11, noon, 1, 2.*

Doffo Winery. This Italian-Argentine wine-making family with a 15-acre property at the Temecula Valley's northeastern edge takes a passionate and quirky approach. Winemaker Damian Doffo and his father, Marcelo, play music for their vines, whose grapes go into small-lot wines, among them a spicy-sharp Muscat, a rich Syrah, and a soft Malbec. Tastings of these and other bottlings take place inside a refurbished garage. The family's racing and vintage motorcycles, which guests can view on free self-guided walking tours, are displayed in an airy showroom nearby. ✉ *36083 Summitville St.* ☎ *951/676–6989* ⊕ *www.doffowines.com* ▣ *Tasting $10, tour $65* ⊙ *Daily 10–5; tours weekdays 11 and 2, weekends 10, 12, 2, and 4* ☞ *Groups of six or more by appointment only.*

Leoness Cellars. Rhône- and Tuscan-style blends—along with killer views—are the specialties of this mountaintop facility. Winemaker Tim Kramer and his staff produce about a dozen and a half wines each year, of which you can select six. If you like reds, be sure to try the Syrahs, which are almost always winners. Winery tours take in the vineyards and the wine-making areas. The tours require a reservation, as do wine-and-food pairing sessions that might include fruits and cheeses or, in the case of dessert wines, some chocolates. ✉ *38311 DePortola Rd.* ☎ *951/302–7601* ⊕ *www.leonesscellars.com* ▣ *Tasting $15–$18, tour with tasting $18–$85* ⊙ *Daily 11–5.*

Miramonte Winery. At Temecula's hippest winery, perched on a hilltop, listen to Spanish-guitar recordings while sampling the slightly pricy Opulente Meritage, a supple Roussanne, or the sultry Syrah. Owner Cane Vanderhoof's wines have earned dozens of awards. While you're enjoying your wine on the deck, order an artisan cheese plate. On Friday and Saturday nights from 7 to 10, the winery turns into a local hot spot with tastings of signature wines ($17) and beer, live music, and dancing that spills out into the vineyards. ✉ *33410 Rancho California Rd.* ☎ *951/506–5500* ⊕ *www.miramontewinery.com* ▣ *Tastings $15–$17, tours $75 (reservations required weekends)* ⊙ *Sun.–Thurs. 11–6, Fri. and Sat. 11–10.*

Mount Palomar Winery. One of the original Temecula Valley wineries, opened in 1969, Mount Palomar introduced Sangiovese grapes, a varietal that has proven perfectly suited to the region's soil and climate. New owners have transformed the homey winery into a grand Mediterranean villa with acres of gardens and trees. Some of the wines are made from grapes brought from Italy nearly 50 years ago. Try the dry Sangiovese or Bordeaux-style Meritage. Shorty's Bistro, open for lunch daily and for dinner Friday through Sunday, presents live entertainment on Friday nights. ✉ *33820 Rancho California Rd.* ☎ *951/676–5047* ⊕ *www.mountpalomar.com* ▣ *Winery free, tasting $12 Mon.–Thurs., $16 Fri.– Sun.* ⊙ *Daily 10:30–6.*

There's no more relaxing way to enjoy Temecula's Wine Country than by taking a peaceful hot-air balloon ride over the vineyards.

Fodor'sChoice ★ **Wiens Family Cellars.** A winery on the rise, Wiens promotes its "Big Reds"—among them the Reserve Primitivo and a Tempranillo–Petite Sirah blend—but many visitors often wind up taking home a bottle of the perky-fruity Amour De L'Orange sparkling wine. Other wines of note include the Ruby Port and the Dulce Maria, made from Chardonnay and Muscat Canelli grapes. The ambience at Wiens is informal, but the cordial tasting-room staffers are well informed about the wines they enthusiastically pour. ✉ *35055 Via Del Ponte* ☎ *951/694–9892* ⊕ *www.wienscellars.com* 🍷 *Tasting $15* ⊙ *Daily 10:30–6.*

Wilson Creek Winery & Vineyards. One of Temecula's busiest tasting rooms sits amid inviting, parklike grounds. Wilson is known for its Almond Champagne, but the winery also produces appealing still wines. The Viognier, Reserve Syrah, Reserve Zinfandel, and late-harvest Zinfandel all merit a taste. The on-site Creekside Grill Restaurant serves sandwiches, salads, and entrées such as Mexican white sea bass and gluten-free vegetable potpie. Dine inside or select a picnic spot, and the servers will deliver your meal to you. ✉ *35960 Rancho California Rd.* ☎ *951/699–9463* ⊕ *www.wilsoncreekwinery.com* 🍷 *Tasting $15 weekdays, $20 weekends and holidays* ⊙ *Daily 10–5, restaurant weekdays 11–4, Sat. 11–5, Sun. 10–3.*

WHERE TO EAT AND STAY

$$$ ✕ **Baily's Front Street Bar & Grill.** The easy-on-the-budget menu lists eight
AMERICAN gourmet burgers, chipotle-braised barbecued ribs, chili-stuffed chicken,
FAMILY and jambalaya. You can also nosh on Irish nachos and jalapeño-calamari tempura. On weekend evenings, the place turns into a locally

popular nightclub. Breakfast is offered on weekends only. It's a good place for casual fare, however, note that some diners have complained about service. $ *Average main: $26* ✉ *28699 Old Town Front St.* ☎ *951/676–9567* ⊕ *www.oldtowndining.com* ⧤ *Reservations essential.*

$$$
MEDITERRANEAN

✕ **Meritage Restaurant at Callaway Vineyards.** Impressively prepared cuisine and stunning Temecula Valley views from a shaded terrace make a visit to the restaurant at Callaway winery a memorable occasion. Pomegranate *pico de gallo* (salsa), radish and ginger vinaigrette, and other inventive flourishes add piquancy and pep to the mostly Mediterranean dishes, which include tapas made from slow-roasted meats and fresh seafood. Try the ceviche mixto or a grass-fed burger from nearby Sage Mt. Farm, or perhaps a thick, smoked pork chop with apple chutney, paired with Callaway's Reserve Syrah or one of the California and international craft beers poured here. With live music and open mic nights, Meritage is consistently hopping. $ *Average main: $25* ✉ *32720 Rancho California Rd., east of Butterfield Stage Rd.* ☎ *951/587–8889* ⊕ *www.callawaywinery.com* ⊘ *No dinner Mon.–Thurs.*

$$
MODERN
AMERICAN
FAMILY

✕ **Public House.** A low-key gastropub inside a restored 1950s home, this Old Town spot with a sunlit patio hosts live music on weekends. A surprisingly light meat loaf with a shallot and hot butter pan sauce is among the standouts here; the grilled romaine wedge salad is also worth trying. Like all Public House dishes, both are prepared with seasonal, locally produced ingredients. Craft beers by innovative Southern California breweries Lost Abbey and The Bruery are among the 20 selections on tap. ■ TIP→ **The choices for kids include a mini Kobe beef burger and a 3-ounce filet mignon.** $ *Average main: $21* ✉ *41971 Main St.* ☎ *951/676–7305* ⊕ *www.publicrestaurants.com/ public-house-temecula.*

$$$
HOTEL

⌑ **Ponte Vineyard Inn.** Slow down in old Californio Rancho style at this delightful hotel that opened in 2012 on the grounds of the Ponte Family Estate winery. **Pros:** huge rooms; lounges everywhere; excellent winery on-site; gracious service. **Cons:** weddings; very, very quiet. $ *Rooms from: $200* ✉ *35001 Rancho California Rd.* ☎ *951/587–6688* ⊕ *www. pontevineyardinn.com* ⇅ *60 rooms* ⦿ *No meals.*

$$
RESORT

⌑ **Temecula Creek Inn.** Each room at this spacious inn has a private patio or balcony overlooking the championship golf course. **Pros:** beautiful grounds; top golf course; great views. **Cons:** simple furnishings; shows its age; location away from Old Town and wineries. $ *Rooms from: $139* ✉ *44501 Rainbow Canyon Rd.* ☎ *951/694–1000, 888/976–3404* ⊕ *www.temeculacreekinn.com* ⇅ *130 rooms, 1 guesthouse* ⦿ *No meals.*

NIGHTLIFE

Pechanga Resort and Casino. Casino gambling is the main attraction here, and there are several entertainment venues. Headliners such as Paul Anka, B.B. King, and Jerry Seinfeld have appeared at the Pechanga Theater; the intimate Comedy Club books up-and-coming talent. HBO and Fox Sports championship boxing matches draw thousands of fans. The largest Indian casino in California, Pechanga has a 517-room hotel, a golf course, a spa, and an RV park. ✉ *45000 Pechanga Pkwy.* ☎ *877/711–2946, 951/770–1819* ⊕ *www.pechanga.com.*

SPORTS AND THE OUTDOORS
GOLF

Temecula has several championship golf courses cooled by the valley's ocean breezes.

Redhawk Golf Club. Considered one of the best 18-hole public golf courses in California, the Ron Fream–designed championship golf course is designed to take advantage of Temecula's tree-studded rolling hills set against craggy mountains. The course holds a bunch of traps to challenge your swing or putt. Watch out for wind, doglegs, skinny sand traps, and tiered greens. Rico's Cantina here offers Mexican and Southwestern items, served up for breakfast or lunch. ⊠ *45100 Redhawk Pkwy.* ☎ *951/302–3850* ⊕ *www.redhawkgolfcourse.com* ⊇ *$30–$50 weekdays; $40–$70 weekends* ⅄ *18 holes, 7110 yards, par 72.*

Temecula Creek Inn Golf Resort. Ted Robinson and Dick Rossen designed this Wine Country resort's three picturesque nine-hole courses. Stonehouse, the most challenging one, demands precise tee shots. ⊠ *44501 Rainbow Canyon Rd.* ☎ *951/676–2405* ⊕ *www.temeculacreekinn.com* ⊇ *$80 weekdays; $95 weekends* ⅄ *Creek: 9 holes, 3348 yards, par 36; Oaks: 9 holes, 3436 yards, par 36; Stonehouse: 9 holes, 3257 yards, par 36.*

Temeku Hills Golf Club. The tiered greens, five lakes, and many blind spots make for challenging rounds at this club's Ted Robinson-designed championship course. ⊠ *41687 Temeku Dr.* ☎ *951/694–9998* ⊕ *www.temekuhillsgolfcourse.com* ⊇ *$55 weekdays; $65 weekends* ⅄ *18 holes, 6636 yards, par 72.*

HOT-AIR BALLOONING

California Dreamin'. Float serenely above Temecula's vineyards and country estates on an early-morning balloon adventure. The ride includes champagne, coffee, a pastry breakfast, and a souvenir photo. ⊠ *Flights depart from La Vindemia Vineyard, 33133 Vista Del Monte Rd.* ☎ *800/373–3359* ⊕ *www.californiadreamin.com* ⊇ *$148 weekdays and Sun., $168 Sat.*

SHOPPING

Temecula Lavender Co. Owner Jan Schneider offers an inspiring collection of the herb that fosters peace, purification, sleep, and longevity. Bath salts, hand soaps, essential oil, even dryer bags to freshen up the laundry—she's got it all. ⊠ *28561 Old Town Front St.* ☎ *951/676–1931* ⊕ *www.temeculalavenderco.com* ☉ *Daily 10–6.*

Temecula Olive Oil Company. While you're shopping in Old Town, stop by the cool tasting room here for a sample of extra-virgin olive oils, flavored balsamic vinegars and sea salts, bath products, and Mission, Ascalano, and Italian olives. Guided tours of the ranch where the olives are grown are available. ⊠ *28653 Old Town Front St., Suite H* ☎ *951/693–0607* ⊕ *www.temeculaoliveoil.com* ☉ *Daily 9:30–6.*

8

PALM SPRINGS

And the Desert Resorts

WELCOME TO PALM SPRINGS

TOP REASONS TO GO

★ **Fun in the sun:** The Palm Springs area has 350 days of sun each year, and the weather is usually ideal for playing one of the area's more than 100 golf courses.

★ **Spa under the stars:** Many resorts and small hotels now offer after-dark spa services, including outdoor soaks and treatments you can savor while sipping wine under the clear, starry sky.

★ **Personal pampering:** The resorts here have it all, beautifully appointed rooms packed with amenities, professional staffs, sublime spas, and delicious dining options.

★ **Divine desert scenery:** You'll probably spend a lot of time taking in the gorgeous 360-degree natural panorama, a flat desert floor surrounded by 10,000-foot mountains rising into a brilliant blue sky.

★ **The Hollywood connection:** The Palm Springs area has more celebrity ties than any other resort community. So keep your eyes open for your favorite star.

1 Palm Springs. A hideaway for celebrities, artists, politicians, sports personalities, and high-profile types since the midcentury, Palm Springs retains the luster of its golden era. Most visitors spend their days lounging poolside at a posh resort or an artsy inn, enjoying a well-crafted meal at an upscale restaurant, or shopping for treasures at the Uptown Design District before heading back to sip martinis under the stars.

2 The Desert Resorts. East of Palm Springs on Highway 111 lie several towns, each containing strip malls, gated communities, and huge resort complexes. Palm Desert is the Coachella Valley's answer to Rodeo Drive in Beverly Hills, with walkable downtown dining options aplenty. The golfing havens of Rancho Mirage, Indian Wells, and La Quinta cater to moneyed outdoor types.

3 Along Twentynine Palms Highway. The towns of Yucca Valley, Joshua Tree, and Twentynine Palms punctuate Twentynine Palms Highway (Highway 62)—the northern highway from the desert resorts to Joshua Tree National Park—and provide visitor information, lodging, and other services to park visitors.

4 Anza-Borrego Desert. If you're looking for a break from the action, you'll find solitude and solace in this 600,000-acre desert landscape.

GETTING ORIENTED

The Palm Springs resort area lies within the Colorado Desert, on the western edge of the Coachella Valley. The area holds seven cities that are strung out along Highway 111, with Palm Springs at the northwestern end of this strip and Indio at the southeastern end. North of Palm Springs, between Interstate 10 and Highway 62, is Desert Hot Springs. Northeast of Palm Springs, the towns of the Morongo Valley lie along Twentynine Palms Highway (Highway 62), which leads to Joshua Tree National Park. Head south on Highway 86 from Indio to reach Anza-Borrego Desert State Park and the Salton Sea. All of the area's attractions are easy day trips from Palm Springs.

Updated by
Michele Bigley

With the Palm Springs area's year-round sunshine, luxurious spas, chef-driven restaurants, and see-and-be-seen pool parties, it's no wonder that Hollywood A-listers and weekend warriors make the desert a getaway. Stretching south and east of the city along Highway 111, the desert resort towns—Cathedral City, Rancho Mirage, Palm Desert, Indian Wells, La Quinta, and Indio, along with Desert Hot Springs to the north—teem with resorts, golf courses, and shopping centers. Yucca Valley, Joshua Tree, and other artistic communities lie farther north and northeast. To the south, the wildflowers of Anza-Borrego Desert State Park herald the arrival of spring.

Well before it became the darling of the current crop of überhip Angelenos, the Palm Springs area was the playground of the celebrity elite. In the 1920s Al Capone opened the Two Bunch Palms Hotel in Desert Hot Springs (with multiple tunnels to help him avoid the police); Marilyn Monroe was discovered poolside in the late 1940s at a downtown Palm Springs tennis club; Elvis and Priscilla Presley honeymooned here—and the list goes on.

In recent years the desert arts scene has blossomed as spectacularly as the wildflowers of Anza-Borrego. For urban-chic contemporary artwork, stop by downtown Palm Springs' Backstreet Arts District, but try to slip away to the rural areas—the aforementioned Yucca Valley but also Joshua Tree, Pioneertown, and Twentynine Palms. Each April attention centers on Indio, where the Coachella Valley Music and Arts Festival, California's largest outdoor concert, generates a frenzy of cultural activity.

PLANNING

WHEN TO GO

Desert weather is best between January and April, the height of the visitor season. The fall months are nearly as lovely, but less crowded and less expensive (although autumn draws many conventions and business travelers). In summer, a popular time with European visitors, daytime temperatures may rise above 110°F (though evenings cool to the mid-70s); some attractions and restaurants close or reduce their hours during this time.

GETTING HERE AND AROUND

AIR TRAVEL

Palm Springs International Airport serves California's desert communities. Air Canada, Alaska, Allegiant, American, Delta, Sun Country, United, Virgin America, US Airways, and WestJet all fly to Palm Springs, some only seasonally. Yellow Cab of the Desert serves the airport, which is about 3 miles from downtown. The fare is $2.50 to enter the cab and about $3.12 per mile.

Airport Information Palm Springs International Airport ✉ *3200 E. Tahquitz Canyon Way, Palm Springs* ☎ *760/323–8299* ⊕ *www.palmspringsairport.com.*

Airport Transfers Yellow Cab of the Desert ✉ *75150 St. Charles Pl., Palm Desert* ☎ *760/340–8294* ⊕ *www.yellowcabofthedesert.com.*

BUS TRAVEL

Greyhound provides service to Palm Springs from many cities. SunBus, operated by the SunLine Transit Agency, serves the entire Coachella Valley, from Desert Hot Springs to Mecca.

Bus Contacts Greyhound ☎ *800/231–2222* ⊕ *www.greyhound.com.* **SunLine Transit Agency** ☎ *800/347–8628* ⊕ *www.sunline.org.*

CAR TRAVEL

The desert resort communities occupy a 20-mile stretch between Interstate 10, to the east, and Palm Canyon Drive (Highway 111), to the west. The region is about a two-hour drive east of the Los Angeles area and a three-hour drive northeast of San Diego. It can take twice as long to make the trip from Los Angeles to the desert on winter and spring weekends because of heavy traffic. From Los Angeles take the San Bernardino Freeway (Interstate 10) east to Highway 111. From San Diego, Interstate 15 heading north connects with the Pomona Freeway (Highway 60), leading to the San Bernardino Freeway east.

To reach Borrego Springs from Los Angeles, take Interstate 10 east past the desert resorts area to Highway 86 south to the Borrego Salton Seaway (Highway S22) west. You can reach the Borrego area from San Diego via Interstate 8 to Highway 79 through Cuyamaca State Park. This will take you to Highway 78 in Julian, which you follow east to Yaqui Pass Road (S3) into Borrego Springs.

TAXI TRAVEL

Yellow Cab of the Desert serves the entire Coachella Valley. The fare is $2.50 to enter a cab and about $3 per mile.

TRAIN TRAVEL

The Amtrak Sunset Limited, which runs between Florida and Los Angeles, stops in Palm Springs.

Train Contact Amtrak ☎ 800/872–7245 ⊕ www.amtrakcalifornia.com.

HEALTH AND SAFETY

Never travel alone in the desert. Let someone know your trip route, destination, and estimated time and date of return. Before setting out, make sure your vehicle is in good condition. Stay on main roads, and watch out for horses and range cattle.

Drink at least a gallon of water a day (three gallons if you're hiking or otherwise exerting yourself). Dress in layered clothing and wear comfortable, sturdy shoes and a hat. Keep snacks, sunscreen, and a first-aid kit on hand. If you suddenly have a headache or feel dizzy or nauseous, you could be suffering from dehydration. Get out of the sun immediately and drink plenty of water. Dampen your clothing to lower your body temperature.

Do not enter mine tunnels or shafts. Avoid canyons during rainstorms. Never place your hands or feet where you can't see them: Rattlesnakes, scorpions, and black widow spiders may be hiding there.

TOURS

Art in Public Places. Several self-guided tours cover the works in Palm Desert's 150-piece Art in Public Places collection. Each tour is walkable or drivable. Maps and information about guided tours (one Saturday each month) are available at the city's visitor center and online. ⊠ Palm Desert Visitor Center, 73-470 El Paseo, Suite F-7, Palm Desert ☎ 760/568–1441 ⊕ www.palm-desert.org/arts-culture/public-art ▣ Free.

Best of the Best Tours. One of the valley's largest outfits leads tours into Andreas Canyon, along the celebrity circuit, or to view windmills up close. ☎ 760/320–1365 ⊕ www.thebestofthebesttours.com ▣ From $40.

Desert Adventures. This outfit's two- to four-hour jeep or van tours explore the San Andreas Fault, local craft breweries, celebrity homes, and gay history. Tours may also go off-road through Joshua Tree National Park. The groups are small and the guides are knowledgeable. Departures are from Palm Springs and La Quinta; hotel pickups are available. ☎ 760/324–5337 ⊕ www.red-jeep.com ▣ From $79.

Trail Discovery Hiking Guides. For more than two decades, this outfit has been guiding hikers of all abilities through the desert canyons of the Palm Springs area. New tours include sections of the Pacific Crest Trail and Whitewater Canyon Preserve and an overnight trip to Joshua Tree. ☎ 760/413–1575 ⊕ www.palmspringshiking.com ▣ From $75.

Palm Springs Tours. Dive into celebrity history or the inner reaches of Joshua Tree with this longtime local operator. ☎ 800/409–3174 ⊕ www.palmspringstours.net ▣ From $100.

The green revolution is proudly on display in many parts of the Palm Springs area.

RESTAURANTS

During the season, restaurants can be busy, as many locals and visitors dine out every night, and some for every meal. An influx of talented chefs has expanded the dining possibilities of a formerly staid scene. The meat-and-potatoes crowd still has plenty of options, but you'll also find fresh seafood superbly prepared and contemporary Californian, Asian, Indian, and vegetarian cuisine, and Mexican food abounds. Most restaurants have early-evening happy hours, with discounted drinks and small-plate menus. Restaurants that remain open in July and August frequently discount deeply; others close in July and August or offer limited service.

HOTELS

In general you can find the widest choice of lodgings in Palm Springs, from tiny bed-and-breakfasts and chain motels to business and resort hotels. Massive resort properties predominate in down-valley communities, such as Palm Desert and Rancho Mirage. You can stay in the desert for as little as $90 or spend more than $1,000 a night. Rates vary widely by season and expected occupancy—a $200 room midweek can jump in price to $450 on Saturday.

Hotel and resort prices are frequently 50% cheaper in summer and fall than in winter and early spring. From January through May prices soar, and lodgings book up far in advance. You should book well ahead for stays during events such as Modernism Week or the Coachella and Stagecoach music festivals.

Most resort hotels charge a daily fee of up to $35 that is not included in the room rate; be sure to ask about extra fees when you book. Many hotels are pet-friendly and offer special services, though these also come with additional fees. Small boutique hotels and bed-and-breakfasts have plenty of character and are popular with hipsters and artsy types; discounts are sometimes given for extended stays. Casino hotels often offer good deals on lodging. Take care, though, when considering budget lodgings; other than reliable chains, they may not be up to par. *Hotel reviews have been shortened. For full information, visit Fodors.com.*

WHAT IT COSTS				
	$	$$	$$$	$$$$
Restaurants	under $16	$16–$22	$23–$30	over $30
Hotels	under $120	$120–$175	$176–$250	over $250

Restaurant prices are the average cost of a main course at dinner or, if dinner is not served, at lunch. Hotel prices are the lowest cost of a standard double room in high season.

NIGHTLIFE

Desert nightlife is concentrated and abundant in Palm Springs, where there are many straight and gay bars and clubs, as well as hotel bars and lively pool parties. Arts festivals occur on a regular basis, especially in winter and spring. *Palm Springs Life* magazine (⊕ *www.palmspringslife.com*), available at hotels and visitor centers, has nightlife listings, as does the *Desert Sun* newspaper (⊕ *www.mydesert.com*).

PALM SPRINGS

A tourist destination since the late 19th century, Palm Springs evolved into an ideal hideaway for early Hollywood celebrities who slipped into town to play tennis, lounge poolside, attend a party or two, and, unless things got out of hand, remain beyond the reach of gossip columnists. But the place really blossomed in the 1930s after actors Charlie Farrell and Ralph Bellamy bought 200 acres of land for $30 an acre and opened the Palm Springs Racquet Club, which soon listed Ginger Rogers, Humphrey Bogart, and Clark Gable among its members.

Today's Palm Springs is embracing its glory days. Owners of resorts, bed-and-breakfasts, and galleries have renovated midcentury modern buildings, luring a new crop of celebs and high-powered executives. LGBT travelers, twentysomethings, and families also sojourn here. Pleasantly touristy Palm Canyon Drive is packed with alfresco restaurants, many with views of the bustling sidewalk, along with indoor cafés and semi-chic shops. Farther west is the Uptown Design District, the area's shopping and dining destination. Continuing east on Palm Canyon Drive just outside downtown lie resorts and boutique hotels that host lively pool parties and house exclusive dining establishments and trendy bars.

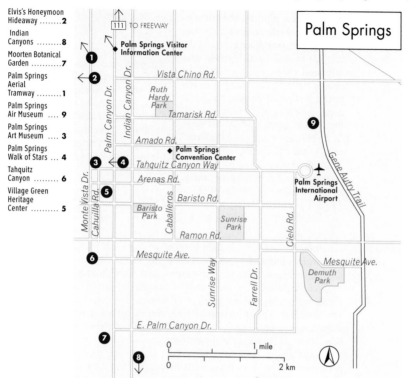

Palm Springs

GETTING HERE AND AROUND

Palm Springs is 90 miles southeast of Los Angeles on Interstate 10. Most visitors arrive in the Palm Springs area by car from the Los Angeles or San Diego area via this freeway, which intersects with Highway 111 north of Palm Springs. Tahquitz Canyon Way marks the division between north and south on major streets (e.g., North and South Palm Canyon Drive).

ESSENTIALS

Visitor Information Greater Palm Springs Convention and Visitors Bureau ✉ *Visitor Center, 70-100 Hwy. 111, at Via Florencia, Rancho Mirage* ☎ *760/770-9000, 800/967–3767* ⊕ *www.palmspringsoasis.com* ⊙ *Weekdays 8:30–5.* **Palm Springs Visitor Information Center** ✉ *2901 N. Palm Canyon Dr., Palm Springs* ☎ *760/778–8418, 800/347–7746* ⊕ *www.palm-springs.org* ⊙ *Daily 9–5.*

EXPLORING

TOP ATTRACTIONS

Elvis's Honeymoon Hideaway. The hideaway where the King of rock 'n' roll and his young bride, Priscilla, lived during the first year of their marriage perches on a hilltop abutting the San Jacinto Mountains. A stunning example of local midcentury modern architecture, the house is rich in Elvis lore, photos, and furnishings. Docents describe the fabulous parties that took place here and the celebrities and local legends who attended them. Built in 1962 by one of Palm Spring's largest developers, Robert Alexander, the house consists of four perfect circles, each set on a different level. At the time, *Look* magazine described the structure as the "house of tomorrow," and indeed many of its features are standard in the homes of today. ✉ *1350 Ladera Circle* ☎ *760/322–1192* ⊕ *www.elvishoneymoon.com* ✉ *$30 weekdays, $35 weekends and holidays* ☉ *Tours daily at 11, 1, and 3:30, by appointment.*

FAMILY
Fodor's Choice
★

Indian Canyons. The Indian Canyons are the ancestral home of the Agua Caliente, part of the Cahuilla people. You can see remnants of their ancient life, including rock art, house pits and foundations, irrigation ditches, bedrock mortars, pictographs, and stone houses and shelters atop cliff walls. Short, easy walks through the canyons reveal palm oases, waterfalls, and, in spring, wildflowers. Tree-shaded picnic areas are abundant. The attraction includes three canyons open for touring: Palm Canyon, noted for its stand of Washingtonia palms; Murray Canyon, home of Peninsula bighorn sheep and a herd of wild ponies; and Andreas Canyon, where a stand of fan palms contrasts with sharp rock formations. Ranger-led hikes to Palm and Andreas canyons are offered daily for an additional charge. The trading post at the entrance to Palm Canyon has hiking maps and refreshments, as well as Native American art, jewelry, and weavings. ✉ *38520 S. Palm Canyon Dr., south of Acanto Dr., Palm Springs* ☎ *760/323–6018* ⊕ *www.indian-canyons.com* ✉ *$9, ranger hikes $3* ☉ *Oct.–June, daily 8–5; July–Sept., Fri.–Sun. 8–5.*

FAMILY
Fodor's Choice
★

Palm Springs Aerial Tramway. A trip on the tramway provides a 360-degree view of the desert through the picture windows of rotating cars. The 2½-mile ascent through Chino Canyon, the steepest vertical cable ride in the United States, brings you to an elevation of 8,516 feet in less than 20 minutes. On clear days, which are common, the view stretches 75 miles—from the peak of Mt. San Gorgonio in the north to the Salton Sea in the southeast. Stepping out into the snow at the summit is a winter treat. At the top, a bit below the summit of Mt. San Jacinto, are several diversions. Mountain Station has an observation deck, two restaurants, a cocktail lounge, apparel and gift shops, picnic facilities, a small wildlife exhibit, and a theater that screens movies on the history of the tramway and the adjacent Mount San Jacinto State Park and Wilderness. Take advantage of free guided and self-guided nature walks through the state park, or if there's snow on the ground, rent skis, snowshoes, or snow tubes (inner tubes or similar contraptions for sliding down hills). The tramway generally closes for maintenance in mid-September. ■TIP→ **Ride-and-dine packages are available in late afternoon. The tram is a popular attraction; to avoid a**

two-hour or longer wait, arrive before the first car leaves in the morning. ⊠ *1 Tramway Rd., off N. Palm Canyon Dr. (Hwy. 111), Palm Springs* ☎ *888/515–8726* ⊕ *www.pstramway.com* ⌷ *$24.95, ride-and-dine package $36* ⊙ *Tramcars depart at least every 30 min from 10 am weekdays and 8 am weekends; last car up leaves at 8 pm, last car down leaves Mountain Station at 9:45 pm.*

FAMILY
Fodor's Choice
★

Palm Springs Air Museum. This museum's impressive collection of World War II aircraft includes a B-17 Flying Fortress bomber, a P-51 Mustang, a Lockheed P-38, and a Grumman TBF Avenger. Among the cool exhibits are model warships, a Pearl Harbor diorama, and a Grumman Goose into which kids can crawl. Photos, artifacts, memorabilia, and uniforms are also on display, and educational programs take place on Saturday. Flight demonstrations are scheduled regularly. Biplane rides are offered on Saturday. ⊠ *745 N. Gene Autry Trail, Palm Springs* ☎ *760/778–6262* ⊕ *palmspringsairmuseum.org* ⌷ *$16* ⊙ *Daily 10–5.*

Palm Springs Art Museum. This world-class art museum focuses on photography, modern architecture, and the traditional arts of the Americas. Galleries are bright and open. The permanent collection includes shimmering works in glass by Dale Chihuly, Ginny Ruffner, and William Morris. You'll also find handcrafted furniture by the late actor George Montgomery, midcentury modern architectural photos by Julius Shulman, enormous Native American baskets, and works by artists like Allen Houser, Arlo Namingha, and Fritz Scholder. The museum also displays significant works of 20th-century sculpture by Henry Moore, Marino Marina, Deborah Butterfield, and Mark Di Suvero. The Annenberg Theater presents plays, concerts, lectures, operas, and other cultural events. ⊠ *101 Museum Dr., off W. Tahquitz Canyon Dr., Palm Springs* ☎ *760/322–4800* ⊕ *www.psmuseum.org* ⌷ *$12.50, free Thurs. 4–8 during Villagefest* ⊙ *Tues., Wed., and Fri.–Sun. 10–5, Thurs. noon–8* ⊙ *Closed Mon.*

Tahquitz Canyon. On ranger-led tours of this secluded canyon on the Agua Caliente Reservation you can view a spectacular 60-foot waterfall, rock art, ancient irrigation systems, and native wildlife and plants. Tours are conducted several times daily; participants must be able to navigate 100 steep rock steps. (You can also take a self-guided tour of the 1.8-mile trail.) A visitor center at the canyon entrance screens a video, displays artifacts, and sells maps. ⊠ *500 W. Mesquite Ave., west of S. Palm Canyon Dr., Palm Springs* ☎ *760/416–7044* ⊕ *www. tahquitzcanyon.com* ⌷ *$12.50* ⊙ *Oct.–June, daily 7:30–5; July–Sept., Fri.–Sun. 7:30–5.*

WORTH NOTING

Backstreet Art District. Galleries and live-work studios just off East Canyon Drive showcase the works of highly acclaimed artists. Joseph and Leena Pilcher—he's a wood sculptor and she's a renowned mixed-media painter—and sculptor Bill Anson are among stars here. The gallery of the Russian-born painter Elena Bulatova displays her modernistic desert landscape paintings. ■TIP→ On the first Wednesday evening of the month, the galleries remain open until 9. ⊠ *2600 S. Cherokee Way, Palm Springs* ⊕ *www.backstreetartdistrict.com* ⌷ *Free* ⊙ *Most galleries closed Mon. and Tues.; check Galleries page on website.*

9

Espresso Cielo. The Coachella Valley's best coffee shop specializes in artfully crafted espresso drinks. There's also a fine selection of teas and pastries, which locals enjoy throughout the day in the sleek interior or outside on the covered patio. ✉ *245 S. Palm Canyon Dr., at W. Baristo Rd., Palm Springs* ☎ *760/327–9050* 🌐 *ps.espressocielo.com* 🕒 *Sun.–Wed. 7–4, Thurs.–Sat. 7–6.*

Moorten Botanical Garden. In the 1920s, Chester "Cactus Slim" Moorten and his wife, Patricia, opened this showpiece for desert plants—now numbering in the thousands—that include an ocotillo, a massive elephant tree, a boojum tree, and vine cacti. Their son Clark now operates the garden. **■TIP→ Take a stroll through the Cactarium to spot rare finds such as the welwitschia, which originated in the Namib Desert in southwestern Africa.** ✉ *1701 S. Palm Canyon Dr., Palm Springs* ☎ *760/327–6555* 🌐 *www.moortengarden.com* 🎟 *$4* 🕒 *Sept.–June, Thurs.–Tues. 10–4; July and Aug., Thurs.–Tues. 9–1.*

Palm Springs Walk of Stars. Along the walk, more than 300 bronze stars are embedded in the sidewalk (à la Hollywood Walk of Fame) to honor celebrities with a Palm Springs connection. Frank, Elvis, Marilyn, Dinah, Lucy, Ginger, Liz, and Liberace have all received their due. Those still around to walk the Walk and see their stars include Nancy Sinatra, Kathy Griffin, and Adam West. ✉ *Palm Canyon Dr., around Tahquitz Canyon Way, and Tahquitz Canyon Way, between Palm Canyon and Indian Canyon Drs., Palm Springs* ☎ *760/320–3129* 🌐 *www.palmsprings.com/stars.*

Village Green Heritage Center. Three small museums at the Village Green Heritage Center illustrate early life in Palm Springs. The **Agua Caliente Cultural Museum,** the centerpiece, traces the culture and history of the Cahuilla tribe with several exhibits. The **McCallum Adobe** holds the collection of the Palm Springs Historical Society. **Rudy's General Store Museum** is a re-creation of a 1930s general store. ✉ *219–221 S. Palm Canyon Dr., Palm Springs* ☎ *760/323–8297* 🎟 *Agua Caliente free, McCallum $2, Rudy's $1* 🕒 *Agua Caliente Sept.–May, Wed.–Sat. 10–5, Sun. noon–5; call for others.*

WHERE TO EAT

$$ MEDITERRANEAN

🍴 **Alicante.** This sidewalk café near the Plaza Theatre is one of the best people-watching spots in Palm Springs. Pasta, pizza, *pollo alla diavolo* (macadamia-crusted chicken breast), and veal scaloppini are among the hearty items on the lunch and dinner menus. A separate tapas menu contains tasty surprises: spicy chickpeas with Mediterranean chicken sausage, chorizo-stuffed calamari, pine nuts with honey topped with blue cheese, or spicy lime-drizzled shrimp. [$] *Average main: $20* ✉ *140 S. Palm Canyon Dr., at La Plaza, Palm Springs* ☎ *760/325–9464* 🌐 *www.alicanteps.com* ✍ *Reservations essential.*

$ AMERICAN Fodor's Choice ★

🍴 **Cheeky's.** The artisanal bacon bar and hangover-halting mimosas attract legions to this breakfast and lunch joint, but brioche French toast and other favorites also contribute to the epic wait on weekends. Huevos rancheros, the goat-cheese scramble, and other farm-centric dishes entice the foodie crowd. Lunch options include a gem salad with green goddess dressing, and there's a burger from grass-fed cows that's becoming a legend in these parts when topped with the famous house bacon. ■TIP➜ **The spacious outdoor patio is a fine perch when the weather's not too hot.** $ *Average main: $10* ✉ *622 N. Palm Canyon Dr., at E. Granvia Valmonte, Palm Springs* ☎ *760/327–7595* ⊕ *www. cheekysps.com* ⊗ *Closed Tues. No dinner.*

$$$

MODERN
AMERICAN

✕**Copley's on Palm Canyon.** Chef Manion Copley prepares innovative cuisine in a setting that's straight out of Hollywood—a hacienda once owned by Cary Grant. Dine in the clubby house or under the stars in the garden. Start with appetizers such as roasted beet and warm goat cheese salad or one of the Hawaiian ahi tacos. Tandoori-spiced salmon is a hit among entrées that also include sesame-seared tofu and lavender-and-parsley-crusted rack of lamb. ■TIP➜ **Save room for Copley's sweet and savory herb ice creams.** $ *Average main: $24* ✉ *621 N. Palm Canyon Dr., at E. Granvia Valmonte, Palm Springs* ☎ *760/327–9555* ⊕ *www. copleyspalmsprings.com* ⟁ *Reservations essential* ⊗ *No lunch.*

$$

MODERN
MEXICAN

✕**El Mirasol at Los Arboles.** Chef Felipe Castañeda owns two Mexican restaurants in Palm Springs—this one, part of Los Arboles Hotel, is outside on a charming patio set amid flower gardens and shaded by red umbrellas. Castañeda prepares classic combinations of tacos, tamales, and enchiladas, along with specialties such as double-cooked pork and *pollo en pipián* (chicken with a pre-Columbian sauce made of ground roasted pumpkin seeds and dry chilies). Vegetarian offerings include delicate spinach enchiladas and a fine chile relleno. ■TIP➜ **Castañeda's more casual café, also called El Mirasol, is 2 miles south at 140 East Palm Canyon Drive.** $ *Average main: $18* ✉ *266 Via Altamira, off N. Indian Canyon Dr., Palm Springs* ☎ *760/459–3136* ⊕ *www. elmirasolrestaurants.com.*

$$$$

STEAKHOUSE

✕**The Falls.** A mile-long martini menu lures a chic, moneyed crowd to this hot spot overlooking Palm Canyon Drive. Reserve well in advance for one of the outdoor balcony tables to get the best view. The restaurant specializes in dry aged beef, but you can also get seafood and chops, and there are vegetarian choices. Steaks and chops are prepared your way with a selection of sides that includes mac and cheese, roasted potatoes, and steamed asparagus with hollandaise sauce. Go early for the nightly happy hour (between 4 and 6:30), when items on the bar menu are half price—or hang around late to catch the action at the Martini Dome bar. $ *Average main: $38* ✉ *155 S. Palm Canyon Dr., near W. Arenas Rd., Palm Springs* ☎ *760/416–8664* ⊕ *thefallsprimesteakhouse. com* ⟁ *Reservations essential* ⊗ *No lunch.*

$$$$

FRENCH

✕**Le Vallauris.** A longtime favorite that occupies the historic Roberson House, Le Vallauris is popular with ladies who lunch, all of whom get a hug from the maître d'. The menu changes daily, and each day it's handwritten on a white board. Lunch entrées might include perfectly rare tuna Niçoise salad, or grilled whitefish with Dijon mustard sauce. Dinner might bring a sublime smoked salmon, sautéed calves' liver, roasted quail with orange sauce, or rack of lamb. There are also weekly prix-fixe menus, with and without wine, for lunch and dinner. The restaurant has a lovely tree-shaded garden. On cool winter evenings, request a table by the fireplace. $ *Average main: $35* ✉ *385 W. Tahquitz Canyon*

9

Way, west of Palm Canyon Dr., Palm Springs ☎ *760/325–5059* ⊕ *www.levallauris.com* ⌕ *Reservations essential* ☉ *Closed July and Aug.*

$$ ✕ **Matchbox Vintage Pizza Bistro.** The name says pizza, but this bistro
ITALIAN also serves interesting salads topped with grilled tuna, and a selec-
FAMILY tion of sandwiches like crab cakes on a toasted brioche. Main courses include bacon-wrapped scallops, macaroni and cheese, a hearty pork chop, and fish-and-chips. The pizzas are made just about any way you'd like, including vegetarian, and are topped with everything from figs to pepperoni. On the second-floor overlooking the action on Palm Canyon Drive, this is a great place to go for cocktails and small plates. ■TIP➔ Kids love the balls of pizza dough the servers dole out. $ *Average main: $22* ✉ *155 S. Palm Canyon Dr., near W. Arenas Rd., Palm Springs* ☎ *760/778–6000* ⊕ *www.matchboxpalmsprings.com* ☉ *No lunch Mon. and Tues.*

$$$$ ✕ **Purple Palm.** The hottest tables in Palm Springs are those that surround
MODERN the pool at the Colony Palms Hotel, where the hip and elite pay homage
AMERICAN to Purple Gang mobster Al Wertheimer, who reportedly built the hotel in the mid-1930s. Now it's a casual, convivial place where you can dine alfresco surrounded by a tropical garden. The dinner menu is heavy on seafood, such as bouillabaisse and roasted barramundi; you can also shuck oysters, crab legs, and prawns. The impressive wine list roams the globe. The restaurant is also open for breakfast, lunch, and dinner. ■TIP➔ The ladies' room features a fabulous black-and-white image of a very young Paul Newman. $ *Average main: $31* ✉ *572 N. Indian Canyon Dr., at E. Granvia Valmonte, Palm Springs* ☎ *800/557–2187* ⊕ *www.colonypalmshotel.com* ⌕ *Reservations essential.*

$$$$ ✕ **Spencer's Restaurant.** The swank dining space inside the Palm Springs
MODERN Tennis Club Resort occupies a historic midcentury modern structure,
AMERICAN but the cuisine of chef Eric Wadlund, a local star with a national rep-utation, is the main attraction. Crab cakes, kung pao calamari, and crispy flash-fried oysters are favorite starters. Filet mignon topped with a Gorgonzola-sage sauce, rack of lamb, and crispy-skin Lake Superior whitefish, are among the crowd-pleasing entrées. Desserts can be hit or miss, though the banana-cream pie in a martini glass is a delight-ful way to end a meal. Spencer's serves breakfast, lunch, and dinner. You can dine inside or on the pet-friendly patio under a massive ficus tree that's strung with lights. $ *Average main: $35* ✉ *701 W. Baristo Rd., Palm Springs* ☎ *760/327–3446* ⊕ *www.spencersrestaurant.com* ⌕ *Reservations essential.*

$$$$ ✕ **Tinto.** Jose Garces, a winner on the Food Network's *Iron Chef America*
BASQUE show and the recipient of a James Beard Foundation award, concocts delightfully exotic tapas at his Basque-inspired wine bar in the Saguaro Hotel. The inventive small plates include bacon-wrapped Coachella dates with almonds and pearl onions in a Valdeón cheese fondue, *jamón ibérico de bellota* (cured Spanish ham made from acorn-fed pigs), and Spanish octopus with potato confit, smoked paprika, and lemon. The chef's tast-ing menu (from $65 per person) is available with wine pairing ($40). Tinto is a fun place with closely spaced tables; dinner becomes a party as the Spanish guitarist plays to the crowd. $ *Average main: $65* ✉ *1800*

E. Palm Canyon Dr., at S. Sunshine Way, Palm Springs ☎ *760/323–1711* 🌐 *palmsprings.tintorestaurant.com* ✍ *Reservations essential.*

$$ MODERN AMERICAN 🍴 **Trio.** The owners of this high-energy Uptown Design District restaurant claim that it's "where Palm Springs eats," and it certainly seems so on nights when the lines run deep near the front door. The menu includes home-style staples such as Yankee pot roast, crawfish pie, and other dishes, along with veggie burgers and other vegetarian and gluten-free items. Eat outside or inside, where colorful works by local artists hang on the walls. Save room for inventive desserts, among them the pumpkin bread pudding. [$] *Average main: $19* ✉ *707 N. Palm Canyon Dr., Palm Springs* ☎ *760/864–8746* 🌐 *www.triopalmsprings.com* ✍ *Reservations essential.*

$$$ INTERNATIONAL 🍴 **The Tropicale.** Tucked onto a side-street corner, the Tropicale is a mid-century–style watering hole with a contemporary vibe. The bar and main dining room hold cozy leather booths, and flowers and water features brighten the outdoor area. The menu spans the globe with small and large plates, from the miso-glazed salmon rice bowl, to the grilled Idaho trout with aioli sauce, to filet mignon with Zinfandel sauce. [$] *Average main: $28* ✉ *330 E. Amado Rd., at N. Calle Encilia, Palm Springs* ☎ *760/866–1952* 🌐 *www.thetropicale.com* ✍ *Reservations essential* ⏲ *No lunch.*

$ AMERICAN FAMILY Fodor's Choice ★ 🍴 **Tyler's Burgers.** Families, singles, and couples head to Tyler's for simple lunch fare that appeals to carnivores and vegetarians alike. Expect mid-20th-century America's greatest hits: heaping burgers, stacks of fries, root beer floats, milk shakes. The sandwiches lure the first-time customers, but everyone comes back for the cole slaw, made in-house and well worth a try. On weekends, be prepared to wait with the masses. ■ **TIP→ Bring cash: this old-school joint doesn't accept credit cards.** [$] *Average main: $6* ✉ *149 S. Indian Canyon Dr., at La Plaza, Palm Springs* ☎ *760/325–2990* 🌐 *tylersburgers.com* 💳 *No credit cards* ⏲ *Closed Sun. late May–mid-Feb.*

$$$ AMERICAN 🍴 **Workshop Kitchen + Bar.** Chef Michael Beckman's Uptown Design District hot spot pairs high-quality California cuisine with creative cocktails in a sleek, almost utilitarian, setting. The outdoor patio lures the oversize sunglasses Sunday brunch crowd, who slurp Cava mimosas and artisanal cocktails. Inside, the sleek concrete booths are topped with black leather cushions. The dinner menu changes with the seasons, but might feature a brussels sprouts salad, whole chicken (ideal for sharing), or pan-roasted scallops atop squash slaw. Deep-pocketed diners will appreciate Beckman's artistry, though be advised that portions are small—three scallops for $36? [$] *Average main: $30* ✉ *800 N. Palm Canyon Dr., at E. Tamarisk Rd., Palm Springs* ☎ *760/459–3451* 🌐 *workshoppalmsprings.com* ✍ *Reservations essential* ⏲ *No lunch Mon.–Sat.*

WHERE TO STAY

$$$ RESORT 🏨 **Ace Hotel and Swim Club.** With the hotel's vintage feel and hippie-chic decor, it would be no surprise to find the Grateful Dead playing in the bar as guests gather around cozy communal fire pits enjoying the feel-good vibe. **Pros:** Amigo Room has late-night dining; poolside

stargazing deck; Sunday DJ scene at the pool. **Cons:** party atmosphere not for everyone; limited amenities; casual staff and service. [$] *Rooms from: $180* ✉ *701 E. Palm Canyon Dr., Palm Springs* ☎ *760/325–9900* 🌐 *www.acehotel.com/palmsprings* 🛏 *180 rooms, 8 suites* 🍴 *No meals.*

$ HOTEL 🏨 **Alcazar Palm Springs.** Amid an area known as the Movie Colony, Alcazar embodies the desert's popular midcentury modern design style; the ample, blazing-white guestrooms here wrap around a sparkling pool. **Pros:** walking distance of downtown; parking on-site; bikes available. **Cons:** limited service; wall air-conditioners; resort fee. [$] *Rooms from: $119* ✉ *622 N. Indian Canyon Dr., Palm Springs* ☎ *760/318–9850* 🌐 *www.alcazarpalmsprings.com* 🛏 *34 rooms* 🍴 *No meals.*

TRIBAL WEALTH

The Agua Caliente Band of Cahuilla Indians owns nearly half the land in the Palm Springs area. Wanting to encourage the railroad to bring their trains through the desert, Congress granted half the land to the railroad and the other half to the Native Americans. The Cahuilla were granted all the even-numbered one-square-mile sections—but they were unable to develop the land for years due to litigation. The resulting patchwork of developed and vacant land can still be seen today, though the Cahuilla are making up for lost time by opening new hotels and casinos.

$$$$ RESORT 🏨 **Avalon Hotel Palm Springs.** A visit to the Avalon, formerly the Viceroy, is like entering a tableau of bright white and yellow, reminiscent of a sun-filled desert day. **Pros:** poolside cabanas; complimentary fitness classes; celebrity clientele; dog-friendly. **Cons:** popular wedding site. [$] *Rooms from: $400* ✉ *415 S. Belardo Rd., Palm Springs* ☎ *844/328–2566* 🌐 *www.avalonpalmsprings.com* 🛏 *67 rooms, 12 villas* 🍴 *No meals.*

$ B&B/INN 🏨 **Casa Cody.** The service is personal and gracious at this historic bed-and-breakfast near the Palm Springs Art Museum; spacious studios and one- and two-bedroom suites hold Santa Fe–style rustic furnishings. **Pros:** family-size digs; friendly ambience; good value. **Cons:** old buildings; limited amenities. [$] *Rooms from: $99* ✉ *175 S. Cahuilla Rd., Palm Springs* ☎ *760/320–9346, 800/231–2639* 🌐 *www.casacody.com* 🛏 *18 rooms, 8 suites, 1 cottage* 🍴 *Breakfast.*

$$$ HOTEL 🏨 **Colony Palms Hotel.** This hotel has been a hip place to stay since the 1930s, when gangster Al Wertheimer built it to front his casino, bar, and brothel. **Pros:** glam with a swagger; attentive staff; all that history. **Cons:** high noise level outside; not for families with young children. [$] *Rooms from: $229* ✉ *572 N. Indian Canyon Dr., Palm Springs* ☎ *760/969–1800, 800/577–2187* 🌐 *www.colonypalmshotel.com* 🛏 *43 rooms, 3 suites, 8 casitas* 🍴 *No meals.*

$$ B&B/INN 🏨 **East Canyon Hotel & Spa.** The vibe is social and the rooms are spacious at this classy resort whose gracious hosts serve a primarily gay clientele. **Pros:** elegant but laid-back feel; attentive service; complimentary poolside cocktails. **Cons:** some guests might find the decor too masculine. [$] *Rooms from: $169* ✉ *288 E. Camino Monte Vista, Palm Springs* ☎ *760/320–1928, 877/324–6835* 🌐 *www.eastcanyonps.com* 🛏 *15 rooms, 1 suite* 🍴 *Breakfast.*

$$ HOTEL Fodor's Choice ★ **Hotel California.** Expect homey accommodations for all budgets at this delightful hotel that's decked out in rustic Mexican furniture. **Pros:** comfortable design; friendly hosts; free limo service in the evenings. **Cons:** away from downtown. [$] *Rooms from: $159* ✉ *424 E. Palm Canyon Dr., Palm Springs* ☎ *760/322–8855* 🌐 *www.palmspringshotelcalifornia.com* 🛏 *7 rooms, 7 suites* 🍴 *No meals.*

$$$ B&B/INN Fodor's Choice ★ **Korakia Pensione.** The painter Gordon Coutts, best known for desert landscapes, constructed this Moroccan villa in 1924 as an artist's studio, and these days creative types gather in the main house and the adjacent Mediterranean-style villa to soak up the spirit of that era. **Pros:** design-minded decor; international vibe; complimentary breakfast; yoga on weekends. **Cons:** might not appeal to those who prefer standard resorts; no TVs or phones in rooms. [$] *Rooms from: $179* ✉ *257 S. Patencio Rd., Palm Springs* ☎ *760/864–6411* 🌐 *www.korakia.com* 🛏 *11 rooms, 9 suites, 8 rental units* 🍴 *No meals.*

$$ B&B/INN **La Maison.** Offering all the comforts of home, this small bed-and-breakfast contains large rooms that surround the terra-cotta–tiled and very comfortable pool area, where you can spend quiet time soaking up the sun or taking a dip. **Pros:** restaurants nearby; quiet; genial hosts. **Cons:** on busy Highway 111; rooms open directly onto pool deck. [$] *Rooms from: $169* ✉ *1600 E. Palm Canyon Dr., Palm Springs* ☎ *760/325–1600* 🌐 *www.lamaisonpalmsprings.com* 🛏 *13 rooms* 🍴 *Breakfast.*

$$ B&B/INN **Movie Colony Hotel.** Designed in 1935 by Albert Frey, this intimate hotel evokes midcentury minimalist ambience; its gleaming white, two-story buildings, flanked with balconies and porthole windows, bring to mind a luxury yacht. **Pros:** architectural icon; happy hour; cruiser bikes. **Cons:** close quarters; off the beaten path; staff not available 24 hours. [$] *Rooms from: $169* ✉ *726 N. Indian Canyon Dr., Palm Springs* ☎ *760/320–6340, 888/953–5700* 🌐 *www.moviecolonyhotel.com* 🛏 *13 rooms, 3 suites* 🍴 *Breakfast.*

$$ B&B/INN Fodor's Choice ★ **Orbit In Hotel.** The architectural style of this hip inn on a quiet backstreet dates back to the late 1940s and '50s—nearly flat roofs, wide overhangs, glass everywhere—and the period feel continues inside. **Pros:** saltwater pool; in-room spa services; Orbitini cocktail hour. **Cons:** best for couples; style not to everyone's taste; staff not available 24 hours. [$] *Rooms from: $159* ✉ *562 W. Arenas Rd., Palm Springs* ☎ *760/323–3585, 877/996–7248* 🌐 *www.orbitin.com* 🛏 *9 rooms* 🍴 *Breakfast.*

$$$$ RESORT Fodor's Choice ★ **The Parker Palm Springs.** A cacophony of color and over-the-top contemporary art assembled by New York City–based designer Jonathan Adler mixes well with the brilliant desert garden, two pools, fire pits, and expansive spa of this hip hotel that attracts a stylish, worldly clientele. **Pros:** fun in the sun; celebrity clientele; on-site Palm Springs Yacht Club Spa; design-centric. **Cons:** pricey drinks and wine; a bit of a drive from downtown; resort fee ($30). [$] *Rooms from: $325* ✉ *4200 E. Palm Canyon Dr., Palm Springs* ☎ *760/770–5000, 800/543–4300* 🌐 *www.theparkerpalmsprings.com* 🛏 *131 rooms, 13 suites* 🍴 *No meals.*

$$$$ RESORT **Riviera Resort & Spa.** A party place built in 1958 and renovated in 2008, the Riviera attracts young, well-heeled, bikini-clad guests who hang out around the pool by day and the Bikini Bar by night. **Pros:**

personal beachy fire pits throughout the property; hip vibe; excellent spa. **Cons:** high noise level outdoors; party atmosphere; location at north end of Palm Springs. [$] *Rooms from: $300* ✉ *1600 N. Indian Canyon Dr., Palm Springs* ☎ *760/327–8311* 🌐 *www.psriviera.com* 🛏 *406 rooms, 43 suites* 🍴 *No meals.*

$$$$ RESORT FAMILY **Smoke Tree Ranch.** A world apart from Palm Springs' pulsating urban village, the area's most under-the-radar resort complex occupies 400 pristine desert acres surrounded by mountains and unspoiled vistas. **Pros:** priceless privacy; simple luxury; recreational choices include horseback riding, lawn bowling, hiking, golfing, a playground, and jogging. **Cons:** no glitz; limited entertainment options; family atmosphere not for everyone. [$] *Rooms from: $400* ✉ *1850 Smoke Tree La., Palm Springs* ☎ *760/327–1221, 800/787–3922* 🌐 *www.smoketreeranch.com* 🛏 *49 cottages, includes 18 suites* ⏲ *Closed Apr.–late Oct.* 🍴 *Multiple meal plans.*

$$ B&B/INN **Sparrows Lodge.** Rustic earthiness meets haute design at the adult-centered Sparrows, just off Palm Springs' main drag. **Pros:** unique design that draws an urban clientele; intimate property; private patios; relaxed ambience. **Cons:** rooms feel a little dark; some guests might deem them charmless. [$] *Rooms from: $149* ✉ *1330 E. Palm Canyon Dr., Palm Springs* ☎ *760/327–2300* 🌐 *www.sparrowslodge.com* 🛏 *18 rooms, 2 suites* 🍴 *Breakfast.*

$$$$ B&B/INN **Willows Historic Palm Springs Inn.** An opulent Mediterranean-style mansion built in the 1920s to host the rich and famous, this luxurious hillside bed-and-breakfast has gleaming hardwood and slate floors, stone fireplaces, frescoed ceilings, hand-painted tiles, iron balconies, antiques throughout, and a 50-foot waterfall that splashes into a pool outside the dining room. **Pros:** luxurious; sublime service; expansive breakfast. **Cons:** closed from June to September; pricey. [$] *Rooms from: $295* ✉ *412 W. Tahquitz Canyon Way, Palm Springs* ☎ *760/320–0771, 800/966–9597* 🌐 *www.thewillowspalmsprings.com* 🛏 *8 rooms* 🍴 *Breakfast.*

NIGHTLIFE AND PERFORMING ARTS

NIGHTLIFE

BARS AND PUBS

Bar. The mural-covered exterior of Bar makes it clear that this hot spot caters to the L.A. crowd. Pulled-pork sandwiches and flatbreads pair well with whiskey drinks and artisan-beer cocktails such as gin, lemon, honey, and pale ale. DJs spin music throughout the week. ■ **TIP→ On most nights there's no cover charge.** ✉ *340 N. Palm Canyon Dr., near E. Amado Rd., Palm Springs* ☎ *760/537–7337* 🌐 *barwastaken.com.*

Hair of the Dog English Pub. Drawing a young crowd that likes to tip back English ales and ciders, this bar is lively and popular. ✉ *238 N. Palm Canyon Dr., near E. Amado Rd., Palm Springs* ☎ *760/323–9890* .

Fodor's Choice ★ **Village Pub.** With live entertainment, DJs, and friendly service, this popular bar caters to a young crowd. Happy hour is fantastic. On weekend days there is live music as well. ✉ *266 S. Palm Canyon Dr., at Baristo Rd., Palm Springs* ☎ *760/323–3265* 🌐 *www.palmspringsvillagepub.com.*

CASINOS

Casino Morongo. A 20-minute drive west of Palm Springs, this casino has 2,000 slot machines, video games, the Vibe nightclub, plus Vegas-style shows. ✉ *49500 Seminole Dr., off I–10, Cabazon* ☎ *800/252–4499, 951/849–3080* ⊕ *www.morongocasinoresort.com.*

Spa Resort Casino. This resort holds 1,000 slot machines, blackjack tables, a high-limit room, four restaurants, two bars, and the Cascade Lounge for entertainment. ✉ *401 E. Amado Rd., at N. Calle Encilia, Palm Springs* ☎ *888/999–1995* ⊕ *www.sparesortcasino.com.*

DANCE CLUBS

Zelda's Nightclub. At this Palm Springs institution the high-energy DJs, dancing, and drinking are still going strong and the dance floor is still thumping with Latin, hip-hop, and sounds from the '60s, '70s, and '80s. Zelda's offers bottle service in the VIP Sky Box. ✉ *611 S. Palm Canyon Dr., at E. Camino Parocela, Palm Springs* ☎ *760/325–2375* ⊕ *www. zeldasnightclub.com* ⊘ *Closed Mon.*

GAY AND LESBIAN

The Dinah. In late March, when the world's finest female golfers hit the links for the Annual LPGA Kraft Nabisco Championship in Rancho Mirage, thousands of lesbians converge on Palm Springs for a four-day party popularly known as The Dinah. ⇨ *Kraft Nabisco Championship in Rancho Mirage.* ✉ *Palm Springs* ☎ *888/923–4624* ⊕ *www. clubskirts.com.*

Hunter's Video Bar. Drawing a young gay and straight crowd, Hunter's is a club-scene mainstay. ✉ *302 E. Arenas Rd., at Calle Encilia, Palm Springs* ☎ *760/323–0700* ⊕ *huntersnightclubs.com.*

Fodor's Choice ★ **Toucans Tiki Lounge.** A friendly place with a tropical–rain forest setting, Toucans serves festive drinks and hosts live entertainment and theme nights. On Sunday it seems as though all of Palm Springs has turned out for drag night. ✉ *2100 N. Palm Canyon Dr., at W. Via Escuela, Palm Springs* ☎ *760/416–7584* ⊕ *www.toucanstikilounge.com.*

White Party Palm Springs. Held during spring break, the White Party draws tens of thousands of gay men from around the world for four days of parties and events. ✉ *Palm Springs* ⊕ *jeffreysanker.com.*

THEMED ENTERTAINMENT

Fodor's Choice ★ **Ace Hotel and Swim Club.** Events are held here nearly every night, including film screenings, full-moon parties, live concerts, and DJ music with dancing. Many are free, and some are family-friendly. The poolside venue makes most events fun and casual. ✉ *701 E. Palm Canyon Dr., at Calle Palo Fierro, Palm Springs* ☎ *760/325–9900* ⊕ *www.acehotel.com.*

PERFORMING ARTS

ARTS CENTERS

Annenberg Theater. Broadway shows, operas, lectures, Sunday-afternoon chamber concerts, and other events take place at the Palm Springs Art Museum's handsome theater. ✉ *101 N. Museum Dr., at W. Tahquitz Canyon Way, Palm Springs* ☎ *760/325–4490* ⊕ *www.psmuseum.org.*

9

Palm Springs is a golfer's paradise: the area is home to more than 125 courses.

FESTIVALS

Modernism Week. Each February the desert communities celebrate the work of the architects and designers who created the Palm Springs "look" in the 1940s, 1950s, and 1960s. Described these days as mid-century modern—you'll also see the term "desert modernism" used—these structures were created by Albert Frey, Richard Neutra, William F. Cody, John Lautner, and other notables. The 11-day event features lectures, a modernism show, films, vintage car and trailer shows, galas, and home and garden tours. ⊠ *Palm Springs* ☎ *760/322–2502* ⊕ *www. modernismweek.com.*

FILM

Palm Springs International Film Festival. In mid-January this 12-day festival brings stars and nearly 200 feature films from several dozen countries, plus panel discussions, short films, and documentaries, to various venues. ⊠ *Palm Springs* ☎ *760/322–2930, 800/898–7256* ⊕ *www. psfilmfest.org.*

SPORTS AND THE OUTDOORS

BIKING

Many hotels and resorts have bicycles available for guest use.

Big Wheel Tours. Rent cruisers, performance road bikes, and mountain bikes from this agency that also offers road tours to La Quinta Loop, Joshua Tree National Park, and the San Andreas Fault. Off-road tours are available, too. The company will pick up and deliver bikes to your hotel and supply you with maps. The guides are first-rate. ⊠ *Palm Springs* 🕾 *760/779–1837* ⊕ *www.bwbtours.com* 🖅 *$95.*

GOLF

Golf a la Carte. Golf specialist David McKeating advises golfers about the best courses for them, then secures tee times at the area's most exclusive greens. ⊠ *Palm Springs* 🕾 *877/887–6900* ⊕ *palmspringsgolf.com.*

Indian Canyons Golf Resort. Operated by the Aqua Caliente tribe, this spot at the base of the mountains includes two 18-hole courses open to the public. In the 1960s this was *the* place to play for celebrities visiting the desert, including presidents Dwight Eisenhower and Lyndon Johnson. The North Course, designed by William F. Bell, is adjacent to property once owned by Walt Disney and has six water hazards. The South Course, redesigned in 2004 by Casey O'Callaghan with input from the LPGA player Amy Alcott, has four ponds, hundreds of palm trees, and five par-5 holes. ⊠ *1097 E. Murray Canyon Dr., at Kings Rd. E, Palm Springs* 🕾 *760/833–8700* ⊕ *www.indiancanyonsgolf.com* 🖅 *North Course, $89; South Course, $109* 🏌 *North Course: 18 holes, 6943 yards, par 72; South Course: 18 holes, 6582 yards, par 72.*

Tahquitz Creek Golf Resort. Conveniently located in Palm Springs near Cathedral City, the resort has two popular courses open to the public. Golfers have been walking the Legend course for more than 50 years—the back nine here are challenging, particularly the greens. The newer Resort course, designed by Ted Robinson, offers sweeping mountain views and scenic waterscapes. ⊠ *1885 Golf Club Dr., at 34th Ave., Palm Springs* 🕾 *760/328–1005* ⊕ *www.tahquitzgolfresort.com* 🖅 *Legend Course, $69; Resort Course, $79* 🏌 *Legend Course: 18 holes, 6815 yards, par 71; Resort Course: 18 holes, 6705 yards, par 72.*

HORSEBACK RIDING

Smoke Tree Stables. At these stables you can explore desert canyons on horseback like the earliest pioneers. One-hour tours depart on the hour and take riders along the base of the Santa Rosa Mountains. Two-hour tours depart four times daily for trips that take in the Aqua Caliente Indian Reservation. ⊠ *2500 Toledo Ave., Palm Springs* 🕾 *760/327–1372* ⊕ *www.smoketreestables.com* 🖅 *$50 for 1 hr, $100 for 2 hrs* ☉ *Daily 8–4.*

SHOPPING

BOUTIQUES

Fodor's Choice
★

Raymond | Lawrence. This colorful concept gallery showcases paintings and sculptures, clothing and accessories, and home-decor and other items by contemporary artists. You can also shop for hand creams from The Body Deli, underwear from Chelsea Lane, and photo prints by William Dey. This gallery has a satellite location in the Ritz-Carlton, Rancho Mirage. ⊠ *830 N. Palm Canyon Dr., Palm Springs* 🕾 *760/322–3344* ⊕ *www.raymond-lawrence.com.*

Trina Turk Boutique. Celebrity designer Trina Turk's empire takes up a city block in the Uptown Design District. Turk, famous for men's and women's outdoor wear, reached out to another celebrity, interior designer

Kelly Wearstler, to create adjoining clothing and residential boutiques. Lively fabrics brighten up the many chairs and couches for sale at the residential store, which also carries bowls, paintings, and other fun pieces to spiff up your home. ⊠ *891 N. Palm Canyon Dr., Palm Springs* ☏ *760/416–2856* ⊕ *www.trinaturk.com.*

OUTLET MALLS

Fodor's Choice
★ **Desert Hills Premium Outlets.** About 20 miles west of Palm Springs lies one of California's largest outlet centers. The 180 brand-name discount fashion shops include Jimmy Choo, Neiman Marcus, Versace, Saint Laurent Paris, J. Crew, Armani, Gucci, and Prada. Home cooks: don't miss the Le Creuset outlet. ⊠ *48400 Seminole Rd., off I–10, Cabazon* ☏ *951/849–6641* ⊕ *www.premiumoutlets.com.*

SHOPPING DISTRICTS

Fodor's Choice
★ **Uptown Heritage Galleries & Antiques District.** A loose-knit collection of consignment and secondhand shops, galleries, and lively restaurants extends north of Palm Springs' main shopping area. The theme here is decidedly retro. Many businesses sell midcentury modern furniture and decorator items, and others carry clothing and estate jewelry. One spot definitely worth a peek is **Shag, the Store,** the gallery of fine-art painter Josh Agle. For antique costume jewelry check out **Dazzles.** If you dig the mid-mod aesthetic, breeze through the furnishings at **Towne Palm Springs.** ⊠ *N. Palm Canyon Dr., between Amado Rd. and Vista Chino, Palm Springs* ⊕ *www.palmcanyondrive.org.*

SPAS

Fodor's Choice
★ **Estrella Spa at the Avalon Hotel Palm Springs.** This spa earns top honors each year for the indoor/outdoor experience it offers with a touch of Old Hollywood ambience. You can enjoy your massage in one of four outdoor treatment canopies in a garden, experience a Vichy shower massage, get a facial or pedicure fireside, or receive a full-body treatment with lemon crystals in the spa's Ice Haus. Whatever the treatment, you can use the spa's private pool, take a break for lunch, and order a drink from the hotel's bar. ⊠ *415 S. Belardo Rd., Palm Springs* ☏ *760/320–4117* ⊕ *www.avalonpalmsprings.com* ☞ *Salon Services: body wrap, facials, specialty massages, prenatal massages, outdoor treatments, wellness classes. $135, 60-min massage; $370, spa package.*

Feel Good Spa at the Ace Hotel. Despite its funkiness, this 21st-century indie hangout takes its services very seriously. The estheticians use local clay, mud, and sea algae, and you can make your own scrub from organic botanicals such as lotions and essential oils. There are a variety of settings where you can get a rubdown, but the most relaxing is poolside. ⊠ *701 E. Palm Canyon Dr., Palm Springs* ☏ *760/866–6188* ⊕ *www.acehotel.com/palmsprings* ☞ *Fully equipped gym. Services: wraps and scrubs, massage, facials, paraffin, manicures, pedicures, in-room treatments, salon, wellness classes, yoga, water aerobics. $95, 60-min massage.*

Palm Springs Yacht Club. It's all about fun at the Parker Palm Springs hotel's yacht club. Guests receive a complimentary cocktail while lounging in a poolside tent. Before spa treatments, you can play video games, use an iPod Touch, or select a book from the spa's library. When you're ready to crash, wander over to the outdoor café for a burger and Pimm's. Treatments might feature local clay or stones. There's a fine Thai massage as well. ⊠ *4200 E. Palm Canyon Dr., Palm Springs* ☎ *760/321–4606* ⊕ *www.theparkerpalmsprings.com/spa* ☞ *Sauna, steam room, indoor pool, library. Services: scrubs and wraps, massage, facials, manicures, pedicures, waxing, salon, fitness center with Cybex equipment, dining and cocktails. $150, 60-min massage.*

Spa Resort Casino. Taking the waters at this resort is an indulgent pleasure. You can spend a full day enjoying a five-step, wet-and-dry treatment that includes a mineral bath with water from the original spring, steam, sauna, and eucalyptus inhalation. The program allows you to take fitness classes and use the gym and, for an extra charge, add massage or body treatments. Bring a swimsuit for sunbathing and swimming in the pool. ⊠ *100 N. Indian Canyon Dr., at E. Tahquitz Canyon Way, Palm Springs* ☎ *760/778–1772* ⊕ *www.sparesortcasino.com* ☞ *Hair and nail salon, sauna, steam room, hot tubs, relaxation room, lounge. Gym with: cardiovascular equipment, free weights, circuit machines. Services: body wraps and scrubs, facials, massage, waxing, salon services. $115, 50-min massage; $285, spa package.*

THE DESERT RESORTS

The term *desert resorts* refers to the communities along or just off Highway 111—Cathedral City, Rancho Mirage, Palm Desert, Indian Wells, Indio, and La Quinta—along with Desert Hot Springs *(⇨ see Along Twentynine Palms Highway)*, which is north of Palm Springs off Highway 62 and Interstate 10.

CATHEDRAL CITY

2 miles southeast of Palm Springs.

Cathedral City is more residential than tourist-oriented, with large and small malls everywhere, but the city has several good restaurants and entertainment venues with moderate prices.

GETTING HERE AND AROUND

Cathedral City lies due east of the Palm Springs International Airport. Main streets north and south are Landau and Date Palm; west to east are Ramon Road, Dinah Shore, and Highway 111.

EXPLORING

FAMILY **Boomers Palm Springs.** At this mini-theme park you can play mini golf, drive bumper boats, climb a rock wall, drive a go-kart, swing in the batting cages, test your skills in an arcade, and play video games. ⊠ *67-700 E. Palm Canyon Dr., at Cree Rd.* ☎ *760/770–7522* ⊕ *www. boomerspalmsprings.com* ⊠ *$9.99 per activity, $29.99 day passes* ⊗ *Mon.–Thurs. 12–8, Fri. 12–11, Sat. 11–11, Sun. 11–8.*

Pickford Salon at the Mary Pickford Theater. This small museum inside a multiplex celebrates silent film star Mary Pickford. Items on display include her 1976 Oscar for contributions to the film industry, a gown she wore in the 1927 film *Dorothy Vernon of Haddon Hall,*

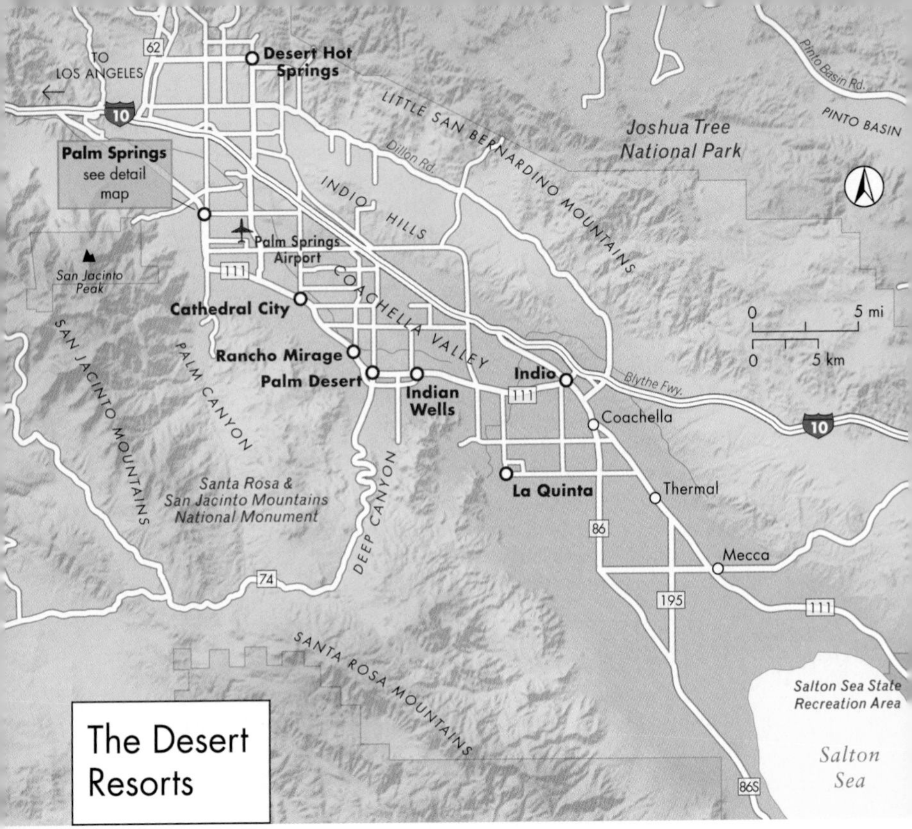

and dinnerware from Pickfair, the Beverly Hills mansion she shared with actor Douglas Fairbanks. Pickford herself produced one of the film bios the Salon screens. ✉ *Mary Pickford Theater, 36-850 Pickfair St., at Buddy Rogers Ave.* ☎ *760/328–7100* 🎟 *Free* 🕒 *Daily 10:30 am–midnight.*

WHERE TO EAT

$$$ BISTRO 🍴 **Cello's.** A favorite of locals and critics, this art-laden café in a strip mall serves modern twists on classics such as the crab Napoleon and onion soup fondue as starters, and liver and onions, chicken caprese, and eggplant Parmesan as main courses. The owner, Bonnie Barley, is as friendly as they come. In 2015 she added the gourmet grocery Cello's Pantry in Rancho Mirage to her empire. [$] *Average main: $30* ✉ *35-943 Date Palm Dr., at Gerald Ford Dr.* ☎ *760/328–5353* 🌐 *www.cellosbistro.com* ✍ *Reservations essential* 🕒 *Closed for 5 wks around Aug.–mid-Sept.*

$$ ITALIAN 🍴 **Trilussa.** Locals gather for delicious food, big drinks, and a friendly welcome. The bar is busy during happy hour, after which diners drift to their nicely spaced tables indoors and out. The long menu changes daily, but staples include antipasti, homemade pasta bathing in rich sauces, expertly crafted pizza, risotto, veal, and fish. All come with an Italian

accent. [$] *Average main: $20* ✉ *68718 E. Palm Canyon Dr., at Monty Hall Dr.* ☎ *760/328–2300* ✍ *Reservations essential.*

RANCHO MIRAGE

4 miles southeast of Cathedral City.

The rich and famous of Rancho Mirage live in beautiful estates and patronize elegant resorts and expensive restaurants. Although many mansions here are concealed behind the walls of gated communities and country clubs, the grandest of them all, Sunnylands, the Annenberg residence, is open to the public as a museum and public garden.

The city's golf courses host many high-profile tournaments. You'll find some of the desert's fanciest resorts in Rancho Mirage, and plenty of peace and quiet. For those truly needing to take things down a notch further, the Betty Ford Center, the famous drug-and-alcohol rehab center, is also here.

GETTING HERE AND AROUND

Due east of Cathedral City, Rancho Mirage stretches from Ramon Road on the north to the hills south of Highway 111. The western border is Da Vall Drive, the eastern one Monterey Avenue. Major east–west cross streets are Frank Sinatra Drive and Country Club Drive. Most shopping and dining spots are on Highway 111.

EXPLORING

The Annenberg Retreat at Sunnylands. The stunning 25,000-square-foot winter home and retreat of the late Ambassador Walter H. and Leonore Annenberg opened to the public in 2012. You can spend a whole day enjoying the 9 glorious acres of gardens, or take a guided 90-minute tour of the residence (reservations essential), a striking midcentury modern edifice designed by A. Quincy Jones. Floor-to-ceiling windows frame views of the gardens and Mount San Jacinto, and the expansive rooms hold furnishings from the 1960s and later, along with impressionist art (some original, some replicas). The history made here is as captivating as the surroundings. Eight U.S. presidents—from Dwight Eisenhower to Barack Obama—and their First Ladies have visited Sunnylands; Ronald and Nancy Reagan were frequent guests. Britain's Queen Elizabeth and Prince Philip also relaxed here, as did Princess Grace of Monaco and Japanese Prime Minister Toshiki Kaifu. Photos, art, letters, journals, and mementos provide insights into some of the history that unfolded here. ✉ *37-977 Bob Hope Dr., south of Gerald Ford Dr.* ☎ *760/202–2222* 🌐 *www.sunnylands.org* 🎟 *Tours $40, tickets available online 2 wks in advance; visitor center and gardens free* 🕒 *Sept.–June, Thurs.–Sun. 9–4.*

FAMILY **Children's Discovery Museum of the Desert.** With instructive hands-on exhibits, this museum contains a miniature rock-climbing area, a magnetic sculpture wall, make-it-and-take-it-apart projects, a rope maze, and an area for toddlers. Kids can paint a VW Bug, work as chefs in the museum's pizza parlor, and build pies out of arts-and-crafts supplies. There's also a racetrack for which kids can assemble their own cars. The museum recently updated its store, making this one of the best spots to pick up educational gifts. ✉ *71-701 Gerald Ford Dr., at Bob Hope Dr.* ☎ *760/321–0602* 🌐 *www.cdmod.org* 🎟 *$8* 🕒 *Jan.–Apr., daily 10–5; May–Dec., Tues.–Sun. 10–5.*

WHERE TO EAT AND STAY

$ MEXICAN FAMILY 🍴 **Las Casuelas Nuevas.** Hundreds of artifacts from Guadalajara, Mexico, lend festive charm to this casual restaurant, which has an expansive garden patio. Tamales and shellfish dishes are among the specialties—expect more traditional Mexican fare, rather than California-influenced creations. The tequila menu lists dozens of aged and reserve selections, served by the shot or folded into a margarita. There's live entertainment on weekends. Another location, Las Casuelas Terraza, does business in downtown Palm Springs. [$] *Average main: $14* ✉ *70-050 Hwy. 111* ☎ *760/328–8844* 🌐 *www.lascasuelasnuevas.com* ✍ *Reservations essential.*

$$$ MEDITERRANEAN 🍴 **Catalan.** At this restaurant known for its beautifully prepared Mediterranean cuisine you can dine inside or under the stars in the atrium. The service here is attentive, and the menu roams the Riviera and beyond. Entrées include seared scallops with wild mushrooms, pan-roasted rainbow trout, and the house special, paella with clams, calamari chorizo, and Laughing Bird shrimp. [$] *Average main: $25* ✉ *70026 Hwy. 111* ☎ *760/770–9508* 🌐 *www.catalanrestaurant.com* ✍ *Reservations essential.*

$ RESORT 🏨 **Agua Caliente Casino, Resort & Spa.** As in Las Vegas, the Agua Caliente casino is in the lobby, but once you get into the spacious, beautifully appointed rooms of the resort, all of the cacophony at the entrance is forgotten. **Pros:** gorgeous; access to high-rollers room offered for $25; value priced. **Cons:** casino ambience; not appropriate for kids. [$] *Rooms from: $109* ✉ *32-250 Bob Hope Dr.* ☎ *888/999–1995* 🌐 *www.hotwatercasino.com* 🛏 *340 rooms, 26 suites* 🍽 *No meals.*

$$$$ RESORT FAMILY 🏨 **Omni Rancho Las Palmas Resort & Spa.** The desert's most family-friendly resort, this large venue holds Splashtopia, a huge water-play zone. **Pros:** family-friendly; trails for hiking and jogging; nightly entertainment. **Cons:** second-floor rooms accessed by very steep stairs; golf course surrounds rooms; resort hosts conventions. [$] *Rooms from: $259* ✉ *41-000 Bob Hope Dr.* ☎ *760/568–2727, 866/423–1195* 🌐 *www.rancholaspalmas.com* 🛏 *422 rooms, 22 suites* 🍽 *No meals.*

$$$$ RESORT FAMILY Fodor's Choice ★ 🏨 **The Ritz Carlton, Rancho Mirage.** On a hilltop perch overlooking the Coachella Valley, this luxury resort spoils guests with exemplary service and comforts that a include a trio of pools, access to the desert's finest spa, and private outdoor sitting areas for each room. **Pros:** outstanding service; cheery staff; comfortable environment; spa that's a destination in itself. **Cons:** hefty rates; some airport noise; resort and parking fees ($30 each). [$] *Rooms from: $549* ✉ *68900 Frank Sinatra Dr.* ☎ *760/321–8282* 🌐 *www.ritzcarlton.com* 🛏 *228 rooms, 16 suites* 🍽 *No meals.*

$$$$ RESORT FAMILY 🏨 **The Westin Mission Hills Golf Resort & Spa.** A sprawling resort on 360 acres, the Westin is surrounded by fairways, putting greens, and time-share accommodations; rooms, in two-story buildings surrounding patios and fountains, have a stylish Arts-and-Crafts look with sleek mahogany furnishings accented with sand-color upholstery and crisp

white linens. **Pros:** gorgeous grounds; first-class golf facilities; daily activity program for kids. **Cons:** rooms are spread out. [$] *Rooms from: $369* ✉ *71333 Dinah Shore Dr.* ☎ *760/328–5955, 800/937–8461* 🌐 *www.westinmissionhills.com* 🛏 *512 rooms, 40 suites* 🍴 *No meals.*

NIGHTLIFE

Agua Caliente Casino. This elegant and surprisingly quiet casino contains 1,400 slot machines, 39 table games, an 18-table poker room, a high-limit room, a no-smoking area, and six restaurants. The Show, the resort's concert theater, presents acts such as Liza Minnelli, ZZ Top, Styx, and Ray Romano, as well as live sporting events. ✉ *32-250 Bob Hope Dr., at E. Ramon Rd.* ☎ *760/321–2000* 🌐 *www.hotwatercasino.com.*

SPORTS AND THE OUTDOORS

GOLF

Kraft Nabisco Championship. The best female golfers in the world compete in this championship held in late March or early April. ✉ *Mission Hills Country Club* ☎ *760/324–4546* 🌐 *www.kncgolf.com.*

Fodor's Choice ★ **Westin Mission Hills Resort Golf Club.** Golfers at the Westin Mission Hills have two courses to choose from, the Pete Dye and the Gary Player Signature. They're both great, with amazing mountain views and wide fairways, but if you've only got time to play one, choose the Dye. The club is a member of the Troon Golf Institute, and has several teaching facilities, including the Westin Mission Hills Resort Golf Academy and the *Golf Digest* Golf School. ■ **TIP→ The resort's Best Available Rate program guarantees golfers (with a few conditions) the best Internet rate possible.** ✉ *71333 Dinah Shore Dr.* ☎ *760/328–3198* 🌐 *www.playmissionhills.com* 🎫 *Gary Player, $74–$180; Pete Dye, $114–$172* ⛳ *Pete Dye Resort: 18 holes, 5525 yards, par 72; Gary Player Signature: 18 holes, 5327 yards, par 70.*

SHOPPING

MALL

The River at Rancho Mirage. This shopping-dining-entertainment complex holds 20 high-end shops, including the So-Cal darling Diane's Beachwear, all fronting a faux river with cascading waterfalls. Also here are a 12-screen cinema, an outdoor amphitheater, and many restaurants including Fleming's Prime Steakhouse and Babe's Bar-B-Que and Brewery. ✉ *71-800 Hwy. 111, at Bob Hope Dr.* ☎ *760/341–2711* 🌐 *www.theriveratranchomirage.com.*

SPAS

Fodor's Choice ★ **The Ritz Carlton Spa, Rancho Mirage.** Two hundred–plus suspended quartz crystals guard the entrance of the desert's premier spa. With private men's and women's areas, a co-ed outdoor soaking tub, food service, and some of the kindest spa technicians around, guests can expect pampering par excellence. The signature Spirit of the Mountains treatment, which starts with a full-body exfoliation, includes a massage, and ends with a body wrap and a scalp massage with lavender oil, is a blissful experience. The gym, equipped with state-of-the-art machines, is open 24/7. Private trainers are available to guide your workout, and there are wellness classes. ✉ *68900 Frank Sinatra Dr.* ☎ *760/321–8282* 🌐 *www.ritzcarlton.*

9

com ☞ Fully equipped gym. Salon. Services: body wraps, body scrubs, facials, mineral baths, specialty massages, outdoor treatments, waxing, wellness classes. $165, 50-min massage; $330, signature package.

The Spa at Mission Hills. The emphasis at this spa in a quiet corner of the Weston Mission Hills Resort is on comfort rather than glitz and glamour. The treatments the attentive therapists administer incorporate coconut milk, lemon balm, mint, thyme, red algae, hydrating honey, and other botanicals. Yoga and other wellness classes are also available. ⊠ *71333 Dinah Shore Dr.* ☎ *760/770–2134* ⊕ *www.spaatmissionhills. com ☞ Steam room. Gym with: machines, cardio, pool. Services: rubs and scrubs, massage, facials, nail services. $125, 50-min massage.*

PALM DESERT

2 miles southeast of Rancho Mirage.

Palm Desert is a thriving retail and business community with popular restaurants, private and public golf courses, and premium shopping along the main commercial drag, El Paseo. Each October, the Palm Desert Golf Cart Parade launches "the season" with a procession of 80 golf carts decked out as floats buzzing up and down El Paseo. The town's stellar sight to see is the Living Desert complex.

GETTING HERE AND AROUND

Palm Desert stretches from north of Interstate 10 to the hills south of Highway 111. West–east cross streets north to south are Frank Sinatra Drive, Country Club Drive (lined on both sides with gated golfing communities), and Fred Waring Drive. Monterey Avenue marks the western boundary, and Washington Street forms the eastern edge.

EXPLORING

Fodor's Choice ★ **El Paseo.** West of and parallel to Highway 111, this mile-long Mediterranean-style shopper's paradise is lined with fountains, courtyards, and upscale boutiques. You'll find shoe salons, jewelry stores, children's shops, two-dozen restaurants, and nearly as many art galleries. The strip is a pleasant place to stroll, window-shop, people-watch, and exercise your credit cards. ■TIP➔ **In winter and spring a free bright-yellow shuttle ferries shoppers from store to store and back to their cars.** ⊠ *Between Monterey and Portola Aves.* ☎ *877/735–7273* ⊕ *www. elpaseo.com.*

FAMILY
Fodor's Choice ★ **Living Desert.** Come eyeball-to-eyeball with wolves, coyotes, mountain lions, cheetahs, bighorn sheep, golden eagles, warthogs, and owls at the 1,800-acre Living Desert. Easy-to-challenging scenic trails traverse desert terrain populated with plants of the Mojave, Colorado, and Sonoran deserts. In recent years the park has expanded its vision to include Australia and Africa. At the 3-acre African WaTuTu village you'll find a traditional marketplace as well as camels, leopards, hyenas, and other African animals. Children can pet African domesticated animals, including goats and guinea fowl, in a "petting kraal." Gecko Gulch is a children's playground with crawl-through underground tunnels, climb-on snake sculptures, a carousel, and a Discovery Center that holds ancient Pleistocene animal bones. Elsewhere, a small enclosure contains

butterflies and hummingbirds, and a cool model train travels through miniatures of historic California towns. ■ **TIP→ A garden center sells native desert flora, much of which is unavailable elsewhere.** ✉ *47900 Portola Ave., south from Hwy. 111* ☎ *760/346–5694* 🌐 *www.livingdesert.org* 🎟 *$17.25* ⏲ *June–Sept., daily 8–1:30; Oct.–May, daily 9–5.*

GREEN PALM DESERT

The City of Palm Desert's ambitious plan to reduce energy consumption includes incentives to install efficient pool pumps, air-conditioners, refrigeration, and lighting. The city has banned drive-through restaurants and made golf carts legal on city streets.

Palm Springs Art Museum in Palm Desert. A satellite branch of the Palm Springs Art Museum, this gallery space tucked into a desert garden at the west entrance to El Paseo exhibits cutting-edge works by contemporary sculptors and painters. ■ **TIP→ The on-site restaurant Cuistot (☎ *760/340–1000,* 🌐 *www.cuistotrestaurant.com*) is a splendid, if pricey, place to enjoy French cuisine.** ✉ *72-567 Hwy. 111* ☎ *760/346–5600* 🌐 *www.psmuseum.org/palm-desert* 🎟 *Free* ⏲ *Tues.–Thurs. and weekends 10–5, Fri. noon–8.*

Santa Rosa and San Jacinto Mountains National Monument. Administered by the U.S. Bureau of Land Management, this monument protects Peninsula bighorn sheep and other wildlife on 280,000 acres of desert habitat. Stop by the visitor center for an introduction to the site and information about the natural history of the desert. A landscaped garden displays native plants and frames an impressive view. The well-informed staffers can recommend hiking trails that show off the beauties of the desert. ■ **TIP→ Free guided hikes are offered on Thursday and Saturday.** ✉ *51-500 Hwy. 74* ☎ *760/862–9984* 🌐 *www.ca.blm.gov/palmsprings* 🎟 *Free* ⏲ *Daily 9–4.*

WHERE TO EAT AND STAY

$ AMERICAN Fodor's Choice ★

🍴 **Bouchee.** This La Quinta favorite disappeared abruptly a few years back, leaving devotees perplexed until it reemerged in a sparkling new space in a Palm Desert strip mall. Order the salads or gorgeous sandwiches—the salmon salad is to die for—at the counter and then retire to the French-inspired dining area. There's some shaded outdoor seating as well. ■ **TIP→ Bouchee closes at 6:30 on weekdays and 5 on weekends; arrive before then to buy wines, cheeses, and premade foods for dinner to go.** [$] *Average main: $8* ✉ *72-785 Hwy. 111* ☎ *442/666–3296* ⏲ *No dinner.*

$ ECLECTIC Fodor's Choice ★

🍴 **Clementine's Gourmet Marketplace and Cafe.** A favorite of families, lunching ladies, and couples enjoying an afternoon tryst, Clementine's presents an artful mix of Mediterranean flavors. Diners at the café perch at long wooden communal tables to tuck into baked egg Ficelle, lamb burgers, and other specialties, but this space's nerve center is the take-out counter and kitchen that brims with pre-made salads, boulangerie-style meats and cheeses, and decadent French-inspired pastries and desserts. A cocktail bar and dinner service add to the appeal. A small retail area sells aprons, glassware, and wines. Check the website to learn about evening events such as Italian-tapas dinners or the tastes

9

of Greece. $ *Average main: $15* ✉ *72990 El Paseo* ☎ *760/834–8814* ⊕ *www.clementineshop.com* ☾ *No dinner.*

$$$$ × **Pacifica Seafood.** Choice seafood, rooftop dining, and reduced prices
SEAFOOD at sunset draw locals and visitors to this busy restaurant on the second floor of the Gardens of El Paseo. Seafood that shines in dishes such as butter-poached Maine lobster tail, grilled Pacific swordfish, and barbecued sugar-spiced salmon arrives daily from San Diego; the menu also includes chicken, steaks, and meal-size salads. Preparations feature sauces such as orange-cumin glaze, Szechuan peppercorn butter, and green curry-coconut. The bar stocks 130 different vodkas. ■ **TIP→ Arrive between 3 and 5:30 to select from the lower-price sunset menu.** $ *Average main: $40* ✉ *73505 El Paseo* ☎ *760/674–8666* ⊕ *www. pacificaseafoodrestaurant.com* ⌕ *Reservations essential* ☾ *No lunch June–Aug.*

$$$$ ⊞ **Desert Springs J. W. Marriott Resort and Spa.** With a dramatic U-shape
RESORT design, this sprawling convention-oriented hotel is set on 450 land-
FAMILY scaped acres and wraps around the desert's largest private lake. **Pros:** gondola rides on the lake to restaurants; Kids' Club daily activities; popular lobby bar; wonderful spa. **Cons:** crowded in-season; high resort fee; extra charges; business-traveler vibe. $ *Rooms from: $449* ✉ *74-855 Country Club Dr.* ☎ *760/341–2211, 888/538–9459* ⊕ *www. desertspringsresort.com* ⇲ *833 rooms, 51 suites* ¶⊘ *No meals.*

PERFORMING ARTS

McCallum Theatre. The principal cultural venue in the desert, this theater hosts productions from fall through spring. *Fiddler on the Roof* has played here; Lily Tomlin, Willie Nelson, and Michael Feinstein have performed, and Joffrey Ballet dancers have pirouetted across the stage. ✉ *73-000 Fred Waring Dr.* ☎ *760/340–2787* ⊕ *www.mccallum theatre.com.*

SPORTS AND THE OUTDOORS

BALLOONING

Fantasy Balloon Flights. Sunrise excursions over the southern end of the Coachella Valley lift off at 6 am and take from 60 to 90 minutes; a traditional champagne toast follows the landing. Afternoon excursions are timed to touch down at sunset. ■ **TIP→ For a unique ballooning experience, book the vessel that's shaped like a bunch of bananas.** ☎ *760/568–0997* ⊕ *www.fantasyballoonflight.com* ⛁ *$195.*

BIKING

Big Wheel Bike Tours. This outfit delivers rental mountain, three-speed, and tandem bikes to area hotels. The company also conducts full- and half-day escorted on- and off-road bike tours. ☎ *760/779–1837* ⊕ *www.bwbtours.com* ⛁ *$95 per person.*

GOLF

Desert Willow Golf Resort. Praised for its environmentally smart design, this public golf resort planted water-thrifty turf grasses and doesn't use pesticides. The Mountain View course has four configurations; Firecliff is tournament quality with five configurations. A public facility, Desert Willow is one of the country's top-rated golf courses. ✉ *38-995 Desert Willow Dr., off Country Club Dr.* ☎ *760/346–0015* ⊕ *www.*

desertwillow.com 🖥 *Mountain View and Firecliff from $55* 🎯 *Mountain View: 18 holes, 7079 yards, par 72; Firecliff: 18 holes, 7056 yards, par 72.*

INDIAN WELLS

5 miles east of Palm Desert.

For the most part a quiet and exclusive residential enclave, Indian Wells hosts major golf and tennis tournaments throughout the year, including the BNP Paribus Open tennis tournament. Three hotels share access to championship golf and tennis facilities, and there are several noteworthy resort spas and restaurants.

GETTING HERE AND AROUND

Indian Wells lies between Palm Desert and La Quinta, with most resorts, restaurants, and shopping set back from Highway 111.

WHERE TO EAT AND STAY

$$$ ✕ **Vue Grille and Bar at the Indian Wells Golf Resort.** This not-so-private
AMERICAN restaurant at the Indian Wells Golf Resort offers a glimpse of how the country-club set lives. The service is impeccable, and the outdoor tables provide views of mountain peaks that seem close enough to touch. Chef Cale Falk's focus is on farm-to-table cuisine, with kale and quinoa salads, diver scallops atop a yuzu puree, and a Jidori chicken breast hugged by cheesy polenta among the offerings. For less adventurous eaters, the flatbreads and burgers are quite tasty. $ *Average main: $28* ✉ *44-500 Indian Wells La.* ☎ *760/834–3800* ⊕ *www.vuegrilleandbar. com* 🍴 *Reservations essential.*

$$$$ 🏨 **Hyatt Grand Regency Indian Wells Resort.** This stark-white resort adja-
RESORT cent to the Golf Resort at Indian Wells is one of the grandest in the
FAMILY desert. **Pros:** spacious rooms; excellent business services; butler service
Fodor's Choice in some rooms; very pet friendly. **Cons:** big and impersonal; spread
★ out over 45 acres; noisy public areas. $ *Rooms from: $350* ✉ *44-600 Indian Wells La.* ☎ *760/341–1000, 800/552–4386* ⊕ *www.indianwells. hyatt.com* 🛏 *454 rooms, 26 suites, 40 villas* 🍴 *No meals.*

$$$ 🏨 **Miramonte Resort & Spa.** A warm bit of Tuscany against a backdrop of
RESORT the Santa Rosa Mountains characterizes the most intimate of the Indian Wells hotels. **Pros:** romantic intimacy; gorgeous gardens; daily wellness classes; one of the desert's best spas. **Cons:** adult-oriented; limited resort facilities on-site; rooms could use some refreshing. $ *Rooms from: $209* ✉ *45000 Indian Wells La.* ☎ *760/341–2200* ⊕ *www.miramonteresort. com* 🛏 *215 rooms* 🍴 *Some meals.*

$$$$ 🏨 **Renaissance Esmeralda Resort and Spa.** The centerpiece of this luxuri-
RESORT ous resort, adjacent to the Golf Resort at Indian Wells, is an eight-story
FAMILY atrium lobby, onto which most rooms open. **Pros:** balcony views; adjacent to golf-tennis complex; kids' club; bicycles available. **Cons:** higher noise level in rooms surrounding pool; somewhat impersonal ambience. $ *Rooms from: $289* ✉ *44-400 Indian Wells La.* ☎ *760/773–4444* ⊕ *www.renaissanceesmeralda.com* 🛏 *538 rooms, 22 suites* 🍴 *No meals.*

9

SPORTS AND THE OUTDOORS

GOLF

Fodor'sChoice **Golf Resort at Indian Wells.** Adjacent to the Hyatt Regency Indian Wells,
★ this complex includes the Celebrity Course, designed by Clive Clark
and twice a host to the PGA's Skins game (lots of water here), and the
Players Course, designed by John Fought to incorporate views of the
surrounding mountain ranges. Both courses consistently rank among
the best public courses in California. ■TIP→ It's a good idea to book
tee times well in advance, up to 60 days. ⊠ 44-500 Indian Wells La.
☎ 760/346–4653 ⊕ www.indianwellsgolfresort.com ⊠ Both courses
$69–$219 ⅄. Celebrity Course: 18 holes, 7050 yards, par 72; Players
Course: 18 holes, 7376 yards, par 72.

TENNIS

BNP Paribas Open. Drawing 200 of the world's top players, this tennis
tournament takes place at Indian Wells Tennis Garden for two weeks in
March. Various ticket plans are available, with some packages including stays at the adjoining Hyatt Regency Indian Wells or Renaissance
Esmeralda resorts. ⊠ 78200 Miles Ave. ☎ 800/999–1585 ⊕ www.
bnpparibasopen.com.

SPA

Fodor'sChoice **The Well.** A luxurious 12,000-square-foot facility, The Well draws on
★ international treatments and ingredients to indulge the senses and relax
the body. Treatments such as wine baths, water massages, table yoga,
and the ancient Ayurvedic Shirodhara experience, which involves liq-
uids poured over the forehead, are well worth the splurge. Diamond
facials and precious stone exfoliating scrubs may well restore the soul
in addition to the skin. ⊠ Miramonte Resort, 45-000 Indian Wells La.
☎ 866/843–9355 ⊕ www.miramonteresort.com ☉ Daily 9–8 ☞ Services: facials, nail care, solo and couple's massages, and scrubs, water,
and other body therapies. $125, 60-min massage.

LA QUINTA

4 miles south of Indian Wells.

The desert became a Hollywood hideout in the 1920s, when La Quinta
Hotel (now La Quinta Resort and Club) opened, introducing the
Coachella Valley's first golf course. Old Town La Quinta is a popular
attraction; the area holds dining spots, shops, and galleries.

GETTING HERE AND AROUND

Most of La Quinta lies south of Highway 111. The main drag through
town is Washington Street.

WHERE TO EAT AND STAY

$$$$ ✕ **Arnold Palmer's.** From the photos on the walls to the trophy-filled
AMERICAN display cases to the putting green for diners awaiting a table, Arnie's
essence infuses this restaurant. It's a big, clubby place where families
gather for birthdays and Sunday dinners, and the service is always
attentive. Among the well-crafted main courses are Arnie's homemade
meat loaf, double-cut pork chops, and the popular mac and cheese. The
wine list is top-notch, and there's entertainment most nights. At Arnie's

Pub the more limited menu focuses on comfort food. $ *Average main: $33* ⊠ *78164 Ave. 52, near Desert Club Dr.* ☎ *760/771–4653* ⊕ *www. arnoldpalmersrestaurant.com* ⌂ *Reservations essential.*

$$$$
BISTRO
Fodor'sChoice
★

✕ **Lavender Bistro.** This romantic bistro gives diners the impression they've been transported to southern France. The spacious outdoor atrium is decked out with flowers, fountains, and twinkling lights. Choices on the large menu include steamed mussels, a honey-brine pork chop, and nori and sesame seed crusted ahi. For dessert you can't go wrong with the baked apple tart with frangipane or the banana walnut brioche bread pudding. Dessert wines and cognacs are also available. $ *Average main: $32* ⊠ *78073 Calle Barcelona* ☎ *760/327–8311* ⊕ *www.lavenderbistro.com* ⌂ *Reservations essential.*

$$$$
RESORT
FAMILY

🏨 **La Quinta Resort and Club.** Opened in 1926 and now a member of the Waldorf-Astoria Collection, the desert's oldest resort is a lush green oasis set on 45 acres. **Pros:** individual swimming pools in some rooms; gorgeous gardens; pet and family friendly. **Cons:** a party atmosphere sometimes prevails; spotty housekeeping/maintenance. $ *Rooms from: $600* ⊠ *49499 Eisenhower Dr.* ☎ *760/564–4111, 800/598–3828* ⊕ *www.laquintaresort.com* ⇆ *562 rooms, 24 suites, 210 villas* ❍❙ *No meals.*

PERFORMING ARTS

La Quinta Arts Festival. More than 200 artists participate each March in a four-day juried show that's considered one of the best in the West. The event, held at La Quinta Civic Center, includes sculptures, paintings, watercolors, fiber art, and ceramics. ⊠ *78495 Calle Tampico* ☎ *760/564–1244* ⊕ *www.lqaf.com* ⊠ *$15; multiday ticket $20.*

SPORTS AND THE OUTDOORS
GOLF

Fodor'sChoice
★

PGA West. A world-class golf destination where Phil Mickelson and Jack Nicklaus play, this private/public facility includes five resort courses and four private ones. Courses meander through indigenous desert landscapes, water features, and bunkers. The Norman, Nick Tournament, and TPC Stadium courses are "shot-makers" courses made for pros. TPC highlights include its two lakes, "San Andreas Fault" bunker, and island green called "Alcatraz." The Norman course has tight fairways and small greens. ⊠ *49-499 Eisenhower Dr.* ☎ *760/564–5729 for tee times* ⊕ *www.pgawest.com* ⛳ *Mountain Course, $159–$229; Dunes, $119–$189; Greg Norman, $159–$229; TPC Stadium, $189–$269; Jack Nicklaus Tournament, $159–$229* ⛳ *Mountain Course: 18 holes, 6732 yards, par 72; Dunes: 18 holes, 6712 yards, par 72; Greg Norman: 18 holes, 7156 yards, par 72; TPC Stadium: 18 holes, 7300 yards, par 72; Jack Nicklaus Tournament: 18 holes, 7204 yards, par 72.*

SHOPPING
SPAS

Spa La Quinta. The gorgeous Spa La Quinta may be the grandest spa in the entire desert. At this huge stand-alone facility you'll find everything from massages to facials to salon services, plus a beautiful garden setting with a large fountain, flowers galore, and plenty of nooks where you can hide out and enjoy the sanctuary. There are four outdoor treatment spaces, showers, secluded soaking tubs, and a Jacuzzi with a waterfall. ■ **TIP→ Spa La Quinta has a Canine Suite where your dog can enjoy a massage. The canine services are also offered in-room.** ✉ *49499 Eisenhower Dr.* ☎ *760/777–4800* 🌐 *www.laquintaresort.com* ☞ *Fitness center with cardio and weight training machines. Services: aromatherapy, body wraps and scrubs, massage, skin care, waxing, salon services, water therapies. $165, 50-min massage; $195, 30-min HydraFacial.*

INDIO

5 miles east of Indian Wells.

Indio is the home of the date shake, which is exactly what it sounds like: an extremely thick milk shake made with dates. The city and surrounding countryside generate 95% of the dates grown and harvested in the United States. If you take a hot-air balloon ride, you will likely drift over the tops of date palm trees.

GETTING HERE AND AROUND

Indio is east of Indian Wells and north of La Quinta. Highway 111 runs right through Indio, and Interstate 10 skirts it to the north.

EXPLORING

FAMILY **Coachella Valley History Museum.** Learn about dates at this museum inside a former farmhouse. The exhibits here provide an intriguing glimpse into irrigation, harvesting, and other farming practices; a timeline and other displays chronicle how the agriculture industry emerged in the desert a century ago. ✉ *82616 Miles Ave.* ☎ *760/342–6651* 🌐 *www.cvhm.org* 🎫 *$10* 🕓 *Oct.–May, Thurs.–Sat. 10–4, Sun. 1–4.*

FAMILY **National Date Festival and Riverside County Fair.** Indio celebrates its raison d'être each February at its date festival and county fair. The mid-month festivities include an Arabian Nights pageant, camel and ostrich races, and exhibits of local dates, plus monster truck shows, a demolition derby, a nightly musical pageant, and a rodeo. ✉ *Riverside County Fairgrounds, 82-503 Hwy. 111* ☎ *800/811–3247, 760/863–8247* 🌐 *www.datefest.org* 🎫 *$9.*

Shields Date Garden and Café. Sample, select, and take home some of Shields's locally grown dates. Ten varieties are available, including the giant super-sweet royal medjools, along with specialty date products such as date crystals, stuffed dates, confections, and local honey. At the Shields Date Garden Café you can try an iconic date shake, dig into date pancakes, or go exotic with a date tamale. Breakfast and lunch are served daily. ✉ *80-225 Hwy. 111* ☎ *760/347–0996* 🌐 *www.shieldsdategarden.com* 🕓 *Store 9–5, café 7–2:30.*

WHERE TO EAT

$ SICILIAN 🍴 **Ciro's Ristorante and Pizzeria.** Serving pizza and pasta since the 1960s, this popular casual restaurant has a few unusual pies on the menu, including cashew with three cheeses. The decor is classic pizza joint, with checkered tablecloths and bentwood chairs. Daily pasta specials vary, but might include red- or white-clam sauce or scallops with parsley and red wine. [$] *Average main: $12* ✉ *81-963 Hwy. 111* ☎ *760/347–6503* 🌐 *www.cirosofindio.com* 🕓 *No lunch Sun.*

$$$ ✕**Jackalope Ranch.** It's worth the drive to Indio to sample flavors of the
AMERICAN Old West, 21st-century style. Inside a rambling 21,000-foot building,
holding a clutch of indoor/outdoor dining spaces, you may be seated
near an open kitchen, a bar, fountains, fireplaces, or waterworks (both
inside and out). Jackalope can be a busy, noisy place; ask for a quiet
corner if that's your pleasure. The large menu favors the West, featur-
ing grilled and barbecued fare of all sorts, spicy and savory sauces,
flavorful vegetables, and sumptuous desserts. Locals like the place,
especially the bar; but some urbanites complain that the quality of the
food doesn't match the setting. $ *Average main: $30* ✉ *80-400 Hwy.
111* ☎ *760/342–1999* ⊕ *www.thejackaloperanch.com* ⌧ *Reservations
essential.*

NIGHTLIFE AND PERFORMING ARTS
MUSIC FESTIVALS

Fodor's Choice **Coachella Valley Music and Arts Festival.** Among Southern California's big-
★ gest parties, the festival draws hundreds of thousands of rock music
fans to Indio each April for two weekends of live concerts. Headlin-
ers include acts such as Arcade Fire, Jack Johnson, Beck, Portishead,
Roger Waters, and Radiohead. Many attendees camp on-site, but to
give your ears a rest post-concert you might want to stay at a nearby
hotel. ■TIP➔ **The festival sells out before the lineup is announced, so
expect to pay big bucks if you haven't purchased tickets by late fall.**
✉ *Empire Polo Club, 81-800 Ave. 51* ⊕ *www.coachella.com.*

EN
ROUTE

Coachella Valley Preserve. For a glimpse of how the desert appeared
before development, head northeast from Palm Springs to this pre-
serve. It has a system of sand dunes and several palm oases that were
formed because the San Andreas Fault lines here allow water flowing
underground to rise to the surface. A mile-long walk along Thousand
Palms Oasis reveals pools supporting the tiny endangered desert pupfish
and more than 183 bird species. Families like the relatively flat trail that
is mostly shaded. The preserve has a visitor center, nature and eques-
trian trails, restrooms, and picnic facilities. Guided hikes are offered.
■TIP➔ **Be aware that it's exceptionally hot in summer here.** ✉ *29200
Thousand Palms Canyon Rd., Thousand Palms* ☎ *760/343–2733*
⊕ *www.coachellavalleypreserve.org* ⌧ *Free* ☉ *Visitor center mid-Oct.–
mid-Apr., daily 8–4; mid-Apr.–May and Sept.–mid-Oct., daily 8–noon.*

9

ALONG TWENTYNINE PALMS HIGHWAY

Designated a California Scenic Highway, the Twentynine Palms High-
way connects two of the three entrances to Joshua Tree National Park
and provides gorgeous high-desert views, especially in winter and spring
when you might find yourself driving beneath snowcapped peaks or
through a field of wildflowers. Park entrances are located at Joshua
Tree and Twentynine Palms. Yucca Valley and Twentynine Palms have
lodging and dining options, and other services. If you see any strange
artworks along the way, they might be created by artists associated with
the avant-garde High Desert Test Sites (⊕ *www.highdeserttestsites.com*).

DESERT HOT SPRINGS

9 miles north of Palm Springs.

Desert Hot Springs's famous hot mineral waters, thought by some to have curative powers, bubble up at temperatures of 90°F to 148°F and flow into the wells of more than 40 hotel spas.

GETTING HERE AND AROUND

Desert Hot Springs lies due north of Palm Springs. Take Gene Autry Trail north to Interstate 10, where the street name changes to Palm. Continue north to Pierson Boulevard, the town's center.

EXPLORING

Cabot's Pueblo Museum. Cabot Yerxa, the man who found the spring that made Desert Hot Springs famous, built a quirky four-story, 35-room pueblo between 1939 and his death in 1965. Now a museum run by the city of Desert Hot Springs—Yerxa was the town's first mayor—the Hopi-inspired adobe structure is filled with memorabilia of his time as a homesteader; his encounters with Hollywood celebrities at the nearby Bar-H Ranch; his expedition to the Alaskan gold rush; and many other events. The home, much of it crafted out of materials Yerxa recycled from the desert, can only be seen on hour-long tours. Outside, walk the grounds to a lookout with amazing desert views. ✉ *67-616 E. Desert View Ave., at Eliseo Rd.* ☎ *760/329–7610* 🌐 *www.cabotsmuseum.org* 🎟 *$11* 🕐 *Tues.–Sun. 9–4; tours 9:30, 10:30, 11:30, 1:30, 2:30.*

WHERE TO STAY

$$$ HOTEL 🏨 **The Spring.** Designed for those who want to detox, lose weight, or chill out in the mineral pools, The Spring delivers quiet and personal service atop a Desert Hot Springs hill. **Pros:** access to mineral pools 24 hours a day; complimentary continental breakfast; spa and lodging packages available. **Cons:** rooms lack character. [$] *Rooms from: $199* ✉ *12699 Reposo Way* ☎ *760/251–6700, 877/200–2110* 🌐 *www.the-spring.com* 🛏 *12 rooms* 🍴 *Breakfast.*

SHOPPING

SPAS

Fodor's Choice ★ **Two Bunch Palms.** This iconic retreat has long been a favorite with Los Angeles yogis for its peaceful, palm-shaded grounds and hot springs pools. Big changes occurred in 2014, with new rooms added and a fresh look for the existing ones. Guests can still purchase a day pass to soak in the grotto, attend yoga classes, lounge on the grounds, and enjoy a spa treatment or two. **■ TIP→ This is an adults-only, whispers-only destination.** ✉ *67-425 Two Bunch Palms Tr.* ☎ *760/329–8791* 🌐 *www.twobunchpalms.com* 🎟 *Day pass $25 weekdays, $40 weekends* 🕐 *Day use daily 10–6* ☞ *Services: facials, nail care, solo and couple's massages, breath work, water, and other therapies; treatments from $135, 60-min massage.*

YUCCA VALLEY

30 miles northeast of Palm Springs.

One of the high desert's fastest-growing cities, Yucca Valley is emerging as a bedroom community for people who work as far away as Ontario, 85 miles to the west. In this suburb you can shop for necessities, get your car serviced, grab coffee or purchase vintage furnishings, and chow down at fast-food outlets. Just up Pioneertown Road you'll find the most-talked-about dining establishment in the desert, Pappy and Harriet's, the famed performance venue that hosts big-name talent.

GETTING HERE AND AROUND

The drive to Yucca Valley on Highway 62/Twentynine Palms Highway passes through the Painted Hills and drops down into a valley. Take Pioneertown Road north to the Old West outpost.

EXPLORING

FAMILY **Hi-Desert Nature Museum.** Creatures that make their homes in Joshua Tree National Park are the focus here. A small live-animal display includes scorpions, snakes, ground squirrels, and chuckwallas (a type of lizard). You'll also find rocks, minerals, and fossils from the Paleozoic era and Native American artifacts. There's also a children's room and art exhibits. ✉ *Yucca Valley Community Center, 57116 Twentynine Palms Hwy.* ☎ *760/369–7212* 🌐 *hidesertnaturemuseum.org* 🎟 *Free* 🕐 *Thurs.–Sat. 10–5.*

Pioneertown. In 1946 Roy Rogers, Gene Autry, the Sons of the Pioneers (the music group for whom the town is named), and Russ Hayden built Pioneertown, an 1880s-style Wild West movie set complete with hitching posts, saloon, and an OK Corral. You can stroll past wooden and adobe storefronts and feel like you're back in the Old West. Or not: Pappy and Harriet's Pioneertown Palace, now the town's top draw, has evolved into a hip venue for indie and mainstream performers such as Dengue Fever, Neko Case, and Robert Plant. ✉ *53688 Pioneertown Rd., 4 miles north of Yucca Valley, Pioneertown* 🌐 *pappyandharriets.com.*

9

WHERE TO EAT AND STAY

$$$ AMERICAN FAMILY Fodor's Choice ★ 🍴 **Pappy & Harriet's Pioneertown Palace.** Smack in the middle of a Western-movie-set town is this Western-movie-set saloon where you can have dinner, relax over a drink at the bar, or check out some great indie and other bands—Leon Russell, Sonic Youth, the Get Up Kids, and Robert Plant have all played here, as have many Cali groups. The food ranges from Tex-Mex to Santa Maria–style barbecue to steak and burgers. No surprises, but plenty of fun. ■ TIP→ **Pappy & Harriet's may be in the middle of nowhere, but you'll need reservations for dinner on weekends, especially on Sunday night.** [$] *Average main: $24* ✉ *53688 Pioneertown Rd., Pioneertown* ☎ *760/365–5956* 🌐 *www.pappyandharriets.com* ✍ *Reservations essential* 🕐 *Closed Tues. and Wed.*

$ HOTEL 🏨 **Best Western Joshua Tree Hotel & Suites.** This hotel has spacious, nicely appointed rooms decorated in soft desert colors. **Pros:** convenient to Joshua Tree National Park; pleasant lounge; newly renovated pool and hot tub. **Cons:** on a busy highway; limited service. [$] *Rooms from: $100* ✉ *56525 Twentynine Palms Hwy.* ☎ *760/365–3555* 🌐 *www.bestwestern.com* 🛏 *95 rooms* 🍽 *Breakfast.*

$ RENTAL

🏨 **Rimrock Ranch Cabins.** The quiet beauty of the surrounding desert attracts Hollywood writers, artists, and musicians to circa-1940s housekeeping cabins, an Airstream trailer, and the newer Hatch House duplex. **Pros:** affordable accommodations in a quiet desert hideaway; fun vibe for music fans. **Cons:** rustic cabins will not appeal to resort seekers; far from most services. [$] *Rooms from: $61* ✉ *53688 Pioneertown Rd., Pioneertown* ☎ *760/228–1297* 🌐 *www.rimrockranchcabins.com* 🛏 *7 rental units* 🍴 *No meals.*

JOSHUA TREE

12 miles east of Yucca Valley.

Artists and renegades have long found solace in the small upcountry desert town of Joshua Tree, home to artsy vintage shops, cafés, and B&Bs and a gateway to Joshua Tree National Park. Those who zip through town might wonder what all the hype is about, but if you slow down and spend time chatting with the folks in this funky community, you'll find much to love.

GETTING HERE AND AROUND

Highway 62 is the main route to and through Joshua Tree. Most businesses are here or along Park Boulevard as it heads toward the park.

ESSENTIALS

Visitor Information **Joshua Tree Visitor Center** ✉ *6554 Park Blvd.* ☎ *760/366–1855* 🕒 *Daily 8–5.*Exploring

Fodor's Choice ★

Noah Purifoy Foundation. This vast 10-acre art installation full of "assemblage art" on a sandy tract of land in the town of Joshua Tree honors the work of artist Noah Purifoy. The sculptures blend with the spare desert in an almost post-apocalyptic way. Purifoy lived most of his life in this desert until his death is 2004. He used found materials to make commentary on social issues. His art has been showcased at LACMA, J. Paul Getty Museum, MOCA, and many more. ✉ *63030 Blair Lane, Joshua Tree* ☎ *213/382-7516* 🌐 *www.noahpurifoy.com* 🎟 *Free* 🕒 *Sunrise to sunset; call for an appointment.*

WHERE TO EAT AND STAY

$ AMERICAN

🍴 **Crossroads Cafe.** Mexican breakfasts, chicken-cilantro soup, and hearty sandwiches are among the draws at this Joshua Tree institution for pre-hike breakfasts, birthday lunches, and early dinners. With its stained-wood bar and black-and-white photos of the national park, the remodeled wooden interior still feels like it's been around for ages. Taxidermied animals and beer-can lights hint at the community's consciousness, while the tattooed waitresses and slew of veggie options make it clear the Crossroads is unlike anywhere else in San Bernardino County. [$] *Average main: $7* ✉ *61715 29 Palms Hwy.* ☎ *760/366–5414* 🌐 *www.crossroadscafejtree.com.*

$$$$ B&B/INN Fodor's Choice ★

🏨 **Sacred Sands.** The dramatic exterior of this strawbale house, atop a mountain near Joshua Tree National Park's western entrance, hints at the design-forward intentions of the friendly owners, Scott and Steve. **Pros:** gorgeous design; extravagant breakfasts; convenient to Joshua Tree. **Cons:** expensive for the area; few nearby dining options. [$] *Rooms* *from: $329* ⊠ *63155 Quail Springs Rd.* ☎ *760/424–6407* ⊕ *www. sacredsands.com* ➥ *2 rooms* ⓧ *Breakfast.*

TWENTYNINE PALMS

12 miles east of Joshua Tree.

The main gateway town to Joshua Tree National Park, Twentynine Palms is also the location of the U.S. Marine Air Ground Task Force Training Center. You can find services, supplies, and lodging in town.

GETTING HERE AND AROUND

Highway 62 is the main route to and through Twentynine Palms. Most businesses here center around Highway 62 and Utah Trail, 3 miles north of Joshua Tree's entrance.

ESSENTIALS

Visitor Information Twentynine Palms Chamber of Commerce and Visitor Center ⊠ *73484 Twentynine Palms Hwy.* ☎ *760/367–6197* ⊕ *www.visit29.org* ⊙ *Weekdays 9–5, weekends 10–4.*

EXPLORING

Oasis of Murals. Twenty murals painted on the sides of buildings depict the history and current lifestyle of Twentynine Palms. If you drive around town, you can't miss the murals, but you can also pick up a free map from the Twentynine Palms Chamber of Commerce.

29 Palms Art Gallery. This gallery features work by local painters, sculptors, and jewelry makers inspired by the desert landscape. If you find yourself inspired as well, sign up for one of the day-long art workshops. ⊠ *74055 Cottonwood Dr.* ☎ *760/367–7819* ⊕ *www.29palmsartgallery. com* ⊙ *Wed.–Sun. noon–3.*

WHERE TO STAY

$$
B&B/INN

Roughley Manor. To the wealthy pioneer who erected the stone mansion now occupied by this bed-and-breakfast, expense was no object, which is evident in the 50-foot-long planked maple floor in the great room, the intricate carpentry on the walls, and the huge stone fireplaces that warm the house on the rare cold night. **Pros:** elegant rooms and public spaces; good stargazing in the gazebo; great horned owls on property. **Cons:** somewhat isolated location; three-story main building doesn't have an elevator. ⓢ *Rooms from: $135* ⊠ *74744 Joe Davis Dr.* ☎ *760/367–3238* ⊕ *www.roughleymanor.com* ➥ *2 suites, 7 cottages* ⓧ *Breakfast.*

$$
B&B/INN
FAMILY
Fodor's Choice
★

29 Palms Inn. The closest lodging to the entrance to Joshua Tree National Park, the funky 29 Palms Inn scatters a collection of adobe and wood-frame cottages, some dating back to the 1920s and 1930s, over 70 acres of grounds that include the ancient Oasis of Mara, a popular destination for birds and bird-watchers year-round. **Pros:** gracious hospitality; exceptional bird-watching; popular with artists. **Cons:** rustic accommodations; limited amenities. ⓢ *Rooms from: $165* ⊠ *73950 Inn Ave.* ☎ *760/367–3505* ⊕ *www.29palmsinn.com* ➥ *18 rooms, 5 suites* ⓧ *Breakfast.*

9

ANZA-BORREGO DESERT

Largely uninhabited, the Anza-Borrego Desert is popular with those who love solitude, silence, space, starry nights, light, and sweeping mountain vistas. This desert lies south of the Palm Springs area, stretching along the western shore of the Salton Sea down toward Interstate 8 along the Mexican border. Isolated from the rest of California by mile-high mountains to the north and west, most of this desert falls within the borders of Anza-Borrego Desert State Park, which at more than 600,000 acres is the largest state park in the contiguous United States.

For thousands of years Native Americans of the Cahuilla and Kumeyaay people inhabited this area, spending their winters on the warm desert floor and their summers in the mountains. The first Europeans—a party led by the Spanish explorer Juan Baptiste de Anza—crossed this desert in 1776. Anza, for whom the desert is named, made the trip through here twice. Roadside signs along Highways 86, 78, and S2 mark the route of the Anza expedition, which spent Christmas Eve 1776 in what is now Anza-Borrego Desert State Park. Seventy-five years later thousands of immigrants on their way to the goldfields up north crossed the desert on the Southern Immigrant Trail, remnants of which remain along Highway S2. Permanent settlers arrived early in the 20th century, and by the 1930s the first adobe resort cottage had been built.

BORREGO SPRINGS

59 miles south of Indio.

The permanent population of Borrego Springs, set squarely in the middle of Anza-Borrego Desert State Park, hovers around 2,500. From September through June, when temperatures stay in the 80s and 90s, you can engage in outdoor activities such as hiking, nature study, golfing, tennis, horseback riding, and mountain biking. If winter rains cooperate, Borrego Springs puts on some of the best wildflower displays in the low desert. In some years the desert floor is carpeted with color: yellow dandelions and sunflowers, pink primrose, purple sand verbena, and blue wild heliotrope. The bloom generally lasts from late February through April. For current information on wildflowers around Borrego Springs, call Anza-Borrego Desert State Park's wildflower hotline (☎ 760/767–4684).

GETTING HERE AND AROUND

You can access Anza Borrego by taking the Highway 86 exit from Interstate 10, south of Indio. Highway 86 passes through Coachella and along the western shore of the Salton Sea. Turn west on Highway S22 at Salton City and follow it to Peg Leg Road, where you turn south until you reach Palm Canyon Drive. Turn west and the road leads to the center of Borrego Springs, Christmas Circle, where most major roads come together. Well-marked roads radiating from the circle will take you to the most popular sites in the state park. If coming from the San Diego area, drive east on Interstate 8 to the Cuyamaca Mountains, exit at Highway 79, and enjoy the lovely 23-mile drive through the mountains until you reach Julian; head east on Highway 78 and follow signs to Borrego Springs.

ESSENTIALS

Visitor Information Borrego Springs Chamber of Commerce ⊠ *786 Palm Canyon Dr.* ☎ *760/767–5555, 800/559–5524* ⊕ *www.borregospringschamber. com.*

EXPLORING

Fodor'sChoice **Anza-Borrego Desert State Park.** One of the richest living natural-history
★ museums in the nation, this state park is a vast, nearly uninhabited wilderness where you can step through a field of wildflowers, cool off in a palm-shaded oasis, count zillions of stars in the black night sky, and listen to coyotes howl at dusk. The landscape, largely undisturbed by humans, reveals a rich natural history. There's evidence of a vast inland sea in the piles of oyster beds near Split Mountain and of the power of natural forces such as earthquakes and flash floods. In addition, recent scientific work has confirmed that the Borrego Badlands, with more than 6,000 meters of exposed fossil-bearing sediments, is likely the richest such deposit in North America, telling the story of 7 million years of climate change, upheaval, and prehistoric animals. Evidence has been unearthed of sabertooth cats, flamingos, zebras, and the largest flying bird in the northern hemisphere beneath the now-parched sand. Today the desert's most treasured inhabitants are the herds of elusive and endangered native bighorn sheep, or borrego, for which the park is named. Among the strange desert plants you may observe are the gnarly elephant trees. As these are endangered, rangers don't encourage visitors to seek out the secluded grove at Fish Creek, but there are a few examples at the visitor center garden. After a wet winter you can see a short-lived but stunning display of cacti, succulents, and desert wildflowers in bloom.

The park is unusually accessible to visitors. Admission to the park is free, and few areas are off-limits. There are two developed campgrounds, but you can camp anywhere; just follow the trails and pitch a tent wherever you like. There are more than 500 miles of dirt roads, two huge wilderness areas, and 110 miles of riding and hiking trails. Many sites can be seen from paved roads, but some require driving on dirt roads, for which rangers recommend you use a four-wheel-drive vehicle. When you do leave the pavement, carry the appropriate supplies: a cell phone (which may be unreliable in some areas), a shovel and other tools, flares, blankets, and plenty of water. The canyons are susceptible to flash flooding, so inquire about weather conditions (even on sunny days) before entering. ■TIP→ **Borrego resorts, restaurants, and the state park have Wi-Fi, but the service is spotty at best. If you need to talk to someone in the area, it's best to find a phone with a landline.**

The sites and hikes listed below are arranged by region of the park and distance from the Visitor Center: in the valley and hills surrounding Borrego Springs, near Tamarisk Campground, along Highway S2, south of Scissors Crossing, and south of Ocotillo Wells.

Stop by the **Visitor Center** to get oriented, to pick up a park map, and to learn about weather, road, and wildlife conditions. Designed to keep

If you think the desert is just a sandy wasteland, the colorful beauty of the Anza-Borrego Desert will be a pleasant surprise.

cool during the desert's blazing-hot summers, the center is built underground, beneath a demonstration desert garden containing examples of most of the native flora and a little pupfish pond. Displays inside the center illustrate the natural history of the area. Picnic tables are scattered throughout, making this a good place to linger and enjoy the view.

A 1½-mile trail leads to **Borrego Palm Canyon,** one of the few native palm groves in North America. The canyon, about 1 mile west of the Visitor Center, holds a grove of more than 1,000 native fan palms, a stream, and a waterfall. Wildlife is abundant along this route. This moderate hike is the most popular in the park.

With a year-round stream and lush plant life, **Coyote Canyon,** approximately 4½ miles north of Borrego Springs, is one of the best places to see and photograph spring wildflowers. Portions of the canyon road follow a section of the old Anza Trail. This area is closed between June 15 and September 15 to allow native bighorn sheep undisturbed use of the water. The dirt road that gives access to the canyon may be sandy enough to require a four-wheel-drive vehicle.

The late-afternoon vista of the Borrego badlands from **Font's Point,** 13 miles east of Borrego Springs, is one of the most breathtaking views in the desert, especially when the setting sun casts a golden glow in high relief on the eroded mountain slopes. The road from the Font's Point turnoff can be rough enough to make using a four-wheel-drive vehicle advisable; inquire about road conditions at the Visitor Center before starting out. Even if you can't make it out on the paved road, you can see some of the view from the highway.

East of Tamarisk Grove campground (13 miles south of Borrego Springs), the **Narrows Earth Trail** is a short walk off the road. Along the way you can see evidence of the many geologic processes involved in forming the canyons of the desert, such as a contact zone between two earthquake faults, and sedimentary layers of metamorphic and igneous rock.

The 1.6-mile round trip **Yaqui Well Nature Trail** takes you along a path to a desert water hole where birds and wildlife are abundant. It's also a good place to look for wildflowers in spring. At the trailhead across from Tamarisk Campground you can pick up a brochure describing what can be seen along the trail.

Traversing a boulder-strewn trail is the easy, mostly flat **Pictograph/ Smuggler's Canyon Trail.** At the end is a collection of rocks covered with muted red and yellow pictographs painted within the last hundred years or so by Native Americans. Walk about ½ mile beyond the pictures to reach Smuggler's Canyon, where an overlook provides views of the Vallecito Valley. The hike, from 2 to 3 miles round-trip, begins in Blair Valley, 6 miles southeast of Highway 78, off Highway S2, at the Scissors Crossing intersection.

Just a few steps off the paved road, **Carrizo Badlands Overlook** offers a view of eroded and twisted sedimentary rock that obscures the fossils of the mastodons, saber-tooths, zebras, and camels that roamed this region a million years ago. The route to the overlook through Earthquake Valley and Blair Valley parallels the Southern Emigrant Trail. It's off Highway S2, 40 miles south of Scissors Crossing.

Geology students from all over the world visit the Fish Creek area of Anza-Borrego to explore the canyon through Split Mountain. The narrow gorge with 600-foot walls was formed by an ancient stream. Fossils in this area indicate that a sea once covered the desert floor. From Highway 78 at Ocotillo Wells, take Split Mountain Road south 9 miles. ⊠ *Visitor Center, 200 Palm Canyon Dr., Hwy. S22* ☎ *760/767–5311, 800/444–7275 campground reservations only, 760/767–4684 wildflower hotline* ⊕ *www.parks.ca.gov* ⊠ *Free* ☉ *Park daily dawn–dusk. Visitor Center Oct.–May 1, daily 9–5.*

Galleta Meadows. Flowers aren't the only things popping up from the earth in Borrego Springs. At Galleta Meadows, camels, llamas, saber-toothed tigers, tortoises, and monumental gomphotherium (a sort of ancient elephant) appear to roam the earth again. These life-size bronze figures are of prehistoric animals whose fossils can be found in the Borrego Badlands. The collection of more than 130 sculptures created by Ricardo Breceda was commissioned by the late Dennis Avery, who installed the works of art on property he owned for the entertainment of locals and visitors. Maps are available from Borrego Springs Chamber of Commerce. ⊠ *Borrego Springs Rd. from Christmas Circle to Henderson Canyon* ☎ *760/767–5555* ⊕ *www.galletameadows.com* ⊠ *Free.*

WHERE TO EAT

$$
MODERN
AMERICAN
✕ **The Arches.** On the edge of the Borrego Springs Resort & Spa's golf course, set beneath a canopy of grapefruit trees, The Arches is a pleasant place to eat. For breakfast you'll find burritos alongside standard

fare such as pancakes, or biscuits and gravy. For lunch, best enjoyed on the patio, or dinner, the options include sandwiches, salads, and entrées such as molasses-Sriracha smothered ribs, fish-and-chips, and Cuban-style roasted pork. [$] *Average main: $19* ✉ *1112 Tilting T Dr.* ☎ *760/767–5700* 🌐 *www.borregospringsresort.com/dining.asp* 🕒 *Summer hrs vary; call ahead.*

$$$ AMERICAN 🍴 **Carlee's Place.** Sooner or later most visitors to Borrego Springs wind up at Carlee's Place for a drink and a bite to eat. It's an all-American type of establishment, where your server might call you "honey" while setting a huge steak in front of you. The extra-large menu has everything: burgers, salads, seafood, sandwiches, and prime rib. At the bar ask for a lemon-drop martini. [$] *Average main: $25* ✉ *660 Palm Canyon Dr.* ☎ *760/767–3262.*

$ MEXICAN 🍴 **Carmelita's Mexican Grill and Cantina.** A friendly, family-run eatery tucked into a back corner of what is called "The Mall," Carmelita's draws locals and visitors all day, whether it's for a hearty breakfast, a cooked-to-order enchilada or burrito, or to tip back a brew at the bar. The menu lists typical combination plates (enchiladas, burritos, tamales, and tacos). Salsas have a bit of zing, and the *masas* (corn dough used to make tortillas and tamales) are tasty and tender. [$] *Average main: $12* ✉ *575 Palm Canyon Dr.* ☎ *760/767–5666.*

$$$ MODERN AMERICAN 🍴 **Coyote Steakhouse/Red Ocotillo.** The owners of the Palms at Indian Head operate these two restaurants together. Red Ocotillo serves breakfast (all the usual suspects) and lunch—burgers, Caesar salads, fish-and-chips, and the like. The more upscale Coyote Steakhouse was recently spruced up to cater to those who want a fancy dinner, particularly hunks of filet mignon or rack of lamb. Dog-lovers will appreciate the canine menu, whose treats include house-made peanut-butter dog cookies. [$] *Average main: $25* ✉ *2220 Hoberg Rd.* ☎ *760/767–7400* 🌐 *www.thepalmsatindianhead.com* ✍ *Reservations essential* 🕒 *Coyote Steakhouse, no breakfast or lunch; Red Ocotillo, no breakfast or lunch July and Aug.*

$ MEXICAN 🍴 **Jilberto's Taco Shop.** A casual local favorite for affordable Mexican dishes, Jilberto's serves up big burritos and meaty enchiladas. [$] *Average main: $5* ✉ *655 Palm Canyon Dr.* ☎ *760/767–1008* 💳 *No credit cards.*

WHERE TO STAY

$$$ RESORT 🏨 **Borrego Springs Resort & Spa.** The large, smart-looking rooms at this quiet resort set around a swimming pool and with golf, tennis, and golf options come with either a shaded balcony or a patio with desert views. **Pros:** golf and tennis; good desert views from most rooms. **Cons:** limited amenities; average service. [$] *Rooms from: $182* ✉ *1112 Tilting T Dr.* ☎ *760/767–5700, 888/826–7734* 🌐 *www.borregospringsresort.com* 🛏 *66 rooms, 34 suites* 🍽 *No meals.*

$$$ B&B/INN Fodor's Choice ★ 🏨 **Borrego Valley Inn.** Those looking for desert landscapes may enjoy the adobe Southwestern-style buildings here that house spacious rooms, which boasts plenty of natural light, original art, pine beds, and double futons facing corner fireplaces, plus have desert gardens of mesquite, ocotillo, and creosote just outside. **Pros:** swimming under the stars in the clothing-optional pool; exquisite desert gardens. **Cons:** potential street

noise in season; not a good choice for families with young children or pets. $ *Rooms from: $235* ✉ *405 Palm Canyon Dr.* ☎ *760/767–0311, 800/333–5810* ⊕ *www.borregovalleyinn.com* ⇵ *15 rooms, 1 suite* †⦿| *Breakfast.*

$$
RESORT
FAMILY
Fodor's Choice
★

⌂ **La Casa Del Zorro.** The draws at this desert hideaway a short drive from Anza Borrego State Park include five public pools, a hot tub, six night-lit tennis courts, a spa, a restaurant, and the lively Fox Den Bar. **Pros:** upscale accommodations that aren't stuffy or overpriced; outdoor activities; on-site spa, bar, and restaurant. **Cons:** service can be spotty. $ *Rooms from: $159* ✉ *3845 Yaqui Pass Rd.* ☎ *760/767–0100* ⊕ *www. lacasadelzorro.com* ⇵ *48 rooms, 19 casitas* †⦿| *No meals.*

SPORTS AND THE OUTDOORS

GOLF

Borrego Springs Resort & Spa Country Club. Formerly part of a trio of three 9-hole courses (one has since closed), the remaining two, Mesquite and Desert Willow, are generally played as an 18-hole round by most golfers, starting with Mesquite. Both courses have natural desert land-scaping and mature date palms. ✉ *1112 Tilting T Dr.* ☎ *760/767–5700* ⊕ *www.borregospringsresort.com* ⊠ *From $30* ⑂ *18 holes, 6760 yards, par 71.*

SHOPPING

Anza-Borrego State Park Store. The Anza-Borrego Foundation, a land conservation group, runs this store that sells guidebooks, maps, clothing, desert art, and gifts for kids. Its enthusiastic staffers also assist with trip planning. Foundation guides organize hikes, naturalist talks, classes, research programs, and nature walks. ✉ *587 Palm Canyon Dr., No. 110* ☎ *760/767–4063* ⊕ *theabf.org/visitor-center-store-sales* ⊘ *June–Sept., weekdays 8–noon; Oct.–May, Fri.–Wed. 9–3.*

Borrego Outfitters. This contemporary general store stocks high-end outdoor gear from Kelty and Columbia, personal care items from Burt's Bees, footwear from Teva and Acorn, Speedo and Fresh Produce swimsuits, and tabletop and home-decor items. You can browse through racks of clothing and piles of hats, all suited to the desert climate. ✉ *579 Palm Canyon Dr.* ☎ *760/767–3502* ⊕ *www.borregooutfitters. com* ⊘ *Sun. 10–4, weekdays 9–5, Sat. 9–6.*

SALTON SEA

30 miles southeast of Indio, 29 miles east of Borrego Springs.

The Salton Sea, one of the largest inland seas on Earth, is the product of both natural and artificial forces. The sea occupies the Salton Basin, a remnant of prehistoric Lake Cahuilla. Over the centuries the Colorado River flooded the basin and the water drained into the Gulf of California. In 1905 a flood once again filled the Salton Basin, but the exit to the gulf was blocked by sediment. The floodwaters remained in the basin, creating a saline lake 228 feet below sea level, about 35 miles long and 15 miles wide, with a surface area of nearly 380 square miles. The sea, which lies along the Pacific Flyway, supports 400 species of birds. Fishing for tilapia, boating, camping, and bird-watching are popular activities year-round.

GETTING HERE AND AROUND

Salton Sea State Recreation Area includes about 14 miles of coastline on the northeastern shore of the sea, about 30 miles south of Indio via Highway 111. The Sonny Bono Salton Sea National Wildlife Refuge fills the southernmost tip of the sea's shore. To reach it from the recreation area, continue south about 60 miles to Niland; continue south to Sinclair Road, and turn west following the road to the Refuge Headquarters.

EXPLORING

FAMILY **Salton Sea State Recreation Area.** This huge recreation area on the sea's north shore draws thousands each year to its playgrounds, hiking trails, fishing spots, and boat launches. Ranger-guided bird walks take place on Saturday; you'll see migrating and native birds including Canada geese, pelicans, and shorebirds. On Sunday there are free kayak tours. ✉ *100–225 State Park Rd., North Shore* ☎ *760/393-3052* ⊕ *www. parks.ca.gov* ▣ *$5* ☉ *Park daily 8–sunset.*

Sonny Bono Salton Sea National Wildlife Refuge. The 2,200-acre wildlife refuge here, on the Pacific Flyway, is a wonderful spot for viewing migratory birds. There's an observation deck where you can watch Canada geese, and along the trails you might view eared grebes, burrowing owls, great blue herons, ospreys, and yellow-footed gulls. ⚠ **Though the scenery is beautiful, the waters here give off an unpleasant odor, and the New River, which empties into the sea, is quite toxic.** ✉ *906 W. Sinclair Rd., Calipatria* ☎ *760/348-5278* ⊕ *www.fws.gov/refuge/ sonny_bono_salton_sea* ▣ *Free* ☉ *Oct.–Feb., Park: daily sunrise–sunset; Visitor center: weekdays 7–3, weekends 8–4:15. Mar.–Sept., weekdays only.*

JOSHUA TREE
NATIONAL PARK

WELCOME TO JOSHUA TREE NATIONAL PARK

TOP REASONS TO GO

★ **Rock climbing:** Joshua Tree is a world-class site with challenges for climbers of just about every skill level.

★ **Peace and quiet:** Savor the solitude of one of the last great wildernesses in America.

★ **Stargazing:** You'll be mesmerized by the Milky Way flowing across the summer sky. For spectacular natural fireworks, visit in mid-August during the Perseid meteor shower and watch shooting stars streak overhead.

★ **Wildflowers:** In spring the hillsides explode in a patchwork of yellow, blue, pink, and white.

★ **Sunsets:** Twilight is a magical time here, especially during the winter, when the setting sun casts a golden glow on the mountains.

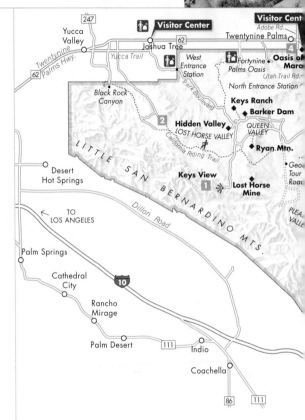

1 Keys View. This is the most dramatic overlook in the park—on clear days you can see Signal Mountain in Mexico.

2 Hidden Valley. Crawl between the big rocks and you'll understand why this boulder-strewn area was once a cattle rustlers' hideout.

3 Cholla Cactus Garden. Come here in the late afternoon, when the spiky stalks of the Bigelow (jumping) cholla cactus are backlit against an intense blue sky.

4 Oasis of Mara. Walk the nature trail around this desert oasis, which the first settlers, the Serrano, dubbed "the place of little springs and much grass."

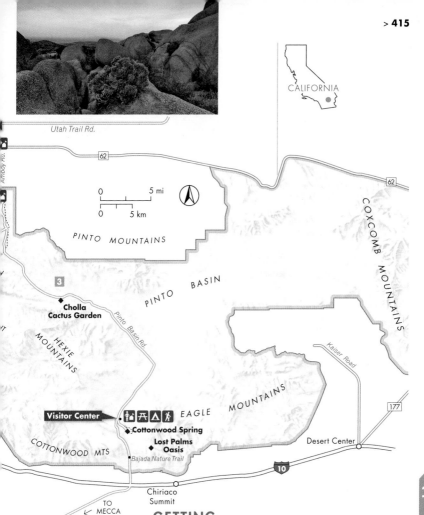

CALIFORNIA

Utah Trail Rd.

62

0   5 mi

0   5 km

PINTO   MOUNTAINS

PINTO   BASIN

COXCOMB   MOUNTAINS

3

◆ **Cholla Cactus Garden**

HEXIE MOUNTAINS

Pinto Basin Rd.

Kaiser Road

EAGLE   MOUNTAINS

177

Visitor Center

◆ **Cottonwood Spring**

COTTONWOOD MTS

Lost Palms Oasis

◆ *Bajada Nature Trail*

Desert Center

10

Chiriaco Summit

TO
← MECCA

10

GETTING ORIENTED

Daggerlike tufts grace the branches of the namesake of Joshua Tree National Park in southeastern California, where the arid Mojave Desert meets the sparsely vegetated Colorado Desert (part of the Sonoran Desert, which lies across California, Arizona, and northern Mexico). Passenger cars are fine for paved areas, but you'll need four-wheel drive for many of the rugged backcountry roadways. At the park's most popular sites, parking is limited. Joshua Tree does not have public transportation.

Updated by
Steve Pastorino

Ruggedly beautiful desert scenery attracts more than a million visitors each year to Joshua Tree National Park, one of the last great wildernesses in the continental United States. Its mountains support mounds of enormous boulders and jagged rock; natural cactus gardens and lush oases shaded by tall fan palms mark the meeting place of the Mojave (high) and Sonoran (low) deserts. Extensive stands of Joshua trees gave the park its name; the plants (members of the yucca family of shrubs) reminded Mormon pioneers of the biblical Joshua, with their thick, stubby branches representing the prophet raising his arms toward heaven.

JOSHUA TREE PLANNER

WHEN TO GO
October through May, when the desert is cooler, is when most visitors arrive. Daytime temperatures range from the mid-70s in December and January to mid-90s in October and May. Lows can dip to near freezing in midwinter, and you may even encounter snow at the higher elevations. Summers can be torrid, with daytime temperatures reaching 110°F.

PLANNING YOUR TIME
JOSHUA TREE IN ONE DAY
After stocking up on water, snacks, and lunch in Yucca Valley or Joshua Tree (you won't find any supplies inside the park), begin your visit at the **Joshua Tree Visitor Center,** where you can pick up maps and peruse exhibits to get acquainted with what awaits you. Enter the park itself at the nearby **West Entrance Station** and continue driving along the highly scenic and well-maintained **Park Boulevard.** Stop first at **Hidden Valley,** where you can relax at the picnic area or hike the easy 1-mile loop trail.

After a few more miles, turn left onto the spur road that takes you to the trailhead for the **Barker Dam Nature Trail.** Walk the easy 1.3-mile loop to view a water tank that ranchers built to quench their cattle's thirst; along the way you'll spot birds and a handful of cactus varieties. Return to Park Boulevard and head south; you'll soon leave the main road again for the drive to **Keys View.** The easy loop trail here is only 0.25 miles, but the views extend for miles in every direction—look for the San Andreas Fault, the Salton Sea, and nearby mountains. Return to Park Boulevard, where you'll find **Cap Rock,** another short loop trail winding amid rock formations and Joshua trees.

Continuing along Park Boulevard, the start of the 18-mile self-guided **Geology Tour Road** will soon appear on your right. A brochure outlining its 16 stops is available here; note that the round trip will take about two hours, and high-clearance vehicles are recommended after stop 9. ⚠ **Do not attempt if it has recently rained.** Back on Park Boulevard, you'll soon arrive at the aptly named **Skull Rock.** This downright spooky formation is next to the parking lot; a nearby trailhead marks the beginning of a 1.7-mile nature trail. End your day with a stop at the **Oasis Visitor Center** in Twentynine Palms, where you can stroll through the historic **Oasis of Mara,** popular with area settlers.

GETTING HERE AND AROUND
CAR TRAVEL
An isolated island of pristine wilderness—a rarity these days—Joshua Tree National Park is within a short drive of 11 million Southern California residents. Most visitors, in fact, make the two-hour drive from the Los Angeles area to enjoy a weekend of solitude in 792,726 acres of untouched desert. The urban sprawl of Palm Springs (home to the nearest airport) is about 40 miles away, but gateway towns Joshua Tree, Yucca Valley, and Twentynine Palms are just north of the park. If you're staying in the Palm Springs area, you can enjoy the highlights of the park in one day, including a stop for a picnic at a scenic spot.

■ **TIP→ If you'd prefer not to drive, most Palm Springs area hotels can arrange a half- or full-day tour that hits the highlights of Joshua Tree National Park.** But you'll need to spend two or three days camping here to truly experience the quiet beauty of the desert.

10

PARK ESSENTIALS
PARK FEES AND PERMITS
Park admission is $15 per car, $5 per person on foot, bicycle, motorcycle, or horse. The Joshua Tree Pass, good for one year, is $30. Free permits—available at all visitor centers—are required for rock climbing.

PARK HOURS
The park is open every day, around the clock.

VISITOR INFORMATION
PARK CONTACT INFORMATION
Joshua Tree National Park ✉ *74485 National Park Dr., Twentynine Palms* ☎ *760/367–5500* ⊕ *www.nps.gov/jotr.*

VISITOR CENTERS

Joshua Tree Visitor Center. This visitor center has interesting exhibits illustrating park geology, cultural and historic sites, and hiking and rock-climbing activities. There's also a small bookstore. Restrooms with flush toilets are on the premises. ⊠ *6554 Park Blvd., Joshua Tree* ☎ *760/366–1855* ⊕ *www.nps.gov/jotr* ⬚ *$15 entrance fee* ☉ *Daily 8–5.*

Oasis Visitor Center. Exhibits here illustrate how Joshua Tree was formed, reveal the differences between the park's two types of desert, and demonstrate how plants and animals eke out an existence in this arid climate. Take the 0.5-mile nature walk through the nearby Oasis of Mara, which is alive with cottonwood trees, palm trees, and mesquite shrubs. Facilities include picnic tables, restrooms, and a bookstore. ⊠ *74485 National Park Dr., Twentynine Palms* ☎ *760/367–5500* ⊕ *www.nps.gov/jotr* ⬚ *$15* ☉ *Daily 8:30–5.*

EXPLORING

SCENIC DRIVES

Park Boulevard. If you have time only for a short visit, driving Park Boulevard is your best choice. Traversing the most scenic portions of Joshua Tree, this well-paved road connects the north and west entrances in the park's high desert section. Along with some sweeping desert views, you'll see jumbles of splendid boulder formations, stands of Joshua trees, and Hidden Valley and Barker Dam, remnants of the area's wild and woolly past. From the Oasis Visitor Center, drive south. After about 5 miles, the road forks; turn right and head west toward Jumbo Rocks (clearly marked with a road sign). ⊠ *Joshua Tree.*

Pinto Basin Road. This paved road takes you from high Mojave desert to low Colorado desert. A long, slow drive, the route runs from the main part of the park to I–10; it can add as much as an hour to and from Palm Springs (round-trip), but the views and roadside exhibits make it worth the extra time. From the Oasis Visitor Center, drive south. After about 5 miles, the road forks; take a left and continue another 9 miles to the Cholla Cactus Garden, where the sun fills the cactus needles with light. Past that is the Ocotillo Patch, filled with spindly plants bearing razor-sharp thorns and brilliant red flowers. Side trips from this route require a 4X4. ⊠ *Joshua Tree.*

HISTORIC SITES

FAMILY **Hidden Valley.** This legendary cattle-rustlers' hideout is set among big boulders, which kids love to scramble over and around. There are shaded picnic tables here. ⊠ *Park Blvd., 14 miles south of West Entrance.*

Fodor's Choice **Keys Ranch.** This 150-acre ranch, which once belonged to William and
★ Frances Keys and is now on the National Historic Register, illustrates one of the area's most successful attempts at homesteading. The couple raised five children under extreme desert conditions. Most of the original

buildings, including the house, school, store, and workshop, have been restored to the way they were when William died in 1969. The only way to see the ranch is on one of the 90-minute walking tours usually offered Friday through Sunday, October to May; advance reservations recommended. ⊠ *2 miles north of Barker Dam Rd.* ☎ *760/367–5500* ⊕ *www. nps.gov* ✉ *$10 tours* ⊗ *Oct.–May, Fri. and Sat. at 2, Sun. at 10 am.*

SCENIC STOPS

Barker Dam. Built around 1900 by ranchers and miners to hold water for cattle and mining operations, the dam now collects rainwater and is a good place to spot wildlife such as the elusive bighorn sheep. Unfortunately, access to the dam itself was eliminated in 2013 after repeated graffiti vandalism. ⊠ *Barker Dam Rd., off Park Blvd., 10 miles south of West Entrance.*

Cholla Cactus Garden. This stand of bigelow cholla (sometimes called jumping cholla, since its hooked spines seem to jump at you) is best seen and photographed in late afternoon, when the backlit spiky stalks stand out against a colorful sky. ⊠ *Pinto Basin Rd., 20 miles north of Cottonwood Visitor Center.*

> ### PLANTS AND WILDLIFE IN JOSHUA TREE
>
> Joshua Tree will shatter your notions of the desert as a wasteland. Life flourishes here, as flora and fauna have adapted to heat and drought. In most areas you'll be walking among native Joshua trees, ocotillos, and yuccas. One of the best spring desert wildflower displays in Southern California blooms here. You'll see plenty of animals—reptiles such as nocturnal sidewinders, birds like golden eagles or burrowing owls, and occasionally mammals like coyotes and bobcats.

Cottonwood Spring. Home to the native Cahuilla people for centuries, this spring provided water for travelers and early prospectors. The area, which supports a large stand of fan palms, is one of the best stops for bird-watching, as migrating birds (and bighorn sheep) rely on the water as well. A number of gold mines were located here, and the area still has some remains, including an *arrastra* (a gold ore–grinding tool) and concrete pillars. Flash floods in 2011 and 2013, however, have necessitated that some areas no longer be open to the public. ⊠ *Cottonwood Visitor Center.*

Fortynine Palms Oasis. A short drive off Highway 62, this site is a bit of a preview of what the park's interior has to offer: stands of fan palms, interesting petroglyphs, and evidence of fires built by early American Indians. Since animals frequent this area, you may spot a coyote, bobcat, or roadrunner. ⊠ *End of Canyon Rd., 4 miles west of Twentynine Palms.*

Fodor's Choice
★ **Keys View.** At 5,185 feet, this point affords a sweeping view of the Santa Rosa Mountains and Coachella Valley, the San Andreas Fault, the peak of 11,500-foot Mount San Gorgonio, the shimmering surface of Salton Sea, and—on a rare clear day—Signal Mountain in Mexico. Sunrise and sunset are magical times, when the light throws rocks and trees into high relief before bathing the hills in brilliant shades of red, orange, and gold. ⊠ *Keys View Rd., 16 miles south of park's west entrance.*

10

Lost Palms Oasis. More than 100 fan palms comprise the largest group of the exotic plants in the park. A spring bubbles from between the rocks, but disappears into the sandy, boulder-strewn canyon. The seven-mile round-trip hike is not for everyone. Don't forget to bring water. ⊠ *Cottonwood Visitor Center.*

SPORTS AND THE OUTDOORS

HIKING

There are more than 190 miles of hiking trails in Joshua Tree, ranging from quarter-mile nature trails to 35-mile treks. Some connect with each other, so you can design your own desert maze. Remember that drinking water is hard to come by—you won't find water in the park except at the entrances. Bring along at least a gallon per person for all but the shortest hikes, more if the weather is hot. Before striking out on a hike or apparent nature trail, check out the signage. Roadside signage identifies hiking- and rock-climbing routes. Ask a ranger about flash flooding during rare rainy times.

EASY

Cap Rock. This 0.5-mile wheelchair-accessible loop—named after a boulder that sits atop a huge rock formation like a cap—winds through fascinating rock formations and has signs that explain the geology of the Mojave Desert. *Easy.* ⊠ *Trailhead at junction of Park Blvd. and Keys View Rd.*

MODERATE

Fodor'sChoice **Ryan Mountain Trail.** The payoff for hiking to the top of 5,461-foot Ryan
★ Mountain is one of the best panoramic views of Joshua Tree. From here you can see Mt. San Jacinto, Mt. San Gorgonio, Lost Horse Valley, and the Pinto Basin. You'll need two to three hours to complete the 3-mile round-trip with 1,000+ feet of elevation gain. *Moderate.* ⊠ *Trailhead at Ryan Mountain parking area, 16 miles southeast of park's west entrance, or Sheep Pass, 16 miles southwest of Oasis Visitor Center.*

DIFFICULT

Mastodon Peak Trail. Some boulder scrambling is required on this 3-mile hike that loops up to the 3,371-foot Mastodon Peak, but the journey rewards you with stunning views of the Salton Sea. The trail passes through a region where gold was mined from 1919 to 1932, so be on the lookout for open mines. The peak draws its name from a large rock formation that early miners believed looked like the head of a prehistoric behemoth. *Difficult.* ⊠ *Trailhead at Cottonwood Spring Oasis.*

ROCK CLIMBING

Fodor'sChoice With an abundance of weathered igneous boulder outcroppings, Joshua
★ Tree is one of the nation's top winter climbing destinations. There are more than 4,500 established routes offering a full menu of climbing experiences—from bouldering for beginners in the Wonderland of Rocks to multiple-pitch climbs at Echo Rock and Saddle Rock. The best-known climb in the park is Hidden Valley's Sports Challenge Rock.

THE MOJAVE DESERT

With Owens Valley

WELCOME TO THE MOJAVE DESERT

TOP REASONS TO GO

★ **Nostalgia:** Old neon signs, historic motels, and restored (or neglected but still striking) rail stations abound across this desert landscape. Don't miss the classic eateries along the way, including Summit Inn in Oak Hills and Emma Jean's Holland Burger Cafe in Victorville.

★ **Death Valley wonders:** Visit this distinctive landscape to tour some of the most varied desert terrain in the world.

★ **Great ghost towns:** California's gold rush brought miners to the Mojave, and the towns they left behind have their own unique charms.

★ **Cool down in Sierra country:** Head up U.S. 395 toward Bishop to visit the High Sierra, home to majestic Mt. Whitney.

★ **Explore ancient history:** The Mojave Desert is replete with rare petroglyphs, some dating back almost 16,000 years.

1 The Western Mojave. Stretching from the town of Ridgecrest to the base of the San Gabriel Mountains, the western Mojave is a varied landscape of ancient Native American petroglyphs, tufa towers, and hillsides covered in bright orange poppies.

2 The Eastern Mojave. Joshua trees and cacti dot a predominantly flat landscape that is interrupted by dramatic, rock-strewn mountains. The area is largely uninhabited, so be cautious when driving the back roads, where towns and services are scarce.

3 Owens Valley. Lying in the shadow of the Eastern Sierra Nevada, the Owens Valley stretches along U.S. 395 from the Mono–Inyo county line, in the north, to the town of Olancha, in the south. Tiny towns punctuate the highway, and the scenery is quietly powerful. If you're traveling between Yosemite National Park and Death Valley National Park or are headed from Lake Tahoe or Mammoth to the desert, U.S. 395 is your north–south corridor.

4 Death Valley National Park. This arid desert landscape is one of the hottest, lowest, and driest places in North America. From the surrounding mountains, you look down on its vast beauty. Among the beautiful canyons and wide-open spaces, you'll find quirky bits of Americana, including the elaborate Scotty's Castle inside the park and eclectic Amargosa Opera House outside.

GETTING ORIENTED

The Mojave Desert, once part of an ancient inland sea, is one of the largest swaths of open land in Southern California. Its boundaries include the San Gabriel and San Bernardino mountain ranges to the south; the areas of Palmdale and Ridgecrest to the west; Death Valley to the north; and Needles and Lake Havasu in Arizona to the east. The area is distinguishable by its wide-open sandy spaces, peppered with creosote bushes, Joshua trees, cacti, and abandoned homesteads. You can access the Mojave via interstates 40 and 15, highways 14 and 95, and U.S. 395.

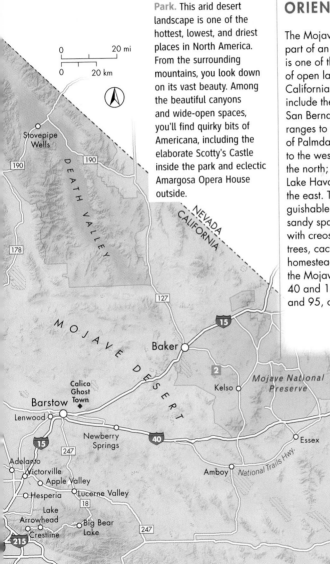

Updated by
Joan Patterson

Dust and desolation, tumbleweeds and rattlesnakes, barren landscapes and failed dreams—these are the bleak images that come to mind when most people hear the word *desert*. Yet the remote regions east of the Sierra Nevada possess a singular beauty, the vast open spaces populated with spiky Joshua trees, undulating sand dunes, faulted mountains, and dramatic rock formations. With a few exceptions the area is not heavily peopled, providing expanses in which visitors can both lose and find themselves.

The topography is extreme; while Death Valley drops to almost 300 feet below sea level and contains the lowest (and hottest) spot in North America, the Mojave Desert, which lies to the south, has elevations ranging from 3,000 to 5,000 feet. Owens Valley is where the desert meets the mountains; its 80-mile width separates the depths of Death Valley from Mt. Whitney, the highest mountain in the contiguous United States.

PLANNING

WHEN TO GO

Spring and fall are the best seasons to tour the desert and Owens Valley. Winters are generally mild, but summers can be cruel. If you're on a budget, be aware that room rates drop as the temperatures rise.

GETTING HERE AND AROUND

AIR TRAVEL

McCarran International Airport in Las Vegas is the nearest airport to many eastern Mojave destinations. Needles Airport and Inyokern Airport serve small, private planes.

Contacts Inyokern Airport ⊠ *1669 Airport Rd., off Hwy. 178, 9 miles west of Ridgecrest, Inyokern* ☎ *760/377–5844* ⊕ *www.inyokernairport.com.* **McCarran**

International Airport ⊠ *5757 Wayne Newton Blvd., Las Vegas, Nevada*
☎ *702/261–5211* ⊕ *www.mccarran.com.* **Needles Airport** ⊠ *711 Airport Rd.,
Needles* ☎ *760/247–2371* ⊕ *cms.sbcounty.gov/airports.*

BUS TRAVEL

Greyhound provides bus service to Barstow, Victorville, and Palmdale;
check with the chambers of commerce about local bus service, which
is generally more useful to residents than to tourists.

Contacts Greyhound ☎ *800/231–2222* ⊕ *www.greyhound.com.*

CAR TRAVEL

The major north–south route through the western Mojave is U.S. 395,
which intersects with Interstate 15 between Cajon Pass and Victorville.
U.S. 395 travels north into the Owens Valley, passing such relatively
remote outposts as Lone Pine, Independence, Big Pine, and Bishop.
Farther west, Highway 14 runs north–south between Inyokern (near
Ridgecrest) and Palmdale. Two major east–west routes travel through
the Mojave: to the north, Interstate 15 to Las Vegas, Nevada; to the
south, Interstate 40 to Needles. At the intersection of the two interstates, in Barstow, Interstate 15 veers south toward Victorville and
Los Angeles, and Interstate 40 gives way to Highway 58 west toward
Bakersfield.

■ TIP → **For the latest Mojave traffic and weather, tune in to the Highway
Stations (98.1 FM near Barstow, 98.9 FM near Essex, and 99.7 FM near
Baker).** Traffic can be especially troublesome Friday through Sunday,
when thousands of Angelenos head to Las Vegas for a bit of R&R.

Contacts Caltrans Current Highway Conditions ☎ *800/427–7623* ⊕ *www.
dot.ca.gov.*

TRAIN TRAVEL

Amtrak trains traveling east and west stop in Victorville, Barstow, and
Needles, but the stations aren't staffed, so you'll have to purchase tickets
in advance and handle your own baggage. The Barstow station is served
daily by Amtrak California motor coaches that stop in Los Angeles,
Bakersfield, Las Vegas, and elsewhere.

Contacts Amtrak ☎ *800/872–7245* ⊕ *www.amtrak.com.*

HEALTH AND SAFETY

Let someone know your trip route, destination, and estimated time of
return. Before setting out, make sure your vehicle is in good condition.
Carry water, a jack, tools, and towrope or chain. Keep an eye on your
gas gauge and try to keep the needle above half. Stay on main roads,
and watch out for wildlife, horses, and cattle.

Drink at least a gallon of water a day (more if you're hiking or otherwise exerting yourself). Dress in layered clothing and wear comfortable, sturdy shoes and a hat. Keep snacks, sunscreen, and a first-aid
kit on hand. If you have a headache or feel dizzy or nauseous, you
could be suffering from dehydration. Get out of the sun immediately
and drink plenty of water. Dampen your clothing to lower your body
temperature. Do not enter abandoned mine tunnels or shafts, of which

there are hundreds in the Mojave Desert. The structures may be unstable, and there may be hidden dangers such as pockets of bad air. Avoid canyons during rainstorms. Floodwaters can quickly fill up dry riverbeds and cover or wash away roads. Never place your hands or feet where you can't see them: rattlesnakes, scorpions, and black widow spiders may be hiding there.

Contacts Barstow Community Hospital ⌂ *820 E. Mountain View St., Barstow* ☎ *760/256–1761* ⊕ *www. barstowhospital.com.* **BLM Rangers** ☎ *916/978–4400* ⊕ *www.blm.gov/ ca.* **San Bernardino County Sheriff** ☎ *760/256–4838 in Barstow, 760/733– 4448 in Baker* ⊕ *cms.sbcounty.gov/ sheriff.*

HIKING IN THE MOJAVE DESERT

Hiking trails are abundant throughout the desert and along the eastern base of the Sierra, meandering toward sights that you can't see from the road. Some of the best trails are unmarked; ask locals for directions. Among the prime hiking spots is the John Muir Trail, which starts near Mt. Whitney. Whether you're exploring the high or low desert, wear sunscreen, protective clothing, and a hat. Watch for tarantulas, black widows, scorpions, snakes, and other creatures.

RESTAURANTS

Throughout the desert and the Eastern Sierra, dining is a fairly simple affair. Owens Valley is home to many mom-and-pop eateries, as well as a few fast-food chains. There are chain establishments in Ridgecrest, Victorville, and Barstow, as well as some ethnic eateries.

HOTELS

Chain hotel properties and roadside motels are the desert's primary lodging options. The tourist season runs from late May through September. Reservations are rarely a problem, but it's still wise to make them. *Hotel reviews have been shortened. For full information, please visit Fodors.com.*

WHAT IT COSTS				
	$	$$	$$$	$$$$
Restaurants	under $16	$16–$22	$23–$30	over $30
Hotels	under $120	$120–$175	$176–$250	over $250

Restaurant prices are the average cost of a main course at dinner or, if dinner is not served, at lunch, excluding sales tax of 7.75%. Hotel prices are the lowest cost of a standard double room in high season, excluding service charges and 7.25% tax.

TOURS

Sierra Club. The San Gorgonio Chapter of the Sierra Club and the chapter's Mojave Group conduct interesting field trips and desert excursions. Activities are often volunteer-run and free, but participants are sometimes required to cover parking and other expenses. ☎ *951/684–6203* ⊕ *content.sierraclub.org/outings/local-outdoors* ▱ *Some free; tour prices vary.*

VISITOR INFORMATION
Contacts Barstow Welcome Center ✉ *2796 Tanger Way, Barstow*
☎ *760/253–4782* ⊕ *www.visitcwc.com/Barstow.* **Bureau of Land Management** ✉ *California Desert District Office, 22835 Calle San Juan De Los Lagos, Moreno Valley* ☎ *951/697–5200* ⊕ *www.blm.gov/ca.* **Death Valley Chamber of Commerce** ☎ *888/600–1844* ⊕ *www.deathvalleychamber.com.*

THE WESTERN MOJAVE

This vast area is especially beautiful along U.S. 395. From January through March, wildflowers are in bloom and temperatures are manageable. Year-round, snowcapped mountain peaks are irresistible sights.

PALMDALE

60 miles north of Los Angeles.

Before proclaiming itself the aerospace capital of the world, the town of Palmdale was an agricultural community. Settlers of Swiss and German descent, moving west from Illinois and Nebraska, populated the area in 1886, and most residents made their living as farmers, growing alfalfa, pears, and apples. After World War II, with the creation of Edwards Air Force Base and U.S. Air Force Plant 42, the region evolved into a center for aerospace and defense activities, with contractors such as McDonnell Douglas, Rockwell, Northrop, and Lockheed establishing factories here. Until the housing crisis and recent recession struck, Palmdale was one of Southern California's fastest-growing cities.

GETTING HERE AND AROUND

From the Los Angeles basin, take Highway 14 to get to Palmdale. From the east, arrive via the Pearblossom Highway (Highway 18/138). Regional Metrolink trains serve the area from Los Angeles. Palmdale attractions are most easily seen by car, but you can see some of the town via local transit.

ESSENTIALS

Contacts Antelope Valley Transit Authority ☎ *661/945–9445* ⊕ *www.avta. com.*

Metrolink ☎ *800/371–5465* ⊕ *www.metrolinktrains.com.*

Visitor Information Palmdale Chamber of Commerce ✉ *817 East Ave., Ste. Q-9* ☎ *661/273–3232* ⊕ *www.palmdalechamber.org.*

EXPLORING

Devil's Punchbowl Natural Area. A mile from the San Andreas Fault, the namesake of this attraction is a natural bowl-shaped depression in the earth, framed by 300-foot rock walls. At the bottom is a stream, which you can reach via a moderately strenuous 1-mile hike. You also can detour on a short nature trail; at the top an interpretive center has displays of native flora and fauna, including live animals such as snakes, lizards, and birds of prey. ✉ *28000 Devil's Punchbowl Rd., south of Hwy. 138, Pearblossom* ☎ *661/944–2743* 💲 *Free* ☉ *Park daily sunrise–sunset; center daily 8–4.*

St. Andrew's Abbey. This Benedictine monastery occupies 760 acres made lush by natural springs. The Abbey Ceramics studio, established here in 1969, sells handmade tile saints, angels, and plaques designed by Father Maur van Doorslaer, a Belgian monk whose work U.S. and Canadian collectors favor. ✉ *31101 N. Valyermo Rd., south of Hwy. 138, Valyermo* ☎ *888/454–5411, 661/944–1047 ceramics studio* 🌐 *www.saintsandangels.org* 🎟 *Free* 🕒 *Mon.–Thurs. 10–4.*

WHERE TO STAY

$ HOTEL 🏨 **Best Western John Jay Inn & Suites.** All rooms at this modern hotel have large desks and ergonomic chairs; some suites have amenities such as balconies, fireplaces, wet bars, and Jacuzzis. **Pros:** clean; good rates; spacious rooms. **Cons:** no on-site restaurant; ambulance noise from the hospital next door. [$] *Rooms from: $89* ✉ *600 W. Palmdale Blvd.* ☎ *661/575–9322* 🌐 *www.bestwestern.com* 🛏 *66 rooms, 13 suites* 🍴 *Breakfast.*

$$ HOTEL 🏨 **Residence Inn Palmdale.** Accommodations here range from studios to one-bedroom suites, all with full kitchens, sitting areas, and sleeper sofas. **Pros:** spacious rooms; close to town. **Cons:** no room service. [$] *Rooms from: $159* ✉ *514 W. Ave. P* ☎ *661/947–4204, 800/331–3131* 🌐 *www.marriott.com* 🛏 *90 suites* 🍴 *Breakfast.*

SPORTS AND THE OUTDOORS

AERIAL TOURS

Brian Ranch Airport. The airport's school offers introductory flights that allow you to pilot (with an instructor) two-seater light-sport aircraft across the Mojave. The annual World's Smallest Air Show, held on Memorial Day weekend, draws many aviation enthusiasts. ✉ *34810 Largo Vista Rd., off Hwy. 138, Llano* ☎ *661/261–3216* 🌐 *www.brianranch.com* 🎟 *$40, 15-min flight; $75, 30 min; $130, 1 hr.*

SKYDIVING

Southern California Soaring Academy. This nonprofit academy, which works with wounded veterans and area schools, operates sailplane rides (no engines!) over the scenic San Gabriel mountains, with views of snow-topped peaks in winter and the Pacific Ocean and Catalina Island in spring/summer. Accompanied by a certified instructor, you'll learn the basics before handling the craft on your own. Reservations are required. ✉ *32810 165th St. E, off Hwy. 138, Llano* ☎ *661/944–1090* 🌐 *www.soaringacademy.org* 🎟 *$109–$250* 🕒 *Fri.–Mon. 9–5.*

LANCASTER

8 miles north of Palmdale.

Lancaster was founded in 1876, when the Southern Pacific Railroad arrived. Before that, several Native American tribes, some of whose descendants still live in the surrounding mountains, inhabited it. Points of interest around Lancaster are far from the downtown area, and some are in neighboring communities.

Mojave Desert

GETTING HERE AND AROUND

From the Los Angeles basin, take Highway 14, which proceeds north to Mojave and Highway 58, a link between Bakersfield and Barstow. Regional Metrolink trains serve Lancaster from the Los Angeles area. Local transit exists, but a car is the best way to experience this area.

ESSENTIALS

Visitor Information Destination Lancaster ✉ 44933 Fern Ave., at W. Lancaster Blvd. ☎ 661/723–6110 ⊕ www.destinationlancasterca.org.

EXPLORING

TOP ATTRACTIONS

Antelope Valley Indian Museum. Notable for its one-of-a-kind artifacts from California, Southwest, and Great Basin native tribes, the museum occupies an unusual Swiss chalet–style building that clings to the rocky hillside of Piute Butte. To get here, exit north off Highway 138 at 165th Street East and follow the signs, or take the Avenue K exit off Highway 14. ✉ 15701 E. Ave. M ☎ 661/946–3055 ⊕ www.avim.parks.ca.gov ✉ $3 ⊗ Weekends 11–4.

Antelope Valley Poppy Reserve. The California poppy, the state flower, can be spotted throughout the state, but this quiet park holds the densest concentration. Seven miles of trails wind through 1,745 acres of hills carpeted with poppies and other wildflowers, including a paved section that allows wheelchair access. ■TIP➜ Peak blooming time is usually March through May. On a clear day at any time of year, you'll be treated to sweeping views of Antelope Valley. ✉ 15101 Lancaster Rd., west off Hwy. 14, Ave. I Exit ☎ 661/724–1180, 661/946–6092 ⊕ www.parks. ca.gov/?page_id=627 ✉ $10 per vehicle ⊗ Visitor center mid-Mar.–mid-May, weekdays 10–4, weekends 9–5.

OFF THE
BEATEN
PATH

Exotic Feline Breeding Compound's Feline Conservation Center. About a dozen species of wild cats, from the weasel-size jaguarundi to leopards, tigers, and jaguars, inhabit this small, orderly facility. You can see the cats (behind barrier fences) in the parklike public zoo and research center. ✉ Rhyolite Ave. off Mojave-Tropico Rd., Rosamond ☎ 661/256–3793 ⊕ www.wildcatzoo.org ✉ $7 ⊗ Thurs.–Tues. 10–4.

WORTH NOTING

Air Flight Test Museum at Edwards Air Force Base. This museum, at what many consider to be the birthplace of supersonic flight, chronicles the rich history of flight testing. Numerous airplanes are on exhibit, from the first F-16B to the giant B-52D bomber. The 3½-hour walking and driving tour is open to the public once a month, and requires a reservation. ■TIP➜ To take the tour, you have to provide basic information for a background check at least a week in advance (a month for non-U.S. residents). On the base's website, click Tours for details. ✉ 405 S. Rosamond Blvd., off Yeager Blvd., Edwards ☎ 661/277–3517 ⊕ www. edwards.af.mil ✉ Free ⊗ 1 day a month, 9–12:30.

Antelope Valley Winery/Donato Family Vineyard. Cyndee and Frank Donato purchased the Los Angeles-based McLester Winery in 1990 and moved it to Lancaster, where the high-desert sun and nighttime chill work their magic on wine grapes such as Merlot, Zinfandel, and Sangiovese.

In addition to tastings, the winery hosts a Saturday Farmers' Market (from May through November between 9 and noon) and sells grass-fed buffalo and other game and exotic meats such as venison, pheasant, and wild boar. ☒ *42041 20th St. W, at Ave. M* ☎ *661/722–0145, 888/282–8332* ⊕ *www.avwinery.com* ☒ *Winery free, tasting $5 to $12* ⊙ *Wed.–Sun. 11–6.*

RED ROCK CANYON STATE PARK

48 miles north of Lancaster.

On the stretch of Highway 14 that slices through Red Rock Canyon State Park, it's easy to become caught up in the momentum of rushing to your "real" destination. But it would be a shame not to stop for this deeply beautiful canyon, with its rich, layered colors and Native American heritage.

GETTING HERE AND AROUND

The only practical way to get here is by car, taking Highway 14 north from the Palmdale-Lancaster area or south from Ridgecrest.

Red Rock Canyon State Park. A geological feast for the eyes with its layers of pink, white, red, and brown rock, this remote canyon is also a region of fascinating biological diversity—the ecosystems of the Sierra Nevada, the Mojave Desert, and the Basin Range all converge here. Entering the park from the south just beyond Red Rock–Randsburg Road, you pass through a steep-walled gorge to a wide bowl tinted pink by volcanic ash. Native Americans known as the Kawaiisu lived here some 20,000 years ago; later, Mojave Indians roamed the land for centuries. Gold-rush fever hit the region in the mid-1800s, and you can still see remains of mining operations in the park. In the 20th century, Hollywood invaded the canyon, shooting westerns, TV shows, commercials, music videos, and movies such as *Jurassic Park* here. Be sure to check out the Red Cliffs Preserve on Highway 14, across from the entrance to the Ricardo Campground. ☒ *Visitor Center, 37749 Abbott Dr., off Hwy. 14, Cantil* ☎ *661/946–6092* ⊕ *www.parks.ca.gov* ☒ *$6 per vehicle* ⊙ *Daily sunrise–sunset; visitor center open in spring and fall, dates vary.*

RIDGECREST

28 miles northeast of Red Rock Canyon State Park; 77 miles south of Lone Pine.

A military town that serves the U.S. Naval Weapons Center to its north, Ridgecrest has scores of stores, restaurants, and hotels. With about 25,000 residents, it's the last city of any significant size you'll encounter as you head northeast toward Death Valley National Park. It's a good base for visiting regional attractions such as the Trona Pinnacles and Petroglyph Canyons.

GETTING HERE AND AROUND

Arrive here by car via U.S. 395 or, from the Los Angeles area, Highway 14. The local bus service is of limited use to tourists.

ESSENTIALS
Transportation Contacts **Ridgerunner Transit** ☎ 760/499–5040
⊕ ridgecrest-ca.gov/transit/transit.

Visitor Information **Ridgecrest Area Convention and Visitors Bureau**
✉ 643 N. China Lake Blvd., Ste. C ☎ 760/375–8202, 800/847–4830 ⊕ www.
racvb.com.

EXPLORING

TOP ATTRACTIONS

Fodor'sChoice **Petroglyph Canyons.** Two canyons in the Coso Mountain range, com-
★ monly called Big Petroglyph and Little Petroglyph, hold a superlative
concentration of ancient rock art, the largest of its kind in the Northern Hemisphere. Thousands of well-preserved images of animals and
humans are scratched or pecked into dark basaltic rocks. The canyons
lie within the million-acre U.S. Naval Weapons Center at China Lake.
Only the drawings of Little Petroglyph can be visited, and only on a
guided tour arranged in advance through the Maturango Museum.
■ TIP→ Tour participants must be U.S. citizens over 10 years of age,
and must supply birthdate, birthplace, and Social Security information
before visiting. Because vehicles caravan during the tour, a valid ID,
vehicle registration, and proof of insurance must be presented upon
arrival. ☎ 760/375–6900 ⊕ www.maturango.org ☛ $40 ☉ Feb.–June,
and mid-Sept. or Oct.–early Dec.; call or check website for times.

Trona Pinnacles National Natural Landmark. Fantastic-looking formations
of calcium carbonate, known as tufa, were formed underwater along
fault lines in the bed of what is now Searles Dry Lake. Some of the
more than 500 spires stand as tall as 140 feet, creating a landscape so
surreal that it doubled for outer-space terrain in the film Star Trek V.

An easy-to-walk ½-mile trail allows you to see the tufa up close, but
wear sturdy shoes—tufa cuts like coral. The best road to the area can
be impassable after a rainstorm. ✉ Pinnacle Rd., 5 miles south of Hwy.
178, 18 miles east of Ridgecrest ☎ 760/384–5400 Ridgecrest BLM
office ⊕ www.blm.gov/ca/st/en/fo/ridgecrest/trona.3.html.

OFF THE
BEATEN
PATH
Indian Wells Brewing Company. After driving through the hot desert,
you'll surely appreciate a cold one at Indian Wells Brewing Company,
where master brewer Rick Lovett lovingly crafts his Lobotomy Bock,
Amnesia I.P.A., and Death Valley Pale Ale, among others. If you have
the kids along, grab a six-pack of his specialty root beer, black cherry,
orange, or cream soda. ✉ 2565 N. Hwy. 14, 2 miles west of U.S. 395,
Inyokern ☎ 760/377–5989 ⊕ www.mojavered.com ☛ $5 beer tasting
☉ Daily 9:30–5.

WORTH NOTING

Maturango Museum. The museum contains interesting exhibits that survey the Upper Mojave Desert area's art, history, and geology, and spon-
sors tours of the amazing rock drawings in Petroglph Canyons. ✉ 100
E. Las Flores Ave., at Hwy. 178 ☎ 760/375–6900 ⊕ www.maturango.
org ☛ $5 ☉ Daily 10–5.

WHERE TO STAY

$$ 🛏 **Hampton Inn & Suites Ridgecrest.** Clean and reliable, the Hampton has a
HOTEL   well-equipped exercise room, spotless Internet service, and a welcoming
breakfast area that help keep guests in shape, in touch, and invigorated.
Pros: attentive, friendly service; good breakfast; big rooms. **Cons:** a
rather strong chain vibe. $ *Rooms from: $149* ⊠ *104 East Sydnor Ave.*
☎ *760/446–1968* 🔊 *93 rooms* ❍❘ *Breakfast.*

$$ 🛏 **SpringHill Suites Ridgecrest.** The bar might not be set that high, but
HOTEL   this is the best hotel in Ridgecrest. **Pros:** clean; good breakfast; help-
ful staff. **Cons:** some guests complain of a bleach smell. $ *Rooms
from: $169* ⊠ *113 E. Sydnor Ave.* ☎ *888/236–2427, 760/446–1630*
⊕ *www.marriott.com/hotels/travel/iyksh-springhill-suites-ridgecrest*
❍❘ *Breakfast.*

RANDSBURG

*21 miles south of Ridgecrest; 26 miles east of Red Rock Canyon State
Park.*

Randsburg and nearby Red Mountain and Johannesburg make up the
Rand Mining District, which first boomed with the discovery of gold in
the Rand Mountains in 1895. Rich tungsten ore, used in World War I to
make steel alloy, was discovered in 1907, and silver was found in 1919.
The boom has gone bust, but the area still has some residents, a few
antiques shops, and plenty of character. Butte Avenue is the main drag
in Randsburg, whose tiny city jail, just off Butte, is among the original
buildings still standing. An archetypal Old West cemetery perched on
a hillside looms over Johannesburg.

GETTING HERE AND AROUND

Arriving by car is the best transportation option. From Red Rock Canyon, drive east on Redrock Randsburg Road. From Ridgecrest, drive
south on South China Lake Road and U.S. 395.

EXPLORING

Rand Desert Museum. The small museum celebrates the Rand Mining
District's heyday with historic photographs and mining paraphernalia and other artifacts. ⊠ *161 Butte Ave.* ☎ *760/371–0965* ⊕ *www.
randdesertmuseum.com* 🎫 *Free* ⊗ *Weekends 10–4, and by appointment.*

**OFF THE
BEATEN
PATH**

Desert Tortoise Natural Area. Between mid-March and mid-June, this
natural habitat of the elusive desert tortoise blazes with desert candles,
primroses, lupine, and other wildflowers. Arrive bright and early to spot
the state reptile, while it grazes on fresh flowers and grass shoots. The
area is also a great spot to see desert kit fox, red-tailed hawks, cactus
wrens, and Mojave rattlesnakes. ⊠ *8 miles northeast of California City
via Randsburg Mojave Rd.* ☎ *951/683–3872* ⊕ *www.tortoise-tracks.
org* 🎫 *Free* ⊗ *Daily.*

General Store. Built as Randsburg's Drug Store in 1896, the General Store
is one of the area's few surviving ghost-town buildings with an original
tin ceiling, light fixtures, and 1904-era marble-and-stained-glass soda
fountain. You can still enjoy a phosphate soda from that same fountain, or lunch on chili dogs, burgers, and barbecue-beef sandwiches.

✉ *35 Butte Ave.* ☎ *760/374–2143* ⊕ *www.randsburggeneralstore.com* ⊗ *Mon., Thurs. and Fri. 11–4, weekends 10–5.*

White House Saloon. One of the Wild West's few surviving saloons, the White House is an atmospheric stop. Step in for a drink and, if you're feeling adventurous and aren't too picky, order some food (burgers, hot dogs, fries, chili). ■TIP→ **Across the street and also worth a peek is another joint—The Joint.** ✉ *168 Butte Ave.* ☎ *760/374–2464.*

THE EASTERN MOJAVE

Majestic, wide-open spaces define this region, with the Mojave National Preserve being one of the state's most remote but rewarding destinations.

VICTORVILLE

87 miles south of Ridgecrest.

At the southwest corner of the Mojave is the sprawling town of Victorville, a town with a rich Route 66 heritage. Victorville was named for Santa Fe Railroad pioneer Jacob Nash Victor, who drove the first locomotive through the Cajon Pass here in 1885. Once home to Native Americans, the town later became a rest stop for Mormons and missionaries. In 1941 George Air Force Base, now an airport and storage area, brought scores of military families to the area, many of which have stayed on to raise families of their own.

GETTING HERE AND AROUND

Drive here on Interstate 15 from Los Angeles or Las Vegas, or from the north via U.S. 395. Amtrak and Greyhound also serve the town. There are local buses, but touring by car is more practical.

ESSENTIALS

Transportation Information The Victor Valley Transit Authority ☎ 760/948–3030 ⊕ www.vvta.org.

Visitor Information Victor Valley Chamber of Commerce ✉ *14174 Green Tree Blvd., at St. Andrews Dr.* ☎ 760/245–6506 ⊕ www.vvchamber.com.

EXPLORING

TOP ATTRACTIONS

California Route 66 Museum. Fans of the Mother Road (as John Steinbeck dubbed Route 66) will love this museum whose exhibits chronicle the famous highway's history. A book sold here contains a self-guided tour of a local stretch of the old Sagebrush Route, including icons such as Bottle Tree Ranch in Oro Grande and the once-rowdy Sagebrush Inn, now a private residence. ✉ *16825 South D St., between 5th and 6th Sts.* ☎ *760/951–0436* ⊕ *www.califrt66museum.org* ▱ *Free* ⊗ *Mon. and Thurs.–Sat. 10–4, Sun. 11–3.*

WORTH NOTING

FAMILY **Mojave Narrows Regional Park.** In one of the few spots where the Mojave River flows aboveground, this park has two lakes surrounded by cottonwoods and cattails. You'll find fishing, rowboat rentals, a bait shop, and equestrian paths. ✉ *18000 Yates Rd., north on Ridgecrest Rd.*

off Bear Valley Rd. ☎ *760/245–2226* 🌐 *cms.sbcounty.gov/parks* 🎟 *$8 weekdays, $10 weekends and holidays.*

Silverwood Lake State Recreation Area. One of the desert's most popular boating and fishing areas, 1,000-acre Silverwood Lake also has campgrounds and a beach with a lifeguard. You can rent boats; fish for trout, largemouth bass, crappie, and catfish; and hike and bike the trails. In winter, bald eagles nest in the tall Jeffrey pines by the shore. ✉ *14651 Cedar Cir., at Cleghorn Rd., off Hwy. 138, Hesperia* ☎ *760/389–2303* 🌐 *www.parks.ca.gov* 🎟 *$10 per car, $10 per boat* 🕓 *May–Sept. daily 6 am–9 pm, Oct.–Apr. daily 7–7.*

WHERE TO EAT AND STAY

$ AMERICAN 🍴 **Emma Jean's Holland Burger Cafe.** This circa-1940s diner sits right on U.S. Historic Route 66, and is favored by locals for its generous portions and old-fashioned home cooking. Try the biscuits and gravy, chicken-fried steak, or the famous Trucker's Sandwich, stuffed with roast beef, bacon, chilies, and cheese. The Brian Burger also elicits consistent praise. [$] *Average main: $10* ✉ *17143 N. D St., at Water Power Housing Dr.* ☎ *760/243–9938* 💳 *No credit cards* 🕓 *Closed Sun. No dinner.*

$ AMERICAN 🍴 **Summit Inn.** Elvis Presley and Pearl Bailey are two of many famous customers who passed through this kitschy diner perched atop the Cajon Pass. Open since 1952, the restaurant is filled with Route 66 novelty items, a gift shop, and a vintage jukebox that plays oldies from the 1950s to 1980s. All-day breakfast, including omelets made with ostrich or emu eggs, and the funky decor and historic significance make it worth a stop. [$] *Average main: $10* ✉ *5970 Mariposa Rd., exit I–15 at Oak Hills, Oak Hills* ☎ *760/949–8688.*

$ HOTEL 🏨 **La Quinta Inn and Suites Victorville.** If you're looking for a clean, comfortable, and no-smoking hotel with reasonable prices, this is a good choice. **Pros:** near shopping mall; clean rooms; hot breakfast. **Cons:** near a busy freeway. [$] *Rooms from: $94* ✉ *12000 Mariposa Rd., Hesperia* ☎ *760/949–9900* 🌐 *www.lq.com* 🛏 *53 rooms, 22 suites* 🍽 *Breakfast.*

BARSTOW

32 miles northeast of Victorville.

Barstow was born in 1886, when a subsidiary of the Atchison, Topeka, and Santa Fe Railway began construction of a depot and hotel here. Outlet stores, chain restaurants, and motels define today's landscape, though old-time neon signs light up the town's main street.

GETTING HERE AND AROUND

Driving here on Interstate 15 from Los Angeles or Las Vegas is the best option, although you can reach Barstow via Amtrak or Greyhound. The local bus service is helpful for sights downtown.

ESSENTIALS

Transportation Information **Barstow Area Transit** ☎ *760/255–3330* 🌐 *www.barstowca.org.*

Visitor Information **Barstow Area Chamber of Commerce and Visitors Bureau** ✉ *681 N. 1st Ave., near Riverside Dr.* ☎ *760/256–8617* 🌐 *www.*

Many of the buildings in the popular Calico Ghost Town are authentic.

barstowchamber.com. **California Welcome Center** ✉ *2796 Tanger Way, Ste. 100, off Lenwood Rd.* ☎ *760/253–4782* ⊕ *www.visitcwc.com* ⊙ *Daily 9–8.*

EXPLORING

TOP ATTRACTIONS

FAMILY **Calico Early Man Site.** The earliest-known Americans fashioned the artifacts buried in the walls and floors of the pits here. Nearly 12,000 stone tools—used for scraping, cutting, and gouging—have been excavated here. The apparent age of some of these items (said to be as much as 50,000 years old) contradicts the dominant archaeological theory that humans populated North America only 13,000 years ago. Noted archaeologist Louis Leakey was so impressed with the Calico site that he became its director in 1963 and served in that capacity until his death in 1972. His old camp is now a visitor center and museum. Self-guided tours can be accompanied by a lecture from a volunteer if desired; guided tours are available on request. ■TIP→ **Volunteers host an open-to-the-public dig the first full weekend of every month from October through May. Digging tools and instructions are provided. Any items found cannot be removed from the site.** ✉ *Off I–15, Minneola Rd. exit, 15 miles northeast of Barstow* ☎ *760/218–0827* ⊕ *www.calicoarchaeology.com* ✉ *$5* ⊙ *Visitor center Wed. 12:30–4:30, Thurs.–Sun. 9–4:30.*

FAMILY **Calico Ghost Town.** Once a wild and wealthy mining town, Calico took off in 1881 when prospectors found a rich deposit of silver in the area, and by 1886 more than $85 million worth of silver, gold, and other precious metals had been harvested from the surrounding hills. Many buildings here are authentic, but the restoration has created a sanitized version of the 1880s. You can stroll the wooden sidewalks of Main Street, browse shops filled with Western goods, roam the tunnels of Maggie's Mine ($2), and take an enjoyable ride on the Calico-Odessa Railroad ($4). Calico, 12 miles northeast of Barstow, is a fun and mildly educational place for families to stretch their legs on the drive between Los Angeles and Las Vegas. Festivals throughout the year celebrate Calico's Wild West theme. ⊠ *36600 Ghost Town Rd., off I–15, Yermo* ☎ *760/254–2122* ⊕ *www.calicotown.com* ⊠ *$8* ☉ *Daily 9–5.*

Casa Del Desierto Harvey House. This distinctive two-story structure—its Spanish name means "house of the desert"—was one of many hotel and restaurant depots opened in the West by the Fred Harvey Co. in the early 20th century. The famous Harvey Girls, the waitresses who served weary travelers in the dining rooms, are the subject of a 1946 musical starring Judy Garland. The building now houses the Route 66 Mother Road Museum and Western America Railroad Museum. ⊠ *681 N. 1st Ave., near Riverside Dr.* ☎ *760/255–1890* ⊕ *www.route66museum.org* ⊠ *Free* ☉ *Fri. and Sat. 10–4, Sun. 11–4; guided tours by appointment.*

FAMILY
Fodor's Choice
★
Goldstone Deep Space Communications Complex. Friendly and enthusiastic staffers conduct guided tours of this 53-square-mile complex. Tours start at the Goldstone Museum, where exhibits detail past and present space missions and Deep Space Network history. From there, you'll drive out to see the massive concave antennas, starting with those used for early manned space flights and culminating with the 24-story-tall "listening" device and its always-staffed mission control room used to track spacecraft that have drifted beyond our solar system. ■ TIP➔ **Appointments are required; contact the complex to reserve a slot.** ⊠ *Ft. Irwin Military Base, Ft. Irwin Rd. off I–15, 35 miles north of Barstow* ☎ *760/255–8688* ⊕ *www.gdscc.nasa.gov* ⊠ *Free* ☉ *Guided tours by appointment only.*

Rainbow Basin National Natural Landmark. Many science-fiction movies set on Mars have been filmed at this landmark 8 miles north of Barstow. Huge slabs of red, orange, white, and green stone tilt at crazy angles like ships about to capsize. Hike the washes, and you might see the fossilized remains of mastodons and bear-dogs, which roamed the basin up to 16 million years ago. At times, only 4-wheel-drive vehicles are permitted. If you have the time, park and hike. ⊠ *Fossil Bed Rd., 3 miles west of Fort Irwin Rd. (head north from I–15)* ☎ *760/252–6000* ⊕ *www.blm.gov/ca/barstow/basin.html.*

Skyline Drive-In Theatre. Check out a bit of surviving Americana at this dusty drive-in, where you can watch the latest Hollywood flicks among the Joshua trees and starry night sky. ⊠ *31175 Old Hwy. 58* ☎ *760/256–3333* ⊕ *www.barstowtheaters.com* ⊠ *$8 per person* ☉ *Showtime 7:45 pm and 10:15 pm* ☉ *Closed for winter season.*

FAMILY
Western America Railroad Museum. For a truly nostalgic experience, check out the old locomotives and cabooses at this museum that houses memorabilia from Barstow's early railroad days, as well as interactive and historic displays on railroad history. ⊠ *Casa Del Desierto, 685 N. 1st Ave., near Riverside Dr.* ☎ *760/256–9276* ⊕ *www.barstowrailmuseum.org* ⊠ *Free* ☉ *Fri.–Sun. 11–4.*

WORTH NOTING

Afton Canyon. Because of its colorful, steep walls, Afton Canyon is often called the Grand Canyon of the Mojave. It was carved over thousands of years by the rushing waters of the Mojave River, which makes one of its few aboveground appearances here. The dirt road that leads to the canyon is ungraded in spots, so it is best to explore it in an all-terrain vehicle. ✉ *Off Afton Rd., 36 miles northeast of Barstow via I–15* 🌐 *www.blm.gov/ca/st/en/fo/barstow/afton.html.*

FAMILY **Desert Discovery Center.** The center's main attraction is Old Woman Meteorite, the second-largest such celestial object ever found in the United States. It was discovered in 1976 about 50 miles from Barstow. The center also has exhibits of fossils, plants, and local animals. Environmental education, history, and the arts are among the topics of workshops and presentations the center hosts. ✉ *831 Barstow Rd.* ☎ *760/252–6060* 🌐 *www.desertdiscoverycenter.com* 🎫 *Free* ⏲ *Tues.–Sat. 11–4.*

Inscription Canyon. With nearly 10,000 petroglyphs and pictographs of bighorn sheep and other Mojave wildlife, Inscription is one of the world's largest natural Native American art galleries. The canyon lies 42 miles northwest of Barstow in the Black Mountains. ✉ *EF373, off Copper City Rd., 10 miles west of Fort Irwin Rd.* ☎ *760/252–6000* 🌐 *www.blm.gov/ca/st/en/fo/barstow/petroglyph1.html.*

FAMILY **Mojave River Valley Museum.** Two blocks from the the intersection of I–15 and Barstow Road, this museum is crowded with exhibits that include American Indian pottery, mammoth bones, and elephant tracks. Worth a look outside are the iron-strap jail, a rare Santa Fe Railroad drover's car, and a 130-year-old log cabin. ✉ *270 E. Virginia Way, at Belinda St.* ☎ *760/256–5452* 🌐 *www.mojaverivervalleymuseum.org* 🎫 *Free* ⏲ *Daily 11–4.*

WHERE TO EAT AND STAY

$ AMERICAN 🍴 **Bagdad Café.** Tourists from all over the world flock to the Route 66 eatery where the 1987 film of the same name was shot. Built in the 1940s, the divey Bagdad Café's walls are crammed with memorabilia donated by visitors famous and otherwise. The menu includes standards such as burgers and chicken-fried steak; the quality of both food and service can be inconsistent. [$] *Average main: $8* ✉ *46548 National Trails Hwy., at Nopal La., Newberry Springs* ☎ *760/257–3101.*

$$$ AMERICAN 🍴 **Idle Spurs Steakhouse.** Since the 1950s this roadside ranch has been a Barstow dining staple, and it's still beloved by locals. Decorated inside with Christmas lights, it's a colorful, cheerful place with a big wooden bar. The menu features prime cuts of meat, ribs, and lobster, and there's a great microbrew list. [$] *Average main: $24* ✉ *690 Old Hwy. 58, at Camarillo Ave.* ☎ *760/256–8888* 🌐 *thespurs.us* ⏲ *Closed Mon.; no lunch weekends.*

$ AMERICAN FAMILY 🍴 **Peggy Sue's 50s Diner.** Checkerboard floors and life-size versions of Elvis and Marilyn Monroe greet you at this funky coffee shop and pizza parlor in the middle of the Mojave. Outside, kids can play by the duck pond before heading in to spin a tune on the jukebox or order from the soda fountain. The fare is basic American—fries, onion rings, burgers, pork chops. [$] *Average main: $10* ✉ *35654 W. Yermo Rd., at*

Daggett-Yermo Rd., Yermo ☎ *760/254–3370* ⊕ *www.peggysuesdiner. com.*

$ ✕ **Slash X Ranch Cafe.** Known as a favorite stop for off-roaders, this
SOUTHERN   rowdy Wild West-esque watering hole named for the cattle ranch that
preceded it serves up burgers, cold beer, and chili-cheese fries in hearty
portions. Shuffleboard tables and horseshoe pits add to the fun, provided it's not too sizzling hot outside. $ *Average main: $10* ⊠ *28040
Barstow Rd., at Powerline Rd.* ☎ *760/252–1197* ⊙ *Closed Mon.–Thurs.*

$$ ▦ **Country Inn & Suites By Carlson.** A friendly and attentive staff makes
HOTEL   this chain hotel stand out in a town that has a sea of them. **Pros:** clean
rooms; engaged management; entirely nonsmoking. **Cons:** pricey for
Barstow. $ *Rooms from: $129* ⊠ *2812 Lenwood Rd.* ☎ *760/307–3121*
⊕ *www.countryinns.com* ⇨ *92 rooms and suites* ⦿ *Breakfast.*

MOJAVE NATIONAL PRESERVE

Visitor center 118 miles east of Barstow, 58 miles west of Needles.

The 1.6 million acres of the Mojave National Preserve hold a surpris-
ing abundance of plant and animal life—especially considering their
elevation (nearly 8,000 feet in some areas). There are traces of human
history here as well, including abandoned army posts and vestiges of
mining and ranching towns.

GETTING HERE AND AROUND

A car is the best way to access the preserve, which lies between inter-
states 15 and 40. Kelbaker Road bisects the park from north to south;
northbound from I–40, Essex Road gets you to Hole-in-the-Wall on
pavement but is graveled beyond there.

EXPLORING

Hole-in-the-Wall. Created millions of years ago by volcanic activity,
Hole-in-the-Wall formed when gases were trapped between layers of
deposited ash, rock, and lava; the gas bubbles left holes in the solidi-
fied material.

You will encounter one of California's most distinctive hiking experi-
ences here. Proceeding clockwise from a small visitor center, you walk
gently down and around a craggy hill, past cacti and fading petroglyphs
to Banshee Canyon, whose pockmarked walls resemble Swiss cheese.
From there you head back out of the canyon, supporting yourself with
widely spaced iron rings (some of which wiggle precariously from their
rock moorings) as you ascend a 50-foot incline that deposits you back
near the visitor center. The one-hour adventure can be challenging but
wholly entertaining. ■ **TIP→ There are no services (gas or food) nearby;
be sure to fill your tank and pack some snacks before heading out here.**
⊠ *From I–40, take Essex Rd. exit, drive north 10 miles to Black Canyon
Rd., and continue north another 10 miles* ☎ *760/928–2572* ⊕ *www.nps.
gov/moja* ⊡ *Free* ⊙ *Visitor center open seasonally, call for hrs.*

Fodor's Choice   **Kelso Dunes.** As you enter the preserve from the south, you'll pass miles
★   of open scrub brush, Joshua trees, and beautiful red-black cinder cones
before encountering the Kelso Dunes. These golden, fine-sand slopes
cover 70 square miles, reaching heights of 600 feet. You can reach

them via a short walk from the main parking area, but be prepared for a serious workout. When you reach the top of a dune, kick a little bit of sand down the lee side and listen to the sand "sing." North of the dunes, in the town of Kelso, is the Mission revival–style **Kelso Depot Visitor Center.** The striking building, which dates to 1923, contains several rooms of desert- and train-themed exhibits. ✉ *For Kelso Depot Visitor Center, take Kelbaker Rd. exit from I-15 (head south 34 miles) or I-40 (head north 22 miles)* ☎ *760/252–6100, 760/252–6108* ⊕ *www. nps.gov/moja* 🎫 *Free* ⊙ *Visitor center daily 9–5.*

NEEDLES

150 miles east of Barstow.

Along Route 66 and the Colorado River, Needles is a decent base for exploring Mojave National Preserve and other desert attractions. Founded in 1883, the town, named for the jagged mountain peaks that overlook the city, served as a stop along the Santa Fe railroad line.

GETTING HERE AND AROUND

Greyhound and Amtrak both pass through town daily, though most travelers arrive by car, either via Interstate 40 (east–west) or Highway 95 (north–south). Needles Area Transit is the local bus service.

ESSENTIALS

Bus Information Needles Area Transit ☎ *866/669–6309* ⊕ *www. cityofneedles.com.*

Visitor Information Needles Chamber of Commerce ✉ *100 G St., at Front St.* ☎ *760/326–2050* ⊕ *www.needleschamber.com.*

EXPLORING

FAMILY

Fodor's Choice

★

Havasu National Wildlife Refuge. In 1941, after the construction of Parker Dam, President Franklin D. Roosevelt set aside Havasu National Wildlife Refuge, a 30-mile stretch of land along the Colorado River between Needles and Lake Havasu City. Best seen by boat, this beautiful waterway is punctuated with isolated coves, sandy beaches, and Topock Marsh, a favorite nesting site of herons, egrets, and other waterbirds. You can see wonderful petroglyphs on the rocky red canyon cliffs of Topock Gorge. The refuge has three points that provide boat access to Topock Marsh, though not to the lower Colorado River. ■ TIP➜ **Spring is by far the best time to visit, as the river is more likely to be robust and wildflowers in bloom.** ✉ *Off I-40, 13 miles southeast of Needles* ☎ *760/326–3853* ⊕ *www.fws.gov/refuge/havasu.*

WHERE TO EAT AND STAY

$

PIZZA

✕ **River City Pizza.** This inexpensive pizza place off Interstate 40 is a local favorite and offers a range of specialty pies. Try a Vegetarian Deluxe or a Teriyaki Chicken with a mug of cold lager or a glass of wine out on the small patio. $ *Average main: $12* ✉ *1901 Needles Hwy.* ☎ *760/326–9191* ⊕ *www.rivercitypizzaco.com.*

$

HOTEL

🛏 **Best Western Colorado River Inn.** The spartan rooms at the best lodging in town are decorated in rich colors; expect the standard Best Western amenities. **Pros:** good rates; clean rooms; nice pool. **Cons:** town's dead at night (and not much livelier during the day); occasional train noise. [$] *Rooms from: $90* ✉ *2371 Needles Hwy.* ☎ *760/326–4552, 800/780–7234* 🌐 *www.bestwestern.com* 🛏 *63 rooms* 🍴 *Breakfast.*

$ RESORT FAMILY 🏨 **Fender's River Road Resort.** On a calm section of the Colorado River, this funky little 1960s-era motel-resort—off the beaten path in a town that's in the proverbial middle of nowhere—caters to families. **Pros:** on the river; clean rooms; peaceful. **Cons:** several minutes from the freeway; rooms could use refreshing. [$] *Rooms from: $66* ✉ *3396 Needles Hwy.* ☎ *760/326–3423* 🌐 *www.fendersresort.com* 🛏 *10 rooms, 27 campsites with full hookups* 🍴 *No meals.*

LAKE HAVASU CITY, AZ

43 miles southeast of Needles.

This wide spot in the Colorado River, created in the 1930s by Parker Dam, is accessed from its eastern shore in Arizona. Here you can swim; zip around on a Jet Ski; paddle a kayak; fish for trout, bass, or bluegill; or boat beneath the London Bridge, one of the desert's oddest sights. During sunset the views are breathtaking. Just be wary of coming here during March, when spring-breaking students definitely change the vibe.

GETTING HERE AND AROUND

Shuttles operate between here and Las Vegas, but as with other desert sites, traveling by car is the only practical way to go.

EXPLORING

London Bridge. The piece-by-piece reconstruction and subsequent reopening of London Bridge in 1971 put Lake Havasu City on the map. Today the circa-1831 bridge connects the city to a small island. Riverbanks on both sides have numerous restaurants, hotels, and RV parks. ☎ *928/855–4115* 🌐 *www.havasuchamber.com* 🎟 *Free* 🕓 *Daily 24 hrs.*

WHERE TO EAT

$$$ AMERICAN 🍴 **Shugrue's.** This lakefront restaurant serves up beautiful views of London Bridge and the English Village, along with fresh seafood, steak, and specialties such as Bombay chicken and shrimp, served with spicy yogurt sauce and mango chutney. [$] *Average main: $24* ✉ *1425 N. McCulloch Blvd.* ☎ *928/453–1400* 🌐 *shugrueslakehavasu.com.*

SPORTS AND THE OUTDOORS

TOURS

London Bridge Watercraft Tours & Rentals. Right on the beach, this outfitter rents personal watercraft such as Jet Skis and Sea-Doos. ✉ *Crazy Horse Campground, 1534 Beachcomber Blvd.* ☎ *928/453–8883* 🌐 *lakehavasubestboatandjetskirentals.com.*

OWENS VALLEY

Along U.S. 395 east of the Sierra Nevada.

In this undervisited region the snowcapped Sierra Nevada range abruptly and majestically rises to the west, and the high desert whistles to the east. In between are a series of roadside towns full of character, history, and outfits that cater to adventurers and other visitors. The best dining and lodging options can be found along U.S. 395 in Lone Pine and Bishop.

LONE PINE

30 miles west of Panamint Valley.

Mt. Whitney towers majestically over this tiny community, which supplied nearby gold- and silver-mining outposts in the 1860s, and for the past century the town has been touched by Hollywood glamour: several hundred movies, TV episodes, and commercials have been filmed here.

GETTING HERE AND AROUND

Arrive by car via U.S. 395 from the north or south, or Highway 190 from Death Valley National Park. No train or regularly scheduled bus service is available.

ESSENTIALS

Visitor Information Lone Pine Chamber of Commerce ⊠ *120 S. Main St., at Whitney Portal Rd.* ☎ *760/876–4444* ⊕ *www.lonepinechamber.org.*

EXPLORING

TOP ATTRACTIONS

Alabama Hills. Drop by the Lone Pine Visitor Center for a map of the Alabama Hills and take a drive up Whitney Portal Road (turn west at the light) to this wonderland of granite boulders. Erosion has worn the rocks smooth; some have been chiseled to leave arches and other formations. The hills have become a popular location for rock climbing. Tuttle Creek Campground sits among the rocks, with a nearby stream for fishing. The area has served as a scenic backdrop for hundreds of films; ask about the self-guided tour of the various movie locations at the visitor center. ⚠ **Traffic will be affected by reconstruction that is tentatively scheduled to begin in 2016 on Whitney Portal Road. Check with the Inyo National Forest Service, or Eastern Sierra Interagency Visitor Center at Lone Pine.** ⊠ *Whitney Portal Rd., 4½ miles west of Lone Pine.*

Mt. Whitney. Straddling the border of Sequoia National Park and Inyo National Forest–John Muir Wilderness, Mt. Whitney (14,496 feet) is the highest mountain in the contiguous United States. A favorite game for travelers passing through Lone Pine is trying to guess which peak is Mt. Whitney. Almost no one gets it right, because Mt. Whitney is hidden behind other mountains. There is no road that ascends the peak, but you can catch a glimpse of the mountain by driving curvy Whitney Portal Road west from Lone Pine into the mountains. The pavement ends at the trailhead to the top of the mountain, which is also the start of the 211-mile John Muir Trail from Mt. Whitney to Yosemite National Park. Day and overnight permits are required to ascend Mt. Whitney. The highly competitive lottery for these permits opens on February 1st. At the portal, a restaurant (known for its pancakes) and a small store cater to hikers and campers staying at Whitney Portal Campground. You can see a waterfall from the parking lot and go fishing in a small trout pond. The portal area is closed from mid-October to early May;

the road closes when snow conditions require. ⚠ Traffic will be affected by reconstruction tentatively scheduled to begin in 2016 on Whitney Portal Road. Check with the Inyo National Forest Service, or Eastern Sierra Interagency Vistior Center at Lone Pine before heading out. There will be traffic delays, significant at times, and limited parking. ✉ *Whitney Portal Rd., west of Lone Pine* ⊕ *www.fs.usda.gov/attmain/inyo.*

WORTH NOTING

Beverly and Jim Rogers Museum of Lone Pine Film History. Hopalong Cassidy, Barbara Stanwyck, Roy Rogers, John Wayne—even Robert Downey Jr.—are among the stars who have starred in Westerns and other films shot in the Alabama Hills and surrounding dusty terrain. The marquee-embellished museum relates this Hollywood-in-the-desert tale via exhibits and a rollicking 20-minute documentary. ✉ *701 S. Main St., U.S. 395* ☎ *760/876–9909* ⊕ *www.lonepinefilmhistorymuseum.org* 🖼 *$5* 🕙 *mid-Nov.–early Apr., Mon.–Sat. 10–5, Sun. 10–4; mid-Apr.–early Nov., Mon.–Wed. 10–6, Thurs.–Sat. 10–7, Sun 10–4.*

WHERE TO STAY

$ | 🏨 **Dow Villa Motel and Dow Hotel.** The Dow Villa Motel and the historic
HOTEL | Dow Hotel sit in the center of Lone Pine. **Pros:** clean rooms; great mountain views; in-room whirlpool tubs in motel. **Cons:** some rooms share bathrooms. 💲 *Rooms from: $110* ✉ *310 S. Main St.* ☎ *760/876–5521, 800/824–9317* ⊕ *www.dowvillamotel.com* 🔁 *92 rooms* 🍴 *No meals.*

INDEPENDENCE

17 miles north of Lone Pine.

Named for a military outpost that was established near here in 1862, sleepy Independence has some wonderful historic buildings and is worth a stop for two other reasons. The Eastern California Museum provides a marvelous overview of regional history, and 6 miles south of the small downtown lies the Manzanar National Historic Site, one of 10 camps in the West where people of Japanese descent were confined during the Second World War.

GETTING HERE AND AROUND

Greyhound passes through town, but most travelers arrive by car on U.S. 395.

ESSENTIALS

Visitor Information Independence Chamber of Commerce ✉ *139 N. Edwards St.* ☎ *760/878–0084.*

EXPLORING

TOP ATTRACTIONS

FAMILY | **Eastern California Museum.** The highlights of this museum dedicated to Inyo County and the Eastern Sierra's history include photos and artifacts from the Manzanar War Relocation Center, Paiute and Shoshone baskets, and a yard full of equipment used by early miners and ranchers. ✉ *155 N. Grant St., at W. Center St.* ☎ *760/878–0258* ⊕ *www.inyocounty.us/ecmsite* 🖼 *Free* 🕙 *Daily 10–5.*

A memorial honors the 11,000 Japanese-Americans who were held at the Manzanar War Relocation Center during World War II.

Fodor's Choice
★
Manzanar National Historic Site. A reminder of an ugly episode in U.S. history, the former Manzanar War Relocation Center is where more than 11,000 Japanese-Americans were confined behind barbed-wire fences between 1942 and 1945. A visit here is both deeply moving and inspiring—the former because it's hard to comprehend that the United States was capable of confining its citizens in such a way, the latter because those imprisoned here showed great pluck and perseverance in making the best of a bad situation. Most of the buildings from the 1940s are gone, but two sentry posts, the auditorium, and numerous Japanese rock gardens remain. One of eight guard towers and two barracks have been reconstructed, and a mess hall has been restored. You can drive the one-way dirt road on a self-guided tour past various ruins to a small cemetery, where a monument stands. Signs mark where the barracks, a hospital, a school, and the fire station once stood. ■TIP→ An outstanding 8,000-square-foot interpretive center has exhibits and documentary photographs and screens a short film. ⊠ *West side of U.S. 395 between Independence and Lone Pine* ☎ 760/878–2194 ⊕ *www. nps.gov/manz* ☜ *Free* ☉ *Park daily dawn–dusk; center daily Nov.–Mar. 9–4:30; April–Oct. 9–5:30.*

WORTH NOTING

FAMILY **Mt. Whitney Fish Hatchery.** A delightful place for a family picnic, the hatchery was one of California's first trout farms. The Tudor Revival–style structure, completed in 1917, is an architectural stunner, its walls nearly 3-feet thick with locally quarried granite. Fish production ceased in 2007 after a fire and subsequent mudslide, but dedicated volunteers staff the facility and raise trout for display purposes in a large pond out front. ■TIP➔ Bring change for the fish-food machines. ✉ *Fish Hatchery Rd., 2 miles north of town* ☎ *760/876–4128* ⊕ *mtwhitneyfishhatchery. org* ✎ *Free* ☉ *Mid-Apr.–mid-Dec., Thurs.–Mon. 10–3:30.*

EN
ROUTE

Ancient Bristlecone Pine Forest. About an hour's drive from Independence or Bishop you can view some of the oldest living trees on earth, some of which date back more than 40 centuries. The world's largest bristlecone pine can be found in Patriarch Grove, while the world's oldest living tree is along Methusula Trail in Schulman Grove. ⚠ **Getting to Patriarch Grove is slow going along the narrow dirt road, especially for sedans with low clearance.** ✉ *Schulman Grove visitor center, White Mountain Rd. (from U.S. 395, turn east onto Hwy. 168 and follow signs for 23 miles)* ⊕ *www.fs.usda.gov/main/inyo/home* ✎ *$3* ☉ *Mid-May–Nov., weather permitting*

BISHOP

43 miles north of Independence.

One of the biggest towns along U.S. 395, bustling Bishop has views of the Sierra Nevada and the White and Inyo mountains. First settled by the Northern Paiute Indians, the area was named in 1861 for cattle rancher Samuel Bishop, who established a camp here. Paiute and Shoshone people reside on four reservations in the area. Bishop kicks off the summer season with its Mule Days Celebration. Held over Memorial Day weekend, the five-day event includes mule races, a rodeo, an arts-and-crafts show, and country-music concerts.

GETTING HERE AND AROUND

To fully enjoy the many surrounding attractions, you must get here by car. Arrive and depart via U.S. 395 or, from Nevada, U.S. 6. Local transit provides limited service to nearby tourist sites.

ESSENTIALS

Bus Information Eastern Sierra Transit Authority ☎ *760/872–1901* ⊕ *www. estransit.com.*

Visitor Information Bishop Chamber of Commerce ✉ *690 N. Main St., at Park St.* ☎ *760/873–8405, 888/395–3952* ⊕ *www.bishopvisitor.com.*

EXPLORING

FAMILY **Laws Railroad Museum.** The laid-back and wholly nostalgic railroad museum celebrates the Carson and Colorado Railroad Company, which set up a narrow-gauge railroad yard here in 1883. Among the exhibits are a self-propelled car from the Death Valley Railroad, a stamp mill from an area mine, and a full village of rescued buildings, including a post office, the original 1883 train depot, and a restored 1900 ranch house. Many of the buildings are full of "modern amenities" of days gone by. ✉ *200 Silver Canyon Rd., off U.S. 6, 4.5 miles north of town* ☎ *760/873–5950* ⊕ *www.lawsmuseum.org* ✎ *$5 suggested donation* ☉ *Daily 10–4.*

11

WHERE TO EAT AND STAY

$ ✕ **Erick Schat's Bakkerÿ.** A bustling stop for motorists traveling to and
BAKERY from Mammoth Lakes, this shop is crammed with delicious pastries,
cookies, rolls, and other baked goods. The biggest draw, though, is
the sheepherder bread, a hand-shaped and stone hearth–baked sourdough that was introduced during the gold rush by immigrant Basque
sheepherders in 1907. That bread and others baked here are sliced to
make the mammoth sandwiches the shop is also famous for. $ *Average
main: $8* ✉ *763 N. Main St., near Park St.* ☎ *760/873–7156* ⊕ *www.
erickschatsbakery.com.*

$$ ⛺ **Bishop Creekside Inn.** The nicest spot to stay in Bishop, this clean
B&B/INN and comfortable mountain-style hotel is a good base from which to
explore the town or go skiing and trout fishing nearby. **Pros:** nice pool;
spacious and modern rooms. **Cons:** pets not allowed. $ *Rooms from:
$150* ✉ *725 N. Main St.* ☎ *760/872–3044, 800/273–3550* ⊕ *www.
bishopcreeksideinn.com* ⇱ *89 rooms* ⦿ *Breakfast.*

SPORTS AND THE OUTDOORS

The Owens Valley is trout country; its glistening alpine lakes and
streams are brimming with feisty rainbow, brown, brook, and golden
trout. Good spots include Owens River, the Owens River gorge, and
Pleasant Valley Reservoir. Although you can fish year-round here, some
fishing is catch-and-release. Bishop is the site of fishing derbies through-
out the year, including the Blake Jones Blind Bogey Trout Derby in
March. Rock-climbing, mountain biking, and hiking are also popular
Owens Valley outdoor activities.

FISHING

Brock's Flyfishing Specialists and Tackle Experts. Whether you want to take a
fly-fishing class or a guided wade trip, Brock's is a valuable resource. Its
website has up-to-date fishing reports. ✉ *100 N. Main St.* ☎ *760/872–
3581* ⊕ *www.brocksflyfish.com.*

TOURS

Sierra Mountain Center. The guided experiences Sierra Mountain offers
include hiking, skiing, snowshoeing, rock-climbing, and mountain-
biking trips for all levels of expertise. ✉ *200 S. Main St.* ☎ *760/873–
8526* ⊕ *www.sierramountaincenter.com.*

DEATH VALLEY
NATIONAL PARK

WELCOME TO DEATH VALLEY NATIONAL PARK

TOP REASONS TO GO

★ **Roving rocks:** Death Valley's Racetrack is home to moving boulders, a baffling phenomenon that scientists have only recently been able to explain.

★ **Lowest spot on the continent:** Stand on the lowest spot on the continent at Badwater, 282 feet below sea level.

★ **Wildflower explosion:** During the spring, this desert landscape is ablaze with greenery and colorful flowers, especially between Badwater and Ashford Mill.

★ **Ghost towns:** Death Valley is renowned for its Wild West heritage and is home to dozens of crumbling settlements including Ballarat, Cerro Gordo, Keeler, Panamint City, and Rhyolite.

★ **Naturally amazing:** From canyons to sand dunes to salt flats and dry lake beds, Death Valley serves up plenty of geological treasures.

NEVADA / CALIFORNIA

Visitor Center

Scotty's Castle
Ubehebe Crater   Grapevine
Mesquite Spring   267

PANAMINT RANGE

The Racetrack

Panamint Dunes   190

TO LONE PINE   Father Crowley Point   Panamint Springs

Darwin Falls   Wildrose Canyon Rd.

Darwin

TO RIDGECREST   178

0 ___ 10 mi
0 ___ 10 km

1 Central Death Valley. Furnace Creek sits in the heart of Death Valley—if you have only a short time in the park, head here. You can visit gorgeous Golden Canyon, Zabriskie Point, the Salt Creek Interpretive Trail, and Artist's Drive, among other popular points of interest.

2 Northern Death Valley. This region is uphill from Furnace Creek, which means marginally cooler temperatures. Be sure to stop by Rhyolite Ghost Town on Highway 374 before entering the park and exploring Moorish Scotty's Castle, colorful Titus Canyon, and jaw-dropping Ubehebe Crater.

3 Southern Death Valley. This is a desolate area, but there are plenty of sights that help convey Death Valley's rich history.

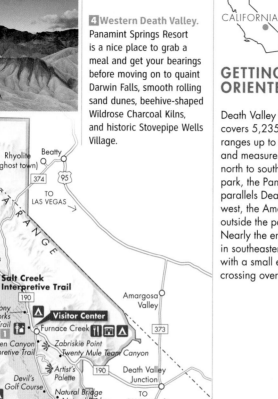

4 **Western Death Valley.**
Panamint Springs Resort
is a nice place to grab a
meal and get your bearings
before moving on to quaint
Darwin Falls, smooth rolling
sand dunes, beehive-shaped
Wildrose Charcoal Kilns,
and historic Stovepipe Wells
Village.

CALIFORNIA

12

GETTING ORIENTED

Death Valley National Park
covers 5,235 square miles,
ranges up to 60 miles wide,
and measures 160 miles
north to south. Within the
park, the Panamint Range
parallels Death Valley to the
west, the Amargosa Range is
outside the park to the east.
Nearly the entire park lies
in southeastern California,
with a small eastern portion
crossing over into Nevada.

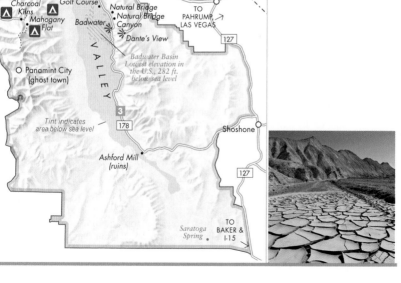

Updated by
Steve Pastorino

The desert is no Disneyland. With its scorching summer heat and vast, sparsely populated tracts of land, it's not often at the top of the list when most people plan their California vacations. But the natural riches of Death Valley—the largest national park outside Alaska—are overwhelming: rolling waves of sand dunes, black cinder cones thrusting up hundreds of feet from a blistered desert floor, riotous sheets of wildflowers, bizarrely shaped Joshua trees basking in the orange glow of a sunset, tiny pupfish that enthrall youngsters, and a silence that is both dramatic and startling.

DEATH VALLEY PLANNER

WHEN TO GO

Most of the park's 1 million annual visitors still come between late fall and early spring, taking advantage of moderate temperatures and the lack of rainfall. During these cooler months you will need to book a room in advance, but don't worry: the park never feels crowded. If you visit during summer, believe everything you've ever heard about desert heat—it can be brutal, with temperatures often topping 120°F. The dry air wicks moisture from the body without causing a sweat, so drink plenty of water. Bring sunglasses, a hat, and sufficient clothing to block the sun's rays and the wind. Flash floods are fairly common; sections of roadway can be flooded or washed away. The wettest month is February, when the park receives an average of 0.5 inch of rain.

GETTING HERE AND AROUND

CAR TRAVEL

It can take more than three hours to cross from one side of the park to another, so it's important to choose an entrance point that makes sense for what you want to see. If you're driving from Los Angeles, enter through the western portion along Highway 395; if you're coming from Las Vegas, enter from the north at Beatty, Nevada, or via the central entrance at Death Valley Junction. Travelers from Orange County, San Diego, and the Inland Empire should access the park via Interstate 15 North at Baker.

When driving in Death Valley, reliable maps are important, as signage is often limited or, in a few places, nonexistent. Other important accessories include a compass, a mobile phone (though these don't always work in remote areas), and extra food and water (at least 1 gallon per person per day is recommended, plus additional radiator water). If you're able to take a four-wheel-drive vehicle, bring it: many of Death Valley's most spectacular canyons are otherwise inaccessible. Be aware of possible winter closures or driving restrictions due to snow.

Driving Information California Highway Patrol. The California Highway Patrol offers the latest traffic incident information for roads outside the park. ☏ *800/427–7623 recorded info, 760/872–5900 live dispatcher ⊕ www.chp. ca.gov.* **California State Department of Transportation Hotline.** Call this hotline for updates on highways and other public road conditions. ☏ *800/427–7623 ⊕ www.dot.ca.gov.*

PARK ESSENTIALS
PARK FEES AND PERMITS
The entrance fee is $20 per vehicle and $10 for those entering on foot, bus, bike, or motorcycle. Payment, valid for seven consecutive days, is collected at the park's entrance stations and at the visitor center at Furnace Creek. (If you enter the park on Highway 190, you won't find an entrance station; remember to pay at a self-service fee station or stop by the visitor center to pay the fee.) Annual park passes, valid only at Death Valley, are $40.

A permit is not required for groups of 19 or fewer, but if you're planning an overnight visit to the backcountry, complete a registration form at the Furnace Creek Visitor Center. Backcountry camping is allowed in areas that are at least 2 miles from maintained campgrounds and the main paved or unpaved roads and ¼ mile from water sources. Most abandoned mining areas are restricted to day use.

PARK HOURS
Most facilities within the park remain open year-round, daily 8–6. Call ahead to see if seasonal changes are in effect.

PRICES

WHAT IT COSTS			
$	$$	$$$	$$$$
Restaurants under $12	$12–$20	$21–$30	over $30
Hotels under $100	$100–$150	$151–$200	over $200

Restaurant prices are the average cost of a main course at dinner or, if dinner is not served, at lunch. Hotel prices are the lowest cost of a standard double room in high season.

TOURS

Death Valley Tours. Choose from a variety of roughly 10-hour tours via all manner of vehicles: luxury motor-coach, SUV, even a Hummer. Tours of the park pass through its most famous landmarks, and include lunch and hotel pickup from designated Las Vegas–area hotels. ☎ *800/719–3768 Death Valley Tours ⊕ www.deathvalleytours.net ⊠ From $199.*

Farabee's Jeep Rentals. At Farabee's Jeep Rentals you can make a reservation for a guided tour into Titus Canyon (4 hours, $145), Badwater Basin (2 hours, $65), or Racetrack (8 hours, $280), or rent a two- or four-door Jeep for a do-it-yourself tour. Daily rates start at $195 and 200 free miles. All Jeeps come equipped with air-conditioning, automatic transmission, and an ice chest filled with water. Maps and off-roading driving instructions are provided, but don't worry if you get lost: your Jeep contains a GPS tracking unit. ⊠ *Across from Inn at Furnace Creek, Hwy. 190, Furnace Creek ☎ 760/786–9872, 877/970–5337 ⊕ www.farabeesjeeprentals.com ⊠ From $65.*

Furnace Creek Visitor Center tours. This center has many tour options, including a weekly 2-mile Harmony Borax Walk and guided hikes to Mosaic Canyon and Golden Canyon. Less strenuous options include wildflower, birding, and geology walks, and a Furnace Creek Inn historical tour. Visit the website for a complete list. The visitor center also shows a movie about the park every half hour daily from 8 to 5. ⊠ *Furnace Creek Visitor Center, Rte. 190, 30 miles northwest of Death Valley Junction ☎ 760/786–2331 ⊕ www.nps.gov/deva/planyourvisit/ tours.htm ⊙ Tours available mid-Nov. through mid-Apr.*

Pink Jeep Tours Las Vegas. Hop aboard a distinctive, pink four-wheel-drive vehicle with Pink Jeep Tours Las Vegas to visit places—the Charcola Kilns, the Racetrack, and Titus Canyon among them—that your own vehicle might not be able to handle. Pink Jeep tours are professionally narrated, and last 9 to 10 hours from Las Vegas (you also can board at Furnace Creek). ⊠ *3629 West Hacienda Ave., Las Vegas, Nevada ☎ 888/900–4480 ⊕ pinkjeeptours.com ⊠ From $244.*

VISITOR INFORMATION

PARK CONTACT INFORMATION

Death Valley National Park ☎ *760/786–3200 ⊕ www.nps.gov/deva.*

VISITOR CENTERS

Furnace Creek Visitor Center and Museum. The exhibits and artifacts here provide a broad overview of how Death Valley formed; you can pick up maps at the bookstore run by the Death Valley Natural History Association. This is also the place to learn about or sign up for ranger-led walks (available November through April) or check out a live presentation about the valley's cultural and natural history. The helpful center offers a 20-minute movie about the park every 30 minutes. Your children are likely to receive plenty of individual attention from the enthusiastic rangers. ⊠ *Hwy. 190, 30 miles northwest of Death Valley Junction ☎ 760/786–3200 ⊕ www.nps.gov/deva ⊙ Oct.–May, daily 8–5; June–Sept., daily 9–6.*

Scotty's Castle Visitor Center and Museum. During your visit to Death Valley, make sure you make the hour's drive north from Furnace Creek to Scotty's Castle. In addition to living-history tours, you'll find a nice display of exhibits, books, self-guided tour pamphlets, and displays about the castle's creators, Death Valley Scotty and Albert M. Johnson. Fuel up with convenience store food or souvenirs (there's no gasoline sold here anymore) before heading back out to the park. ⊠ *Rte. 267, 53 miles northwest of Furnace Creek and 45 miles northwest of Stovepipe Wells Village* ☎ *760/786–2392* ⊕ *www.nps.gov/deva* ☻ *Daily 9:45–3:45 (hours vary seasonally).*

EXPLORING

SCENIC DRIVES

Artist's Drive. This 9-mile, one-way route skirts the foothills of the Black Mountains and provides intimate views of the changing landscape. Once inside the palette, the huge expanses of the valley are replaced by the small-scale natural beauty of pigments created by volcanic deposits or sedimentary layers. It's a quiet, lonely drive, and shouldn't be rushed. Reach Artist's Palette by heading south on Badwater Road from its intersection with Rte. 190. ⊠ *Death Valley National Park.*

HISTORIC SITES

FAMILY **Scotty's Castle.** This Moorish-style mansion, begun in 1924 and never completed, takes its name from Walter Scott, better known as Death Valley Scotty. An ex-cowboy, prospector, and performer in Buffalo Bill's Wild West Show, Scotty always told people the castle was his, financed by gold from a secret mine. In reality, there was no mine, and the house belonged to a Chicago millionaire named Albert Johnson, whom Scott had finagled into investing in the fictitious mine. Despite the con, Johnson and Scott became great friends. The house functioned for a while as a hotel and still contains works of art, imported carpets, handmade European furniture, and a tremendous pipe organ. To see both floors of the house, you must book a tour—purchase tickets in advance to reserve a space during holidays and some weekends. Park rangers dressed in period attire re-create life at the castle circa 1939. Check out the Underground Tour (separate admission ticket required), which takes you through a ¼-mile tunnel in the castle basement. ⊠ *Scotty's Castle Rd. (Hwy. 267), 53 miles north of Salt Creek Interpretive Trail* ☎ *760/786–2392* ⊕ *www.nps.gov/deva* ☛ *$15* ☻ *Daily 8:30–4:15; tours daily 10–3:30 (hours vary seasonally).*

SCENIC STOPS

Artist's Palette. So called for the contrasting colors of its volcanic deposits and sedimentary layers, this is one of signature sights of Death Valley. Artist's Drive, the approach to the area, is one-way heading north off Badwater Road, so if you're visiting Badwater from Furnace Creek, come here on the way back. The drive winds through foothills of sedimentary and volcanic rocks. About 4 miles into the drive, a short side road veers right to a parking lot that's a few hundred feet before the "palette," whose natural colors include shades of green, gold, and pink. ✉ *Off Badwater Rd., 11 miles south of Furnace Creek.*

Badwater. At 282 feet below sea level, Badwater is the lowest spot on land in North America—and also one of the hottest. Stairs and wheelchair ramps descend from the parking lot to a wooden platform that overlooks a sodium chloride pool, a small but remarkably persistent reminder that the valley floor used to contain a lake. You can continue past the platform on a broad, white path that peters out after a half-mile or so. Badwater is one of the most popular and easily accessible sites within the park. From this lowest point, be sure to look across to Telescope Peak, which towers more than 2 miles above the valley floor. ✉ *Badwater Rd., 19 miles south of Furnace Creek.*

Fodor's Choice
★

Dante's View. This lookout is 5,450 feet above sea level in the Black Mountains. In the dry desert air you can see across most of 160-mile-long Death Valley. The view is astounding. Take a 10-minute, mildly strenuous walk from the parking lot toward a series of rocky overlooks, where with binoculars you can spot some of Death Valley's signature sites. A few interpretive signs point out the highlights below in the valley and across, in the Sierra. Getting here from Furnace Creek takes about an hour—time well invested. ✉ *Dante's View Rd., off Hwy. 190, 35 miles from Badwater, 20 miles south of Twenty Mule Team Canyon.*

Devil's Golf Course. Thousands of miniature salt pinnacles carved into surreal shapes by the desert wind dot this wildly varied landscape. The salt was pushed up to the earth's surface by pressure created as underground salt- and water-bearing gravel crystallized. Get out of your vehicle and take a closer look; you'll see perfectly round holes descending into the ground. ✉ *Badwater Rd., 13 miles south of Furnace Creek. Turn right onto dirt road and drive 1 mile.*

Racetrack. Getting here involves a 28-mile journey over a rough dirt road, but the reward is well worth the trip. Where else in the world do rocks move on their own? This phenomenon has baffled scientists for years, but in a paper published in August 2014, UC San Diego scientists proposed that freezing and melting water was causing giant rocks to "race" across the basin. You have to see this landscape to draw your own conclusions. The trek to the Racetrack can be made in a sedan, but beware—sharp rocks can slash tires; a truck or SUV with thick tires, high clearance, and a spare tire are suggested. ✉ *27 miles west of Ubehebe Crater via dirt road.*

Sand Dunes at Mesquite Flat. These dunes, made up of minute pieces of quartz and other rock, are ever-changing products of the wind-rippled hills, with curving crests and a sun-bleached hue. The dunes are the most photographed destination in the park, and you can see them at their best at sunrise and sunset. Keep your eyes open for animal tracks—you may spot a coyote or fox—and rattlesnakes on warm evenings. Bring plenty of water, and note where you parked your car: it's easy to become disoriented in this ocean of sand. If you lose your bearings, climb to the top of a dune and scan the horizon for the parking lot. ✉ *19 miles north of Hwy. 190, northeast of Stovepipe Wells Village.*

Titus Canyon. The most popular scenic drive in the park, this one-way, 27-mile route starts at Nevada Highway 374 (Daylight Pass Road), 2 miles from the park's boundary. Along the way you'll see Leadville Ghost Town and spectacular limestone and dolomite narrows at the end of the canyon. Toward the end, a two-way-section of gravel road leads you into the mouth of the canyon from Scotty's Castle Road. High-clearance vehicles are strongly recommended. ⊠ *Access road off Nevada Hwy. 374, 6 miles west of Beatty, NV.*

Zabriskie Point. This is one of Death Valley National Park's most scenic spots, overlooking a striking panorama of wrinkled, multicolor hills. Although only 710 feet in elevation, Zabriskie Point is a great place to watch the sunrise, but it can be bustling any time of day. Pair it with a drive out to magnificent Dante's View. ⊠ *Hwy. 190, 5 miles south of Furnace Creek.*

SPORTS AND THE OUTDOORS

BIRD-WATCHING

Approximately 307 bird species have been identified in Death Valley. The best place to see the park's birds is along the Salt Creek Interpretive Trail, where you can spot ravens, common snipes, killdeer, spotted sandpipers, and great blue herons. Along the fairways at Furnace Creek Golf Club, you can see kingfishers, peregrine falcons, hawks, Canada geese, yellow warblers, and the occasional golden eagle. Scotty's Castle attracts wintering birds from around the globe that are attracted to its running water, shady trees, and shrubs. Other good spots to find birds are at Saratoga Springs, Mesquite Springs, Travertine Springs, and Grimshaw Lake near Tecopa. You can download a complete park bird checklist, divided by season, at ⊕ *www.nps.gov/deva/naturescience/birds.htm.* Rangers at Furnace Creek Visitor Center often lead birding walks nearby between November and March.

FOUR-WHEELING

Maps and SUV guidebooks for four-wheel-drive and other backcountry roads (including the popular Cottonwood/Marble canyons, Racetrack, Eureka Dunes, Saratoga Springs, and Warm Springs Canyon) are offered at the Furnace Creek Visitor Center. Remember: Never travel alone and be sure to pack plenty of water and snacks. Driving off established roads is strictly prohibited in the park.

HIKING

Plan to hike before or after midday in the spring, summer, or fall; note that park rangers strongly discourage hiking during these seasons because of the heat. Carry plenty of water, wear protective clothing, and keep an eye out for black widows, scorpions, snakes, and other potentially dangerous creatures. Some of the best trails are unmarked; if the opportunity arises, ask for directions.

EASY

FAMILY Fodor's Choice ★ **Darwin Falls.** This lovely 2-mile round-trip hike rewards you with a refreshing waterfall surrounded by thick vegetation and a rocky gorge. No swimming or bathing is allowed, but it's a beautiful place for a picnic. Adventurous hikers can scramble higher toward more rewarding views of the falls. *Easy.* ✉ *Access the 2-mile graded dirt road and parking area off Hwy. 190, 1 mile west of Panamint Springs Resort.*

FAMILY **Salt Creek Interpretive Trail.** This trail, a ½-mile boardwalk circuit, loops through a spring-fed wash. The nearby hills are brown and gray, but the floor of the wash is alive with aquatic plants such as pickleweed and salt grass. The stream and ponds here are among the few places in the park to see the rare pupfish, the only native fish species in Death Valley. Animals such as bobcats, foxes, coyotes, and snakes visit the spring, and you may also see ravens, common snipes, killdeer, and great blue herons. *Easy.* ✉ *Off Hwy. 190, 14 miles north of Furnace Creek.*

MODERATE

Fall Canyon. This is a 3-mile, one-way hike from the Titus canyon parking area. First, walk ½ miles north along the base of the mountains to a large wash, then go 2½ miles up the canyon to a 35-foot dry fall. You can continue by climbing around to the falls on the south side. *Moderate.* ✉ *Access road off Scotty's Castle Rd., 33 miles northwest of Furnace Creek.*

FAMILY **Mosaic Canyon.** A gradual uphill trail (4 miles round-trip) winds through the smoothly polished, marbleized limestone walls of this narrow canyon. There are dry falls to climb at the upper end. *Moderate.* ✉ *Access road off Hwy. 190, ½ mile west of Stovepipe Wells Village.*

DIFFICULT

Fodor's Choice ★ **Telescope Peak Trail.** The 14-mile round-trip begins at Mahogany Flat Campground, which is accessible by a rough dirt road. The steep and at some points treacherous trail winds through pinyon, juniper, and bristlecone pines, with excellent views of Death Valley and Panamint Valley. Ice axes and crampons may be necessary in winter—check at the Furnace Creek Visitor Center. It takes a minimum of six grueling hours to hike to the top of the 11,049-foot peak and then return. Getting to the peak is a strenuous endeavor; take plenty of water and only attempt it in fall unless you're an experienced hiker. *Difficult.* ✉ *Off Wildrose Rd., south of Charcoal Kilns.*

WHERE TO EAT

$$ CAFÉ FAMILY 🍴 **Forty-Niner Cafe.** This casual coffee shop serves basic American fare for breakfast, lunch, and dinner. It's done up in a rustic mining style with whitewashed pine walls, vintage map-covered tables, and prospector-branded chairs. Past menus and old photographs decorate the walls. [$] *Average main: $20* ✉ *Ranch at Furnace Creek, Hwy. 190, Furnace Creek* ☎ *760/786–2345* 🌐 *www.furnacecreekresort.com.*

$$$$ AMERICAN Fodor's Choice ★ 🍴 **Inn at Furnace Creek Dining Room.** Fireplaces, beamed ceilings, and spectacular views provide a visual feast to match the inn's ambitious ever-evolving menu of California cuisine. Entrées range from filet mignon to salmon to sablefish, complemented with decidely non-desert sides

"I'd always wanted to photograph this remote location, and on my drive into Death Valley I was rewarded at Zabriskie Point with this amazing view." —photo by Rodney Ee, Fodors.com member

such as pearl barley risotto and savoyard potatoes. There's a seasonal menu of vegetarian dishes, too. There's a nominal evening dress code (no T-shirts or shorts). Lunch is served, too, and you can always have afternoon tea in the lobby, an inn tradition since 1927. Breakfast and Sunday brunch are also served. Reservations are essential for dinner only. $ *Average main: $38* ⊠ *Inn at Furnace Creek, Hwy. 190, Furnace Creek* ☎ *760/786–3385* ⊕ *www.furnacecreekresort.com* ⋒ *Reservations essential* ☉ *Closed Mother's Day–mid-Oct.*

WHERE TO STAY

During the busy season (November through March) you should make reservations for lodgings within the park several months in advance.

$$$$
HOTEL
Fodors Choice
★

☷ **The Inn at Furnace Creek.** Built in 1927, this adobe-brick-and-stone lodge nestled in one of the park's greenest oases is Death Valley's most luxurious accommodation, going so far as to have valet parking. **Pros:** refined; comfortable; great views. **Cons:** a far cry from roughing it; expensive. $ *Rooms from: $399* ⊠ *Furnace Creek Village, near intersection of Hwy. 190 and Badwater Rd.* ☎ *760/786–2345* ⊕ *www. furnacecreekresort.com* ⬗ *66 rooms* ☉ *Closed Mother's Day–mid-Oct.* ⁑*Breakfast.*

$
HOTEL

☷ **Panamint Springs Resort.** Ten miles inside the west entrance of the park, this low-key resort overlooks the sand dunes and peculiar geological formations of the Panamint Valley. **Pros:** slow-paced; friendly; there's a glorious amount of peace and quiet after sundown. **Cons:** far from the park's main attractions. $ *Rooms from: $79* ⊠ *40440*

CLOSE UP

Plants and Wildlife in Death Valley

There's a general misconception that Death Valley National Park consists of mile upon endless mile of flat desert sands, scattered cacti, and an occasional cow skull. Many people don't realize that across the valley floor from Badwater—the lowest point in North America—Telescope Peak towers at 11,049 feet above sea level. The extreme topography of Death Valley is a lesson in geology. Two hundred million years ago seas covered the area, depositing layers of sediment and fossils. Between 3.5 million and 5 million years ago faults in the Earth's crust and volcanic activity pushed and folded the ground, causing mountain ranges to rise and the valley floor to drop. The valley was then filled periodically by lakes, which eroded the surrounding rocks into fantastic formations and deposited the salts that now cover the floor of the basin.

Most animal life in Death Valley (51 mammal, 36 reptile, 307 bird, and 3 amphibian species) is found near the limited sources of water. The bighorn sheep spend most of their time in the secluded upper reaches of the park's rugged canyons and ridges. Coyotes often can be seen lazing in the shade next to the golf course and have been known to run onto the fairways to steal a golf ball. The only native fish in the park is the pupfish, which grows to slightly longer than 1 inch. In winter, when the water is cold, the fish lie dormant in the bottom mud, becoming active again in spring. Because they are wary of large moving shapes, you must stand quietly over a pool at Salt Creek to see them.

Botanists say there are more than 1,000 species of plants here (21 exist nowhere else in the world), though many annual plants lie dormant as seeds for all but a few months in spring, when rains trigger a bloom. The rest congregate around the few water sources. Most of the low-elevation vegetation grows around the oases at Furnace Creek and Scotty's Castle, where oleanders, palms, and salt cedar grow. At higher elevations you will find pinyon, juniper, and bristlecone pine.

Hwy. 190, 28 miles west of Stovepipe Wells ☎ 775/482–7680 🌐 www.panamintsprings.com 🛏 14 rooms, 1 cabin 🍴 No meals.

$$ HOTEL 🏨 **Stovepipe Wells Village.** If you prefer quiet nights and an unfettered view of the night sky and nearby sand dunes and Mosaic Canyon, this property is for you. **Pros:** intimate; relaxed; no big-time partying; authentic desert-community ambience. **Cons:** isolated; a bit dated. [$] *Rooms from: $117 ✉ 51880 Hwy. 190, Stovepipe Wells ☎ 760/786–2387 🌐 www.escapetodeathvalley.com 🛏 83 rooms 🍴 No meals.*

THE CENTRAL VALLEY

Highway 99 from Bakersfield to Lodi

WELCOME TO
THE CENTRAL VALLEY

TOP REASONS TO GO

★ **Down under:** The handiwork of an Italian immigrant who helped dig New York City's subway, Forestiere Underground Gardens is an oddly inspirational attraction.

★ **Grape escape:** In the past two decades, Lodi's wineries have grown sufficiently in stature for the charming little town to become a must-sip destination.

★ **Utopian spirit:** A century ago, a small but resourceful group of citizens established the state's first all–African American town. Colonel Allensworth State Historic Park celebrates their utopian spirit.

★ **Go with the flow:** Whitewater rafting will get your blood pumping, and maybe your clothes wet, on the Kern River near Kernville.

★ **Hee haw!:** Kick up your heels and break out your drawl at Buck Owens' Crystal Palace in Bakersfield, a city some believe is the heart of country music.

1 Southern Central Valley. When gold was discovered in Kern County in the 1860s, settlers flocked to the southern end of the Central Valley. Black gold—oil—is now the area's most valuable commodity; the county provides two-thirds of California's oil production. Kern is also among the country's five most productive agricultural counties. From the flat plains around Bakersfield, the landscape grows gently hilly and then graduates to mountains as it nears Kernville, which lies in the Kern River valley.

2 Mid-Central Valley. The Mid-Central Valley extends over three counties—Tulare, Kings, and Fresno. Bustling Visalia is mostly off the tourist-traffic radar but has its charms. From Visalia, Highway 198 winds east 35 miles to Generals Highway, which passes through Sequoia and Kings Canyon national parks. Highway 180 snakes east 55 miles to Sequoia and Kings Canyon. From Fresno, Highway 41 leads north 95 miles to Yosemite National Park.

3 North Central Valley. The northern section of the valley cuts through Merced, Madera, Stanislaus, and San Joaquin counties, from the flat, abundantly fertile terrain between Merced and Modesto north to the edges of the Sacramento River delta and the fringes of the Gold Country. Modesto serves as a gateway to Yosemite, and Lodi lures lovers of old-vine Zinfandels and other robust wines.

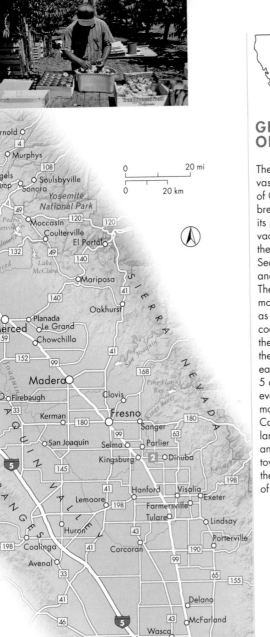

GETTING ORIENTED

The Central Valley is the vast geographical center of California and, from a breadbasket perspective, its proverbial heart. Many vacationers travel through the region on the way to Sequoia, Kings Canyon, and Yosemite national parks. The valley's flat landscapes may not appear as scenic as those along the dramatic coastline to the west and the spectacular peaks of the Sierra Nevada to the east. Beyond busy Interstate 5 and Highway 99, however, the region reflects the more subtle beauty of rural California: bountiful farmland, miles of gentle hillsides and wildlife areas, and small towns that have preserved the heritage and character of the state's early history.

Updated by Cheryl Crabtree

In California's family of diverse regions, the 225-mile-long Central Valley is literally and figuratively a middle sibling. Cradled between the popular coastal communities to the west and the national parks in the mighty Sierra Nevada to the east, the "Big Valley" is among the world's most fertile working lands, filled with orchards, vineyards, and farms. The area also supports myriad bird and other animal species.

The Central Valley encompasses all or part of eight counties. Vineyards, especially in the northern valley around Lodi, and almond orchards, whose white blossoms make February a brighter month, are pleasant sights out motorists' windows. In the towns, historical societies display artifacts of the region's eccentric past, concert halls and restored theaters showcase samplings of contemporary culture, and museums provide a blend of both. Country-music enthusiasts will find a lot to appreciate on the radio and on stages, especially in the Bakersfield area. Summer nights spent at a minor-league baseball park—Bakersfield, Fresno, Modesto, and Visalia have teams—can be a relaxing, affordable experience. Whether you're on back roads or main streets, you'll find the locals proud to help outsiders explore the area.

PLANNING

WHEN TO GO
Spring, when wildflowers are in bloom and the scent of fruit blossoms is in the air, and fall, when the air is brisk and leaves turn red and gold, are the best times to visit. Many festivals take place during these seasons. (If you suffer from allergies, though, beware of spring, when stone-fruit trees blossom.) Summer, when temperatures often top 100 degrees F, can be oppressive, though area water parks and lakes provide respite. Many attractions close in winter. Thick, ground-hugging tule fog is a common driving hazard at this time.

GETTING HERE AND AROUND

AIR TRAVEL

The area's main airport is Fresno Yosemite International Airport (FAT), served by AeroMexico, Alaska, Allegiant, American, Delta, Frontier, United/United Express, US Airways, and Volaris. Bakersfield's Meadows Field Airport (BFL), served by United and US Airways, is the southern air gateway to the Central Valley.

Airport Contacts **Fresno Yosemite International Airport** (FAT) ✉ *5175 E. Clinton Way, Fresno* ☎ *800/244–2359 automated info, 559/454–2052 terminal info desk* ⊕ *www.flyfresno.com.* **Meadows Field Airport** (BFL) ✉ *3701 Wings Way, off Merle Haggard Dr., Bakersfield* ☎ *661/391-1800* ⊕ *www.meadowsfield. com.*

BUS TRAVEL

Greyhound provides bus service to several cities; Orange Belt Stages to Bakersfield, Visalia, and other towns; KART (Kings Area Rural Transit) throughout Kings County; Kern Transit in Bakersfield and the Kern River valley; and YARTS (Yosemite Area Rapid Transit System) to Yosemite Valley from Fresno, Merced, and other towns.

Bus Contact **Greyhound** ☎ *800/231-2222* ⊕ *www.greyhound.com.* **KART** ☎ *559/584-0101* ⊕ *mykartbus.com.* **Kern Transit** ☎ *800/323-2396* ⊕ *kerntransit.org.* **Orange Belt Stages** ☎ *800/266-7433 toll-free Fresno/ Bakersfield, 559/733-4408 Visalia* ⊕ *www.orangebelt.com.* **YARTS** ☎ *877/989–2787, 209/388-9589* ⊕ *www.yarts.com.*

CAR TRAVEL

Highway 99 is the main route between the valley's major cities and towns. Interstate 5 runs roughly parallel to it to the west but misses the major population centers; its main use is for quick access to San Francisco or Los Angeles. Major roads that connect the interstate with Highway 99 are highways 58 (to Bakersfield), 198 (to Visalia), 140 (to Merced), 132 (to Modesto), and 120 (to Manteca).

Road Conditions **Caltrans** ☎ *800/427-7623* ⊕ *www.dot.ca.gov.*

TRAIN TRAVEL

The Central Valley stops of Amtrak's daily *San Joaquin* train include Bakersfield, Fresno, Merced, Modesto, Stockton, and Lodi, with connections to YARTS (⇨ *Bus Travel, above*) in Fresno and Merced.

Train Contact **Amtrak** ☎ *800/872-7245* ⊕ *www.amtrakcalifornia.com.*

RESTAURANTS

Fast-food and chain restaurants are omnipresent, but homegrown bistros and fine restaurants take advantage of the local produce and meats. Superb Mexican food abounds, and Chinese, Italian, Armenian, and Basque cuisines are amply represented.

HOTELS

Chain motels and hotels predominate, but there are upscale lodgings, small inns, and Victorian-style bed-and-breakfasts. *Hotel reviews have been shortened. For full information, visit Fodors.com.*

WHAT IT COSTS			
$	**$$**	**$$$**	**$$$$**
Restaurants	under $16	$16–$22	$23–$30	over $30
Hotels	under $120	$120–$175	$176–$250	over $250

Restaurant prices are the average cost of a main course at dinner, excluding sales tax of 7%–10% (depending on location). Hotel prices are in the lowest cost of a standard double room in high season, excluding service charges and 8%–13% tax.

SOUTH CENTRAL VALLEY

BAKERSFIELD

110 miles north of Los Angeles; 110 miles west of Ridgecrest.

Bakersfield's founder, Colonel Thomas Baker, arrived with the discovery of gold in the nearby Kern River valley in 1851. With 364,000 residents, including the country's largest Basque community, his namesake town, nicknamed Nashville West, is closely affiliated with country-music performers Buck Owens, who died here, and Merle Haggard, who was born here. It has an up-and-coming arts district and some fine museums. Historic sites and other downtown attractions are a short walk from the Amtrak station.

GETTING HERE AND AROUND

Arrive here by car via Highway 99 from the north or south, or via Highway 58 from the east or west. Amtrak and Greyhound provide train and bus service. GETbus operates local buses.

ESSENTIALS

Bus Contact GETbus ☎ 661/869–2438 ⊕ www.getbus.org.

Visitor Information Bakersfield Convention & Visitors Bureau ✉ 515 *Truxtun Ave.* ☎ 661/852–7282, 866/425–7353 ⊕ *visitbakersfield.com* ☉ *Weekdays 8–5.* **VisitKern** ✉ 2101 Oak St. ☎ 661/868–5376, 661/861–2017 ⊕ www. visitkern.com.

EXPLORING

FAMILY **California Living Museum.** At this combination zoo, botanical garden, and Fodor'sChoice natural history museum, the emphasis is on the zoo. Within the reptile ★ house lives every species of rattlesnake found in California. The landscaped grounds—about a 20-minute drive northeast of Bakersfield—also shelter captive bald eagles, tortoises, coyotes, black bears, and foxes. Additions in 2015 include a touch tank and jellyfish exhibit, a zip line, and a high ropes challenge course. ✉ *10500 Alfred Harrell Hwy., Hwy. 178 east to Harrell Hwy. north* ☎ 661/872–2256 ⊕ *calmzoo.org* 🖾 *$9* ☉ *Mar.–Oct., daily 9–5; Nov.–Feb., daily 9–4.*

FAMILY **Kern County Museum and Lori Brock Children's Discovery Center.** This 16-acre Fodor'sChoice site is one of the Central Valley's top museum complexes. The indoor-★ outdoor Kern County Museum is an open-air, walk-through historic

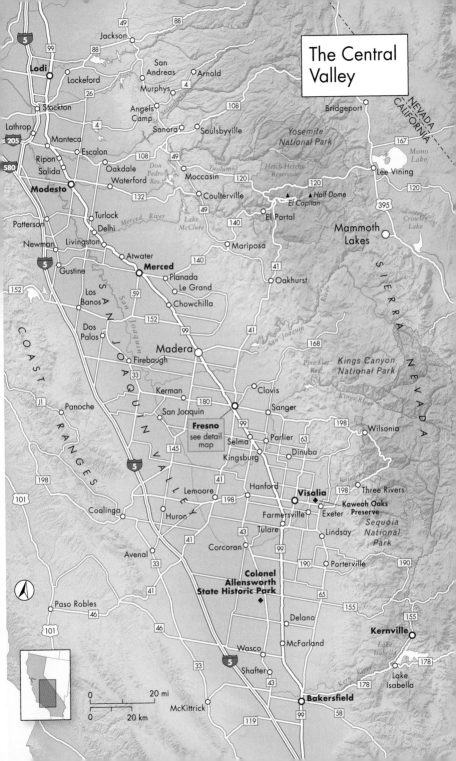

The Central Valley

village with more than 55 restored or re-created buildings dating from the 1860s to the 1940s. "Black Gold: The Oil Experience," a permanent exhibit, shows how oil is created, discovered, extracted, and transformed for various uses. The Lori Brock Children's Discovery Center, for ages eight and younger, has hands-on displays and an indoor playground. ✉ *3801 Chester Ave., at 38th St.* ☎ *661/437–3330* 🌐 *www.kcmuseum.org* 🎟 *$10* ⏲ *Mar.–Nov., Mon.–Sat. 10–5, Sun. noon–5; Dec.–Feb., Mon.–Sat. 10–4, Sun. noon–4.*

FAMILY **Murray Family Farms.** You can partake of the southern Central Valley's agricultural bounty at the farm's Big Red Barn location—owners Steve and Vickie Murray promise more free samples than Costco, and they deliver. You'll find whatever's in season, including peaches, plums, apricots, and 18 cherry varieties. There are prepared foods, too, and activities for kids (jumping pillow, petting zoo, hay rides, AstroTurf sledding hill). The Cal-Okie Kitchen sells tasty fry pies filled with eggs and other ingredients for breakfast and pulled chicken and other meats for lunch and dinner. ✉ *6700 General Beale Rd., off Hwy. 58, 18 miles south of downtown* ☎ *661/330–0100* 🌐 *www.murrayfamilyfarms.com* 🎟 *Store: free; Farm tours: $6 weekdays, $10 Sat., and $8 Sun.* ⏲ *Daily 8–8 most months, call for seasonal hrs; farm visits close at dusk.*

WHERE TO EAT

$ THAI 🍴 **Chef's Choice Noodle Bar.** Aromatic pan-Asian spices, healthful ingredients, and inventive cocktails have made this arts-district eatery a local fave. Chef Preeda Piamfa, who hails from Thailand's east coast, focuses on Thai cuisine, including traditional curries, soups, and noodles (try the drunken noodles with duck), but he also prepares dishes from Japan, Singapore, and Vietnam. Preeda even puts an Asian twist on American standards. Case in point: the citrus-marinated rib-eye steak, served with carrot fried rice and steamed vegetables and topped with tamarind sauce. [$] *Average main: $13* ✉ *1534 19th St., at Eye St.* ☎ *661/325–1234* 🌐 *www.ccnoodlebar.com* ⏲ *Closed Sun.*

$$ ITALIAN Fodor's Choice ★ 🍴 **Luigi's.** The same family has operated this popular restaurant, bar, and delicatessen at the same site since 1910. Feast on generous portions of pastas and sauces made from old family recipes. The extensive menu also includes sandwiches, steaks, salads, and daily specials such as prime rib and lasagna. Plates are served family style in several casual rooms, reminiscent of a Tuscan trattoria and decorated with local sports photos. **TIP→ Luigi's isn't open for dinner, but you can order to-go items, or pick up meal fixings at the adjacent deli.** [$] *Average main: $16* ✉ *725 E. 19th St.* ☎ *661/322–0926* 🌐 *www.shopluigis.com* ✍ *Reservations not accepted* ⏲ *Closed Sun. and Mon. No dinner.*

$$ MODERN AMERICAN 🍴 **The Mark.** An upscale restaurant and bar in the downtown arts district, The Mark specializes in fresh seafood, hand-cut steaks, pastas, homemade soups, and comfort foods such as chicken potpie. Though the dishes are straightforward, they're skillfully executed. The wine list favors California but includes representatives from France, Italy, and elsewhere abroad. At the bar, which hosts live music, you can sink into leather high-back chairs and booths and order creative cocktails. [$] *Average main: $19* ✉ *1623 19th St.* ☎ *661/322–7665* 🌐 *www.atthemark.com* ⏲ *Closed Sun. No lunch Sat.*

WHERE TO STAY

$$ **Bakersfield Marriott Convention Center.** A safe choice, the full-service
HOTEL Marriott caters to the business and convention crowd with spacious,
tech-updated rooms that also serve vacationing families well. **Pros:**
clean; large pool; good fitness center; convenient to convention cen-
ter; business services; discounted weekend rates often available online.
Cons: not much character; service can be spotty. $ *Rooms from:*
$159 ⊠ *801 Truxtun Ave.* ☎ *661/323–1900, 844/745–6336* ⊕ *www.*
bakersfieldmarriott.com ⬳ *250 rooms, 9 suites* ⊙⃒ *No meals.*

$$ **Four Points by Sheraton.** Fountains, lush lawns, and exotic plants pro-
HOTEL vide a spectacular setting for this hotel. **Pros:** clean; good neighborhood.
Cons: somewhat impersonal; far from main attractions. $ *Rooms from:*
$129 ⊠ *5101 California Ave.* ☎ *661/325–9700, 800/368–7764* ⊕ *www.*
fourpointsbakersfield.com ⬳ *198 rooms* ⊙⃒ *No meals.*

$$ **Padre Hotel.** Erected in 1928 during the Oil Rush era, the eight-story
HOTEL Padre is a sophisticated contemporary haven. **Pros:** in the heart of his-
Fodor's Choice toric downtown; hip urban vibe; 24-hour room service. **Cons:** noise
★ from the bars and lounges travels to some rooms; service sometimes
inconsistent. $ *Rooms from: $169* ⊠ *1702 18th St.* ☎ *661/427–4900*
⊕ *www.thepadrehotel.com* ⬳ *109 rooms, 2 suites* ⊙⃒ *No meals.*

NIGHTLIFE AND PERFORMING ARTS

Buck Owens' Crystal Palace and Museum. The late Buck Owens is Bakers-
field's local boy made good, and this venue is a combination nightclub,
restaurant, souvenir store, and country music memorabilia showcase.
Country-and-western entertainers perform here, as Owens himself
did countless times. A dance floor beckons patrons who can still twirl
after sampling the menu of steaks, burgers, nachos, and gooey desserts.
⊠ *2800 Buck Owens Blvd., off Hwy. 178* ☎ *661/328–7560* ⊕ *www.*
buckowens.com ⬳ *Cover charge some weeknights, most weekends*
⊙ *Closed Mon. No dinner Sun.*

KERNVILLE

50 miles northeast of Bakersfield.

The wild Kern River, which flows through Kernville en route from Mt.
Whitney to Bakersfield, delivers some of the most exciting white-water
rafting in the state. Kernville (population 1,400) rests in a mountain val-
ley on both banks of the river and at the northern tip of Lake Isabella,
a dammed portion of the river used as a reservoir and for recreation.

Old West–style buildings line Kernville's main streets, reflecting the
city's heritage as a rough-and-tumble gold-mining town once known
as Whiskey Flat. Present-day Kernville dates from the 1950s, when it
was moved upriver to make room for Lake Isabella. The road from
Bakersfield includes stretches where the rushing river is on one side and
granite cliffs are on the other.

GETTING HERE AND AROUND

Highway 178 connects Kernville and Bakersfield; take Highway 155
if coming from Delano.

ESSENTIALS

Visitor Information **Kern County Board of Trade** ☎ *661/868–5376, 661/868–2017* 🌐 *www.visitkern.com.*

EXPLORING

Fodor's Choice ★ **Kern Valley Museum.** A cadre of sweet, well-informed volunteers runs this jam-packed throwback of a museum that's bigger than it looks from the outside. With exhibits about Lake Isabella, minerals and gems, old tools and farming implements, pioneer and native life, and Hollywood Westerns shot in the area, you'll likely find something to intrigue you. ✉ *49 Big Blue Rd., off Kernville Rd.* ☎ *760/376–6683* 🌐 *www.kernvalleymuseum.org* 🎫 *Free* 🕓 *Thurs.–Sun. 10–4.*

WHERE TO EAT AND STAY

$ ITALIAN 🍴 **That's Italian.** For northern Italian cuisine in a no-frills trattoria, this is the spot. Try the braised lamb shanks in a Chianti wine sauce, grilled rib eye with chef's seasonal sauce, or the filet mignon with shrimp, roasted pepper, and onions in a demiglaze sauce. To drift back to old Italy—or 1950s Kernville, perhaps—sample the spaghetti and meatballs. [$] *Average main: $15* ✉ *9 Big Blue Rd., at Kernville Rd.* ☎ *760/376–6020* 🕓 *Closed Mon. year-round, Tues. mid-Sept.–Mar. No lunch.*

$$$ B&B/INN 🏨 **Whispering Pines Lodge.** On the banks of the Kern River, this 8-acre property has units that are motel-style or in duplex bungalows; all have fireplaces, king-size beds, Wi-Fi access, large-screen TVs, and traditional pine and oak furnishings. **Pros:** rustic setting; big breakfasts; great views; very clean. **Cons:** bungalows are pricey; town is remote. [$] *Rooms from: $189* ✉ *13745 Sierra Way* ☎ *760/376–3733, 877/241–4100* 🌐 *pineskernville.com* 🛏 *17 rooms* 🍽 *Breakfast.*

SPORTS AND THE OUTDOORS

BOATING AND WINDSURFING

The Lower Kern River, which extends from Lake Isabella to Bakersfield and beyond, is open for bass, trout, and other fishing year-round. Lake Isabella is popular with anglers, water-skiers, sailors, and windsurfers.

French Gulch Marina. The marina has moorings, boat rentals, and a full-service general store. ✉ *Western shore, near dam* ☎ *760/379–8774* 🌐 *www.frenchgulchmarina.com.*

North Fork Marina. This west-shore operation rents slips and boats and has bait and tackle at its general store. ✉ *100 Tuttle Rd., Wofford Heights* ☎ *760/376–1812* 🌐 *www.northforkmarina.com.*

WHITE-WATER RAFTING

The three sections of the Kern River—known as the Lower Kern, Upper Kern, and the Forks—add up to nearly 50 miles of white water, ranging from Class I (easy) to Class V (expert). The Lower and Upper Kern are the most popular and accessible sections. Rafting season usually runs from late spring until the end of summer.

Kern River Tours. This outfit leads rafting tours—from half a day or less on Class II or III rapids to three-day excursions on Class V ones. ✉ *2712 Mayfair Rd., Lake Isabella* ☎ *800/844–7238, 760/379–4616* 🌐 *www.kernrivertours.com* 🎫 *From $38.*

Mountain & River Adventures. The lineup here includes calm-water kayaking and stand-up paddleboard tours, white-water rafting trips, and mountain-bike excursions. The company also has a campground, a climbing wall, and a ropes course. ✉ *11113 Kernville Rd.* ☎ *760/376–6553, 800/861–6553* ⊕ *www.mtnriver.com* ✎ *From $40.*

Sierra South. Half-day Class II and III white-water rafting trips are emphasized at Sierra South, which also offers kayaking classes and calm-water excursions. ✉ *11300 Kernville Rd.* ☎ *760/376–3745, 800/457–2082* ⊕ *www.sierrasouth.com* ✎ *From $45.*

13

MID-CENTRAL VALLEY

COLONEL ALLENSWORTH STATE HISTORIC PARK

45 miles north of Bakersfield.

GETTING HERE AND AROUND
The easiest way to get here is by car. The park is off Highway 43, a 15-minute drive west of Highway 99.

Fodor'sChoice **Colonel Allensworth State Historic Park.** It's worth the slight detour off
★ Highway 99 to learn about and pay homage to the dream of Allen Allensworth and other black pioneers who in 1908 founded Allensworth, the only California town settled, governed, and financed by African Americans. At its height, the town prospered as a key railroad transfer point, but after cars and trucks reduced railroad traffic and water was diverted for Central Valley agriculture, the town declined and was eventually deserted. Today the restored and rebuilt schoolhouse, library, and other structures commemorate Allensworth's heyday, as do festivities that take place each October. ■TIP→ **The parking lot is open only on Thursday, Friday, and weekends, but daily you can park nearby, walk over to the buildings, and peek in.** ✉ *4129 Palmer Ave., off Hwy. 43; from Hwy. 99 at Delano, take Garces Hwy. west to Hwy. 43 north; from Earlimart, take County Rd. J22 west to Hwy. 43 south* ☎ *661/849–3433* ⊕ *www.parks.ca.gov* ✎ *$6 per car* ☉ *Daily sunrise–sunset; visitor center Thurs.–Sun. 10–4; buildings open by appointment.*

VISALIA

75 miles north of Bakersfield.

Visalia's combination of a reliable agricultural economy and civic pride has produced the Central Valley's most vibrant downtown. If you're into Victorian and other old houses, drop by the visitor center and pick up a free map of them. A clear day's view of the Sierra from Main Street is spectacular, and even Sunday night can find the streets bustling with pedestrians. Visalia provides easy access to grand Sequoia National Park and the serene Kaweah Oaks Preserve.

GETTING HERE AND AROUND
Highway 198, just east of its exit from Highway 99, cuts through town (and proceeds up the hill to Sequoia National Park). Greyhound stops here, but not Amtrak. KART buses serve the locals, and in summer the

Sequoia Shuttle travels between Visalia and Sequoia National Park with a stop in Three Rivers.

Sequoia Shuttle ☎ *877/287–4453* ⊕ *www.sequoiashuttle.com* ✉ *$15 round-trip* ⊗ *Late May–early Sept.*

ESSENTIALS

Visitor Information Visalia Convention & Visitors Bureau ⊠ *Kiosk, 303 E. Acequia Ave., at S. Bridge St.* ☎ *559/334-0141, 800/524-0303* ⊕ *www. visitvisalia.org* ⊗ *Weekdays 8–5.*

EXPLORING

TOP ATTRACTIONS

Kaweah Oaks Preserve. Trails at this 344-acre wildlife sanctuary off the main road to Sequoia National Park lead past majestic valley oak, sycamore, cottonwood, and willow trees. Among the 134 bird species you might spot are hawks, hummingbirds, and great blue herons. Bobcats, lizards, coyotes, and cottontails also live here. The Sycamore Trail has digital signage with QR codes you can scan with your smartphone to access plant and animal information. ⊠ *Follow Hwy. 198 for 7 miles east of Visalia, turn north on Rd. 182, and proceed ½ mile to gate on left side* ☎ *559/738-0211* ⊕ *www.sequoiariverlands.org* ✉ *Free* ⊗ *Daily sunrise–sunset.*

WORTH NOTING

FAMILY   **Bravo Farms Traver.** For one-stop truck-stop entertainment, pull off the highway in Traver, where at Bravo Farms you can try your luck at an arcade shooting gallery, watch cheese being made, munch on barbecue and ice cream, play a round of mini golf, peruse funky antiques, buy produce, visit a petting zoo, and climb a multistory tree house. Taste a few "squeekers" (fresh cheese curds, so named because chewing them makes your teeth squeak), and then be on your way. ⊠ *36005 Hwy. 99, 9 miles north of Hwy. 198 and Visalia, Traver* ☎ *559/897-5762* ⊕ *www.bravofarms.com* ✉ *Free* ⊗ *Daily 7–7.*

FAMILY
Fodor's Choice
★   **McKellar Family Farms.** Taste, touch, and feel your way through orange and mandarin groves on a guided tour of this 180-acre working citrus farm. Tours last from 60 to 90 minutes. McKellar Family Farms also has the nation's only orange-grove maze. Kids and adults love the challenge of navigating it, answering questions at a series of checkpoints to earn a prize at the end. ⊠ *32985 Rd. 164, north of Hwy. 216, Ivanhoe* ☎ *559/798-0557* ⊕ *www.mckellarfamilyfarms.com* ✉ *Tour $10, maze $3* ⊗ *Tours daily, by appointment.*

FAMILY   **Mooney Grove Park.** Amid shady oaks you can picnic alongside duck ponds, rent a boat and tool around the lagoon, and view a bronze replica of James Earl Fraser's iconic *End of the Trail* sculpture, which depicts a Native American warrior on horseback. The indoor-outdoor **Tulare County Museum** contains several re-created environments from the pioneer era, displays of Yokuts tribal artifacts (basketry, arrowheads, clamshell-necklace currency), and exhibits that chronicle farm history and labor. ⊠ *27000 S. Mooney Blvd., off Hwy. 63, 5 miles south of downtown* ☎ *559/733-6616 museum* ⊕ *www.tularecountyhistoricalsociety. org* ✉ *$7 per car, free in winter* ⊗ *Park: daily 8–sunset, sometimes closed Tues. and Wed.; Museum: Thurs.–Mon. 10–4.*

13

WHERE TO EAT

$$ MODERN AMERICAN 🍴 **Café 225.** High ceilings and contemporary decor create a relaxed elegance at this popular downtown restaurant. Chef-owner Karl Merten can often be spotted at area markets seeking out locally grown ingredients for his seasonally changing dishes. Meats and fish grilled on a wood-fired rotisserie figure prominently on the menu, which also includes pastas and unusual treats such as artichoke fritters and slow-roasted pork loin adobo. The green-chili burger, grilled over oak coals and served with sharp cheddar and chipotle aioli, is a town favorite. [$] *Average main: $19* ✉ *225 W. Main St.* ☎ *559/733–2967* 🌐 *www.cafe225.com* 🕒 *Closed Sun.*

$ AMERICAN 🍴 **The Lunch Box.** A casual downtown café and bakery, the Lunch Box serves healthful meals at reasonable prices. Choose from nearly 50 types of hot and cold sandwiches and wraps, more than 20 different salads, and soups such as chicken noodle and Tuscan tomato. Tandoori-seasoned salmon fillet and chicken verde enchiladas are typical daily specials. **TIP→ This is a good place for a quick bite or to pick up picnic items before or after a visit to Sequoia National Park.** [$] *Average main: $10* ✉ *112 N. Court St., at Main St.* ☎ *559/635–8624* 🌐 *lunchboxcateringcompany.com* 🕒 *Closed Sun.*

$$$$ EUROPEAN Fodor's Choice ★ 🍴 **The Vintage Press.** Built in 1966, this is the best restaurant in the Central Valley. Cut-glass doors and bar fixtures decorate the artfully designed rooms. The California–continental cuisine includes dishes such as crispy veal sweetbreads with a port-wine sauce and filet mignon with a cognac-mustard sauce. The chocolate Grand Marnier cake is a standout among the homemade desserts and ice creams. The wine list has more than 900 selections. [$] *Average main: $32* ✉ *216 N. Willis St.* ☎ *559/733–3033* 🌐 *www.thevintagepress.com.*

WHERE TO STAY

$ HOTEL 🏨 **Hampton Inn Visalia.** In a town with a fair share of outmoded properties the Hampton stands out as a clean, well-run facility with a friendly staff. **Pros:** clean; friendly staff; complimentary breakfast; 24-hour business center; less than an hour's drive from Sequoia National Park. **Cons:** on a service road and hard to find; some guests may find rooms facing freeway too noisy. [$] *Rooms from: $118* ✉ *4747 W. Noble Ave., off Hwy. 198 Akers exit* ☎ *559/732–3900, 800/426–7866* 🌐 *hamptoninn.hilton.com* 🛏 *88 rooms* 🍽 *Breakfast.*

$ B&B/INN 🏨 **The Spalding House.** This restored Colonial Revival inn is decked out with antiques, oriental rugs, handcrafted woodwork, and glass doors. **Pros:** warm feel; old-time atmosphere; great place for a twilight stroll. **Cons:** no TVs in rooms. [$] *Rooms from: $95* ✉ *631 N. Encina St.* ☎ *559/739–7877* 🌐 *www.thespaldinghouse.com* 🛏 *3 suites* 🍽 *Breakfast.*

Each spring the fruit orchards along the Blossom Trail, near Fresno, burst into bloom.

FRESNO

44 miles north of Visalia.

Fresno, with half a million people, is the center of the richest agricultural county in the United States. Cotton, grapes, and tomatoes are among the major crops; poultry and milk are also important. About 75 ethnic groups, including Armenians, Laotians, and Indians, live here. The city has a relatively vibrant arts scene, several public parks, and many low-price restaurants. The **Tower District**—with its restaurants, coffeehouses, and performance venues—is the town's arts and nightlife nexus.

GETTING HERE AND AROUND

Highway 99 is the biggest road through Fresno. Highways 41 and 180 also bisect the city. Amtrak trains stop here daily (and often). Fresno Area Express (FAX) provides comprehensive local bus service.

ESSENTIALS

Transportation Contacts FAX ☎ *559/621–7433* ⊕ *www.fresno.gov/fax.*

Visitor Information Fresno / Clovis Convention & Visitors Bureau ✉ *1550 E. Shaw Ave.* ☎ *559/981–5500, 800/788–0836* ⊕ *playfresno.org.*

EXPLORING

TOP ATTRACTIONS

FAMILY
Fodor's Choice
★

Forestiere Underground Gardens. Sicilian immigrant Baldassare Forestiere spent four decades (1906–46) carving out an odd, subterranean realm of rooms, tunnels, grottoes, alcoves, and arched passageways that once extended for more than 10 acres between Highway 99 and

Fresno Area

13

KEY

🛈 *Tourist information*

0 — 4 miles
0 — 6 km

busy, mall-pocked Shaw Avenue. Though not an engineer, Forestiere called on his memories of the ancient Roman structures he saw as a youth and on techniques he learned digging subways in New York and Boston. Only a fraction of his prodigious output is on view, but you can tour his underground living quarters, including bedrooms (one with a fireplace), the kitchen, living room, and bath, as well as a fishpond and auto tunnel. Skylights allow exotic full-grown fruit trees to flourish more than 20 feet belowground. ⊠ *5021 W. Shaw Ave., 2 blocks east of Hwy. 99* ☎ *559/271–0734* ⊕ *www.undergroundgardens.com* ⛁ *$15* ⊙ *Tours June–Aug., Wed.–Sun. on the hour 10–4 (weather permitting); Sept.–Nov. and Mar.–May, hrs vary.*

Fresno Art Museum. The museum's key permanent collections include pre-Columbian Mesoamerican art, Andean pre-Columbian textiles and artifacts, Japanese prints, Berkeley School abstract expressionist paintings, and contemporary sculpture. Temporary exhibits include important traveling shows. ⊠ *Radio Park, 2233 N. 1st St., at E. Yale Ave.* ☎ *559/441–4221* ⊕ *www.fresnoartmuseum.org* ⛁ *$5* ⊙ *Thur.–Sun. 11–5.*

WORTH NOTING

> **LOCAL LITERARY LEGENDS**
>
> The Central Valley's cultural diversity and agricultural roots have woven a textured social fabric that has been chronicled by some of the country's finest writers, including Fresno native William Saroyan, Stockton native Maxine Hong Kingston, and *The Grapes of Wrath* author John Steinbeck.

Blossom Trail. The 62-mile self-guided Blossom Trail driving tour takes in Fresno-area orchards, citrus groves, and vineyards during spring blossom season. The trail passes through small towns and past rivers, lakes, and canals. The most colorful and aromatic time to go is from late February to mid-March, when almond, plum, apple, apricot, and peach blossoms shower the landscape with shades of white, pink, and red. After the blossoms mature, the route is known as the Fruit Trail. ☎ *559/600–4271* 🌐 *goblossomtrail.com.*

Fresno Chaffee Zoo. The zoo's most striking exhibit is its tropical rain forest, where you'll encounter exotic birds along paths and bridges. Elsewhere at the zoo live tigers, sloth bears, sea lions, tule elk, camels, elephants, and siamang apes. The facility has a high-tech reptile house and there's a petting zoo. ✉ *Roeding Park, 894 W. Belmont Ave., east of Hwy. 99* ☎ *559/498–5910* 🌐 *www.fresnochaffeezoo.org* 🎟 *$7* 🕒 *Apr.–Aug., daily 9–6; Sept.–Oct., weekdays 9–4, weekends 9–6; Nov.–Mar., daily 9–4.*

Woodward Park. The Central Valley's largest urban park, with 300 acres of jogging trails, picnic areas, and playgrounds, is especially pretty in spring, when plum and cherry trees, magnolias, and camellias bloom. Outdoor concerts take place in summer. The **Shinzen Friendship Garden** *(🌐 shinzenjapanesegarden.org)* has a teahouse, a koi pond, arched bridges, a waterfall, and Japanese art. ✉ *Audubon Dr. and Friant Rd., off Hwy. 41* ☎ *559/621–2900, 559/840–1264 Shinzen garden* 🌐 *www.fresno.gov* 🎟 *$5 per car; $3 additional for Shinzen garden* 🕒 *Apr.–Oct., daily 6 am–10 pm; Nov.–Mar., daily 6 am–7 pm. Call for Shinzen garden hrs.*

WHERE TO EAT AND STAY

$$ ITALIAN 🍴 **Café Via.** Sharing a strip of a strip mall with a massage parlor and a mattress retailer, this restaurant couldn't have a more humble location, but the mostly Italian cuisine here more than compensates. Chef-owner Matthew Babcock displays a fine touch with calzones and pizzas, and pasta standards such as fettuccine Alfredo and shrimp scampi. Non-Italian dishes include a flavorful Southwestern barbecue pulled pork sandwich served on a baguette. Locals adore the homemade desserts, especially the coconut cake, banana cream tart, and crème brûlée. [$] *Average main: $16* ✉ *6640 N. Blackstone Ave., near Herndon Ave.* ☎ *559/447–8706* 🌐 *cafeviafresno.com* 🕒 *Closed Sun.*

$$ AMERICAN 🍴 **Elbow Room.** A classic San Francisco–style steak house and bar, the Elbow Room has been a Fresno social hub since opening in 1955. The steak sandwich, served open face on jalapeño cheese bread, has been a menu staple since the beginning; other classics include deviled eggs and an iceberg wedge with blue cheese. Among the more contemporary

dishes are grilled Alaskan salmon and a salad with quinoa, mixed greens, asparagus, and artichoke hearts. The restaurant has indoor seating areas and a covered patio with year-round temperature controls, a boon in summer. $ *Average main: $22* ⊠ *Fig Garden Village Shopping Center, 731 W. San Jose Ave., near W. Shaw Ave.* ☎ *559/227–1234* ⊕ *elbowroomfresno.com.*

$$$

MODERN

AMERICAN

13

✕ **School House Restaurant & Tavern.** A Wine Country–style establishment that sources ingredients from the on-site gardens and surrounding farms and orchards, this popular restaurant occupies a red-brick 1921 schoolhouse in the town of Sanger. Chef Ryan Jackson, who grew up on local fruit farms, returned home after stints cooking at prestigious Napa Valley restaurants to create seasonal menus from the bounty of familiar backyards. The fare might include salmon ratatouille with summer vegetables, braised duck Stroganoff in a mushroom-Cabernet sauce, or lobster salad tossed with local peaches, arugula, goat cheese, almonds, and roasted peach vinaigrette. With salads, pizza, pasta, and sandwiches, lunch is more basic. You can eat in the main dining room (the former school auditorium), the more casual tavern, or by the outdoor patio's fire pits. $ *Average main: $25* ⊠ *1018 S. Frankwood Ave., at Hwy. 180 (King's Canyon Rd.), 20 miles east of Fresno, Sanger* ☎ *559/787–3271* ⊕ *schoolhousesanger.com* ☉ *Closed Mon. and Tues.*

$

HOTEL

🛏 **Best Western Plus Fresno Inn.** With a location near Highway 41 (the main route to Yosemite), Fresno State, and a big mall, this well-run hotel is popular with families, businesspeople, and parents with offspring at the university. **Pros:** convenient location; attentive staff; 24-hour business center. **Cons:** mildly sterile feel. $ *Rooms from: $105* ⊠ *480 E. Shaw Ave.* ☎ *559/475–9539* ⊕ *bestwesternfresnoinn.com* ➪ *55 rooms* ⃒⃝ *Breakfast.*

$$

HOTEL

🛏 **La Quinta Fresno Riverpark.** Reasonably clean if not spotless, with a spacious lobby and an accommodating staff, this four-story chain property is right off Highway 41, which leads north into Yosemite National Park. **Pros:** reasonably clean; amenities for business travelers and families; just off highway to Yosemite; filling breakfasts. **Cons:** not much in the way of character; far from downtown Fresno. $ *Rooms from: $144* ⊠ *330 E. Fir Ave.* ☎ *559/449–0928* ⊕ *www.laquintafresnoriverpark. com* ➪ *56 rooms* ⃒⃝ *Breakfast.*

$

HOTEL

🛏 **Piccadilly Inn Shaw.** This two-story property has 7½ attractively landscaped acres and a big swimming pool. **Pros:** big rooms; nice pool; on-site restaurant/pub. **Cons:** some rooms show mild wear; neighborhood is somewhat sketchy. $ *Rooms from: $109* ⊠ *2305 W. Shaw Ave.* ☎ *559/348–5520* ⊕ *www.piccadillyinn.com* ➪ *183 rooms, 4 suites* ⃒⃝ *Breakfast.*

NIGHTLIFE AND PERFORMING ARTS

Roger Rocka's Dinner Theater. This Tower District venue stages Broadway-style musicals. ⊠ *1226 N. Wishon Ave., at E. Olive Ave.* ☎ *559/266–9494* ⊕ *www.rogerrockas.com.*

Tower Theatre for the Performing Arts. The restored 1930s art-deco movie house, the namesake of the Tower District of theaters, clubs, restaurants, and cafés, presents theater, ballet, concerts, and other cultural events. ✉ *815 E. Olive Ave., at N. Wishon Ave.* ☎ *559/485–9050* 🌐 *www.towertheatrefresno.com.*

SPORTS AND THE OUTDOORS

WHITE-WATER RAFTING

Kings River Expeditions. This outfit arranges one- and two-day white-water rafting trips on the Kings River. ✉ *1840 W. Shaw Ave., Clovis* ☎ *559/233–4881, 800/846–3674* 🌐 *www.kingsriver.com* 🎟 *From $110.*

NORTH CENTRAL VALLEY

MERCED

50 miles north of Fresno.

The 2005 debut of a branch of the University of California helped spur redevelopment in Merced County's seat of government. The transformation has resulted in a brewpub, new restaurants, a multiplex, the restoration of historic buildings, and foot traffic won back from outlying strip malls.

GETTING HERE AND AROUND

Most people arrive in Merced by car via Highway 99, but Amtrak also stops several times daily. The Bus provides local transit service. Get oriented at the visitor center—which does double duty as a California Welcome Center—at the Bus/Greyhound transit station downtown.

ESSENTIALS

Bus Contact The Bus ☎ *209/725–3813* 🌐 *www.mercedthebus.com.*

Visitor Information Merced Visitor Services/California Welcome Center ✉ *710 W. 16th St.* ☎ *209/724–8104, 800/446–5353* 🌐 *visitmerced.travel.*

EXPLORING

Merced County Courthouse Museum. Built in 1875, the courthouse is a striking example of Victorian Italianate style. The upper two floors contain a museum of early Merced history whose highlights include ornate restored courtrooms and an 1870 Chinese temple with carved redwood altars. ✉ *621 W. 21st St., at N St.* ☎ *209/723–2401* 🌐 *www.mercedmuseum.org* 🎟 *Free* 🕒 *Wed.–Sun. 1–4.*

Merced Multicultural Arts Center. The center displays paintings, sculpture, and photography and presents plays and concerts. ✉ *645 W. Main St., at N St.* ☎ *209/388–1090* 🌐 *www.artsmerced.org* 🎟 *Free* 🕒 *Tues.–Fri. 11–6, Sat. 10–2.*

WHERE TO EAT AND STAY

$$ ITALIAN 🍴 **Bella Luna Bistro & Bar.** In a downtown Tuscan-theme bakery, bar, and bistro, chef Vincent DeAngelo, a graduate of the Culinary Institute of America, brings his considerable skills to chicken Parmesan, calamari steak dore, and other Italian favorites. All breads, buns, cakes, pizzas, and other baked delights are made on-site in a New York brick oven. [$] *Average main: $20* ✉ *350 W. Main St.* ☎ *209/383–1700* 🌐 *bellalunabakerycafe.com* 🕒 *Closed Sun. and Mon.*

$$ \
MODERN \
AMERICAN

✕ **Five Ten Bistro.** Elegant yet unpretentious Five Ten serves upscale bistro-style meals at reasonable prices. Sit at candlelit tables and watch the cooks in the open kitchen craft dishes on a seasonal menu that always includes soups (try the mushroom bisque), salads, pastas (among them chicken penne with bacon and tomato), and chicken marsala and other bistro staples. Local vintages and bottlings from around the globe grace the impressive wine list. The on-site After 5 Bar & Lounge lures locals with craft-beer flights and creative martinis. ■TIP→ **In fair weather, ask for a table outside under the stars.** $ *Average main: $19* ⊠ *510 W. Main St.* ☎ *209/381–0280* ⊕ *www.fivetenbistro.com* ⊘ *Closed Sun.*

$$ \
B&B/INN

⬚ **Bear Creek Inn.** This 1931 neocolonial home stands regally along M Street; rooms are appointed with antiques and big, soft beds. **Pros:** historic charm; good breakfast; convenient to downtown and train station. **Cons:** front rooms can be noisy. $ *Rooms from: $129* ⊠ *575 W. North Bear Creek Dr., at M St.* ☎ *209/723–3991* ⊕ *www.bearcreekinnmerced. com* ⇆ *4 rooms, 1 cottage* ⦿| *Breakfast.*

EN ROUTE

Castle Air Museum. You can stroll among dozens of restored military aircraft at this outdoor facility. The vintage war birds include the B-25 Mitchell medium-range bomber—best known for the Jimmy Doolittle raid on Tokyo after the attack on Pearl Harbor—and the speedy SR-71 Blackbird, used for reconnaissance over Vietnam and Libya. A recently arrived star is an aircraft that from 1974 to 2006 was known as Air Force One whenever it transported the U.S. president. ⊠ *Castle Airport, 5050 Santa Fe Dr., 6 miles north of Merced, Buhach Rd. exit off Hwy. 99, Atwater* ☎ *209/723–2178* ⊕ *www.castleairmuseum.org* ⦿ *$10* ⊘ *Apr.–Sept., daily 9–5; Oct.–Mar., daily 10–4.*

MODESTO

38 miles north of Merced.

Among the most striking "welcome to downtown" signs you'll see, the Modesto Arch, at 9th and I streets, bears the city's motto: "Water, Wealth, Contentment, Health." A gateway to Yosemite National Park, Modesto, population 205,000, was founded in 1870 to serve the Central Pacific Railroad. The tree-lined town was originally to be named after a railroad baron, but as the story goes, he modestly declined—thus the name Modesto. The city is the birthplace of producer-director George Lucas, creator of *American Graffiti* and the *Star Wars* film series.

GETTING HERE AND AROUND

Highway 99 is the major traffic artery; Highway 132 heads east from here toward Yosemite National Park. Several Amtrak trains arrive daily. Modesto Area Express (MAX) is the local bus service.

ESSENTIALS

Bus Contact MAX ☎ *209/521–1274* ⊕ *www.modestoareaexpress.com.*

Visitor Information Modesto Convention & Visitors Bureau ⊠ *1150 9th St., Suite C* ☎ *209/526–5588, 888/640–8467* ⊕ *www.visitmodesto.com.*

The Central Valley is California's agricultural powerhouse.

EXPLORING

Historic Graffiti Cruise Route. A downtown walking tour follows the iconic 1950s-era cruise route portrayed in Modesto native George Lucas's 1973 film *American Graffiti*. The path's 25 historic kiosk markers provide details about the filmmaker, the people and places that inspired him, and Modesto's history. ■TIP→ **The tour loops around 10th and 11th streets between K and G streets—start at 10th and K.** ⊠ *10th and 11th Sts., between K and G Sts.* ☎ *209/526–5588* ⊕ *modestocruiseroute.com.*

McHenry Mansion. A rancher and banker built the 1883 McHenry Mansion, the city's sole surviving original Victorian home. The Italianate mansion has been decorated to reflect Modesto life in the late 19th century. Its period-appropriate wallpaper is especially impressive. ⊠ *15th and I Sts.* ☎ *209/549–0428 gift shop* ⊕ *www.mchenrymansion.org* ☞ *Free* ☉ *Tours Sun.–Fri. noon–4.*

McHenry Museum. The best exhibits at this repository of early Modesto and Stanislaus County memorabilia include the re-creations of an old-time dentist's office, a blacksmith's shop, and a schoolroom. Also worth a peek are the extensive doll collection and a general store stocked with period goods such as hair crimpers and corsets. ⊠ *1402 I St., at 14th St.* ☎ *209/577–5235* ⊕ *www.mchenrymuseum.org* ☞ *Free* ☉ *Tues.–Sun. noon–4.*

WHERE TO EAT AND STAY

$$$$

MODERN
AMERICAN

✕ **Dewz.** Modestans hankering for a fine-dining experience—especially one involving prime rib or filet mignon—often head to this handsome dining room. Chef Vincent Alvarado introduces French influences (by way of the sauces) and Asian ones (by way of the spices) to beef, chicken, and seafood standards. Beef predominates, but the sea bass is a good alternative, as is the pan-roasted pork tenderloin, served with a sweet and spicy plum sauce. *$ Average main: $31* ⊠ *1505 J St.* ☎ *209/549–1101* ⊕ *dineatdewz.com* ⚐ *Reservations essential* ☉ *Closed Sun. No lunch Sat.*

$
HOTEL
🏨 **Best Western Town House Lodge.** Its downtown location is the lodge's primary draw—the McHenry Mansion and the McHenry Museum are nearby, and the county historical library is across the street. **Pros:** convenient location; updated. **Cons:** staff's limited knowledge of town. *$ Rooms from: $85* ⊠ *909 16th St.* ☎ *209/524–7261, 800/772–7261* ⊕ *www.centralvalleybwhotels.com* ⌁ *55 rooms* ⦿ *Breakfast.*

LODI

41 miles north of Modesto; 34 miles south of Sacramento.

Founded on agriculture, Lodi was once the watermelon capital of the country. Today it's surrounded by fields of asparagus, pumpkins, beans, safflowers, sunflowers, kiwis, melons, squashes, peaches, and cherries. With about 100,000 acres of mostly rich alluvial soils planted to more than six-dozen grape varietals—more types than in any other California viticultural area—Lodi is a major a wine-making grape hub, particularly for Zinfandel. Eighty or so wineries do business in Lodi and neighboring Acampo, Lockeford, and Woodbridge. Lodi itself retains an old rural charm. You can stroll downtown or visit a wildlife refuge, all the while benefiting from a Sacramento River delta breeze that keeps this microclimate cooler in summer than anyplace else in the area.

GETTING HERE AND AROUND

Most of Lodi lies to the west of Highway 99, several miles east of Interstate 5. Buses and Amtrak trains stop here frequently. Although the GrapeLine bus (☎ *209/333–6806*) can get you around town and to many of the wineries, you are better off with your own vehicle.

ESSENTIALS

Visitor Information Lodi Conference & Visitors Bureau ⊠ *25 N. School St.* ☎ *209/365–1195, 800/798–1810* ⊕ *www.visitlodi.com.*

EXPLORING

TOP ATTRACTIONS

Lodi Wine & Visitor Center. A fine place to sample Lodi wines, the center has a tasting bar and viticultural exhibits. You can also buy wine and pick up a free winery map. The knowledgeable pourers can suggest wineries to explore. ⊠ *2545 W. Turner Rd., at Woodhaven La.* ☎ *209/365–0621* ⊕ *www.lodiwine.com* ⛃ *Tasting $7* ☉ *Daily 10–5.*

Lucas Winery. David Lucas was one of the first local producers to start making serious wine, and today his Zinfandels are among Lodi's most sought-after vintages. In addition to fruity Zins, Lucas makes a light Chardonnay with subtle oaky flavors. The 90-minute tour and tasting ($20) will get you up to speed on the Lodi wine appellation. ⊠ *18196 N. Davis Rd., at W. Turner Rd.* ☎ *209/368–2006* ⊕ *www.lucaswinery.*

com 🍷 *Tastings $10–$50, tour (includes tasting) $55* ⊙ *Thurs.–Sun. noon–4:30.*

Fodor's Choice
★

M2 Wines. With its translucent polycarbonate panels, concrete floor, and metal framing, this winery's high-ceilinged tasting room strikes an iconoclastic, industrial-sleek pose along an otherwise relentlessly rural lane north of Lodi. Willfully splashy, the space is an apt visual metaphor for the flights of fancy that founding partner Layne Montgomery, M2's largely self-taught winemaker, takes in crafting his deliciously sophisticated mostly red wines. The Soucie Vineyard old-vine Zinfandel—among Lodi's best and like few others made here—and the Trio Red Wine blend are the flagships, and the Tempranillo, a smart Syrah from Sierra foothills grapes, and the Clockstopper blend are also worth trying. ⊠ *2900 E. Peltier Rd., Acampo* ☎ *209/339–1071* ⊕ *www. m2wines.com* 🍷 *Tasting $10* ⊙ *Thurs.–Mon. 11–5.*

Fodor's Choice
★

Michael David Winery. Fifth-generation farmers turned winery owners Michael and David Phillips operate their tasting room at the rustic roadside **Phillips Farms Fruit Stand,** where they also sell their family's gorgeous produce. Michael David is well known for Zinfandels, among them 7 Deadly Zins, but the Freakshow Cabernet Sauvignon and the daring Petite Petit (mostly Petite Sirah with some Petit Verdot) are also popular. ■TIP➜ **Breakfast or lunch at the café here is a treat.** ⊠ *4580 W. Hwy. 12, at N. Ray Rd.* ☎ *209/368–7384* ⊕ *www. michaeldavidwinery.com* 🍷 *Tastings $5–$10* ⊙ *Daily 10–5, reserve tasting Fri.–Sun. only.*

WORTH NOTING

Berghold Estate Winery. The tasting room at Berghold recalls an earlier wine era with its vintage Victorian interior, including restored, salvaged mantelpieces, leaded glass, and a 26-foot-long bar. The wines—among them Viognier, Cabernet Sauvignon, Merlot, Syrah, and Zinfandel—pay homage to French winemaking styles. ⊠ *17343 N. Cherry Rd., off E. Victor Rd./Hwy. 12* ☎ *209/333–9291* ⊕ *bergholdvineyards.com* 🍷 *Tasting $7* ⊙ *Thurs.–Sun. 11–5.*

Jessie's Grove Winery. Shaded by ancient oak trees, an 1870s farm building houses the tasting room of this winery whose vineyards and horse ranch have been in the same family since 1863. In addition to producing old-vine Zinfandels, it presents blues, country, and rock concerts on some summer Saturdays. ■TIP➜ **A second tasting room, open on Friday and weekends, is downtown at 27 East Locust Street.** ⊠ *1973 W. Turner Rd., west of Davis Rd.* ☎ *209/368–0880* ⊕ *www.jessiesgrovewinery. com* 🍷 *Tasting $5* ⊙ *Daily noon–5.*

FAMILY

Micke Grove Regional Park. This 258-acre, oak-shaded park has a Japanese tea garden, picnic tables, children's play areas, an agricultural museum, a zoo, a golf course, and a water-play feature. **Fun Town at Micke Grove,** a family-oriented amusement park, is geared toward younger children. ⊠ *11793 N. Micke Grove Rd., off Hwy. 99 Armstrong Rd. exit, 5 miles south of downtown* ☎ *209/953–8800 park info, 209/369–7330 Fun Town, 209/331–2010 zoo* 🍷 *Parking $5 weekdays, $6 weekends and holidays; pets $1 (leash required); Fun Town*

Lodi Lake Park is a great place to escape the Central Valley heat in summer.

ride prices vary; zoo $5 ⏲ Park daily 8–sunset; Fun Town daily 11–5, weekends and holidays Apr.–Sept. 11–6; zoo daily 10–5.

Van Ruiten Family Vineyards. For an affordable experience of what Lodi's hardworking old Zinfandel vines can produce, sample the Van Ruiten Old Vine Zin and the Reserve Sideways Lot 69 Old Vine Zin. Other wines of note include the Chardonnays and the Cabernet-Shiraz blend. ✉ *340 W. Hwy. 12* ☎ *209/334–5722* 🌐 *www.vrwinery.com* 🎟 *Tastings $10–$15* ⏲ *Daily 11–5.*

Woodbridge Winery. At huge Woodbridge, you can take a 45-minute tour of the vineyard and barrel room and learn about the label's legendary founder, the late Robert Mondavi. In the tasting room, look for hard-to-find and exclusive offerings such as the Lodi Old Vine Zinfandel and the well-aged Port. ✉ *5950 E. Woodbridge Rd., east of N. Hildebrand Rd., Acampo* ☎ *209/365–8139* 🌐 *www.woodbridgewines.com* 🎟 *Tasting $5, tour $5* ⏲ *Daily 10:30–4:30, tour 9:30 and 1:30.*

WHERE TO EAT

$$ AMERICAN 🍴 **The Dancing Fox Winery and Bakery.** A good downtown stop for coffee and fresh pastries, a granola parfait, or more filling breakfast selections, the Dancing Fox also serves lunch (sandwiches, salads, and wraps) and dinner (eclectic plates from tempeh tacos to bangers and mash). The restaurant, its decor ashimmer with fairy-tale whimsy, has more than a dozen beers on tap, and there's a tasting room for its eponymous wines. [$] *Average main: $19* ✉ *203 S. School St.* ☎ *203/366–2634* 🌐 *www.dancingfoxwinery.com* ⏲ *Closed Mon. No lunch Sun.*

$$ ITALIAN 🍴 **Pietro's Trattoria.** Lodi's go-to spot for Italian-American classics wins fans for its quality ingredients, Tuscan-courtyard ambience, and

plant-filled outdoor patio. Expect straightforward, well-executed renditions of chicken and veal piccata, filling lasagna and fettucine Alfredo (with chicken or prawns), pizzas, and the like, all delivered with informal good cheer by the cadre of servers. The meatball and chicken pesto with cheese sandwiches are good bets for lunch. The wine list favors local vintages. ■TIP→ **Reservations are essential on weekends.** $ *Average main: $22* ⊠ *317 E. Kettleman La.* ☎ *209/368–0613* ⊕ *www. pietroslodi.com* ⊘ *Closed Sun. No lunch Mon.*

$$$ ✕**Rosewood Bar & Grill.** The folks at the Wine and Roses complex oper-
AMERICAN ate this low-key downtown spot that serves American fare such as meat loaf wrapped in bacon, pizzas, and blackened salmon. Some locals come here just for the potent cocktails, others for steak, particularly the "the trifecta" special with three different cuts, each topped with a separate side such as cheddar-dipped cauliflower or mushroom risotto with shrimp. $ *Average main: $29* ⊠ *28 S. School St., at W. Oak St.* ☎ *209/369–0470* ⊕ *rosewoodbarandgrill.com* ⊘ *No lunch Mon.–Thurs.*

$$$$ ✕**Towne House Restaurant.** Lodi power breakfasts and lunches and spe-
MODERN cial-occasion dinners often take place in the distinguished rooms of this
AMERICAN former residence behind, and part of, the Wine and Roses hotel. Painted
Fodor'sChoice in rich, textured hues offset by wide white molding, the rooms exude
★ a subtle sophistication matched by the cuisine of executive chef John Hitchcock. The smoked salmon scramble at breakfast comes with crème fraîche; the tamale pancake for lunch is made from true masa (the rye for the corned-beef Reuben is the real deal, too); and evanescent leek foam tops the seared day boat scallops. Jazz musicians perform nightly in the lounge, noteworthy for its specialty cocktails and selection of local wines by the glass. $ *Average main: $40* ⊠ *2505 W. Turner Rd., at Woodhaven La.* ☎ *209/371–6160* ⊕ *winerose.com/towne-house-restaurant* ⌂ *Reservations essential.*

WHERE TO STAY

$$ 🏠 **The Inn at Locke House.** Built between 1862 and 1882, the inn occu-
B&B/INN pies a pioneer doctor's family home that rates a listing on the National Register of Historic Places. **Pros:** friendly; quiet; lovely. **Cons:** remote; can be hard to find. $ *Rooms from: $155* ⊠ *19960 Elliott Rd., Locke-ford* ☎ *209/727–5715* ⊕ *www.theinnatlockehouse.com* ⟿ *4 rooms, 1 suite* ⎮◉⎮ *Breakfast.*

$$$$ 🏠 **Wine & Roses Hotel and Restaurant.** Set on 7 acres amid a tapestry of
HOTEL informal gardens, this hotel has cultivated a sense of refinement typically associated with Napa or Carmel. **Pros:** luxurious; relaxing; quiet. **Cons:** expensive; some guests mention that walls are thin. $ *Rooms from: $259* ⊠ *2505 W. Turner Rd.* ☎ *209/334–6988* ⊕ *www.winerose. com* ⟿ *60 rooms, 6 suites* ⎮◉⎮ *No meals.*

SPORTS AND THE OUTDOORS

Lodi Lake Park. Shaded by grand old elms and oaks, the lake's banks are much cooler in summer than other spots in town. You can swim, watch birds, picnic, and rent a kayak, canoe, or pedal boat here. ⊠ *1101 W. Turner Rd., at Mills Ave.* ☎ *209/333–6742* ⊕ *www.lodi.gov/prcs/ lodilake.html* ⎘ *$5 vehicle entrance fee, $3 public swimming.*

THE SOUTHERN SIERRA

Around Sequoia, Kings Canyon,
and Yosemite National Parks

WELCOME TO THE SOUTHERN SIERRA

TOP REASONS TO GO

★ **Hiking:** Whether you walk the paved loops in the national parks or head off the beaten path into the backcountry, a hike through groves and meadows or alongside streams and waterfalls will allow you to see, smell, and feel nature up close.

★ **Winter Fun:** Famous for its incredible snowpack—some of the deepest in the North American continent—the Sierra Nevada has something for every winter-sports fan.

★ **Live it up:** Mammoth Lakes is eastern California's most exciting resort area.

★ **Pamper yourself:** Tucked in the hills south of Oakhurst, the elegant Château du Sureau will make you feel as if you've stepped into a fairy tale.

★ **Go with the flow:** Three Rivers, the gateway to Sequoia National Park, is the launching pad for white-water trips down the Kaweah River.

1 South of Yosemite National Park. Several gateway towns to the south and west of Yosemite National Park, most within an hour's drive of Yosemite Valley, have food, lodging, and other services.

2 Mammoth Lakes. A jewel in the vast Eastern Sierra Nevada, the Mammoth Lakes area lies just east of the Sierra crest, on the backside of Yosemite and the Ansel Adams Wilderness. It's a place of rugged beauty, where giant sawtooth mountains drop into the vast deserts of the Great Basin. In winter, 11,053-foot-high Mammoth Mountain offers the finest skiing and snowboarding in California—sometimes as late as June or even July. Once the snows melt, Mammoth transforms itself into a warm-weather playground, with fishing, mountain biking, golfing, hiking, and horseback riding. Nine deep-blue lakes are spread throughout the Mammoth Lakes Basin, and another 100 lakes dot the surrounding countryside.

3 East of Yosemite National Park. The area to the east of Yosemite National Park includes some ruggedly handsome, albeit desolate, terrain, most notably around Mono Lake. The area is best visited by car, as distances are great and public transportation is negligible. U.S. 395 is the main north–south road on the eastern side of the Sierra Nevada, at the western edge of the Great Basin. It's one of California's most beautiful highways; plan to snap pictures at roadside pullouts.

GETTING ORIENTED

The transition between the Central Valley and the rugged Southern Sierra may be the most dramatic in California sightseeing; as you head into the mountains, your temptation to stop the car and gawk will increase with every foot gained in elevation. Although you should spend most of your time here in the nearby national parks, be sure to check out some of the mountain towns on the parks' fringes—in addition to being great places to stock up on supplies, they have worthy attractions, restaurants, and lodging options.

14

4 South of Sequoia and Kings Canyon. Scenic Three Rivers is the main gateway for Sequoia and Kings Canyon National Parks.

Updated by Cheryl Crabtree

The Southern Sierra's granite peaks and giant sequoias bedazzle heart and soul so completely that for many visitors the experience surpasses that at more famous urban attractions. Most of the Sierra's wonders lie within national parks, but outside them deep-blue Mono Lake and its tufa towers never cease to astound. The megaresort Mammoth Lakes, meanwhile, lures skiers and snowboarders in winter and hikers and mountain bikers in summer, and the town of Three Rivers delivers laid-back hospitality with a smile.

The national parks are accessed most easily via gateway towns that include Oakhurst, Fish Camp, and Lee Vining for Yosemite and Visalia and Three Rivers for Sequoia and Kings Canyon. Pristine lakes and rolling hills outside the parks offer year-round opportunities for rest and relaxation. Or not. In winter the thrill of the slopes—and their relative isolation compared to busy Lake Tahoe—draws a hearty breed of outdoor enthusiast. In summer a hike through groves and meadows or alongside streams and waterfalls allows you to see, smell, and feel nature up close.

PLANNING

GETTING HERE AND AROUND

AIR TRAVEL

Three main airports provide access to the Southern Sierra: Fresno Yosemite International (FAT), on the western side, and, on the eastern side, Mammoth-Yosemite (MMH), 6 miles east of Mammoth Lakes, and Reno–Tahoe (RNO), 130 miles north of Mammoth Lakes via U.S. 395. Alaska, Allegiant, American, Delta, Frontier, United, and a few other carriers serve Fresno and Reno. Alaska and United serve Mammoth Lakes.

Airports **Fresno Yosemite International Airport** (*FAT*) ✉ *5175 E. Clinton Ave., Fresno* ☎ *800/244–2359 automated information, 559/454–2052 terminal info desk* ⊕ *www.flyfresno.com*. **Mammoth Yosemite Airport** ✉ *1200 Airport Rd., Mammoth Lakes* ☎ *760/934–2712, 888/466–2666* ⊕ *www.visitmammoth. com*. **Reno–Tahoe International Airport** ✉ *2001 E. Plumb La., Reno, Nevada* ☎ *775/328–6400* ⊕ *www.renoairport.com*.

BUS TRAVEL

Greyhound serves Fresno, Madera, and other Central Valley towns west of the Sierra. Madera County Connection buses travel between Madera and Oakhurst/Bass Lake. Eastern Sierra Transit Authority buses serve Mammoth Lakes and other eastern Sierra towns. YARTS (Yosemite Area Regional Transportation System) connects Yosemite National Park with surrounding towns, including Fresno, Merced, Oakhurst, Fish Camp, and Lee Vining; this is a good option during summer, when parking in Yosemite Valley and elsewhere in the park can be difficult.

Bus Contacts **Eastern Sierra Transit Authority** ☎ *760/872–1901 general, 760/914–1315 Mammoth Lakes* ⊕ *www.estransit.com*. **Greyhound** ☎ *800/231– 2222* ⊕ *www.greyhound.com*. **Madera County Connection** ✉ *Madera* ☎ *559/661–3040* ⊕ *www.maderactc.org/public-transit*. **YARTS** ☎ *877/989– 2787, 209/388–9589* ⊕ *www.yarts.com*.

CAR TRAVEL

Interstate 5 and Highway 99 travel north–south along the western side of the Sierra Nevada. U.S. 395 follows a roughly parallel route on the eastern side.

From San Francisco: Head east on Interstate 80 to 580 to 205E to connect with Interstate 5 and Highway 99. To best reach the eastern side, take Interstate 80 to U.S. 395, then head south.

From Los Angeles: Head north on Interstate 5, continuing north on the interstate (or Highway 99) for the western side and exiting north onto Highway 14 and later onto U.S. 395.

■TIP→ Gas stations are few and far between in the Sierra, so fill your tank when you can. Between October and May heavy snow may cover mountain roads. Always check road conditions before driving. Carry tire chains, and know how to install them. On Interstate 80 and U.S. 50 chain installers assist travelers (for $35), but elsewhere you're on your own.

Travel Reports **Caltrans Current Highway Conditions** ☎ *800/427–7623* ⊕ *www.dot.ca.gov*.

TRAIN TRAVEL

The Southern Sierra stops of Amtrak's daily *San Joaquin* train include Fresno and Merced, where you can connect to YARTS for travel to Yosemite National Park and smaller gateway towns.

Train Contact **Amtrak** ☎ *800/872–7245* ⊕ *www.amtrak.com*.

RESTAURANTS

Most small towns in the Sierra Nevada have at least one restaurant. Standard American fare is the norm, but you'll also find sophisticated cuisine. With few exceptions, dress is casual. Local grocery stores and delis stock picnic fixings, good to have on hand should the opportunity for an impromptu meal under giant trees emerge.

HOTELS

The lodgings nearest the national parks generally fill up the quickest; book hotels in the western Sierra Nevada well in advance in summer. Booking far ahead is less crucial for Eastern Sierra accommodations, except in Mammoth Lakes. *Hotel reviews have been shortened. For full information, visit Fodors.com.*

Hotel Contacts Mammoth Reservations ⊠ *Mammoth Lakes* ☎ *800/223–3032* ⊕ *www.mammothreservations.com.*

WHAT IT COSTS				
	$	**$$**	**$$$**	**$$$$**
Restaurants	under $16	$16–$22	$23–$30	over $30
Hotels	under $120	$120–$175	$176–$250	over $250

Restaurant prices are the average cost of a main course at dinner or, if dinner is not served, at lunch. Hotel prices are the lowest cost of a standard double room in high season.

TOUR OPERATORS

Discover Yosemite. This outfit operates daily tours to Yosemite Valley, Mariposa Grove, and Glacier Point in 14- and 29-passenger vehicles. The Highway 41 route stops in Bass Lake, Oakhurst, and Fish Camp, and the Highway 140 route departs from Mariposa, Midpines, and El Portal. Rates include lunch. Sunset tours to Sentinel Dome are additional summer options. ☎ *559/642–4400, 800/585–0565* ⊕ *www. discoveryosemite.com* ✉ *From $124.*

Mammoth All Weather Shuttle. This outfit operates summer tours from Mammoth Lakes to Yosemite; north to June Lake, Mono Lake, and Bodie Ghost Town; and around the lakes region. The company also runs charters to Los Angeles, Reno, and Las Vegas airports—useful when inclement weather causes flight cancellations at Mammoth's airport. ⊠ *Mammoth Lakes* ☎ *760/709–2927* ⊕ *www.mawshuttle.com* ✉ *From $60.*

VISITOR INFORMATION

Mammoth Lakes Tourism ⊠ *Mammoth Lakes* ☎ *760/934–2712, 888/466–2666* ⊕ *www.visitmammoth.com.*

Mono County Tourism ⊠ *Mammoth Lakes* ☎ *800/845–7922* ⊕ *mono-county.org.*

SOUTH OF YOSEMITE NATIONAL PARK

People heading to Yosemite National Park, especially those interested in seeing the giant sequoias on the park's south side, pass through Oakhurst and Fish Camp on Highway 41.

OAKHURST

40 miles north of Fresno.

Motels, restaurants, gas stations, and small businesses line Highway 41 in Oakhurst, the last sizeable community before Yosemite National Park and a good spot to find provisions. The park's southern entrance is 23 miles north of Oakhurst on Highway 41.

GETTING HERE AND AROUND

At the junction of highways 41 and 49, Oakhurst is about an hour's drive north of Fresno. It's the southern gateway to Yosemite, so many people fly into Fresno and rent a car to get here and beyond.

ESSENTIALS

Visitor Information Yosemite Sierra Visitors Bureau ☎ *559/683–4636* 🌐 *www.yosemitethisyear.com.*

EXPLORING

Fresno Flats Historical Village and Park. For a dose of colorful foothills history, make a quick stop at this engaging local museum centered around two 1870s houses. ✉ *School Rd. and Indian Springs Rd.* ☎ *559/683–6570* 🌐 *www.fresnoflatsmuseum.org.*

Yosemite Gateway Gallery Row. Find out what mountain art is all about at this enclave of five galleries representing dozens of painters, sculptors, and other artists. ✉ *40982 Hwy. 41, 1¼ mile north of Hwy. 49* ☎ *559/683–5551* 🌐 *www.yosemitegatewaygalleryrow.com* 🎟 *Free* 🕒 *Daily 10–5 (days and hrs vary for some galleries).*

WHERE TO EAT

$$$$ EUROPEAN Fodor's Choice ★

🍴 **Erna's Elderberry House.** Erna Kubin-Clanin, the grande dame of Château du Sureau, created this culinary oasis, stunning for its understated elegance, gorgeous setting, and impeccable service. Earth-tone walls and wood beams accent the dining room's high ceilings, and arched windows reflect the glow of candles. The seasonal six-course prix-fixe dinner ($108) can be paired with superb wines, with each course delivered in perfect synchronicity by the elite waitstaff. **■ TIP→ Diners can also order à la carte, and a shorter bar menu is offered in the former wine cellar.** [$] *Average main: $48* ✉ *Château du Sureau, 48688 Victoria La., off Hwy. 41* ☎ *559/683–6800* 🌐 *www.elderberryhouse.com* ✍ *Reservations essential* 🕒 *No lunch Mon.–Sat.*

$ AMERICAN Fodor's Choice ★

🍴 **South Gate Brewing Company.** Locals pack this family-friendly, industrial-chic restaurant to socialize and savor small-lot beers, crafted on site, along with tasty meals. The creative pub fare runs a wide gamut, from shepherd's pie Wellington and thin-crust brick-oven pizzas to fish tacos, fish-and-chips, vegan black-bean burgers, and slow-roasted pulled-pork sandwiches. Save room for the house-made root-beer float or the brownie sundae, both topped with a scoop of locally made vanilla ice cream. When the weather's good, musicians perform on most weekends and on some weekday evenings. [$] *Average main: $13* ✉ *40233 Enterprise Dr., off Hwy. 49, north of Von's shopping center* ☎ *559/692–2739* 🌐 *southgatebrewco.com.*

WHERE TO STAY

$$
HOTEL
FAMILY

Best Western Plus Yosemite Gateway Inn. Perched on 11 hillside acres, Oakhurst's best motel has carefully tended landscaping and rooms with stylish contemporary furnishings and hand-painted murals of Yosemite. **Pros:** close to park's southern entrance; on-site restaurant; indoor and outdoor swimming pools; frequent deer and wildlife sightings. **Cons:** some rooms on the small side; Internet connection can be slow. $ *Rooms from: $150* ⊠ *40530 Hwy. 41, Oakhurst* ☎ *800/545–5462, 559/683–2378* ⊕ *www.yosemitegatewayinn.com* ⤵ *133 rooms, 16 suites* ⦿ *No meals.*

$$$$
RESORT
Fodor'sChoice
★

Château du Sureau. You'll feel pampered from the moment you drive through the wrought-iron gates of this fairy-tale castle. **Pros:** luxurious; great views; sumptuous spa facility. **Cons:** expensive; cost might not seem worth it to guests not spa-oriented. $ *Rooms from: $385* ⊠ *48688 Victoria La., Oakhurst* ☎ *559/683–6860* ⊕ *www.chateausureau.com* ⤵ *10 rooms, 1 villa* ⦿ *Breakfast.*

$$$
B&B/INN

Homestead Cottages. Set on 160 acres of rolling hills that once held a Miwok village, these cottages (the largest sleeps six) have gas fireplaces, fully equipped kitchens, and queen-size beds. **Pros:** remote location; quiet setting; friendly owners. **Cons:** might be too quiet for some. $ *Rooms from: $179* ⊠ *41110 Rd. 600, 2½ miles off Hwy. 49, Ahwahnee* ☎ *559/683–0495* ⊕ *www.homesteadcottages.com* ⤵ *6 cottages* ⦿ *Breakfast.*

NIGHTLIFE

Queen's Inn Wine Bar & Beer Garden. A combination wine bar, tasting room, and small inn, this popular hangout on a bluff above the Fresno River serves about 100 wines by the glass or flight, plus microbrews and imported beers. At the tasting room, open from Wednesday through Sunday between 11 and 5, you can sample ($5 tasting fee) Tempranillo, Pinot Gris, and other limited-production wines. ⊠ *41139 Hwy. 41, Oakhurst* ☎ *559/683–4354* ⊕ *queensinn.com* ⊙ *Closed Sun.–Tues.*

SPORTS AND THE OUTDOORS

FAMILY

Zip Yosemite. Fly through ponderosa and sugar pine trees and gaze at Fresno Dome and giant sequoias on a 1½-hour guided tour at this Sierra National Forest complex. The progressively challenging course, at elevation 5,000 feet, includes several zip lines, a suspension bridge, and daring rope lowers from 100-foot-high platforms. Participants should be at least 10 years old and weigh between 75 and 270 pounds. ⊠ *Calvin Crest Retreat Center, 45800 Calvin Crest Rd., 11 miles northeast of Oakhurst via Highway 41 and Sierra Sky Ranch Rd. (632), Oakhurst* ☎ *559/642–6688* ⊕ *zipyosemite.com* ⤳ *From $125* ⊙ *Closed Dec.–Mar.*

FISH CAMP

14 miles north of Oakhurst.

As you climb in elevation along Highway 41 northbound, you see nothing but trees until you get to Fish Camp, where there's a post office and general store, but no gasoline. (For gas, head 7 miles north to Wawona, in Yosemite, or 14 miles south to Oakhurst.)

GETTING HERE AND AROUND

Highway 41 is the main drag here. YARTS public transit stops in Fish Camp on its route between Fresno and Yosemite Valley.

EXPLORING

FAMILY **Yosemite Mountain Sugar Pine Railroad.** Travel back to a time when powerful steam locomotives hauled massive log trains through the Sierra. This 4-mile, narrow-gauge railroad excursion takes you near Yosemite's south gate. There's a moonlight special ($55), with dinner and entertainment, and you can pan for gold ($10) and visit the free museum. ✉ *56001 Hwy. 41, 8 miles south of Yosemite, Fish Camp* ☎ *559/683–7273* 🌐 *www.ymsprr.com* 🎟 *$22* 🕒 *May–Sept., daily; Apr. and Oct., weekends and selected weekdays.*

WHERE TO STAY

$$$ B&B/INN 🏨 **Narrow Gauge Inn.** The well-tended rooms at this family-owned property have balconies with views of the surrounding woods and mountains. **Pros:** close to Yosemite's south entrance; nicely appointed rooms; wonderful balconies. **Cons:** rooms can be a bit dark; dining options are limited, especially for vegetarians. [$] *Rooms from: $209* ✉ *48571 Hwy. 41, Fish Camp* ☎ *559/683–7720, 888/644–9050* 🌐 *www.narrowgaugeinn.com* 🛏 *26 rooms* 🍴 *Breakfast.*

$$$$ RESORT FAMILY Fodor's Choice ★ 🏨 **Tenaya Lodge.** One of the region's largest hotels, Tenaya Lodge is ideal for people who enjoy wilderness treks by day but prefer creature comforts at night. **Pros:** rustic setting with modern comforts; exceptional spa and exercise facility; close to Yosemite; activities for all ages. **Cons:** so big it can seem impersonal; pricey during summer. [$] *Rooms from: $295* ✉ *1122 Hwy. 41, Fish Camp* ☎ *559/683–6555, 888/514–2167* 🌐 *www.tenayalodge.com* 🛏 *282 rooms, 20 suites* 🍴 *No meals.*

$$$ B&B/INN 🏨 **Yosemite Lodging at Big Creek Inn.** A romantic bed-and-breakfast in a woodsy setting south of the park, the inn offers perks that place it ahead of the competition. **Pros:** friendly, knowledgeable innkeeper; hearty home-cooked breakfast; intimate setting. **Cons:** with only three rooms it books up quickly; no pets allowed. [$] *Rooms from: $239* ✉ *1221 Hwy. 41, Fish Camp* ☎ *559/641–2828* 🌐 *www.yosemiteinn.com* 🛏 *3 rooms* 🍴 *Breakfast.*

MAMMOTH LAKES

30 miles south of the eastern edge of Yosemite National Park.

International real-estate developers joined forces with Mammoth Mountain Ski Area to transform the once sleepy town of Mammoth Lakes (elevation 7,800 feet) into an upscale ski destination. Relatively sophisticated dining and lodging options can be found at the Village at Mammoth complex, and multimillion-dollar renovations to tired motels and restaurants have revived the "downtown" area of Old Mammoth Road. Also here is the hoppin' Mammoth Rock 'n' Bowl, a two-story

Twin Lakes, in the Mammoth Lakes region, is a great place to unwind.

activity, dining, and entertainment complex. Winter is high season at Mammoth; in summer, the room rates drop.

GETTING HERE AND AROUND
The best way to get to Mammoth Lakes is by car. The town is about 2 miles west of U.S. 395 on Highway 203, signed as Main Street in Mammoth Lakes and Minaret Road west of town. In summer and early fall (until the first big snow) you can drive to Mammoth Lakes east through Yosemite National Park on scenic Tioga Pass Road; signed as Highway 120 outside the park, the road connects to U.S. 395 north of Mammoth. In summer YARTS provides once-a-day public-transit service between Mammoth Lakes and Yosemite Valley. The shuttle buses of Eastern Sierra Transit Authority serve Mammoth Lakes and nearby tourist sites.

ESSENTIALS
Visitor Information Mammoth Lakes Visitor Center ⊠ *Welcome Center, 2510 Main St., near Sawmill Cutoff Rd.* ☎ *760/934–2712, 888/466–2666* ⊕ *www. visitmammoth.com.*

EXPLORING

TOP ATTRACTIONS
Fodor'sChoice **Devils Postpile National Monument.** Volcanic and glacial forces sculpted
★ this formation of smooth, vertical basalt columns. For a bird's-eye view, take the short, steep trail to the top of a 60-foot cliff. To see the monument's second scenic wonder, **Rainbow Falls,** hike 2 miles past Devils Postpile. A branch of the San Joaquin River plunges more than 100 feet over a lava ledge here. When the water hits the pool below, sunlight

turns the resulting mist into a spray of color. ■TIP➔ **From mid-June to early September, day-use visitors must ride the shuttle bus from the Mammoth Mountain Ski Area to the monument.** ⊠ *13 miles southwest of Mammoth Lakes off Minaret Rd. (Hwy. 203)* ☎ *760/934–2289, 760/872–1901 shuttle* ⊕ *www.nps.gov/depo* ⊠ *$10 per vehicle (allowed early Sept.–mid-Oct.), $7 per person shuttle* ☉ *Park mid-June–mid-Oct.; shuttle mid-June–early Sept.*

Fodor'sChoice ★ **Mammoth Lakes Basin.** Mammoth's seven main lakes are popular for fishing and boating in summer, and a network of multi-use paths connects them to the North Village. First comes Twin Lakes, at the far end of which is Twin Falls, where water cascades 300 feet over a shelf of volcanic rock. Also popular are Lake Mary, the largest lake in the basin; Lake Mamie; and Lake George. ■TIP➔ **Horseshoe Lake is the only lake in which you can swim.** ⊠ *Lake Mary Rd., off Hwy. 203, southwest of town.*

Mammoth Rock 'n' Bowl. A sprawling complex with sweeping views of the Sherwin Mountains, Mammoth Rock 'n' Bowl supplies one-stop recreation, entertainment, and dining. Downstairs are 12 bowling lanes, a band stage and dance floor, Ping-Pong and foosball tables, dartboards, and a casual bar-restaurant ($$) serving burgers, pizzas, and small plates. The upstairs floor has three golf simulators, a pro shop, and Mammoth Rock Brasserie ($$$), an upscale dining room and lounge. ■TIP➔ **If the weather's nice, sit on the outdoor patio or the upstairs deck and enjoy the unobstructed vistas.** ⊠ *3029 Chateau Rd., off Old Mammoth Rd.* ☎ *760/934–4200* ⊕ *mammothrocknbowl. com* ⊠ *Bowling: $7 per game per person evenings and weekends, $5 before 5 pm and after 10 pm; $3 shoe rental* ☉ *Hrs vary by venue; call or check website.*

FAMILY
Fodor'sChoice ★ **Panorama Gondola.** Even if you don't ski, ride the gondola to see Mammoth Mountain, the aptly named dormant volcano that gives Mammoth Lakes its name. Gondolas serve skiers in winter and mountain bikers and sightseers in summer. The high-speed, eight-passenger gondolas whisk you from the chalet to the summit, where you can read about the area's volcanic history and take in top-of-the-world views. Standing high above the tree line, you can look west 150 miles across the state to the Coastal Range; to the east are the highest peaks of Nevada and the Great Basin beyond. You won't find a better view of the Sierra High Country without climbing. ■TIP➔ **The air is thin at the 11,053-foot summit; carry water, and don't overexert yourself.** ⊠ *Boarding area at Main Lodge, off Minaret Rd. (Hwy. 203), west of village center* ☎ *760/934–2571* ⊠ *$25* ☉ *July 4–Oct., daily 9–4:30; Nov.–July 3, daily 8:30–4.*

WORTH NOTING

Minaret Vista. The glacier-carved sawtooth spires of the Minarets, the remains of an ancient lava flow, are best viewed from the Minaret Vista. Pull off the road, park your car in the visitors' viewing area, and walk along the path, which has interpretive signs explaining the spectacular peaks, ridges, and valleys beyond. ⊠ *Off Hwy. 203, 1¼ mile west of Mammoth Mountain Ski Area.*

14

Village at Mammoth. This huge complex of shops, restaurants, and luxury accommodations is the town's tourist center, and the venue for many special events—check the website for the weekly schedule. The complex is also the transfer hub for the free public transit system, with fixed routes throughout the Mammoth Lakes area. The free village gondola starts here and travels up the mountain to Canyon Lodge and back. ■ TIP→ **Unless you're staying in the village and have access to the on-site lots, parking can be very difficult here.** ✉ *100 Canyon Blvd.* ☎ *760/924–1575* 🌐 *villageatmammoth.com.*

WHERE TO EAT

$$$ STEAKHOUSE FAMILY

🍴 **The Mogul.** Come here for straightforward steaks—top sirloin, New York, filet mignon, and porterhouse. The only catch is that the waiters cook them, and the results vary depending on their experience. But generally things go well, and kids love the experience. The knotty-pine walls lend a woodsy touch, and suggest Mammoth before all the development. ■ TIP→ **There's an extensive salad bar—all you can eat, with hot bread included.** [$] *Average main: $24* ✉ *1528 Tavern Rd., off Old Mammoth Rd., Mammoth Lakes* ☎ *760/934–3039* 🌐 *www.themogul.com* ⏲ *No lunch.*

$$$ AMERICAN

🍴 **Petra's Bistro & Wine Bar.** The ambience at Petra's—quiet, dark, and warm (there's a great fireplace)—complements its seductive meat and seafood entrées and smart selection of mostly California-made wines. The service is top-notch. With its pub grub, whiskies, and craft beers and ales, the downstairs Clocktower Cellar bar provides a lively, if sometimes rowdy, alternative. [$] *Average main: $28* ✉ *Alpenhof Lodge, 6080 Minaret Rd.* ☎ *760/934–3500* 🌐 *www.petrasbistro.com* ✍ *Reservations essential* ⏲ *Closed Mon. No lunch.*

$$$$ AMERICAN Fodor's Choice ★

🍴 **Restaurant at Convict Lake.** The lake is one of the most spectacular spots in the Eastern Sierra, and the food here lives up to the view. Beef Wellington, rack of lamb, and pan-seared local trout, all beautifully prepared, are among the chef's specialties. The woodsy room has a vaulted knotty-pine ceiling and a copper-chimney fireplace. Natural light abounds in the daytime, but if it's summer, opt for a table outdoors under the white-barked aspens. Service is exceptional, as is the wine selection, which includes reasonably priced European and California bottlings. ■ TIP→ **The restaurant offers shuttle service from Mammoth Lakes for groups of four or more (reservations required).** [$] *Average main: $32* ✉ *Convict Lake Rd. off U.S. 395, 4 miles south of Mammoth Lakes* ☎ *760/934–3803* 🌐 *www.convictlake.com* ✍ *Reservations essential* ⏲ *No lunch early Sept.–mid-June.*

$$ AMERICAN

🍴 **The Stove.** Down-to-earth, folksy cooking is the hallmark of this casual place known for hearty comfort—prime-rib hash, fried chicken, meat loaf, and other standbys. Breakfast is served all day; the mainstays include chicken and waffles. Save room for the pie, baked daily in-house. The dining room here is cozy, with gingham curtains and dark-wood booths, and the service is friendly. ■ TIP→ **Reservations are accepted for dinner only.** [$] *Average main: $16* ✉ *644 Old Mammoth Rd., south off Meridian Blvd.* ☎ *760/934–2821* 🌐 *www.thestoverestaurantmammoth.com* ⏲ *No dinner occasionally during off-season; call for hrs.*

$$ ╳**Toomey's.** A passionate baseball fan, chef Matt Toomey designed this
MODERN casual space near the Village Gondola to resemble a dugout, and deco-
AMERICAN rated it with baseball memorabilia. At breakfast, don't miss the coconut
FAMILY mascarpone pancakes. After a day outdoors, relax over lobster taquitos,
giant chicken wings, fish tacos, and Angus beef sliders. Lunch and din-
ner entrées include buffalo meat loaf, seafood jambalaya, and a New
Zealand elk rack chop. Save room for homemade, organic, gluten-free
pie and other desserts. ■TIP→ **If you're in a hurry, phone in your order
for curbside delivery to your car.** $ *Average main: $20* ⊠ *6085 Mina-
ret Rd., at the Village* ☎ *760/924–4408* ⊕ *www.toomeyscatering.com.*

WHERE TO STAY

14

$$ ⛄ **Alpenhof Lodge.** Across from the Village at Mammoth, this mom-and-
B&B/INN pop motel offers basic comforts and a few niceties such as the attractive
pine furniture. **Pros:** convenient for skiers; reasonable rates. **Cons:** some
bathrooms are small; rooms above pub can be noisy. $ *Rooms from:
$159* ⊠ *6080 Minaret Rd., Box 1157* ☎ *760/934–6330, 800/828–0371*
⊕ *www.alpenhof-lodge.com* ⇆ *54 rooms, 3 cabins* ❍❘ *Breakfast.*

$$$ ⛄ **Double Eagle Resort and Spa.** Lofty pines tower over this very fine spa
RESORT retreat on the June Lake Loop. **Pros:** pretty setting; spectacular indoor
Fodor'sChoice pool; 1½ mile from June Mountain Ski Area. **Cons:** expensive; remote.
★ $ *Rooms from: $249* ⊠ *5587 Hwy. 158, June Lake* ☎ *760/648–7004*
⊕ *www.doubleeagle.com* ⇆ *17 2-bedroom cabins, 16 rooms, 1 3-bed-
room house* ❍❘ *No meals.*

$$$ ⛄ **Juniper Springs Resort.** Tops for slope-side comfort, these condominium-
RESORT style units have full kitchens and ski-in ski-out access to the moun-
tain. **Pros:** bargain during summer; direct access to the slopes; good
views. **Cons:** no nightlife within walking distance; no air-conditioning.
$ *Rooms from: $199* ⊠ *4000 Meridian Blvd.* ☎ *760/924–1102, 800/
626–6684* ⊕ *www.juniperspringsmammoth.com* ⇆ *10 studios, 99
1-bedrooms, 92 2-bedrooms, 3 3-bedrooms* ❍❘ *No meals.*

$$ ⛄ **Mammoth Mountain Inn.** If you want to be within walking distance
RESORT of the Mammoth Mountain Main Lodge, this is the place. **Pros:** great
location; big rooms; a traditional place to stay. **Cons:** can be crowded
in ski season. $ *Rooms from: $134* ⊠ *1 Minaret Rd.* ☎ *760/934–2581,
800/626–6684* ⊕ *www.themammothmountaininn.com* ⇆ *124 rooms,
91 condos* ❍❘ *No meals.*

$$$ ⛄ **Sierra Nevada Resort & Spa.** A full-service resort in the heart of Old
RESORT Mammoth, the Sierra Nevada has it all: three restaurants, four bars, a ded-
icated spa facility, on-site ski and snowboard rentals, a pool and Jacuzzi,
miniature golf, and room and suite options in three buildings. **Pros:** many
on-site amenities; walk to restaurants on property or downtown; complimentary shuttle service. **Cons:** must drive or ride a bus or shuttle to the
slopes; thin walls in older rooms. $ *Rooms from: $189* ⊠ *164 Old Mammoth Rd.* ☎ *760/934–2515, 800/824–5132* 🖷 *760/934–7319* ⊕ *thesier-
ranevadaresort.com* ⇆ *143 rooms, 6 townhomes* ❍❘ *No meals.*

$$$ ⛄ **Tamarack Lodge Resort & Lakefront Restaurant.** On the edge of the John
RESORT Muir Wilderness Area, where cross-country ski trails lace the woods,
Fodor'sChoice this 1924 lodge looks like something out of a snow globe. **Pros:** rus-
★ tic; eco-sensitive; many nearby outdoor activities. **Cons:** pricey; shared

bathrooms for some main lodge rooms. [$] *Rooms from: $239* ✉ *Lake Mary Rd., off Hwy. 203* ☎ *760/934–2442, 800/626–6684* 🌐 *www.tamaracklodge.com* 🛏 *11 rooms, 35 cabins* 🍴 *No meals.*

$$$ RESORT 🏨 **The Village Lodge.** With their exposed timbers and peaked roofs, these four-story condo buildings at the epicenter of Mammoth's dining and nightlife scene pay homage to Alpine style. **Pros:** central location; clean; big rooms; good restaurants nearby. **Cons:** pricey; can be noisy outside. [$] *Rooms from: $239* ✉ *1111 Forest Trail* ☎ *760/934–1982, 800/626–6684* 🌐 *www.thevillagelodgemammoth.com* 🛏 *277 units* 🍴 *No meals.*

$$$$ RESORT 🏨 **Westin Monache Resort.** On a hill just steps from the Village at Mammoth, the Westin provides full-service comfort and amenities close to restaurants, entertainment, and free public transportation. **Pros:** upscale amenities; prime location; free gondola to the slopes is across the street. **Cons:** long, steep stairway down to village; added resort fee. [$] *Rooms from: $349* ✉ *50 Hillside Dr.* ☎ *760/934–0400, 888/627–8154 reservations* 🌐 *www.westinmammoth.com* 🛏 *109 rooms, 121 suites* 🍴 *No meals.*

SPORTS AND THE OUTDOORS

BIKING

Mammoth Mountain Bike Park. The park opens when the snow melts, usually by July, and has 100-plus miles of single-track trails—from mellow to super-challenging. Chairlifts and shuttles provide trail access, and rentals are available. ✉ *Mammoth Mountain Ski Area* ☎ *760/934–0677, 800/626–6684* 🌐 *www.mammothmountain.com* 🎟 *$49 day pass.*

FISHING

The fishing season runs from the last Saturday in April until the end of October. Crowley Lake is the top trout-fishing spot in the area; Convict Lake, June Lake, and the lakes of the Mammoth Basin are other prime spots. One of the best trout rivers is the San Joaquin, near Devils Postpile. Hot Creek, a designated Wild Trout Stream, is renowned for fly-fishing (catch-and-release only).

Kittredge Sports. This outfit rents rods and reels and conducts guided trips. ✉ *3218 Main St., at Forest Trail* ☎ *760/934–7566* 🌐 *kittredgesports.com.*

Sierra Drifters Guide Service. To maximize your time on the water, get tips from local anglers, or better yet, book a guided fishing trip, contact Sierra Drifters. ☎ *760/935–4250* 🌐 *www.sierradrifters.com.*

HIKING

Hiking in Mammoth is stellar, especially along the trails that wind through alpine scenery around the Lakes Basin. Carry lots of water; and remember, the air is thin at 8,000-plus feet.

U.S. Forest Service Ranger Station. Stop at the ranger station, just east of the town of Mammoth Lakes, for an area trail map and permits for backpacking in wilderness areas. ✉ *2510 Main St., Hwy. 203* ☎ *760/924–5500* 🌐 *www.fs.usda.gov/main/inyo.*

HORSEBACK RIDING

Stables around Mammoth are typically open from June through September.

Mammoth Lakes Pack Outfit. This company runs day and overnight horseback trips and will shuttle you to the high country. ⊠ *Lake Mary Rd., between Twin Lakes and Lake Mary* ☎ *888/475–8747* ⊕ *www. mammothpack.com.*

McGee Creek Pack Station. These folks customize pack trips or will shuttle you to camp alone. ⊠ *2990 McGee Creek Rd., Crowley Lake* ☎ *760/935–4324 summer, 760/878–2207, 800/854–7407* ⊕ *www. mcgeecreekpackstation.com.*

SKIING

In winter, check the On the Snow website or call the Snow Report for information about Mammoth weather conditions.

FAMILY **June Mountain Ski Area.** Snowboarders especially dig June Mountain, a compact, low-key resort north of Mammoth Mountain. Three beginner-to-intermediate terrain areas—the Surprise Fun Zone, Mambo Playground, and Bucky's Adventure—are for both skiers and boarders. There's rarely a line for the lifts here: if you must ski on a weekend and want to avoid the crowds, this is the place to come, and in a storm it's better protected from wind and blowing snow than Mammoth is. (If it starts to storm, you can use your Mammoth ticket at June.) The services include a rental-and-repair shop, a ski school, and a sports shop. There's food, but the options are better at Mammoth. ■TIP➔ **Kids 12 and under ski and ride free.** ⊠ *3819 Hwy. 158/June Lake Loop, off U.S. 395, 22 miles northwest of Mammoth, June Lake* ☎ *760/648–7733, 888/586–3686* ⊕ *www.junemountain.com* ⊠ *From $72* ⌁ *35 trails on 1,400 acres, rated 35% beginner, 45% intermediate, 20% advanced. Longest run 2 miles, base 7,545 feet, summit 10,190 feet. Lifts: 7.*

Fodor's Choice **Mammoth Mountain Ski Area.** One of the West's largest and best ski areas, ★ Mammoth has more than 3,500 acres of skiable terrain and a 3,100-foot vertical drop. The views from the 11,053-foot summit are some of the most stunning in the Sierra. Below, you'll find a 6½-mile-wide swath of groomed boulevards and canyons, as well as pockets of tree-skiing and a dozen vast bowls. Snowboarders are everywhere on the slopes; there are three outstanding freestyle terrain parks of varying difficulty, with jumps, rails, tabletops, and giant super pipes—this is the location of several international snowboarding competitions, and, in summer, mountain-bike meets. Mammoth's season begins in November and often lingers into May. Lessons and equipment are available, and there's a children's ski and snowboard school. Mammoth runs free shuttle-bus routes around town and to the ski area, and the Village Gondola runs from the Village complex to Canyon Lodge. However, only overnight guests are allowed to park at the Village for more than a few hours. ⚠ **The main lodge is dark and dated, unsuited in almost every way for the crush of ski season.** ⊠ *Minaret Rd., west of Mammoth Lakes* ☎ *760/934–2571, 800/626–6684, 760/934–0687 shuttle* ⊕ *www.mammothmountain.com* ⊠ *From $95* ⌁ *150 trails on 3,500 acres, rated 25% beginner, 40% intermediate, 20% advanced, 15%*

14

expert. Longest run 3 miles, base 7,953 feet, summit 11,053 feet. Lifts: 28, including 11 high-speed and 3 gondolas.

Tamarack Cross Country Ski Center. Trails at the center, adjacent to Tamarack Lodge, meander around several lakes. Rentals are available. ✉ *Lake Mary Rd., off Hwy. 203* ☎ *760/934–5293, 760/934–2442* ⊕ *tamaracklodge.com* ➲ *$56 all-inclusive day rate.*

SKI RENTALS AND RESOURCES

Fodor's Choice ★ **Black Tie Ski Rentals.** Skiers and snowboarders love this rental outfit whose staffers will deliver and custom-fit equipment for free. They also offer slope-side assistance. ☎ *760/934–7009* ⊕ *mammothskis.com.*

Footloose. When the U.S. Ski Team visits Mammoth and needs boot adjustments, everyone heads to Footloose, the best place in town—and possibly all California—for ski-boot rentals and sales, as well as custom insoles. ✉ *3043 Main St., at Mammoth Rd.* ☎ *760/934–2400* ⊕ *www.footloosesports.com.*

Kittredge Sports. Advanced skiers should consider this outfit, which has been around since the 1960s. ✉ *3218 Main St.* ☎ *760/934–7566* ⊕ *kittredgesports.com.*

Mammoth Sporting Goods. This company rents good skis for intermediates and sells equipment, clothing, and accessories. ✉ *452 Old Mammoth Rd.* ☎ *760/934–3239* ⊕ *www.mammothoutdoorsports.com.*

OntheSnow.com ⊕ *www.onthesnow.com/california/mammoth-mountain-ski-area/ski-resort.html.*

Snow Report. For information on winter conditions around Mammoth, call the Snow Report. ☎ *760/934–7669, 888/766–9778.*

EAST OF YOSEMITE NATIONAL PARK

Most people enter Yosemite National Park from the west, having driven out from the Bay Area or Los Angeles. The eastern entrance on Tioga Pass Road (Highway 120), however, provides stunning, sweeping views of the High Sierra. Gray rocks shine in the bright sun, with scattered, small vegetation sprinkled about the mountainside. To drive from Lee Vining to Tuolumne Meadows is an unforgettable experience, but keep in mind that the road tends to be closed for at least seven months of the year.

LEE VINING

20 miles east of Tuolumne Meadows, 30 miles north of Mammoth Lakes.

Tiny Lee Vining is known primarily as the eastern gateway to Yosemite National Park (summer only) and the location of vast and desolate Mono Lake. Pick up supplies at the general store year-round, or stop here for lunch or dinner before or after a drive through the high country. In winter the town is all but deserted, except for the ice climbers who come to scale frozen waterfalls.

GETTING HERE AND AROUND

Lee Vining is on U.S. 395, north of the road's intersection with Highway 120 and on the south side of Mono Lake. In summer YARTS public transit can get you here from Yosemite Valley, but you'll need a car to explore the area.

ESSENTIALS

Visitor Information Lee Vining Chamber of Commerce ☎ 760/647–6629 ⊕ www.leevining.com. **Mono Basin National Forest Scenic Area Visitor Center** ⊠ Visitor Center Dr., off U.S. 395, 1 mile north of Hwy. 120 ☎ 760/647–3044 ⊕ www.monolake.org/visit/vc ⊙ Mid-May–mid-Oct., daily 8–5; early Apr.–mid-May and mid-Oct.–Nov., Thurs.–Mon. 9–4:30.

EXPLORING

14

Fodor's Choice
★

Mono Lake. Since the 1940s Los Angeles has diverted water from this lake, exposing striking towers of tufa, or calcium carbonate. Court victories by environmentalists have meant fewer diversions, and the lake is rising again. Although to see the lake from U.S. 395 is stunning, make time to visit South Tufa, whose parking lot is 5 miles east of U.S. 395 off Highway 120. There in summer you can join the naturalist-guided **South Tufa Walk,** which lasts about 90 minutes. The **Scenic Area Visitor Center,** off U.S. 395, is a sensational stop for its interactive exhibits and sweeping Mono Lake views. In town at U.S. 395 and 3rd Street, the **Mono Lake Committee Information Center & Bookstore,** open from 9 to 5 daily, has more information about this beautiful area. ⊠ *Hwy. 120, east of Lee Vining, Lee Vining* ☎ *760/647–3044 visitor center, 760/647–6595 info center* ⊕ *www.monolake.org* 🖃 *Free* ⊙ *Visitor center early Apr.–Nov., daily 8–5; hrs vary at other times* .

EN
ROUTE

June Lake Loop. Heading south from Lee Vining, U.S. 395 intersects the June Lake Loop. This gorgeous 17-mile drive follows an old glacial canyon past Grant, June, Gull, and other lakes before reconnecting with U.S. 395 on its way to Mammoth Lakes. ■TIP→ The loop is especially colorful in fall. ⊠ *Hwy. 158 W.*

WHERE TO EAT AND STAY

$$
AMERICAN

✕**Tioga Gas Mart & Whoa Nelli Deli.** This might be the only gas station in the United States serving craft beers and lobster taquitos, but its appeal goes beyond novelty. Succulent fish tacos with mango salsa and barbecued ribs with a huckleberry glaze are among the many well-executed dishes. ■TIP→ Order at the counter and grab a seat inside, or sit at one of the picnic tables on the lawn outside and take in the distant view of Mono Lake. 🖇 *Average main: $16* ⊠ *Hwy. 120 and U.S. 395* ☎ *760/647–1088* ⊕ *www.whoanelliedeli.com* ⊙ *Closed early Nov.–late Apr.*

$
B&B/INN

🏠 **Lake View Lodge.** Enormous rooms and landscaping that includes several shaded sitting areas set this motel apart from its competitors in town. **Pros:** attractive; peaceful; clean; friendly staff. **Cons:** could use updating. 🖇 *Rooms from: $109* ⊠ *51285 U.S. 395* ☎ *760/647–6543, 800/990–6614* ⊕ *www.lakeviewlodgeyosemite.com* 🛏 *76 rooms, 12 cottages* ᠀ *No meals.*

BODIE STATE HISTORIC PARK

31 miles northeast of Lee Vining.

The town of Bridgeport is the gateway to Bodie State Historic Park, and the only supply center for miles around. The scenery is spectacular, with craggy, snowcapped peaks looming over vast prairies. Bridgeport's claim to fame is that most of the 1947 film-noir classic *Out of the Past,* starring Robert Mitchum in his prime as a private eye whose past catches up with him, was filmed here. In winter, much of Bridgeport shuts down.

GETTING HERE AND AROUND

A car is the best way to reach this area. Bodie is on Highway 270 about 13 miles east of U.S. 395.

EXPLORING

Fodor'sChoice **Bodie Ghost Town.** The mining village of Rattlesnake Gulch, abandoned
★ mine shafts, and the remains of a small Chinatown are among the sights at this fascinating ghost town. The town boomed from about 1878 to 1881, but by the late 1940s all its residents had departed. A state park was established here in 1962, with a mandate to preserve everything in a state of "arrested decay." Evidence of Bodie's wild past survives at an excellent museum, and you can tour an old stamp mill where ore was crushed into fine powder to extract gold and silver. Bodie lies 13 miles east of U.S. 395 off Highway 270. The last 3 miles are unpaved, and snow may close the highway from late fall through early spring. ■TIP➔ No food, drink, or lodging is available in Bodie. ⊠ *Bodie Rd., off Hwy. 270* ☏ *760/647–6445* ⊕ *www.parks.ca.gov/bodie* ☉ *$5* ☉ *Mid-Apr.–Oct., daily 9–6; Nov.–mid-Apr., daily 9–4.*

SOUTH OF SEQUOIA AND KINGS CANYON

Numerous towns and cities tout themselves as "gateways" to Sequoia and Kings Canyon national parks, but one that merits the distinction is frisky Three Rivers, a foothills hamlet along the Kaweah River.

THREE RIVERS

7 miles south of Sequoia National Park's Foothills Visitor Center.

Close to Sequoia National Park's Ash Mountain and Lookout Point entrances, Three Rivers is a good spot to find a room when park lodgings are full. Either because residents here appreciate their idyllic setting or because they know that tourists are their bread and butter, you'll find them eager to share tips about the best spots for "Sierra surfing" the Kaweah's smooth, moss-covered rocks or where to find the best cell-phone reception (it's off to the cemetery for Verizon customers).

GETTING HERE AND AROUND

Driving is the easiest way to get to and around Three Rivers, which straddles a long stretch of Highway 198. In summer the Sequoia Shuttle connects Three Rivers to Visalia and Sequoia National Park.

BUS CONTACTS

Sequoia Shuttle ☏ *877/287–4453* ⊕ *www.sequoiashuttle.com* ☉ *$15 round-trip* ☉ *Late May–early Sept.*

WHERE TO EAT AND STAY

$
CAFÉ
✕ **Antoinette's Coffee and Goodies.** For smoothies, well-crafted espresso drinks, and pumpkin chocolate-chip muffins and other homemade baked goods, stop for a spell at this convivial coffee shop next door to Sierra Subs and Salads. ■**TIP**➔ **There's Wi-Fi here, too.** $ *Average main: $6* ✉ *41727 Sierra Dr., Three Rivers* ☎ *559/561–2253* ⊕ *www. antoinettescoffeeandgoodies.com* ⌓ *Reservations not accepted* ⊘ *Closed Tues. No dinner.*

$$$
AMERICAN
✕ **Gateway Restaurant and Lodge.** The view's the draw at this roadhouse that overlooks the Kaweah River as it plunges out of the high country. The Gateway serves everything from osso buco to shrimp in Thai chili sauce. Some menu items are pricey, but you can also order a pizza or a beef or salmon burger. For the best results, stick to the simpler preparations. Dinner reservations are essential on summer weekends. $ *Average main: $29* ✉ *45978 Sierra Dr., Three Rivers* ☎ *559/561–4133* ⊕ *www.gateway-sequoia.com.*

$
AMERICAN
✕ **Sierra Subs and Salads.** This well-run sandwichery satisfies carnivores and vegetarians alike with crispy-fresh ingredients prepared with panache. Depending on your preference, the centerpiece of the Bull's Eye sandwich, for instance, will be roast beef or a Portobello mushroom, but whichever you choose, the accompanying flavors—of ciabatta bread, horseradish-and-garlic mayonnaise, roasted red peppers, Havarti cheese, and spinach—will delight your palate. $ *Average main: $8* ✉ *41717 Sierra Dr., Three Rivers* ☎ *559/561–4810* ⊕ *www. sierrasubsandsalads.com* ⊘ *Closed Mon. No dinner.*

$$
B&B/INN
⊞ **Buckeye Tree Lodge.** Every room at this two-story motel has a patio facing a sun-dappled grassy lawn, right on the banks of the Kaweah River. **Pros:** near the park entrance; fantastic river views; friendly staff; kitchenette in some rooms. **Cons:** can fill up quickly in the summer; could use a little updating. $ *Rooms from: $139* ✉ *46000 Sierra Dr., Hwy. 198, Three Rivers* ☎ *559/561–5900* ⊕ *www.buckeyetree.com* ⤴ *11 rooms* ⦿| *Breakfast* ☞ *2-night minimum on summer weekends.*

$$
B&B/INN
Fodor's Choice
★
⊞ **Rio Sierra Riverhouse.** Guests at Rio Sierra come for the river views, the sandy beach, and the proximity to Sequoia National Park (6 miles away), but invariably end up raving as much about the warm yet laidback hospitality of proprietress Mars Roberts as they do about location. **Pros:** seductive beach; winning hostess; river views from all rooms; contemporary ambience; full kitchen in one room, kitchenette in another. **Cons:** books up quickly in summer; some road noise audible in rooms. $ *Rooms from: $170* ✉ *41997 Sierra Dr., Hwy. 198, Three Rivers* ☎ *559/561–4720* ⊕ *www.rio-sierra.com* ⤴ *5 rooms* ⊘ *Closed Jan.* ⦿| *No meals* ☞ *2-night minimum stay on summer weekends.*

SPORTS AND THE OUTDOORS

RAFTING

Kaweah White Water Adventures. Kaweah's trips include a two-hour excursion (good for families) through Class III rapids, a longer paddle through Class IV rapids, and an extended trip (typically Class IV and V rapids). ✉ *40443 Sierra Dr.* ☎ *559/740–8251, 800/229–8658* ⊕ *www. kaweah-whitewater.com* ⊟ *$50–$140 per person.*

YOSEMITE
NATIONAL PARK

WELCOME TO YOSEMITE NATIONAL PARK

TOP REASONS TO GO

★ **Wet and wild:** An easy stroll brings you to the base of Lower Yosemite Falls, where roaring springtime waters make for misty lens caps and lasting memories.

★ **Tunnel vision:** Approaching Yosemite Valley, Wawona Road passes through a mountainside and emerges before one of the park's most heart-stopping vistas.

★ **Inhale the beauty:** Pause to smell the light, pristine air as you travel about the High Sierra's Tioga Pass and Tuolumne Meadows, where 10,000-foot granite peaks just might take your breath away.

★ **Walk away:** Leave the crowds behind—but do bring along a buddy—and take a hike somewhere along Yosemite's 800 miles of trails.

★ **Powder your nose:** Winter's hush floats into Yosemite on snowflakes. Lift your face to the sky and listen to the trees.

1 Yosemite Valley. At an elevation of 4,000 feet, in roughly the center of the park, beats Yosemite's heart. This is where you'll find the park's most famous sights and biggest crowds.

2 Wawona and Mariposa Grove. The park's southern tip holds Wawona, with its grand old hotel and pioneer history center, and the Mariposa Grove of Big Trees, filled with giant sequoias. These are closest to the South Entrance, 35 miles (a one-hour drive) south of Yosemite Village.

3 Tuolumne Meadows. The highlight of east-central Yosemite is this wildflower-strewn valley with hiking trails, nestled among sharp, rocky peaks. It's a 1½-hour drive northeast of Yosemite Valley along Tioga Road (closed mid-October through late May).

4 Hetch Hetchy. The most remote, least visited part of Yosemite accessible by automobile, this glacial valley is dominated by a reservoir and veined with wilderness trails. It's near the park's western boundary, about a half-hour drive north of the Big Oak Flat Entrance.

CALIFORNIA

GETTING ORIENTED

Yosemite is so large that you can think of it as five parks. Yosemite Valley, famous for waterfalls and cliffs, and Wawona, where the giant sequoias stand, are open all year. Hetch Hetchy, home of less-used backcountry trails, is most accessible from late spring through early fall. The subalpine high country, Tuolumne Meadows, is open for summer hiking and camping; in winter it's accessible via cross-country skis or snowshoes. Badger Pass Ski Area is open in winter only. Most visitors spend their time along the park's southwestern border, between Wawona and Big Oak Flat Entrance; a bit farther east in Yosemite Valley and Badger Pass Ski Area; and along the east–west corridor of Tioga Road, which spans the park north of Yosemite Valley and bisects Tuolumne Meadows.

15

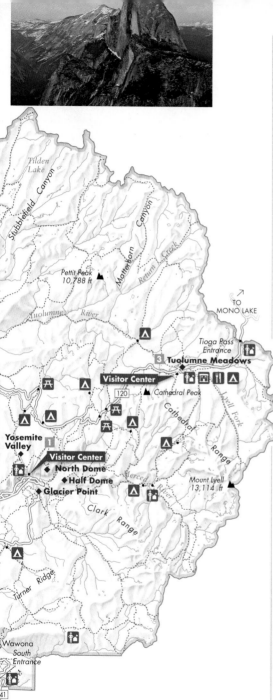

Updated by
Steve Pastorino

By merely standing in Yosemite Valley and turning in a circle, you can see more natural wonders in a minute than you could in a full day pretty much anywhere else. Half Dome, Yosemite Falls, El Capitan, Bridalveil Fall, Sentinel Dome, the Merced River, white-flowering dogwood trees, maybe even bears ripping into the bark of fallen trees or sticking their snouts into beehives—it's all in Yosemite Valley.

In the mid-1800s, when tourists were arriving to the area, the valley's special geologic qualities and the giant sequoias of Mariposa Grove 30 miles to the south so impressed a group of influential Californians that they persuaded President Abraham Lincoln to grant those two areas to the state for protection. On October 1, 1890—thanks largely to lobbying efforts by naturalist John Muir and Robert Underwood Johnson, the editor of *Century Magazine*—Congress set aside 1,500 square miles for Yosemite National Park.

YOSEMITE PLANNER

WHEN TO GO

During extremely busy periods—such as July 4—you will experience delays at the entrance gates. For smaller crowds, visit midweek. Or come mid-April through Memorial Day or mid-September through October, when the park is a bit less busy and the days usually are sunny and clear.

Summer rainfall is rare. In winter heavy snows occasionally cause road closures, and tire chains or four-wheel drive may be required on the roads that remain open. The road to Glacier Point beyond the turnoff for Badger Pass is closed after the first major snowfall; Tioga Road is closed from late October through May or mid-June. Mariposa Grove Road is typically closed for a shorter period in winter.

GETTING HERE AND AROUND
BUS TRAVEL
Once you're in Yosemite you can take advantage of the free shuttle buses, which operate on low emissions, have 21 stops, and run from 7 am to 10 pm year-round. Buses run about every 10 minutes in summer, a bit less frequently in winter. A separate (but also free) summer-only shuttle runs out to El Capitan. Also in summer, you can pay to take the morning "hikers' bus" from Yosemite Valley to Tuolumne or the bus up to Glacier Point. Bus service from Wawona is geared to people who are staying there and want to spend the day in Yosemite Valley. Free and frequent shuttles transport people between the Wawona Hotel and Mariposa Grove. During the snow season, buses run regularly between Yosemite Valley and Badger Pass Ski Area.

CAR TRAVEL
Roughly 200 miles from San Francisco, 300 miles from Los Angeles, and 500 miles from Las Vegas, Yosemite takes a while to reach—and its many sites and attractions merit much more time than what rangers say is the average visit: four hours. Most people arrive via automobile or tour bus, but public transportation (courtesy of Amtrak and the regional YARTS bus system) also can get you to the valley efficiently.

Of the park's four entrances, Arch Rock is the closest to Yosemite Valley. The road that goes through it, Route 140 from Merced and Mariposa, is a scenic western approach that snakes alongside the boulder-packed Merced River. Route 41, through Wawona, is the way to come from Los Angeles (or Fresno, if you've flown in and rented a car). Route 120, through Crane Flat, is the most direct route from San Francisco. The only way in from the east is Tioga Road, which may be the best route in terms of scenery—though due to snow accumulation it's open for a frustratingly short amount of time each year (typically early June through mid-October).

There are few gas stations within Yosemite (Crane Flat, Tuolumne Meadows, and Wawona; none in the valley), so fuel up before you reach the park. From late fall until early spring, the weather is especially unpredictable, and driving can be treacherous. You should carry chains.

PARK ESSENTIALS
PARK FEES AND PERMITS
The admission fee, valid for seven days, is $30 per vehicle (April through October), $25 during the off-season (November through March), or $10 per individual.

If you plan to camp in the backcountry or climb Half Dome, you must have a wilderness permit. Availability of permits depends upon trailhead quotas. It's best to make a reservation, especially if you will be visiting May through September. You can reserve two days to 24 weeks in advance by phone, mail, or fax (✉ *Box 545, Yosemite, CA 95389* ☎ *209/372–0740* 🖷 *209/372–0739*); you'll pay $5 per person plus $5 per reservation if and when your reservation is confirmed. Requests must include your name, address, daytime phone, the number of people in your party, trip date, alternative dates, starting and ending trailheads, and a brief itinerary. Without a reservation, you may still get a free permit on a first-come, first-served basis at wilderness permit offices at Big Oak Flat, Hetch Hetchy, Tuolumne Meadows, Wawona, the Wilderness Center in Yosemite Village, and Yosemite Valley in summer. From fall to spring, visit the Valley Visitor Center.

PARK HOURS
The park is open 24/7 year-round. All entrances are open at all hours, except for Hetch Hetchy Entrance, which is open roughly dawn to dusk.

PRICES

WHAT IT COSTS			
$	$$	$$$	$$$$
Restaurants	under $12	$12–$20	$21–$30	over $30
Hotels	under $100	$100–$150	$151–$200	over $200

Restaurant prices are the average cost of a main course at dinner or, if dinner is not served, at lunch. Hotel prices are the lowest cost of a standard double room in high season, excluding taxes and service charges.

TOURS

Fodor's Choice ★   **Ansel Adams Photo Walks.** Photography enthusiasts shouldn't miss these 90-minute guided camera walks offered four mornings (Mon., Tues., Thurs., and Sat.) each week by professional photographers. All are free, but participation is limited to 15 people. Meeting points vary, and advance reservations are essential. ☎ *209/372–4413* ⊕ *www. anseladams.com* ✉ *Free.*

FAMILY   **Wee Wild Ones.** Designed for kids under 7, this 45-minute program includes animal-theme games, songs, stories, and crafts. The event is held outdoors before the regular Yosemite Lodge or Curry Village evening programs in summer and fall; it moves to the Ahwahnee's big fireplace in winter and spring. All children must be accompanied by an adult. ☎ *209/372–8243* ⊕ *www.yosemitepark.com* ✉ *Free.*

VISITOR INFORMATION

PARK CONTACT INFORMATION
Yosemite National Park ☎ *209/372–0200* ⊕ *www.nps.gov/yose.*

VISITOR CENTERS
Le Conte Memorial Lodge. This small but striking National Historic Landmark, with its granite walls and steeply pitched shingle roof, is Yosemite's first permanent public information center. Step inside to see the cathedral-like interior, which contains a library and environmental exhibits. To find out about evening programs, check the kiosk out front. ⊠ *Southside Dr., about ½ mile west of Curry Village* ⊕ *vault.sierraclub. org/education/leconte* ⊗ *May–Sept., Wed.–Sun. 10–4.*

Valley Visitor Center. Learn about Yosemite Valley's geology, vegetation, and human inhabitants at this visitor center, which is also staffed with helpful rangers and contains a bookstore with a wide selection of books and maps. Two films, including one by Ken Burns, alternate on the half-hour in the theater behind the visitor center. ⊠ *Yosemite Village* ☎ *209/372–0200* ⊕ *www.nps.gov/yose* ⊗ *Late May–early Sept., daily 9–7; early Sept.–late May, daily 9–5.*

Plants and Wildlife in Yosemite

Dense stands of incense cedar and Douglas fir—as well as ponderosa, Jeffrey, lodgepole, and sugar pines—cover much of the park, but the stellar standout, quite literally, is the *Sequoiadendron giganteum,* the giant sequoia. Sequoias grow only along the west slope of the Sierra Nevada between 4,500 and 7,000 feet in elevation. Starting from a seed the size of a rolled-oat flake, each of these ancient monuments assumes remarkable proportions in adulthood. In late May the valley's dogwood trees bloom with white, starlike flowers. Wildflowers, such as black-eyed Susan, bull thistle, cow parsnip, lupine, and meadow goldenrod, peak in June in the valley and in July at higher elevations.

The most visible animals in the park—aside from the omnipresent western gray squirrels, which fearlessly attempt to steal your food at every campground and picnic site—are the mule deer. Though sightings of bighorn sheep are infrequent in the park itself, you can sometimes see them on the eastern side of the Sierra Crest, just off Route 120 in Lee Vining Canyon. You may also see the American black bear, which often has a brown, cinnamon, or blond coat. The Sierra Nevada is home to thousands of bears, and you should take all necessary precautions to keep yourself—and the bears—safe. Bears that acquire a taste for human food can become very aggressive and destructive, and often must be destroyed by rangers, so store all your food and even scented toiletries in the bear lockers located at many campgrounds and trailheads, or use bear-resistant canisters if you'll be hiking in the backcountry.

Watch for the blue Steller's jay along trails, near public buildings, and in campgrounds, and look for golden eagles soaring over Tioga Road.

15

EXPLORING

HISTORIC SITES

Ahwahneechee Village. This solemn smattering of structures, accessed by a short loop trail behind the Yosemite Valley Visitor Center, is a look at what Native American life might have been like in the 1870s. One interpretive sign points out that the Miwok people referred to the 19th-century newcomers as "Yohemite" and "Yohometuk," which have been translated as meaning "some of them are killers." ✉ *Northside Dr., Yosemite Village* 🖃 *Free* ☉ *Daily sunrise–sunset.*

Pioneer Yosemite History Center. Some of Yosemite's first structures—those not occupied by Native Americans, that is—were relocated here in the 1950s and 1960s. You can spend a pleasurable and informative half-hour walking about them and reading the signs, perhaps springing for a self-guided-tour pamphlet (50¢) to further enhance the history lesson. Weekends and some weekdays in the summer, costumed docents conduct free blacksmithing and "wet-plate" photography demonstrations, and for a small fee you can take a stagecoach ride. ✉ *Rte. 41, Wawona*

Yosemite's Valley Floor

KEY

🏠 Ranger Station
🏕 Campground
🏞 Picnic Area
🍴 Restaurant
🏨 Lodge
🚶 Trailhead
🚻 Restrooms
✺ Scenic Viewpoint
····· Walking/Hiking Trails
– – – John Muir Trail
········ Bicycle Path
▢ Valley Floor

Half Dome
8,836 ft

Liberty Cap

Mist Trail

Nevada Fall

Emerald Pools

Footbridge

Vernal Fall

Mist Trail

John Muir Trail

Clark Point

Panorama Cliff

Grizzly Peak

Sierra Point

John Muir Trail

Illilouette Gorge

Mirror Lake

Washington Column

Road open only to bicycles and Shuttlebuses

bicycle path

Royal Arches

North Pines

Clarks Bridge

Upper Pines

Happy Isles Bridge

Nature Center at Happy Isles

Road open only to bicycles and Shuttlebuses

Royal Arch Cascade

Lower Pines

CURRY VILLAGE

Curry Village Store

Glacier Point
7,214 ft

Panorama Trail

Ahwahnee Hotel

bicycle path

Housekeeping Camp

Maricopa Falls

Four Mile Trail

Glacier Point Road

Pohono Trail

1/2 mi

1/2 km

Medical Clinic

Village Store

Auto Repair

Le Conte Memorial Lodge

Moran Point

Union Point

0

YOSEMITE VILLAGE

Wilderness Office

P.O.

Ansel Adams Gallery

Ahwahneechee Village

Valley Visitor Center

Chapel

Sentinel Rock

Four Mile Trail

Sentinel Fall

Yosemite Fall

Lower Yosemite Fall

Yosemite Lodge at the Falls

Merced River

Road open only to bicycles and Shuttlebuses

bicycle path

Sentinel Fall

☎ *209/375–9531* ✉ *Free* ☉ *Building interiors are open mid-June–Labor Day, Wed. 2–5, Thurs.–Sun. 10–1 and 2–5.*

SCENIC STOPS

El Capitan. Rising 3,593 feet—more than 350 stories—above the valley, El Capitan is the largest exposed-granite monolith in the world. Since 1958, people have been climbing its entire face, including the famous "nose." You can spot adventurers with your binoculars by scanning the smooth and nearly vertical cliff for specks of color. ⊠ *Off Northside Dr., about 4 miles west of the Valley Visitor Center.*

Fodor's Choice ★

Glacier Point. If you lack the time, desire, or stamina to hike more than 3,200 feet up to Glacier Point from the Yosemite Valley floor, you can drive here—or take a bus from the valley—for a bird's-eye view. You are likely to encounter a lot of day-trippers on the short, paved trail that leads from the parking lot to the main overlook. Take a moment to veer off a few yards to the Geology Hut, which succinctly explains and illustrates what the valley looked like 10 million, 3 million, and 20,000 years ago. ⊠ *Glacier Point Rd., 16 miles northeast of Rte. 41* ☎ *209/372–0200* ☉ *Late May–late Oct.*

Fodor's Choice ★

Half Dome. Visitors' eyes are continually drawn to this remarkable granite formation that tops out at more than 4,700 feet above the valley floor. Despite its name, the dome is actually about three-quarters intact. You can hike to the top of Half Dome on an 8.5-mile (one-way) trail whose last 400 feet must be ascended while holding onto a steel cable. Permits are required (and checked on the trail), and available only by lottery. Call ☎ *209/372–0826* or visit ⊕ *www.recreation.gov* well in advance of your trip for details. Back down in the valley, see Half Dome reflected in the Merced River by heading to Sentinel Bridge just before sundown. The brilliant orange light on Half Dome is a stunning sight. ⊕ *www.nps.gov/yose/planyourvisit/halfdome.htm.*

Hetch Hetchy Reservoir. When Congress approved the O'Shaughnessy Dam in 1913, pragmatism triumphed over aestheticism. Some 2.5 million residents of the San Francisco Bay Area continue to get their water from this 117-billion-gallon reservoir. Although spirited efforts are being made to restore the Hetch Hetchy Valley to its former, pristine glory, three-quarters of San Francisco voters in 2012 ultimately opposed a measure to even consider draining the reservoir. Eight miles long, the reservoir is Yosemite's largest body of water, and one that can be seen up close from several trails. ⊠ *Hetch Hetchy Rd., about 15 miles north of the Big Oak Flat entrance station.*

Mariposa Grove of Big Trees. Mariposa Grove is closed until Spring 2017 for a restoration project. Check their website for details on the closure. Of Yosemite's three sequoia groves—the others being Merced and Tuolumne, both near Crane Flat well to the north—Mariposa is by far the largest and easiest to walk around. Grizzly Giant, whose base measures 96 feet around, has been estimated to be one of the largest in the world. Perhaps more astoundingly, it's about 1,800 years old. Up the hill, you'll find more sequoias, a small museum, and fewer people. Summer weekends are usually crowded here.

15

"This is us taking a break before conquering the top of Lembert Dome, while enjoying the beautiful view over Yosemite's high country." —photo by Rebalyn, Fodors.com member

Please note that due to major reconstruction the lower grove, which includes Grizzly Giant, Fallen Monarch, and the California Tunnel Tree, will be closed through November 2016. The upper grove may be open intermittently during this time. Shuttle service from Wawona will not be available in 2016. ■TIP→ Check the Yosemite website before visiting this area in 2016 or 2017. ⊠ *Rte. 41, 2 miles north of the South Entrance station* ⊕ *www.nps.gov/yose/planyourvisit/mariposagrove.htm.*

Tuolumne Meadows. The largest subalpine meadow in the Sierra (at 8,600 feet) is a popular way station for backpack trips along the Pacific Crest and John Muir trails. The setting is not as dramatic as Yosemite Valley, 56 miles away, but the almost perfectly flat basin, about 2½ miles long, is intriguing, and in July it's resplendent with wildflowers. The most popular day hike is up Lembert Dome, atop which you'll have breathtaking views of the basin below. Keep in mind that Tioga Road rarely opens before June and usually closes by mid-October. ⊠ *Tioga Rd. (Rte. 120), about 8 miles west of the Tioga Pass entrance station.*

WATERFALLS

Yosemite's waterfalls are at their most spectacular in May and June. When the snow starts to melt (usually peaking in May), streaming snowmelt spills down to meet the Merced River. By summer's end, particularly in recent drought years, some falls, including the mighty Yosemite Falls, trickle or dry up. Their flow may increase in late fall, and in winter they may be hung dramatically with ice. Even in drier months, the waterfalls can be breathtaking. If you choose to hike any

GOOD READS

■ *The Photographer's Guide to Yosemite*, by Michael Frye, is an insider's guide to the park, with maps for shutterbugs looking to capture perfect images.

■ John Muir penned his observations of the park he long advocated for in *The Yosemite*.

■ *Yosemite and the High Sierra*, edited by Andrea G. Stillman and John Szarkowski, features beautiful reproductions of landmark photographs by Ansel Adams,

accompanied by excerpts from the photographer's journals written when Adams traveled in Yosemite National Park in the early 20th century.

■ An insightful collection of essays accompanies the museum-quality artworks in *Yosemite: Art of an American Icon*, by Amy Scott.

■ Perfect for budding botanists, *Sierra Nevada Wildflowers*, by Karen Wiese, identifies more than 230 kinds of flora growing in the Sierra Nevada region.

15

of the trails to or up the falls, be sure to wear shoes with no-slip soles; the rocks can be extremely slick. Stay on trails at all times.

■TIP→ **Visit the park during a full moon and you can stroll without a flashlight and still make out the ribbons of falling water, as well as silhouettes of the giant granite monoliths.**

Bridalveil Fall. This 620-foot waterfall is often diverted dozens of feet one way or the other by the breeze. It is the first marvelous site you will see up-close when you drive into Yosemite Valley. ⊠ *Yosemite Valley, access from parking area off Wawona Rd.*

Nevada Fall. Climb Mist Trail from Happy Isles for an up-close view of this 594-foot cascading beauty. If you don't want to hike (the trail's final approach is quite taxing), you can see it—albeit distantly—from Glacier Point. ⚠ **Stay safely on the trail, as there have been fatalities in recent years after visitors have fallen and been swept away by the water.** ⊠ *Yosemite Valley, access via Mist Trail from Nature Center at Happy Isles.*

Ribbon Fall. At 1,612 feet, this is the highest single fall in North America. It's also the first waterfall to dry up in summer; the rainwater and melted snow that create the slender fall evaporate quickly at this height. Look just west of El Capitan for the best view of the fall from the base of Bridalveil Fall. ⊠ *Yosemite Valley, west of El Capitan Meadow.*

Vernal Fall. Fern-covered black rocks frame this 317-foot fall, and rainbows play in the spray at its base. You can get a distant view from Glacier Point, or hike to see it close up. You'll get wet, but the view is worth it. ⊠ *Yosemite Valley, access via Mist Trail from Nature Center at Happy Isles.*

Fodor'sChoice ★ **Yosemite Falls.** Actually three falls, they together constitute the highest waterfall in North America and the fifth-highest in the world. The water from the top descends a total of 2,425 feet, and when the falls run hard, you can hear them thunder across the valley. If they dry up—that sometimes happens in late summer—the valley seems naked without the wavering tower of spray. ■ TIP→ If you hike the mile-long loop trail (partially paved) to the base of the Lower Falls in spring, prepare to get wet. You can get a good full-length view of the falls from the lawn of Yosemite Chapel, off Southside Drive. ⊠ *Yosemite Valley, access from Yosemite Lodge or trail parking area.*

EDUCATIONAL OFFERINGS

CLASSES AND SEMINARS

Art Classes. Professional artists conduct workshops in watercolor, etching, drawing, and other mediums. Bring your own materials or purchase the basics at the Art Activity Center, next to the Village Store. Children under 12 must be accompanied by an adult. ⊠ *Art Activity Center, Yosemite Village* ☎ *209/372–1442* ⊕ *www.yosemiteconservancy.org* ✑ *$10* ⊙ *Early Apr.–early Oct., Mon.–Sat. 10–2.*

Yosemite Outdoor Adventures. Naturalists, scientists, and park rangers lead multi-hour to multiday educational outings on topics from woodpeckers to fire management to pastel painting. Most sessions take place spring through fall, but a few focus on winter phenomena. ☎ *209/379– 2317* ⊕ *www.yosemiteconservancy.org* ✑ *From $99.*

RANGER PROGRAMS

Junior Ranger Program. Children ages 7 to 13 can participate in the informal, self-guided Junior Ranger program. A park activity handbook (about $4) is available at the Valley Visitor Center or the Nature Center at Happy Isles. Once kids complete the book, rangers present them with a certificate and a badge. ⊠ *Valley Visitor Center or the Nature Center at Happy Isles* ☎ *209/372–0299.*

Ranger-Led Programs. Rangers lead entertaining walks and give informative talks several times a day from spring to fall. The schedule is more limited in winter, but most days you can find a program somewhere in the park. In the evenings at Yosemite Lodge and Curry Village, lectures, slide shows, and documentary films present unique perspectives on Yosemite. On summer weekends, Camp Curry and Tuolumne Meadows Campground host sing-along campfire programs. Schedules and locations are posted on bulletin boards throughout the park as well as in the indispensable *Yosemite Guide*, which is distributed to visitors as they arrive at the park. ⊕ *www.yosemitepark.com.*

SPORTS AND THE OUTDOORS

BIKING

One enjoyable way to see Yosemite Valley is to ride a bike beneath its lofty granite monoliths. The eastern valley has 12 miles of paved, flat bicycle paths across meadows and through woods, with bike racks at convenient stopping points. For a greater challenge but at no small risk, you can ride on 196 miles of paved park roads—but bicycles are not allowed on hiking trails or in the backcountry. Kids under 18 must wear a helmet.

TOURS AND OUTFITTERS

Yosemite bike rentals. You can arrange for rentals from Yosemite Lodge and Curry Village bike stands. Bikes with child trailers, baby-jogger strollers, and wheelchairs are also available. The cost for bikes is $11.50 per hour, or $32 a day. ⊠ *Yosemite Lodge or Curry Village* ☎ *209/372–1208* ⊕ *www.yosemitepark.com* ⊙ *Apr.–Oct.*

BIRD-WATCHING

More than 250 bird species have been spotted in the park, including the sage sparrow, pygmy owl, blue grouse, and mountain bluebird. Park rangers lead free bird-watching walks in Yosemite Valley a few days each week in summer; check at a visitor center or information station for times and locations. Binoculars are sometimes available for loan.

HIKING

TOURS AND OUTFITTERS

Wilderness Center. This facility provides free wilderness permits, which are required for overnight camping (advance reservations are available for $5 per person plus $5 per reservation and are highly recommended for popular trailheads in summer and on weekends). The staff here also provides maps and advice to hikers heading into the backcountry, and rents bear-resistant canisters, which are required if you don't have your own. ⊠ *Between the Ansel Adams Gallery and the post office, Yosemite Village* ☎ *209/372–0308* ⊙ *May–Oct., daily 8–5; permits at Valley Visitor's Center Nov.–Apr.*

Yosemite Mountaineering School and Guide Service. From April to November, you can learn to climb, hire a guide, or join a two-hour to full-day trek with Yosemite Mountaineering School. They also rent gear and lead backpacking and overnight excursions. Reservations are recommended. In winter, cross-country ski programs are available at Badger Pass. ⊠ *Yosemite Mountain Shop, Curry Village* ☎ *209/372–8344* ⊕ *yosemitemountaineering.com.*

EASY

Yosemite Falls Trail. This is the highest waterfall in North America. The upper fall (1,430 feet), the middle cascades (675 feet), and the lower fall (320 feet) combine for a total of 2,425 feet, and when viewed from the valley appear as a single waterfall. The ¼-mile trail leads from the parking lot to the base of the falls. Upper Yosemite Fall Trail, a strenuous 7.2-mile round-trip climb rising 2,700 feet, takes you above the top of the falls. Lower trail: *Easy.* Upper trail: *Difficult.* ⊠ *Trailhead off Camp 4, north of Northside Dr.*

MODERATE

Mist Trail. Except for Lower Yosemite Falls, more visitors take this trail (or portions of it) than any other in the park. The trek up to and back from Vernal Fall is 3 miles. Add another 4 miles total by continuing up to 594-foot Nevada Fall; the trail becomes quite steep and slippery in its final stages. The elevation gain to Vernal Fall is 1,000 feet, and to Nevada Fall an additional 1,000 feet. The Merced River tumbles down both falls on its way to a tranquil flow through the Valley. *Moderate.* ⊠ *Trailhead at Happy Isles.*

Fodor'sChoice **Panorama Trail.** Few hikes come with the visual punch that this 8½-mile
★ trail provides. It starts from Glacier Point and descends to Yosemite
Valley. The star attraction is Half Dome, visible from many intriguing
angles, but you also see three waterfalls up close and walk through a
manzanita grove. ⚠ **If you take the last bus from the valley floor to
Glacier Point before starting your hike, you might run out of daylight
before you finish.** *Moderate.* ⊠ *Trailhead at Glacier Point.*

DIFFICULT

Fodor'sChoice **John Muir Trail to Half Dome.** Ardent and courageous trekkers continue on
★ from Nevada Fall to the top of Half Dome. Some hikers attempt this
entire 10- to 12-hour, 16¾-mile round-trip trek in one day; if you're
planning to do this, remember that the 4,800-foot elevation gain and the
8,842-foot altitude will cause shortness of breath. Another option is to
hike to a campground in Little Yosemite Valley near the top of Nevada
Fall the first day, then climb to the top of Half Dome and hike out the
next day. Get your wilderness permit (required for a one-day hike to
Half Dome, too) at least a month in advance. Be sure to wear hiking
boots and bring gloves. The last pitch up the back of Half Dome is very
steep—the only way to climb this sheer rock face is to pull yourself up
using the steel cable handrails, which are in place only from late spring
to early fall. Those who brave the ascent will be rewarded with an
unbeatable view of Yosemite Valley below and the high country beyond.
⚠ **Only 300 hikers per day are allowed atop Half Dome, and they all
must have permits, which are distributed by lottery, one in the spring
before the season starts and another two days before the climb. Contact www.recreation.gov for details.** *Difficult.* ⊠ *Trailhead at Happy
Isles* ⊕ *www.nps.gov/yose/planyourvisit/halfdome.htm.*

15

HORSEBACK RIDING

Reservations for guided trail rides must be made in advance at the hotel
tour desks or by phone. Scenic trail rides range from two hours to a
half day; four- and six-day High Sierra saddle trips are also available.

TOURS AND OUTFITTERS

Tuolumne Meadows Stables. Tuolumne Meadows Stables runs two- and
four-hour trips that start at $65, as well as four- to six-day camping
treks on mules that start at $1,000. Reservations are required at least
one day in advance. ⊠ *Off Tioga Rd., 2 miles east of Tuolumne Meadows Visitor Center* ☎ *209/372–8427* ⊕ *www.yosemitepark.com.*

Wawona Stables. Two-hour rides at these stables start at $65, and
half-day rides are $88.50. Reservations are recommended. ⊠ *Rte. 41,
Wawona* ☎ *209/375–6502.*

Yosemite Valley Stables. You can tour the valley on two-hour and four-
hour rides starting from the Yosemite Valley Stables. Reservations are
strongly recommended for the trips, which start at $65. ⊠ *At entrance
to North Pines Campground, 100 yards northeast of Curry Village*
☎ *209/372–8348* ⊕ *www.yosemitepark.com.*

RAFTING

Rafting is permitted only on designated areas of the Middle and South forks of the Merced River. Check with the Valley Visitor Center for closures and other restrictions.

OUTFITTERS

Curry Village raft stand. The per-person rental fee ($31) at Curry Village raft stand covers the four- to six-person raft, two paddles, and life jackets, plus a return shuttle at the end of your trip. ⊠ *South side of Southside Dr., Curry Village* ☎ *209/372–4386* ⊕ *www.yosemitepark. com* ⊠ *$31* ☉ *Late May–July.*

ROCK CLIMBING

Fodor's Choice
★

The granite canyon walls of Yosemite Valley are world-renowned for rock climbing. El Capitan, with its 3,593-foot vertical face, is the most famous, but there are many other options here for all skill levels.

TOURS AND OUTFITTERS

Yosemite Mountaineering School and Guide Service. The one-day basic lesson at Yosemite Mountaineering School and Guide Service includes some bouldering and rappelling, and three or four 60-foot climbs. Climbers must be at least 10 years old and in reasonably good physical condition. Intermediate and advanced classes include instruction in first aid, anchor building, multi-pitch climbing, summer snow climbing, and big-wall climbing. There's a nordic program in the winter. ⊠ *Yosemite Mountain Shop, Curry Village* ☎ *209/372–8344* ⊕ *www. yosemitemountaineering.com* ⊠ *From $148* ☉ *Apr.–Nov.*

WINTER SPORTS

ICE-SKATING

Curry Village Ice Rink. Winter visitors have skated at this outdoor rink for decades, and there's no mystery why: it's a kick to glide across the ice while soaking up views of Half Dome and Glacier Point. ⊠ *South side of Southside Dr., Curry Village* ☎ *209/372–8319* ⊠ *$10.50 per session, $4 skate rental* ☉ *Mid-Nov.–early Mar., hrs vary.*

SKIING AND SNOWSHOEING

Badger Pass Ski Area. California's first ski resort has five lifts and 10 downhill runs, as well as 90 miles of groomed cross-country trails. Free shuttle buses from Yosemite Valley operate between December and the end of March, weather permitting. Lessons, backcountry guiding, and cross-country tours are also available. You can rent downhill, telemark, and cross-country skis, plus snowshoes and snowboards. ⊠ *Badger Pass Rd., off Glacier Point Rd., 18 miles from Yosemite Valley* ☎ *209/372–8430* ⊕ *www.yosemitepark.com/BadgerPass.aspx* ⊠ *Lift tickets from $48.50.*

Yosemite Cross-Country Ski School. The highlight of Yosemite's cross-country skiing center is a 21-mile loop from Badger Pass to Glacier Point. You can rent cross-country skis for $25 per day at the Cross-Country

Ski School, which also rents snowshoes ($24 per day) and telemarking equipment ($29.50). ☎ 209/372–8444 🌐 *www.yosemitepark.com.*

Yosemite Ski School. The gentle slopes of Badger Pass make Yosemite Ski School an ideal spot for children and beginners to learn downhill skiing or snowboarding for as little as $45.50 for a group lesson. ☎ *209/372–8430* 🌐 *www.yosemitepark.com.*

Yosemite Mountaineering School. This branch of the Yosemite Mountaineering School, open at the Badger Pass Ski Area during ski season only, conducts snowshoeing, cross-country skiing, telemarking, and skate-skiing classes starting at $35.50. ✉ *Badger Pass Ski Area* ☎ *209/372–8344* 🌐 *www.yosemitepark.com.*

WHERE TO EAT

In addition to the dining options listed here, you'll find fast-food grills and cafeterias, plus temporary snack bars, hamburger stands, and pizza joints lining park roads in summer. Many dining facilities in the park are open summer only.

$$$$ | EUROPEAN | Fodor's Choice ★

🍴 **Ahwahnee Hotel Dining Room.** Rave reviews about the dining room's appearance are fully justified—it features towering windows, a 34-foot-high ceiling with interlaced sugar-pine beams, and massive chandeliers. Although many continue to applaud the food, others have reported that they sense a dip in the quality both in the service and what is being served. Diners must spend a lot of money here, so perhaps that inflates the expectations and amplifies the disappointments. In any event, the lavish $45 Sunday brunch is a popular way to experience the grand room. Reservations are always advised, and the attire is "resort casual." [$] *Average main: $38* ✉ *Ahwahnee Hotel, Ahwahnee Rd., about ¾ mile east of Yosemite Valley Visitor Center, Yosemite Village* ☎ *209/372–1489* 🌐 *www.yosemitepark.com* ✍ *Reservations essential.*

$$$ | AMERICAN | Fodor's Choice ★

🍴 **Mountain Room.** Though good, the food becomes secondary when you see Yosemite Falls through this dining room's wall of windows—almost every table has a view. The chef makes a point of using locally sourced, organic ingredients whenever possible, so you can be assured of fresh vegetables to accompany the hearty main courses, such as steaks and seafood, as well as vegetarian and even vegan options. The Mountain Room Lounge, a few steps away in the Yosemite Lodge complex, has about 10 beers on tap. Weather permitting, take your drink out onto the small back patio. [$] *Average main: $24* ✉ *Yosemite Lodge, Northside Dr. about ¾ mile west of the visitor center, Yosemite Village* ☎ *209/372–1403* 🌐 *www.yosemitepark.com* ⏲ *No lunch.*

$ | FAST FOOD

🍴 **Tuolumne Meadows Grill.** Serving continuously throughout the day until 5 or 6 pm, this fast-food eatery cooks up basic breakfast, lunch, and snacks. It's possible that ice cream tastes better at this altitude. Stop in for a quick meal before exploring the meadows. [$] *Average main: $8* ✉ *Tioga Rd. (Rte. 120), 1½ mile east of Tuolumne Meadows Visitor Center* ☎ *209/372–8426* ⏲ *Closed Oct.–Memorial Day. No dinner.*

$$ | AMERICAN

🍴 **Tuolumne Meadows Lodge.** At the back of a small building that contains the lodge's front desk and small gift shop, this restaurant serves a menu of hearty American fare at breakfast and dinner. The decor is woodsy, with dark-wood walls, red-and-white-checkered tablecloths, and a handful of communal tables, which give it the feeling of an old-fashioned summer camp. The menu is small, often featuring a few meat and seafood dishes and one pasta or other special, including a vegetarian choice. If you have any dietary restrictions, let the front desk know in advance and the cooks will not let you down. Order box lunches from here for before hikes. $ *Average main: $20 ⊠ Tioga Rd. (Rte. 120)* ☎ *209/372–8413 ⊕ www.yosemitepark.com ⚏ Reservations essential* ☉ *Closed late Sept.–mid-June. No lunch.*

$$$

AMERICAN

✕ **Wawona Hotel Dining Room.** Watch deer graze on the meadow while you dine in the romantic, candlelit dining room of the whitewashed Wawona Hotel, which dates from the late 1800s. The American-style cuisine favors fresh ingredients and flavors; trout and flatiron steaks are menu staples. There's also a brunch on some Sunday holidays, like Mother's Day and Easter, and a barbecue on the lawn Saturday evening in summer. $ *Average main: $28 ⊠ 8308 Wawona Rd., Wawona* ☎ *209/375–1425 ☉ Closed most of Dec., Jan., Feb., and Mar.*

PICNIC AREAS

Considering how large the park is and how many visitors come here—some 4 million people every year, most of them just for the day—it is somewhat surprising that Yosemite has so few formal picnic areas, though in many places you can find a smooth rock to sit on and enjoy breathtaking views along with your lunch. The convenience stores all sell picnic supplies, and prepackaged sandwiches and salads are widely available. Those options can come in especially handy during the middle of the day, when you might not want to spend precious daylight hours in such a spectacular setting sitting in a restaurant for a formal meal.

WHERE TO STAY

Hotel reviews have been shortened. For full information, visit Fodors. com.

$$$$

HOTEL

Fodor's Choice

★

▦ **Ahwahnee Hotel.** A National Historic Landmark, the hotel is constructed of sugar-pine logs and features Native American design motifs; public spaces are enlivened with art deco flourishes, oriental rugs, and elaborate iron- and woodwork. **Pros:** best lodge in Yosemite; helpful concierge. **Cons:** expensive rates; some reports that service has slipped in recent years. $ *Rooms from: $471 ⊠ Ahwahnee Rd., about ¾ miles east of Yosemite Valley Visitor Center, Yosemite Village ☎ 801/559–4884 ⊕ www.yosemitepark.com ⇨ 95 lodge rooms, 6 suites, 24 cottage rooms ♍ No meals.*

$$

HOTEL

▦ **Curry Village.** Opened in 1899 as a place for budget-conscious travelers, Curry Village has plain accommodations: standard motel rooms, simple cabins with either private or shared baths, and tent cabins with shared baths. **Pros:** close to many activities; family-friendly atmosphere. **Cons:** not that economical after a recent price surge; can be crowded; sometimes a bit noisy. $ *Rooms from: $124 ⊠ South side of Southside Dr. ☎ 801/559–4884 ⊕ www.yosemitepark.com ⇨ 18 rooms, 485 cabins ♍ No meals.*

Best Campgrounds in Yosemite

If you are going to concentrate solely on valley sites and activities, you should endeavor to stay in one of the "Pines" campgrounds, which are clustered near Curry Village and within an easy stroll from that busy complex's many facilities. For a more primitive and quiet experience, and to be near many backcountry hikes, try one of the Tioga Road campgrounds.

National Park Service Reservations Office. Reservations are required at many of Yosemite's campgrounds, especially in summer. You can book a site up to five months in advance, starting on the 15th of the month. Unless otherwise noted, book your site through the central National Park Service Reservations Office. If you don't have reservations when you arrive, many sites, especially those outside Yosemite Valley, are available on a first-come, first-served basis. ☎ 877/444–6777 ⊕ www.recreation. gov ⏰ Daily 10–10.

Bridalveil Creek. This campground sits among lodgepole pines at 7,200 feet, above the valley on Glacier Point Road. From here, you can easily drive to Glacier Point's magnificent valley views. ⊠ From Rte. 41 in Wawona, go north to Glacier Point Rd. and turn right; entrance to campground is 25 miles ahead on right side.

Camp 4. Formerly known as Sunny-side Walk-In, and extremely popular with rock climbers who don't mind that a total of six are assigned to each campsite, no matter how many are in your group, this is the only valley campground available on a first-come, first-served basis. ⊠ Base of Yosemite Falls Trail, just west of Yosemite Lodge on Northside Dr., Yosemite Village.

Housekeeping Camp. Composed of three concrete walls and covered with two layers of canvas, each unit has an open-ended fourth side that can be closed off with a heavy white canvas curtain. You can rent "bedpacks," consisting of blankets, sheets, and other comforts. ⊠ Southside Dr., ½ mile west of Curry Village.

Porcupine Flat. Sixteen miles west of Tuolumne Meadows, this campground sits at 8,100 feet. If you want to be in the high country, this is a good bet. ⊠ Rte. 120, 16 miles west of Tuolumne Meadows.

Tuolumne Meadows. In a wooded area at 8,600 feet, just south of its namesake meadow, this is one of the most spectacular and sought-after campgrounds in Yosemite. ⊠ Rte. 120, 46 miles east of Big Oak Flat entrance station.

Upper Pines. This is one of the valley's largest campgrounds and the closest one to the trailheads. Expect large crowds in the summer—and little privacy. ⊠ At east end of valley, near Curry Village.

Wawona. Near the Mariposa Grove, just downstream from a popular fishing spot, this year-round campground has larger, less densely packed sites than campgrounds in the valley. ⊠ Rte. 41, 1 mile north of Wawona.

White Wolf. Set in the beautiful high country at 8,000 feet, this is a prime spot for hikers from early July to mid-September. ⊠ Tioga Rd., 15 miles east of Big Oak Flat entrance.

15

$$$ ▥ **Wawona Hotel.** This 1879
HOTEL National Historic Landmark at
Yosemite's southern end is an
old-fashioned New England–style
estate, with whitewashed build-
ings, wraparound verandas, and
pleasant, no-frills rooms decorated
with period pieces. **Pros:** lovely
building; peaceful atmosphere.
Cons: few modern amenities, such
as phones and TVs; an hour's drive
from Yosemite Valley. ⓢ *Rooms
from: $159* ✉ *8308 Wawona Rd.,
Wawona* ☎ *801/559–4884* ⊕ *www.
yosemitepark.com* ⇱ *104 rooms,
50 with bath* ⊘ *Closed Dec.–Mar., except mid-Dec.–Jan. 2* ⍟⊘ *Breakfast.*

> **LODGING TIP**
>
> Reserve your room or cabin in
> Yosemite as far in advance as
> possible. You can make a reserva-
> tion up to a year before your
> arrival (within minutes after the
> reservation office makes a date
> available, the Ahwahnee, Yosemite
> Lodge, and Wawona Hotel often
> sell out their weekends, holiday
> periods, and all days between May
> and September).

$$ ▥ **White Wolf Lodge.** Set in a subalpine meadow, the rustic accommoda-
HOTEL tions at White Wolf Lodge make it an excellent base camp for hiking
the backcountry. **Pros:** quiet location; near some of Yosemite's most
beautiful, less crowded hikes; good restaurant. **Cons:** far from the valley. ⓢ *Rooms from: $124* ✉ *Off Tioga Rd. (Rte. 120), 25 miles west of
Tuolumne Meadows and 15 miles east of Crane Flat* ☎ *801/559–4884*
⇱ *24 tent cabins, 4 cabins* ⊘ *Closed mid-Sept.–mid-June* ⍟⊘ *No meals.*

$$$$ ▥ **Yosemite Lodge at the Falls.** This 1915 lodge near Yosemite Falls more
HOTEL closely resembles a 1960s resort with its numerous two-story structures
tucked beneath the trees, and it doesn't help that the brown buildings
are surrounded by large parking lots. **Pros:** centrally located; dependably
clean rooms; lots of tours leave from out front. **Cons:** can feel impersonal; appearance is a little dated; prices recently skyrocketed. ⓢ *Rooms
from: $250* ✉ *9006 Yosemite Lodge Dr., Yosemite Village* ☎ *801/559–
4884* ⊕ *www.yosemitepark.com/yosemite-lodge.aspx* ⇱ *245 rooms*
⍟⊘ *No meals.*

SEQUOIA AND KINGS CANYON NATIONAL PARKS

WELCOME TO SEQUOIA AND KINGS CANYON NATIONAL PARKS

TOP REASONS TO GO

★ **Gentle giants:** You'll feel small—in a good way—walking among some of the world's largest living things in Sequoia's Giant Forest and Kings Canyon's Grant Grove.

★ **Because it's there:** You can't even glimpse it from the main part of Sequoia, but the sight of majestic Mt. Whitney is worth the trek to the eastern face of the High Sierra.

★ **Underground exploration:** Far older even than the giant sequoias, the gleaming limestone formations in Crystal Cave will draw you along dark, marble passages.

★ **A grander-than-Grand Canyon:** Drive the twisting Kings Canyon Scenic Byway down into the jagged, granite Kings River Canyon, deeper in parts than the Grand Canyon.

★ **Regal solitude:** To spend a day or two hiking in a subalpine world of your own, pick one of the 11 trailheads at Mineral King.

1 **Giant Forest–Lodgepole Village.** The most heavily visited area of Sequoia lies at the base of the "thumb" portion of Kings Canyon National Park and contains major sights such as Giant Forest, General Sherman Tree, Crystal Cave, and Moro Rock.

2 **Grant Grove Village–Redwood Canyon.** The "thumb" of Kings Canyon National Park is its busiest section, where Grant Grove, General Grant Tree, Panoramic Point, and Big Stump are the main attractions.

3 **Cedar Grove.** The drive through the high-country portion of Kings Canyon National Park to Cedar Grove Village, on the canyon floor, reveals magnificent granite formations of varied hues. Rock meets river in breathtaking fashion a few miles beyond Cedar Grove in Zumwalt Meadow.

4 **Mineral King.** In the southeast section of Sequoia, the highest road-accessible part of the park is a good place to hike, camp, and soak up the unspoiled grandeur of the Sierra Nevada.

5 **Mount Whitney.** The highest peak in the Lower 48 stands on the eastern edge of Sequoia; to get there from Giant Forest you must either backpack eight days through the mountains or drive nearly 400 miles around the park to its other side.

General Grant Tree
Visitor Center
180
Grant Grove Village
180
2
Pinehurst
Montecito-Sequoia Lodge
245
Badger

Three Rivers

General Highway

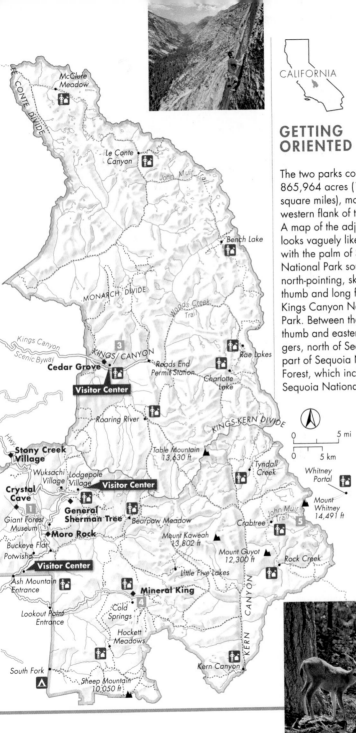

CALIFORNIA

16

GETTING ORIENTED

The two parks comprise 865,964 acres (1,353 square miles), mostly on the western flank of the Sierra. A map of the adjacent parks looks vaguely like a mitten, with the palm of Sequoia National Park south of the north-pointing, skinny thumb and long fingers of Kings Canyon National Park. Between the western thumb and eastern fingers, north of Sequoia, lies part of Sequoia National Forest, which includes Giant Sequoia National Monument.

0 — 5 mi
0 — 5 km

McClure Meadow

LE CONTE DIVIDE

Le Conte Canyon

John Muir Trail

Bench Lake

MONARCH DIVIDE

Woods Creek Trail

Kings Canyon Scenic Byway

KINGS / CANYON   3

Cedar Grove

Visitor Center

Roads End Permit Station

Rae Lakes

Charlotte Lake

Roaring River

KINGS-KERN DIVIDE

Stony Creek Village

Hwy

Table Mountain 13,630 ft

Tyndall Creek

Whitney Portal

Wuksachi Village   Lodgepole Village

Visitor Center

Crystal Cave   1

General Sherman Tree

Giant Forest Museum

Bearpaw Meadow

Mount Kaweah 13,802 ft

Crabtree

John Muir Trail   5

Mount Whitney 14,491 ft

Moro Rock

Buckeye Flat

Potwisha

Visitor Center

Ash Mountain Entrance

Mineral King   4

Little Five Lakes

Mount Guyot 12,300 ft

Rock Creek

Lookout Point Entrance

Cold Springs

KERN CANYON

Hockett Meadows

South Fork

Sheep Mountain 10,050 ft

Kern Canyon

Updated by
Steve Pastorino

Although *Sequoiadendron giganteum* is the formal name for the redwoods that grow here, everyone outside the classroom calls them sequoias, big trees, or Sierra redwoods. Their monstrously thick trunks and branches, remarkably shallow root systems, and neck-craning heights are almost impossible to believe, as is the fact they can live for more than 2,500 years. Many of these towering marvels are in the Giant Forest stretch of Generals Highway, which connects Sequoia and Kings Canyon national parks.

Next to or a few miles off the 43-mile Generals Highway are most of Sequoia National Park's main attractions and Grant Grove Village, the orientation hub for Kings Canyon National Park. The two parks share a boundary that runs from the Central Valley in the west, where the Sierra Nevada foothills begin, to the range's dramatic eastern ridges. Kings Canyon has two portions: the smaller is shaped like a bent finger and encompasses Grant Grove Village and Redwood Mountain Grove (the two parks' largest concentration of sequoias), and the larger is home to stunning Kings River Canyon, whose vast, unspoiled peaks and valleys are a backpacker's dream. Sequoia is in one piece and includes Mt. Whitney, the highest point in the Lower 48 states (although it is impossible to see from the western part of the park and is a chore to ascend from either side).

SEQUOIA AND KINGS CANYON PLANNER

WHEN TO GO

The best times to visit are late spring and early fall, when temperatures are moderate and crowds thin. Summertime can draw hordes of tourists to see the giant sequoias, and the few, narrow roads mean congestion at peak holiday times. If you must visit in summer, go during the week. By contrast, in wintertime you may feel as though you have the parks all to yourself. But because of heavy snows, sections of the main park roads can be closed without warning, and low-hanging clouds can move in and obscure mountains and valleys for days. From mid-November to late April, check road and weather conditions before venturing out.

GETTING HERE AND AROUND

CAR TRAVEL

Sequoia is 36 miles east of Visalia on Route 198; Grant Grove Village in Kings Canyon is 56 miles east of Fresno on Route 180. There is no automobile entrance on the eastern side of the Sierra. Routes 180 and 198 are connected by Generals Highway, a paved two-lane road that sometimes sees delays at peak times due to ongoing improvements. The road is extremely narrow and steep from Route 198 to Giant Forest, so keep an eye on your engine temperature gauge, as the incline and congestion can cause vehicles to overheat; to avoid overheated brakes, use low gears on downgrades.

If you are traveling in an RV or with a trailer, study the restrictions on these vehicles. Do not travel beyond Potwisha Campground on Route 198 with an RV longer than 22 feet; take straighter, easier Route 180 instead. Maximum vehicle length on Generals Highway is 40 feet, or 50 feet combined length for vehicles with trailers.

From May through September, the Sequoia Shuttle offers free transportation within the park along four routes in and around the Giant Forest and Lodgepole areas. Buses run every 15 minutes.

Generals Highway between Lodgepole and Grant Grove is sometimes closed by snow. The Mineral King Road from Route 198 into southern Sequoia National Park is closed 2 miles below Atwell Mill either on November 1 or after the first heavy snow. The Buckeye Flat–Middle Fork Trailhead Road is closed from mid-October to mid-April, when the Buckeye Flat Campground closes. The lower Crystal Cave Road is closed when the cave closes in November. Its upper 2 miles, as well as the Panoramic Point and Moro Rock–Crescent Meadow roads, close with the first heavy snow. Because of the danger of rockfall, the portion of Kings Canyon Scenic Byway east of Grant Grove closes in winter. For current road and weather conditions, call ☎ *559/565–3341.*

■ TIP➔ **Snowstorms are common from late October through April. Unless you have a four-wheel-drive vehicle with snow tires, you should carry chains and know how to install them.**

PARK ESSENTIALS

PARK FEES AND PERMITS

The admission fee is $20 per vehicle and $10 for those who enter by bus, on foot, bicycle, motorcycle, or horse; it is valid for seven days in both parks. U.S. residents over the age of 62 pay $10 for a lifetime pass, and permanently disabled U.S. residents are admitted free.

If you plan to camp in the backcountry, you need a permit, which costs $15 for hikers or $30 for stock users (e.g., horseback riders). One permit covers the group. Availability of permits depends upon trailhead quotas. Reservations are accepted by mail or fax for a $15 processing fee, beginning March 1, and must be made at least 14 days in advance

16

(☎ 559/565–3766). Without a reservation, you may still get a permit on a first-come, first-served basis starting at 1 pm the day before you plan to hike. For more information on backcountry camping or travel with pack animals (horses, mules, burros, or llamas), contact the Wilderness Permit Office (☎ 530/565–3761).

PARK HOURS

The parks are open 24/7 year-round.

PRICES

WHAT IT COSTS			
$	**$$**	**$$$**	**$$$$**
Restaurants	under $12	$12–$20	$21–$30	over $30
Hotels	under $100	$100–$150	$151–$200	over $200

Restaurant prices are the average cost of a main course at dinner or, if dinner is not served, at lunch. Hotel prices are the lowest cost of a standard double room in high season, excluding taxes and service charges.

VISITOR INFORMATION

NATIONAL PARK SERVICE

Sequoia and Kings Canyon National Parks ⊠ 47050 Generals Hwy.(Rte. 198), Three Rivers ☎ 559/565–3341 ⊕ www.nps.gov/seki.

SEQUOIA VISITOR CENTERS

Foothills Visitor Center. Exhibits here focus on the foothills and resource issues facing the parks. You can pick up books, maps, and a list of ranger-led walks, and get wilderness permits. ⊠ 47050 Generals Hwy., Rte. 198, 1 mile north of Ash Mountain entrance, Sequoia National Park ☎ 559/565–4212 ☉ Daily 8–4:30.

Lodgepole Visitor Center. Along with exhibits on the area's history, geology, and wildlife, the center screens an outstanding 22-minute film about bears. You can buy books, maps, and tickets to cave tours and the Wolverton barbecue here. ⊠ Generals Hwy. (Rte. 198), 21 miles north of Ash Mountain entrance, Sequoia National Park ☎ 559/565–4436 ☉ Late May–early Sept., daily 7–7; Apr.–late May and early Sept.–Dec., days and hrs vary ⊂ Shuttle: Giant Forest or Wuksachi-Lodgepole-Dorst.

KINGS CANYON VISITOR CENTERS

Cedar Grove Visitor Center. Off the main road and behind the Sentinel Campground, this small ranger station has books and maps, plus information about hikes and other activities. ⊠ Kings Canyon Scenic Byway, 30 miles east of Rte. 180/198 junction, Kings Canyon National Park ☎ 559/565–3793 ☉ Late May–early Sept., Tues.–Sun. 9–5.

Kings Canyon Park Visitor Center. The center's 15-minute film and various exhibits provide an overview of the park's canyon, sequoias, and human history. Books, maps, and weather advice are dispensed here, as are (if available) free wilderness permits. ⊠ Grant Grove Village, Generals Hwy. (Rte. 198), 3 miles northeast of Rte. 180, Big Stump entrance, Kings Canyon National Park ☎ 559/565–4307 ☉ Daily 9–4:30; may vary seasonally.

SEQUOIA NATIONAL PARK

EXPLORING

SCENIC DRIVES

Fodor's Choice ★ **Generals Highway.** One of California's most scenic drives, this 43-mile road is the main asphalt artery between Sequoia and Kings Canyon national parks. Some portions are also signed as Route 180, others as Route 198. Named after the landmark Grant and Sherman trees that leave so many visitors awestruck, Generals Highway runs from Sequoia's Foothills Visitor Center north to Kings Canyon's Grant Grove Village. Along the way, it passes the turnoff to Crystal Cave, the Giant Forest Museum, Lodgepole Village, and other popular attractions. The lower portion, from Hospital Rock to the Giant Forest, is especially steep and winding. If your vehicle is 22 feet or longer, avoid that stretch by entering the parks via Route 180 (from Fresno) rather than Route 198 (from Visalia or Three Rivers). ■TIP→ **Take your time on this road—there's a lot to see, and wildlife can scamper across at any time.**

SCENIC STOPS

Sequoia National Park is all about the trees, and to understand the scale of these giants you must walk among them. But there is much more to the park than the trees. Try to access one of the vista points that provide a panoramic view over the forested mountains. Generals Highway (on Routes 198 and 180) will be your route to most of the park's sights. A few short spur roads lead from the highway to some sights, and Mineral King Road branches off Route 198 to enter the park at Lookout Point, winding east from there to the park's southernmost section.

Crescent Meadow. A sea of ferns signals your arrival at what John Muir called the "gem of the Sierra." Walk around for an hour or two and you might decide that the Scotland-born naturalist was exaggerating a wee bit, but the verdant meadow is quite pleasant and you just might see a bear. ■TIP→ **Wildflowers bloom here throughout the summer.** ⊠ *End of Moro Rock–Crescent Meadow Rd., 2.6 miles east off Generals Hwy.* ↪ *Shuttle: Moro Rock–Crescent Meadow.*

Fodor's Choice ★ **Crystal Cave.** One of more than 200 caves in Sequoia and Kings Canyon, Crystal Cave is composed largely of marble, the result of limestone being hardened under heat and pressure. It contains several eye-popping formations. There used to be more, but some were damaged or obliterated by early-20th-century dynamite blasting. You can only see the cave on a tour. The Daily Tour ($15), a great overview, takes about 50 minutes. To immerse yourself in the cave experience—at times you'll be crawling on your belly—book the exhilarating Wild Cave Tour ($130). ■TIP→ **Purchase Daily Tour tickets at either the Foothills or Lodgepole visitor center; they're not sold at the cave itself.** ⊠ *Crystal Cave Rd., off Generals Hwy.* ☎ *559/565–3759* ⊕ *www.sequoiahistory.org* 🎟 *$15* 🕙 *Mid-May–Nov., daily 10–4.*

Fodor's Choice ★ **General Sherman Tree.** The 274.9-foot-tall General Sherman is one of the world's tallest and oldest sequoias, and it ranks No. 1 in volume, adding the equivalent of a 60-foot-tall tree every year to its approximately

16

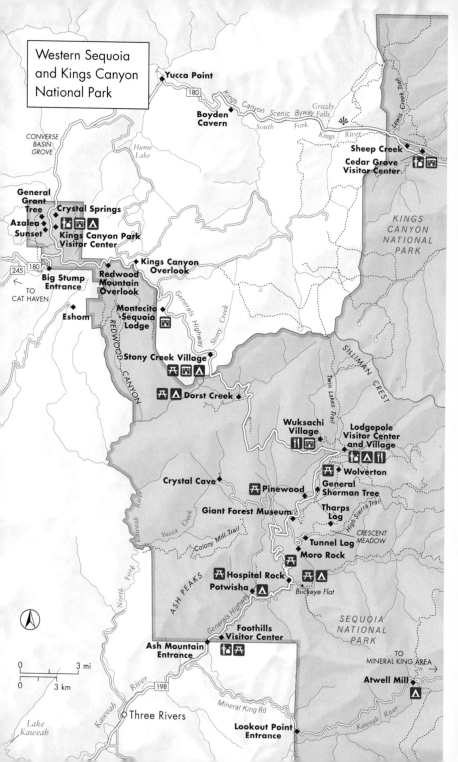

Western Sequoia
and Kings Canyon
National Park

Yucca Point

Boyden Cavern

Kings Canyon Scenic Byway

Grizzly Falls

Kings River

South Fork

Sheep Creek
Cedar Grove Visitor Center

CONVERSE BASIN GROVE

Hume Lake

KINGS CANYON NATIONAL PARK

General Grant Tree

Azalea Sunset

Crystal Springs

Kings Canyon Park Visitor Center

Kings Canyon Overlook

245

180

Big Stump Entrance

TO CAT HAVEN

Eshom

Redwood Mountain Overlook

Montecito Sequoia Lodge

Generals Highway

Stony Creek

REDWOOD CANYON

Stony Creek Village

Dorst Creek

SILLIMAN CREST

Twin Lakes Trail

Wuksachi Village

Lodgepole Visitor Center and Village

Wolverton

Crystal Cave

Pinewood

General Sherman Tree

Giant Forest Museum

Kaweah River

Yucca Creek

Colony Mill Trail

North Fork

ASH PEAKS

Tharps Log

High Sierra Trail

CRESCENT MEADOW

Tunnel Log

Moro Rock

Hospital Rock

Potwisha

Buckeye Flat

SEQUOIA NATIONAL PARK

TO MINERAL KING AREA

Foothills Visitor Center

Ash Mountain Entrance

Generals Highway

198

Three Rivers

Mineral King Rd

Atwell Mill

Lake Kaweah

Kaweah River

Kaweah River

Lookout Point Entrance

0   3 mi
0   3 km

52,500 cubic feet of mass. The tree doesn't grow taller, though—it's dead at the top. A short, wheelchair-accessible trail leads to the tree from Generals Highway, but the main trail (½ mile) winds down from a parking lot off Wolverton Road. ■ TIP→ **The walk back up the main trail is steep, but benches along the way provide rest for the short of breath.** ⊠ *Main trail Wolverton Rd. off Generals Hwy. (Rte. 198)* ⌖ *Shuttle: Giant Forest or Wolverton–Sherman Tree.*

Mineral King Area. A subalpine valley of fir, pine, and sequoia trees, Mineral King sits at 7,500 feet at the end of a steep, winding road. This is the highest point to which you can drive in the park. It is open only from Memorial Day through late October. ⊠ *Mineral King Rd., 25 miles east of Generals Hwy. (Rte. 198)* ☽ *June–late Oct., daily.*

Fodor'sChoice **Moro Rock.** Sequoia National Park's best non-tree attraction offers pan-
★ oramic views to those fit and determined enough to mount its 350 or so steps. In a case where the journey rivals the destination, Moro's stone stairway is so impressive that it's on the National Register of Historic Places. The rock's 6,725-foot summit overlooks the Middle Fork Canyon, sculpted by the Kaweah River and approaching the depth of Arizona's Grand Canyon, although smoggy, hazy air often compromises the view. ⊠ *Moro Rock–Crescent Meadow Rd., 2 miles east off Generals Hwy. (Rte. 198) to parking area* ⌖ *Shuttle: Moro Rock–Crescent Meadow.*

Tunnel Log. This 275-foot tree fell in 1937, and soon a 17-foot-wide, 8-foot-high hole was cut through it for vehicular passage (not to mention the irresistible photograph) that continues today. Large vehicles take the nearby bypass. ⊠ *Moro Rock–Crescent Meadow Rd., 2 miles east of Generals Hwy. (Rte. 198)* ⌖ *Shuttle: Moro Rock–Crescent Meadow.*

EDUCATIONAL OFFERINGS

PROGRAMS AND SEMINARS

Evening Programs. The Sequoia Natural History Association presents film and slide shows, hikes, and evening lectures during the summer and winter. From May through October the popular Wonders of the Night Sky programs celebrate the often stunning views of the heavens experienced at both parks. ☎ *559/565–3341* ⊕ *www.sequoiahistory.org/snhacalendar.asp* ☽ *Locations and times vary.*

Free Nature Programs. Almost any summer day, half-hour to 1½-hour ranger talks and walks explore subjects such as the life of the sequoia, the geology of the park, and the habits of bears. Giant Forest, Lodgepole Visitor Center, Wuksachi Village, and Dorst Creek Campground are frequent starting points. Look for less frequent tours in the winter from Grant Grove. Check bulletin boards throughout the park for the week's offerings.

Seminars. Expert naturalists lead seminars on a range of topics, including birds, wildflowers, geology, botany, photography, park history, backpacking, and pathfinding. Reservations are recommended. Information about times and prices is available at the visitor centers or through the Sequoia Natural History Association. ☎ *559/565–3759* ⊕ *www.sequoiahistory.org.*

16

TOURS

Fodor's Choice ★ **Sequoia Field Institute.** The Sequoia Natural History Association's highly regarded educational division conducts single-day and multi-day "EdVenture" tours that include backpacking hikes, natural-history walks, and kayaking excursions. ✉ *47050 Generals Hwy., Unit 10, Three Rivers* ☎ *559/565–4251* ⊕ *www.sequoiahistory.org.*

Sequoia Sightseeing Tours. This operator's friendly, knowledgeable guides conduct interpretive sightseeing tours in a 10-passenger van. Reservations are essential. The company also offers private tours of Kings Canyon. ✉ *Three Rivers* ☎ *559/561–4189* ⊕ *www.sequoiatours.com* 🖃 *From $69 tour of Sequoia; from $129 tour of Kings Canyon.*

SPORTS AND THE OUTDOORS

The best way to see Sequoia is to take a hike. Unless you do so, you'll miss out on the up-close grandeur of mist wafting between deeply scored, red-orange tree trunks bigger than you've ever seen. If it's winter, put on some snowshoes or cross-country skis and plunge into the snow-swaddled woodland. There are not too many other outdoor options: no off-road driving is allowed in the parks, and no special provisions have been made for bicycles. Boating, rafting, and snowmobiling are also prohibited.

BIRD-WATCHING

More than 200 species of birds inhabit Sequoia and Kings Canyon national parks. Not seen in most parts of the United States, the white-headed woodpecker and the pileated woodpecker are common in most mid-elevation areas here. There are also many hawks and owls, including the renowned spotted owl. Species are diverse in both parks due to the changes in elevation, and range from warblers, kingbirds, thrushes, and sparrows in the foothills to goshawks, blue grouse, red-breasted nuthatches, and brown creepers at the highest elevations. Ranger-led bird-watching tours are held on a sporadic basis. Call the park's main information number to find out more about these tours. The Sequoia Natural History Association (☎ *559/565–3759* ⊕ *www.sequoiahistory. org*) also has information about bird-watching in the southern Sierra.

CROSS-COUNTRY SKIING

Wuksachi Lodge Rentals. Rent cross-country skis and snowshoes here. Depending on snowfall amounts, instruction may also be available. Reservations are recommended. Marked trails cut through Giant Forest, about 5 miles south of the lodge. ✉ *Off Generals Hwy. (Rte. 198), 2 miles north of Lodgepole* ☎ *559/565–4070* ☉ *Nov.–May (unless no snow), daily 9–4* ⌇ *Shuttle: Wuksachi-Lodgepole-Dorst.*

HIKING

The best way to see the park is to hike it. Carry a hiking map and plenty of water. Visitor center gift shops sell maps and trail books and pamphlets. Check with rangers for current trail conditions, and be aware of rapidly changing weather. As a rule of thumb, plan on covering about a mile per hour.

EASY

Fodor's Choice
★

Congress Trail. This 2-mile trail, arguably the best hike in the parks in terms of natural beauty, is a paved loop that begins near General Sherman Tree. You'll get close-up views of more big trees here than on any other Sequoia hike. Watch for the clusters known as the House and Senate. The President Tree, also on the trail, supplanted the General Grant Tree in 2012 as the world's second largest in volume (behind the General Sherman). ■TIP→ An offshoot of the Congress Trail leads to Crescent Meadow, where in summer you can catch a free shuttle back to the Sherman parking lot. *Easy. ⊠ Trail begins off Generals Hwy. (Rte. 198), 2 miles north of Giant Forest ☞ Shuttle: Giant Forest.*

Crescent Meadow Trails. A 1-mile trail loops around lush Crescent Meadow to Tharp's Log, a cabin built from a fire-hollowed sequoia. From there you can embark on a 60-mile trek to Mt. Whitney, if you're prepared and have the time. ■TIP→ Brilliant wildflowers bloom here in midsummer. *Easy. ⊠ Trail begins at the end of Moro Rock–Crescent Meadow Rd., 2.6 miles east off Generals Hwy. (Rte. 198) ☞ Shuttle: Moro Rock–Crescent Meadow.*

MODERATE

Tokopah Falls Trail. This trail with a 500-foot elevation gain follows the Marble Fork of the Kaweah River for 1.75 miles one way and dead-ends below the impressive granite cliffs and cascading waterfall of Tokopah Canyon. The trail passes through a mixed-conifer forest. It takes 2½ to 4 hours to make the round-trip journey. *Moderate. ⊠ Trail begins off Generals Hwy. (Rte. 198), ¼ mile north of Lodgepole Campground ☞ Shuttle: Lodgepole-Wuksachi-Dorst.*

DIFFICULT

Mineral King Trails. Many trails to the high country begin at Mineral King. Two popular day hikes are Eagle Lake (6.8 miles round-trip) and Timber Gap (4.4 miles round-trip). ■TIP→ At the Mineral King Ranger Station (559/565–3768) you can pick up maps and check about conditions from late May to late September. *Difficult. ⊠ Trailheads at end of Mineral King Rd., 25 miles east of Generals Hwy. (Rte. 198).*

HORSEBACK RIDING

TOURS AND OUTFITTERS

Grant Grove Stables. Grant Grove Stables (⇨ *Horseback Riding in Kings Canyon National Park*) isn't too far from parts of Sequoia National Park, and is perfect for short rides from June to September. Reservations are recommended. ⊕ *www.visitsequoia.com/grant-grove-stables.aspx* ⊠ *From $40 per person.*

Horse Corral Pack Station. One- and two-hour trips through Sequoia are available for beginning and advanced riders. ⊠ *Big Meadow Rd., 12 miles east of Generals Hwy. (Rte. 198) between Sequoia and Kings Canyon national parks* ☎ *559/565–3404* ⊕ *www.highsierrapackers.org* ⊠ *From $45* ⊙ *May–mid.-Sept.*

KINGS CANYON NATIONAL PARK

EXPLORING

SCENIC DRIVES

Fodor's Choice ★ **Kings Canyon Scenic Byway.** The 30-mile stretch of Route 180 between Grant Grove Village and Zumwalt Meadow delivers eye-popping scenery—granite cliffs, a roaring river, waterfalls, and Kings River Canyon itself—much of which you can experience at vista points or on easy walks. The canyon comes into view about 10 miles east of the village at **Junction View.** Five miles beyond, at **Yucca Point,** the canyon is thousands of feet deeper than the more famous Grand Canyon. **Canyon View,** a special spot 1 mile east of the Cedar Grove Village turnoff, showcases evidence of the area's glacial history. Here, perhaps more than anywhere else, you'll understand why John Muir compared Kings Canyon vistas with those in Yosemite. ■ TIP→ Driving the byway takes about an hour each way without stops. ⊠ *Rte. 180 north and east of Grant Grove village.*

HISTORIC SITES

Fallen Monarch. This toppled sequoia's hollow base was used in the second half of the 19th century as a home for settlers, a saloon, and even to stable U.S. Cavalry horses. As you walk through it (assuming entry is permitted, which is not always possible), notice how little the wood has decayed, and imagine yourself tucked safely inside, sheltered from a storm or protected from the searing heat. ⊠ *Grant Grove Trail, 1 mile north of Kings Canyon Park Visitor Center.*

SCENIC STOPS

General Grant Tree. President Coolidge proclaimed this to be the "nation's Christmas tree," and 30 years later President Eisenhower designated it as a living shrine to all Americans who have died in wars. Bigger at its base than the General Sherman Tree, it tapers more quickly. It's estimated to be the world's third-largest sequoia by volume. ■ TIP→ A spur trail winds behind the tree, where scars from a long-ago fire remain visible. ⊠ *Trailhead 1 mile north of Grant Grove Visitor Center.*

Redwood Mountain Sequoia Grove. One of the world's largest sequoia groves, Redwood contains within its 2,078 acres nearly 2,200 sequoias whose diameters exceed 10 feet. You can view the grove from afar at an overlook or hike 6 to 10 miles down into the richest regions, which include two of the world's 25 heaviest trees. ⊠ *Drive 6 miles south of Grant Grove on Generals Hwy. (Rte. 198), then turn right at Quail Flat; follow it 2 miles to the Redwood Canyon trailhead.*

SPORTS AND THE OUTDOORS

The siren song of beauty, challenge, and relative solitude (by national parks standards) draws hard-core outdoors enthusiasts to the Kings River Canyon and the backcountry of the park's eastern section. Backpacking, rock-climbing, and extreme-kayaking opportunities abound, but the park also has day hikes for all ability levels. Winter brings

16

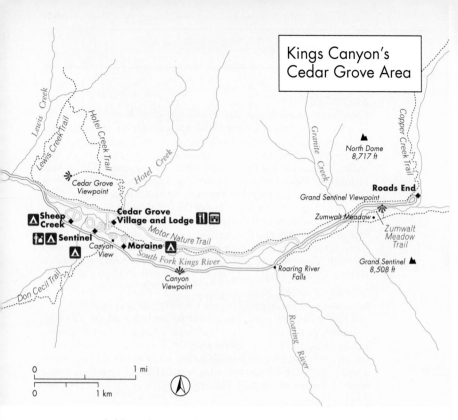

Kings Canyon's
Cedar Grove Area

sledding, skiing, and snowshoeing fun. No off-road driving or biking is allowed in the park, and snowmobiling is also prohibited.

CROSS-COUNTRY SKIING

Roads to Grant Grove are accessible even during heavy snowfall, making the trails here a good choice over Sequoia's Giant Forest when harsh weather hits.

HIKING

You can enjoy many of Kings Canyon's sights from your car, but the giant gorge of the Kings River Canyon and the sweeping vistas of some of the highest mountains in the United States are best seen on foot. Carry a hiking map—available at any visitor center—and plenty of water. Check with rangers for current trail conditions, and be aware of rapidly changing weather. Except for one trail to Mt. Whitney, permits are not required for day hikes.

Roads End Permit Station. You can obtain wilderness permits, maps, and information about the backcountry at this station, where bear canisters, a must for campers, can be rented or purchased. When the station is closed, complete a self-service permit form. ⊠ *Eastern end of Kings Canyon Scenic Byway, 6 miles east of Cedar Grove Visitor Center* ☉ *Mid-May–Sept., daily 7–4.*

CLOSE UP

Plants and Wildlife in Sequoia and Kings Canyon

The parks can be divided into three distinct zones. In the west (1,500–4,500 feet) are the rolling, lower elevation foothills, covered with shrubby chaparral vegetation or golden grasslands dotted with oaks. Chamise, red-barked manzanita, and the occasional yucca plant grow here. Fields of white popcorn flower cover the hillsides in spring, and the yellow fiddleneck flourishes. In summer, intense heat and absence of rain cause the hills to turn golden brown. Wildlife includes the California ground squirrel, noisy blue-and-gray scrub jay, black bears, coyotes, skunks, and gray foxes.

At middle elevation (5,000–9,000 feet), where the giant sequoia belt resides, rock formations mix with meadows and huge stands of evergreens—red and white fir, incense cedar, and

ponderosa pines, to name a few. Wildflowers like yellow blazing star and red Indian paintbrush bloom in spring and summer. Mule deer, golden-mantled ground squirrels, Steller's jays, mule deer, and black bears (most active in fall) inhabit the area, as does the chickaree.

The high alpine section of the parks is extremely rugged, with a string of rocky peaks reaching above 13,000 feet to Mt. Whitney's 14,494 feet. Fierce weather and scarcity of soil make vegetation and wildlife sparse. Foxtail and whitebark pines have gnarled and twisted trunks, the result of high wind, heavy snowfall, and freezing temperatures. In summer you can see yellow-bellied marmots, pikas, weasels, mountain chickadees, and Clark's nutcrackers.

16

EASY

Fodor's Choice ★ **Zumwalt Meadow Trail.** Rangers say this is the best (and most popular) day hike in the Cedar Grove area. Just 1.5 miles long, it offers three visual treats: the South Fork of the Kings River, the lush meadow, and the high granite walls above, including those of Grand Sentinel and North Dome. *Easy.* ⊠ *Trailhead 4½ miles east of Cedar Grove Village turnoff from Kings Canyon Scenic Byway.*

MODERATE

Big Baldy. This hike climbs 600 feet and 2 miles up to the 8,209-feet summit of Big Baldy. Your reward is the view of Redwood Canyon. Round-trip the hike is 4 miles. *Moderate.* ⊠ *Trailhead 8 miles south of Grant Grove on Generals Hwy. (Rte. 198).*

Redwood Canyon Trails. Two main trails lead into Redwood Canyon Grove, the world's largest sequoia grove. The 6.5-mile **Hart Tree and Fallen Goliath Loop** passes by a 19th-century logging site, pristine Hart Meadow, and the hollowed-out Tunnel Tree before accessing a side trail to the grove's largest sequoia, the 277.9-foot-tall Hart Tree. The 6.4-mile **Sugar Bowl Loop** provides views of Redwood Mountain and Big Baldy before winding down into its namesake, a thick grove of mature and young sequoias. *Moderate.* ⊠ *Trail begins off Quail Flat ✛ Drive 5 miles south of Grant Grove on Generals Hwy. (Rte. 198), turn right at Quail Flat and proceed 1½ miles to trailhead.*

Mt. Whitney

At 14,494 feet, Mt. Whitney is the highest point in the contiguous United States and the crown jewel of Sequoia National Park's wild eastern side. The peak looms high above the tiny, high-mountain desert community of Lone Pine, where numerous Hollywood Westerns have been filmed. The high mountain ranges, arid landscape, and scrubby brush of the eastern Sierra are beautiful in their vastness and austerity.

Despite the mountain's scale, you can't see it from the more traveled west side of the park because it is hidden behind the Great Western Divide. The only way to access Mt. Whitney from the main part of the park is to circumnavigate the Sierra Nevada via a 10-hour, nearly 400-mile drive outside the park. No road ascends the peak; the best vantage point from which to catch a glimpse of the mountain is at the end of Whitney Portal Road. The 13 miles of winding road lead from U.S. 395 at Lone Pine to the trailhead for the hiking route to the top of the mountain. Whitney Portal Road is closed in winter.

DIFFICULT

Hotel Creek Trail. For gorgeous canyon views, take this trail from Cedar Grove up a series of switchbacks until it splits. Follow the route left through chaparral to the forested ridge and rocky outcrop known as Cedar Grove Overlook, where you can see the Kings River Canyon stretching below. This strenuous 5-mile round-trip hike gains 1,200 feet and takes three to four hours to complete. *Difficult.* ⊠ *Trailhead at Cedar Grove Pack Station, 1 mile east of Cedar Grove Village.*

HORSEBACK RIDING

One-day destinations by horseback out of Cedar Grove include Mist Falls and Upper Bubb's Creek. In the backcountry, many equestrians head for Volcanic Lakes or Granite Basin, ascending trails that reach elevations of 10,000 feet. Costs per person range from $35 for a one-hour guided ride to around $250 per day for fully guided trips for which the packers do all the cooking and camp chores.

TOURS AND OUTFITTERS

Cedar Grove Pack Station. Take a day ride or plan a multiday adventure along the Kings River Canyon with Cedar Grove Pack Station. Popular routes include the Rae Lakes Loop and Monarch Divide. ⊠ *Kings Canyon Scenic Byway, 1 mile east of Cedar Grove Village* ☎ *559/565–3464* ⊕ *www.nps.gov/seki/planyourvisit/horseride.htm* ✈ *From $40 per hour or $100 per day* ⊙ *Late May–early Sept.*

Grant Grove Stables. A one- or two-hour trip through Grant Grove leaving from the stables provides a taste of horseback riding in Kings Canyon. ⊠ *Rte. 180, ½ mile north of Grant Grove Visitor Center* ☎ *559/335–9292 mid-June–Sept.* ⊕ *www.nps.gov/seki/planyourvisit/horseride.htm* ✈ *From $45* ⊙ *June–Labor Day, daily 8–6.*

Hiking in the Sierra Mountains is a thrilling experience, putting you amid some of the world's highest trees.

SLEDDING AND SNOWSHOEING

In winter Kings Canyon has a few great places to play in the snow. Sleds, inner tubes, and platters are allowed at both the Azalea Campground area on Grant Tree Road, ¼ mile north of Grant Grove Visitor Center, and at the Big Stump picnic area, 2 miles north of the lower Route 180 entrance to the park.

Snowshoeing is good around Grant Grove, where you can take naturalist-guided snowshoe walks on Saturdays and holidays from mid-December through mid-March as conditions permit. For a small donation, you can rent snowshoes at the Grant Grove Visitor Center for the guided walks. Grant Grove Market rents sleds and snowshoes.

WHERE TO EAT

SEQUOIA

$ CAFÉ 🍴 **Lodgepole Market and Snack Bar.** The choices here run the gamut from simple to very simple, with the three counters only a few strides apart in a central eating complex. For hot food, venture into the snack bar. The deli sells prepackaged salads, sandwiches, and wraps along with ice cream scooped from tubs. You'll find other prepackaged foods in the market. [$] *Average main: $6* ✉ *Next to Lodgepole Visitor Center* ☎ *559/565–3301* 🕒 *Closed late Sept.–mid-Apr.*

$$$ MODERN AMERICAN 🍴 **The Peaks.** Huge windows run the length of the Wuksachi Lodge's high-ceilinged dining room, and a large fireplace on the far wall warms both body and soul. The diverse dinner menu—by far the best at both

parks—reflects a commitment to locally sourced and sustainable products. The menu might include venison, pan-seared mountain trout, and vegetarian options like pho and chili. The wine selection is serviceable but lacks imagination. Breakfast and lunch are also served. $ *Average main: $28 ⊠ Wuksachi Village ☏ 559/565–4070 ⊕ www.visitsequoia. com/the-peaks-restaurant.aspx ⌂ Reservations essential.*

$$$ ✕**Wolverton Barbeque.** Weather permitting, diners congregate nightly on a
BARBECUE wooden porch that looks directly out onto a small but strikingly verdant meadow. In addition to the predictable meats such as ribs and chicken, the all-you-can-eat buffet has sides that include baked beans, corn on the cob, and potato salad. Following the meal, listen to a ranger talk and then clear your throat for a campfire sing-along. Purchase tickets at Lodgepole Market, Wuksachi Lodge, or Wolverton Recreation Area's office. $ *Average main: $25 ⊠ Wolverton Rd., 1½ mile northeast off Generals Hwy. (Rte. 198) ☏ 559/565–4070 ⊗ No lunch. Closed early Sept.–mid-June.*

KINGS CANYON

$$ ✕**Cedar Grove Snack Bar.** The menu here is surprisingly extensive, with
AMERICAN dinner entrées such as pasta, pork chops, trout, and steak. For breakfast, try the biscuits and gravy, French toast, pancakes, or cold cereal. Burgers (including vegetarian patties) and hot dogs dominate the lunch choices. Outside, a patio dining area overlooks the Kings River. $ *Average main: $14 ⊠ Cedar Grove Village ☏ 559/565–0100 ⊗ Closed Oct.–May.*

$$ ✕**Grant Grove Restaurant.** In a no-frills, open room, this restaurant offers
AMERICAN utterly standard American fare such as pancakes for breakfast or hot sandwiches and chicken for later meals. Take-out service is available year-round, and during the summer there's also a pizza parlor. $ *Average main: $16 ⊠ Grant Grove Village ☏ 559/335–5500.*

WHERE TO STAY

SEQUOIA

$$$$ ▥**Wuksachi Lodge.** The striking cedar-and-stone main building is a fine
HOTEL example of how a structure can blend effectively with lovely mountain
Fodor's Choice scenery. **Pros:** best place to stay in the parks; lots of wildlife. **Cons:**
★ rooms can be small; main lodge is a few-minutes' walk from guest rooms. $ *Rooms from: $229 ⊠ 64740 Wuksachi Way, Wuksachi Village ☏ 559/565–4070, 888/252–5757 ⊕ www.visitsequoia.com/ lodging.aspx ⇆ 102 rooms ⎮○⎮ No meals.*

KINGS CANYON

$$$$ ▥**John Muir Lodge.** This modern, timber-sided lodge occupies a wooded
HOTEL area in the hills above Grant Grove Village. **Pros:** open year-round; common room stays warm; lodge is far enough from the main road to be quiet. **Cons:** check-in is down in the village. $ *Rooms from: $205 ⊠ Kings Canyon Scenic Byway, ¼ mile north of Grant Grove Village, 86728 Highway 180 ☏ 559/335–5500 ⊕ www.visitsequoia.com/John-Muir-Lodge.aspx ⇆ 36 rooms ⎮○⎮ No meals.*

TRAVEL SMART SOUTHERN CALIFORNIA

GETTING HERE AND AROUND

Wherever you plan to go in California, getting there will likely involve driving, even if you fly. Major airports are usually far from main attractions. For example, four airports serve the Los Angeles area—but three of them are outside the city limits. California's major airport hubs are LAX in Los Angeles and SFO in San Francisco, but you can find satellite airports around most major cities. When booking flights, it pays to check these options for more convenient times and a better location in relation to your hotel.

FROM LOS ANGELES TO:	BY AIR	BY CAR
San Diego	55 mins	2 hrs
Death Valley		5 hrs
San Francisco	1 hr 30 mins	5 hrs 40 mins
Monterey	1 hr 10 mins	5 hrs
Santa Barbara	50 mins	1 hr 40 mins
Big Sur		5 hrs 40 mins
Sacramento	1 hr 30 mins	5 hrs 30 mins

▮ AIR TRAVEL

Flying time to California is about 5½ hours from New York and 4 hours from Chicago. Travel from London to either Los Angeles or San Francisco is 11 hours and from Sydney approximately 15. Flying between San Francisco and Los Angeles takes about 90 minutes.

AIRPORTS

Southern California's gateways are Los Angeles International Airport (LAX) and San Diego International Airport (SAN), as well as the smaller Long Beach (LGB), Bob Hope Airport (BUR), LA/Ontario (ONT), and John Wayne Airport (SNA).

Airport Information Bob Hope Airport ✉ Burbank ☎ 818/840–8840 ⊕ www. burbankairport.com. **John Wayne Airport** ☎ 949/252–5200 ⊕ www.ocair.com. **LA/**

Ontario International Airport ☎ 909/937–2700 ⊕ www.lawa.org. **Long Beach Airport** ☎ 562/570–2600 ⊕ www.lgb.org. **Los Angeles International Airport** ☎ 310/646–5252 ⊕ www.lawa.org. **San Diego International Airport** ☎ 619/400–2404 ⊕ www.san.org.

FLIGHTS

With hubs in San Francisco and Los Angeles, United has the greatest number of flights into and within California. But most national and many international airlines fly to the state. Southwest Airlines and United Airlines connect smaller cities within California, often from satellite airports near major cities.

Airline Contacts Air Canada ☎ 888/247–2262 ⊕ www.aircanada.com**Alaska Airlines/ Horizon Air** ☎ 800/252–7522 ⊕ www. alaskaair.com. **American Airlines** ☎ 800/433–7300 ⊕ www.aa.com. **British Airways** ☎ 800/247–9297 ⊕ www.britishairways.com. **Cathay Pacific** ☎ 800/233–2742 ⊕ www. cathaypacific.com. **Delta Airlines** ☎ 800/221–1212 for U.S. reservations, 800/241–4141 for international reservations ⊕ www.delta. com. **Frontier Airlines** ☎ 800/432–1359 ⊕ www.flyfrontier.com. **Japan Airlines** ☎ 800/525–3663 ⊕ www.jal.com. **JetBlue** ☎ 800/538–2583 ⊕ www.jetblue.com. **Qantas** ☎ 800/227–4500 ⊕ www.qantas.com. au. **Southwest Airlines** ☎ 800/435–9792 ⊕ www.southwest.com. **Spirit Airlines** ☎ 801/401–2200 ⊕ www.spirit.com. **United Airlines** ☎ 800/864–8331 for U.S. reservations, 800/538–2929 for international reservations ⊕ www.united.com. **US Airways** ☎ 800/428–4322 for U.S. and Canada reservations, 800/622–1015 for international reservations ⊕ www.usairways.com.

▮ BOAT TRAVEL

CRUISES

A number of major cruise lines offer trips that begin or end in California. Most voyages sail north along the Pacific coast to Alaska or south to Mexico. Southern

California cruise ports include Los Angeles and San Diego.

Cruise Lines Carnival Cruise Line ☎ 305/599–2600, 888/227–6482 ⊕ www.carnival.com. **Celebrity Cruises** ☎ 800/647–2251, 800/437–3111 ⊕ www.celebritycruises.com. **Crystal Cruises** ☎ 310/785–9300, 888/722–0021 ⊕ www.crystalcruises.com. **Disney Cruise Line** ☎ 800/951–3532 ⊕ www.disneycruise.disney.go.com. **Holland America Line** ☎ 206/281–3535, 877/932–4259 ⊕ www.hollandamerica.com. **Norwegian Cruise Line** ☎ 305/436–4000, 866/234–7350 ⊕ www.ncl.com. **Princess Cruises** ☎ 661/753–0000, 800/774–6237 ⊕ www.princess.com. **Regent Seven Seas Cruises** ☎ 954/776–6123, 844/473–4368 ⊕ www.rssc.com. **Royal Caribbean International** ☎ 305/539–6000, 866/562–7625 ⊕ www.royalcaribbean.com. **Silversea Cruises** ☎ 954/522–4477, 877/276–6816 ⊕ www.silversea.com.

▌ BUS TRAVEL

Greyhound is the major bus carrier in California. Regional bus service is available in metropolitan areas.

Bus Information Greyhound ☎ 800/231–2222 ⊕ www.greyhound.com.

▌ CAR TRAVEL

There are two basic north–south routes in California: Interstate 5 runs inland most of the way from the Oregon border to the Mexican border; and U.S. 101 hugs the coast for part of the route from Oregon to Mexico. A slower but much more scenic option is to take California State Route 1, also referred to as Highway 1 and the Pacific Coast Highway, which winds along much of the California coast and provides an occasionally hair-raising, but breathtaking, ride.

From north to south, the state's east–west interstates are Interstate 80, Interstate 15, Interstate 10, and Interstate 8. Much of California is mountainous, and you may encounter winding roads, frequently cliff-side, and steep mountain grades. In winter, roads crossing the Sierra from east to west may close at any time due to weather. Also in winter, Interstate 5 north of Los Angeles closes during snowstorms.

FROM LOS ANGELES TO:	ROUTE	DISTANCE
San Diego	I–5 or I–405	127 miles
Las Vegas	I–10 to I–15	270 miles
Death Valley	I–10 to I–15 to Hwy. 127 to Hwy. 190	290 miles
San Francisco	I–5 to I–580 to I–80	382 miles
Monterey	U.S. 101 to Salinas, Hwy. 68 to Hwy. 1	320 miles
Santa Barbara	U.S. 101	95 miles
Big Sur	U.S. 101 to Hwy. 1	349 miles
Sacramento	I–5	391 miles

GASOLINE

Gasoline prices in California vary widely, depending on location, oil company, and whether you buy it at a full-service or self-serve pump. It's less expensive to buy fuel in the southern part of the state than in the north. If you're planning to travel near Nevada, you can sometimes save a bit by purchasing gas over the border. Gas stations are plentiful throughout the state. Most stay open late (24 hours along major highways and in big cities), except in rural areas, where Sunday hours are limited and where you may drive long stretches without a chance to refuel.

ROAD CONDITIONS

Rainy weather can make driving along the coast or in the mountains treacherous. Some of the smaller routes over mountain ranges and in the deserts are prone to flash flooding. When the rains are severe, coastal Highway 1 can quickly become a slippery nightmare, buffeted by strong winds and obstructed by falling debris from the cliffs above. When the weather is particularly bad, Highway 1 may be closed due to mud and rock slides.

Many smaller roads over the Sierra Nevada are closed in winter, and if it's snowing, tire chains may be required on routes that are open. From October through April, if it's raining along the coast, it's usually snowing at higher elevations. Consider renting a four-wheel-drive vehicle, or purchase chains before you get to the mountains. (Chains or cables generally cost $40 to $70, depending on tire size; cables are easier to attach than chains, but chains are more durable.) If you delay and purchase them in the vicinity of the chain-control area, the cost may double. Be aware that most rental-car companies prohibit chain installation on their vehicles. If you choose to risk it and do not tighten them properly, they may snap—your insurance likely will not cover any resulting damage.

Always carry extra clothing, blankets, water, and food when driving to the mountains in the winter, and keep your gas tank full to prevent the fuel line from freezing.

Road Conditions Caltrans Current Highway Conditions ☎ *800/427-7623* ⊕ *www.dot. ca.gov.*

Weather Conditions National Weather Service ☎ *805/988-6610 Los Angeles area, 858/675-8700 San Diego area* ⊕ *www. weather.gov.*

ROADSIDE EMERGENCIES

Dial 911 to report accidents and to reach the police, the California Highway Patrol (CHP), or the fire department. On some rural highways and on most interstates, look for emergency phones on the side of the road.

In Los Angeles, the Metro Freeway Service Patrol provides assistance to stranded motorists under nonemergency conditions. Dial 511 from a cell phone and choose the "motorist aid" option to reach them 24 hours a day.

RULES OF THE ROAD

All passengers must wear seat belts at all times. It is illegal to leave a child six years of age or younger unattended in a motor vehicle. A child must be secured in a federally approved child passenger restraint system and ride in the back seat until at least eight years of age or until the child is at least 4 feet 9 inches tall. Children who are eight but don't meet the height requirement must ride in a booster seat or a car seat. Unless indicated, right turns are allowed at red lights after you've come to a full stop. Left turns between two one-way streets are allowed at red lights after you've come to a full stop.

Drivers with a blood-alcohol level higher than 0.08 who are stopped by police are subject to arrest, and those under 21 convicted of driving with a level of 0.01 or more can have their driving privileges revoked for a year. California's drunk-driving laws are extremely tough—violators may have their licenses immediately suspended, pay hefty fines, and spend the night in jail.

The speed limit on many interstate highways is 70 mph; unlimited-access roads are usually 55 mph. In cities, freeway speed limits are between 55 mph and 65 mph. Many city routes have commuter lanes during rush hour.

You must turn on your headlights whenever weather conditions require the use of windshield wipers.

Those 18 and older must use a hands-free device for their mobile phones while driving; those under 18 may not use mobile phones or wireless devices while driving. Texting on a wireless device is illegal for all drivers. Smoking in a vehicle where a minor is present is an infraction. For more information, refer to the Department of Motor Vehicles driver's handbook at ⊕ *www.dmv.ca.gov.*

CAR RENTAL

When you reserve a car, ask about cancellation penalties, taxes, drop-off charges (if you're planning to pick up the car in one city and leave it in another), and surcharges (for being under or over a certain age, for additional drivers, or for driving across state or country borders or beyond a specific distance from your point of rental). All these things can add substantially to your costs. Request car seats and extras such as GPS when you book.

Rates are sometimes—but not always—better if you book in advance or reserve through a rental agency's website. There are other reasons to book ahead, though: for popular destinations, during busy times of the year, or to ensure that you get certain types of cars (vans, SUVs, exotic sports cars).

■ TIP➔ Make sure that a confirmed reservation guarantees you a car. Agencies sometimes overbook, particularly for busy weekends and holiday periods.

A car is essential in most parts of California. In sprawling cities such as Los Angeles and San Diego, you'll have to take the freeways to get just about anywhere.

Rates statewide for the least expensive vehicle begin as low as $30 a day, usually on weekends, and less than $200 a week (though they increase rapidly from here, especially in some of the larger metropolitan areas). This does not include additional fees or the tax on car rentals, which is 9.50% in Los Angeles and 8% in San Diego. Be sure to shop around—you can get a decent deal by shopping the major car-rental companies' websites. Compare prices by city before you book, and ask about "drop charges" if you plan to return the vehicle in a city other than the one where you rented it. If you pick up at an airport, there may also be a facility charge of as much as $12 per rental, plus higher tax rates; ask when you book.

In California you must have a valid driver's license and be 21 to rent a car; rates may be higher if you're under 25. Some agencies will not rent to those under 25; check when you book. Non-U.S. residents must have a license with text in the Roman alphabet that is valid for the entire rental period. Though it need not be entirely written in English, it must have English letters that clearly identify it as a driver's license. In addition, most companies also require an international license; check in advance.

If you dream of driving down the coast with the top down, or you want to explore the desert landscape not visible from the road, consider renting a specialty vehicle. Agencies that specialize in convertibles and sport-utility vehicles will often arrange airport delivery in larger cities. Unlike most of the major agencies, the following companies guarantee the car class that you book.

Specialty Car Agencies Enterprise Exotic Car Rentals ☎ *800/400-8412, 866/458-9227 locations in Los Angeles and other Southern California locations ⊕ exoticcars.enterprise. com.* **Beverly Hills Rent a Car** ☎ *800/479-5996 San Francisco and several locations in Los Angeles, 310/274-6969 ⊕ www.bhrentacar. com.* **Midway Car Rental** ☎ *866/717-6802 several locations in Los Angeles and Southern California ⊕ www.midwaycarrental.com.*

Major Rental Agencies Alamo ☎ *800/462-5266 ⊕ www.alamo.com.* **Avis** ☎ *800/331-1212 ⊕ www.avis.com.* **Budget** ☎ *800/527-0700 ⊕ www.budget.com.* **Hertz** ☎ *800/654-3131 ⊕ www.hertz.com.* **National Car Rental** ☎ *877/222-9058 ⊕ www. nationalcar.com.*

▌ TRAIN TRAVEL

One of the most beautiful train trips in the country, Amtrak's *Coast Starlight* begins in Los Angeles and hugs the Pacific Coast to San Luis Obispo before it turns inland for the rest of its journey to Portland and Seattle. The *Pacific Surfliner* connects San Diego and San Luis Obispo via Los Angeles and Santa Barbara with multiple departures daily; the *Sunset Limited* runs from Los Angeles to New Orleans via Arizona, New Mexico, and Texas.

Information Amtrak ☎ *800/872-7245 ⊕ www.amtrak.com.*

ESSENTIALS

∎ ACCOMMODATIONS

The lodgings we review are the top choices in each price category. ⇨ *For an expanded review of each property, please see ⊕ www.fodors.com.* We don't specify whether the facilities cost extra; when pricing accommodations, ask what's included and what costs extra. ⇨ *For price information, see the planner in each chapter.*

Most hotels require you to give your credit-card details before they will confirm your reservation. If you don't feel comfortable emailing this information, ask if you can fax it or call and give details over the phone. However you book, get confirmation in writing and have a copy of it handy when you check in.

Be sure you understand the hotel's cancellation policy. Some places allow you to cancel without any kind of penalty—even if you prepaid to secure a discounted rate—if you cancel at least 24 hours in advance. Others require you to cancel a week in advance or penalize you the cost of one night. Small inns and B&Bs are most likely to require you to cancel far in advance. Most hotels allow children under a certain age to stay in their parents' room at no extra charge, but others charge for them as extra adults; find out the cutoff age for discounts.

Many B&Bs are entirely no-smoking, and hotels and motels are decreasing their inventory of smoking rooms; if you require one, ask when you book if any are available.

BED-AND-BREAKFASTS

California has more than 1,000 bed-and-breakfasts. You'll find everything from simple homestays to lavish luxury lodgings, many in historic hotels and homes. The California Association of Boutique and Breakfast Inns has about 300 member properties that you can locate and book through its website.

Reservation Services Bed & Breakfast.com ☎ *512/322-2710, 800/462-2632* ⊕ *www. bedandbreakfast.com.* **Bed & Breakfast Inns Online** ☎ *800/215-7365* ⊕ *www.bbonline. com.* **BnB Finder.com** ☎ *212/480-0414, 888/547-8226* ⊕ *www.bnbfinder.com.* **California Association of Boutique and Breakfast Inns** ☎ *800/373-9251* ⊕ *www.cabbi.com.*

∎ COMMUNICATIONS

INTERNET

Internet access is widely available in urban areas, but it's usually more difficult to get online in the state's rural communities. Most hotels offer some kind of connection—usually broadband or Wi-Fi. Many hotels charge a daily fee (about $10) for Internet access. Cybercafés are located throughout California.

∎ EATING OUT

California has led the pack in bringing natural and organic foods to the forefront of American dining. Though rooted in European cuisine, California cooking sometimes has strong Asian and Latin influences. Wherever you go, you're likely to find that dishes are made with fresh produce and other local ingredients.

The restaurants we list are the cream of the crop in each price category. ⇨ *For price information, see the planner in each chapter.*

CUTTING COSTS

∎ TIP➜ If you're on a budget, take advantage of the "small plates" craze sweeping California by ordering several appetizer-size portions and having a glass of wine at the bar, rather than having a full meal. Also, the better grocery and specialty-food stores have grab-and-go sections, with prepared foods on a par with restaurant cooking, perfect for picnicking (remember, it infrequently rains between May and October). At resort areas in the off-season you can often find two-for-one dinner specials at upper-end restaurants; check coupon apps or local papers or with visitor bureaus.

RESERVATIONS AND DRESS

Regardless of where you are, it's a good idea to make a reservation if you can. We only mention reservations specifically when they are essential (there's no other way you'll ever get a table) or when they are not accepted. For popular restaurants, book as far ahead as you can (often 30 days), and reconfirm as soon as you arrive. (Large parties should always call ahead to check the reservations policy.) We mention dress only when men are required to wear a jacket or a jacket and tie.

Online reservation services make it easy to book a table before you even leave home. OpenTable covers many California cities.

Contacts OpenTable ⊕ www.opentable.com.

WINES, BEER, AND SPIRITS

Throughout the state, you can visit wineries, many of which have tasting rooms and offer tours. Microbreweries are an emerging trend in the state's cities. The legal drinking age is 21.

▌ HEALTH

Smoking is illegal in all California bars and restaurants, including on outdoor dining patios in some cities. If you have an existing medical condition that may require emergency treatment, be aware that many rural and mountain communities have only daytime clinics, not hospitals with 24-hour emergency rooms.

Outdoor sports are a huge draw in California's moderate climate, but caution, especially in unfamiliar areas, is key. Drownings occur each year because beach lovers don't heed warnings about high surfs with their deadly rogue waves. Do not fly within 24 hours of scuba diving.

▌ HOURS OF OPERATION

Banks in California are typically open weekdays from 9 to 6 and Saturday morning; most are closed on Sunday and most holidays. Smaller shops usually operate from 10 to 6, with larger stores remaining open until 8 or later. Hours vary for museums, historical sites, and state parks, and many are closed one or more days a week, or for extended periods during off-season months. It's a good idea to check before you visit a tourist site.

▌ MONEY

Los Angeles and San Diego tend to be expensive cities to visit, and rates at coastal and desert resorts are almost as high. A day's admission to a major theme park can run as much as $99 per person, though you may be able to get discounts by purchasing tickets in advance online. Hotel rates average $150 to $250 a night (though you can find cheaper places), and dinners at even moderately priced restaurants often cost $20 to $40 per person. Costs in the Death Valley/Mojave Desert region are considerably less—many motels in the Mojave charge $70 to $90.

CREDIT CARDS

It's a good idea to inform your credit-card company before you travel. Otherwise, unusual activity might prompt the company to put a hold on your card—not a good thing halfway through your trip. Record all your credit-card numbers—as well as the phone numbers to call if your cards are lost or stolen—in a safe place, so you're prepared should something go wrong. Both MasterCard and Visa have general numbers you can call (collect if you're abroad) if your card is lost or not working.

Reporting Lost Cards **American Express** ☎ 800/528–4800 in U.S., 715/343–7977 collect from abroad ⊕ www.americanexpress. com. **Discover** ☎ 800/347–2683 in U.S., 801/902–3100 collect from abroad ⊕ www. discover.com. **Diners Club** ☎ 800/234–6377 in U.S., 514/877–1577 collect from abroad ⊕ www.dinersclub.com. **MasterCard** ☎ 800/627–8372 in U.S., 636/722–7111 collect from abroad ⊕ www.mastercard.com. **Visa** ☎ 800/847–2911 in U.S., 303/967–1096 collect from abroad ⊕ www.visa.com.

▮ SAFETY

California is a safe place to visit, as long as you take the usual precautions. In large cities ask the concierge or desk clerk to point out areas on your map that you should avoid. Lock valuables in a hotel safe when you're not using them. (Some hotels have in-room safes large enough to hold a laptop computer.) Keep an eye on your handbag when you're out in public. Security is high (but mostly invisible) at theme parks and resorts.

▮ TAXES

Sales tax in the state of California is 7.5%, but local taxes vary and may be as much as an additional 2%. Sales tax applies to all purchases except for food bought in a grocery store; food consumed in a restaurant is taxed, but take-out food is not. Hotel taxes vary widely by region, from about 8% to 15.5%.

▮ TIME

California is in the Pacific time zone. Pacific daylight time (PDT) is in effect from mid-March through early November; the rest of the year the clock is set to Pacific standard time (PST).

▮ TIPPING

Most service workers in California are fairly well paid compared to those in the rest of the country, and extravagant tipping is not the rule here. Exceptions include wealthy enclaves such as Beverly Hills and La Jolla in Southern California, as well as the most expensive resort areas.

TIPPING GUIDELINES FOR CALIFORNIA	
Bartender	$1 per drink, or 10%–15% of tab per round of drinks
Bellhop	$1–$2 per bag, depending on the level of the hotel
Hotel Concierge	$5–$10, if he/she performs a service for you
Hotel Doorman	$1–$2 if he/she helps you get a cab
Valet Parking Attendant	$3–$5 when you get your car
Hotel Maid	$2–$5 per day; more in high-end hotels
Waiter	15%–20% (20%–25% is standard in upscale restaurants); nothing additional if a service charge is added to the bill
Skycap at Airport	$1–$2 per bag
Hotel Room-Service Waiter	15%–20% per delivery, even if a service charge was added since that fee goes to the hotel, not the waiter
Taxi Driver	15%–20%, but round up the fare to the next dollar amount
Tour Guide	15% of the cost of the tour, more depending on quality

▮ TOURS

Guided tours are a good option when you don't want to do it all yourself. You travel along with a group (sometimes large, sometimes small), stay in prebooked hotels, eat with your fellow travelers (the cost of meals is sometimes included in the price of your tour, sometimes not), and follow a schedule.

But not all guided tours are an if-it's-Tuesday-this-must-be-Yosemite experience. A knowledgeable guide can take you places that you might never discover on your own, and you may be pushed to see more than you would have otherwise. Tours aren't for everyone, but they can be just the thing for trips to places where making travel arrangements is difficult or time-consuming.

Whenever you book a guided tour, find out what's included and what isn't. A "land-only" tour includes all your travel (by bus, in most cases) in the destination, but not necessarily your flights to and from or even within it. Also, in most cases prices in tour brochures don't include fees and taxes. And remember that you'll be expected to tip your guide (in cash) at the end of the tour.

SPECIAL-INTEREST TOURS

BIKING

Biking is a popular way to see the California countryside, and commercial tours are available throughout the state. Most three- to five-day trips are all-inclusive—you'll stay in delightful country inns, dine at good regional restaurants, and follow experienced guides. When booking, ask about level of difficulty, as nearly every trip will involve some hill work. Tours fill up early, so book well in advance. ■ TIP→ Most airlines accommodate bikes as luggage, provided they're dismantled and boxed.

Bicycle Adventures. Based in Washington state, this outfitter plans all the meal, lodging, and travel details of multiday bike trips through some of California's most engaging scenery, including the redwoods, wine country, the North Coast, Big Sur, and rugged Death Valley. ✉ *29700 S.E. High Point Way, Issaquah, Washington* ☎ *800/443–6060, 425/250–5540* ⊕ *www. bicycleadventures.com.*

▌ VISITOR INFORMATION

The California Travel and Tourism Commission's website takes you to each region of California, with digital visitor guides in multiple languages, driving tours, maps, welcome center locations, information on local tours, links to bed-and-breakfasts, and a complete booking center. It also links you—via the Destinations menu—to the websites of city and regional tourism offices and attractions. ⇨ *For the numbers and websites of regional and city visitor bureaus and chambers of commerce, see the Planning section in each chapter.*

Contacts California Travel and Tourism Commission ✉ *Sacramento* ☎ *916/444–4429 CA Tourism Commission office, 800/862–2543 brochures and information* ⊕ *www. visitcalifornia.com.*

INDEX

PHOTO CREDITS

Front cover: Della Huff / Alamy. [Description: Rodeo Drive, Beverly Hills, California]. 1, Greg Epperson/Shutterstock. 2, Unclejay l Dreamstime.com. 5, Epukas/Wikimedia Commons. Chapter 1: Experience Southern California: 8–9, Doug Lemke/Shutterstock. 11, Lisa M. Hamilton. 12, Robert Holmes. 13 (left), Vincent Thompson, Fodors.com member. 13 (right), Charlie_Oregon, fodors.com member. 14, Stas Volik/Shutterstock. 15 (left), Robert Holmes. 15 (right), dgassa, fodors.com member. 16 (left), Lorcel / Shutterstock. 16 (top right), f11photo / Shutterstock. 16 (bottom right), Joshuaraineyphotography l Dreamstime.com. 17 (top left), Linda Moon / Shutterstock. 17 (bottom left), Gary C. Tognoni / Shutterstock. 17 (right), Nadia Borisevich / Shutterstock. Chapter 2: Southern California's Best Road Trips: 21, Paul Giamou/iStockphoto. 18, Robert Holmes. 19, Geir Olav Lyngfjell/Shutterstock. 21, Paul Gamou/iStockphoto. 22 (top), Janine Bolliger/iStockphoto. 22 (bottom), Lise Gagne/iStockphoto. 23, iStockphoto. 24 (top right), Evan Meyer/iStockphoto. 24 (center right), Kyle Maass/iStockphoto. 24 (left), iStockphoto. 24 (bottom right), Lise Gagne/ iStockphoto. 25, Tom Baker/Shutterstock. 26 (left), SuperStock/age fotostock. 26 (top right), CURAphotography/Shutterstock. 26 (bottom right), Michael Almond/iStockphoto. 27 (top), iStockphoto. 27 (bottom), Lise Gagne/iStockphoto. 28 (left), TebNad/Shutterstock. 28 (top right), Ross Stapleton-Gray/ iStockphoto. 28 (bottom right), Jay Spooner/iStockphoto. 29 (top), Jay Spooner/iStockphoto. 29 (bottom), Lise Gagne/iStockphoto. Chapter 3: San Diego: 41, Brett Shoaf/Artistic Visuals Photography. 42, frogger256, Fodors.com member. 43 (top), rkkwan, Fodors.com member. 43 (bottom), Steve Rabin/iStockphoto. 44 and 50, Brett Shoaf/Artistic Visuals Photography. 59 (top), Dreyer Peter / age fotostock. 59 (bottom), Epukas/Wikimedia Commons [Public Domain]. 60, Robert Holmes. 61, Steve Snodgrass/Flickr. 62 (left and top center), fPat/Flickr. 62 (top right), Jim Epler/ Flickr. 62 (bottom center), Matthew Field/wikipedia.org. 62 (bottom right), RENAULT Philippe / age fotostock. 63, lora_313/Flickr. 64 (left), Cburnett/wikipedia.org. 64 (right), Susann Parker / age fotostock. 65 (top), George Ostertag / age fotostock. 65 (bottom right), Sally Brown/age Fotostock. 650 (bottom left), Stefano Panzeri/Shutterstock. 74, Howard Sandler/iStockphoto. 78, Brett Shoaf/Artistic Visuals Photography. 112, Legoland California Resort. 114, Merryl Edelstein, Fodors.com member. Chapter 4: Orange County and Catalina Island: 117, Robert Holmes. 118, Marc Pagani Photography/Shutterstock. 119 (top), Robert Holmes. 119 (bottom), Brent Reeves/Shutterstock. 120, Robert Holmes. 129, www.ericcastro.biz/Flickr. 137, Robert Holmes. 143, Scott Vickers/iStockphoto. 146, www.rwongphoto.com / Alamy. 149, Brett Shoaf/Artistic Visuals Photography. 154, Lowe Llaguno/Shutterstock. Chapter 5: Los Angeles: 161, California Travel and Tourism Commission/Andreas Hub. 162, Kenna Love/LACVB. 163 top), Wendy Connett/ age fotostock. 163 (bottom), Scott Frances/Esto/J. Paul Getty Trust. 164, Jeff Morse/iStockphoto. 165 (top), Yelo34 l Dreamstime.com. 165 (bottom), wando studios inc/iStockphoto. 166, Nstanev l Dreamstime.com. 174, S. Greg Panosian/iStockphoto. 182, Alvaro Leiva/age fotostock. 190, NOIZE Photography/Flickr. 220, Thomas Barrat/Shutterstock. Chapter 6: The Central Coast: 225, Shippee l Dreamstime.com. 226, Stephen Walls/iStockphoto. 227, Robert Holmes. 228, David M. Schrader/Shutterstock. 242, S. Greg Panosian/iStockphoto. 243, Ruben G. Mendoza. 244 (top), Richard Wong/www.rwongphoto.com/ Alamy. 244 (bottom), Ruben G. Mendoza. 245 (top left), Witold Skrypczak/Alamy. 245 (top right), S. Greg Panosian/iStockphoto. 245 (bottom), Janet Fullwood. 246 (top left), GIPhotoStock Z/Alamy. 246 (top right), Craig Lovell/Eagle Visions Photography/Alamy. 246 (bottom) and 247 (top), S. Greg Panosian/iStockphoto. 247 (bottom), Eugene Zelenko/wikipedia.org. 252, David M. Schrader/Shutterstock. 258, Doreen Miller, Fodors.com member. 270, Aimee M Lee / Shutterstock. 288–89, Valhalla l Design & Conquer, Fodors.com member.

Chapter 7: The Monterey Bay Area: 293, mellifluous, Fodors.com member. 295 (top), vittorio sciosia/ age fotostock. 295 (bottom), Jeff Greenberg/ age fotostock. 296, Brent Reeves/Shutterstock. 304, Robert Holmes. 311, Holger Mette/iStockphoto. 318, laurel stewart/iStockphoto. Chapter 8: The Inland Empire: 339, Mission Inn Hotel & Spa. 340, Hartford Family Wines. 341 (top), Robert Holmes. 341 (bottom), stevekc/Flickr. 342, Edward Lin/ iStockphoto. 350, Glen Ivy Hot Springs. 363, Brett Shoaf/ Artistic Visuals Photography. Chapter 9: Palm Springs: 367, Carol M. Highsmith/Visit California. 368, JustASC/Shutterstock. 369 (top and bottom), Robert Holmes. 370, iStockphoto. 373, William Royer/ iStockphoto. 386, David Falk/ iStockphoto. 408, Brett Shoaf/Artistic Visuals Photography. Chapter 10: Joshua Tree National Park: 413, Eric Foltz/iStockphoto. 414 (top), Loic Bernard/iStockphoto. 414 (bottom), Eric Foltz/iStockphoto. 415 (top), Justin Mair/Shutterstock. 415 (bottom), Mariusz S. Jurgielewicz/Shutterstock. 416, Eric Foltz/iStockphoto. Chapter 11: The Mojave Desert: 421, Robert Holmes. 422, amygdala imagery/ Shutterstock. 423, Robert Holmes. 424, San Bernardino County Regional Parks. 430, Merryl Edelstein, Fodors.com member. 437, Robert Holmes. 445, Paul Erickson/ iStockphoto. Chapter 12: Death Valley National Park: 449, Rodney Ee, Fodors.com member. 451 (top), Igor Karon/Shutterstock. 451 (bottom), iofoto/Shutterstock. 452, Paul D. Lemke/iStockphoto. 458-59,

NOTES

NOTES

NOTES

NOTES

NOTES

NOTES

NOTES

NOTES